Hume's Challenge and the Renewal of Modern Philosophy

Leslie Dewart

Hume's Challenge and the Renewal of Modern Philosophy

Leslie Dewart

Print ISBN: 978-1-48357-206-2

eBook ISBN: 978-1-48357-207-9

One half of this work, or less, I dedicate

to my beloved

Doreen Moore Dewart

Already hers, as of right, and well-earned

Is the other half and more.

Table of Contents

Foreword

Leslie Dewart, my friend and mentor, died in December 2009 with his *magnum opus* unfinished. Recently his daughter, Elizabeth Dewart, approached me with a challenge and a proposal: would I pour over the many drafts and notes of her father's work with a mind to prepare a final version for publication? I considered her request an honour and a privilege, to say nothing of an enormous undertaking. However, before I gave any consideration to an affirmative reply, I asked my beloved wife, Deana Albertini, if she was willing to engage in such a time consuming enterprise with me.

While I was investigated the many versions of the unfolding emersion of Leslie's profound thought, Deana spent countless hours at the computer incorporating these "thoughts" into electronic language. The final electronic version of Professor Dewart's provocative thought is because of her dedicated and talented commitment. I am profoundly grateful to my wife for her loving and uncomplaining devotion to an enterprise that reached far beyond our collective imagination.

Spell-check had a field day with run-on sentences, passive voice, dangling modifiers, sentences beginning with And or But. I chose deliberately not to adjust any of these journalistic maladies for a very specific reason. While Leslie had published several previous books on philosophy and consciousness, his thoughts had continued to evolve and he had a great deal more to say. The spontaneity of his style bespeaks a man in a hurry to convey his message. It has a conversational as opposed to a polished professional style. I felt it important for the reader to sense the urgency and imperative nature of what he was seeking to share.

Sadly, he did not quite complete his mission. That is where I have stepped in. Every word of the ensuing text is authentic. However, no single version has been left intact. I have attempted to put together the clearest and most comprehensive exposition of Professor Dewart's long considered and incredibly precise insights into one of philosophy's greatest challenges: the understanding of consciousness. Two versions of his work do not contain the final Chapter IV. I have included it because

I feel it rounds out much of his thought and provides even further food for consideration among the most curious of those who delve into this his final expression of ideas.

I recall at the memorial of his death, an acquaintance was asked to speak. He began by saying "When I first met Leslie, I asked him what was his field of interest? The simple reply, 'consciousness.'" For the thirty-five years I shared ideas with and learned from Professor Dewart, his primary interest was in understanding the nature of consciousness. He undertook a law degree and was called to the bar (though he never practiced law) in order to achieve a broader perspective on consciousness from a different field of scholarship. In this work he has drawn upon his very broad intellectual acumen, developed over many years of rumination, to enrich our understanding and appreciation of the nature of consciousness. He truly dreamed of surpassing the intellectual stagnation into which he saw philosophy had fallen. Till his dying day he was determined to achieve the realization of that dream. This work is testimony to that devotion.

The ensuing book may not appear on the NY Times best sellers' list. Relatively few readers will have the stamina to grasp the depth of insight buried in every paragraph. The extent of his delving into physics, evolution, linguistics, psychology, theology, morality and particularly into the historical development of philosophical thought offer profound and often disturbing insights for future consideration. In a stunning and incisive analysis of what constitutes a human being, this work opens the floodgates for moral and medical reappraisal of traditional values and taboos. Political and social implications are rife as one reflects on exactly what the author is suggesting as our most fundamental responsibilities in a world where we are fully and engagingly conscious.

While some fellow philosophers may not agree with all of his findings, none can question nor deny the depth, breadth, and thorough understanding of the witnesses that Dewart has called upon to substantiate his insights. What is most significant about this work is the depth to which the author has gone into many different fields of study in order to show how profoundly a renewed sense of philosophical understanding will effect each of these disciplines. Readers who do not particularly consider themselves students of philosophy will, nevertheless, come away with a much deeper and more incisive appreciation of their own discipline because of the philosophical implications that Dewart has unearthed and offered as an incentive to ever more profound investigation. While this work is the end of Leslie Dewart's contribution to the richness of philosophical study, it is actually the prologue to far greater study and commitment by those who are inspired and motivated by his relentless desire to bring philosophy, once again, into the forefront of intellectual curiosity and understanding.

This was a man who loved philosophy as a mental exercise and as the door through which clear and focused thought in nearly every field of serious study must pass. What he calls "the stagnation of philosophy" was unmistakably his greatest sorrow and concern. That he looked to the "existential skepticism" of David Hume as the jumping off point for his probing, from which he explores backward and projects forward in history, testifies to the thoroughness of his quest. The depth of insight into the history of philosophy and the impact of its mistakes provides a very solid foundation for the modern interpretation he gives to such bugbears as 'representationism' and 'dualism' to name just two. For many, his conclusions will seem extreme, even unbelievable. But belief calls for faith; the scholarship of this exercise calls for open-minded cognition.

A word of caution to the curious and committed reader: keep a dictionary close at hand! Leslie's rather wry and dry sense of humour shows itself in the occasionally unconventional vocabulary he will use to most accurately express or identify an idea. To fail to grasp the precise meaning of these words is to miss the clever turn of phrase intended by the author. He was indeed a textualist of the first order. Be prepared to frequently confront one of Leslie's favourite expressions: "willy-nilly".

Despite death, because of the dedication of his wife, Doreen, his daughter, Elizabeth, his granddaughters, Karen and Alison, Elizabeth's partner George McLauchlan, and the loving devotion and talented hard work of my wife, Deana, Leslie Dewart's deepest and most significant contribution to the enrichment and powerful impact upon contemporary philosophical thought lives on, in the pages to which you are about to turn, as a challenge to every field of serious intellectual inquiry.

Cajetan J. Menke, PhD (University of St. Michael's College, Toronto)
Montréal 2016

Preface

Soon after philosophy was revived in modern times by René Descartes and given an empirical orientation by John Locke, anglophone philosophy ceased to make much progress in its understanding of the human mind and its conscious quality. Many philosophers today are likely to agree that, regretfully, although the attempts of modern philosophy to fathom the mind have never come to a standstill, generation after generation the most promising beginnings have in the fullness of time invariably foundered. Quite to the contrary, however, on a very different issue 'a Great Divide'[1] bisects today's philosophical community into irreconcilable factions: is it true, as the advocates of 'cognitivism' maintain, that with the advent of this school of thought the stagnation of philosophy and its inability to deal effectively with consciousness have come to an end?

The proponents of philosophical cognitivism judge that modern philosophy, having enlisted in the service of cognitive science, has finally come of age and now faces a bright future. The reason, they say, is that cognitivism has at long last discovered how to study human cognition as what it truly is, namely, as one among many possible 'realizations' or 'instantiations' of the 'mentality' of processes that can be observed not only in human beings and infrahuman animals, but even among non-living entities such as computing machines. This, they say, is necessary, because it is the only way in which philosophy can avoid dualism. The more traditionally-minded amongst us, however, continue to uphold the autonomous, science-independent nature and unique value of philosophical knowledge, as well as the empirically-based conviction that human organisms exhibit mental functions that, on the one hand, are vested in exclusively material organisms, but which nonetheless, on the other, are truly real and conscious as well as distinct from, and irreducible to, the organism's non-mental functions. Now, if this should turn out to be true — and time will probably tell — philosophical cognitivism, like the many other philosophical shooting stars that have risen and fallen in the last two hundred years, is likely to dry out and ultimately evaporate. But that is yet to come, if ever it will. In

---

1   David J. Chalmers, *The Conscious Mind: In Search of a Fundamental Theory* (New York: Oxford University Press, 1996), p. xiii.

the meantime, those of us who contest the validity of cognitivism are challenged to account for the causes of what we take to be the stagnation of modern philosophy throughout modern times. How did it come about? Why is there no end of it in sight? What is the remedy, if there is one? And how should philosophy reorient itself once it overcomes the obstacles that bar its way to progress? These are the questions that this work has undertaken to investigate.

A sidelight of what we shall find is unusual enough to be worth mentioning before we proceed. Most often, a search for the causes of a phenomenon envisages positive, active factors. Nevertheless, everyday experience teaches us that sometimes an event's not-happening, its *absence*, has a decisive causal role within a larger process. But as we shall conclude, one of the prime causes at work in the historical process that yielded the stagnation of modern philosophy — a process that began with Descartes but which was completed only with the philosophical community's response to Hume's contributions — was plain and unwitting *unawareness*, on the part of the philosophers of the seventeenth and eighteenth centuries, of several important philosophical developments that had taken place at various earlier times during the late middle ages. Neither Descartes nor others in the modern tradition had little [much?] accurate collective recollection of the events surrounding the calamity that had overtaken late scholasticism when in the fourteenth century it succumbed to the prevailing opinion that human reason was radically

impotent to demonstrate the existence of the world. All that had survived in the memory of European culture was the aftermath of the catastrophe — namely, the disrepute into which philosophy had fallen once it had been generally agreed that philosophy, and in the first place the human mind, were powerless to establish as little as the bare existence of the world. More specifically, the premises from which such bleak conclusion had followed, and the process through which existential skepticism had gained general acceptance, had been almost entirely forgotten. This was the condition in which philosophy was still to be found when Descartes was inspired to come to its rescue — but unfortunately, on the basis of the same misconceptions that had originally generated skepticism and destroyed scholastic thought.

Unsurprisingly, the earlier misfortunes of philosophy threatened to descend upon it once again: the prospect of existential skepticism and terminal philosophical impotence were soon raised by

Hume. Now, this time the reaction of the philosophical community was very different from the last — but for all that, it was no less inadequate than it had been originally. Existential skepticism was almost universally rejected, but unawareness of how the first wave of philosophical destruction had become unleashed played a key role: the false premises on which skepticism had originally depended continued to be generally supposed. And so, widespread existential skepticism was averted, but philosophy had been maimed: the study of the mind was predicated thereafter on the very suppositions that had once presided over the ruin of scholasticism, and whose fallaciousness, though not obvious, undermined every effort to understand the human mind. Philosophy stagnated. Therefore, as we shall have occasion to verify, the historical events that shall concern us in this investigation amount to a case study illustrating the truth of George Santayana's aphorism:

> Progress depends on retentiveness. When … experience is not retained …
> infancy is perpetual. Those who cannot remember the past are condemned
> to repeat it.[2]

Strictly speaking, however, one cannot forget what one has never known. Stated precisely and positively, the point of Santayana's insight is that, since one cannot overcome one's mistakes unless one becomes conscious of them, and since one cannot so become unless one looks back upon past events, one can correct one's mistakes only in retrospect. This is why reflection upon the *history* of philosophy can play not simply a useful, but a crucial role, in the investigation of philosophical problems. In the absence of historical retrospection, philosophical investigations cannot but perpetuate whatever earlier inadequacies might have hindered, if not indeed prevented, progress. However, the advances made by historians of philosophy in the last century or so can reveal, to those who take them into account, how the stagnation of modern philosophy is rooted in failures of an earlier age. Thus, the historians have given us back what we had, as it were, 'forgotten' — or more exactly, what

---

2   George Santayana, *The Life of Reason: or The Phases of Human Progress*, vol. 1. (New York: Scribner's, 1906), 284. Note well: unawareness of the history of philosophy during the thirteenth and fourteenth centuries explains why the events were repeated (in essential respects) during the eighteenth; the original appearance of existential skepticism in the fourteenth century requires, of course, a different explanation, namely, the original adoption of the premises that generated existential skepticism.

had been absent from our consideration but which is now ours to benefit from. But only if we care to use it, of course.

There's the rub. Modern philosophers have not always taken advantage of as much historical memory as we have regained; for philosophers are human beings, and their attitudes and habits, like their prejudices, change only slowly. True to the orientation modern thought was given by René Descartes at the time of its foundation, modern philosophy has long presupposed that the history of philosophy can never be of much, if indeed any, help towards the solution of philosophical problems. I argue, on the contrary, that the key to overcoming the stagnation of philosophy is to understand the historical process through which the malaise logically came about. This is why in the introductory Chapter of this work I devote as much attention to the issue of how the problem should be approached as I do to an elucidation of the nature of the problem itself.

And yet, I have done no independent research on the historical process that eventually led to the unfortunate outcome; for none is indispensable for grasping at least the fundamentals of the case. The principal historical facts regarding Greek and mediaeval philosophy on which my argument depends reflect the well-established consensus arrived at by historians of philosophy during the first half of the twentieth century regarding a relatively few Greek and mediaeval ideas that, as it happens, were transmitted to modern philosophy by Descartes. My contribution to the solution of the problem is limited to pointing out that, when the historical facts that are now known are put together, they explain the stagnation of modern philosophy as the logically unavoidable effect of historical causes. For when certain traditional ideas were pursued to their logical consequences, the unintended effect, given the absence of what had been 'forgotten', was that modern philosophy's endeavour to understand the conscious mind became mired in assumptions whose mutual contradiction was not readily apparent. If the historians themselves have not remarked on this, it is probably because, as specialists are notoriously wont to do, the historians of the three main philosophical ages have not always been in touch with each other. They have not always considered the consequences that the philosophical thought of their favourite period may have had when it was imported by a later age into a new intellectual environment.

I gladly acknowledge the source of my inspiration to turn to the history of philosophy for an explanation of the difficulties in which modern philosophy has increasingly found itself since Descartes and Hume: it was John R. Searle's remarkable study of *The Rediscovery of the Mind*. [3] The philosophical investigation of the mind, he suggested, had become disoriented and should not expect to make true progress unless it became conscious of the assumptions that impeded its understanding the mind, and unless it identified correctly what it had to explain. Searle's insightful work was squarely on target, I thought, insofar as it looked to history to teach us how philosophy had lost its way and why was likely to regain its bearings only after learning how its waywardness had come about. In my estimation, however, Searle's strategy was unnecessarily restricted in scope. Being highly conscious (as my philosophical education had, by chance rather than design, made me) of the continuity of the history of philosophy throughout its three major epochs, it seemed to me that in order to understand the situation of philosophy today it would be essential, first, to go back to the very beginning of the tradition, and, second, to pay special attention to the transition from mediaeval to modern philosophy. Only then could one begin to grasp the inexorable logic of the process whereby modern philosophy unwittingly condemned itself, in the end, to having to explain the mind on the basis of assumptions that make it impossible to do so.

Philosophy owes it to itself to remember where it has been and how it got to where it is now, before it decides in which direction it should strike next. However, in this essay I have barely touched on the high points of a rather complex sequence of intellectual events. The general structure of the causal historical process as I have set it down is, I think, fairly clear, but many of its details remain tantalizingly obscure. As for the suppositions that I propose here concerning cognition, reality, and causality as replacements of the traditional versions of these concepts, I recognize they may amount only to an uncertain and unhelpful step towards the reconstruction of modern philosophy. Nevertheless, if this work arouses the interest of open-minded scholars and stimulates them to investigate in depth the questions I raise here but which I answer only superficially, and if it moves them to reset the compass of philosophy on a more promising course than I have been able to suggest, my fondest objectives in writing this book will have been attained.

---

3   John R. Searle, *The Rediscovery of the Mind* (Cambridge, Mass.: MIT press, 1992).

Acknowledgements

Comments on portions of this work at various early stages of composition contributed by Thomas Duddy and Alastair Hannay have been most useful to me. So have been the exchanges I have had with Gregory Nixon over many years, and my correspondence with Timo Järvilehto. My gratitude to Richard Hinners for comments, suggestions, inspiration, and for the example of his devotion to philosophical thought, is deep as our lifetime friendship has been long. Of course, neither agreement with my views nor approval of my recommendations regarding the orientation that philosophy should be given in the future is to be inferred from these acknowledgements.

I

The Challenge of Hume and Philosophy's Failure to Meet It

Three hundred and fifty years after the death of René Descartes, the elementary issues raised by the founder of modern philosophy about the nature of the mental functions and activities of human organisms - or the 'mind,' as he thought of such functions, and as we, somewhat ambiguously, still refer to them in their collectivity - could not be said to have been resolved. Questions about the nature of consciousness are the prime example. Descartes himself was concerned with consciousness only incidentally -- namely, insofar as the self-observability of the mind, which is manifested by the *cogito*, demonstrated the existence of the mind. For by so demonstrating, Descartes would have fulfilled his great ambition: to refute the long-prevailing opinion that philosophy was incapable of establishing the existence of the world of which we take ourselves to be part, much less understand its nature. However, to the philosophers who answered his call for the establishment of a new, reformed, and strictly rational mode of inquiry that should restore confidence in philosophy, the *cogito* suggested that the ancient problems of philosophy about the mental life of human beings pertained to a mind characterized by what in the ordinary vocabulary of European culture had recently become known as 'consciousness.'[4]

This was a philosophical novelty. The French *conscience* and the Latin *conscientia* (and their equivalents in the various European vernaculars) antedate Descartes by far; but before the seventeenth century, these terms had referred solely to moral self-awareness. In early modern times, however, *conscience* became accepted in French, and its equivalents in the other Romance languages, with more general reference to a person's awareness of its mental life. (In English, however, the wider

---

4   According to the *Oxford English Dictionary*, the earliest known record of the word dates from 1632.

meaning of 'conscience' was signified separately by the neologism 'consciousness,' while 'conscience' continued to be restricted to moral self-awareness.) Well, the Cartesian *cogito* presupposes the human mind's awareness of its mental functions and not only moral self-awareness. Thus, the *cogito* tended to draw 'consciousness' to the attention of philosophers as a fundamental characteristic of the human mind; the *cogito* is the origin of the supposition of John Locke - and thereafter by many others to the present - that consciousness is the mind's awareness of its awareness.[5] In short, modern philosophy was from the outset dedicated to the proposition that to understand the human mind it was necessary to understand its consciousness.

Unfortunately, consciousness has proven 'notoriously difficult to pin down.'[6] Most contemporary philosophers would probably agree with Daniel C. Dennett that '[c]onsciousness stands alone today as a topic that often leaves even the most sophisticated thinkers tongue-tied and confused.'[7] Indeed, a few philosophers have actually concluded that 'consciousness is… not readily amenable to ordinary scientific or philosophical explanation.'[8] But perhaps the best measure of the lack of progress in philosophy of mind[9] regarding consciousness is the fact, noted by William G. Lycan, that 'a clear sense of what is meant by "consciousness" has been sadly lacking'[10] among modern philosophers.

In evidence of it, Lycan cited the expression that during the previous two decades had been widely accepted as the proper definition of the *explicandum* of consciousness:

> What... of 'what it's like'? That phrase... [has become] an umbrella term for
> whatever one finds puzzling about consciousness, subjectivity, etc... It is
> long past time to recognize...that the phrase... is now worse than useless: it is

---

5   Although the human mind is indeed able to observe itself, it is not my view that consciousness may be reduced to the selfobservability of the human mind. The two should not be confused. The nature of consciousness and its relationship to the self-observability of the conscious mind will be fully discussed in due course.

6   David J. Chalmers, *The Conscious Mind: In Search of A Fundamental Theory* (New York: Oxford University Press, 1996), 3.

7   Daniel C Dennett, *Consciousness Explained* (Boston: Little, Brown, 1991), 22.

8   Reported by Guven Guzeldere, 'The many faces of consciousness,' in Ned Block, Owen Flanagan, and Guven Guzeldere, (eds.) *The Nature of Consciousness: Philosophical Debates* (Cambridge, Mass.: MIT Press, 1998), 3.

9   Following common usage, I accept the term 'philosophy of mind' as referring to the study of our *cognitive* mental functions exclusively, ignoring the fact that the human 'mind' comprises also our affective mental life.

10   William G. Lycan, *Consciousness and Experience* (Cambridge, Mass.: MIT Press, 1996), 1-2.

positively pernicious and harmful, because nothing whatever is clarified or explained by reference to it.[11]

Lycan was referring to a widely echoed contribution of Thomas Nagel, which to the sustained acclaim of many had suggested that 'the fact that an organism has conscious exper-ience at all means, basically, that there is something it is like to be that organism... [For instance,] the essence of the belief that bats have experience is that there is something that it is like to be a bat.'[12] But remarkably few philosophers demurred, as Alastair Hannay did, that the same could be said of a stone.[13] For there is something it is like to be a stone. Indeed, there seems to be hardly anything of which it could not be said that there is something that it is like to be it.

Puzzlement has not come to an end. There is among philosophers, it seems, 'no consensus on what the term consciousness denotes.'[14] But if this is true, it should be sobering. Only unawareness of the simple fact that human beings are conscious could be a more disadvantageous point of departure for the investigation of the conscious mind by philosophers, than their being aware of the fact, but so indistinctly as to find it difficult to agree on what it is that they want to explain.

Besides, not only consciousness, but most other aspects of human cognition continue to baf-fle us. The so-called 'body mind' problem has not completely ceased to divide opinion. Nor is it a rare comment that '[w]e have at present no conception of how a single event or thing [such as a human organism] could have both physical and phenomenological aspects, or how, if it did, they might be related.'[15] The 'explanatory gap' between these two aspects of the mind has yet to be closed. Thus, centuries of modern philosophical effort to understand the human, conscious mind have been ineffective.

---

11   Lycan, *Consciousness and Experience*, 77.

12   Thomas Nagel, *Mortal Questions* (Cambridge: Cambridge University Press, 1974), 165-180, 166,168 italics in the original).

13   Alastair Hannay, *Human Consciousness* (London: Routledge, 1990), 186, note 2.

14   Guzeldere, 'The many faces of consciousness,' 7. The same is true among psychologists; see David Cohen, *The Secret Language of Mind: A Visual Enquiry into the Mysteries of Consciousness* (London: Duncan-Baird, 1998), 67.

15   Thomas Nagel, *The View from Nowhere* (New York: Oxford University Press, 1986), 47.

Moreover, the defeat of philosophy of mind reverberates throughout philosophy; for the human mind occupies a cardinal position in relation to every other subject of philosophical investigation. Since every philosophical claim about the nature of the world is a claim regarding what we know about the world, the assumptions of philosophers regarding the nature of human cognition are always relevant to the formulation and investigation of every other philosophical problem. When philosophy of mind fails to meet with success, all philosophical thought is adversely affected.

The current situation of philosophy of mind is a remarkable state of affairs. There is, of course, no reason to suppose that the success of the tradition founded in Greece more than two and a half millennia ago and continued during the middle ages had been guaranteed at the outset. Nor should we suppose that a fixed timetable governed the progress of philosophy when, after mediaeval philosophy had come to a disreputable end, Descartes tried to reform it and make it relevant to modern times. Nevertheless, the recurrent failures of modern philosophy to understand the conscious mind amount to stagnation, and contrast unfavourably with the advances of experimental science during the same period. And so, when one balances the widely acknowledged fact that consciousness remains 'just about the last surviving mystery'[16] against the enormous industry and ingenuity invested in the project over three and a half centuries by a large number of dedicated and capable thinkers, one may well wonder: is the stagnation of philosophy of mind not sufficiently striking a phenomenon to provoke us to ask why it should be so?

Moreover, philosophy results from the exercise of the human 'cognitive' functions - by which I mean simply the mental functions that yield 'knowledge.' Or more precisely, the functions that yield the state of actively knowing. For the philosophical study of the mind is hindered, or so I suggest, if we do not observe that what we call 'knowledge' is a reification of the *active organic* state that is the actual outcome of the discharge of our mental functions. Our cognitive activities do not bring a commodity called 'knowledge' into our minds; they bring about the peculiar active relationship of cognitively endowed organisms to the world and its objects, a relationship that consists in 'knowing' them. At any rate, from the fact that the process of 'cognition' has 'knowledge' for its outcome, it follows that the assumptions of philosophers regarding cognition, whatever they may be, will affect

---

16   Dennett, *Consciousness Explained*, 21.

their conception of the nature of philosophical *knowledge*. In short, the reliability of our philosophical *knowledge of the world* can never be greater than the reliability of our philosophical knowledge *of our cognitive processes.*

But further, and for the same reason – that philosophy is a form of knowledge – our knowledge of the nature of philosophy, too, can never be more profound than our understanding of the nature of our cognitive mental functions. This is why, as we have gradually learned to appreciate in modern times, although philosophy is not reducible to the study of mind, the whole of philosophy turns on philosophy of mind. And so, when modern philosophy of mind fails to achieve its most elementary objectives, it compromises an indispensable part of the infrastructure of all philosophy. The stagnation of modern philosophy of mind is, in effect, the stagnation of modern philosophy as a whole.

There may be other reasons as well,[17] but the foregoing remarks should suffice to support the suggestion that it would be appropriate for today's philosophers to consider whether the unsatisfactory progress of modern philosophy since Descartes's time – but as we shall see, most markedly after Hume's—does not present a philosophical problem that bears investigating. For if it does, and if we could solve it, we could look forward to the end of the stagnation and to philosophy's regaining the reasonable expectation of future progress.

The road to that goal begins with our determining, in the first section of this introductory chapter, the nature of the problem. In subsequent sections we shall formulate a hypothesis towards its solution, and then consider the procedure we might follow to reach it. But first, two preliminary terminological stipulations should be made.

I dissent from the Lockean convention that prevails in some philosophical circles, which restricts the terms 'cognition' and 'knowledge' to 'the domain of thought and inference, marking the contrast

---

17   There is indeed another reason, but its weight should become apparent only below, when we verify that our understanding *of* the *world* and *of* the way in which world events come about is directly related to our understanding of ourselves and the conscious nature of our cognition. If we misperceive ourselves and how we understand ourselves, we shall unavoidably misperceive also the nature of reality and of causality.

with perceptual experience and other [similar] mental phenomena.'[18] I side with Galen Strawson, who suggests that:

> [We should] not speak of thoughts *or* experiences, opposing them in the way that some do... The spectrum of experience ranges from the most purely sensory experiences to the most abstractly cognitive experiences... [T]here is such a thing as "understanding-experience", just as there is such a thing as visual experience.[19]

Thus, in my usage of the term, the 'spectrum of experience' is also the spectrum of cognition, of knowledge, and of awareness. Both sense perception and understanding are levels of 'cognition.' In this work, however, we shall be interested almost exclusively in the more basic level of cognition we call sense perception.

As for 'mind,' the term is notoriously more than a little ambiguous. Since 'mind' is grammatically a substantive, and substantive nouns are often used to refer to separate and independent existents, 'mind' tends to connote to most of us (as it denoted to Descartes) reference to a supposed agent of our mental functions, distinct from the human organism, rather than to the mental functions themselves. I make no such supposition. As I use it, 'mind' does not refer to a distinct agent, but to a set of organic, bodily functions and activities of human organisms; the agent of the mental functions is the organism. Of course, human organisms discharge non-mental functions as well as the kind we call 'mental,' and all the functions that we human beings are capable of discharging, mental and non-mental, are integrated in the physiology of the organism. Now, such organic functions are distinguishable by the various effects they achieve. It follows that none of our organic functions is reducible to any other; if they were, they would not be different functions. And so, the human mental functions are irreducible to any of our non-mental functions; for unlike our non-mental functions,

---

18   Barry C. Smith, 'Cognition,' in Ted Honderich, (ed.), *The Oxford Companion to Philosophy* (Oxford: Oxford University Press, 1995), 138.

19   Galen Strawson, *Mental Reality* (Cambridge, Mass.: MIT Press, 1994), 4, 5.

they achieve mental states. But our mental functions are organic functions, and the mental states they achieve are states of the organism.

1. The stagnation of modern philosophy as a philosophical problem

The facts that oblige us to recognize the unsatisfactory situation of philosophy today are widely acknowledged, but they are not usually perceived[20] as raising questions that merit philosophical attention. The more typical reaction of many of today's philosophers of mind to two and a half centuries of sterility and stagnation seems limited to estimating that, if we press on - as surely we shall - eventually we shall almost certainly understand the conscious mind. The underlying assumption seems to be that, meanwhile, there is nothing that need or can be done to hasten the process - other than, of course, to renew our efforts. For philosophy has failed to fulfil its promise only in the negative sense that success has eluded it so far. The possibility of future success is very much alive, and nothing stands in the way of the eventually favourable outcome of the philosophical quest.

If one were to suggest, therefore, that the lack of progress in philosophy warrants a study of its past performance as well as of the future it now faces and of what we can do today to enhance its prospects, a likely rejoinder would be that no inquiry is needed, because the failure is a purely primitive absence of success. The temporary failure has, therefore, a negative and obvious cause: we do not know the answers to our questions about the human mind simply because we have not yet found them. And we have not found them because, like an undiscovered petroleum field or a yet-to-be-found cure for cancer, the nature of the human mind is hidden from sight; we have investigated possibilities that seemed likely, but which ultimately did not yield what we had hoped. Therefore, revisiting our unsuccessful efforts would be pointless; it would be somewhat like returning to a dry oil well or repeating experiments that failed. All we can do is rather to keep searching new ground

---

20 In current general English usage, 'to perceive' and 'perception' refer to the mental activity of apprehending, grasping, or becoming aware of something, without reference to how such apprehension takes place; the terms include, therefore, not only what psychologists mean strictly by 'perception' but also 'sensation' as well as the knowledge we gain through thinking and understanding. In this work, in passages where strict reference to either sentience or to understanding is important and the context does not make my intention clear, I will either specify 'sense perception,' or use 'to sense' and 'sensation,' in one case, or else 'to understand,' in the other. Otherwise, as in this instance, I will use 'to perceive' and 'perception' in their unrestricted non-technical meaning, covering indistinctly every mental function that yields awareness of anything.

until we find the buried truth and bring it to the surface. Our lack of success may frustrate our wishes, but does not present a problem of the sort that philosophy could solve. Now, is this true?

a) The 'difficulty' of the problem

Underlying the view that persistence is all that is needed to surmount the futility of philosophy's attempts to understand the human mind, certain questionable assumptions can be detected. The supposition is sometimes made, usually tacitly, that human judgments regarding the development of philosophical knowledge measure an unchanging truth against the approximations to it made by various individual philosophers at various times. That is, human beings can make mistakes, but the truth that the human mind seeks to discover is predetermined and unchanging. Thus, failures are possible, and have to be corrected; but the truth about the world and ourselves resides objectively in things themselves, and pre-exists our discovery of it.

In the past, since it is clear that our knowledge does not create the world, and since it seems likely on its face that nothing can be known unless some mind knows it, questions about the nature of such pre-existing truth residing in things themselves were readily answered by reference to the existence of a 'higher' Mind in accordance with which the universe had been created. The truth immanent in the natures of real things was the truth of God's creative knowledge of them. However, such higher Mind is no longer generally acceptable as a premise for further philosophical reasoning, either to most modern philosophy or to modern science. Therefore, the question is no longer asked either by philosophers or by science: whence comes the pre-existing truth embedded in objects? But if the question is not asked, philosophers are hardly entitled to assume that the changing truth of human knowledge of the world is an approximation of the unchanging truth of a higher Mind's creative knowledge of the world. In the absence of a transcendent Mind, the only truth that remains is the truth of the knowledge of those actually existing minds that are able to know the world. And clearly, the truth of our knowledge is not unchanging; one hopes it increases, though sometimes it does not. Sometimes our knowledge is off target, and sometimes it is positively confused.

The true nature of truth shall occupy our attention only later. So shall the reason why the inconsistency I have just pointed out tends to go unnoticed. At this time, my concern is rather that, if I have depicted correctly the prevailing suppositions of modern philosophy, it is not surprising that inquiries into the failure of philosophy to make much progress have been scarce. For in the view of many, the history of knowledge is by definition a history of discards, a safe disposal location where outright mistakes are to be stowed away out of public sight, along with still current or superseded defective truths that have given way to more comprehensively true human knowledge. If what one searches for is the objectively existing truth that still remains to be ascertained, it does not make sense either to rummage through the refuse accumulated by the history of philosophy, or to confirm discoveries previously made. Nothing that we can possibly find within history is of any conceivable use to us.

There is a different way to look at the matter. When oil explorers or medical researchers fail, they do not merely try and try again at random. They usually *review* their observations, procedures, and reasoning; they *search* for what might have been done differently, in order to enhance the likelihood of better results next time. Should we suppose that philosophy is different? That it is a lottery with truth as the prize, and that the persistent lack of success of modern philosophy indicates nothing more remarkable than a centuries-long run of bad luck?

We might consider instead that philosophy's failure to understand the mind even after centuries of effort is a historical event. And in the causation of historical events, human decisions play a predominant role: the possibility that the philosophical tradition may bear responsibility for its record and its present condition should not be discarded offhand. Perhaps it would be useful to investigate whether the absence of progress may not be the result of choices, misperceptions, or misinterpretations that have escaped criticism or decisive rejection; for if this should have been the case, it would follow, of course, that as long as the missteps remained uncorrected they would continue to prevent success. Is it not possible that this has happened already? That it accounts for the stagnation of philosophy?

Contrasting with the more common indifference to the question why philosophy of mind should not have fulfilled its promises is therefore what at one time was the much-discussed work of Colin McGinn. With enviable originality, he called attention to the question why the efforts of modern philosophy of mind to the present should have been futile. His question was insightful – for, contrary to the more common assumption, it supposed that the failure obeyed ascertainable causes – but his answer was less so. For it seems that in order to answer the questions he did not inquire into the adequacy of the past performance of philosophy; instead, he argued that the cause of the disappointingly low level of success was the 'cognitive closure'[21] of the human mind in respect of itself as an object of study. Therefore, he concluded, 'the time has come to admit candidly that we cannot resolve'[22] the problems of the mind.

However, to support the hypothesis that 'cognitive closure' regarding the mind itself was an actual characteristic of the human mind, the only evidence alleged by McGinn was the paucity of philosophy's success in solving the problems of the mind. McGinn's argument bordered on Panglossian circularity; few philosophers have been persuaded by it.

Some philosophers might agree that it is appropriate to ask for the causes of the bleak record of philosophy of mind, but estimate that the absence of progress could be explained by the hypothesis that although the human mind has the capability to understand itself, the mind is 'inherently difficult' to understand; as we often say, it resists our efforts to penetrate its secrets; its nature is elusive, not easily grasped, and the like. Therefore, the argument goes, there would be little point in reviewing the unsuccessful attempts made by philosophy in the past, because it would not affect the inherent difficulty of the mind as the subject of philosophical study. Therefore, no further inquiry into the absence of progress is necessary. Again, persistence is the route to success.

Well, when we attempt to achieve a certain objective and attain it only after much labour, or not at all, we are prone to say that we were held back, or defeated, by the 'difficulty' we ran into. But 'difficulty' is what we experience in such circumstances; it is not an obstacle that actively defies and thwarts our efforts. We do not actually 'wrest' nature's secrets from their rightful owner, because otherwise she will not give them up. Our failure to satisfy our desire to understand any given event or aspect of the world has its cause in ourselves: we have exercised our power to understand but have nevertheless failed to reach our goal. This is simply to recognize that, in what pertains to our

---

21   Colin McGinn, *The Problem of Consciousness: Essays Towards a Resolution* (Oxford: Blackwell, 1991), 3.

22   McGinn, *Problem of Consciousness*, 1.

cognitive power – as indeed in every other dimension - we are, on the one hand, *active agents*, but endowed, on the other, *with finite powers* the efficacy of which will vary from one person to another, and the exercise of which may require greater or lesser effort and yield greater or lesser results in various situations, If we were to suppose instead that 'difficulty' was truly an active characteristic of the object, we would have *projected* the cause of our disappointment onto the object of our disappointed wanting or striving.

Projection is sometimes characterized as a so-called 'ego defence mechanism,' a means to avoid vexatious feelings, such as the unpleasantness of having to acknowledge responsibility for one's failures. But it need not always obey such motivation, and in this work, I do not use the term in that sense. Projection can also describe a form of fallacious reasoning resulting from simple absence of due discrimination. For example, the attribution of *gravity* to certain bodies and *levity* to others by philosophers and non-philosophers alike between Greek and modern times - and by scientists before Newton - was a projection onto such bodies of what we human beings experience in ourselves when we manipulate 'heavy' and 'light' objects. That one has to make an effort to hold up a rock, and that to lift it one has to activate one's muscles to take advantage of their power to contract, is true. But it is true of ourselves; it is what we perceive in ourselves when we lift a rock. To attribute to rocks a quality that enables them to oppose what we do when we lift them is a projection. Such ascription is not justified by anything that is empirically evident to us in them.[23]

---

23   It is enlightening that among the theological and other condemnations of Galileo and his defence of heliocentrism in the early seventeenth century, sensible and weighty objections to it were to be found. Although Copernicus had denied the immobility of the Earth and its location at the centre of the universe, most of the other features of his system repeated the assumptions of the Ptolemaic. The latter went back, through Hipparchus, Eudoxus, and Callipus, to the hierarchical universe of Aristotle, which incorporated, among others, the doctrine that some bodies possessed the quality of 'heaviness;' this property of material beings, Aristotle had said, was the cause of their tendency to move towards the centre of the universe. Neither Copernicus nor Galileo challenged this. And yet, if it was true that the Sun was at the centre of the universe, why did heavy objects on Earth nevertheless tend to move towards the centre of the Earth? They should have fallen towards the Sun. As Aristotle had explained, 'if the Earth were to be moved to where the Moon now is, the various bodies on Earth would move not towards the Earth but towards the place where the Earth now is;' Aristotle, On the Heavens, 4.3.310b3. The Copernicans had no reasonable answer. Or rather, not until fifty years later when Newton had discarded, besides the immobility of the Earth, other Ptolemaic assumptions that had not been rejected by Copernicanism: that the universe had a centre, that it ended at the outermost, 'empyrean' shell, and in the first place that 'gravity' was a property of certain bodies; see Alexandre Koyre, From the Closed World to the Infinite Universe (New York: Harper 1958), passim. According to Newton, gravity was a universal 'force' rather than a quality of some bodies, which was distinct from all bodies and which acted upon bodies from without so as to

I have dwelt on the vacuity of supposing that the 'difficulty' of the object of study accounts at least in part for the absence of progress in philosophy of mind, because projection illustrates a particularly insidious defect of human reasoning that sometimes leads philosophical argumentation astray. If we agree to study the causes of the lack of success of philosophy of mind, the ascription of 'difficulty' to the mind as the object of philosophical study is not the only fallacious projection against which we should forewarn ourselves. Projection, I suggest, is a recurring hazard of which students of the human mind must beware. Occasions to verify this will arise as we proceed, but one instance should be singled out immediately because of its crucial importance.

When one considers the roles played in cognition, respectively, by the object and by the mind that tries to attain the object, it is not difficult to ascribe to the one what is actually true only of the other. We have to look at the matter twice before we recognize that objects do not do our perceiving (and much less our understanding): we do our own. The object is that which we try to perceive or understand, and our understanding or perceiving the object is rather what is done by us. But to grasp the full significance of this, it is necessary to discriminate, within the unity of our experience, between what we experience (often described as the 'contents' of the experience, although for reasons we shall explore later, this is an ambiguous and potentially misleading expression), and the performance of the activity of experiencing. But the former is obvious and to the fore, whereas the latter is in the background and easily escapes notice: to fail to discriminate between any two given things, one will of course identify them. Thus, if discrimination is made between what we experience and our experiencing it, the mind's experiential activity will be projected onto the object. Projection, as I shall argue below, also accounts for our frequently ascribing to objects the quality of truth that is actually possessed by our cognition of objects. The truth is about reality, but should not be identified with reality. It is the truth of our knowledge of reality.

There is an additional reason why the activity of cognizing seems particularly elusive or difficult to detect – namely, that the brain and other organs of our cognitive apparatus have no proprioceptive capability. Ample proprioceptive capability leaves us in no doubt of, for example, our motive

---

overcome and modify the natural inertial motion of material entities within an infinite universe that had no centre; see Isaac Newton, The Mathematical Principles of Natural Philosophy, Second edition, (New York: Philosophical Library, 1964).

activities. However, we can detect our perceptual activity mostly through indirect and equivocal signs. For example, the fact that we cannot have visual sensation at all unless we open our eyes should suggest to seers that they have to do their own seeing. The active nature of cognition is therefore easily overlooked, and the causation of perception is projected onto the objects perceived. I stress, therefore, that as we proceed we should guard against lapsing into projection. Insufficient discrimination in our observations regarding the mind and its cognition of reality can result in attributing to reality what in truth should be attributed to the mind, and vice versa.

And so, as Alastair Hannay has also said -- referring specifically to 'the mind-body problem, but with general applicability to the wider problem of the human mind – the fact that the mind 'remains a mystery' comes from our own cognitive limitations, not from any objective eeriness in the world.'[24] The human mind may be safely presumed to have the requisite ability to understand itself; the success or defeat of our philosophical study of the mind depend on how adequately (or otherwise) we exercise our mental functions when we investigate and try to understand their nature.

The defective use of our cognitive powers may derive from any of a large number of possible reasons. Neither lack of ability nor of diligence on the part of philosophers need be implied; moreover, recognition of our fallibility is not an admission of fault, but of fact. But in any event, since we alone are the agents of our efforts to understand – or, for that matter, to strike oil, or to force an uncooperative virus to reveal its vulnerabilities - the success or failure of our efforts to understand is also ours. Needless to say, it would be pedantic to forbid ourselves on that account the usual idiomatic conventions and refrain from the metaphorical attribution of 'difficulty,' 'elusiveness,' and 'resistance' to what we fail to understand. As long as we do not take ourselves literally, no harm need be done. But only as long.

To differentiate between attributing difficulty to that which one tries to understand but unsuccessfully, and attributing the lack of success to the insufficient or inappropriate exercise of one's mental powers, may at first blush smack of pettifoggery. But there is a true difference, and the difference is important because it determines, among other things, the procedure we should adopt to enhance the likelihood of philosophy's future success. One possibility is to forge ahead, which to many seems

---

24   Alastair Hannay, *Human Consciousness* (London: Routledge, 1990), 10.

obvious. The other is to look back and ensure, so far as may be possible, that one is facing the right direction before one forges ahead. The assumption that continued effort will sooner or later overcome the 'difficulty' of understanding the conscious mind would be naive, unless it were preceded by a deliberate and searching inquiry into the reasons for the lack of success. Once we determined the causes of philosophy's waywardness, we should find it possible to avoid them; only then, we could face the future with a reasonable expectation of success.

b) The position of cognitivism

So far, I have considered only the less radical among the objections that could be raised against my suggestion that the stagnation of philosophy presents us with a true philosophical problem, and that the problem might be solved by re-examining the past history of philosophy. More disturbing would be the criticism that might come from what may currently be the single most populous school of thought among philosophers of mind, namely cognitivism. Their opposition would take a very different form.

Cognitivist philosophizing comes in varieties and subvarieties, but they share a minimum common denominator, which shall alone concern us here. Cognitivist philosophers uniformly acknowledge, and freely join philosophers of other persuasions in judging, that until recently the past efforts of philosophers since Descartes had yielded little more than recurrent failures. In the eyes of cognitivists, this unfortunate outcome has had ascertainable causes, principally the tradition's widespread and persistent acceptance of certain errors. The critical one has been dualism. The remedy is to be found in the first place, therefore, in a rigorous and comprehensive rejection of dualism. And so, unlike those who suppose that time and perseverance will suffice to bring success to philosophy, cognitivists believe that something has stood - and in significant ways still stands - in the way of philosophical progress. If nevertheless they estimate that success will not continue to elude philosophy, it is because cognitivist thought has already begun to make a promising course correction.

The obstacle, they believe, is philosophy's traditional objective regarding the mind, and in particular, the ancient supposition of the long-prevailing school of 'mental realism,' as we may call it, that philosophy is charged with explaining consciousness as a real and distinctive characteristic of the mind.

In the opinion of most cognitivists, the reason why the reality of consciousness obstructs progress is that the 'realist' conception of the *explicandum* of philosophy of mind necessarily implies dualism. Therefore, it must be rejected but decisively and radically, as only cognitivism does. Consciousness may *seem* real, but it is more like a mirage, an illusion that can and should be explained. And indeed, it can and should be explained, but as such illusion, rather than under the assumption that it is real.

In the opinion of cognitivist philosophers, therefore, the arrival of cognitivism brought about – or at least, promised to bring about—the transcendence of the historical antecedents of philosophy of mind. It engendered thereby the well-grounded estimate that a new philosophical epoch had dawned. Working throughout the second half of the twentieth century under the inspiration of cognitive science, cognitivist philosophy of mind has begun to develop a new understanding of the philosophical problems that the human mental functions present to themselves. But since cognitive philosophy of mind proposes a new conception of the *explicandum*, the earlier efforts of philosophy are altogether irrelevant to its present concerns and future success. A further reason why the ill-considered convictions of the past are best forgotten is that the reformulation of the problem of the mind has brought about a new vision of the nature and methods of philosophy of mind. Philosophy of mind is now allied with science and charged with ancillary scientific functions: it is a branch of the philosophy of science concerning itself with the conceptual foundation and problems of the sciences of the mind.[25]

Philosophical cognitivism rightly points out, I think, that the study of the mind has been chronically prejudiced in the past by the assumption of dualism. Even today, dualism continues to be deliberately supposed by some philosophers (for example, by David J. Chalmers); upon occasion, it is accepted unwittingly, merely by inadvertence to the implications of other positions taken. (An illustration of this will be discussed later in this chapter.) However, dualism has not been the only miscalculation hindering the tradition; cognitivism continues to accept other doubtful assumptions whose waywardness it does not seem to have detected. (Evidence of this, too, will be alleged in due course.) Moreover, cognitivism attempts to redefine the problem of the mind by appealing to a methodologically (as well as substantively) illegitimate 'principle' – the so-called 'multiple realizability of

---

25   Daniel C. Dennett, *Brainstorms: Philosophical Essays on Mind and Psychology* (Cambridge, Mass.: MIT Press, 1978), xiii.

mind' - which depends on baseless assumptions and arbitrariness. (Again, reasons to affirm this will be advanced.)

Moreover, cognitivists take representationism for granted. It is openly acknowledged to be a fundamental and indispensable supposition of cognitivist research. Representations are indeed, in a sense, the basic subject of study of cognitive science and philosophy of mind. But representationism does not disturb the cognitivists. It is not a problem. The possibility that representationism might entail existential skepticism - as I shall henceforth refer to the opinion that the human mind is powerless to support the supposition that the external world exists – is simply given no serious attention and requires no refutation. It is as if Hume had never lived.

Besides, in addition to its procedural and substantive fatal defects, cognitivism proposes a conception of philosophy and its study of the human mind that, as noted above, fails to do justice to the self-sufficiency of philosophy and which ignores the radical impotence of science to investigate the nature of cognition by scientific methods, and *a fortiori* also the nature of science and philosophy. Cognitivism is a form of 'scientism,' a trend to which no philosopher seems to have been converted by rational considerations alone, since it depends on excessive admiration for science: as Hilary Putnam and others have said, scientism can be described as 'science worship'[26] and as an 'infatuation with science.'[27]

Nevertheless, cognitivist convictions cast their shadow over the current philosophical landscape; they cannot be ignored. Nor would it be proper, in view of the elaborate self justification of philosophical cognitivism, to give short shrift to its claims and to the objections it can be presumed to offer to my suggested investigation of the causes of the stagnation of philosophy. I propose, therefore, to by-pass all further consideration of cognitivism at this point, in order to discuss the topic in an Appendix to this chapter in which I shall consider at slightly greater leisure why I evaluate it

---

26   Hilary Putnam, *Renewing Philosophy* (Cambridge, Mass.: Harvard University Press, 1992), p. ix.

27   Tom Sorell, *Scientism: Philosophy and the Infatuation with Science* (London: Routledge, 1991). Seeking an explanation for the origin of scientism, Frederick A. Olafson has commented that it may be related to changes in the relative prestige and influence of philosophy and the natural sciences that took place in the twentieth century, and on 'the impact these changes have had on the morale of the philosophical community... [A] kind of antecedent improbability began to attach to any philosophical thesis that seemed to say something about the world that could not be put to the test by the procedures of natural science,' 'Brain Dualism,' *Inquiry* (Oslo) 37 (1994): 253-265; 253-4.

adversely. I shall then explain, first, how cognitivism emerged in the history of modern philosophy in opposition to the older, but still highly popular, traditional view of the nature of the problem of the mind, or 'mental realism.' Then I shall spell out my reasons for judging that philosophical cognitivism is, no more than mental realism, an effective attempt to obviate the problem of the stagnant situation of philosophy. Indeed, in my estimation, cognitivism should be considered a confirmation of the failure.

But as I shall also underline, to cognitivism must nevertheless be granted that it has rightly objected to the dualism that, unnecessarily and unwisely, has long been allowed to contaminate mental realism. The reality of the conscious mind may be upheld, I think, within the strict limits of monism. But 'monism' is not to be confused with 'reductionism.' And the distinction between mental and nonmental functions is not to be erased by the empirically gratuitous postulation of the concept that is the theoretical basis of cognitivism: the 'multiple realizability of mind.'

c) Hume's challenge: its nature and magnitude

From the foregoing discussion we may conclude not only that to entrust the future of philosophy to mere perseverance, with the simple passage of time in aid, is to take improvident position from which to try to overcome the defeat of modern philosophy's efforts to understand the conscious mind. Projecting onto the nature of the mind our deficient exercise of our mental abilities is not a procedure in which we can reasonably place any confidence. But more conclusive considerations than mere prudence support the view that the current condition of philosophy poses a true and real metaproblem - a philosophical problem about the causes of the chronic failure of philosophy to solve the problem of the mind. Philosophers might well want to devote some attention to such metaproblem before they return to the problem of the mind and its cognition of 'objects'[28] and tackle it in the reasonable expectation of success. What is the evidence that such problem exists? And what is the nature of the problem?

---

28   Throughout this work I assume that 'objects' - that is, the targets, as it were, of cognition - can be either external to the organism or internal to it, such as mental activities, processes, and states.

The fact that even after repeated attempts modern philosophy has been unable to understand the human mind and its consciousness is not the problem. Stagnation is rather, in my suggestion, a consequence and a manifestation of a deeper affliction. The underlying problem is all the more insidious because its reality is usually unrecognized; sometimes it is positively denied. Before philosophy tries to solve the problem, it must advert to it and face it. To bring it to light is the task immediately before us.

The diagnosis of a malady normally begins with a study presenting its symptoms. The earliest indication available to modern philosophy of the ailment whose repercussions remain with us today appeared in 1740 with the publication of David Hume's *Treatise of Human Nature* and its various skeptical conclusions. Such conclusions, I shall argue, spelled the failure of Hume's attempt to understand the nature of the human mind. However, the philosophical community did not make Hume's mistake; both in his time and thereafter to the present, his skepticism has been rejected by practically all but a few modern philosophers. The philosophical community' response to Hume was inadequate, but its infelicity was of a very different sort from that of Hume's thought. Hume deliberately concluded and accepted that philosophical knowledge was an idle dream; the community assumed that it was not, but felt free to ignore Hume's demonstration of the necessary link between representationism and existential skepticism. It was the latter - accepting representationism hoping blindly that its skeptical consequences could be avoided - that resulted in the stagnation of modern philosophy.

The most notorious of Hume's conclusions pounced on the traditionally accepted concepts of 'causality' as the necessitation of effects, and of 'reality' as the non-perceptible substance that underlies the perceptible appearances of things. For present purposes, however, the *Treatise's* most important announcement, because it pronounced the equivalent of a sentence of death upon philosophy, was existential skepticism: philosophy was powerless to establish whether the extramental world actually existed. *A fortiori*, philosophy was also unable to yield reliable knowledge about the nature of anything in the world. However, Hume's work did not begin to cause severe discomfort to many philosophers until years later, especially after 1780, when Immanuel Kant had recognized its importance in his *Critique of Pure Reason*. Thereafter, it has steadily disturbed modern philosophy to some degree at all times, though never enough to have precipitated an acknowledged crisis. Experimental cures that have invariably turned out to be unsuccessful have been tried, of which the best known, most elaborate, and seemingly closest to success was that proposed by Kant. Otherwise, the complaint has always been treated with anodynes.

Symptoms point to underlying pathological conditions. The immediately antecedent condition of modern philosophy prior to the appearance of the overt signs of the disease reported by Hume was philosophy's acceptance of 'representationism.' Hume's existential skepticism was a direct and necessary consequence of his representationism. By this term I mean the supposition (a) that cognition consists in the mind's coming into vicarious mental possession of the inherently knowable 'contents' of reality, which thereby become the 'contents' of cognition; (b) that such possession is achieved, of course, not by bodily absorption of objects, but by means of representations, existing in the mind, of the reality that exists outside the mind; and (c) that such representations are the effect caused by the action of objects on our receptive, passive sense organs and nervous system. To be sure, it is usually granted by proponents of representationism that, once the perceiving mind has been impressed by objects with representations of themselves, the mind becomes active in various ways so as to accept, process, and take advantage of the information it has received. But in the long philosophical tradition, the active role in the causation of perception has always been played by the world and its objects. Now, according to Hume, if one assumes that representationism correctly describes the phenomenon we call perception, one must also accept that philosophy cannot demonstrate the existence of the world or its objects, nor therefore, determine the nature of anything. Representationism implies *universal* and *total* skepticism. Its enormity does *not* depend on its making the mind impervious *to* the characteristics of everything in the world, but in the first place to their *existence*. Thus, the ascription of pathology to representationalism is not a rhetorical exaggeration; if Hume's argument is valid – and no one has yet found fault with his logic – to say that representationalism spells the death of philosophy is a sober truth.

The representationist account of perceptual cognition has been a fixture of modern philosophy from its Cartesian beginnings.[29] Indeed, it antedated Descartes, though it does not go as far back as

---

29   See, e.g., Descartes, *Dioptric,* Fourth, Fifth, and Sixth Discourses; in Norman Kemp Smith, (ed.), *Descartes' Philosophical Writings* (London: Macmillan, 1952), 167 ff., where Descartes rejects the supposition that representations depend for their representative value on resemblance to the represented objects, but otherwise accepts them.

Greek philosophy; it originated in the high middle ages. Modern representationism came into its own, however, only when John Locke made it seem self-evident by proposing, in effect, the conception of consciousness that since then has tended to predominate in empiricist thought. In part, such conception repeated the meaning ordinarily assigned by common sense to the word 'consciousness' when it became part of the English vocabulary earlier in the seventeenth century. As the *Oxford English Dictionary* explains, it was coined at that time to signify 'internal knowledge or conviction; knowledge as to which one has the testimony within oneself.' (How this had come to light and become the common conviction of European culture will be discussed also in the next chapter.) But to the ordinary, popular notion Locke attached a further precision: the mind's awareness of its awareness - its 'consciousness' - was the mind's ability 'to look into itself' and behold the ideas and perceptions that it contains. Namely, ideas and perceptions that represented real objects. (We shall have occasion to verify that this conception of 'consciousness' was questionable.[30]) Locke's interpretation of 'consciousness' implied that we are not immediately and directly conscious of objects, but of the interior world of our awareness of objects; we are aware of the extramental world only immediately, by being aware of our representational ideas about it. With the blessing of Locke, consciousness (as he understood it) and representationism had become joined in philosophical wedlock.

I call attention parenthetically to an aspect of Locke's reasoning that is easily overlooked. Representationism seemed self-evident to Locke, but why? In my estimation, possibly because representationism seemed to him, as it later did to Hume and to many other empirically-minded modern

---

30   In the meantime I merely mention in passing, in case it should be useful, what I think is the source of the confusion. On the one hand, it is an observable fact that the human mind is capable of observing itself; it is capable of 'reflecting.' That is, it can take a prior cognitive act of an object as the target of a *second* cognitive act. Such second, or reflexive, cognitive act reveals the same 'content' as that of the first act, but insofar as it exists within the mind. In other words, reflection reveals our 'ideas' as such. (This is what allows us, for example, to analyse them.) On the other hand, it is a different observable fact that normally all our perceptual experiences -and not only our reflections -reveal to us their 'experiential' character. Then one experiences an object, one does not have to reflect upon one's experience in order to be aware of the fact that one has experienced it. This, not reflexive self-observation, is the distinctive aspect of 'consciousness.' It follows that whereas reflection is conscious, consciousness need not be reflexive. When we reflect, we use our memory and imagination to experience *our prior experience* of an object; this is why we can *imagine* the object as if it existed in our mind in the form of a representation of the object. When we have an ordinary (i.e., non-reflexive) conscious experience, however, we experience an object as *other than* our experience of it, and thus as existing in itself and independently of our experience of it. Avoidance of the confusion of reflection with consciousness is essential to understanding the nature of the conscious mind. The confusion was first remarked upon, so far as I know, by Jean-Paul Sartre, as will be discussed in chapter III.

philosophers to the present, to be the conception of cognition that is revealed by conscious experience and its ability to 'look into itself,' its 'introspection.' If, as just noted, we are immediately and directly *conscious of our awareness* of objects, it seems to follow that, as our own experience teaches us, we are aware of the interior world of our ideas directly; it follows, supposedly, that we are aware of external objects only indirectly. This reasoning, however, does not seem quite correct to me. What makes it appear plausible, if not indeed unavoidable, is the previously mentioned 'confusion of consciousness' and the self-observability of the conscious mind when it 'reflects' upon itself. The confusion results in treating 'consciousness'·and the mind's 'self-observation' as synonyms. Which they are not.

But be that as it may, what is immediately relevant to our present subject is rather that in the mid-eighteenth century David Hume became aware of an implication of the representationist conception of cognition that is fairly easily noticeable once attention is drawn to it, but which, somehow, no modern philosopher had stumbled upon, or even suspected, before Hume did. (George Berkeley had come close, though not close enough.) As already noted, what Hume realized was that, if we gain all our knowledge of extramental reality through the mediation of mental representations existing in the mind, it follows that nothing can ever be known by the mind except itself and its ideas, impressions, or perceptions. Why? Because all we can ever know directly is the representations of objects. Since we do not know the world and its objects themselves, it is only a guess that the representation actually represents the object. But the guess cannot possibly be verified. Therefore, far from explaining how we gain acquaintance with the world, representationism implies that human beings cannot know whether the extramental world exists. Philosophers may conjecture, and they may believe, that it exists, but they cannot *know*. *A fortiori*, they cannot know what the real world is like in reality. Thus, according to Hume:

> [A] blind and powerful instinct of nature [leads us to] suppose the very images, presented by the senses, to be the external objects, and never entertain any suspicion that the one are nothing but representations of the other... But this universal and primary opinion of all men is soon destroyed by the slightest philosophy, which teaches us, that nothing can

ever be present to the mind but an image or perception, and that the senses are only the inlets, through which these images are conveyed, without being able to produce any immediate intercourse between the mind and the object.'[31]

Moreover, representationism does not merely imply the impotence of philosophy to establish the existence and the nature of the world; it also renders reasonable the supposition of solipsism. And indeed, solipsism in respect of one's mind; for even the existence of one's own body is mediated by representative sense perceptions. We cannot claim to have knowledge of the extramental world even to the small extent of being certain of the existence of our own bodies:

> [It may seem] that no other faculty is required, beside the senses, to convince us of the external existence of body. But to prevent this inference, we need only... [consider that] properly speaking, it is not our body we perceive, when we regard our limbs and members, but certain impressions, which enter by the senses; so that the ascribing a real and corporeal existence to these impressions, or to their objects, is an act of the mind as difficult to explain, as [the existence of external bodies]'[32]

If we analyse critically Hume's reasoning, we may verify that it mixes truth and falsity. His thinking begins with his assuring himself of the truth of a position that he seems to have deemed obvious and from which he never retreated: that the representationist concept of cognition stated correctly the nature of the process of sense perception. The paradox that this supposition involves - namely, that a correct description of our perceptual cognition of the world should imply skepticism, so that it is an account of our perception of the world according to which we cannot perceive the world - seems never to have quite struck him with sufficient force. The concept may even have seemed to him to be empirically derived. For as Locke had taught, our ability to describe cognition

---

31   David Hume, *An Enquiry Concerning Human Understanding*, XII, 1.

32   Hume, *A Treatise of Human Nature*, I, iv, 2.

depended on our consciousness (as Locke understood it) – that is, on our ability to reflect upon our awareness of objects,[33] and thus on our ability to become aware of our awareness of objects. And so, we look inwards and we behold our ideas and perceptions of objects. At first glance, we may take them for ideas and perceptions of objects. But if any doubt should arise, a further consideration is equally clear: when we know objects, the objects themselves do not come physically into our minds; the object I see does not take up abode within my eyes and brain. Thus, my ideas and my perceptions exist only in my mind, and are representations of the external reality which we suppose to exist in the world, but whose existence is forever beyond our grasp.

Hume was aware, of course, that such description was at variance with the 'universal and primary opinion of all men' that they beheld extramental objects themselves. The representationist description of cognition was not readily apparent to anyone, who should have been innocent of all philosophy; but in Hume's estimation, it would seem irrefutable to anyone who might have been willing to reason it out. It was obvious, invulnerable, and empirically grounded. Thus, the contradiction of philosophy by common sense seemed to Hume to cast no valid doubt upon representationism; the objections of common sense should be discarded. After all, philosophy was, by definition, rationally cultivated knowledge, and was to be contrasted, as it had been since at least the time of Parmenides, with the imaginative, undisciplined conclusions of the blind but powerful 'instinct of nature ' to which we now more often refer as our culture's 'common sense.'

Nevertheless, Hume was in a quandary. It was brought about by the theretofore unnoticed but now unwelcome implication of representationism that human cognition was radically incapable of producing 'any immediate intercourse between the mind and the object.' We have seen why. If it is true that we know extramental objects by means of mental representations, then all we can rightly claim to know are the mental representations of objects. Of course, common sense could suppose nonetheless that the world existed; if so, it would not be the first time that common sense had held fast to opinions whose lack of rationality philosophy had revealed. But philosophical, reliable knowledge of the existence of the world (and, *a fortiori,* of its nature) was impossible. This conclusion might

---

33   I remind us again that consciousness should not be identified with reflexive awareness of one's awareness, or of oneself, or of other objects.

be most unpalatable, but there was no reasonable way to avoid it. Existential skepticism must be accepted. Quandary resolved.

Well, more or less. For despite the seeming rationality of this conclusion, Hume long remained reluctant fully to credit, without more, his existential skepticism. But the nature of his reluctance should be noted. He had no doubt, it must be stressed, that representationism correctly described cognition. Throughout the section of the *Treatise* where he expounded his skeptical conclusions, he repeatedly asserted that:

> [T]he only existences, of which we are certain, are perceptions, which being immediately present to us by consciousness, command our strongest assent, and are the first foundation of all our conclusions... Whoever would explain the origin of the common opinion concerning the continued and distinct existence of body... must proceed upon the supposition, that our perceptions are our only objects.[34]

What puzzled him nevertheless was the harrowing, diametric opposition between the testimony of philosophy and the insistent, clamorous protestations of common sense. He thought, on the one hand, that he had no choice but to advert to the philosophically observable fact (as he took it to be) that the human mind did not actually perceive existing objects, but only its ideas and perceptions of objects. But he also knew, and pointed out, on the other, that 'whatever may be the reader's opinion at this present moment... an hour hence he will be persuaded that there is both an external and internal world.'[35]

Well, to Hume the objections of common sense were, as such, no insuperable obstacle to the acceptance of representationism. But the *obviousness* of the common sense conviction was enough to give him pause. He seems to have felt, therefore, that in order to defend the rationality of his skeptical conclusion he had to explain the 'manner, in which these two systems, though directly contrary, are

---

34   Hume, *Treatise*, I, iv, 2.

35   Hume, *Treatise*, I, iv, 2.

connected together.'[36] Most of his discussion 'Of skepticism with regard to the senses' (the second Section of the fourth Part of the first Book of the *Treatise*) is devoted to explaining how contradiction arises between the irrefragable 'instinct of nature' (which he deemed erroneous) and the logic that generates the representationist concept of cognition (which he held to be true). His explanation of the conflict was much lengthier, more detailed, and more complicated than our consideration of it must needs be; only part of it is relevant to present purposes. Nor need we be detained, therefore, by whether his explanation is correct, or plausible - though actually it is an ingenious but fanciful and questionable construction. However, we may not ignore it altogether, because it touches, albeit incidentally, upon a question that does concern us intimately, namely, the fundamental reason why representationism should be deemed wide off the mark. Thus, from the viewpoint of our investigation of the causes of the stagnation of modern philosophy, the passage in question may be among the most important single contributions of Hume, since it helps us understand quite precisely the specific reason why representationism necessarily implies existential skepticism. Hume's explanation of the unwelcome mutual contradiction between philosophy and common sense was that, on the one hand, our imagination has the 'propension to bestow an identity on our resembling perceptions, [which] produces the fiction of a continued existence'[37] - while reason, on the other, tells us that 'our perceptions have no more a continued than an independent existence.'[38] But the mutual contradiction between the 'systems' constructed respectively by common sense and philosophy generates mental discomfort, and therefore:

> In order to set ourselves at ease in this particular, we contrive a new hypothesis which seems to comprehend both principles of reason and imagination. This hypothesis is the philosophical one of the double existence of perceptions and objects; which pleases our reason, in allowing, that our dependent perceptions are interrupted and different; and at the same time is agreeable

---

36   Hume, *Treatise*, I, iv, 2.

37   The 'continued existence' of objects after we perceive them is not necessarily a 'fiction.' If we perceive objects again, after having ceasing to perceive them, we can *deduce* that they existed while we were not perceiving them; and if the deduction is made validly, their 'continued existence' may not be said to have been fictional, but real.

38   Hume, *Treatise*, I, iv, 2.

to the imagination, in attributing a continu' d existence to something else, which we call *objects.* This philosophical system, therefore, is the monstrous offspring of two principles, which are contrary to each other, which are both at once embrac' d by the mind, and which are unable mutually to destroy each other.[39]

Thus, according to Hume, considerations that in isolation from each other seem normal and innocent enough, when taken together add up to a misbegotten and misshapen 'monster ' - namely, the philosophical supposition of the 'double existence of perceptions and objects.' Such 'double existence' is the essential basis of representationism: it means that whereas objects exist in reality, and only in reality, representative ideas exist in the mind, and only in the mind. Now, when we study in the next chapter the original doctrine of the 'double existence of perceptions and objects,' we shall verify that, in point of historical fact, when representationism first appeared in the history of philosophy - namely, in the fourteenth century - this supposition emerged for entirely different reasons from those advanced by Hume. It had nothing to do with the morganatic coupling of patrician reason and plebeian imagination; it followed rather, as we shall see, from the teaching of Thomas Aquinas regarding the nature of the reality of the world and its objects. Nevertheless, quite correctly, and with astonishing depth of insight, Hume put his finger on the very nub of the reason why representationism must necessarily produce existential skepticism when its implications are pursued: this is the aspect of his doctrine that interests us.

The reason is that the 'double existence of perceptions and objects' is, in part, the doctrine that both perceptions and objects may be said to exist *independently* of each other. As all of us, philosopher and layman alike, have understood the term throughout modern times and earlier, 'to exist' is the same as to exist by *one's own existence.* Hume understood it in the same sense. Perceptions do not, of course, have substantive existence apart from the perceiving organism; they are mental events,

---

39   Hume, *Treatise*, I, iv, 2. In other words, according to Hume, our imagination compels us to suppose that objects continue to exist uninterruptedly when they are not perceived by us, although we have no way of knowing whether this is so; from reason and observation comes the fact that our perceptions are interrupted and discontinuous. Actually, nothing compels us so to suppose, although it is true, as already noted, that our perceiving again an object that had previously disappeared may lead to our deducing that it had continued to exist in reality during its disappearance.

activities, and states of the organism, and exist by the existence of the organism. But the existence of perceptions in the mind of the organism is distinct from the existence of the object in reality. Each has its own existence: the existence of one is not the existence of the other. Well, the *separate* existence of perceptions and objects is what isolates objects from their representations into two *mutually exclusive* realms, namely, the existing mind and the existing external world of objects. To make the point crystal clear, Hume might have referred, more precisely, to the '*double independent* existence of perceptions and objects;' but even without the adjective, the point is clear enough. Nothing exists by the existence of another, but only *by its own*. This is how both philosophers and common sense have interpreted the reality of the world and its objects since the fourteenth century. Thus, the perceptions existing in our minds are one thing, whereas the objects existing in reality are another. The existence of each is what makes both independent of each other. Therefore, there can be 'no intercourse' between the mind and reality.

There is good reason, therefore, to speak of the 'double existence of perceptions and objects' as one would of a villain. It may be aptly described as a monster - though not precisely in Hume's sense, whose metaphor alludes to the congenitally malformed 'new hypothesis' sired by philosophy on common sense, but in the looser acceptation of the term, which is popularly applied to any ugly and frightening imaginary creature. For the supposition of the 'double existence' contains a necessary implication - existential skepticism - that is repugnant even to those who (like Hume) deem it true, and which poses a mortal danger to philosophy.

We may put it in different terms, but the outcome is the same. Objects exist in the world and only in the world; they are not transported bodily to the mind when they are known. Therefore, according to representationism what exists in the mind is not the real bodily object, but a representation of it. But since the representation exists in the perceiving organism, whose existence is independent of the existence of the external reality, there is no way for the perceiver to tell whether the representation does in fact represent the external reality or even whether it was caused by it. The representation may well have been caused by the mind itself, or by an agency other than the object – for instance, by Descartes's hypothetical *malin génie*.

And so:

By what argument can it be proved, that the perceptions of the mind must be caused by external objects, entirely different from them, though resembling them (if that be possible) and could not arise either from the energy of the mind itself, or from the suggestion of some invisible and unknown spirit, or from some other cause still more unknown to us?[40]

By his own witness, therefore, it was only after much anguish that Hume accepted the skepticism that necessarily accompanied representationism, thereby putting at stake the viability of philosophy in its entirety; this is the magnitude of the issue he brought before the philosophical community. To be sure, his skepticism was 'mitigated,' in the sense that he allowed that demonstrative mathematical knowledge was possible; for, Pythagoreans to the contrary, Hume was right when he thought that mathematical knowledge does not concern any extramentally existing reality. But regarding every 'matter of fact and existence'[41] to be philosophically studied, his skepticism was absolute.

The problem for the philosophical community was how to react to Hume. But before we consider the consensus that emerged in reply to the troubling dilemma, we should briefly evaluate Hume's work.

Hume was mistaken in some respects, I suggest, but right in others, and it is important that we do not confuse the two. Hume was right when he reasoned that the representationist conception of cognition, which had always been assumed in modern times since Descartes, necessarily implied existential skepticism. His original discovery of this implication challenged philosophers, therefore, to respond to his argument that, if philosophy accepted the representationist conception of cognition, philosophy was logically required to declare itself an invalid, pointless, vacuous, illusion. Was this true, or was it false? And if it was not true, what was amiss with Hume's reasoning? Hume was also right when he said that the reason why representationism so implied was 'the double existence of perceptions and objects.' Existential skepticism is the direct consequence of the representationist

40   Hume, *Enquiry*, XII, 1.

41   Hume, *Enquiry*, XII, 3.

supposition that both perceptions and objects exist, each by its own distinct and separate existence and in its own separate domain, i.e. one in the mind, the other in reality.

Now Hume 's skeptical conclusion may have been incorrect. But even if one acknowledges that it was, one must recognize that Hume was undoubtedly correct when he proposed that existential skepticism *followed necessarily* from the assumption that perceptual cognition takes place by means of representations of reality existing in the mind. In other words, Hume's inference was, beyond all reasonable doubt, *formally valid*, and therefore unassailable from the viewpoint of logic. However, formal logical validity provides, of itself, no evidence of the *truth* of an inference; such truth also demands materially true premises - specifically, in this case, the supposition that perception takes place through the mediation of representations. Unless this is true, Hume's conclusion of existential skepticism could not be said to be true. Well, then, was Hume's representationist concept of perception true or false? For the answer one must turn, of course, to the available evidence. But the available evidence is that representationism is indeed false. Why should we say so?

Existential skepticism is incredible. But it would be methodologically impermissible to reason that representationism must be deemed a false description of cognition because existential skepticism is incredible; surely no philosopher should acknowledge that he or she had rejected a validly drawn inference arbitrarily, or merely because he or she disapproved of the substance of the inference. To reject representationism, one must have a good reason. But if we search carefully, we have, I think, good and conclusive reason. Indeed, we have two.

The first is that representationism involves a self contradiction. For representationism is a conception of *our perception of the world* that necessarily, directly, and immediately implies that *we cannot perceive the world*. It is an absurd concept. Moreover, let us take special note of the fact that no syllogism is needed to draw such inference. An *immediate* inference is enough. It is, more specifically, an immediate *modal* inference: representations are, supposedly, the *necessary* means whereby to perceive objects, whereas representations make the perception of objects *impossible*. The self-contradiction is clear. And Hume actually perceived it, but he still managed to misinterpret it. Which was much to his misfortune: according to his own description of the emotional upheaval he underwent, it brought him close to mental breakdown. But in the end, he was unable to reject the representationism that implied such contradiction. He treated the absurdity, in effect, as if it were an unfathomably mysterious truth. Now, if it is true that representationism is a self-contradictory concept, the adoption of representationism makes it impossible for philosophy to explain the nature of the human mind. The stagnation of philosophy is the unavoidable result.

Neither Hume nor, apparently, many later philosophers, appear to have appreciated the significance of the logical means - immediate inference rather than syllogistic reasoning - whereby the absurdity of representationism is demonstrated. It is most important. For a valid syllogistic conclusion is, in principle, always open to contradiction by the conclusion of another syllogism; one can always hope, perhaps even reasonably, that an unwelcome conclusion arrived at in this manner may in the future be refuted by additional reasoning in the light of new observations or discoveries. But this is not true of a *concept* that has been found to harbour self-contradiction. If an immediate inference is self-contradictory, it is forever irredeemable. And so, unless one were willing to entertain the possibility that perhaps one day it will be discovered that there is no contradiction between 'knowing' and 'not-knowing,' – or between 'we can perceive the real world' and 'we cannot perceive the real world' – it would be self-deceptive to hope that Hume's argument might in the future be found to be in error. It is a small wonder that in two and a half centuries it has never been so found.

For the second and equally fundamental reason why representationism must be decisively rejected we must turn to the empirical evidence. Again, it will be discussed in greater detail later, when we attempt to determine how the nature of cognition might be more adequately conceived than representationism supposes. At this point, I merely sum up the empirical evidence that contradicts it: namely, that the 'double existence of perceptions and objects' is a delusion born of simple confusion. Far from having been generated by the mating of reason and the imagination, it embodies a muddling of the two. Objects exist in reality, and the only location in which they exist and are perceived is the real and objectively existing world. No one has ever *perceived* an object, or a representation of an object, existing in the mind. What one can easily do is to *imagine* any reality one has previously perceived, and call one's imaginative reproduction of it a 'representation' of reality. The point is that perception does not consist in possessing objects mentally; they do not exist in the mind at all, in any way, at any time. What can exist in the mind is our imaginative retrospections of our perceptions.

But of course, we should not ascribe to *perception* what we *imagine*. To suppose that when we *imagine* it, the object has 'come into the mind 'in a fancied 'incorporeal,' 'intentional,' or 'subjective' mode of existence, and now 'exists in the mind,' would be a delusion. It would be at best a tangled thought. If it were truly believed in, it would amount to a hallucination.

But the delusion is beguiling and the befuddlement is seductive; we shall have to investigate how the confusion originates and why it takes possession of philosophers furtively, before they realize that they have stumbled onto a well camouflaged pitfall. But even now, those who are open to the possibility that in accepting representationism they might have missed their footing, are invited to perform a simple experiment that – if they are open to conviction – may settle the issue. They might look at an external object and then ask themselves: where is the object I am perceiving at this moment? Let us not stop to consider what the object is; let us attend only to *where* it is. Well, if one does not confuse one's *perception* with one's *imagination*, one will verify that (a) one *perceives* the object as existing 'out there,' and (b) one *does not perceive* a duplicate of the object existing anywhere, and least of all within one's mind. Now, one may well *imagine* that a perceived object has come to exist in one's mind; but one's ability to *imagine* should not be confused with one's ability to *perceive*.

Of course, once we reach this conclusion, the question arises: what is the nature of perceptual cognition, if it does not consist in our beholding a mental representation of reality? But by recognizing that it does not involve mental representation, we have voided the implication of existential skepticism and have thereby laid open the possibility of reaching a more adequate conception of the nature of sense perception. In the meantime, if one is unable to determine the answer and finds it necessary to admit to oneself that one does not know what perception consists in, or how it is achieved, one *might* console oneself with the thought that no loaf is better than a poisoned loaf. There is no shame in admitting ignorance, but there can be little valid pride in making philosophy depend on the hope, against all reasonable hope, that evidence will one day be discovered to justify representationism while avoiding existential skepticism.

No interpretation of anything, like every objection to it, can ever seem valid except to someone who is open to the possibility that it might be so. Hume's commitment to representationism – like that of many others today – seems to have been unconditional enough to preclude his having ever considered, however speculatively, the supposition that representationism might not describe correctly our perception of objects. Whence came his inability to question it? Perhaps he was influenced by the greater reliance that the philosophical tradition since Greek times had placed on logic than on observation. To the present, philosophy undergraduates are usually required to study logic, but receive little if any training on philosophical observation and analysis; the assumption seems to be that these skills come naturally to everyone. Hume may well have been more deeply impressed by the formal logic of his skeptical conclusion than by the material absurdity of the representationist concept of cognition from which skepticism necessarily followed. If so, he failed to recognize that reason is more than formal logic, and that formal logic should, no more than the bubble reputation, be pursued even onto the cannon's mouth.

Regardless of whether faith in logic played a role in Hume's philosophy, if he had not professed a blind, heedless faith in representationism, he might have been open to the thought that perhaps an alternative to representationism should be given consideration. For as W. T. Jones, a historian of philosophy, has said:

> [W]hen one gets oneself in the kind of jam into which Hume was led by following out the Lockean premises [and] one remains confident in the power of reason as an instrument, one concludes that something is wrong with the premises from which one started, however plausible they may at first sight have seemed to be.[42]

But Hume did not pause to consider rejecting representationism. If he - and if not he, those who came after him - had perceived that such rejection was imperative, he might have then tried to replace representationism with a self consistent, empirically based, but more thoroughly worked out, concept of cognition. In fairness to Hume, however, it must be said that the times were not ripe for any such undertaking; for nothing anyone had actually observed suggested it. Besides, even if Hume had suspected that the trouble lay in the material falsity of his represent-ationist premises, it would have been difficult for him to search for reasonable, empirically sup-ported alternatives to it. For he

---

42   W.T. Jones, *A History of Western Philosophy* (New York: Harcourt, Brace, 1952), 802.

would have required that he do two things, neither of which was in practice feasible at the time; they were the very things we should do today to the same end.

First, instead of assuming that representationism was an obvious, natural, and unavoidable human 'intuition' and that therefore it had always been presupposed by all philosophers, Hume would have had to go back in history and investigate when and how the representationist conception of cognition originated; if so, he would have found that before the appearance of representationism in the late middle ages, different presuppositions had prevailed. Given the circumstances of the day, however, it is unrealistic to imagine that Hume could have discovered this; the resources regarding the history of philosophy available to philosophers today were severely limited before the explosion of historical scholarship of the nineteenth and twentieth centuries. But if it should have happened, it could have led to the discovery of yet earlier but grievous infelicities - such as supposing that perception is passive and receptive of objects—which in conjunction with the idea that everything in the world had its own existence eventually produced representationism.

Second, Hume would have then been required to observe closely the human cognitive functions in order to verify whether cognition might not be properly and fully described without resorting to the supposition that it involved the representation of objects. But this, too, would have been unlikely: in the mid - eighteenth century philosophy depended on Locke's oversimple idea of consciousness according to which our observation of our mental processes revealed only our awareness of our awareness of objects. It was assumed that conscious experience did not reveal our awareness of objects. Besides, in the days before scholars had become accustomed to entertaining daring new ideas - Darwin, Freud, and Einstein immediately come to mind - it might have been much too daunting to recognize the *mental activity* revealed by experience when it is conscious. As we shall see, the supposition of the Greek philosophers that the human mind's role in perception was essentially passive and receptive had been one of the earliest points at which philosophy of mind had first gone astray.

But speculation is idle. The fact is that, in any event and for whatever reason, neither Hume nor his successors found it possible to pursue the alternative that W.T. Jones suggested. And so, by his own admission, Hume's 'desponding reflections' plunged him, 'affrighted and confounded with forlorn solitude,' into the 'melancholy and delirium' precipitated by the contradiction between common sense and philosophy:

> How then shall we adjust those principles together? Which of them shall we prefer? Or in case we prefer neither of them, but successively assent to both, as is usual among philosophers, with what confidence can we afterwards usurp that glorious title, when we thus knowingly embrace a manifest contradiction?'[43]

Hume's explanation of how the 'monstrous offspring' had been conceived helped him make sense of the contradiction; thereafter, practicality won the remainder of the resolve he needed in order 'to live, and talk, and act like other people in the common affairs of life.'[44] And so, with but traces of misgiving at renouncing his 'former disposition,' Hume stood' ready to throw all [his] books and papers into the fire.'[45] The same sentiment was repeated by the very last words of his later *Enquiry*: that philosophy should be committed 'to the flames: for it can contain nothing but sophistry and illusion.'[46]

Nor did Hume inspire many later philosophers to search for alternative concepts of cognition; significantly, the one who searched the hardest, Immanuel Kant, did not manage, for all his titanic efforts, to cope with the problem of how to dispense with *Vorstellungen.* But if modern philosophers were not inspired to respond to Hume's challenge by searching for alternatives to representationism, what was instead their response?

d) The response of modern philosophy to Hume

Hume succumbed to existential skepticism, but few modern philosophers did, either at the time or since; if they have been injudicious, it has been in other respects. For the near-universal reaction of modern philosophers to Hume's thought, until Kant took it seriously enough to propose an alternative

---

43   Hume, *Treatise,* I, iv, 7.

44   Hume, *Treatise*, I, iv, 7.

45   Hume, *Treatise*, I, iv, 7.

46   Hume, *Enquiry*, XII, iii.

but unworkable interpretation of cognition, can be characterized as an effort to ignore Hume and his gloomy contribution. The philosophical community decisively rejected existential skepticism and the impossibility of philosophical knowledge, but it reaffirmed representationism – quite as if Hume had never demonstrated that the latter necessarily implied such skepticism.

Exceptionally few modern philosophers, either in Hume's time or since, have agreed with Hume that knowledge of the existence of the world, and *a fortiori* of its properties, is impossible. At the same time, however, the negative but most valuable contribution of Hume — namely, establishing that representationism necessarily issued in existential skepticism (which, if taken advantage of would have prevented the decline and stagnation of modern philosophy) — has been consistently disregarded. Setting Hume's demonstration aside is what has allowed modern philosophers to couple the rejection of existential skepticism with their continued acceptance of representationism; it has enabled them to retain representationism without accepting the existential skepticism it logically entails. Representationism has been widely treated, therefore, as if Hume had never demonstrated that it necessarily implied such skepticism. And yet so far as I know, no one has found fault with Hume's demonstration of such a necessary link, or offered reasonable justification for by-passing it. I need hardly point out that setting evidence aside arbitrarily is not an acceptable philosophical procedure.

And so, instead of recognizing that Hume was right when he proposed that skepticism necessarily follows from representationism, but wrong when he supposed that representationism was untouchable, all but a few philosophers have opted instead for the opposite: to follow Hume where he was wrong (namely, in accepting representationism), while hoping that he was wrong where he actually was right (that is, in concluding that skepticism necessarily follows from representationism). The respective positions of both Hume and of most modern philosophers, however, share a common element: neither Hume nor most modern philosophers have found it possible to purge their representationist assumptions from their minds. In essence, therefore, the problem that contemporary philosophy must solve before it can reasonably expect to make progress in the study of the human mind is how to conquer its addiction to representationism and begin to develop a viable, self-consistent, and empirically well grounded idea of perception.

The reaction of philosophers to the work of Hume is puzzling; one tries to explain it to oneself as best one can. Part of the reason why skepticism was unhesitatingly rejected without consideration being given to the implications of representationism may well have been that, as Hume himself had noted, the existential reality of the real world is irrepressible. It is not true, however, that our awareness of the existence of the world comes to human beings, as Hume said, from 'a blind and powerful instinct of nature;' the existence of the world is learned, as I hope to demonstrate below, in the same way in which we learn many other things about the world, i.e., through experience. But it is true that denial of the existence of the world does not carry much conviction with anyone: a philosopher, Hume said, might at this moment accept representationism and conclude that existential skepticism is unavoidable, yet 'an hour hence he will be persuaded' that the external world actually exists. But although irrepressibility would not have been a sound and sufficient reason on which to stake modern philosophy's rejection of skepticism, irrepressibility may well have been an effective factor in the decision of those philosophers who refused to follow Hume. If so, one may further speculate that, once the imminent threat of existential skepticism had been put out of sight (and therefore out of mind), it would not have been strange if philosophers had slipped into supposing that the danger posed by representationism had receded. But if so, it would have been easy then, in the absence of an urgent reason to reject representationism, to fall back on the hope that one day in the future Hume's finding of a necessary link between representationism and skepticism should be proven to have been a false alarm.

One might also remember, however, that the philosophical community is a human society, and that the behaviour of human groups is not reducible to the simple resultant of individual decisions. Perhaps part of the explanation of why modern philosophy took the post-Humean turn it did may have less to do with logic than with sociology. Spontaneous mass reactions to startling and unwelcome events (as would have been Hume's invoking the spectre of existential skepticism) are not always guided by thoughtful reflection; getting rid of unpleasantness at any cost is always a tempting course for most of us. And it is an elementary fact of human life that whatever 'everyone' thinks does not need to be justified by anyone. The safety afforded by numbers may be spurious, but the satisfaction that spurious safety affords is real just the same.

Of course, one could only guess whether considerations of this sort were what in fact persuaded the generality of philosophers to accept representationism while ignoring Hume's clear warning of its skeptical consequences. What is beyond reasonable doubt is that whereas representationism had been quietly taken for granted by modern philosophers since Descartes, after Hume it was consciously and deliberately affirmed by just about everyone. Only isolated dissenters have refused to accept it, claiming instead that objects are perceived 'directly;' the views of the principal objectors will be considered below. Their work, however, has not prospered, possibly for two reasons. First, they have not provided a credible alternative to representationism that would explain how perception takes place 'directly;' they assert that it does so, which is indeed true, but which does not suggest how we should understand the mechanism of perception. And second, they have not explained why to so many philosophers the idea that perception is mediated by representations has long seemed to be 'obvious' although it is false. How could so many have been lulled into accepting representationism? But there is, I think, an explanation: in the light of certain incorrect though plausible presuppositions representationism can take on the deceptive appearance of self-evidence. To understand how easily one can be deceived into representationism one must understand the process through which, in point of historical fact, representationism was created.

What should we think of this turn of affairs? I assume, for reasons I have explained, that there is ample and conclusive reason for declaring representationism an unredeemable mistake. From one viewpoint, therefore, we may judge that accepting representationism while ignoring its skeptical implication may be described as the failure of modern philosophers to seize the opportunity to correct the course on which philosophy had been set by Descartes; for it was he, of course, who, unaware of how representationism had originated, supposing instead that it was a universal, true, and timeless intuition of the mind, and unaware of the disaster that it had loosened upon medieval scholasticism, introduced representationism into modern philosophy, as one of its unquestionable, obvious assumptions.[47] But this meant, in effect, that modern philosophy, without adverting to the fact that it had done so, had put itself into the untenable position of having to explain the nature of the conscious

---

47   W. T. Jones. *A History of Western Philosophy* (New York: Harcourt, Brace, 1952), 802.

mind and its perception of the world on the basis of a presupposition that made success impossible: representationism was both self-contradictory and contrary to the empirical evidence.

From a longer-range perspective, however, it could be wryly argued that the reaction of the philosophical community was less inadequate than Hume's. For the acceptance of representationism crippled philosophy, but the rejection of existential skepticism allowed philosophy to survive. Self-immolation, if philosophers generally had accepted Hume's skepticism, would have been permanent, whereas mere stagnation left open the possibility of a more adequate understanding of the nature of perception in the future.

Part of the reason why skepticism was rejected, it seems, was that, as Hume himself had admitted, the reality of the real world is irrepressible: a philosopher might conclude that existential skepticism was unavoidable, but 'an hour hence he will be persuaded' that the external world actually exists. I am not saying that this was, by itself, among the sound philosophical reasons to reject skepticism, but that it was probably an important factor. For unlike representationism, Hume's great and original contribution -namely, the necessary link between skepticism and representationism -could not be made to disappear, but it could be ignored. In the result, the representationism that thereto had been quietly taken for granted by modern philosophers since Descartes now became consciously and deliberately affirmed by most of the philosophical community. In later times to the present, consuetude has made it unnecessary for modern philosophers to justify their simultaneous acceptance of representationism and their rejection of existential skepticism.

This was, of course, from one viewpoint, a worse position than simply having failed to seize the opportunity that Hume had cracked open -- namely, the occasion to correct the course on which philosophy had been set by Descartes. Without adverting to the fact that it had done so, modern philosophy had managed to put itself into the untenable position of having to explain the nature of the conscious mind on the basis of a presupposition - representationism - that made success impossible. From another viewpoint, however, the reaction of the philosophical community was much preferable to Hume's: it hobbled philosophy, but allowed it to survive until another day, keeping thus open the possibility of a more adequate future response.

We have dealt with Hume 's problem as he himself faced it: it was how to resolve the contradiction between the realism suggested by common sense, and philosophy's representationism. Which he dealt with, even if not to his unmixed satisfaction, by dismissing common sense and accepting that representationism entailed existential skepticism. Indeed, he seems to have been convinced that his skepticism was a most important truth that he had contributed to philosophy. As indeed it was, though not in the sense he took it, but insofar as it contained the implication that philosophy should seek an alternative to representationism. However, as it has been framed after Hume to the present by many later philosophers who have read Hume – and who has not? – the problem is different. In some ways, it is the opposite. Their problem is how to accept representationism while rejecting the existential skepticism and solipsism that representationism logically entails. Sometimes the problem is treated as if it were more like a mildly annoying loose end that, one hopes, will someday be neatly tied up; meanwhile, its solution can be postponed indefinitely. For example, according to Daniel Dennett, a cognitivist:

> [A]n argument that has bedeviled philosophers and psychologists for over two hundred years... [begins with the premise that] the only psychology that could possibly succeed... must posit internal representations. This premise has been deemed obvious by just about everyone... [and] is quite invulnerable, or at any rate it has an impressive mandate... [S]ome philosophers and psychologists who have appealed *to* internal representations over the years have believed in their hearts that somehow Hume's problem could be solved.[48]

---

48   Dennett, *Brainstorms,* 119, 122. (Italics in the original.) More fully quoted, the last sentence continued as follows: 'but I am sure no one had the slightest idea *how to do this,* until AI ... came along'. Apart from the question whether AI's idea of how to solve 'Hume's problem' is viable, Dennett' s satisfaction with AI's 'solution' depends on his reducing 'Hume's problem' to skepticism regarding the existence of an 'inner self' that should perform the function of understanding and manipulating the mental representations existing in the mind. This was indeed one component of Hume's existential skepticism, but hardly all of it. For Hume cast doubt not merely on the capability of philosophy to demonstrate the existence of the self but, more fundamentally, to demonstrate the existence of an objectively real world. I am unaware of any philosopher since Hume's day to the present who has successfully explained how Hume's skepticism regarding the existence of the external world can be removed once representationism is premised.

Dennett's statement is correct on all counts (though to be precise, it was not so much 'Hume's problem' as it was the problem of modern philosophers.) But it is true that representationism has been accepted by 'just about everyone' in the modern philosophical community for more than two centuries. And most frequently it has been adopted without any attempt having been made by philosophers or psychologists to explain why they deem themselves free to 'posit internal representations' while rejecting existential skepticism. They justify their setting Hume aside, if at all, by their simply believing 'in their hearts' that 'somehow' the skeptical consequences of representationism shall one day be avoided.

A very few philosophers have followed Hume in affirming both representationism and skepticism, with or without additional qualifications of their own.[49] But even fewer appear to have considered the possibility that Hume was right when he proposed that skepticism necessarily follows from representationism, but wrong when he supposed that representationism was untouchable. 'Just about everyone' has opted instead for the opposite: they have chosen to follow Hume where he was wrong (namely, in accepting representationism), while hoping that he was wrong where he actually was right (that is, in concluding that skepticism necessarily follows from representationism.) The respective positions of both Hume and of modern philosophers, however, share a common element: neither Hume nor modern philosophers have found it possible to purge their representationist assumptions from their minds.

This turn of events is not easily explained. Of course, to anyone who rejects representationism and faces the prospect of searching *ab initio* for a believable, cogent, empirically grounded, viable conception of perception, the task must appear daunting. But cognitivist and other philosophers have had the audacity to explore the most daring hypotheses. Why not in this case? One might also remember, however, that the philosophical community is a society, and that human group behaviour is not reducible to the simple resultant of individual decisions. Perhaps part of the explanation of modern philosophy's having taken the post-Humean turn it did, has less to do with logic than with sociology. But there is no need to enter into further speculation along such lines, because in any event the principal factor was of a different order: it was a sort of collective 'amnesia,' as it were. Or more

---

49   See, for example, Richard Rorty, *Philosophy and the Mirror of Nature* (Princeton, N.J.: Princeton University Press, 1979).

exactly, collective lack of awareness of certain facts in the absence of which other observations were unavoidably misunderstood. Modern philosophy was launched by Descartes's conviction that existential skepticism could be conquered, but neither he nor those who responded to his call to revive the discipline had any idea of how existential skepticism had come to be generally accepted at the end of the middle ages in the first place. He, and they, repeated earlier mistakes out of plain unawareness of how they had been generated. Nor did they remember – or, rather, they had never learned – how perception had been understood before the advent of representationism. In short, Hume's work challenged philosophy to remember its history and to renew itself in its light. But Hume's gauntlet was not picked up, and modern philosophy committed itself instead to representationism, while ignoring its necessary implication of existential skepticism. There it has remained since, and there it will remain, as one must suppose, as long as it continues to ignore the challenge of Hume.

It need not be so. To vindicate philosophy and help it regain its bearings we might begin by remembering that philosophy is a tradition, and that it depends in large part on much that philosophers have accepted from earlier generations. A critical analysis of the historical record-undertaken for philosophical rather than merely antiquarian historical purposes-should enable us to determine the events that brought modern philosophy to the condition in which it has existed for the last two centuries and a half. But if we understood the causes of stagnation, perhaps we could find it possible to avoid them. And if so, we can conceive the possibility of rejecting not only existential skepticism, but also, and in the first instance, the conception of perception that necessarily leads to it, and thereupon determine viable alternatives to representationism. Is this a sensible and realistic plan of action? What obstacle stands immediately in its way?

e) The consequences of ignoring Hume's challenge, and how to avoid them

I have characterized the condition of modern philosophy after Hume as stagnation. But absence of progress is not the same as absence of effort; philosophical activity has never flagged throughout modern times, but it has been simply futile. What modern philosophy ails from, to put it more precisely, is *persistent* stagnation, a *chronic* failure that has not been recognized as such. And yet, if one reflects on the various approaches to the study of the mind proposed *seriatim* in the last half-century by cognitivists and other philosophers, one may perceive, as John R. Searle has observed, a cyclical, 'compulsive neurotic... pattern.'[50] The analogy may be harsh but is not inappropriate. For somewhat like the unfortunate lifestrategies that persistently precipitate self-defeating neurotic behaviour in most of us at least upon occasion, the game plan of modern philosophy has often amounted to philosophy's attempting to solve the problems of the mind by recycling its failures. Before we tackle the causes of the stagnation, we should consider briefly the mechanism that tends to make the stagnation difficult to recognize and acknowledge.

The pattern of compulsion traced by the last fifty years of philosophy of mind has been explained by Searle as the logical outcome of a dilemma that inheres in the denial of the distinctive reality of the mind. One horn of the dilemma is the fact that the perception of the reality of consciousness comes naturally, spontaneously, and inevitably to all of us; this is why cognitivists and other anti-realists must grant that the conscious mind seems, though in fact it is not, real. The other is the assumption that philosophy is obliged to deny the reality of the mind (mostly for fear that otherwise dualism would be countenanced). But this antithesis creates, as Searle remarks:

> [A] recurring tension between the urge to give an account of reality that leaves out any reference to the special features of the mental... and at the same time account for our "intuitions" about the mind. It is, of course, impossible to do these two things. So there are a series of attempts... to cover over the fact that some crucial element about mental states is being left out.[51]

But since such attempts can be made, *ex hypothesi*, only at the cost of failing to explain the most elementary mental facts, all such movements eventually fade away: once again, consciousness has 'resisted' our efforts to understand it. And so, as the once-rosy hopes of the latest anti-realist program decline and ultimately vanish, new stabs at the impossible are made. But the unanswered questions eventually reassert themselves. When promising new ways are then excogitated to try to justify the

---

50   John R. Searle, *The Rediscovery of the Mind* (Cambridge, Mass.: MIT Press, 1992), 31.

51   Searle, *Rediscovery*, 52. But as will become plain below, Searle's understanding of the 'special features of the mental.' is not the same as mine.

omission of the stubborn, unaccommodating mental facts, the vicious circle is complete and a new cycle begins.

Searle's claim that the failure of philosophy exhibits a repetitive pattern seems to me essentially correct. The mechanism he describes, however, may apply to modern philosophy on a much larger scale than he envisaged. The modern pattern of repetition-compulsion began soon after Hume; and the cycle is powered not only by an unthinking, elemental fear of dualism and by the denial of the reality of the distinctively mental functions of human organisms; two other factors also are fundamental. One is the recurrent effort to make representationism work in the face of Hume's demonstration of its necessary skeptical consequences; the other is that, when such efforts predictably fail and new hypotheses are entertained, they are inspired by the old assumptions but in new garb. To be exact, therefore, the pattern is not exactly that of a closed cycle, but that of a spiral. The unsuitable hypotheses are never exactly the same; they are ingeniously different, devilishly clever, laboriously excogitated, technically accomplished, and ever more raring attempts to escape, in the light of previous failures, the implications of assumptions that remain in the dark or have acquired the status of self-evident facts. Also to be noted, moreover, is that representationism has been retained not only by cognitivism. The current incarnations of mental realism continue mostly to take representationism for granted assuming that it is a viable option for philosophy.

The acceptance of representationism by 'just about everyone' and not only by cognitivists seems to have become a permanent condition of the discipline. And of course, as long as the failure to meet Hume's challenge is not reversed, so that perception is explained without resorting to representationism, nothing of much importance can change in philosophy. Which is not at all to say, however, that to correct the orientation of modern philosophy is an unrealistic goal.

When prudent persons suspect that perhaps they have made a mistake, the first step they usually take is to verify whether they have made it. And in order to do so, as well as to correct it, they try to determine how and why they may have made it. Suspecting, therefore, if not indeed knowing, that representationism may have been a serious mistake rather than an unquestionable 'intuition,' we want to investigate how it made its way into philosophy and why, once it did, it was deemed inescapable. In the next chapter we shall inquire into the sequence of philosophical events that ultimately brought about the general acceptance of representationism whence ultimately followed the inability of modern philosophy to make significant progress. Understanding the causes should teach us to avoid them and may help us seek alternative interpretations of human perception.

Stating and explaining the hypothesis that will steer such investigation will be the burden of the second section of this chapter. Our work, however, would be hindered by a prejudice that was introduced into modern philosophy by Descartes himself, but which continues to affect the modern tradition: that knowledge of the history of philosophy is not relevant to the philosopher's attempt to solve philosophical problems. The inquiry will therefore require a prior refutation of this opinion and a consideration of the procedure we might appropriately follow in order to take advantage of current historical knowledge to understand and overcome the causes of the inability of modern philosophy to progress. This shall be the topic of the third section of this chapter. In keeping with the depth of the stagnation, we seek to conquer, and with the length of the period during which it has remained unchecked, the discussion will have to enter into some detail. In the fourth and last section, the agenda to be followed in the remainder of this work will end this introductory chapter. In the second chapter we shall then consider the historical evidence that should support the hypothesis. In the third chapter we shall begin to consider the general features of a revitalized philosophical approach to the study of the mind based on alternatives to representationism and to the assumptions on which representationism depends.

2. The causes of the stagnation of modern philosophy: a hypothesis

All human beings perceive the world and its objects; moreover, ordinarily they do so consciously - that is, with simultaneous awareness of the perceived object and of the perceiver's own perceptual activity. Therefore, all mature human beings in all cultures conceive both 'perception' and 'reality' as they focus their attention, alternatively, on each of the two aspects that integrate the one event of 'perceiving an object.' For in addition to our more or less perspicuous awareness of the various perceptual functions and of the objects on which the functions are exercised, we human beings also are able clearly to grasp that, try as we might, we cannot make objects appear by willing that they *be there*, and that we lack altogether the power to annihilate by ignoring them or willing that they *not be there* at all. In other words, all human beings normally learn from an early stage of development that the world and its objects are not created by their perception of them. The experience of their independence from us reveals to us what we in our culture call the 'reality' of the world. If the culture has developed philosophical institutions, then, as the common sense concepts are critically refined, philosophical interpretations of both perception and reality follow. The language used to conceive and interpret both perception and the reality of objects of perception varies from one culture to another, of course - as do the accuracy, sufficiency, sophistication, and connotations of the concepts we thus frame. For example, where modern philosophers in our tradition speak of the 'reality of objects' (or to the 'existence of the world'), the Greek philosophers referred to the 'beingness of beings' (the *ousia* of *ta onta*). Both are concepts of 'reality,' but they are not identical concepts of 'reality.' Indeed, they voice very different philosophical interpretations of 'reality.' Let us keep this in mind as we proceed.

After I state the hypothesis, I shall add some remarks explaining certain aspects of the relationship between perception and reality that both the mediaeval scholastics and Hume failed to recognize, but which, *if* taken into account, might have enabled them to reject representationism. This may be useful, because what they might have noticed, but did not, is also what we ourselves might take into consideration today as we confront the question whether representationism should not be rejected, and an alternative interpretation of perception sought.

a) The hypothesis

Reduced to its simplest terms, the hypothesis to be investigated is that important inaccuracies - erroneous though plausible approximations to the truth rather than purely mythological fantasies - crept into certain basic observations and deductions of the Greek philosophers regarding the nature of 'perception' and of 'reality.' The inaccuracies were passed on to Christian thinkers, where they remained undetected and unchallenged for centuries. At a certain point in history, however, under unique and unpredictable circumstances created by the emergence of a new philosophical idea of the nature of 'reality,' the long traditional conception of perception was transformed into representationism. But representationism implies existential skepticism. Thereupon the cultivation of philosophical knowledge was brought to a halt by the existential skepticism that representationism implied. Indeed, such outcome afflicted the history of philosophy twice, first in the late middle ages, when representationism appeared for the first time, and then again early in modern times, with Hume, when unawareness of the earlier crisis brought about by representationism led to the renewed adoption of representationism, thence to the rediscovery of existential skepticism, and ultimately to the stagnation of modern philosophy.

When the Greek philosophers proceeded to interpret the meaning of the concepts of perception and reality, they abided by a consensual assumption that even today is widely concurred in by many philosophers. Namely, that the efficient cause of our perception of the world is the world itself, the objects we perceive. For perception, they generally agreed, is essentially receptive and passive – though once the object has worked its effect on the mind, the mind is normally active in reaction to the perceptual effect caused by the object. Their interpretations of the nature of reality also were constrained by the assumption that objects caused our perception.

This assumption is questionable. I shall argue that the efficient causation of perception is to be attributed solely to the mental functioning of suitably- endowed organisms; objects do indeed act upon our senses in much the same way that they act upon each other, but not specifically so as to procure perception. (A falling object impacts in the same way on the ground and one's head, but the ground does not perceive the object.) But the common sense assumption was not subjected by the Greek philosophers to sufficiently rigorous criticism, and therefore it was allowed to colour their otherwise varied interpretations of both perception and reality.

A crude version of how objects caused perception was that of Leucippus, who supposed that 'effluences' of such objects entered the soul through the 'pores' provided by the senses.[52] Later accounts were increasingly sophisticated; according to Heraclitus reality and the mind were united when their 'contiguity' (*synapsis*) brought about their 'fitting together' (*harmonia*). Of special interest to us, given the singular influence it exerted on mediaeval thought, was Aristotle's elaborate theory. It was grounded on 'hylomorphism.' It proposed that objects were integrated by 'form' and 'matter,' and that perception consisted in the mind's union with, through acquisition and *possession* of, the object's perceptible and intelligible 'forms' (whether substantial or accidental) after they had been

_____

52   John Burnet, *Greek Philosophy: Thales to Plato* (London: Macmillan, 1950), 75.

stripped of their matter. Thus, the perceiving mind acquired - albeit only 'formally,' not 'materially'- the perceptible properties that belonged to the object. The mind became the object by becoming *one* with the object's properties. In Aristotle's own words, '[a]ctual knowledge is identical with its object;'[53] Hellenists agree that he meant this literally. For example, according to W.D. Ross, Aristotle taught that '[t]he actualization of perception is at the same time the actualization of the object. Actual sound and actual hearing are merely distinguishable aspects of a single event.'[54] It is for the same reason that, as Aristotle thought, '[t]he soul is in a way all things... [U]nderstanding is in a way what is understood, and sensation is in a way what is sensible.'[55]

This interpretation of perception, I also comment in passing, is no more correct than the presupposition regarding the causation of perception from which it descends. And not simply because of the oversimple doctrine of hylomorphism. A deeper objection is that the mind's supposed acquisition and possession of the characteristics of objects depends on a projection of our perceptual activity onto objects. Such activity, as we have noted, is difficult to detect and may pass unobserved; but sustained reflection on our experience can lead to our recognition of it. More fundamentally still, the idea that perception *unites* the mind and the object, by *acquiring* and *possessing*, however 'immaterially,' the properties of the object, is questionable. For a crucial part of our perception of an object, when it is conscious, is that the object is not the perceiver. And that the perceiver is not the object. That is why we can perceive the reality of real objects, their independence from whichever mind experiences them. Conscious perception includes the perceiver's *self-differentiation* from the object, and the *otherness* of the object to oneself. This is why no conscious perceiver mistakes itself for the object, or the object for itself. Perception achieves the very opposite of what the Greek philosophers and their successors have thought.

The Greeks also tended to conceive the *reality* of objects under the influence of the same assumption regarding the causation of perception. They seem to have relied on the idea that objects must possess in themselves what they cause us to possess when we have knowledge. Conversely, they

---

53   Aristotle, *De Anima*, 3.5.430a20.

54   W.D. Ross, *Aristotle* (London: Methuen, 1949), 138.

55   Aristotle, *De Anima*, 3.7.431b21-23.

could suppose that perception was the acquisition and 'formal' (i.e., immaterial) possession of the 'contents' of objects, only if objects had such 'contents' in themselves. Thus, the reality of objects – their independence from our perception of them - was assumed by most Greek philosophers to be identical with the properties and characteristics that we predicate of the objects themselves as what they truly 'are.' As Aristotle might well have said, the reason why we cannot confuse ourselves with the objects we perceive is that we perceive their properties as *their own*, even as we acquire such properties mentally for ourselves. Thus, perception of the *properties* of objects is the same as perception of their *reality*; and the *reality* of what we perceive is the same as the *properties* we perceive in them.

To this conception of reality may be objected that it implies that reality is predestined to become known; it is inherently knowable even before it is actually known by a mind. Only a few Greek philosophers, the best known of whom was Anaxagoras, seem to have dissented; he appears to have reasoned that the world can be said to be knowable only in relation to an actual mind that knows it; he therefore supposed a sort cosmic Mind that knew the world and made objects knowable. Most Greek philosophers, however, did not suppose such Mind. They supposed nevertheless the *inherent* knowability - or in their own expression, the *inherent* 'watchability' (*to theion*) of the world and its objects. And from the inherent 'watchability' of objects, they deduced that there was an order of reality 'higher' than that which the human mind could know. This was the origin of 'dualism,' the widely shared supposition of the Greek philosophers, later welcomed by the Christian, that there was a 'higher,' mind-like level of reality: it was the level, if not also (as in the Christian version) the entirely distinct *world*, of the 'divine.'

Their inaccuracies notwithstanding, the concepts of 'perception' and 'reality' on which the Greeks relied as they inquired into the nature of the human mind were mutually consistent. Their compatibility was a reflection of their common descent from the assumption that perception was caused by objects. Therefore, the use of these concepts enabled the philosophers to devise plausible, rational theoretical explanations of (a) how human beings perceived the real world and its objects, and (b) the nature of such world and its reality. Now, awareness of inconsistencies in one's thinking is one the most unsettling warnings to philosophers that their reasoning has gone astray. In the absence of contrary indications, the mutual consistency of the Greek (and later, the Christian) philosophers' ideas of perception and reality tended to prevent a critical reassessment of their adequacy. This explains why defective interpretations of both reality and perception could have perpetuated themselves and remain undetected over a period of many centuries. They did so, indeed, and most probably would have continued to remain undisturbed, until an unforeseeable event in the high middle ages stood in the way. The result was the generation of representationism and the insoluble problems that are its inevitable sequelae.

Into the peaceful co-existence (or blissful ignorance) of the ancient traditional concepts of perception and reality irrupted an unprecedented proposal of Thomas Aquinas in the thirteenth century: it was an altogether new idea regarding the reality of the world. I shall refer to it as the 'existential interpretation.' However, Thomas did not propose at the same time - or at any other time - a new interpretation of *perception*. By default the old one remained generally accepted, at least to begin with.

The existential interpretation included a theological component that demands religious faith, but from which non-believers can readily abstract; its omission does not change what the doctrine proposes about the reality of the world. The aspect of the doctrine that particularly concerns us -not least of all because it was a far-reaching truth which marked the beginning of the eventual transition from the mediaeval to the typically modern *Weltanschauung* can be summed up in the proposition that the 'reality' of the world *inhered* in real beings and was distinct from their properties. In other words, *in addition* to their various characteristics - that is, over and above their having whatever properties may have been truly predictable of them -real objects would count also on what the fourteenth century philosophers learned to call their 'existence.' Everything in the world *did* its own existing, and its existing was therefore *its own*. Conversely, nothing was real unless it should have *its own* 'existence.' This was most clearly evident in living beings, whose existence is the same as their 'life,' and whose life was not a property, but a contingent and temporally limited fact. But it was – and is – true of everything in the world.

For in addition to being whatever it is, and having whatever characteristics it has, a real being *'is there.'* And its 'being there' is actively performed, as it were, by the being itself. The central point of the teaching is that the real objects that make up the real world count on *something else* besides their properties - a resource or asset, as it were - which makes them the unique 'being' they are. We still call it by the name it was given in the fourteenth century, namely, 'existence.' (Before that time, the word had a somewhat different meaning.) Thus, without 'existence,' a 'being' is only a possible 'being.' An actual 'human being' is one that has not only human properties, but also 'existence.'

Now, if this sounds unremarkable, perhaps even trivial, the reason is that Thomas's existential interpretation of the reality of the world was eventually accepted not only by philosophers, but also by our culture at large. It is the idea of reality that most of us take for granted today.

Thomas was, of course, not about to give up his belief in the creation of the world by God; in his proposal, although creatures did their own existing, God gave them the wherewithal to act out or 'perform,' as it were, their own existence. In his view, therefore, God continued to be ultimately responsible for the reality of the world, but no longer directly; the reality of creatures was their own doing; human beings led their own lives. Likewise, their powers were effective in themselves. Human beings were able to take initiatives, and their decisions were truly effective, rather than a reflection and confirmation of what the divine will had disposed from all eternity - although of course, human decisions remained subject to the omnipotent Will of God. (How these two propositions could be reconciled has never been made completely clear by Thomists, but somehow both were to be affirmed at the same time.)

The difference between Thomas's and the traditional Greek, as well as the Christian ideas of reality is therefore clear. It may be summed up in the formula that whereas (a) to Aristotle and the Greek philosophers the 'reality' of a real being was reducible to the being's being whatever it was (i.e., to its properties, powers, and characteristics), and whereas (b) to the Christian philosophers before Thomas it was reducible to God's willing that they be whatever they were and that they have such properties as they actually had, (c) to Thomas (and to those who eventually agreed with him), the 'reality' of the real being was not so reducible, but was distinct from, and additional to the being 's properties, *and* it was the being's own. The world in general, and human beings specifically, were, simply speaking, real, and their reality was their own. In Thomas's own words: 'everything whatever has within itself its own existence [*esse proprium*], which is distinct from that of all others.'[56]

---

56   Aquinas, *Contra Gentiles*, I, 14.

The existential interpretation of the reality of the world had numerous unforeseen repercussions for European culture, including its religious beliefs. But the immediate and fateful consequence was felt in philosophy. Once the existential interpretation had been assumed, it followed that both *perceivers* and *objects of perception* 'existed.' And this meant that the existence of each was *its own*, and therefore independent of the existence of the other. No belief in God or reference to him was required before anyone could agree with this. But if so, the earlier Greek supposition that perception brought about the mind's reception and possession of real objects – which had been retained by the scholastics - had acquired a new meaning. It had morphed into the supposition that perception resulted in the reception and possession of objects when the latter came to *exist* in the mind, at the same time that they continued to *exist,* of course, in the world, outside the mind. And in both cases, their existence in the one was independent of their existence in the other. Which is to say that the Aristotelian mental acquisition and possession of, and union with, the properties of objects had become representationism.

It was granted, to be sure, that real objects did not exist physically within the mind; they existed in the mind by the existence of the organism; they had only a 'subjective' or 'intentional' existence, as duplicates, copies, (or representations) of the object. ('Intentionality' was the neologism coined *ad hoc* in the fourteenth century to characterize the vicarious existence of objects in an existing mind.) And so, the mediaeval scholastics never realized it, but the reason why Thomas's existential interpretation had the effect of converting the Aristotelian idea of perception into representationism was what Hume would a few centuries later describe as the 'monstrous offspring,' that is, 'the double *existence* of perceptions and objects.'

It was in this manner - simply by melding the new interpretation of *reality* into the traditional interpretation of *perception* - that philosophy had condemned itself to the Sisyphean task of trying to explain the nature of perception while harbouring a presupposition, representationism, that made such project impossible. For representationism necessarily implied, of course, existential skepticism. Scholasticism was therefore plunged into a crisis as the scholastics tried hard but could think of no way to avoid representationism. It did not occur to them that a re-interpretation of the nature of reality called for a re-interpretation of the nature of perception; evidently, they did not realize that the concepts of perception and of reality must be consistent with each other, since perception would be meaningless unless it be understood in relation to that which is perceived. However reluctantly, therefore, they felt compelled to accept that philosophy was radically powerless to establish the existence of the world. And so, before the end of the century representationism had brought the scholastic tradition to an inglorious end, as most scholastics agreed that philosophy was useless, since it was incapable of establishing that the world existed – and *a fortiori* what it was like. Though Platonism survived in some places, as reason took refuge in mysticism and faith, philosophy in general, but particularly Aristotelianism, became utterly discredited.

Thereafter the uselessness of philosophy and its impotence to demonstrate the existence of the world were generally taken for granted.

However, the process through which this bleak assessment of the value of philosophy had been arrived at was eventually forgotten. Far from forgotten, on the other hand, was the existential interpretation of the reality of the world; on the contrary, it throve, until it became the interpretation of the reality of the world that almost every one of us takes for granted today. What is likely to come as a surprise to most of us (apart from the provenance of *our* current secular idea of reality in the thought of Aquinas), is, therefore, not the assumption that real beings have their own existence, but that this is neither a natural 'intuition' nor the only interpretation of 'reality' ever held either by our common sense or by our philosophical tradition. But if one supposes the contrary and assumes that philosophy has always since Greek times interpreted the reality of the world as we do today, it is not difficult to misread Aristotle as an anticipation of Thomas and to identify the 'beingness of beings' with the 'existence of the world.' The truth, as twentieth century historians discovered, is that the expression 'the beingness of beings ' meant to the Greeks that the reality of real objects was reducible to their properties, whereas the expression 'the existence of objects' meant to Thomas (and to modern culture) that the existence of existing objects was not reducible to their properties and was their own. Which is to say, precisely the opposite of what Aristotle and other Greek philosophers thought.

If the Thomistic origin of our common assumption regarding reality is not widely known, the reason is at least in part that the popular acceptance of the existential interpretation of the reality of the world followed simply from the popular adoption of the vocabulary of 'existence' and 'to exist' in the peculiar and novel acceptation of these words developed by the fourteenth century scholastics in an effort to make sense of the doctrine of Thomas. (The words themselves were older; they went back to Middle English.) As 'existence' and 'to exist' passed from their philosophical use in the fourteenth century into the European vernaculars, their new meaning became part of the culture's common sense; the process can be compared to the popular adoption of the concept of 'consciousness' originally bruited about by philosophers in early modern times, but soon picked up by everyone.

And so, in time it was commonly assumed by our civilization that the existential interpretation of the reality of the world had always been supposed; it seemed so natural and 'intuitive' a notion that must be deemed self-evident. It was the construction of the 'reality ' of the world taken for granted by Descartes, Locke, and Hume in their day. It was also assumed by Gottlob Frege in the nineteenth century in his partial and somewhat garbled rediscovery of part of Thomas's teaching; Frege described 'existence' as a 'property of the properties' of a real being.[57] (Bertrand Russell agreed.) But when Thomas formulated the idea that the reality of a real being is not one of its properties, he had done so accurately, resorting to the formula first used by Alfarabi, that there was a 'distinction between the *essence* [i.e., the properties[58]] and the *"to be"* [i.e., the existence]' of the beings that make up the created world.

Very much alive remained also, however, the memory of the *outcome* of the fourteenth century crisis, namely, existential skepticism - as contrasted with memory of what had provoked the crisis. And as all modern philosophers know, Descartes's ambition from an early age was to rescue philosophy from the shame of having to admit that it could not establish as little as the existence of the world. What not all modern philosophers apparently have known is (a) why and how philosophy had reached such an abject condition, (b) that neither the existential interpretation nor representationism

---

57   Frege recognized that 'existence' is not a property of existents. However, to say, as he did, that it was rather a property of the properties of a being was imprecise. Existence is not a property at all, and specifically not a property of the properties of the existent; it is rather a contingent fact, state, or condition that betokens the finitude and temporality of the world and its objects. As such fact, the existence of real objects must be said to be distinct from their properties. The nature of existence will be more fully discussed in chapter III.

58   In Aristotelianism, the term 'essence' (to ti en einai, essentia) is not to be understood as if it were an exact synonym for the 'properties' or 'characteristics' attributable to a being; it includes in its denotation the 'necessity' that they be so. But only one aspect of the denotation of essentia is relevant to the limited purposes of this investigation, namely, the knowability of the Aristotelian 'essences.' To simplify my exposition, therefore, I take the term 'essence' as referring to the perceptible and intelligible characteristics, features, or properties of a real being, whether in respect of the abiding substantive nature of the being or the transitory 'accidental' qualities and events that accrue to it.

had always been accepted as part of our philosophical tradition, and (c) that, therefore, these may not be considered 'intuitions' that come naturally and unavoidably to all human beings.

Unfortunately, Descartes himself did not know either. Little historical memory had survived of the reason why mediaeval philosophy had long been deemed incapable of establishing the existence of the world, and of the circumstances under which philosophy had therefore earned widespread opprobrium; it was only in the twentieth century that historical scholarship managed to recover it.

Worse yet, Descartes thought he knew the cause of philosophy's impotence to demonstrate the existence of the world. But he was mistaken; it had had very little to do, as he supposed, with the failure of observe the logical discipline demanded by the 'foundationalist' nature of philosophy. Besides, having lacked as little as a glimmer of suspicion that representationism had figured in the creation of the existential skepticism he sought to vanquish, he assumed it unhesitatingly and without discussion, quite as if it were self-evident. And so did those other modern philosophers who rallied to his call for the restoration of philosophy - including, of course, Hume. Thus, the Cartesian reformation of philosophy was doomed from the start and the dream of Descartes, the restoration of philosophy, could not but have remained unfulfilled. The same conjunction of fundamentally (yet not obviously) incompatible assumptions that had several centuries earlier precipitated existential skepticism obtained once again. It was only a question of time before David Hume did some hard thinking and noticed that not all was well in the modern empiricist paradise.

This time, however, the same causes produced only partly the same effect: existential skepticism did not bring unmitigated havoc to philosophy a second time, because one important circumstance intervened. Hume had discovered not only, as the late mediaeval scholastics had, that existential skepticism necessarily followed from representationism. As already noted, he had the further insight that such skepticism followed, more specifically, from the 'double existence of perceptions and objects.' This brought him a step closer to the truth that representationism should be rejected, though not close enough to persuade him to reject it. On the other hand, the philosophical community of the eighteenth century was sufficiently strongly impressed by the existential reality of the world to refuse to follow Hume into existential skepticism. Perhaps they supposed that such refusal left them free to agree otherwise with Hume; but in any event and for whatever reason, what is clear is that 'just about everyone' accepted representationism. The philosophical community's reaction to Hume is what explains the difference in outcome between the mediaeval and the modern outbreaks of existential skepticism.

The collective decision of modern philosophers to accept representationism while rejecting existential skepticism was far from ideal, but from a practical viewpoint should nevertheless be evaluated as preferable to Hume's. For the calamitous outcome of the original crisis of existential skepticism was averted; the aftermath of its modern replay was subdued, and philosophy survived. For which we can be grateful - even if philosophy had thereby also condemned itself to attempting an impossibility: to account for perception on the basis of representationism, while avoiding the existential skepticism that is implicit in representationism. Stagnation was the logically necessary result.

A coda should be added. The principal consequences of the original existential interpretation of Thomas were felt beyond philosophy; some shall be briefly discussed in the next chapter. At this time I only mention that before the existential interpretation of the reality of the world became the norm, a human being's awareness of its own reality was evidence of the existence of God as the direct, hands-on creator of the world; for its own reality was but the direct effect of the Will of God. However, awareness of the *inherent* reality of human beings took away all such evidence; we have within ourselves all the 'reality' we need to make us truly and unqualifiedly real. To be sure, one might accept the existential interpretation and nevertheless continue to *believe* in the existence of God and of the 'other world.' But now one had to justify it to oneself.

The inherent reality of the world took away thus the rationality of every possible attempt to demonstrate a transcendent order of reality. *Nothing* in the world can be seen as a demonstration of God's work. For every such attempt, if it appeals to reason, must reach its conclusion on the basis of premises regarding what we know about the world and ourselves - whose reality inheres in ourselves. Thus, awareness of the reality of the world and of ourselves reveals the utterly imaginary nature of every supposed transcendent reality; it shows up the self-contradiction of the concept of a 'real-world-that-is-less-real-than-the-real world.' Believers have therefore had to fall back on the admissibility of paradox as valid form of reasoning, in order to argue, for instance, that the divine 'existence' is 'analogous' (i.e., proportional) to earthly existence, though we cannot know the nature of the proportion. In sum, the existential interpretation does not of itself argue against the existence of God, but rendered him irrelevant to the existing world and made possible thus the 'secularity' of the modern world.

b) The asymmetric relationship between perception and reality

The hypothesis explains at what point, in my estimation, the philosophical tradition first strayed: it was at the very beginning of the attempt of the Greek philosophers to understand the

human mind. And it also explains why, once human beings had the opportunity to perceive their own inherent reality, the existence of God ceased to be obvious. The reasoning of the philosophers had been based on lack of sensitivity to the active role of the human mental functions in cognition; this was the root from which their inadequate conceptions of both 'perception' and 'reality' flowed. But when eventually the existential interpretation of reality appeared, the self-contradiction of representationism - a concept of perception that makes perception impossible - should have provoked a critical reappraisal and revision of the traditional interpretation of the nature of perception. But it did not. The philosophers seem to have remained unaware that there was any need for such re-evaluation. It was quite as if perception could be interpreted independently of an interpretation of the reality of the world and its objects. Their mistake consisted in assuming that perception and reality are symmetrically related, whereas in fact they are not. I will explain.

The concepts of 'perception' and 'reality' are not generated separately from each other, but only as a pair and in relation to each other; they are derived out of the *single* fact that human beings have the ability to perceive real objects and indeed to do so consciously; their consciousness enables them to be aware of their powers in relation to the real world. And when they become aware of it, they conceive simultaneously *both* 'perception' and the 'reality' of the world. Neither can be conceived in the total absence of the other. Why must we say so?

For the double reason (a) that we cannot possibly 'perceive' without perceiving some-thing that 'is perceived' (i.e., what we ordinarily call an 'object' or more generally, the 'world'[59] and (b) that

---

59   Not even Buddhists or other mystics claim that it is possible to *perceive* without perceiving anything. They only claim that it is possible to *think* without thinking an object of thought.

nothing can 'be perceived' unless by a perceiver's act of 'perception.' Nevertheless, the two concepts are radically distinct from each other. No conscious human being can fail altogether to notice the difference between its perception, which is the perceiver's own activity, and the target of its perceptual activity, which is what the activity is trained upon. What is possible, and indeed not at all rare, is to notice the activity only dimly and confusedly, by contrast with the reality of the object, which is invariably to the fore and cannot be missed. But however distinct, the two concepts are at the same time closely related. The relationship is one of opposition: for when we experience the world, we become aware (a) that the 'object' is *other than* our 'perception,' and (b) that our perception is *other than* the 'world' of 'objects.' This, I stress, is put in evidence by our experience. It is the reason why no one who is sane ever finds it possible to confuse a perceived object with him- or herself. Within a small fraction of a millimeter, all of us are capable of pointing out unerringly where our body ends and the non-self, or the 'world,' begins. But these features are not all we can observe regarding the relationship between perception and reality. A further and most important aspect of their relationship is something else: its *asymmetry*.

Perception is so related to reality that it cannot take place in the absence of a reality that is cognized;[60] therefore, if we tried to explain perception without reference to reality, the impossibility would be obvious. This is easily understood by everyone. But the relationship is asymmetric, which is not always clear to everyone. Nevertheless, on the one hand, in the absence of reality there can be no perception; but on the other hand, the reality of the world and its objects is not affected by the absence of any mind's perception of it. Reality would be misunderstood, if we tried to explain it by reference to cognition.

Which is, in effect, what most Greek philosophers did when they identified the reality of objects with their inherent 'watchability,' and what the mediaeval Christian philosophers did when they identified the 'beingness' of objects ' with God's willing that certain 'ideas' in his Mind come to be. Thus,

---

60   The objection might be raised that hallucinations demonstrate that perception can take place in the absence of reality. Actually, objects of hallucination are not 'perceived;' they are *imagined*. Ordinarily, our discharge of our mental functions, if conscious, provides information regarding which function is at work; we can tell the difference between imaging and perceiving an object. When a defect in the organ or its function prevents awareness of such information, a hallucination is the result. Objects of hallucinations may not be properly said to have been perceived, but only imagined.

the concepts of perception and reality must be consistent with each other, but their relationship is not symmetric. Perceptually equipped minds depend upon real objects for perception, but the world does not depend on any mind's perception for its reality. In other words, we cannot perceive the world without a real world, but the world can be real regardless of whether it is known by any mind: minds presuppose reality, but reality does not presuppose minds. No account of perception can be true if it fails to respect this fact. For there is no reason why we should suppose otherwise - except, of course, a prior gratuitous commitment to the existence of either Anaxagoras' cosmic Mind or other equivalent source of the (supposedly) derivative reality of the empirically-given world, such as is imagined in Buddhism, in the biblical religions, and in a few other religions.

Corroboration of the asymmetric relationship between perception and reality is provided to us today by our awareness of the origin of human perception in biological evolution. Such evidence would not have been available to philosophers in the fourteenth century, of course, or even in the eighteenth. But evolution selected the characteristics of animal perception for their aptness to promote the adjustment of the human organism to the world. When the human mind appeared, the world was already in place; it was the background against which sentience and human nature evolved. Therefore, human life was required to adjust to it -rather than the other way about. This is why one's understanding of, say, the physiology of respiration could not contradict with impunity one's understanding of the chemistry of the atmosphere that earth-dwellers breathe. For example, since evolution created the physiology of respiration in a world that has an oxygen-nitrogen atmosphere, an interpretation of the physiology of respiration must be deemed *a priori* incorrect if it were to suggest that breathing our oxygen nitrogen atmosphere was unhealthy. Well, no less ludicrous than this is, in effect, the suggestion that we should hold fast onto a conception of our perception of the reality of the world according to which it is impossible to perceive the reality of the world. Why? Because the world *was there* before there were any minds. One's understanding of perception may not contradict with impunity one's understanding of the reality of the world within which perception appeared, but must accommodate it.[61]

But self-contradictory though representationism is, it is not always obviously so; confusion about, or unawareness of, the asymmetry of the relationship between perception and reality may hide its absurdity. Both in the fourteenth century and in the eighteenth, the existential interpretation of the reality of the world should have exposed the weakness of the traditional interpretation of perception. But it did not. And it still has not. Adherence to the idea that perception transfers the contents of reality into the mind, where they exist by the existence of the mind, continues to generate representationism. To be sure, representationism implies existential skepticism. But such implication need not disturb anyone. For it can be ignored, and if necessary, denied.

To conclude, if the historical evidence should confirm the proposed hypothesis, we could then proceed to determine how we should conceive perception, if not as the mind's 'reception' and 'possession' of, and 'union' with, objects. The beckoning possibility that perception is not caused by objects, but by minds, may or may not turn out to be correct, but it is worth exploring. Which we shall do after we first attempt to explain, in the next chapter, the sequence of relatively few but momentous and literally epochal events in the history of philosophy that led from the Greek foundation of the discipline to Hume's challenge, and to the subsequent stagnation of modern philosophy when the challenge was not met.

But the question how the stagnation of modern philosophy came about is one issue; why two and a half centuries later it has yet to be overcome is a different one. The above hypothesis may account for the *inception* of the stagnation of modern philosophy, but we also have to explain the *continuation* of the stagnation from Hume to the present. For that purpose, we may invoke two factors:

---

61   To my knowledge, this point has not been made by any philosopher at any time, but it is not original with me. It was first made by a scientist, Antonio R. Damasio, when he noted that '[t]aken literally "I think therefore I am" illustrates precisely the opposite of ... [the truth] about the ... relationship between mind and body ..... Yet long before the dawn of humanity, beings were beings. At some point, came a simple mind; with greater complexity of mind came the possibility of thinking and, even later, of using language to communicate and organize thinking,' *Descartes' Error: Emotion, Reason, and the Human Brain* (New York: Putnam, 1994), 248. The criticism, however - that there is no reason to think that reality demands mentality - applies not only to Descartes, but to the entire philosophical tradition since the Greeks.

unawareness of the history of philosophy, and unawareness of the role that history can play in the solution of philosophical problems.

Oblivion of the historicity of philosophy was part of the legacy bequeathed by Descartes to Hume and later modern philosophers. Unawareness of the historical facts that (a) the existential interpretation of the reality of the world had been first proposed only in the thirteenth century and (b) representationism only in the fourteenth, fostered the illusion that these were natural, primitive, unavoidable and *inalterable* 'intuitions' of the human mind. Once it had been generated, the metaproblem of modern philosophy seems to have been perpetuated, in substantial part, by misprision of the historicity of philosophical knowledge.

The truth that human beings can discover their mistakes *only* in retrospect (an issue that shall be the object of further discussion below) has not been given sufficiently serious consideration by modern philosophy either in Descartes's or Hume's time, or since. The stagnation can be overcome, I suggest, but only by a retrospective *philosophical* study of the history of philosophy. Which brings us to the question how we should proceed to conduct such study, and why philosophy is capable of doing so.

3. Approaching the problem

Disregard for the history of philosophy by modern philosophers began with Descartes, but it is now institutionalized. Albeit by indirection, it is inculcated in philosophers during the earliest stages of their education. As Robert Pasnau has remarked, attitudes are created and perpetuated when, for example:

> [O]ur histories of philosophy … tend to skip, with a few apologetic murmurs,
> from the fourth century B.C. to the seventeenth century. So, too, run our phi-
> losophy curriculum and the research interests of the professors who teach in
> our universities.[62]

---

62   Robert Pasnau, *Theories of Cognition in the Later Middle Ages* (Cambridge: Cambridge University Press, 1997), vii.

It is indeed incongruous that many of us are introduced to philosophy by learning, on the one hand, of the foundation of modern philosophy when Descartes's resorted to the *cogito* to refute the prevailing opinion that philosophy was incapable of yielding knowledge of the existence of the world, but that ordinarily, on the other, little is said about how such opinion had come to prevail. The impression is taken from an early stage of our usual philosophical education, if not also deliberately given, that modern philosophy had little or no continuity with its mediaeval past —the very period one should have suspected of having conditioned modern thought most directly of all. But for the beginning of the trend we should go back to Descartes. Since neither he himself nor many of his contemporaries could count on any memory of how representationism had originated, or of its connection with existential skepticism, his attempt to reform and renew philosophy was based on a false diagnosis of the causes of its disrepute. He blamed philosophy's having strayed from the strict methods demanded by foundationalism.

But among the other unfortunate assumptions of the Cartesian reformation for which Descartes was responsible, one shall interest us most particularly, because it has been preserved in the ahistoricism that is still with us today and which militates strongly against the idea that philosophy should review its history with a view to detecting and correcting its missteps – or what I have [called?] the prejudice of 'ahistoricism'. For Descartes's appreciation of the temporal, evolving nature — the 'historicity' — of all knowledge and culture, and specifically that of philosophy, appears to have been deficient. And this had a decisive and lasting influence upon the modern philosophical tradition he founded.

Descartes's ahistoricism was superimposed upon certain views regarding the nature of philosophy which he probably derived from the scholasticism in which he was educated in his youth. He seems to have taken for granted that the world was structured by a set of fixed, timeless truths, and that the source of such truth was the creative thinking of the world by the divine Mind. The latter was necessary to support the former, because truths need minds to think them, and only the truths thought by an eternal Mind would be eternal truths. The eternal and unchanging truth thus created and embedded in the nature of the world could be gradually discovered by the human mind, but human knowledge was the passive reception or mirroring of previously existing truth. In other words, Descartes does not seem to have realized that human knowledge in general, and philosophy in particular, were *alive;* much less did he recognize that as philosophical knowledge evolves, the truth of our knowledge *evolves.* (Galileo, a Platonist,[63] had made, before Descartes, much the same assumption regarding knowledge and science, and transmitted it to the tradition of experimental science.) According to this view, what changed was not the eternal truth, but only the degree to which human beings uncovered and perceived the truth that philosophy (and experimental science) managed to uncover.

Descartes' disregard for the historicity of human knowledge was vigorous enough to bear comparison with that of cognitivists today. Consistently, he appears to have envisioned the history of philosophy, therefore, merely as the record, at any given time, of the triumphs and failures of individual thinkers in their quest for discovering as much of the eternal, unchanging truth as possible. Throughout his life he remained unmindful of the influence of the past — I mean, the past that comprises both the biography of the individual mind and the history of the culture within which the individual mind thinks — upon what human individuals and societies think at any given time. This attitude has persisted to the present as part of the modern philosophical tradition — though much less consistently now than in Descartes's time. For eternal truths make sense if an eternal Mind who thinks them is supposed, but not if they are deemed to exist in empty ethereal space and in gossamer form as the truth of no mind's thoughts. Nevertheless, Descartes's ahistoricism became part of the modern philosophical tradition.

To determine how we should best approach the interpretation of our problem, we need at a minimum a little historical background regarding the Cartesian foundation of modern philosophy. We must begin, therefore, by considering how Descartes imported representationism into modern philosophy, and how in the course of doing so he linked ahistoricism and representationism. For it is the addition of ahistoricism to representationism that confirms and reinforces the insolubility of 'Hume's problem.' Representationism locks the mind within itself and isolates it from the existing world; but if it is true that the key to escaping representationism is to go back and undo philosophy's immuring the mind within itself, ahistoricism is the equivalent of doing away with the key. Thus,

---

63   See Alexandre Koyré, 'Galileo and Plato,' *Journal of the History of Ideas*, 4 (1943) 400-22.

learning how representationism came to the modern world should give us some indications of why the solution might be found in philosophy's reviewing its past history with a view to steering itself in a new direction. The remainder of this section will therefore attempt to justify, in the face of much current opinion and practice to the contrary, how and why we can make use of the history of philosophy in order to investigate the problem that concerns us.

a) The importation of representationism into modern philosophy

Four hundred years before the publication of Hume's *Treatise of Human Nature,* mediaeval philosophy entered a period of steep decline when the conviction became widespread among scholastics that philosophy and reason were utterly useless for the purpose of gaining knowledge about anything in the world, since it could not establish even the existence of the world. A devastating, demoralizing tide to that effect had been set in motion by the philosophical work of several scholastic thinkers, the best known of whom were William of Ockham and Nicholas of Autrecourt. A trend among the scholastics towards abdicating reason in favour of faith followed directly. Philosophy became an object of scorn, and eventually was practiced mostly in a few religious communities — such as that at La Flèche, in France, now so familiar to modern philosophers —that were isolated from the intellectual (and increasingly secular) mainstream of modern European culture. But three centuries after Ockham and Autrecourt, the sea of anti-reason was still rising when Michel de Montaigne, for example, was advocating in his influential *Essais* the superiority of faith over reason — while Pierre Charron, the principal promoter of Montaigne's work, was arguing, somewhat archly, that given the impotence of the human mind to gain knowledge there was no reason for disbelieving in God: Christianity might as well be believed in, since it demanded only faith. But before the last of Montaigne's works had been published, René Descartes had been born. And in the ripeness of time Descartes, unlike every other critic of philosophy in his age, came to believe that he knew what should be done to rescue philosophy from the infamy into which it had fallen at some indeterminate time in the past.

Unfortunately, during the hiatus between the collapse of mediaeval philosophy and Descartes's attempt to reform and revive it in the mid-seventeenth [century?], little memory had been preserved of precisely how the disgrace of philosophy had come about. If nothing else, the epochal split of

Western Christianity in the sixteenth century would have sufficed to ensure that the collective mind of Europe turned to broader matters than the perceptual function of the human mind. Descartes knew that universal existential doubt had been the immediate cause of philosophy's disrepute, but not much more. He was unaware of, specifically, the premises and reasoning concerning the nature of perception and of the existential reality of the world that had led fourteenth century scholastics to a logically faultless, yet utterly incredible, absolute skepticism. Nor did he know that mediaeval philosophy had broken down and all but disappeared because the 'double existence of perceptions and objects' had had the incidental effect of generating representationism. He was not wrong when he divined that the sterility of philosophy was rooted in an ancient failure, but his interpretation of the causes of existential skepticism was not the outcome of a critical investigation of its historically factual origin. He had deduced it instead from what is now known as the 'foundationalist' conception of philosophical knowledge, which he seems to have absorbed as part of his scholastic education.

The central idea of foundationalism, the germ of which goes back to Aristotle,[64] is that philo-sophical knowledge is a structure of deductions that depends, as a building does upon a foundation, on a few original *a priori* 'principles' whose truth is certain beyond all possible doubt because they are self-evident. Behind Aristotle's proto-foundationalism was the claim of Plato that philosophy was 'trustworthy knowledge,' *episteme*, (which was translated into Latin as *scientia)*, as distinct from the unreliable 'opinions' *(doxa)* of common sense. The belief that certitude was the mark of philosophical knowledge of the causes of phenomena had generated the lapidary definition of philosophical *scien-tia* by the scholastics: philosophy was *cognito certa per causas.* The causal conclusions of philosophy were certain if, when logically drawn, they were continuous with 'first principles' or 'foundations' that were themselves certain by virtue of their self-evidence.[65] Therefore, Descartes estimated that the cause of philosophy's humiliation had been that the philosophers had tried to build philosophical knowledge without the benefit of an absolutely indubitable 'foundation' whence the certainty of its conclusions might derive.

---

64   Aristotle, *Posterior Analytics,* 1.2.71b3ff.

65   A modern restatement of the self-evident scholastic 'principles' which serve as the 'foundations' of philosophy is to be found in Jacques Maritain, *A Preface to Metaphysics: Seven Lectures on Being* (London: Sheed & Ward, 1948).

This was not true; foundationalism may have done no justice to the nature of philosophy, but cannot be blamed for representationism or for existential skepticism. The scholastics of the fourteenth century had *not* reasoned that, since philosophy could not achieve certitude, nothing could be said to exist. They had argued the other way about: philosophy was a useless quest for knowledge, because it was powerless to establish as little as the existence of the world. Coupled with his assumption of representationism and the existence of the world, Descartes's failure to address the true cause of existential skepticism ensured that existential skepticism would sooner or later rear its head again. Which it did, within one hundred years of Descartes's death, when Hume realized that representationism necessarily issued in existential skepticism.

Meditating instead on how reason might be able to attain to absolutely indubitable knowledge of the existence of the world, on November 10, 1619, at the age of 23, Descartes had a reverie in which the insight came to him that there was one instance, the human mind — or more exactly, the thinking activity of the conscious self — the existence of which could be affirmed with unqualified certainty and self-evidence. Eventually he proposed that a radically reformed philosophy could be built upon the 'entirely indubitable'[66] foundation of the *cogito.* From the existence of the mind, the existence of God and of the world could then be proven, he thought, and philosophy would be capable of obtaining fully trustworthy knowledge of the world.

The first step towards the implementation of this project was clear. Since all the presumed philosophical knowledge that had been 'cultivated for many centuries [should be] accounted as well-nigh false,'[67] it had to be replaced 'starting entirely anew, and building from the foundations up:'[68] Descartes's reformation would begin with the 'general overthrow'[69] of the entire philosophical tradition. If modern philosophers assume that modern philosophy was an absolute beginning, it is because Descartes's himself told them as much and they took his word for it. But how would the overthrow be achieved?

---

66   René Descartes, *Discourse on Method* in Norman Kemp Smith (ed.), *Descartes' Philosophical Writings* (London: Macmillan, 1952), 140.

67   Descartes, *Discourse,* in Kemp Smith, 121.

68   René Descartes, *Meditations on First Philosophy* in Norman Kemp Smith (ed.), *Descartes' Philosophical Writings* (London: Macmillan, 1952), 196.

69   Descartes, *Meditations,* in Kemp Smith, 196.

Apparently, if we may judge by what Descartes actually did, by no more elaborate procedure than by consigning the tradition to oblivion: his assumptions regarding the nature of philosophy counselled, in effect, that there was no need to examine critically the history of philosophy with a view to determining why it had gone astray.

It seems clear, therefore, that Descartes was not highly conscious of the *traditional* or *socio-cultural,* and *evolving* nature of philosophy, and indeed of all knowledge. Had he been mindful of it, he would have realized the naiveté of his supposition that he could have overcome what his tradition had taught him by no more burdensome procedure than resolving to set it aside. He seems to have assumed that he could have unlearned it without any need to determine and specify to himself precisely what he thus erased and what not, and why.

The first consequence of these cascading misconceptions was that Descartes's idea of how to reform philosophy foreclosed the possibility of his making a critical determination of the true causes of the decline of philosophy at the end of the middle ages. The second was that his reformation effectively tended to perpetuate such causes. For by ingenuously assuming that he had no need to determine the causes, and that he had created a philosophy that owed very little to the past, he denied himself the possibility of consciously re-examining what he had retained from his scholastic education, along with the doctrine of foundationalism, the concept of representationism, and the defining role of unqualified certainty in the production of philosophical knowledge. In this manner, he failed to advert to all that he had accepted and retained from scholasticism, supposing that it was his own independent knowledge and discovery. And what he thus retained was not a little; Étienne Gilson catalogued most of it.[70] For Gilson, however, who was not only one of the greatest historians of mediaeval philosophy, but also a convinced, skilled, and committed Thomistic philosopher, they were not mistakes or delusions. In his judgment, the errors of modern philosophy did not originate with the scholastics; they stemmed from the corruption of sound scholastic doctrines by the hand of Descartes and later modern philosophers.

As it turns out, however, the flaws of modern philosophy are not invariably original. Mostly they repeat those of mediaeval scholasticism as transmitted through Descartes, the seed of some of

---

70   Étienne Gilson, Études sur le rôle de la pensée médiévale dans la formation du système cartésien (Paris: Vrin, 1930).

which, however, can be traced back to Greece. Most fateful of all, the legacy included the very ideas regarding perception and reality that had brought mediaeval philosophy to ruin. Descartes took for granted that representationism correctly described perception; the point was beyond discussion. Representationism, he might well have said, was obvious, invulnerable, and true.

Richard Rorty has remarked that recent philosophers evince less 'interest in the history of philosophy, or more generally in the history of thought than in solving philosophical problems.'[71] But the trend goes back to Descartes, whose ahistoricism was inherited by modern philosophy at large. The bequest was inherited through a simple but most effective mechanism, namely, the tacit transmission of tacit assumptions from teacher to pupil. To adopt ahistoricism, Descartes' contemporaries had to do little more than to follow Descartes' example. And to preserve it, later modern philosophers have had to do nothing but what philosophers had 'always' done. Silently and inertially, they seem to have absorbed the idea that, since philosophy is interested in the truth, which is timeless and always self-same (which was another gratuitous assumption, for truth is not the value of *reality*, but the value of *our knowledge* of reality, a value that evolves as knowledge evolves), the missteps we may have taken in the past during our temporal search for the unchanging truth are best ignored and forgotten.

Ahistoricism seems to have taken root in the modern philosophical tradition with little debate; its adoption does not seem to have been deliberately intended, or even consciously noted by many. Typical of twentieth-century philosophers in this respect was Ludwig Wittgenstein, who for all his extraordinarily valuable, though negative, contributions on the nature of language — i.e. his critique of the idea of 'language' as the encoding of pre-linguistic thoughts — seems to have 'had no great respect for most of the philosophers of the past.'[72]

But to be precise, lack of respect is not the issue; it is lack of *attention*. Ahistoricism now is among the unspoken presuppositions that shape the attitudes and procedures of much modern philosophical thought. And because it is a presupposition, the possibility of using the history of philosophy in

---

71   Richard Rorty, *Consequences of Pragmatism: Essays 1972-1980* (Minneapolis: University of Minnesota Press, 1982), 215.

72   George Pitcher, *The Philosophy of Wittgenstein* (Englewood Cliffs, N.J.: Prentice-Hall, 1964), 324, who based his conclusion on the testimony of Karl Britton, who in his 'Portrait of a Philosopher,' *The Listener*, 53 (1955): 1372, 1072, (quoted by Pitcher, 325), reported Wittgenstein's admissions that 'no assistant lecturer in philosophy in the country had read fewer books on philosophy than he had,' and that he 'had never read a single word of Aristotle, although he had lately read much of Plato.'

a different manner and for philosophical purposes does not occur readily to many of us. I would like to argue that it should.

Before I do, however, I clarify that when I suggest that Descartes's dismissal of scholasticism was indiscriminate and imprudent, I do not mean that he should have rejected only certain elements of it that were false and preserved others that were true. For one can easily imagine that after centuries of elaborate speculation based on the supposition that 'this world' is not the one and only world, the Augean stables of European philosophy did stand in need of an overhaul and renovation of Herculean proportions. What I have in mind is rather that Descartes failed to distinguish between *rejecting* the inadequacies of scholasticism (and of Greek philosophy in the first place) and *ignoring* their historical role in the formation of modern Western European thought, including Descartes's own.

The historicity of the human philosophical mind and its cognitive processes suggests that, once we reasonably wonder whether past events may not have taken philosophy off the scent of the truth, the best, if not the only, way we can reasonably hope to verify our suspicion and redirect philosophy accordingly is to resort to a critical examination of the history of philosophy. But since the legitimacy of this procedure is widely rejected, our study of the causes of the precarious condition of modern philosophy will be preceded, in the remainder of this section, with an attempt to establish: (a) how the historicity of philosophy can be made use of for philosophical purposes, (b) the handicap under which we would proceed if we were to philosophize without taking the historicity of philosophy into account, and (c) the disadvantages under which Greek philosophy laboured by reason of the fact that the creation of philosophy was an aboriginal, unprecedented cultural development.

b) The historicity of philosophy and how to make use of it

The prevailing ahistoricism of modern philosophy relies on the distinction between philosophy and the history of philosophy, and presumes that the difference suggests the irrelevance of the latter to the former. Now, the difference is real; for it is a fact, albeit a thin and dry one, that whereas philosophy is concerned with problems such as the nature of the mind, the discipline known as the history of philosophy is interested in what philosophers have thought about such problems. This is true, but we should avoid choking on the conclusion that supposedly follows, namely, that if one wants to understand, say, mental phenomena, one should turn one's attention to the mental phenomena themselves; and that if one wants help, inspiration or correction one should seek it in what one's contemporaries think about the subject. In either event, philosophers need pay little or no attention to what philosophers of other ages have thought. As Peter Hare has reported, philosophers and historians of philosophy tend to agree 'that a philosopher cannot at once make a contribution to the solution of current philosophical problems and a contribution to the history of thought.'[73]

This, I think, is not true. The reason is that history can reveal much more than the philosophical thinking of past ages. For the history of philosophy may be studied historically, simply as the record of past philosophical events; and if all we ask of history is that it teach us what philosophers have thought in the past, history will not volunteer additional information. But the history of philosophy can also be read philosophically — that is, for narrowly philosophical ends. This way to read it takes advantage of the fact that the past is not only what has ceased to be, but also the time out of which the present emerges. Past history can help our present and future philosophical endeavours. How?

To answer this question, let us go back briefly to the remote origin of the ahistoricist trend of philosophical thought; it is to be found in the difficulties experienced by Greek philosophers when they tried to account for the nature of 'becoming' or change.

In the predominant Greek tradition, the proper name of what we today call 'reality' (i.e. either an existent, or the totality of existents known as the 'world') was 'being,' *(to on)*. And since 'being' denotes self-identity or self-sameness — for a 'being' surely *is* whatever it is, and *is not* whatever it is not — the Greeks had difficulty reconciling the 'being' of the world with the observable fact that nothing in the world is self-same, since it changes. For whatever changes, ceases to be the same as it was and *becomes* different. Though modern European civilization today is generally much more conscious of the reality of becoming than in ages past, the identification of 'reality' as 'being' continues to influence philosophical thought.

According to Parmenides — whom Plato called his intellectual 'father' — the criterion of truth was conceivability, since 'it is the same thing that can be thought and can be.'[74] We cannot think

---

73   Peter H. Hare, (ed.), *Doing Philosophy Historically* (Amherst, NY: Prometheus, 1988), 12.

74   Herman Diels and Walther Kranz, *Die Fragmente der Vorsokratiker* (Zurich: Weidmann, 1985), 28B3.

of anything unless we conceive it as that which 'is.' Thus, only 'being' (or 'that which is') is real. 'Becoming' is impossible: 'How could Being perish? How could it come into being?'[75] Plato's *Phaedo* illustrates graphically how some Greek philosophers distorted the correct observation that nothing is exactly self-same, given the constancy of change, into the supposition that the empirically given world is less than truly real. But according to Heraclitus, at the other extreme, the *'logos'* (that is, 'the intelligible Law of the universe,' as Freeman translates the term,[76]) determines that nothing can be at rest: 'the river I step in is not the same river I stand in.'[77] (Translations of this famous phrase vary; the sense does not.) Therefore, nothing can be truly said 'to be.' And from this follows that '[w]e cannot *know* anything about particular objects; when we examine them, they dissolve into a part of the process of change.'[78]

A remnant of the same style of thinking is still at work in those of us who try to deduce the meaning of temporality from the concept of time implicit in our culture's linguistic conventions — which begin with the supposition that reality can be envisaged as 'that which *is*.' Consequently, we think that only the present time is truly real. In this view, the past never has any reality unless as a present memory; it is always that which is 'gone' and cannot be changed. And so, we think of the past as having totally disappeared and the present as a replacement of the past. But what we actually observe in the world is not quite so. Philosophers may wring their hands when they try to reconcile being and becoming; and if they take their cues from their concepts rather than from what the world exhibits to us, they will do so endlessly. But the world itself shows no sign of the supposed incompatibility of being and becoming, reality and change, novelty and permanence, sameness and difference. What observation of the world makes plain, if we are open to reading its message, is the mutual relativity of the two: the reality of 'being' is its 'becoming.' There is no 'being' but 'that which becomes.' And nothing 'becomes' unless by 'being.'

---

75   Diels-Kranz, *Fragmente*, 28B8.

76   Kathleen Freeman, *Ancilla to the Pre-Socratic Philosophers: A Complete Translation of the Fragments in Diels, Fragmente der Vorsokratiker* (Oxford: Blackwell, 1948), 24.

77   Diels-Kranz, 22B49a. And again, 'one cannot step into the same river twice,' Diels-Kranz, 22B91.

78   Kathleen Freeman, *The Pre-Socratic Philosophers: A Companion to Diels*, Fragmente der Vorsokratiker (Oxford: Blackwell, 1949), 115. Italics in the original.

This implies, of course, that reality is thoroughly *temporal.* There is no atemporal, or immutable, or eternal reality; these would be oxymorons. But many people, including many philosophers, find difficult to accept this implication. Interestingly, the reason is not necessarily that contemporary philosophers (other than neo-scholastics) normally profess religious belief in a world of eternity beyond the world of time. The reason is rather that they continue to think of 'reality' and 'world' as our cultural tradition has long supposed[79] — although such suppositions implicitly assume that the world in which we live and die is not the standard of reality. Inertia suffices to perpetuate this assumption, even after the religious beliefs that support it are no longer affirmed. We should recognize instead, or so I suggest, that the only meaning with which the words 'reality' and 'world' can be rationally and sensibly taken refers to the reality of the world that is our environment. Every other meaning is crafted by our imagination by the simple expedient of negating the characteristics of the real world. It is thus that we invent 'another world' — that is, a 'non-material', 'non-temporal', 'non-spatial', and 'non-mutable' world.

The agnosticism of much modern philosophy is an unwitting self-contradiction. If one is a philosopher, but one neither affirms the existence nor denies the possibility of a 'higher' level of eternal reality, one has failed to accept that the temporal world is unqualifiedly real. For one may not have adverted to it, but one has implicitly supposed that the empirically given world may be less than pure and simply 'real.' And if so, one has failed to take the world as the measure of 'reality,' despite the fact that it is the only world from which we can learn what the concept of 'reality' can truly mean.

We might well refer to philosophical suppositions of this sort as *orphan assumptions.* They survive and prosper indefinitely, even after the parent opinions that generated them and gave them a semblance of justification have gone the way of all flesh — but without much awareness, on the part of those who adopt them, that in the absence of legitimate lineage such assumptions are delusions. The supposition that there are, for instance, eternal and unchanging 'laws of nature' inherent in the world that rule the operation of the world is an orphan assumption. Unless one also supposes an eternal Legislator of the 'laws of nature,' it is an implicit self-contradiction. A variant of this orphan assumption is the idea that

---

79   For example, that the world is inherently intelligible. The objections to this view, and possible alternative interpretations of the matter, will be discussed below.

the world contains inherent universal and eternal truths – a proposition that would make sense only on the prior supposition of an omniscient and eternal Mind that knows it.

The unity of being and becoming is found in that characteristic of the world — or better, of the world *process* — to which we usually, but equivocally, refer as 'time.' Equivocally, I say, because the substantive noun, 'time,' solidifies the flow of becoming and thereby distorts our vision of the reality to which the concept refers. But however we may put it, the observable fact is that the world is temporal (or more precisely, spatio-temporal), although the fact is twisted out of shape by our inherited syntax (which prompts us to think of reality as 'that which *is*,' in the timeless instant of the present [80]), and by our consequent vocabulary (which dichotomizes reality into 'being,' which alone is real *simpliciter,* and 'becoming,' which is less than really real). To understand the relevance of the past to the present, and how the *philosophical* study of the history of philosophy has philosophical value, let us consider what is meant by the 'temporality' of the events that describe the course of the world as it 'becomes.'

The present situation of the world as a whole is, at any given time, different from the immediately preceding state of affairs. This includes the events that have issued in the present situation of the individual human mind, and in the current configuration of the societies and cultures created by the interaction of individual minds; in all cases the present is always different from its antecedents, and the past never continues unchanged into the present. But this is only part of what we observe. Quite as clearly visible, if we credit our eyes, is the other part: that the present is always conditioned by the immediately preceding moment out of which the present emerged. Therefore, the degree to which at any given moment the present differs from the immediate past is, though variable, always limited. Events do not succeed or replace each other, but flow from one to another; they neither appear nor disappear with digital instantaneity, but fade in and out in a continuous analogue stream.

---

80   The syntax of English and all other Indo-European languages makes it difficult for a philosopher to avoid hypostatizations and reifications such as are involved in speaking of 'time' as if it existed in and by itself, and *within which* the world is supposed to exist and *in relation to which* it changes. What observation shows is rather that 'timing' — or becoming — is a characteristic of reality. When I speak of the 'temporality' of the world I intend to describe one of the observable properties that is common to all real things in the world; time does not exist by itself, separately from such things or from the real world.

It is the latter aspect of the temporality of events that is especially relevant to present purposes — a temporality that, insofar as it refers to human events is more particularly called 'historicity.' It means that the new can never be so absolutely new as to exclude the traces of the past out of which it came. This is true of all worldly processes without exception, and it applies both to the individual and to society; but the fact that becoming involves both the emergence of a degree of difference and the preservation of a degree of sameness is especially evident in the seamless continuity of life and its evolution — and therefore in human history — in which the new differs from, but bears the mark of, the old out of which it came. Historical temporality qualifies human nature and all its activities and institutions.

This is important for appreciating the role that historical perspective can play in philosophy. The temporality of the real means that when we look upon past philosophical events we are looking not only at events that have ceased to be, but also at events that have brought about the situation in which *present* philosophical events take place. This is why, as a few philosophers have recently pointed out,[81] the history of philosophy of mind may be read as an instrument of philosophical criticism. It can help us understand and judge, instead of accepting without question, the conditions under which we *today* undertake philosophical investigation of, for instance, the mind.

Such conditions bear upon not a few aspects of every philosopher's thinking. They influence one's formulation of the problems one wishes to solve, the orientation of one's enquiries, one's acceptance of whatever starting points one chooses to reason from, one's decisions to make certain assumptions and reject others, and one's decisions (or one's non-decisions) to take certain truths as unquestionably self-evident. The historical background of one's present thinking includes even a more or less vague, a more or less conscious, expectation of the general sort of answer that one is likely to find satisfactory for one's purposes.

And so, if one does not read the history of philosophy expecting it to tell one solely about the past, but if, instead, one interrogates it appropriately and for philosophical purposes, the history of philosophy of mind can tell one much about what one *already* thinks at present concerning the mind — that is, *before* one begins to investigate the mind. Regardless of whether one thinks it clearly

---

81   Hare, (ed.), *Doing Philosophy Historically.*

or confusedly, rightly or wrongly, one will *already* think it, by way of either conscious or non-conscious assumption. For one's present philosophical thinking is only the latest episode in a history of philosophical thinking that began more than twenty-five centuries ago — a philosophical thinking, indeed, that was itself conditioned by the *pre-philosophical,* common sense development of the culture that produced it. Learning how we came by our assumptions makes it possible for us to cast a critical eye on them. We can hardly correct our missteps until we become conscious of them.

The last thought provokes a supplementary question that is not asked very often, possibly because the answer seems obvious —though the truth is not. The question is: precisely how do we human beings correct our mistakes? We all have had the experience of changing our opinions; do we not do it almost 'by instinct'? Perhaps we do. But the question remains: exactly how?

It is a common supposition that the only way is to try again. This is the procedure that modern philosophy of mind has invariably followed whenever it has been forced to acknowledge that the latest hypothesis hopefully entertained until not so long ago has proven unworkable. It is the procedure that comes to mind naturally to those who think that the persistent renewal of efforts will in time bring success to philosophy. But if this procedure has not worked — and if we, therefore, should search for a new one — the reason is that it is inadequate. And it is inadequate not only for previously discussed reasons, but also because it presupposes a questionable idea of the nature of mistakes; it assumes, therefore, a questionable idea of how philosophy's mistakes can be discovered and corrected.

Our inadequate conception of a mistake — which is the mirror image of our inadequate conception of truth — depends not only on our previously noted tendency to project our cognitive activities onto the world, but also on our overlooking the fact that cognition, and indeed all aspects of human life, are *processes.* We therefore tend to construe both our cognition, and the reality of the world that is its object, as if neither cognition nor the world of objects were inherently temporal. To recall a Bergsonian metaphor, we misperceive them as if the world's events were comparable to a cinematographic film, which enables us to experience an illusion of motion, although it is actually made up of successive instantaneous static images. The empirically observable fact is rather that the becoming world is not a series of timeless instants, but an unbroken and unbreakable flow of continuous events. Nevertheless, the outcome of conceiving our mental processes as a succession of distinct instants, rather than as a continuous *activity,* is that we find it difficult to observe what otherwise would be a fairly easily noticed feature of our mistakes. Namely, that although we can make a mistake at any time, we can *advert* to the mistakes we have made only by means of a *backwards* glance at an earlier stage of our mental life. Observing how our human mental life actually unfolds demonstrates that we cannot think of our mistakes as mistakes, unless in *hindsight.*

From an early stage of their development, all human beings have occasion to experience that their cognitive activities seem to have met with success; they experience that they 'are right,' or that their perceptions or judgments seem to be 'correct.' This enables them to develop, whether adequately or distortedly, the concept of 'truth.' Actually, truth is a quality that is enjoyed by our cognitive functions when — or rather, to the degree that — such functions effectively fulfil their cognitive purpose, namely, to relate ourselves to reality as it actually is by becoming informed, to a greater or lesser extent, of what it actually is. Sometimes, however, human beings have the contrary experience; their senses or their mental efforts to understand give evidence or at least indications of having failed. They therefore conceive 'falsity,' 'error,' 'mistake,' and so on. If we compare the two experiences, however, we may note a curious disparity between the experience of 'being right,' and what we usually call, but inaccurately, the experience of 'being wrong' or 'being mistaken.' For strictly speaking, none of us ever experiences '*being* wrong' or '*being* mistaken' (i.e., now, at present). What we actually experience is rather '*having been* mistaken' (i.e. in the past). To experience that our present cognitive activity '*is* mistaken' is impossible; for without exception, the concomitant of every conscious assertion, perception, thought, judgment, or interpretation of ours is the experience of 'being right' or of having succeeded in reaching the 'truth.'[82] We can never experience our errors as such *unless in retrospect.* The temporality of the conscious mind asserts itself in this manner, even if usually we are deaf to its message. 'Being in error' *always* refers to a mental event that happened in the past — the kind that cannot be spoken of in the present tense without its being thereby distorted and misunderstood.

---

82   One can lie, of course, by misrepresenting what in fact one thinks is the truth; but one cannot very well simultaneously lie and think that the lie is true. One can, on the other hand, persuade oneself that one is not lying, though in fact one is. In other words, self-deception is perfectly possible. But it does not affect my suggestion that the experience of error is always retrospective.

These are, no doubt, intriguing facts, and no theory of the nature of 'truth' could be at all adequate unless it took them into account. But what matters at this point is rather that they are observable facts and that therefore they must be respected as such. But if we accept them, then we should be able to understand why mere persistence is unlikely to help us correct our mistakes. Repeated observation of the facts may, at best, create suspicion that the truth may have escaped us — though even this is less likely than our reaffirming instead, with greater or lesser dogmatism, what we already believe or suppose to be true. To learn otherwise, we have to look back towards to our original experience; retrospection creates the opportunity to perceive anew, and hopefully to correct, what we had previously perceived incorrectly or misinterpreted. We change our minds only when *retrospection* — looking backwards in time — tells us that we must.

In short, even our daily experience in minor respects teaches us the same lesson as the study of the most complex philosophical questions. If we wish to undo our mistakes, first we must become aware that they are mistakes. And to become aware of it, there is no alternative procedure to looking backwards in time.

c) The handicap of ahistoricism

Ahistoricism, on the contrary, handicaps philosophy in several ways. It discourages radical criticism, since it tends to suggest, in effect, that criticism be limited to recent developments: past errors need not be revived, but are best forgotten, since they have already been detected and discarded. Therefore, ahistoricism also tends to promote intellectual endogamy — which is of course not less unhealthy than its biological counterpart. The gravity of this danger cannot be overstressed; for as L. Jonathan Cohen has remarked, it is easy 'for a philosopher who takes his problems exclusively from other philosophers to believe that these problems merit discussion just because they are also discussed by other philosophers.'[83] To the extent that this happens, the course of philosophy is governed by trends — occasionally, perhaps, even by fads. Most unfortunate may be that ahistoricism tends to render our inherited prejudices inaccessible, and therefore self-perpetuating. Why?

---

83   Jonathan Cohen, *The Dialogue of Reason: An Analysis of Analytic Philosophy* (Oxford: Clarendon Press, 1986), 138.

Because assumptions of which one is not conscious — presuppositions that are only implicit in what one consciously thinks — cannot be examined, of course, as long as they remain outside the purview of consciousness. The philosophical study of the history of philosophy, however, may help us bring our assumptions and their implications to light. Besides, this is not the only boon that historical perspective brings; its most important contribution has to do with *consciously held* assumptions one has inherited from the past but of whose origin one is not aware. Unawareness *of their being inherited* will make them seem indubitable, perhaps even self-evident, because they would seem to have been arrived at spontaneously: quite as Descartes did, one will think that one, in the guise of Everyman, has discovered them for oneself, or that they are among the 'intuitions' that all human beings 'naturally' come by. The opportunity to judge them, and the possibility of ultimately relying instead on assumptions that one has evaluated deliberately as best one could, has been taken away by default. Representationism is, of course, one such assumption.

At the same time, however, it is true, and one must grant, that neither individual philosophers nor entire philosophical generations can reasonably expect to have more than limited success in criticizing the concepts with which they came to be equipped at various stages of life. We are finite and fallible. And of course, if philosophers are reluctant, for whatever reason, to criticize what they have been brought up to deem true — and practical considerations abound why it might be inconvenient to criticize it — it will be difficult for them to overcome the limitations of their beginnings. But it would be next to impossible, if one of the prejudices they inherited — but had forgotten that they had inherited it, and from whom — were the consciously held assumption that philosophy's past misperceptions were best laid to rest. For such strategy had paid off, supposedly, when it was first adopted by Descartes at the beginning of modern times, when it restored philosophy to innocence and opened for it, at long last, the path of true *scientia*. Next to impossible, I say, because the baptismal waters of Lethe would more likely set than remove the stain of originally defective assumptions. As Santayana said, one will have condemned oneself to repeating one's mistakes.

We often speak of history as 'unfolding,' but since historical events, as I argue, are not ruled by deterministic causation, this metaphor tends to distort the truth. A better figure would be that history folds the past into the present as the future emerges. In this respect, history is like biological evolution: it is creative. To be sure, the creativity of biological evolution does not imply that evolution is either progressive or regressive in relation to a predetermined end: evolution does not tend either to bring about or to avoid a predetermined outcome. But the parallel between biological evolution and human history is not fortuitous. Human history is only the continuation, through cultural means, of the evolution of human beings through genetic means. Both forms of evolution follow a causal logic. And like the logic of biological evolution, the logic of historical processes — the logic of cultural evolution — can be ascertained only after the processes have taken place. Biological evolution and human history make sense, but only retrospectively; they cannot be deduced prospectively. And missteps, as already noted, can be seen to be such only in retrospect.

The usefulness of historical perspective for philosophy has to do only in part —though in vitally important part —with the correction of assumptions whose adequacy or truth becomes doubtful upon historical retrospection. Historical perspective also has positive value; it contributes to the evolution of philosophy by helping philosophers envision novel possibilities. When the past is left unexamined, unanalyzed, and unevaluated, even its positive achievements tend to hobble progress; for it is easier to repeat what one already knows rather than to try to improve upon it. Awareness of the dependence of the present on the past tends, on the contrary, to inspire innovative ways to improve on the present. Critical reflection upon the history of the philosophical treatment of a problem provides a background against which the old problem may be seen in a new light. The light cast by historical perspective is indispensable to any philosophical attempt to study the human mind.

d) The disadvantaged origins of philosophy

Finally, before we turn to history to study the causes of the parlous condition of philosophy after Hume, we should give some attention to a further consideration. When the early Greek philosophers discovered the possibility of thinking philosophically — that is, when they discovered that the human mind could be used to peculiar advantage if it followed certain procedures and adhered to certain rules that were not generally followed by the culture — it was most likely — indeed, practically speaking certain — that they would make some miscalculations, especially regarding the characteristics of the philosophical enterprise and its procedures. Beginners can be expected to make mistakes; we should be taken by surprise only when they do not.

The cultural conditions under which the Greeks founded philosophy are not the same as our own today, and neither were those under which the scholastics continued the tradition; even as recently as the seventeenth century they were not. So far as concerns understanding the world and human nature, two and a half millennia ago, Hellenic civilization was in its earliest stages. Its citizens had learned how to use their imagination to answer mythologically the questions that all human societies raise at a certain level of the evolution of the human mind. But they had not yet brought to light the possibility of using reason systematically to derive more reliable, rigorously reasoned, interpretations of human nature and the world than mythology had. The philosophers invented the institution of scholarship *ab initio,* by taking advantage of the characteristics of the human mind. That they did invent scholarship at all, was a feat of ingenuity and creativity; relatively few early human cultures ever developed, on their own, the idea of using the mind in a disciplined, rigorously rational manner. For contrary to a widespread assumption of our own culture, there is ample historical and anthropological evidence that although human cultural progress is possible and desirable (if sensibly and rationally managed), it is not inevitable. It was entirely possible that Greek culture might never have instituted a philosophical tradition *at all*; but if so, it should not amaze us that, having succeeded, it nevertheless stumbled as it took its first steps. Misunderstanding and confusion would have been all the easier at a time when philosophers had not yet honed their philosophical skills and could not count on the benefit of accumulated experience. Inventors, innovators, pioneers, and original thinkers operate under the disadvantage of being such.

But there is a more specific and more portentous circumstance we must take into account if we are to understand why the Greek philosophers should have, almost inevitably, failed to interpret, quite correctly, certain aspects of the human mind.

We today are conscious, and so were the Greeks; there can be little doubt on the point.[84] Based on the evidence provided, for instance, by Upper Palaeolithic art, we can estimate that members of

84   Julian Jaynes, in *The Origin of Consciousness in the Breakdown of the Bicameral Mind* (Toronto: University of Toronto Press, 1976)., 67-83, claims that the absence of theories of mind in classical Greek philosophical texts before the 5th century

our species have been conscious since at least about 25,000 years ago. (To portray what one remembers or imagines, it is necessary to be reflexively aware, at least to a degree, of the cognitive activity of one's mind; it demands introspection.) But the conditions under which we today are conscious are not the same as those in which the Greeks were conscious. We today not only *are* conscious; we also *know* that we are. This is not to say that we also *understand* the nature of consciousness; this is a yet higher level of accomplishment. But there are more than passing indications that neither the Greek nor the mediaeval cultures, nor their philosophers, were *aware* of the conscious character that their cognition in fact enjoyed. Unawareness of it would have put the Greeks and the mediaevals at a disadvantage when they undertook to study the human mind.

It may be difficult for us to understand the difference between one's *being* conscious and one's *knowing* that one is conscious; but the point is essential if we are to read the history of philosophy with at least a modicum of perspective. To *be* conscious, one needs only (a) to have the sort of organism that is capable of the kind of cognition that is called conscious, and (b) to be in actual conscious states as a result of one's having exercised one's organic capacity for experiencing consciously. To *know* that one is conscious, on the other hand, depends on whether one has learned about one's cognitive powers, and how much. It may be nothing; one may be completely unaware of one's being conscious; young children illustrate the point. And knowing that one is conscious may amount to as little as knowing the fact that one's cognition has the quality of being conscious, without one's understanding in what consciousness consists, and even without one's being at all sure of what it means. But it may also include further understanding of the nature of conscious cognition. Organic evolution made us conscious beings, capable of discharging cognitive functions that in fact are conscious, and of having conscious states. But what we know about our consciousness does not depend on organic evolution, but on the degree to which we may have *learned* it — either independently, as individuals, or as members of a culture that has evolved and in which it is common knowledge that we are conscious, and that being conscious 'has something to do' with being aware of one's cognitive powers. Well, how

---

B.C. indicates that their authors were not conscious. Jaynes does not appear to have considered that the absence of explanation may indicate *unawareness,* rather than *absence,* of consciousness.

much had the Greeks learned about the conscious, human mind when a few of them conceived the rudiments of the idea of philosophy? As it happens, very little.

Human cultural evolution began prehistorically, of course. The efforts of human beings to understand themselves and the world predate civilization and philosophy; anthropological studies of surviving primitive cultures provide evidence to that effect. The efforts probably go back to the time when our species first became human; that is, when it attained to 'consciousness.' For conscious cognition, I assume, is one of the two defining indicia of humanity, the other being speech.

We need not be concerned with the question whether the cognitive powers of the higher infra-human species developed consciousness. This is possible in principle: if some non-conscious hominids developed consciousness as our species came into being, others could have, too. But we are interested here only in the mind of our species; and our understanding of it depends on what we observe in ourselves, not on whether we share it with other species. Nevertheless, to judge by the consequences that consciousness brought to human behaviour and to the human mode of life, it is, in my view, exceedingly unlikely that conscious cognition has appeared in other species even in rudimentary form; for we do not observe in any of them the sort of behaviour that in ourselves demands consciousness. The best estimate of which we are capable is that, if by consciousness we mean the quality that our experience ordinarily exhibits to itself— namely, the quality whereby it experiences its own experiential character — then consciousness is uniquely ours.

This position seems to scandalize many psychologists and other scientists. But it is difficult to understand why it should, if they accept the idea of biological evolution through the somewhat ambiguously denominated mechanism of 'natural selection.'[85] For evolution is supposed to produce *differences* from one species to another, and *only* differences; the similarities are what *do not* evolve. As differences appear, they accumulate so as to separate not only species but even 'kingdoms' — that

---

85   Why ambiguous? Because in the context of ordinary human affairs, the noun 'selection' ordinarily presupposes a criterion of differentiation, and thus to imply finality, whereas the 'selection' involved in evolutionary 'natural selection' excludes finality. Thus, the concept of 'natural selection' is easily misunderstood, because the adjective 'natural' alludes only weakly to the exclusion of finality from the evolutionary process of 'natural selection.'

is, the vegetative, sentient, and human forms of life,[86] — each of which preserves the basic features of preceding stages of development but adds a novelty. Thus, *something* must be found in the human species that makes it unique; otherwise we should not be deemed a distinct species. Reductionists, however, confusing continuity with indistinctness, would have us suppose otherwise.

One of the characteristics of cognition when it reaches the level of consciousness in human beings is that the cognitive powers become able to observe themselves. Human beings can observe that they have the ability to become aware of the world and its objects. But as previously mentioned, the self-observability of the conscious mind should not to be confused with consciousness, the typical quality of human cognition. The self-observability of the conscious mind means only that, once human beings have matured and developed consciousness, they cannot altogether fail to apprehend that they are endowed with cognitive powers, because they can reflect upon their cognitive activities — that is, they can make a prior cognitive act the object of a second cognitive act. Consciousness, however, endows us with something else before it yields self-observability. It gives us the ability to perceive our cognitive agency (as well as many of our non-cognitive and non-mental activities), and the reality of our organisms and of the world. (The relationship between consciousness and self-observability will be discussed in detail in Chapter III.)

The self-observability of consciousness is the reason why the vocabularies of even the most primitive cultures of which we have notice include terms and expressions signifying mental functions: 'to see,' 'to think,' 'to imagine,' 'to understand,' 'to speak,' and so on are invariably found in the languages of primitive peoples. To that extent at least, all mature human beings are aware of their cognition; they could scarcely speak about it, if they were not. And such cognition must be conscious in quality, since they are aware of the experiential nature of their experience. What they are not necessarily aware of is that their cognition is conscious — or, *a fortiori,* that there is a difference between cognition and conscious cognition. Or which is the same, they are not always aware that not all cognition is conscious.

---

86   The classical tripartite division of living beings is an oversimplification, but it suffices for most ordinary philosophical purposes.

The same self-observability of the conscious mind enables even the most ignorant and unsophisticated human societies to grasp the fact that their mental abilities put them in touch with the world and its objects; they develop concepts for 'things,' 'objects,' the 'world,' and 'reality.' Likewise, elementary conscious experience is all that is needed before conscious experiencers learn that at least some of the changes that take place in the world are brought about by other events or actions without which the changes would not take place; they conceive 'agency,' 'responsibility,' 'causality,' and the like. Thus, in all cultures the conscious nature of the human mind enables human beings to develop concepts of cognition, causality, and reality — not necessarily, of course, in those very terms, or abstractly —without their necessarily developing awareness of the conscious nature of their mind.

Of course, the conscious mind's awareness of its cognitive activities, as well as its experience of the reality of objects and events that take place in the world, can be more or less shallow or profound, accurate or inaccurate. The anthropologically documented ability of all human beings to conceive cognition, causality, and reality at an early stage of their cultural development does not imply that their observations and their thinking in the matter are well thought out or free from error. It does imply, however, that the emergence of philosophy is necessarily preceded by a socio-culturally mediated casual acquaintance with, and interpretation of, ourselves and the world. Philosophy presupposes pre-philosophical experience. Such casual knowledge is especially evident in the repertoire of concepts, judgments, and categories embodied in the specific language learned and used by philosophers before they become philosophers; in their absence, philosophizing and improving upon common sense knowledge would be absurdly impossible. Philosophy comes into being as an attempt to improve the quality of our pre-philosophical experience. But it is easy to suppose that philosophy is rather an attempt to develop a different order of knowledge. If so, philosophy risks becoming esoteric. If it did so become, it would be at its peril.

Thus, philosophers today try to understand the real world, the causes of phenomena, and the nature of cognition, but they do not conceive for the first time the 'reality' of the world, or the 'causality' of causes when they enquire into their nature: their investigations are invariably preceded by their acquisition of these notions in the normal course of everyday human life, and indeed at a fairly early stage in the mental development of human beings. This is a result of their individual experience under the guidance of the culture into which they are inducted soon after birth. The same is true of the concepts of 'cognition' and 'mind' and their countless variations and cognates. Those philosophers who might deny that philosophical inquiry is necessarily preceded by, and continuous with, the culture's common sense, might do well to remember that when they entered into their first philosophical discussion of 'causality,' 'reality,' or 'cognition' as undergraduates, they were not altogether uninformed of what the conversation was about.

In fact, they had learned to use these words meaningfully years earlier, even in childhood, to assert the experienced (or the imagined) reality signified by the words; willy-nilly, they would have brought their common-sense opinions with themselves to their philosophical studies. The degree to which their understanding progressed thereafter would depend, of course, on the degree to which they meditated critically on their original opinions. But first impressions are notoriously deep-rooted. Like the experiences of early childhood in other respects, which not infrequently mark one for life, both for better and for worse, the conditions under which philosophy came to be are more easily forgotten than overcome. If one supposes discontinuity between common sense and philosophy, one risks mistaking for philosophical insight what in fact may be an error or a prejudice of a culture that has escaped critical review.

We can estimate, therefore, how much, and what, the members of classical Greek culture had learned simply by virtue of their *being* conscious at the time when they were beginning to discover how to use their minds philosophically. What they had learned was all that philosophy had at its disposal as its initial intellectual capital — the savings of common sense, as it were. They knew that they were capable of cognition, that the world was real, and that changes in the world and in themselves were the effects of causes; and they could count on whatever additional observations on these subjects had been preserved by the culture's common sense. But they did not realize that their cognition was conscious. The closest the Greek philosophers ever came to it was when they became aware that the self-observability of the mind made possible, as Aristotle said,[87] the disciplined, rational study of the mind.

---

87   Aristotle, *Metaphysics*, 12.7.1072b19-23.

The evidence of unawareness of the conscious nature of human cognition on the part of the Greek philosophers (and of Greek culture generally) is necessarily negative, of course; but it is hefty. What attests to it is the absence of all discussion of the subject of consciousness, whether by that or by another name, from the surviving classical Greek literature, both philosophical and non-philosophical. Indeed, there was no word in classical Greek to signify what in modern English is meant by 'consciousness,' and by equivalents thereof in the other modern European languages. Much less were the Greeks able to differentiate between 'conscious' and 'non-conscious cognition.' By way of exception, awareness of consciousness has been attributed, with some superficial plausibility, to Aristotle. However, the textual evidence usually cited[88] shows only awareness of the self-observability of the mind — which as I have suggested, is not quite the same thing.[89] And neither Aristotle nor any other Greek philosopher attributed self-observability (or any other aspect of the human mind) to the conscious character of human cognition.

There are two classical Greek words that at first glance may appear to signify 'consciousness,' and which indeed are used in modern Greek with such meaning. The principal one is *syneidesis* (etymologically, 'knowing with'), which was therefore rendered literally into classical Latin as *conscientia*. The other is *synesis* (etymologically, 'withness,' i.e., 'intimacy.'). But neither was used in classical Greek to mean 'consciousness;' they both meant 'conscience.' Their etymologies may be a little misleading: 'knowing with' is sometimes held to connote 'knowing jointly with another person.' For what little it may matter, I do not think this is warranted; and in any event, the denotation is clear. A free idiomatic English translation of both *syeneidesis* and *synesis* would be 'confrontation with oneself' — but strictly in the tacitly understood context of the moral value of one's conduct. The 'withness' in question alludes to the identity of the moral judge and the morally judged, or to the 'interiority' of the process. Both terms describe the process of owning up to, usually with regret and shame or else self-satisfaction, one's past actions, intentions, decisions, and feelings.[90]

---

88   Aristotle, *On the Soul*, 3.2.425b12; *Metaphysics*, 12.7.1072b19-23; and *Nichomachean Ethics*, 9.9.1170a25-1170b-10.

89   Not as easily dismissed is the passage where Aristotle postulates the controversial second *nous* that Hellenists have distinguished from the *nous pathetikos* by referring to it as the 'active intellect,' *De Anima*, 3.5.430a15 ff. However, apart from the other well-known ambiguities and obscurities of the doctrine of the 'active *nous*,' Aristotle himself, as Ross has pointed out, did not actually refer to it as 'active;' Ross, *Aristotle*, 148.

90   An illustration of how *synesis* is used in Greek may be found in Hannay, *Consciousness*, 188.

The question could be raised whether absence of a term from the vocabulary of a culture necessarily indicates absence of the object that the term asserts. It might be argued, for instance, that 'although the Eskimo [sic] vocabulary contains no word for art, that does not prevent a brisk trade in what dealers in North America refer to as Eskimo [sic] art.'[91] By the same token, the absence of 'consciousness' from classical Greek need not indicate absence of consciousness in reality.

True, but the question goes beyond whether the Greeks *were* conscious; their behaviour, their being able to speak, and their ability to recount their experiences and to discuss their mental processes leave no reasonable doubt about it. The further issue is whether absence of the term indicates absence of the *experience* signified by the term; the North American dealers' calling it 'art' does not mean that the Inuit *think* of their artistic works as 'art.' Thus, the question is whether the Greek philosophers, who *were* conscious, *adverted* to the fact that they were conscious and took it into account as they studied the human mind. As Alastair Hannay's discussion of the subject has made clear, what ultimately matters for philosophical purposes is the difference between the Greek and the modern understanding of the problem of the mind. The essential point, as Hannay says, is that in modern times 'philosophy has hit upon problems of a certain very fundamental nature that require more radical solutions than we are ordinarily willing, able, or required to envisage.'[92] Or, I add, than either the Greek or the mediaeval philosophers realized. Thus, according to Hannay, regardless of whether the Greeks had a distinct concept of consciousness:

> What is true is that they did not possess a concept of consciousness with the Cartesian and Lockean connotations of our own concept … [E]ven if the Greeks were excellent psychologists, and their language contained all the distinctions they needed, their conception of the human mind nevertheless lacked something of theoretical importance that would have been available to them had they adopted the "reflective" point of view which has given birth to a concept of consciousness as broad and general as our own.[93]

---

91   Hannay, *Consciousness*, 16.

92   Hannay, *Consciousness*, 14.

93   Hannay, *Consciousness*, 16, 20.

We may conclude that the Greek philosophers were denied a vital piece of the puzzle of the human mind, and that it was therefore unlikely that they could have avoided every inaccuracy on the subject. They distinguished between the human and the infrahuman mind by reference to the human ability to reason, instead of the more fundamental human capacity for conscious cognition. Unawareness of the conscious nature of human cognition was not, of course, a mistake; it was only a disadvantage under which they studied human cognition. But the handicap had consequences: it facilitated their inaccurate interpretations of the human mind.

The precise way in which it did so will be explained below. I mention even now, however, in case it should be useful, the principle involved; I have already broached it and shall have occasion to do so again. Awareness of the conscious nature of our cognitive functions, renders possible (though it does not ensure) our observation of the *active* nature of the cognizing mind. If one is conscious but does not know that one is conscious, one's ability to experience the object consciously remains intact, but it is especially difficult for us to observe the role played in cognition by the *activity* of the mind. And if one does not observe such activity, one can only suppose the passivity of the mind. Which is the first of a series of misinterpretations regarding the conscious mind that historically ended up in representationism. In other words, because the Greek philosophers *were* conscious, they could observe —and therefore undertake to study — the nature of the mind, quite as Aristotle said. But since they did not *know* that they were conscious, their understanding of the human mind had to be correspondingly deficient. For, of course, they were in no position to investigate, analyse, and understand what they were unaware of.

The foregoing remarks notwithstanding, it may still seem unlikely to some of us that a conscious human being should not be automatically conscious of its consciousness. If so, perhaps the following reflection on our ordinary, present-day experience should make it a little more plausible. The fact that we today are conscious during our waking hours makes a prodigious difference to us. If one says that one loves life, one is speaking, whether one realizes it or not, of one's conscious life; one does not have in mind one's biochemical life, which is of course necessary for one's conscious life, and which one prizes on that account, but not for its own sake. What we truly value is the consciously experiential life we live. Nevertheless, unless one is a philosopher deeply concerned with the study of consciousness or is otherwise endowed with a highly abnormal personality, one will be conscious of one's consciousness only rarely. Our experience of ourselves and of the world around us is continuously conscious, but unless special circumstances should require that we face the conscious nature of our experience, we will not remark to ourselves, much less to others, upon its being conscious. It is likely that many members of our culture go for months on end, if not years, without consciously adverting to the fact that they are conscious. If the same was true of the Greeks, it would have been perfectly normal.

4. Agenda

I have proposed that philosophy stands in need of reform at a radical level. But do the words 'radical reform' not exaggerate, perhaps, the inadequacies of contemporary philosophy? Against the thought that they might, I find comfort in Hilary Putnam's estimate 'that the present situation in philosophy is one that calls for a revitalization, a renewal, of the subject.'[94] Putnam bases this assessment on his conviction that 'philosophy … has become agonized, tormented by the weight of its past, burdened by predecessors whom it cannot escape.'[95] And John R. Searle is not alone[96] when he dismisses all the principal philosophical vogues since the mid-twentieth century as 'immensely depressing … pointless and unnecessary.'[97] But of course, this situation did not come about at random; the failure of philosophy is the natural consequence of a process that has unfolded logically, as effect followed cause. We should be able to understand it. To study the philosophical problem posed by the failure of modern philosphy to understand the human mind, and in particular its conscious character, with a veiw to determining the causes of its lack of success, is the first and fundamental purpose of this work.

---

94   Hilary Putnam, *Renewing Philosophy* (Cambridge, MA: Harvard University Press, 1992), ix.

95   Hilary Putnam, *Realism with a Human Face* (Cambridge, MA: Harvard University Press, 1990), 53.

96   See, for example, Mario A. Bunge, *Philosophy in Crisis: The Need for Reconstruction* (Amherst, NY: Prometheus, 2001); Michael M. McCarthy, *The Crisis of Philosophy* (Albany: State University of New York, 1989); Avner Cohen and Marcelo Dascal, (eds.), *The Institution of Philosophy: A Discipline in Crisis?* (LaSalle, IL: Open Court, 1989). These authors' interpretation of the nature of the crisis are not uniform.

97   Searle, *Rediscovery,* 54.

To that end, an analysis of the history of philosophy should reveal the principal stages in the developing logic of the historical process that led modern philosophy to stagnation. In chapter II, we shall remember how it came about that Christian philosophy faltered, even as it began, when it re-interpreted what Plato and Aristotle had called *theologia*, (later to become known as 'metaphysics') in accordance with Christian beliefs; and how it broke down in the fourteenth century and almost disappeared; how it was revived, but ineptly, by Descartes; and how within a hundred years it began to collapse once again under Hume's criticism and the unfortunate inability of modern philosophy to profit from his thought. However, unlike the first time that philosophy fell prey to existential skepticism, the second time it entered into a state of ahistoricist denial that has enabled it to deceive itself into thinking that it is still well grounded, and indeed, that with the advent of cognitivism in recent times it is healthier than ever.

If the attempt to determine the causes of the self-misinterpretation of the human mind and the consequent stagnation of philosophy is successful, the possibility will thereby be opened for contemporary philosophers to attempt to correct Descartes's misguided efforts to reform philosophy. Asking how the reconstruction of modern philosophy might begin, Chapter II shall end with the suggestion that, perhaps the answer is: by learning from Hume. For Hume may have concluded, unfortunately, that philosophy was a vain pursuit, but he also understood enough about the true nature of philosophical reasoning to give us some indications of how philosophy should be conducted if it were capable of providing true knowledge of the world.

His skepticism, it will be remembered, found fault not only with what had become the common assumption of philosophers regarding the nature of *perceptual cognition,* but also the nature of *reality* and of *causation.* He explained, in effect, what we must avoid, besides representationism, to ensure that we reorient ourselves in accordance with what our nature and the world truly are. From his work we can derive, therefore, if only as a faint suggestion, that if philosophical knowledge should be possible, it would have to make sure at the very beginning of its investigations that three basic philosophical concepts — namely, cognition, reality, and causality — had been determined *critically,* i.e., in strict conformity with what we actually observe in ourselves and in the world. For 'mind,' 'world,' and the 'causal events' that take place within the 'mind,' within the 'world,' and across 'mind' and 'world,' comprise all that exists. The basis of the reconstruction of philosophy will have been established thus.

The general objective of the third chapter will be, therefore, to try to determine empirically-justified, post-Humean concepts of cognition, reality, and causality that might thereafter be assumed by philosophy as the basis for its further investigations of the world and of human nature. However, chapter III will dwell only on the principal features of the cognitive function we share with other members of the animal kingdom, namely, *perceptual cognition*, and on the specifically conscious quality that perception exhibits in human beings. A more complete treatment of the nature of the human mind than is contemplated here would continue thereafter to study the cognitive functions that began to supplement and perfect our conscious perception when evolution produced a new form of animal life whose cognitive abilities exceeded that of our ancestor species. I refer to the function of *thinking* and *understanding*, which is made possible by the human peculiarity of *speech*, and to the integration of thought and understanding, along with conscious perception. into the 'stream of consciousness' and the fullness of the human conscious cognitive life.

I point out, however, that modern philosophy has stagnated not only as a consequence of its assumption of the representational nature of perception. Also debilitating may have been Locke's somewhat crude and oversimple commingling of the two levels of cognition of which human beings are capable. According to the classical division of Aristotle, human beings are endowed with two quite distinct cognitive powers, *aesthesis* and *noesis,* sense perception and understanding. This division is empirically based and indispensable to understanding the entire nature of the conscious mind; surely all of us recognize the difference between sensing an object and understanding an explanation of an event.

But part of Locke's legacy has been the separation of the two and the eclipse of understanding by perception. According to him, sense perception yields 'ideas,' and the mind's working out the connections among ideas yields understanding. This 'working out' function is now ascribed to 'language.' In my view, if 'language' is understood as a mental function, as the function of *speaking*, as contrasted with its product — such ascription is correct. However, in spite of Wittgenstein's demonstration that language — or rather, speech — is not representational and passive in nature, it continues to be treated as the encoding of our experience of the intelligible 'contents' of the world and its objects in conventional signs for the purpose of communicating it (or representing it) to others. The active, architectonic role of speech in the *construction* of thought and our understanding of explanations is not usually recognized.

A full reconstruction of modern philosophy would call, therefore, for a critical revision of the nature of speech and thought as a representational form of cognition. However, the problem on which this work focuses is not exactly the nature of the human mind, but the causes of the inability of modern philosophy to deal adequately with the mind. And such stagnation, according to my hypothesis, was reached when early modern philosophy was brought up short by its failure to respond adequately to Hume's challenge and thereby became powerless to explain the nature of *perception*. This work will therefore focus on such objective, and shall, arbitrarily, consider the nature of understanding, speech, and thought in Chapter IV. If this limited goal is reached and philosophy develops a viable and empirically-grounded understanding of perception, the further study of the human mind's mental function of thinking and its culmination in understanding will have become once again an open field.

II

The Causes of the Stagnation of Modern Philosophy: the Historical Evidence

The philosophical study of our mental functions owes its existence to the desire of human beings to understand themselves. All of us experience this need, though to be sure, not all with the same degree of urgency. To those who try to satisfy it, experiencing the want suffices to reveal that their ability to understand is not so powerful that their wish to understand themselves is fulfilled immediately upon its being conceived; we can understand ourselves only by *learning* about ourselves. But our ignorance about ourselves is, to begin with, so profound that it is not immediately clear to us what it is that we are required to study in order to understand ourselves. We have to find out even what the problem is. It is almost as if philosophy of mind were a cleverly plotted mystery novel where a supersleuth solves the mystery only when he discovers that the solution depended on his first solving the problem of what the mystery actually was. Strained metaphor aside, the human mind is a puzzle, because *what* we are investigating, our conscious mind, is also the *means* to investigate it; we have to learn how to use our mind appropriately to understand our mind before we can use it successfully to understand the nature of our mind.

Not surprisingly, we progress slowly. And we make mistakes. For we cannot find out how to learn about ourselves all at once, but only by successive approximations. This is, of course, the usual way in which we learn any but the simplest truths; it is a manifestation of our temporality and historicity, and it should not be different when what we learn about is our own far-from-simple nature. Accordingly, learning about our nature does not begin with philosophy or with sophisticated enquiry. Individually as well as socio-culturally, our cultivated knowledge regarding how our cognitive functions operate is preceded, in the course of our ordinary, everyday life, by an elementary, unsophisticated awareness of our existence and of ourselves as the agents of our cognitive activities. Our own reality is all the more perplexing because the obverse of our awareness of it is the further, gradually dawning intelligence that, unavoidably, we and indeed all living beings shall eventually return to the earth that bore us. Thus, because human beings are conscious of their reality, and of the further fact that they exist only for a time, they wonder about the significance of their existence. This is the situation in which we find ourselves when our interest in understanding ourselves awakens.

And so, when the human species emerged in the course of the evolution of life, the question would have emerged spontaneously in every primitive human society — not necessarily in these terms but nevertheless keenly felt — what does it mean to be human? What is the significance of mortal life? We want to identify ourselves. And we do so by defining our relationship to the world and our fellow humans, and by describing to ourselves the place we occupy in the world and the office we discharge within it. And so, in the history of all human societies of which we have any notice, human self-understanding and self-identification make their first appearance at the level of the culture's common sense. The human mind must learn to walk before it can learn to fly.

At the level of primitive common sense the human search for self-identity usually takes the form of traditional imaginative legends and folklore embodying the observations and accumulated reflections of the community regarding the world to which we are born and our position within it. In other words, our capacity for self-understanding generates what we in our culture call 'religion.' In other cultures, it goes by other names; frequently it is called simply 'our tradition,' or 'our ways,' or 'our customs.' And it is from Greek religion specifically — the 'Greek customs,' as they called it — that our philosophical tradition descends.

Why do I bring this up as we begin to search for the causes of philosophy's stagnation? Did the institutionalization of philosophy by the Greeks not amount to leaving Greek religion behind? Only up to a point. Besides, if it is true that every present moment of history bears the traces of the past and its consequences, it follows that in order to understand why Greek philosophy took the course it did — and hence the course on which later philosophical ages were launched — we need to have some idea of the common sense of the culture that the Greek philosophers were trying to correct. Well, it was a common sense suffused with beliefs that only can be described as 'religious:' they had to do with their understanding of the human situation and the significance of human life, particularly in view of its mortality. Only then could we perceive the degree to which the Greek philosophers transcended their religious antecedents — as well as the large degree to which they did not. Even modern philosophy has not transcended them. Not altogether.

The questions that prompt 'religion' are universal, but 'religions' take many different forms. We should caution ourselves against our natural tendency to think of all religions as if they followed the same pattern as the religions that have long been familiar to most of us. Which means, of course, Judaism and Christianity — although Islam, the third 'biblical religion,' has in very recent times entered into our everyday consciousness as well. Our thinking about 'religion' is likely to be distorted, because these religions (along with a few others, almost all of Indo-European origin), share characteristics that make them atypical of the genus. Indeed, they are highly unusual.

The biblical religions paint a picture of the human situation that may be likened to a planetary system of beliefs describing an ellipse with a sun at each focus. One sun is God, an omnipotent and omniscient Mind characterized by infinity and eternity, but who also is a human-like Person, endowed with consciousness, will, and emotions. Occupying the other focus is Life After Death. And orbiting around these are major and minor astral bodies and moons: 'dogmas,' 'orthodoxy,' 'revelation,' 'authority,' 'scriptures,' 'church,' 'priesthood,' the 'supernatural,' and numberless asteroid practices and rites. But holding all these together is the gravitational force of 'faith' — that is, the profession of belief not merely in the sense that one has developed a settled and reasonably confident opinion about the truth of the matter, but in the sense that one has committed oneself unconditionally to its truth. For in the absence of evidence in its favour, and even when confronted with indications to the contrary, those who share this 'faith' do not merely 'believe,' or 'guess,' or 'suppose,' or 'estimate,' but positively *affirm,* with the utmost assurance and devotion, the truth of their beliefs. In these religions, therefore, believing becomes itself an object of belief: faith is believed to be a gift from God, and a possible sign of the believer's 'election.' Therefore, one does not believe because one chooses to believe; one believes because one has been chosen to believe.[98] It follows that believers feel obliged to believe, and

98   This is true of both Protestant and Roman Christianity, but tends to be more heavily stressed by the former than by the latter, especially at the level of popular interpretation; not a few Catholics appear to think that belief in 'predestination'

that they fear the possibility of losing their faith. They may even pray that they may be spared such calamity, and hope that they shall not be abandoned by God. Without this kind of faith, the ellipse would collapse.

Faith of this sort demands, therefore, a special motive besides one's wanting to understand oneself: it demands unwavering adherence to beliefs that have been adopted — or at least acquiesced in — for motives that are far from simple, but which usually include in the forefront the alleviation of anxiety. For the all-absorbing goal and constantly explicit preoccupation of these religions is 'salvation,' that is, avoidance of the extinction of oneself at death, and enjoyment of a perfect and eternal life of happiness thereafter. As Paul the apostle himself acknowledged, faith provides not only 'the evidence of things unseen,' but also ' the substance of things hoped for.'[99] The kind of faith that these religions solicit and promote, generates absolute certainty, since the faith is God-given. And it is not at all difficult to misinterpret the experience of certainty for the discovery of truth.

The first feature of Greek religion[100] we must keep in mind is that not one of the foregoing religious concepts was part of it. Having been cast in the more usual mould, Greek religion was made up of the customs, practices, vocabulary, and idiomatic expressions that concretized, and the 'stories' (*mythoi*) that unsystematically and not very consistently illustrated, what 'everybody' took to be obvious about the world and about the significance of everyday human life within it. The 'Greek way' was built out of nothing but the demisemiquaver rationality of common sense; its beliefs flowed from the apprentice's variety of logic, in which imagination plays senior advisor to undisciplined and callow reason. Nevertheless, it was a logic that was not displaced by unreasoning faith. The transition from religion to philosophy may have been much facilitated by this circumstance.

To grasp the sense in which our word 'religion' is applicable to the culture out of which philosophy came to be, we should be aware that the traditional Greek interpretation of the human situation

---

is a Protestant heresy from which Roman Catholicism has been providentially spared; in fact, it is part of every Christian orthodoxy.

99   St. Paul, *Hebrews,* 11:1.

100   By 'Greek religion' I mean the so-called 'civic religion' of the Greeks, the traditional beliefs taken for granted by almost all Greeks simply because they were traditional. Minority 'cults' and 'mysteries' imported from other cultures differed from the civic religion in many respects, but had limited impact on the civic religion.

did not have to do with 'gods' in the sense in which we usually take this word — namely, as an approximation of the personal biblical God. Like the usual 'gods' of most primitive religions, the so-called Greek 'gods' were not supernatural entities, but imperfect, finite fellow-citizens of our world; the 'gods' were more powerful than humans, but decidedly neither omnipotent nor transcendent. And generally speaking, the Greeks did not believe in 'life after death.' Death was the permanent and obviously irreversible separation of the *psyche* or 'soul' (that is, the 'breath [of life]') from the body that it had previously made to be alive. Just as the body continued in existence after separation from its soul at death, though only for a relatively short period, the soul also continued in existence after its separation from the body, but indefinitely. However, the Greeks did not assume, as we today commonly do, that the surviving soul was the *self* or the *person* of whom it had once been the life; only the *empsychon soma* (the 'besouled [i.e. living] body') was identifiable with the human self. Thus, the continued existence of the separated soul could no more save human selves from dissolution at death than the preservation of the former person's corpse could have. All this seemed obvious to almost every Greek citizen; the likely exceptions were those who might have adopted a foreign religion. The most important of these was Orphism, whose influence on Greek philosophy was limited, but which included having suggested to Pythagoras, Socrates and Plato the immortality and the transmigration of the soul *(metempyschosis)* — a belief that seemed ridiculous to most citizens.[101]

Belief in the mortality of the self was not peculiar to the Greeks; far from it, it is commonly found in most primitive religions. But despite Emile Durkheim's warning that 'the immortality promised by [primitive] religions … is not personal,'[102] anthropologists who study primitive societies sometimes fail to make the appropriate distinction between the soul and the self. It would be technically correct, therefore, to say that most primitive cultures believe in the 'immortality of the soul.' But almost certainly it would be misleading, since the latter expression is likely to be understood by us in the sense in which Judaism, Christianity and Islam (and some but not all of the other principal religions

---

101   When Socrates seriously considered whether these possibilities might not be true, Aristophanes made fun of him in one of his plays.

102   Emile Durkheim, *The Elementary Forms of the Religious Life* (London: Allen & Unwin, 1964), 267.

of the world,[103] and a few primitive ones) have given to it. The point is that what typically concerned the Greeks, but intensely, was not what might happen to them after they died, but the significance of human life in a world they deemed hostile, demanding, and cruel, and which from birth until its termination in death frustrated human desires. Now, death brings unhappiness to all peoples, but not necessarily a feeling of outrage, as it did to the Greeks. But that was because, in their case, belief in the finality of death was accompanied by belief in Fate. It was Fate, rather than death as such, that provoked bitterness, hopelessness, and rebellion. Presently we shall see why. By contrast, the preoccupation of the biblical religions with mortality have been no less burdensome, despite their superficially opposite manifestations; in these religions mortality is tamed by acceptance of a Fate that is no less unswerving than that of the Greeks, but which is believed to issue, or so believers hope, in an eternally happy ending beyond 'this world' — not for everyone, to be sure, but only for those among the 'elect' who have 'kept the faith.'

I have stressed the differences between the Greek and the biblical religions, but we must remember also that many Greek philosophers, notably Plato and Aristotle, developed, in several somewhat different versions and as part of their attempt to make sense out of popular beliefs, a doctrine that they deemed implicit in the common-sense imagination as well as philosophically true, namely, that there were *degrees of reality*. (The reasoning that yielded this conclusion shall be explained below.) The doctrine was to play a most important role in the history of European culture, when, after the conversion of the Hellenistic world, and then the Roman Empire, to Christianity, the Christian 'apologists' made use of Greek philosophical scholarship to defend the reasonableness and plausibility of Christianity. They thought that the Greek philosophical doctrine stated more or less correctly part of the ancient and fundamental biblical teaching; it seemed to be a rational confirmation of the biblical belief in the unbridgeable, transcendental difference between the world and the 'higher order' of 'divine' forces. Accordingly, at the councils of Nicea in 325 AD, and again, more fully, in 381 AD, the doctrine that there were degrees of reality — and indeed, two incommensurably different 'worlds,' i.e., 'heaven and earth'— was declared part of the authoritative Christian Creed. In brief, religious

---

103   See S.G.F. Brandon, *Man and His Destiny in the Great Religions: An Historical and Comparative Study* (Manchester: Manchester University Press, 1962).

beliefs were in the background of both Greek and Christian thought from the outset, and so far have never ceased to exert some influence over philosophy. In modern times, however, the influence is exerted indirectly, often through adherence to assumptions whose religious origin or significance is not known to those to make them. (Illustrations of this phenomenon also will be studied below.)

In this chapter we shall be concerned with the historical evidence that supports the hypothesis I have advanced to explain the stagnation and sterility of modern philosophy. More specifically than my hypothesis has already anticipated, the evidence will show, first, how Greek philosophy grew out of Greek religion,[104] but preserving some of the basic ideas of the latter; and second, how Greek philosophy then proceeded to interpret certain features of the human mind and of the reality that provided the objects of human cognition so as to rationalize them. Though the Greek philosophers did succeed to a large extent in substituting logically argued explanations of the nature of the world for the imaginative 'stories' of the religious common sense, they did not transcend the traditional supposition that reality had a sort of invisible and fuller 'dimension' — namely, the 'divine' — than the sort of reality with which we are directly familiar by means of our senses. Reality obtained in degrees, and the standard of 'reality' was not the perceptible, 'material' level of reality, but 'the divine' *(to theion)*. The idea that the world was somewhat less than 'really real' provided much of the continuity from the classical to the Christian world; unless we keep this in mind, we shall find it difficult to appreciate the magnitude of the impact upon our tradition of the thirteenth-century idea that the reality of the world is definable as its *inherent* existence.

We shall then consider how Christianity, for all its opposition to Greek religion and to its Roman twin, but inspired by the example of Greco-Roman scholarship, came to establish, after the conversion of the Greco-Roman world, the institutions of Christian 'theology,' and much later 'scholasticism,' which conceived the ideal of reconciling Christian faith and Greek reason. The latter goal became an overriding preoccupation; early in the second millennium, one of the principal common purposes of most 'schoolmen' was to develop an explanation of how and why it was possible to obtain the kind of knowledge of human nature and the world that was derived by purely rational means, but which at the same time was fully compatible with the 'revealed' doctrines of Christianity. It was in

---

104   See Drew A. Hyland, *The Origins of Philosophy: Its Rise in Myth and the Pre-Socratics* (New York: Putnam, 1973).

predominant part in order to solve this problem that Thomas Aquinas proposed his unprecedented doctrine regarding the nature of the world and its inherent reality.

The novelty of Aquinas's doctrine, however, and the terminology he used to explain it, made it controversial and difficult to understand at first; it was only many decades later that it achieved the status of a generally recognized, empirically sustainable fact. Representationism having then appeared and been generally accepted, existential skepticism brought scholasticism to the end of a long and, in its own way, noble history that had begun with the establishment of monastic schools as early as the sixth century. Until it was revived in the nineteenth, the scholastic tradition was kept alive only by a few Catholic religious communities isolated from the times — one of which, however, founded by the Society of Jesus in 1603, would one day become well-known to modern philosophers. It was located in the French town of La Flèche.

Thomas's doctrine of reality made a positive and most important contribution to European culture throughout modern times. It played a crucial role in the modern world's awakening to the complex of ideas we call 'modernity,' which followed from the 'secularization' of the culture, and which was later reinforced by the discovery of our culture that the human mind was 'conscious.' We shall examine how this came about. When we then review how Descartes's artless attempt to restore philosophy set the conditions for the inevitable repetition of the earlier mediaeval calamity, we should have become acquainted with the principal causes of the stagnation of modern philosophy. We could then begin to think about possible directions in which we should turn with a reasonable hope of future success.

1. Greek religion and the origin of Greek philosophy

Hardly any modern philosopher is unaware that Greek philosophy emerged out of Greek religion; what may not be quite as generally known is the degree to which the latter survived in the former and was directly reflected in the most fundamental philosophical concepts, notably in the concept of 'nature.' Contrary to modern usage, in the common sense culture of Greece 'nature' was a religious concept, which philosophy adopted, with some important modifications.

Responding to the typical concerns of the Greeks, Greek religion was concentrated on the concept of *Fate* — or as the Greeks called it, the 'allotment' *(heimarmene)*. The importance of this idea for our intellectual tradition cannot be exaggerated; its shadow still lurks behind suppositions that continue to be at work in philosophy today. In the religion of the Romans, which descended from the same prehistoric Indo-European culture as the Greek, 'the allotment' was called *fatum* — the word from which the English 'Fate' comes — which literally translated means 'what has been spoken.' However, neither the Greek belief in the 'allotment' nor the Roman in 'what has been spoken' included the supposition that there was an Allotter who allotted the 'allotment' or a Speaker who spoke 'what has been spoken.' Fate was an abstract, impersonal cosmic force — but no less real, powerful, and pervasive for all that, than Yahweh was for the Israelites and God for the Christians. The reality and power of Fate was the first and absolutely fundamental of the two principal beliefs that defined Greek (as well as Roman) religion.

Fate was also referred to by several other names, including the 'share' *(moira),* the 'due portion' or 'fair share' *(aisa),* and 'what befalls one' *(potmos)*. But all these expressions clustered around the single idea that whatever happened to each and every entity in the world, but signally to human beings, had been predetermined totally and in minute detail by the mysterious, overwhelming, frightening, frustrating, and completely impersonal and abstract natural force of Fate.[105] Fate is accomplished in the world and in human beings because 'what befalls them' has been 'allotted' to them as their 'fair share.'

Fate may be said to be one's 'fair share,' however, not because it takes justice into account, but in the sense that there are no grounds on which human beings could reasonably complain about it; Fate could not be judged by reference to human values. For whatever happened to, or befell, human beings, as well as everything else that happened throughout the world, happened with absolute 'necessity' or 'stringency' *(ananke)*. Fate operated blindly, without regard to conseq-uences or to justice or fairness, and without aiming at any particular end: it 'was not credited with foresight, purpose, [or] design.'[106] Fate was related to morality only in the sense that the 'physical order is guarded by the same powers

---

105 William Chase Greene, *Moira: Fate, Good, and Evil in Greek Thought* (Cambridge, Mass.: Harvard University Press, 1944).

106 Maurice Cornford, *From Religion to Philosophy: A Study in the Origins of Western Speculation* (New York: Harper & Row, 1957), 20.

[i.e., Fate] that punish moral transgression'[107] in the human order. Fate was a sort of quasi-mechanical legislating will that regulated all world events.

Naturally, the Greeks found it difficult to reconcile themselves to the invincibility, unpredictability, arbitrariness, and amorality of Fate. But realism required that the inevitability of Fate, like that of death, be recognized as such. Indeed, death being the final imposition of Fate upon human beings against their will, it was perhaps the most evocative symbol of Fate. Most modern European languages preserve the association of Fate and death in the denotation of words such as 'fatal' and 'fatality.'

At the origin of the idea of Fate is a distorted form of an elementary, primitive, and universal human experience. All conscious human beings are aware that they have some sort of executive power or will: they reach decisions, take initiatives, and act upon them. Based on their experience of themselves, sooner or later they will necessarily conceive *causality*. This is not to say that they will necessarily understand causality correctly; they may well, for instance, project their own causality onto all objects and events, and attribute all causality, even in the case of inanimate objects, to the exercise of compelling force. But in any event, they will also experience that often enough their attempt to achieve certain purposes by causing certain effects does not succeed; other causal agencies are also at work in the world, many of which may be more powerful than oneself. Frustration is a normal human experience.

The Greeks, however, found it overwhelming: they reacted to frustration with the innocent outrage typical of young children — but also with all the creative imagination that was typically theirs in so many cultural respects. They felt persecuted; they believed that they were *totally* helpless before the dictates of the irresistible opposing will of Fate. Why totally? Because in their view it was not true that human beings were free to pursue their chosen purposes; their will only *seemed* to be capable of achieving its intended goals at least some times. In fact, the human will was radically ineffective; it had no true causal power, but was a delusion. Worse than a delusion, it was a cruel cosmic jest. For the fantasy that one was free to achieve one's purposes by using one's causal power prompted one to refuse one's Fated 'portion,' and to try instead to determine for oneself what would and would not

---

107   Cornford, *Religion to Philosophy, p. 19.*

'befall' one. But since Fate was unavoidable, to rely on one's own power to achieve one's ends was to fall prey to *hubris*.

The word *hubris* is sometimes still translated into English as 'pride.' At one time this rendering would have been fully adequate, but nowadays it is apt to mislead. To understand why, let us remember that Christianity, too, has always included, and to the present continues to include, belief in Fate. In Christianity, however, the term 'Fate' is used only rarely; the more usual term is 'predestination.'[108] But by whatever name, the point is that whatever happens has been willed by God. But since whatever God wills happens necessarily, everything that happens happens necessarily. Therefore, like Greek religion, Christianity has always included also a doctrine of '*hubris*,' which is the outcome of resisting the course of Fate.

In the traditional Christian vocabulary of Middle English, 'pride' conveyed exactly the same as *hubris*. It was the name of one of the seven 'deadly sins' and consisted in choosing to do one's will disregarding or defying God's predestination of events, and therefore deeming oneself the equal of God. This was, of course, not only evil, but also foolish, since it is impossible actually to thwart God's will successfully. However, in contemporary English, 'pride' most commonly means self-satisfaction with one's accomplishments, and is usually considered a virtue. Thus, *hubris* should not be translated today as 'pride,' but more exactly, if also more clumsily, as 'foolishly countervailing self-reliance.' It amounted to arrogating to oneself an authority that one did not actually have, namely, the authority and the freedom to try to determine one's life. *Hubris* was therefore also a false assessment of one's importance in the scheme of the world — which in reality was nil. Indeed, the supposition that we human beings might conceivably defeat the force of Fate was like kicking against a goad; it only made worse the plight of human existence.

The reason was that the corollary of the paranoid, self-alienating logic that generated the idea of Fate —the reaction of indignation, the feeling of *lèse-majesté*, when one's presumed right to have one's way was thwarted — was that one's Fate was accomplished by the very actions that strove to prevent it. Fate was called the 'due [or proper] portion' because what human beings deserved, if anything, was

---

108   'Fate' is used, for example, by Thomas Aquinas in his *Summa Theologiae* at I, 23, 8.

their Fate. This self-evident truth provided the inspiration for one of the greatest of the great artistic accomplishments of Greece: the literary form known as 'tragedy' *(tragoidia).*

The typical leitmotiv of Greek tragedy is the attempt of the hero to avoid his or her Fate, but whose actions have the effect of fulfilling a Fate that is entirely deserved, because, swollen with *hubris,* he (or sometimes she) had relied on him- or herself and tried to escape his or her Fate.[109] Since we entrap ourselves in it, Fate was, by definition, the 'fair share' allotted to every one of us. The supreme truth of the human situation was therefore that human beings are Fated to conspire with Fate against themselves. If one wishes to understand the Greek outlook upon the world which was presupposed by Greek philosophy, one could do no better than to read, for instance, Sophocles's *Oedipus Rex,* imagining oneself at the centre of the situation it describes. Even a brief synopsis evokes the kind of emotion the play dwells upon.[110]

---

109 The Greek word for 'goat' is *tragos. Tragoidia* means literally a 'goat poem [or song].' This may seem strange, but it does make some sense. *Tragos* comes from the same Indo-European root as English 'drink.' (Cf. German *trinken,* 'to drink,' and Spanish *tragar,* 'to swallow.') Goats were called *tragoi* in Greek, i.e. 'swallowers,' because they were ruminants, animals that seemed to have difficulty digesting their food since they could do so only after repeatedly swallowing it. And Fate was very difficult to 'swallow.' It is possible that *tragoidea* alluded to the purpose of the play: ruminating (i.e., meditating) upon the 'tragic' human situation helps the spectator achieve the 'purging,' *catharsis,* of the indigestible lump of Fate.

110   In **Oedipus Rex,** Fate decrees that Laius, King of Thebes, shall be murdered by Oedipus, his son, who shall then take to wife Iocasta, Laius's Queen and Oedipus's mother. Laius is warned by an oracle about his Fate. But he refuses to accept his 'share' and tries to have Oedipus killed while the latter is still an infant. Laius's very attempt to evade his Fate, however, ensures that Oedipus shall live; indeed, the same attempt renders possible, years later, his return to Thebes as a stranger who was capable of killing his father without recognizing him either as his father or as the King, and to marry the widowed Queen without realizing she was his mother or the wife of the man he killed. Now, all this has already happened before the play begins; the audience learns about it only later. For like the true meaning of Fate itself, which was supposed to become clear to the individual retrospectively at the time of death, the moral lesson of the tragedy is revealed to the audience only at the **dénouement** of the play.

As the action begins, a plague is afflicting Oedipus's kingdom and an oracle warns him of his Fate as King: Thebes shall suffer the plague until Oedipus avenges the murder of Laius by punishing the offender. Oedipus promises to obey Fate, but when the seer Tiresias informs him, at Oedipus's insistence, that he is guilty of incest, parricide, and regicide, Oedipus refuses to consider the possibility that the accusation might be true. Indeed, he tries to divert suspicion onto Creon, his brother-in-law, and charges him with having conspired with Tiresias. By so doing, however, he has chosen, albeit unwittingly, to let the murder of Laius go unavenged; unintentionally, but in actual fact just the same, he has defied Fate. However, his pursuit of the case against the supposed conspirators precipitates (partly with Iocasta's help, who is herself tempting Fate by trying to protect Oedipus from his Fate) an incremental series of revelations that ultimately force him to see the truth. Iocasta hangs herself, and Oedipus blinds himself out of remorse and self-loathing. The self-inflicted punishment is justified, because his actions had attempted to contravene Fate. But at the same time, by punishing himself, he has avenged Laius's murder after all. His cruel Fate is thus fulfilled by his own hand. And so, the plague subsides. Fate 'has indeed contrived all, but … through the character and the acts of Oedipus himself' (Greene, **Moira,** 156.)

The Greeks were well aware that causal processes are part of the world; belief in Fate did not take away their capacity for conceiving causality and becoming aware of its operation in the world. They knew that human beings conceive purposes and proceed to execute them, and that other causal agents produce other effects. Thus, at first glance, human actions *seem* to achieve what human beings (or other causal agents) have intended to achieve. But the appearance is deceptive, since what is actually achieved is not the effect of the human cause, but a predetermined effect. Their belief was, therefore that Fate overshadowed causal processes to rob them of their true efficacy.

Now, the question may be raised how it is possible for sane and intelligent human beings to believe in Fate, even when nothing they perceive in the world provides evidence of it; the answer may be, at least in part, that our perception of reality is closely related to our perception of ourselves. We shall come back to this later. At the moment I merely point out that when experience is conscious, as it is in human beings, one's vision of the world will be filtered through one's emotional reaction to what one actually perceives; for one will be aware of one's emotions and will have to take them into account as one makes one's decisions. And so, when concern for oneself is conscious, it may interfere with one's perception of what one is concerned about. The Greek belief in Fate was part of a perception of the world as the Kingdom of Necessity, a realm of phenomena every one of which had to be understood by reference to force, power, and compulsion. Whence comes such compulsion?

At a certain level of evolution, animal life developed the ability of the organism to react emotionally to its perceptions; emotions energized the organism, and if the emotion remained below a critical level, the organism's behavioural adjustment to the environment could be modulated and regulated in accordance with accumulated prior experience rather than automatically; above a certain level, emotion could trigger emergency responses such as the 'fight or flee' reflex. This did not change when humans became conscious experiencers. But the addition of consciousness to cognition meant that when human beings experienced the world, both their experience of the world and their emotional reaction to their experience of the world were conscious. Consciousness brings the two experiences together, and both have to be managed by the one human mind so as to produce one response that takes both into account. Thus, consciousness brought to human beings a problem that infrahuman animals were spared: the problem of having to manage their emotions. But it is notoriously difficult for us human beings to maintain a strict distinction between what we in fact experience, and the emotions evoked in us by what we actually experience. We naturally tend to project our emotions — and most obviously our negative emotions, fear and hostility — unto the object that evokes them. There are probably not many of us who have not done as much at some time or another in our lifetime; and all but the more obtuse of us admit it to ourselves and even to others.

So far as I can see, however, nothing we actually experience about the world warrants the supposition of Fate. The Greek belief in Fate seems to have been, at bottom, a projection of extreme human frustration onto the world; it was an immoderate, unreasoning, overwhelming, fear of the utterly unavoidable mortality of the self after a lifetime of the undoubted asperities of a human existence that, on balance, can be trying as well as rewarding, but which in any event, could seem 'unfair' only to someone who presumed that human beings have the right to command that reality conform to their desires. The truth is, of course, that sometimes the two coincide, but sometimes not. Belief in Fate was a miscalculation of Greek culture that, as will be discussed in a moment, Greek philosophy corrected only in part — but the ghost of which has lingered over us, their intellectual descendants, to this day. But in different guises at different times.

Thus, when Christian civilization emerged in Europe out of the ruins of its Greco-Roman predecessor, belief in Fate was retained, but only after it had undergone a critical adaptation. It ceased to be an abstract, impersonal, and amoral cosmic force and was now identified with the concrete, personal, fair, and indeed *merciful* Will of God. The Christian theologians did not deny, of course — not any more than the Greek philosophers had — that human and other causal agents could be said to *cause* events. Instead, they attempted to rationalize the doctrine by excogitating *ad hoc,* for example, the concept of God's 'physical premotion.' That is, the First Cause willed that the effect of 'secondary causes' such as the human will actually take place. Nicholas Malebranche's 'occasionalism' was a modern philosophical version of much the same idea. From early times Christianity experienced great difficulty reconciling the omnipotence of God with the effectiveness and freedom of human causality. Two thousand years later, the theological controversies have yet to arrive at any but paradoxical results.

The second fundamental Greek religious belief, commensurate with the first -and indeed, the corroborative support of belief in Fate — was also a distorted form of another universal human experience. For it is as a result of nothing but their ordinary experience that all human beings develop not only some idea of *causality* (as contrasted with mere sequences of causally unrelated events), but also some idea of (as *we* call it) *reality.* The reason is that, by whatever name and with whatever variations, and more or less perspicuously, all conscious experienceers are acquainted with the fact that when human beings experience the 'world' and its objects, *what* they experience — the object — is independent of their *experiencing* of it. In other words, they perceive that their mind has not created the world. If the object is external to ourselves, it is experienced as *other-than* ourselves. If it is internal, it is experienced as *other-than* our experiencing of it. For instance, when I think about the headache I feel, I know the headache is not imaginary; the headache is perceived as *other-than* my thinking about and experiencing the pain.

The otherness-to-each-other of experience and mind is a reciprocal relationship: nothing can be 'other-than' by itself. I write not simply 'other,' but 'other-than,' to underline such reciprocity. Thus, the object is other-than our experience of it, and, simultaneously, the experience is other-than the object. The evidence of this is that no one who has the experience of looking at any object and seeing it, has ever been in any doubt about which is the object and which is his or her experience; anyone who were to confuse the two would risk certification. And so, when we use our senses to perceive an object, we discover simultaneously that the object is 'n o t - w e' and that we are 'n o t - i t.' This experience is what teaches us to conceive the 'reality' of the world — though not all human cultures necessarily express it by means of this very term, of course. Nor do they always interpret in the same way what the concept means. For example, we moderns, unlike the Greeks (who referred to reality as 'being'), also describe reality as 'existing.' The reality of the world is the 'existence' of the world. Our use of the latter expression obeys important historical reasons which we shall consider later. Now, in view of the reciprocity of our empirical discovery of the reality of the world and the reality of our perception of it, it is a small wonder that, as our chief hypothesis states, our conceptions of the reality of the world and the reality of the experiencer and its perceptual functions must be mutually consistent, and that otherwise logical thought is impossible.

The concept of 'reality' is not part of the innate equipment of human beings; like all other ideas, it is based on experience. I have outlined above how all human beings develop it; but the universal experience of the reality of the world need not be universally correct. In the history of religions more than one culture has demonstrated this, and one of them is pre-philosophical Greece; its idea of reality was somewhat distorted. But before we consider why we should say so, let us raise a prior question. How and why is it possible for the experience of reality by human beings to become distorted?

The reason why reality can be perceived with distortion is that in order to perceive the reciprocal otherness-to-each-other of object and experience, one must be able to perceive the difference between the two — that is, one must observe the difference between *what* one experiences, and the mind's *activity* of experiencing it. But whereas the object — *what* is experienced — is to the forefront of the conscious experiencer's awareness and cannot be missed, the experiencer's mental *activity* is not easily discernible. The mental activity of the human organism is diffuse and subtle. Additional difficulty in observing the difference between the object in reality and the activity in the mind stems from the physiological fact that neither the brain nor the other organs directly involved in sense perception have interoceptive capability; we detect our organism's cognitive activity only through indirect, equivocal, and mystifying signs. However, if one cannot differentiate reasonably clearly between the otherness-to the object that characterizes one's experience, and the otherness-to one's experience that characterizes the object, one will confuse the two. And if one does, one is likely to project onto objects the otherness-to-the-world that we actually perceive only *in ourselves* and only as part *of our experience.* That is, *our mind's* otherness-to-the-world will be attributed *to the world.* And so, instead of perceiving the reality of the world — its otherness-to — as relative to our experiencing activity, we perceive it as if it were relative to *an experiencing activity other than our own.*

Two consequences follow. One is that the world will seem to one as if, before the world is real in relation to us, it is real in relation to a *viewpoint other than ours.* The world is a *watchable* or *knowable* world. And it is knowable not only in the sense that human beings and all sentient organisms are able to perceive it; since it can be seen from *another* viewpoint than ours, the world is knowable *in itself,* regardless of whether it is known by us. Knowability then is deemed to *inhere* in the reality of the world.

It is true, of course, that we know objects, and that they are 'knowable' in the sense that they can be known *by perceivers.* What is not true is that they are knowable *in themselves,* or *inherently,* or that the reason we can know them is that they are pre-adapted for being known. This would amount to saying that all objects are mind-like; or that whatever is real is either mind or mind-like. Idealist interpretations of reality are based on this assumption. Without this presupposition in the background of the culture, Greek philosophy would not have come to be; for philosophy was conceived as the attempt to make it possible for the human mind to receive, possess, and appropriate for itself the supposed inherent knowability of the world. This assumes that nature contains an inner 'knowledge' that we may be able to tap for our consumption and benefit; it has secrets in its possession that we may be able to 'wrest' from her, if we approach her correctly. This way of thinking was inherited by the Greek philosophers from the common sense of the culture, but it is not exactly foreign to us even today. From Kant we learn indeed that the experience of the wondrous mystery of the world that inheres in the world is most revealing and forceful when it takes place during a clear, starry night. It is 'awesome.'

The further consequence is that, if knowability *inheres* in the world, the viewpoint from which the world is watchable is not only other-than ours, but also *anterior* to ours. Thus, the world is not simply *watchable;* it is a *watched* world. But this is not to say that there is a *Watcher* who watches it. The idea is rather that our experience of the world points towards a *superior degree* of reality that can be perceived only from a viewpoint other than ours. Thus, 'this world,' 'our world,' the world we experience, has only a secondary, or dependent, or derived, sort of reality. The world has *more dimensions,* so to speak, than those which we humans can perceive. Beyond the region of the world that was readily apparent to us, therefore, a higher and invisible province or parameter of reality — perhaps an entirely separate world — can be glimpsed, although it is closed to us. The possibility that there may be an entire series of 'other worlds' parallel to ours, which is seriously considered by some of the more imaginative theoretical physicists today, may be the outcome of a similar subliminal mental process which begins with similar assumptions regarding the inherent knowability of the world.

Conversely, according to the common sense of Greek culture, the visible level of reality was under the scrutiny or watch of the invisible. The Greek literature depicts a recurring preoccupation in everyday life with the subtly felt, but unseen, presence of the invisible to the visible. Now, the Greek verb for 'to look at, to watch, to observe,' is *theorein*. The Greeks therefore coined the nouns *to theion* and *ho theos* —'the watchfulness' and 'the watch,' respectively, if translated literally — to refer to the process whereby Fate holds sway over the visible world. *To theion* referred in the abstract to the invisible province beyond the visible world, and *ho theos* alluded to the same, but concretely. Though to be sure, impersonally.

Although *to theion* and *ho theos* were no more concrete, individual, substantial, or personal than Fate, in the past they have been not infrequently rendered into English, respectively, as 'the divine' and 'the god.' Some translators have indeed insisted in translating *ho theos* as 'God,' so as to avoid confusion with the thoroughly human and finite 'gods' and 'goddesses' of Greek mythology. For Christianity introduced into our culture an idea that Greek philosophy did not generally so much as suspect: namely, that, if the world is 'watched,' the reason is that there is a cosmic Mind that watches it, a *'Watcher'* of the world.

We may find it difficult to credit that *ho theos,* a concrete singular noun, should not have actually referred, in the thinking of the Greeks, to an individual concrete entity rather than to an abstract, impersonal process. But if we should find it strange, the reason would be our prejudice about what a 'god' should look like, not that idioms of this kind are unknown in English. For example, in the anglophone world, the *Wehrmacht* was at one time frequently referred to as 'the Hun.' And when black Americans today in certain contexts speak of 'the man,' they do not have in mind either an individual person or anything more concrete than an entire socio-economic order.

I comment in a brief aside that, in my view, once one projects the human mind's unrecognized viewpoint onto the world and supposes that the world is 'watched,' it makes somewhat better sense to suppose a 'Watcher' than not. Belief in the Christian God seems to me unwarranted; but if one chooses to believe that God exists, it could be argued that it would be less irrational to suppose that God is a concrete agent who performs the activity of 'watching' over the world, than to conceive 'the divine' as an abstract 'watching' done by no one. What makes, in my opinion, least sense of all, is what seems to have happened in our civilization in modern times, when belief in the Christian God having been abandoned by many citizens — not positively rejected, but more like put out of sight — they nevertheless continue to suppose the most absurd superstitions whose common characteristic is that they manifest the 'unknown,' or that which is 'beyond human ken,' or the 'mysterious.' They seem to have regressed and, in effect, reverted to belief in, approximately, the Greek version of the 'divine.'

Confusingly, the Olympian and the other mythological 'gods' and 'goddesses' that were the protagonists of the popular and highly entertaining adventures narrated by Greek mythology, were also 'divine,' albeit in a much weaker sense than Fate. They were much like the 'gods' of many primitive religions, which do not suppose that the 'gods' belong to a world or a level of reality other than the empirically-given world. The 'gods' were imagined by the Greeks as concrete and personal entities, human-like in almost every regard including the less admirable ones. The limitations of their divinity are best signified by their having been subject to the jurisdiction of Fate; even Zeus, the 'father' of the Olympian gods, did not escape its oversight. In short, the 'gods' differed from human beings mostly in two important ways: they were immortal (because they kept a healthy diet of nectar and ambrosia) and they enjoyed a few superhuman, though decidedly finite, powers — which they frequently misused. (But for which, to the *Schadenfreude* of mortals, unpleasant consequences frequently ensued.)

Well, philosophy was created by a few unusually perceptive Greeks who judged that the common language of the culture betokened vagueness and confusion, but who also felt that underneath the scattered thinking of the twofold doctrine of 'Fate' and 'the divine' lay important and salvageable truths. The pre-Socratic philosophers' was the first attempt, only partly successful, to do what Rudolf Bultmann and other scholars would propose many centuries later: that religion be 'demythologized'[111] in order that it better satisfy the desire of human beings to understand themselves, to help them become reconciled to their mortality, and thus to facilitate their leading a fruitful, worthwhile, and reasonably enjoyable life. Modern philosophy's contributions to this programme have been exceedingly modest, having been confined for the most part to monotonous demonstrations that the traditional arguments for the existence of God are not probative, and to a few alternative offerings, no less trite, which argue that, on the contrary, they are.

But of course, before the Greek philosophers became philosophers they were already members of Greek culture, educated in the usual beliefs of Greek common sense. This would have been the

---

111　See Rudolf Bultmann, *Jesus Christ and Mythology* (London: SCM Press, 1966).

starting point of their philosophical meditations; no other possibility was open to them. And so, the seeds of Greek philosophy were, in effect, the religious concepts of the *hiddenness of the reality of the real* — which lurks out of sight behind its appearances to us, obscure and mysterious — and the *relentless dominion of necessity,* which enslaves us but does not conquer our rebellious spirit. The philosophers undertook to revise the common sense version of these concepts, modifying them in accordance with what reason and observation suggested, but retaining what nonetheless seemed true. Neither cognition nor the mind was a preoccupation of the popular culture at any time, and even the philosophers did not take an interest in the mind until about 500 B.C., that is, well after the philosophical tradition had burgeoned. When the philosophers turned their attention to it, however, they estimated that reality cannot be understood in isolation from cognition — or cognition in isolation from reality, or either in isolation from causality. But this is not wholly correct, I think. Although cognition cannot be conceived unless in relation to the real world that supplies its objects, reality does not have to be cognized in order to be real. I refer to this as the *asymmetry* of the relationship between cognition and reality.

Finally, to understand how the common sense belief in Fate was transformed into a philosophical doctrine by the pre-Socratics, we must remember another item of Greek religion. To the Greeks, death was the final imposition on human life coming from without, the culmination of all that necessarily befell one during one's life. (I need scarcely point out that in fact death comes to living beings from within, not from without.) But a human being's Fate was unleashed when the individual was born into the world; therefore the entire history of every human being's fated lifetime was virtually precontained in its birth. Moreover, according to the Greeks, this was true not only of human beings and other living entities whose biological 'birth' was literally so-called; the Greeks used the same word, 'birth,' to refer more generally to 'the origin and growth of the things we find about us … [and to] their source of origin — that from which they have grown, and from which their growth is constantly renewed.'[112] Thus, the Greek word for 'birth' being *physis,* the Greeks commonly spoke of everything that happened to a human being (or to any other entity) during its sojourn in the world

---

112   Werner Jaeger, *The Theology of the Early Greek Philosophers* (Oxford: Clarendon Press, 1947), 20.

as having happened *kata physis,* that is, 'in accordance with its birth.' And so, in the everyday speech of non-philosophical Greek, Fate was 'almost equivalent to *Physis.*'[113]

The inspiration of the pre-Socratics that generated the philosophical tradition was the visionary thought that, although there was indeed an agency or 'power' *(dynamis)* that compelled all things to do as they in fact did, as well as an 'invigoration' *(energeia)* that made the world work as it did, Fate did not exist 'somewhere else,' in an invisible realm of reality: the power of necessitation resided within things themselves. Fate was not 'allotted' to the world from outside the world, but resulted from the operation of the *physis* of each and every agent in the world. By the same token, causal processes obeyed the inherent necessity *(ananke)* that structured every being from within. Thus, the Greek belief in Fate led directly to the idea of rational enquiry into the 'birthness' of things — or in Latin, into their *natura.* Nowadays, of course, 'nature' need not be taken with the same meaning as *physis* or *natura,* but as signifying merely 'what we want to understand' about a given being or phenomenon; this is the sense in which I use the term 'nature' when I speak in my own behalf.

According to the early Greek philosophers, therefore, the common sense of Greek culture had understood correctly, but only in part, the rule of necessity over world events. Common sense had been at fault most obviously regarding the *location* of Fate and thus about the location of the power that was responsible for bringing about world events. The source of necessity was relocated by philosophy to the interiority of the things that made up the world meant. This meant, however, that the rule of Fate was no longer inscrutable. The 'dictates' of Fate were nearby, close at hand, and its 'decrees' were ascertainable in principle by studying the 'nature' of things. 'Certain knowledge' *(episteme,* or in Latin, *scientia)* — as contrasted with the unreliable 'opinions' of common sense — was the result of reading the cryptic messages, written in the book of the natural world, which revealed the 'principle' or 'rule' *(arche)* involved in the causation of events. This was, of course, a giant step towards the injection of rationality into the study of the world and ourselves. It was the birth of scholarship. But let us note well: if I have correctly described the cultural-historical process that generated philosophy, the foundation of scholarship was the presumption of determinism.

---

113   Greene, *Moira,* 14.

In other words, the philosophers disabused themselves fairly easily of the cruder aspects of the common sense belief in Fate, but in what pertained to the fundamental *reality* of Fate they did not fare so well: they accepted the absolute determinism implied by Fate. There may have been a few isolated attempts by the early philosophers to question its universal dominion, but none that was successful. For example, Anaximenes has been interpreted by some Hellenists as having attempted to reduce *physis* to one of the natural elements; but even in his system '*physis* does not really shake off its metaphysical character.'[114] And Aristotle could be read as having tried to soften the stringency of Fate by arguing that some events take place not *kata physis* but 'by chance,' or in accordance with 'luck' *(tyche)*.[115] But as Hellenists have pointed out, Aristotle's argument does not actually question determinism, but merely explains why some exceptional events appear to us to escape determinism though in fact they do not. In the end Aristotle did not demonstrate 'the existence of contingency … Chance is simply a name for the unforeseen meeting of two [or more] chains of rigorous [deterministic] causation … [W]e have no reason to attribute indeterminism to Aristotle.'[116] Determinism remained, and was vested in the *physis* of things.

The advent of philosophy did not change the subjection of Greek life to the imperium of necessity. Since the end of the middle ages its yoke has been loosened, but it has not been thrown off. The endurance of this tradition is illustrated by its having indeed survived into modern times in the milder and relatively harmless, academic form of scientific determinism — which unlike the power of Fate and the Will of God is less than fully relevant to real life. At first, the scientists of the sixteenth and seventeenth centuries (who were almost unanimously Christian believers), simply detached science from theology and deemed science a parallel realm of scholarship. As secularity prevailed in the eighteenth and nineteenth centuries, however, 'the God hypothesis' was increasingly deemed superfluous, and therefore rejected by scientists. But strangely, determinism did not disappear. Having lost both its Greek grandparents and its Christian parents, it survived as an orphan assumption. To many scientists and to not a few modern philosophers, it remains an article of faith. Theirs is a secular faith, to be sure, but a faith nonetheless.

---

114   Cornford, *Religion to Philosophy*, 50.

115   Aristotle, *Physics*, 2.5-6.196b10-198a12.

116   W.D. Ross, *Aristotle* (London: Methuen, 1949), 77-8.

In Greek religion, the idea of Fate and the idea of *to theion,* 'the divine,' were inseparable. Greek philosophy's rationalization of Fate demanded a corresponding rationalization of 'the divine.' And as in the case of *physis,* Greek philosophy's version of 'the divine' did not disturb the vernacular terminology. Philosophy had no quarrel with the characterization of Fate as 'the god,' and of the *ananke* of Fate as 'divine.' It objected only to the crudeness, confusion and inconsistency of the popular interpretations of 'the divine.' Thus, if Thales actually said, as tradition has it, that 'all things are full of the gods,' we can be sure he meant it literally — though not with the other-worldly connotations we may take from the same words today.

Nevertheless, a dash of the popular mystical quality of *physis* lingered in philosophical thinking for some time: 'when the Gods were eliminated, a moral or sacred character still clung to the framework of the world itself.'[117] But if neither Thales nor the Milesians, then at least later philosophers eventually stripped *physis* bare of most of the old connotations. When Heraclitus asked some visitors to come into his kitchen (a place not dedicated to religious rituals, of course, or associated with the Olympian, Thalassian, or other 'divinities') he said, reportedly, 'Here, too, are gods.' He was conveying graphically that the philosophical idea of 'the gods' purified, because it rationalized, what common sense had imaginatively understood by the same term. After the beginning of the 5th century B.C. a philosopher's saying that something was 'divine' was in most instances to say that it pertained to the supra-sensible, purely intelligible order of reality: philosophically, *'theion* is thus equivalent to *kata physis.'*[118]

Rationalizing *to theion,* however, was to prove more difficult, and more contentious, than rationalizing Fate; there was a reason for this. For at this juncture in the history of Greek philosophy, a new consideration emerged: the nature of cognition. Preoccupation with cognition brought to an end the age of Greek 'physics' and marked the beginning of what first Plato, and then Aristotle, called 'theology'[119] *(theologia)* before it became known as 'metaphysics.' A division came about between those philosophers — principally the Pythagoreans, Socrates, and Plato — who had been influenced

---

117   Cornford, *Religion to Philosophy,* 42.

118   Greene, *Moira,* 268n.

119   Plato, *Republic,* II, 379A; Aristotle, *Metaphysics,* 6.1.1026a19.

by foreign religions such as Orphism, which promised the continuation of life after death, and those philosophers who, like Heraclitus and Aristotle, deemed that the human self was mortal and that there was a single world (but within which there were degrees of reality). These events and their consequences for philosophy's treatment of cognition are the subject of the next section.

The continuity from Greek religion to Greek philosophy is understandable. The Greeks' professed their religious beliefs for only one reason: because they made sense to them. The intention of Greek philosophy was from the outset to perfect, not to destroy, whatever reason deemed true in the Greek 'customs.' The transition from the religious to the philosophical notion of *physis* may have been daring but it was not a break with religion; in many but not all respects the philosophical mind subordinated its imagination to reason. Sometimes the changes proposed by philosophers were so radical as to provoke the charge, and punish the offence, of unHellenic proclivities, as one might say today — namely, lack of respect for the ancient wisdom of the Hellenic tradition. But Greek philosophy should not be contrasted with Greek religion as secular knowledge might be with religious belief: Greek religion was secular, and Greek philosophy was religious. Hellenists differ in the degree to which they find uninterrupted consecution from Greek religion to philosophy, but even John Burnet, a member of the school of thought that 'stressed … the empirical and scientific character of the early [Greek] thinkers,'[120] agreed that Greek philosophy, notwithstanding its secularity and its commitment to the demythologization of Greek religion, 'includes most of what we should now call religion.'[121]

2. Greek philosophy and the nature of the human mind

Having been single-mindedly preoccupied with the unsatisfactory situation of humanity in a world characterized by the tyranny of Fate and the unpredictability of invisible divine forces, Greek religion did not have much to say about the nature of the human mind. And for a time, following suit,

---

120   Jaeger, *Theology of the Early Greek Philosophers*, 7.

121   John Burnet, *Early Greek Philosophy* (London: Black, 1920), 12. Elsewhere Burnet states that the Greek philosophers' 'non-religious use of the word "god" … does not bear witness to any theological origin of Greek science, but rather to its complete independence of religious tradition. No one who has once realised the utterly secular character of Ionian civilisation will ever be tempted to look for the origins of Greek philosophy in primitive cosmogonies,' 29. This does not actually contradict his earlier statements; for as I have explained, Greek civilization, including its religion, was indeed 'utterly secular.' The contradiction is rather between what Burnet means by 'religion' in the earlier and in this context; he now reverts to the idea that 'religion' is definable by the doctrines it teaches rather than by its socio-cultural function.

neither did Greek philosophy; the undertaking of the early philosophers to demythologize the concepts of Fate and the divine absorbed all their attention. But the developing thought of the 'physicists' about the nature of the world landed philosophy in deep antinomies. The problem of how to reconcile Being and Becoming cast a shadow of uncertainty over the reliability of our mental faculties, and therefore over that of philosophy as well. Gradually, the philosophers were drawn to the study of the mind.

For example, Zeno's paradoxes illustrated the conflict between ordinary sense experience, which assures us that things both 'are' and 'become,' and logic, which suggests that if they 'are' then they cannot 'become,' and that if they 'become' then they cannot 'be.' The philosophers were discovering also that the problems of philosophy were closely interrelated, and judged that philosophy should widen its scope; as Heraclitus said, philosophers 'must be inquirers into very many things.'[122] And for what it may be worth, we may also note, with Burnet, that by the early 5th century B.C. '[t]he Delphic precept "Know thyself" was a household word.'[123] If this was a factor in the philosophers' directing their attention towards the inner aspects of human nature, it would not be the last time that developments in the culture at large played a role in stimulating philosophical awareness and speculation. But regardless of where he drew his inspiration from, Heraclitus, whose thought marked the beginning of the serious study of the mind by Greek philosophers, did as the oracle recommended. As he himself tells us, 'I searched into myself.'[124]

The delay in the study of the mind of about a century after the institution of philosophy by the Milesians ensured that, when the philosophers undertook to explain the nature of cognition, their original assumptions — their imperfectly demythologized version of the Greek religious beliefs — had acquired the inertial energy of a tradition that may have been relatively recent but which was not inconsiderable. No philosopher questioned the suppositions that everything in the world was ruled by the necessity of its *physis*, or that 'reality' (i.e., 'being,' *to on*), had a dimension that exceeded the

---

122   Herman Diels and Walther Kranz, *Die Fragmente der Vorsokratiker* (Zurich: Weidmann, 1985), 22B35. See also Kathleen Freeman, *Ancilla to the Pre-Socratic Philosophers: A Complete Translation of the Fragments in* Diels, Fragmente der Vorsokratiker (Oxford: Blackwell, 1948).

123   Burnet, *Greek Philosophy,* 59.

124   Diels-Kranz, 22B101.

aspect of the world that was perceptible by the senses. And once these presuppositions were deemed true, they would have tended, of course, to discourage any hypothesis that did not conform to them. Thus, when the philosophers inquired into the cause of cognition, they did not have to think twice: the cause was the world and its objects. Why?

For two reasons. The first was that, in the light of the conventional assumptions of Greek culture, which tended to make human beings the passive victims of higher forces, it made sense to suppose that objects *impose* themselves on us. An ordinary citizen proclaiming the popular wisdom might well have said — if he had thought about it — that since Fate compels us to experience whatever we experience, cognition was the channel through which our 'allotment' was allotted to us. A philosopher would have demythologized this with the explanation that we learn about the *physis* that necessitates things from within when they cause us willy-nilly to 'suffer,' or when they make us forcibly to 'undergo,' their shaping of our minds. When they do so, their 'natures' become apparent to us. Thus, even the philosophers ascribed to objects the causation of cognition. Indeed, many modern philosophers today still tell us that 'experience is passive. In experience one finds oneself *saddled* with content.'[125] The common sense of Greek culture suggested that cognition was the effect wrought on the mind by the causal, necessitating power that inhered in the objects that make up the world.

But the underlying and more powerful second reason was that not even the philosophers among the Greeks were able to discriminate clearly and sharply between the object of cognition and the cognitive activity of the cognizing organism. I have already mentioned, in the context of the Greek philosophers' misperception of reality, the difficulty all of us have in detecting our organism's bodily activity when it discharges its mental functions; we shall continue to run into the same phenomenon in a variety of contexts. But at this point I call attention to the misidentification of the cause

---

125   John McDowell, *Mind and World* (Cambridge, Mass.: Harvard University Press, 1994), 10; italics mine. In a footnote to this text McDowell further explains his reasons: 'one's control over what happens in experience has limits … [I]t is not up to one what … one will experience.' But this is only partly true; much of what we actually experience has been selected by us for being experienced; most human efforts are directed towards rearranging the world so as to experience what we would prefer to experience. But even if McDowell's statement were unqualifiedly true, it would be a mistake to project onto objects the causation of cognition. It is not up to one whether one will digest the food one has consumed, or fail to digest it if it is indigestible; but in no case does the food do one's digesting of it. Sometimes we cannot avoid seeing what is immediately before our eyes — though we can arrange somehow to pretend to ourselves that we have not seen it — but in any case the activity of 'seeing' is done by us.

of cognition that follows directly from the failure to perceive the difference between the object cognized and the mind's cognitive activity. If one cannot recognize one's organic activity when the brain and the other organs involved cause cognition, one has failed to identify the true cause of cognition (i.e. the cognizer's organic activity); one is conscious only of the effect brought about by cause (i.e., one is aware only of one's cognition *of the object)*. But one cannot suppose that one's cognition of the object has no cause; one must suppose one. And if one's activity is not the cause, the most obvious (and indeed sole) candidate for the office is the object. In brief, one will *project* one's own activity onto the object.

The inability to perceive that the human organism's organic activities are related to the cognitive state of the organism as cause is to effect, is responsible also for what has been called in modern times the 'explanatory gap' between the organism and its experience. Naturally, if one fails to perceive that an organism's cognitive state is the *effect* caused on the organism by the activity of our cognitive organs as their *cause*, one has created a gap between the two. One has created it by projecting one's inability to perceive how the two are related, and then calling one's inability to perceive it a 'gap' between the organism and its cognitive states. One will then suppose instead that two unrelated processes are involved; one is an organic, bodily process and the other is a mental process. Thus, dualism is inevitable once one has failed to observe that there is a single process — namely, an activity of the organism that causes effects on the organism itself. For in causal processes there is a difference, but no gap, between the cause and the effect.

Or to put it conversely, nothing in our experience suggests that, when we perceive an object, or indeed when we witness the causation of any effect, one process (the causing of the effect) is succeeded by another process (the effectuation of the effect). There is a single process, the causation of the effect. Nevertheless, there is a difference between the cause and the effect, because the cause *changes* the subject of the process. In the case of perception, as noted earlier, the process that begins with the causation of perception (the nature of which we have yet to determine) results in a change in the perceiving organism, namely, from the prior state of not-perceiving into the state of actually perceiving. If, however, one reifies the activity of *knowing* into a substantive entity, *knowledge,* it would be difficult to avoid supposing that the causation of cognition involves two different processes and two different subjects, each of which undergoes a distinct process. One will have supposed that cognition is the effect worked by the object, through the mediation of the body's sense organs, on a non-bodily receptor, namely, a 'mind' to which the body is somehow joined.

And so, one and the same deficiency (i.e. the inability to perceive the difference between the cognitive organs' discharge of their cognitive function, and the resulting organic state of cognizing the object) is responsible for three classical misperceptions regarding the mind: (a) that objects cause our cognition, (b) that there is an 'explanatory gap' between cognitive organ and cognitive state, and (c) that the cognitive state is not an organic state of one's own organism, but a non-organic state of a substantive 'mind' that is other than the organism.

The Greek supposition that the cause of cognition is the world and its objects has had a remarkable longevity; it is widely accepted by philosophers and non-philosophers alike even today. Nevertheless, it is questionable, and in the next chapter I shall discuss in detail a possible alternative. But first we should recognize a further but highly prejudicial consequence it had for Greek philosophy which has also survived to the present in some philosophers. The supposition that objects caused cognition in the mind of knowers, distorted the Greek philosophers' attempts to interpret the nature of the reality of the world.

Let us amplify earlier remarks. The distortion consisted in fusing together indistinguishably the *reality* of the real and its *knowability.* Equating the two yields the idea that reality is knowable — but not merely in the plain sense that it *can be known,* which is of course quite true. The supposition is rather that the reality and its knowability are one and the same thing. Reality is knowable *in itself;* it is inherently *cognoscible,* if I may so put it. Unawareness that the cause of cognition is the cognitive activity of cognitively-endowed organisms, distorts the truth that reality is independent not only of *our* mind, but of *every* possible mind's cognition of it. For cognition, as our empirical acquaintance with it demonstrates, is a relationship: it requires the duality of two terms, a knower and a known (although these may be two different aspects of a single being). Contrary to the assumption that has come down to us from the Greeks, our empirical acquaintance with cognition entitles us to say not only that reality is whatever it itself is, independently of every mind's cognition of it; but also, on the other, that reality is knowable *only* by minds, not 'in itself.' That anything is knowable absolutely

— that is, even in the absence of any minds that might possibly know it, does not seem to me to make much sense. Of course, if we admit that the world is not knowable 'in itself,' philosophy faces the problem of how *we can* know it. But so be it. This is a proper philosophical question, and like every other philosophical question, dogmatism should not be allowed to prevent its investigation. It will be discussed in Chapter III.

Moreover, the inherent knowability of the world implies that even *before* sentience and consciousness appeared anywhere in the universe, the world was already *prepared* for them. That is, if the world is inherently knowable, then it was already knowable fore the appearance of any minds that might know it. Now, the Greeks would not have been disturbed if this implication of the inherent cognoscibility of the world had been called to their attention; for their universe did not evolve. Nor would it have troubled the scholastics, who would have invoked God's planned creation of the world by thinking it, and his having intended to create it for the sake of mankind. For them, the world was indeed inherently knowable, because it is eternally known by God's Mind, and predestined by God eventually to become known by us. It is more difficult to imagine how it is inherently knowable, if one supposes that life, sentience, and consciousness have not always existed, but emerged in the random course of the world's evolution through natural selection. In other words, there is no reason to suppose that the world was destined one day to be perceptible to the animal form of life that was yet to appear; and there is even less reason to suppose that the world was destined from the outset to be intelligible to future humans.

From all we know regarding the appearance of minds on Earth, the indication is, on the contrary, that when minds evolved, it was *they* that were adapted to the world that already existed, not that the universe was primed to receive the newcomer and make it feel at home. In other words, the assumption of universal evolution professed by many if not most of today's scholars is subliminally contradicted by the assumption of the same scholars of the inherent knowability of the world; the latter implies that from the outset the world was destined eventually to issue forth in human nature and in minds. The inherent knowability of the world is rather an orphan assumption that survived the death of the parent assumptions — which in the Greek version was that reality was 'divine', and in the Christian that the reality of the world consisted in its being thought by God.

The confusion between the reality and the cognoscibility of the real is reflected in the ambiguity of the concept of 'objectivity,' which now covers indistinctly the independence of reality from every mind's cognition of it (which is true), and the inherent cognoscibility of the world (which is not true). The supposed inherent cognoscibility of reality is of a piece with the fantasy that we can envisage reality not only from our own viewpoint as perceivers, but also from *reality's own viewpoint.* But to ascribe a viewpoint to the objects we cognize is implicitly to suppose that the objects we know are themselves *knowers* of our knowledge of them. This subject, too, will be more fully discussed later; meanwhile I make clear that in this work, I use the term 'objectivity' to refer exclusively to the 'otherness' of reality, insofar as it is the *object* — i.e., the target — of the mind's cognitive activities. The notions that reality is inherently knowable and has its own viewpoint, as contrasted with the 'subjective' viewpoint of the human mind does not strike me as having been sufficiently well thought out.

To be sure, the empirically supported opinions I have defended — that the reality of the real is independent of all cognition by all minds, and that reality is knowable only by minds — do not of themselves add up to an interpretation of either cognition or reality. But they have to be respected by any interpretation of reality that seeks to avoid the difficulties created by the Greek confusion of the two. Meanwhile, suffice it to conclude that Greek philosophy set the standard regarding both the *cause of cognition* and the *cognoscibility of reality* by which mediaeval scholasticism and modern philosophy have generally abided.

Finally, before we turn to the philosophical age that was to succeed the Greek, it should be useful to consider critically and mark well two items of Aristotelian thought that have caused a few Hellenists to wonder whether we do not owe 'representationism' to Aristotle. The importance of the subject is clear, given the role in which my hypothesis casts representationism. The first item concerns a remark made by Aristotle only once and incidentally: the point, which was made in what may have been a late work,[126] was not developed or even mentioned by him elsewhere. The passage concerns mostly the nature of language, and is noted for its introduction of the separation of thought

---

126   Hellenists have debated whether *On Interpretation* was not 'the latest of all the extant works' of Aristotle; Ross, *Aristotle,* 19.

from speech which is often taken for granted in modern philosophy; but it includes a statement about cognition:

> Vocal sounds [127] *{ta en te phone]* are the signs *[symbola]* of experience *[ton en te psyche pathematon,* 'the undergoing in the soul'] and written words *{ta gra-phomena}* are the signs *[semeia]* of what is voiced *[ton en te phone].* Like writ-ing *[grammata],* speech is not the same for all peoples. But the experiences *[pathemata tes psyches]* of which vocal sounds are primarily signs *[semeia protos]* are the same for all, as are also those things of which experiences are the likenesses *[homoiomata].* [128]

According to W.D. Ross, the view that experiences are the 'likenesses' of real things indicates 'a frankly 'representative' view of knowledge.' [129] Now, a representationist view of speech was indeed part of Aristotle's intention, but not *of knowledge.* It is the latter I deem questionable. There can be no doubt, of course, that in this text Aristotle stated openly that experiences are 'likenesses' of things.

---

127   The Greek *ta en te phone,* translated here as 'vocal sounds' is sometimes rendered as 'spoken words', which is of course quite correct also — because in English today 'to speak' means primarily 'to use vocal sounds' — but which fails to inform the English reader that the 'words' in question are not *logoi,* but signs of *logoi,* which was a novelty introduced by Aristotle in this text. The innovation separated speech from thought (which implies that speech has no role in human experience, but is posterior to experience), and reduces speech to the encoding of thoughts in subsequent audible and visible signs used to represent one's thoughts to others. It is significant that by so doing Aristotle simultaneously assimilated speaking to writing; for writing is indeed posterior to, and truly encodes, the speech it represents. As Marshall McLuhan said, literacy gave human beings 'an eye for an ear;' *The Gutenberg Galaxy* (Toronto: University of Toronto Press, 1962), p. 27. Or at least, it seems to have done so to Aristotle.

128   Aristotle, *On Interpretation,* 1.16a4-9. Aristotle uses the Greek words for 'sign' *(semeion)* and 'symbol' *(symbolon)* inter-changeably; the two mean the same in Greek, though *symbolon* adds to *semeion* the connotation of 'correspondence' between the sign and the signified. *Symbolon* (which etymologically means 'casting together') originally designated a tablet on which an agreement was inscribed in duplicate and then broken into halves whose indentations matched, and thus verified, each other. Some modern attempts to obviate the difficulties that attend the Aristotelian interpretation of speech depend on differenti-ating between signs and symbols and attributing to the indirectness of the latter (as contrasted with the supposed directness of the former) the aptness of symbols for representing meanings. The effort, I think, is wasted; the difficulties are caused by supposing that speech represents thought, not how it represents thought.

129   Ross, *Aristotle,* 25. At one time I agreed with Ross on this point, but now I am of the opinion that Ross does not seem to have taken into account that Aristotle's doctrine could amount to representationism only if his doctrine of the nature of reality had separated the reality of the knowing mind and the reality of the object — which is precisely what Aristotle took care not to do.

But he stated it baldly, offering no elucidation or explanation; nor did he follow up the bare statement, or amplify it, or refer to it, either later in this work or elsewhere; and nothing indicates that he ever tried to relate it to his elaborate and detailed account of cognition in his treatise *On the Soul,* although representationism would be in tension, if not outright contradiction, with the latter work. In brief, Aristotle did none of the things he would almost certainly have done if the statement had been intended as a modification of his earlier teaching, namely, that cognition was the union of the object and the active mind as the mind gained possession of the 'forms' of objects.

The treatise *On Interpretation* contains some of the elements that are necessary for representationism, but it lacks one that is indispensable. Representationism supposes that when reality is cognized, its characteristics come to *exist* in the knower's mind in a peculiarly mental manner, without ceasing to *exist* in reality. But without the 'monstrous offspring,' the 'double existence of perceptions and objects,' there can be no representationism. And yet, it is well established among Hellenists that the Greeks never developed an idea of 'existence' to signify the reality of a real being, as distinct from the reality of the characteristics of the being. That is, they were not acquainted with the possibility of using the verb 'to be' *existentially,* as grammarians put it, as well as predicatively or *copulatively.* For them, 'to be' meant the same as 'to be something.' And so, they simply did not think of the real as 'that which exists,' but as 'that which is whatever it is,' or 'that which is it itself.' As we have seen, the Greek philosophers estimated that what we call the 'reality' of a being (as contrasted with its 'existence'), consisted in its having a certain perceptible and intelligible structure; its reality was identical with its knowable 'contents,' or its 'essence.'

Elsewhere Ross himself agrees with this, which is the usual modern interpretation of Aristotle's conception of reality. What Ross does not seem to have considered, therefore, is that representationism demands not only 'likenesses' of objects; it demands 'likenesses' *that exist* in the mind. It requires the 'double existence of perceptions and objects.' Ross was aware that a superficial and anachronistic reading of certain texts of Aristotle[130] in which he contrasts questions regarding 'what something is' and 'whether something is,' may yield the impression that Aristotle thought that real beings 'existed.' But as Ross himself explained (and as most contemporary Hellenists agree), for Aristotle 'to ask

---

130   See his *Posterior Analytics,* 2.1-2. 89b21-90a24; 2.7.92b3-92b26.

whether A is, is to ask whether there is an intelligible essence answering to the name, and … to ask *what* A is is to seek to unfold this essence in a definition.'[131] In classical Greek, 'to be' does not mean the same as 'to exist' does in modern English or in any of the other modern European languages.

In short, the theory of cognition in *On the Soul* is not a version of representationism. The treatise *On the Soul* depends, as Heraclitus had previously proposed, on the *unity* or *identity* of the *logos* of reality with the *logos* of cognition. The point is explicitly made by Aristotle: 'actually knowing is identical with its object.'[132] Aristotle clearly recognized, of course, that reality and the mind (i.e., the knower and the object) are two, not one. But when cognition took place, he thought, although the object and the mind remained distinct entities, the *logos* of reality became *one* with the *logos* in the mind. And without the double existence of the *logos* in the mind and the *logos* in reality there can be no representationism. 'Likenesses' of reality do not necessarily imply representationism.

The other item concerning Aristotle's thought that calls for further comment is that, according to some philosophers, Aristotle was aware of the nature of consciousness, or at least of the fact that human cognition was conscious. This would contradict my suggestion that the Greek philosophers were disadvantaged in both these regards. It has been argued that Aristotle's is a special case, but most of the evidence that supposedly indicates awareness of consciousness is controversial.[133] It is nonetheless significant that Aristotle himself explicitly noted that when we perceive, we perceive that we perceive;[134] that the mind can understand itself[135]; that when we think, we perceive that we think; that, indeed, when we so perceive, we perceive our reality; and that perceiving our reality is

---

131   Ross, *Aristotle,* 50.

132   Aristotle, *On the Soul,* 3.5.430a20.

133   For example, Aristotle criticizes his predecessors for their interpretation of sensation as a passive process, but does not disagree that it is an alteration of the sense organs caused by objects (*On the Soul,* 2.5.416b32-418a6. See also Ross's commentary, *Aristotle,* 136-139). Aristotle merely reinterprets the passivity of sensation in a new way. Aristotle also teaches that understanding and rational thought require an active power to process the potential intelligibility of intelligible forms; but apart from the absence of all explanation of how this is done and of the uncertain status of exactly who or what does it, there is no question but that for him, in the end, '[t]hought is receptive of intelligible form, as sense was of sensible form,' Ross, *Aristotle,* 146.

134   Aristotle, *On the Soul,* 3.2.425b12.

135   Aristotle, *Metaphysics,* 12.7.1072b19-23.

the ground of our finding life valuable.[136] However, these remarks need not indicate awareness of the fact that human cognition is conscious; they merely indicate awareness of the self-observability of the human mind.

Consciousness is not to be confused (as it was by Locke) with the mind's self-observability. The reasons why we must say so will be further discussed below; meanwhile I note that at the higher levels of infrahuman life, animals are capable of making use of previous experiences to improve their behavioural responses to their environment. If they are not endowed with consciousness, they could not reflect deliberately, or intending to do so; but if their brains make use of previous experience, their brains must be able to bring up past experience for new consideration affecting current experience. Such *reflection* will be achieved autonomically rather than voluntarily, but achieved none the less. However, if the mental functions of such animals do not have the capacity for attaining conscious quality, their reflections upon prior experience will follow suit: they will not be conscious. The human mind's experience, on the other hand, normally has conscious quality; not surprisingly, its reflexive self-observations also will normally have conscious quality also. But the human mind's capacity for observing itself by reflecting upon itself — i.e., by making itself, or its previous activities, the target or object of a subsequent activity — is not to be identified with its consciousness. Rather, self-observability is a consequence of the conscious quality of the typical form of human cognition. Human cognition has conscious quality when perceptual awareness of an object is accompanied by awareness of the perceptual activity of the perceiver — and thus, awareness of the experiential character of the experience.

Thus, Aristotle's remarks do not seem to me to indicate awareness of the conscious nature of human cognition. They did not result in his raising new questions about the nature of the mind; they played no role in his account of the mind; and they did not affect his conception of the *explicandum*. Besides, even if we were to go to the length of supposing that Aristotle became aware of the conscious nature of the human mental functions, and even if he understood that the foregoing observations changed the *explicandum* of the mind substantially, we would have to say also that his insight died with him. For his awareness of the conscious nature of the mind, if such it was, was not followed

---

136   Aristotle, *Nichomachean Ethics,* 9.9.1170a25-1170b10.

up by him or his disciples, or referred to by later philosophers. His awareness of consciousness, if it existed, played no role in the history of philosophy. It was only many centuries later that consciousness became an important part of the philosophical study of the mind.

To sum up, I underline what I judge to have been the fundamental contribution of the Greek interpretations of cognition and reality to the ultimate inability of modern philosophy to respond adequately to Hume's challenge.

As to cognition, the contribution was simply the basic supposition that cognition was the effect caused by reality upon the mind. Various Greek philosophers interpreted the effect in somewhat different ways, but historically the most important version was that of Aristotle. According to him, the perceptible and intelligible 'contents' of objects entered the mind through our senses and, upon reaching the mind's receptive powers, were absorbed, assimilated into, and *integrated with,* the mind. As to reality, the Greek contribution was the basic supposition that reality has mind-like 'contents' — that is, inherently perceptible and intelligible characteristics — that are ready in themselves to become actually known.

Let us not forget, however, that behind these misinterpretations regarding cognition and reality was their common source: the prior failure to perceive the *activity* of experiencing the object as distinct from the object experienced, and the consequent projection of the mental activity onto the object. Or in other words, the root of the misinterpretations was the assumed *receptivity* and *passivity* of the mind.

3. *Christianity and the emergence of scholasticism*

With the growing ascendancy of Rome and the Augustans, Greek philosophy extended its reach to become the philosophy of the Greco-Roman world — a world, however, that was about to change its religious allegiance. Christianity deemed itself in competition not only with the popular Greco-Roman religion, but most particularly with philosophy, whose rationality made it the more likely contender. Indeed, Christianity deemed itself the 'true philosophy' — which is to say, the true 'theology.' And so, for the best part of half a millennium the two existed side by side — although as Christianity flourished and developed its own 'theology,' Greco-Roman philosophy gradually declined and was practiced by dwindling numbers. The theology of the Christians was erected, however, on the framework provided by the basic concepts of Greek philosophy, adapted as required in order to conform to Christian beliefs. Philosophy had entered a new age, within which the basic concepts of Greek philosophy survived. Much was added, but continuity in respect of such fundamental concepts was carefully and consciously preserved.

Some historians have marvelled that an obscure Jewish sect at the confines of what was then ethnocentrically known as the *oikumene,* the 'inhabited world,' should have captured the allegiance of Hellenistic mankind, and eventually that of the entire Greco-Roman empire, and to have done so peacefully — the use of force being the more usual means whereby mass conversions on this scale are effected. The process, however, is understandable when we consider two factors. First, what the apostle Paul proposed to the Gentiles did not require them to give up any of their *important* pagan religious beliefs, or to change the general outline of their pagan vision of the world. It was rather what they were required to *add* to their earlier beliefs that made all the difference in the world: it made their conversion to Christianity all the easier. They were asked to give up a few things, of course, but most of it was good riddance: the pantheon, and a few beliefs of little practical consequence, such as the supposition that the world had had no beginning or end. And if the Greek gods and their Roman counterparts should have been missed, it would have been mostly on account of the amusement value of their fabled antics. Converts to Christianity were specifically *not* called upon to reject the idea that human beings and their visible world had only a qualified or conditioned reality, or that they depended absolutely on Fate to determine what happened to them. On the contrary, they were asked to reaffirm it. But to be sure, with a twist.

This was the second factor, the fillip that made Christianity not simply acceptable, but positively attractive — which is why its adherents called the message of the Christian preachers the *euangelion,* the 'good news.' The 'news' was, first, that Fate was not an abstract and impersonal force: *ho theos* was to be understood as the proper name of a concrete and personal entity who had created the world — and indeed, for its own good rather than his. And God was kind, merciful, forgiving, and deeply concerned with human welfare; indeed, it had been out of love and compassion for mankind that at a certain point in history he had chosen to share our own human nature, together with its vicissitudes, reverses, and even temptations, and to sacrifice his only begotten Son so as to forgive mankind's betrayal of him. Why this should have placated God is a different question. The culture's normal assumption at the time seems to have been that crime and betrayal could be redeemed by the counterbalance of pain and suffering. But if so, it made sense to suppose that the death of the Christ manifested, and solicited emulation of, the boundless love and compassion of God for mankind. It does not make quite as much sense today, but somehow the 'redemption' of mankind by the passion and death of Jesus remains the centre of Christianity.

But surely the best news was, second, that the Christian *ho theos* promised delivery from the nothingness of death. Mortal human beings could aspire to 'eternal life,' including bodily resurrection, if they were chosen by God to be his friends. And his friends were those who believed in him, loved him, reposed their trust in him, obeyed his commands, and loved one another. Christian evangelists stressed therefore that the Christian God was the *Deus ignotus,* the God who responded to the yearning that the Gentiles had always had for him, but whose true name they had not known. Thus, to those who already were familiar with the concept that an omnipotent divine force worked in mysterious ways so as to rule their lives from birth to death and to enforce its will over theirs and the world's, Christianity made an offer that would have been difficult to turn down: trade the pitiless, pointless, and capricious omnipotence of a cosmic force that determines all events, for the omnipotence of a personal divine Will that determines all events, but mercifully, fairly, and wisely, and who offers delivery from death and an eternity of bliss thereafter. To accept it made perfect sense; to refuse it would have been egregious folly. Much the same considerations would account, a few centuries later, for the conversion of Arabia to the preaching of Muhammad and his updating of the biblical 'revelation.' To be sure, Christianity became renowned also for preaching the brotherhood of man under the fatherhood of God, and for its social conscience. But the appeal that the prospect of 'salvation' held for Christians seems to have been, and to have to the present remained, the overriding motivating force of Christian belief.

Though Christianity transformed much of Greco-Roman culture, acculturation is almost invariably a two-way trade; Christianity also received much from the new environment in which the originally foreign, Jewish belief had taken root. Intellectually speaking, Christianity became thoroughly hellenized. Not the least important of the institutions it adopted was, as noted earlier, the use of reason in order to try to gain knowledge about 'the divine' — and eventually, indeed, about everything else. The Christians were members of a culture where scholarship had been an integral part of civilized, responsible citizenship, and which had accumulated more than a little experience in the cultivation of intellectual skills. Theological/metaphysical/philosophical thinking came naturally to them. Thus, Christianity 'established contact with [Greek] philosophy in the second century … from the time when there were converts whose culture was Greek.'[137] This speaks of an ancient, traditional, atavistic Christian motivation that explains much of the intellectual ferment that eventually stirred the high middle ages — though not until the right conditions prevailed.

Mediaeval thought spans two quite distinct and very different phases. At first, Christian theology was, in what concerned its philosophical foundations, much like the theology of Plato and the Neo-Platonists upon which the particularities of Christianity were superimposed. Of course, all Christian theology must be 'theocentric,' but during its first phase, up to the end of the first millennium A.D., the center absorbed the whole. Nothing mattered, and nothing was true or real, unless as a faint and finite reflection of the divinity of the Christian God. Theology was allowed not only to override reason if necessary, but also to guide it, to inspire it, and to shape it, even in relation to what otherwise would have been called 'philosophical' questions regarding the world 'here below.' Typical of this Christian period was the work of Augustine of Hippo, who emerged in the fifth century A.D. as the most influential theologian in Christendom for nearly the next thousand years. His orientation is well illustrated by his 'God-centered'[138] theory of knowledge. We should take a moment to recall this and one other among his doctrines, as they should enable us to appreciate the difference between the two stages of mediaeval Christian thought and facilitate our understanding of later philosophical events.

---

137 Étienne Gilson, *La philosophie au moyen age: des origines patristiques a la fin du XIVe siecle* (Paris: Payot, 1947), 9.

138 Whitney J. Oates, 'Introduction' to *The Basic Writings of Saint Augustine* (New York: Random House, 1948), vol. 1, xxiii.

Augustine's explanation of human cognition was obviously indebted to Platonism. It is commonly known as the doctrine of 'divine illumination,' because 'it supposes that just as the sun is the source of the physical light that renders things visible, God is the source of the spiritual light that renders the sciences intelligible by thought.'[139] In effect, we do not actually do our own cognizing; God does it for us. We simply reap the benefit of his mind when we receive in our mind the effect of the 'illumination' of which he alone is the active cause. The Greek passivity of the mind is assumed; indeed, it is redoubled.

Most important for understanding later historical developments is also Augustine's interpretation of how God created the world. It begins with the notion that God's infinite mind has 'ideas.' The divine 'ideas' are the thoughts conceived by the divine Thinker regarding the many finite and partial ways in which his infinite and total perfection could be participated in by creatures:

> These ideas are the archetypes of every species and every individual created
> by God ... [E]ach thing has thus been created in accordance with its proper
> model, and since all things have been created by God, these models of things,
> or ideas, could not subsist unless in God's thought.[140]

Thus, the divine 'ideas' in the mind of God were identical with the universal 'essences' of things, as supposed by Greek philosophy. Real beings were created — i.e. made to be real — if, when, and only as long as, God further willed that a certain divine idea be actually realized in a concrete individual being. Therefore, the continuing reality of created beings, including their life (if they were alive) and their whole being, depended on — or more exactly, *consisted in* —God's continuing to will that his thinking of them should be realized: 'we subsist because we bathe, so to speak, in the divine power that makes us be.'[141]

Let us mark well, because we shall need to refer to it later, that both the Greek philosophers and the Christian theologians who typically followed Augustine, used the same terminology — namely,

---

139   Étienne Gilson, *Introduction a l'étude de Saint Augustin* (Paris: Vrin, 1949), 117.

140   Gilson, *Saint Augustin,* 109.

141   Gilson, *Saint Augustin,* 111.

the vocabulary of 'being' and 'to be' — to account for what we today are more likely to call the 'reality' of a real being (which we first conceive when we experience the otherness of the world in relation to ourselves.) They did not account for it by invoking (as we now do) the fact that, over and above their properties, real beings have what we call their own 'existence.' For the Christian interpretations had absorbed from Greek philosophy — but also expanded — the idea that the reality of a real being was its 'beingness' *(ousia);* that is, it was identical with the knowability of the being, since it was identical with properties that could be truthfully predicated of it as what the being *was.*

The principal difference between the Greek and the Christian accounts had to do with whether the knowable properties of the being presupposed a mind that knew them. For the Christians, the Mind that made every 'being' to have the characteristics it had was the personal divine mind of God. He had created the world by the *fiat* of his Will, when he willed that the creature he had conceived become concretized or congealed in matter, so to speak. Creatures were thus real because God willed that they be whatever they were. Conversely, what made a being real was the knowability' that inhered or resided in it because God had conceived it and willed that it *be.* Among the Greek philosophers, however, only a very few had supposed that the constitution of a real being by a set of knowable characteristics predicable of it as 'what it was' pointed towards a cosmic force or principle of Mind as the ultimate explanation of the reality of the world. Such Mind was, of course, of uncertain nature and particulars, but in any event not a singular or personal Being or one who had any regard for the world.

In the thirteenth century, however, at the height of scholasticism, Thomas Aquinas modified the traditional Augustinian doctrine in ways that we shall consider in the next section of this chapter. But until then, the Augustinian interpretation of the reality of man and world had remained for centuries the fixed standard of mediaeval thought regarding the reality of creation. This is why we need not be further concerned here with the history of Christian thought for the next six or seven hundred years after Augustine — that is, until the early part of the second millennium. Let us turn instead to the historical events that led to the transition of Christian thought to a second intellectual age: the age dominated by the institution of scholasticism.

Although Christians had always admired scholarship and reason, they had never been well disposed towards those aspects of Greek philosophy that contradicted Christian beliefs. Apart from practices such as Emperor cult, Christians found abhorrent, for example, the bland assumption of the Greek philosophers that the world had neither beginning nor end; the philosophers' opinion contradicted, of course, the Christian belief that the world had been created *ex nihilo* at a certain specific time 'in the beginning' — that is, exactly so many years ago — by the *fiat* of God. Now, the belief that the truth of the Christian faith is guaranteed by a higher wisdom than the human does not of itself imply intolerance of other religious views. Thus, the baptism of the emperor Constantine in 337 established Christianity as the official religion of the empire, but the teaching of pagan philosophy was not proscribed. The same policy of toleration was continued by later emperors. However, Christians at all times have been known to chafe at the possibility that error might lead astray the innocent and the credulous among the faithful. In the year 529, the emperor Justinian, attempting to bring unity to the divided empire into Christian and pagan factions, reversed the Constantinian policy of toleration and decreed the closure of the philosophical schools of Athens. The philosophers departed, taking with them as much of their libraries as they could, and re-established themselves in various cities in the middle east, mostly in Syria. Syria was then heretical territory outside the control of both the emperor — now no longer in Rome, but in Constantinople — and of the pope in Rome.

By this time, however, the Roman empire was a crumbling shell: in the year 285 it had been divided into Eastern and Western halves by Diocletian, to the detriment and decline of the Western. In 410 Rome had been sacked by the Goths, and in 430 by the Vandals; and with the abdication of Romulus Augustus in 476 the Western Empire had ceased to exist. Darkness was descending over Western European culture; what survived of classical Greece and Rome was concentrated in Byzantium and the Eastern Empire. Literacy was fast declining; it is a symbol of the age that Charlemagne, who was famous for the 'enlightenment' he brought to the early ninth century, was illiterate. The memory of Greek and Roman civilized life had faded, and Europe endured the five-centuries-long period of history up to the end of the first millennium that is known by historians as the 'dark ages.' But of course, the history of mankind did not stop; on the contrary, in another part of the world it was about to take off.

In 622 the Prophet Muhammad fled from Mecca to Medina. A mere twelve years later, in an explosion of proselytizing fervour, Islam had already subjugated Arabia's neighbouring states: Egypt, Persia, and not least important, Syria. For in Syria the Arabs found a treasure trove: the sizeable amount of Greek philosophical literature that had long ceased to be readily available in Christendom, as well as a living tradition of philosophical scholarship. And upon their conquest of Syria, the Arabs had quickly begun to incorporate Greek learning into Islamic culture. In time, the conceptually lean, predominantly homiletic message of Muhammad was developed into a sophisticated, full-fledged theology; the Greek example inspired the creation of an elaborate Islamic legal system, the Shari'a; the creative development of Greek mathematics gave us algebra, positional notation, and possibly zero. And stimulated by Aristotle's numerous 'physical' and 'biological' treatises and his 'natural history' writings, the Arabs' observation of the natural world resulted in advances in medicine and astronomy.

But most important from our viewpoint is that the Arabs were the intermediaries through which Greek philosophy, including most of the philosophical *corpus* of Aristotle, would eventually 'pass … to Jewish and Western Christian philosophers'[142] For Islamic civilization flourished, and by 700 it had reclaimed for God and his imperishable glory a world that stretched eastwards into parts of India and westwards along North Africa to Morocco. In 711 the Jihad crossed the strait of Gibraltar into Spain, almost all of which soon became an Arab state. The advance of Islam into Europe was not checked until 732, when Charles Martel defeated the attempt of the Moors to conquer the French cities of Tours and Poitiers. But the Arab occupation of Spain was protracted. The last of the Moorish invaders was not to leave until earlier the same year that Columbus set sail towards the New World.

Contact among Moorish scholars and their Christian and Jewish counterparts in Spain during the eleventh and the following century brought new ideas to Europe. One of the best known Arabic philosophers of the age, Averroes, was a native of Córdoba; and so was Moses Maimonides, the renowned Jewish thinker, who dates from the same period. Latin translations of the Arabic trans-lations of Aristotle and Plato, and of the Arab philosophers Alfarabi, Avicenna, and Averroes, and the extensive commentaries of the last two on Aristotle, were published in Toledo early in the 12th century and soon circulated throughout Western Europe. It was in this way that Greek philosophy,

---

142   Gilson, *Philosophie au moyen age,* 345.

and Aristotle specifically, were rediscovered by Western Christendom after centuries of very limited access to Greek sources. The 'dark ages' came to an end. The love of learning of Greece and Rome had never been quite allowed to die in Christendom; the spark had been kept alive in monastery schools. But now it flared. In short, the Arabs rescued Western Europe from the intellectual penury to which it had descended. Renewed cultivation of letters promoted the foundation of the European universities, first Bologna in 1119, then Paris in 1150 and Oxford in 1167. And Greek thought now came hand in hand with Arabic thought, which had some original ideas of its own. The institution of 'scholasticism' — the pursuit of theological knowledge not merely for 'pastoral' but principally for intellectual purposes — had been spontaneously engendered much earlier by the practice of theologians. But now Christian philosophy was about to undergo a sea change.

During its first period, Christian thinkers had practiced 'philosophy' mostly under the assumption that it was identical with 'theology' in the sense originally given to the term by Plato and Aristotle. Besides, the Greek (and Roman) resources from which they could draw were severely limited. Of Aristotle, in particular, they knew mostly some logical commentaries such as Porphyry's *Isagoge*, but not much outside the field of logic. In the late eleventh and early twelfth centuries, however, they became exposed to a much more comprehensive view of Greek philosophy; for instance, the *Physics* and the natural treatises of Aristotle now became available to them for the first time. They continued to practice 'theology', but now *scientia* could not be reduced to the use of Platonic and Neo-Platonic concepts so as to understand, so far as possible, the otherwise impenetrable 'mysteries' of the Christian faith. Thus, the recovery of Greek philosophy presented Christian scholars with a new challenge:

> Up to the last years of the twelfth century … Christian theology had never
> had to concern itself with the fact that a non-Christian interpretation of the
> world as a whole, including man and his destiny, was … an open possibil-
> ity … By [the mid-century] every Christian university teacher knew that a
> non-Christian explanation of the world was possible.[143]

---

143 Étienne Gilson, *Elements of Christian Philosophy* (New York: Doubleday, 1960), 11.

Such explanation, moreover, notwithstanding its depending solely on the exercise of reason seemed to most theologians to be true. [144] The challenge that confronted the scholastics has been frequently described, therefore, as the problem of reconciling faith and reason,[145] in which vigorous interest was thereafter taken by most theologians. But we must understand exactly what such 'reconciliation' was expected to achieve.

What moved the theologians was not merely an apologetic interest in fending off possible objections to Christian doctrine by appealing to the compatibility of the truths of Christian faith with rationally established truths; nor was it only the possibility of taking advantage of reason's discoveries to enhance the believer's understanding of the 'revealed' truth. Also at stake was the question of the validity of reason, *independently of revelation,* as a means to obtain knowledge about ourselves and about the world. Granted, as most scholastics agreed, that revelation teaches the believer truths that reason unaided by faith could never aspire to reach — such as the various doctrines that concern 'salvation' from eternal death, or worse — it remains that the scope of revelation is fairly narrow. Christianity had much to say about man and world in their relationship to God, but very little about man and world in themselves apart from such relationship. The assumption in earlier centuries had always been that, apart from such relationship, there was nothing to be said of much importance about anything in the world. But Aristotle's writings seemed to demonstrate the feasibility of investigating the natural world independently of revelation, as well as the importance of doing so.

And so, Christian scholars became aware of the value of *episteme,* or *scientia,* for its own sake: 'the idea of a true scientific study of nature was conceived' by Christian thinkers.[146] But they needed to justify it, and to do so in a manner that safeguarded the 'higher' and more important truth of revelation and faith. They needed, and they sought, in effect, a theory of the relationship between reason and revelation that satisfied such condition.

The nub of the difficulty was that the basis of *scientia* was of course the Greek concept of *physis,* which construed the 'nature' of things as the source of their causal power to necessitate effects.

---

144 Gilson, *Elements,* 14.

145 See Étienne Gilson, *Reason and Revelation in the Middle Ages* (New York: Scribner's, 1948).

146 Étienne Gilson, *The Spirit of Mediaeval Philosophy* (New York: Scribner's, 1949)*,* 367.

Aristotelian *scientia* was definable as *cognitio certa per causas* — 'knowledge [that is] certain through [the ascertainment of] causes' — only because *scientia* discovered the literally *natural* or *physical* and *inherent* causes of events. This, however, if taken literally, conflicted with Christian dogma in several ways. From the viewpoint of the Christian faith the principal and most obvious objection was that a natural world operating by virtue of the *physis* of things was self-sufficient in every way; it needed nothing outside itself to be itself and to operate as it operated. But not much less unwelcome was the Greek philosophical supposition that the world was intelligible *inherently*, rather than because it had been intelligently crafted by the Divine Intellect. After all, such self-sufficiency had been exactly what the Greek philosophers had intended in order to liberate the world from the dominion of the extraneous force of Fate. The transition from Greek religion to Greek philosophy had been achieved through the reduction of mythological 'gods' to the *causal* powers of the immanent *logos* — i.e. the *knowable* content — of worldly entities.

Christianity, on the contrary, had taught since time out of mind that creatures depended from moment to moment for their reality and for their secondary, conditional causal powers on God and his 'physical premotion' of the changes that took place in the world; conversely, the world's causal powers were conditional upon the permissive will of God, the true though unseen cause of all visible effects. Thus, the causal powers of creatures were not independently effective, but only the instruments through which God exercised his will. Likewise, the intelligibility of the world was a mute testimony to the wisdom of the God who had designed it. Moreover, Christianity had done so with emphatic assurance only after Augustine had elucidated how creatures depended on God for their 'being' whatever they were: creatures were but divine ideas made real by God's willing that they 'be.' Of themselves, man and world were therefore literally *nothing;* they had no reality *of their own*. And whereas for Greek philosophy the world's Fate inhered in the world itself, for Christians the Fate of the world was identical with the 'divine plan' for the world. An additional difficulty was that for Christians the world was not everlasting; Christians knew that God had created it a specific (though not readily ascertainable) number of years ago. Besides, God had not been compelled to create the world; the world he had freely created was contingent on his deciding to keep it in existence. The inwardly necessitated world of the Greeks, on the contrary, had always 'been there.' And it had always *had* to be, and to be such as it was.

Arab philosophers, being followers of the Judaeo-Christian Bible, had encountered the same difficulties when they tried to harmonize Aristotle and Islam. But as most Christian thinkers understood it, the best the Arabs had been able to do to come to terms with the issue was not satisfactory; it was the controversial theory, controversially attributed to Averroes — and therefore widely known as 'Averroism' — that revelation and *scientia* could both be equally true though contradictory. Could Christian thinkers do better? There were not many scholastics from the late twelfth century onwards who did not try their hand at improving upon 'Averroism' by attempting to justify an epistemically sound philosophical study of the world that at the same time did not conflict with Christian belief.

From the outset, the ecclesiastical authorities were unconvinced that the new theological trends of the scholastics could be fully orthodox. Then, in the early thirteenth century, as the popularity of Aristotle mushroomed, the Church repeatedly issued restrictions and eventually outright prohibitions against the study of his works; ultimately pope Gregory IX intervened in 1231 to forbid it until it could be determined what might and what might not be acceptable to Christians in Aristotle's legacy. But it was too late. The measure was ineffective: 'henceforth, the writings of Aristotle on physics and metaphysics insinuated themselves everywhere and did not cease to gain ground.'[147] Later Popes, Innocent IV in 1245, and Urban IV in 1263, renewed the prohibitions, but 'their decrees arrived obviously too late, and had no effect.'[148]

The history of the problem of how to justify the possibility of purely rational and natural knowledge of the world 'without offending pious Christian ears' is in itself of no interest to us here. But one of the various proposed solutions — namely, that of Thomas Aquinas — is directly relevant to our topic because it had major and lasting effects on the history of philosophy, and indeed, on the history of Western civilization as a whole. His solution was based on a new philosophical doctrine concerning the nature of the reality of the world; his new teaching modified substantially what both the Greek and the Christian Augustinian traditions had previously held.

---

147 Gilson, *Philosophie au Moyen Age,* 388.

148 Gilson, *Philosophie au Moyen Age,* 388.

It is not my suggestion that Thomas's reinterpretation of the reality of the created world was motivated solely by the wish to solve the problem of justifying the compatibility of Christian faith and natural *scientia*. Since the same doctrine also contained a new conception of the reality of God, it affected every aspect of theology and not only the relationship between faith and reason. Nevertheless, Thomas's reinterpretation of the nature of reality supported such compatibility, because it enabled him to make two key assertions regarding the world and its objects, notwithstanding his beliefs that they had been created by God and that they were subject to the all-powerful will of their creator. Naturally, these beliefs demanded faith — whereas Thomas's suggestion regarding the reality of the world did not.

The two crucial provisions of Aquinas's proposal were that the creatures that made up the world (a) were inherently real (that is, both their reality and their nature were truly *their own)* and (b) had truly effective causal powers *of their own,* which they could exercise on their own initiative. However, Aquinas's doctrines of the inherent reality, inherent nature, and inherent causal powers of the world had the potential to affect philosophy's understanding of cognition. It is not completely clear to pre-cisely what degree Aquinas became aware of the logically necessary implications of his teaching about the reality of the world; but in any event, as his doctrine of the nature of reality became increasingly acceptable, such implications came to the attention of later scholastics and affected their treatment of cognition — and in the first place their interpretation of perception. It was in this manner, indirectly, quietly, and unostentatiously — but decisively — that the thought of Aquinas affected the history of philosophy. It was instrumental in the creation of philosophical representationism when to the earlier assumption about perception — that it consisted in the reception and possession of the 'con-tents' of objects — the doctrine of 'existence' was added. For such addition meant that the 'contents' of objects *existed* both in reality, or objectively, but also in the mind, or 'subjectively,' by virtue of the existence of the mind. The outcome of the 'double existence of perceptions and objects' was, of course, existential skepticism.

Quite as important, moreover, Thomas's existential interpretation also affected the history of European civilization, insofar as it changed the way in which all of us came to think of the reality of the world and of ourselves. When we today, both philosophers and non-philosophers, signify the reality of anything real by saying that it 'exists,' we are supposing, whether we know it or not, a conception of reality originally proposed by Thomas Aquinas. It was he who first taught European culture to think of reality as we now do — namely, as 'existing.' Well, then, exactly what was the doctrine that held such potential?

4. Thomas Aquinas and the existence of the world

Christianity had brought numerous and deep changes to the self-understanding of Europeans; but for all the vital differences between Greco - Roman and Christian Europe a degree of continuity in fundamentals underlay the divergences. Christians lived under the immediate, direct, personal, and minute supervision of a watchful God, and under the strict and omnipotent regime of a caring rather than an uncaring Fate. Theirs was a God with whom they could negotiate, rather than the unapproachable, despotic *ho theos* of old. Above all, they could look forward to cheating death and coming back to life one day, instead of having to look forward to the nothingness of nothingness. But two thousand years after the Milesian initiative, the structure of the world and the situation of human beings in the Christian culture of Europe remained, in all fundamental matters other than God and 'salvation,' much the same as they had been in Homeric and Hesiodic times.

For the world remained an inferior level of reality. It was 'a valley of tears' in which we existed while 'in exile,' overshadowed by an invisible ceiling beyond which true reality and true life were alone to be found. 'This world' was not our home, even if was our native land; it was the location we inhabited temporarily while awaiting real and eternal life to begin after our death 'here below.' Since we did not belong in it; we should not expect to be comfortable or happy while enduring it. After all, it was not unqualifiedly real; the measure of true reality was the 'next' world, the world where God reigned, and where human beings could indeed aspire to participate in his divinity. Moreover, although we were, in a sense, free to decide our Fate, our freely-made decisions merely confirmed God's will for us. This was, of course, a 'mystery,' but God and his ways are supposed to be 'mysterious.' However, these and indeed all other Christian convictions were about to be tested. Scholasticism had prepared the ground for the cultural revolution that in time would bring European civilization into the modern age. But the revolution itself could be said to have taken its first step, quietly and unspectacularly, only when Aquinas proposed his solution to the problem of the reconciliation of faith and reason that turned on a new interpretation of the nature of the reality of the created world.

To prepare ourselves for studying such interpretation we should consider in a little greater detail than previously how the human mind becomes aware of the reality of the real; and in particular how it comes about that, although the mental functions of all human beings are in all essential respects identical throughout the species, not all cultures share identically the same conception of reality. Nor are their various such conceptions of equal adequacy; the degree to which different human communities understand correctly the meaning of 'reality' is no less variable than their understanding of anything else.

Since cognition relates us to reality, and reality is relevant to our mental life only because we can become cognitively aware of it, our understanding of reality cannot be separated from our understanding of cognition. How we understand each will impinge on how we understand the other. But we understand both empirically. We can experience the 'reality' of the real only because, when our experience is conscious, we perceive simultaneously, within the singularity of one and the same experience, both the object and our cognitive activity: therefore, whatever we experience is, at one and the same time, and by one and the same organic activity, both (a) experienced, and (b) known to have been experienced.[149] Therefore, when we experience the world and the objects that make it up, we have the opportunity to experience the difference between the *object* and our *act of experiencing* the object.

It is a *radical* difference. For as we have seen, an integral aspect of every conscious perception of an object is that the object is perceived as *other-than* the mental activity whereby we perceive it. Thus, external objects are always perceived as being 'out there.' (Internal objects are not perceived 'out there,' of course, but nevertheless as other-than, or as 'outside' our experiencing activity.) This is why

---

149 Consciousness is therefore, as we have repeatedly noted, to be distinguished from the self-observability of the mind that results when one mental act is made the object of a second act. The first act informs us not only of the object, but also of the fact that object is being experienced; this is why we cannot confuse the object and our mind. This accounts for the conscious quality of the experience. The second act 'reflects' upon the first, and informs us of the fact that our mind has been informed by the object; this is why we can not only perceive the world, but can study, analyse, manipulate, and explain our perceptions of the world; it is also why we can *imagine* that our perceptions of the world *exist* in the mind, in the guise of 'ideas' of the world that repeat or represent the real world.

it is so perfectly clear to all of us, even to skeptics, that the objects we perceive are not created by our perception of them, not even in the case of 'internal' objects. (Our experiencing a headache does not create the headache.) For a few philosophers may have insisted that existential skepticism is a valid and true philosophical conclusion; but not one of them, so far as I am aware, has also affirmed the opinion that in point of fact the world does not exist.

The externality of external objects can be verified by the reader himself with the aid of a minor experiment. Unless he or she should have fortified him- or herself with one of the many toxic substances available for the purpose of distorting one's mental processes, or suffered from any of the several diseases that have the same effect, he or she will grasp with the utmost clarity both the fact that the book he or she is currently reading *is not he* or *not she*. At the same time, he or she will experience that he or she *is not the book*. Right? Well, this aspect of our experience is the basis of our conceiving 'reality' — both the reality of objects and our own reality as experiencers of objects. Objects are themselves; they are *not* me, and they are *not* my experience of them. To affirm this is to affirm that they are real — or which is the same, that they are 'objective.' To experience the world as real is to experience, in part, that its reality is not our responsibility, but its own. And in another part it is to experience that ours is our own.

The primordial experience of 'reality,' however, is conceptualized and interpreted more or less profoundly, and more or less correctly, by different cultures and philosophers — and expressed in different terms. To understand the interpretations of 'reality' that preceded our own we have to translate from one vocabulary to another. This will offer relatively little difficulty when different terms are used to refer to much the same idea of reality. But in a key case — the case at hand — the same words have been used at different times to express different interpretations of reality. This is the difficulty we now confront.

Aquinas's doctrine of the nature of reality is very different from that of earlier scholasticism and of Greek philosophy, but it was expressed by him in terms that, in most instances, are identical to those of the earlier doctrines. Though this was not the only factor, it is not to be wondered at, therefore, that it took more than one generation before his meaning was taken, and longer still until it was accepted. This happened in the fourteenth century, when a new terminology was introduced to refer to what philosophers had learned from Aquinas. It is easy to become confused, but let us try to dismantle the terminological hazards and consider the various stages of the process through which we came to think of reality as we do today.

When we today wish to say that something is real, we resort to either of two vocabularies. One is that of 'existence:' a real thing is one that 'exists' or that 'has existence.' We take for granted that this means, more precisely, that all real things have *their own* existence; for to us it is beyond doubt that no being can do another being's existing in its place. In other words, the reality or 'existence' of the real *inheres* in the real. Even those of us today who believe in a creator God and are firmly convinced that we owe our reality to him, do not ordinarily think that God does our existing for us. If he did, it would be he, not we, who existed. Likewise, when we speak of imaginary things we say that they are not real beings, because they 'do not exist.' They 'have no existence' *in themselves,* but only in our imagination and as our mental creation. The other way in which we today express reality is much older; it is by means of the verb 'to be.' We now use 'to be' mostly *predicatively,* that is, to attribute a predicate to a subject (e.g. 'roses are beautiful'); but sometimes we use it *existentially,* that is, to signify reality, e.g., 'God *is,*' 'there *are* roses in the garden.' The meaning is clear: 'God exists,' and 'the roses in the garden exist.'

We are apt to suppose that both our culture and our philosophical tradition have always understood reality as 'existence,' but the fact is not so. This is a relatively recent way of thinking. We think of reality in this manner and by means of the vocabulary of 'existence' only because about seven hundred and fifty years ago Thomas Aquinas offered his suggestions about the reality of the world, the essential part of which was adopted by modern philosophers and eventually by European culture as well. However, to express his view of the nature of reality, Aquinas never used the verb 'to exist' or the noun 'existence' in our sense. *Existere* and *existentia* were available as part of the established Latin lexicon, and in the fourteenth century would gain philosophical currency to mean much the same as we now mean; thereafter they passed into the European vernaculars and became part of our everyday speech. But there was a reason why Thomas did not use *existere* or *existentia.* Their ordinary meaning and usual connotations at the time made them less than ideal for Thomas's purposes. Why?

Etymologically, *existere* means 'to stand outside [something].' Before the fourteenth century, therefore, it was apt to be used to refer to an effect as distinct from, or without regard to, the causes or conditions whence the effect derived. Effects might be said to 'stand outside' their causes, because once the effects took place they had become reality; nothing could change the fact that they had taken place; they 'stood' on their own. This is obvious in the case of, for instance, the generation of offspring by parents. Once the young have been procreated, they exist by themselves; unlike the gametes from which they come, they have ceased to depend for their reality, their life, on their procreators. They develop their own life. The child's behaviour may continue to be influenced by, but is independent from, its parents and their existence.

However, this is true not only of the effect of sexual reproduction; it is true of every effect. Once an effect has been caused, it is real: it 'exists.' It cannot not-be, and it cannot not-have-been. In other words, the fact that causation has taken place is irreversible; for causation is integral part of the temporality and the 'becoming' of the real world. The irreversibility of causation is identical with the irreversibility of time. One could glue together the shards of a broken glass, say, and 'restore' the original so skillfully that it would seem as if it had never been broken; but if one did so, one would not have *un-caused* the breakage; one would have simply caused a new effect.

Accordingly, in the earlier ordinary use of *existere,* the weight of the affirmation fell on the *independence* of effects from their causes. Since according to Christianity creatures are in no way independent of God (a point that had to be upheld by Thomas's doctrine of reality) *existere* would almost certainly have seemed to Thomas unsuitable for signifying the inherent reality of creatures, the effect of the First Cause — if indeed, he ever considered it. It would have connoted that the world had not been created by God.

Corroboration of the inadequacy of 'existence' to convey Thomas's existential interpretation (if its original connotations should have been retained) is afforded by Thomas's statement that it would have been inappropriate to say that 'God exists.' The reason is that God is not the effect of a cause: 'God is 'above existence.'[150] Most scholastics would have probably agreed. But whatever his reason may have been, Thomas did not use the terminology of 'existence' to refer to the inherent reality of

---

150   Aquinas, *Summa Theologiae,* I, 12, 1, ad 3.

the world. In the fourteenth century, however, largely as a result of Thomas's doctrine of the nature of reality, *existere* and *existentia* came to signify the inherent reality of the world and its objects in abstraction from any consideration of whether they had been created by God. This is the meaning that 'to exist' has retained in the modern European languages to the present, according to which Christians and other follower of biblical monotheism attribute 'existence' to all real beings — including God.

Instead of 'to exist,' Thomas used exclusively the verb 'to be' *(esse),* but sometimes in an uncommon manner that 'surprised his contemporaries,'[151] yet made perfect sense as a means to convey exactly what he wanted to convey. That is, he used 'to be' in the two different ways that have been preserved to the present — which we, therefore, should have little difficulty understanding — though one is no longer fully idiomatic. Mostly he used 'to be' *predicatively,* as had been done by members of the Indo-European linguistic family as far back as can be traced, for the purpose of attributing to subjects of predication whatever the speaker deemed attributable to them as their characteristics — and thus, as their cognoscibility. But sometimes Aquinas used 'to be' *existentially,* as today's grammarians refer to it, saying that something 'was,' but meaning that it 'existed.' This is possible today, though unusual; if we were to say 'the roses in the garden are' (meaning that 'the roses in the garden exist') we would be understood, but not readily. Intelligible, but still unusual, would be to say 'God is' instead of 'God exists.'

To mean that something has 'existence,' however, we never say that it *has* or *possesses'* 'to be;' whereas Aquinas, using the infinitive verb as a noun (which was permissible in mediaeval Latin, as it is in modern English), did not hesitate to say that something 'possesses to be,' *habet esse* — meaning that it 'has existence.' Peculiarly and most originally, however, he would frequently refer to what we call a being's 'existence' as its 'act of being' *(actus essendi).* Our own peculiarity today is to think of existence in active terms — i.e., as something that real things *do* — only in the case of the existence of living beings, when we equate 'existence' and 'life.' Thus, when an animal's life is taken, we say that the animal has ceased 'to exist.'

---

151   Étienne Gilson, *History of Christian Philosophy in the Middle Ages* (New York: Random House, 1955), 381.

The novelty of Aquinas's language is a reflection of the novelty of the vision of reality it was intended to communicate. To appreciate the depth of its tranquil subversiveness we must remember what it superseded. It replaced the perception of the human situation as immediate and direct subjection to absolute Necessity: it was, therefore, liberating. In the popular Greek culture, reality and the world were not identified as that which actually happened, but as that which happened *necessarily,* as determined by Fate. The supposition that reality implied necessity — i.e., that reality was 'what had to be' — was demythologized by the philosophers, and then softened by the Christian attribution of a degree of humaneness and tractability to the otherwise imperious will of God. But necessity remained a feature of reality even after Aristotle had reworked the concept of 'being' as much as the Greek philosophers ever would, and even after the Christian theologians insisted that God was compassionate and merciful. However, the disruption of European culture as a whole by the doctrine of 'existence' shall interest us only later. At this time, our concern is rather its potential impact on the philosophical study of the nature of reality and the nature of the human mind.

To grasp in detail how Thomas's doctrine differed from Aristotle's interpretation of the reality of the world, let us remember the latter's definition of 'beingness' or 'essence' as *to ti en einai,*[152] which translated word by word means 'what a thing was to be.' This makes little sense in English; the reason is that ordinarily today we do not understand 'to be' to include either in its denotation or its connotation the idea that 'whatever is, is what it must necessarily be.' In Greek, however, the necessity is indicated by the use of the past tense of 'to be.' The rationale is that from the time of a being's 'birth' it already 'was' under the compulsion of Necessity.[153] Thus, when Aristotle spoke of the 'beingness' of 'beings,' the *ousia* of *ta onta* (where we would say either 'the reality of the real,' or 'the existence of the existent'), he had in mind the 'essence' of the being. He did not differentiate, as we do (and as Thomas

---

152   Aristotle, *On the Soul,* 3.6.430b28; *Metaphysics,* 7.3.1028b34.

153   According to Joseph Owens, *The Doctrine of Being in the Aristotelian 'Metaphysics:' A Study in the Greek Background of Mediaeval Thought* (Toronto: Pontifical Institute of Mediaeval Studies, 1948), 184, in the phrase *to ti en einai,* 'the necessity [is] implied rather than expressed.' But perhaps it would be more exact to say that necessity seems implicit to an unwary English reader of a literal translation, because in modern English necessity is no part of either the denotation or the connotation of 'to be.' In Greek, however, the necessity is made explicit by the use of the past tense. For Fate is outside time. It is not only *what is* and *what shall be,* but also *what has always had to be.*

first proposed), between the reality of the being and the knowable structure or cognoscible content of the being. The expression 'what a being necessarily was' applied to both indistinctly.

Now, since the Greek philosophers did not distinguish between the reality of a being, and 'what the thing necessarily was' *(to ti en einai,* i.e. its 'essence'), they used 'to be' accordingly. That is, they did not make a distinction that to us today seems obvious,[154] namely, between *what* a thing is, and *whether* it exists.[155] For example, as Ross explained, according to Aristotle 'to ask *whether* A is, is to ask whether there is an intelligible essence answering to the name, and … to ask *what* A is, is to seek to unfold this essence in a definition.'[156] It is difficult for us to comprehend it, but neither the Greeks nor the scholastics before Thomas saw any difference 'between the being of existence and that of predication … For [Aristotle], to say that a just man exists, or that a man is just, was always to say that a man exists with the determination: to be just. It all came to the same thing.'[157]

But to fail to discriminate between two things that in fact are distinct is to confuse them. The result was that the 'beingness' (or reality) of real 'beings' was ascribed by Aristotle and other Greek philosophers to the inherent knowability of the necessary properties (or 'essences') of things. The fact that beings were real independently of their aptness for becoming known was not denied; it was simply ignored. But the consequence of ignoring it was that the experience that for us indicates the *inherent existence* of the world and its objects, to the Greeks indicated their *inherent knowability,*

---

154   Why did it not seem obvious to them, if they were able to experience the 'out thereness' of real objects? Because they were unable to discriminate between the object 'out there' and their own mental activity. As I have stressed, the object is always clear and to the fore of our experience, whereas the perceiver's activity is in the background and easily overlooked.

155   As previously mentioned, certain passages of Aristotle's *Posterior Analytics* (at 2.1-2.89b21-90a24 and 2.7.92b3-92b26), if incautiously translated, may give a modern reader the impression that Aristotle distinguished between a being's essence and its existence. For in these passages Aristotle contrasts 'what [a thing] is' *(ti esti)* with 'whether [or if] it is' *(ei esti)* and with 'the fact that it is' *(hoti esti).* Thus, he says, 'what man is is other than to be man' (92b11); and 'it is impossible for those who do not know whether a being is, to know what it is' (93a20). But it will be remembered that in classical Greek 'to be' meant 'to be necessarily;' every being is necessarily whatever it was. Aristotle's intention is to distinguish between (a) our knowing the fact that a thing is ruled by necessity, and (b) our understanding what the necessity (or essence) of the thing is. Accordingly, the meaning of the first of the two foregoing quotations is that the intelligible essence of, say, 'man,' is not the same as the sensible object 'man;' one can know that a given entity is of human nature without having philosophical knowledge of what human nature is. The meaning of the second is that merely factual acquaintance (through sense cognition) with an entity is the pre-condition of understanding philosophically its necessary, although it not a sufficient condition (because the necessity of the essence is not sensible but intelligible).

156   Ross, *Aristotle,* 50.

157   Gilson, *Christian Philosophy of St. Thomas,* 42.

or their inherent aptness for being thought. We have already analysed the mental processes that resulted in identifying the reality of the real and its inherent knowability. This projection involved an absurdity: in effect, it construed the reality of the real as its aptness for being known regardless of whether anyone could know it. Since projections naturally tend to pass unnoticed, it is not strange that the irrationality of this proposition should have escaped scrutiny. As previously noted, Galileo's Platonism promoted what at present is the conviction of many scientists and some philosophers: that scientific knowledge and scientific truths exist in reality regardless of whether they are known by anyone. Few if any scientists find this assumption at all puzzling, much less suspect.

Thus, what Aquinas needed in order to make Aristotelian *scientia* possible without straying from orthodoxy was (a) a world constituted, quite as Aristotle thought, by 'essences,' characteristics that inhered in worldly entities and gave them their own effective causal powers; but at the same time (b) a world that remained, as the Christian faith demanded, totally contingent on the will of God. It seemed like an impossible assignment. And it would have been, were it not for faith's ability to reconcile contradictories by declaring that in some mysterious way they are somehow compatible. Aquinas reinterpreted the traditional Augustinian doctrine of creation so as to result in creatures in which, once faith was granted, both these two requirements were 'compatibly' joined.

According to Aquinas,[158] creation is not achieved by God in exactly the way Augustine had proposed. God does indeed conceive eternal 'ideas' of the various ways in which real creatures can participate finitely in his infinite reality. And he creates his creatures, or makes them 'be,' in accordance with such 'ideas.' But he does not create them by simply willing that they 'be.' What he does when he creates them, is to give them the wherewithal actually 'to be.' That is, he gives them an 'act of to be,' an *actus essendi,* which they exercise by and for themselves. When given and received, the 'act of being' brings the creature into the state of actually 'being.' Or as we say today, it has come into existence. It is now part of the real world In other words, instead of 'doing' their existing for them, God provides creatures with the means to *actualize by and for themselves* the 'act' that God has given to them for

---

158   The doctrine is argued in many of Aquinas's writings, beginning with his early work *De Ente et Essentia,* IV. Embellishments of it can found in his *De Veritate,* 8, 8; *Contra Gentiles,* II, 52; and *Summa Theologiae,* I, 44, 1.

that purpose. Without such actualization, their characteristics and powers would remain no more than a mere idea of a *possible* being in the mind of God — whereas

> '[a]ctually existing individual beings are "beings" because of their own exist-ing *(esse)*. In other words, they are real "beings" because they *do* their "to be".'[159]

The same is true of their causal powers. Thomas's existential interpretation of the reality of real beings means that human beings and other creatures are able to act on their own with true and orig-inal *initiative;* they actually *effect* changes in the reality of the real world, because their efficacy is that of a real and existing being:

> '[Aquinas's] philosophy … confer[s] upon second causes [i.e. creatures] the full share of being and efficacy to which they are entitled.'[160] But accord-ing to Thomas, the capability to exercise their reality and their efficacy is given to them by God.

Now, apart from whatever hesitation to play fast and loose with the traditional Augustinian interpretation of creation may have influenced Thomas's contemporaries, it was difficult for them to understand the true import of his doctrine of 'being.' A teaching that altered substantially the earlier understanding of the 'being' of creatures was being expressed with only slight changes in the terminology long used to convey the old. And so, his 'synthesis … was not in fact accepted by his contemporaries.'[161] In reverse, given our habits of modern speech, some pre-Thomistic Latin con-structions look to us so obviously existential that the fact that they are not intended existentially is difficult to accept. For example, many a scholastic before Thomas had asked the question *Utrum Deus sit* — literally, 'whether God is.' What else could it mean but 'does God exist'? Well, not exactly. The pre-Thomistic meaning of these words was closer to: 'Is God God?' or 'Is God divine?' The question

---

159   Étienne Gilson, *Being and Some Philosophers* (Toronto: Pontifical Institute of Mediaeval Studies, 1949), 171.

160   Gilson, *Christian Philosophy of St. Thomas,* 181.

161   C.J.F. Martin, *An Introduction to Medieval Philosophy* (Edinburgh: Edinburgh University Press, 1996), 125.

asks whether our concept of God — *what* we think God is — is *true*. As Gilson said, and as most contemporary Thomists agree: the problem of the *existence* of God was not known before Aquinas: '[i]t was he who made it what we … rightly call … the problem of the *existence* of God.'[162] But by the same token, before Thomas no philosopher had called attention to the fact the world and its objects actually exist, and that their existence is their own.

Aquinas's alternative reading of the basic observations we today interpret in terms of the 'reality of existents' seems to have been inspired in him by a formula that had originated with the Arab philosopher Alfarabi (though Alfarabi's meaning probably was somewhat different from Aquinas's). Alfarabi's formula seems to have awakened in Thomas an insight that contradicted directly what in fact had been the Aristotelian identification of the reality of objects and their properties: it proposed that the 'essences' of creaturely entities were really distinct from their 'existence'.[163] In evidence of it he alleged that the concept of an object did not include reference to its actually existing: 'Every essence … can be understood without anything being understood of its 'to be' *[esse]*. I can know what "a man" or "a phoenix" is, and nevertheless be unaware whether it has 'to be' *[an esse habeat]* in reality *[in rerum natura]*. From this it is clear that [in creatures] 'to be' *[esse]* is other than the essence.'[164]

This was exactly what Thomas needed in order to achieve his purpose. He wanted to preserve the Aristotelian doctrine regarding the 'essences' of things, because 'essences' made possible the purely rational investigation of their characteristics, functions and causal powers. He also needed, of course, to preserve their dependence on God's creation of them in order to ensure orthodoxy; this could be achieved simply by supposing that God gave creatures the power to exercise their existence.

---

162   Gilson, *Christian Philosophy of St. Thomas,* 58. Italics in the original.

163   Thomas does not seem to have been aware of the contradiction, and throughout his life expressed himself as if his doctrine faithfully reproduced Aristotle's. He probably believed it did; for as discussed above, it is not difficult to project Thomas's existential interpretation into Aristotle, *On the Soul,* 3.6.430b28, and *Metaphysics,* 7.3.1028b34.

164   Aquinas, **De Ente et Essentia,** IV. Conceivably, Thomas might have argued **e converso** that we can know that something exists without knowing what it is. For example we can perceive an existing object that appears to be a human being, without knowing whether the object is an actually existing human being or an existing mannequin — although in either event, I know it is something that 'exists,' since it is 'other-than' my experience of it. All of us have had experiences of this sort. It would have been a stronger argument, since it was grounded on experience. If this possibility did not occur to Thomas, it may have been because he did not realize that we conceive reality as a result of our **perception** of objects. Misdirected perhaps by Aristotle, he thought existence was an intelligible characteristic of objects which we grasp only by means of 'the second operation of the mind,' namely, judgment.

Aquinas's doctrine hinged, therefore, on making a clear-cut distinction between the characteristics and the existence of the world so as to assign them different roles. It was, therefore, by this label — 'the distinction between essence and existence in creatures' — that Aquinas's reinterpretation of the reality of creatures would eventually become known.[165] As a theological bonus, the distinction suggested also a reinterpretation of the reality of God. Whereas created beings are not simple, since they are composed of really distinct essence and existence, God is absolutely simple. In him, his essence and his act of existing are one and the same. Since he is uncreated, he does not receive an act of existing: he *is* his act of existing.

And so, the blueprint, as it were, of the necessary characteristics and causal powers of creatures was designed by God, but the *factual* reality (i.e., the existence or *actus essendi)* of a creature having certain properties and causal powers, was enjoyed by the creature — though, supposedly, only if God had gratuitously given such act to it. This condition, of course, is scarcely grounded in experience; it requires faith. But no faith is necessary to observe that we human beings actually exist and that we *own* our reality, in much the same way in which we own, say, the fruits of our labour, the opinions we hold, and the benefits of our learning — as well as the consequences of our stupidities and the shame of our inhumanities. Ordinary experience suffices.

To sum up, then, in Aquinas's redaction, Alfarabi's formula meant that the demands of Aristotelian *scientia* were met; for once it exists, every being in the world is exactly as Aristotle described it: the 'import of this doctrine is that the created world of Thomas Aquinas is identically the intrinsically necessary world of [Aristotelian] science.'[166] To be sure, Aquinas agreed with the theological tradition that a creature did not have '*of itself*' the wherewithal to exist.'[167] But it was also true that a creature *could* have such wherewithal, if it received it from God:

---

165 See John F. Wippel, 'Essence and existence.,' In Norman Kretzman, Anthony Kenny, Jan Pinborg (eds.), *The Cambridge History of Later Mediaeval Philosophy: From the Rediscovery of Aristotle to the Disintegration of Scholasticism* (Cambridge: Cambridge University Press, 1982); Battista Mondin, *A History of Mediaeval Philosophy* (Rome: Urbaniana University Press, 1991) Frederick C. Copleston, *A History of Mediaeval Philosophy* (London: Methuen, 1972).

166 Gilson, *Elements,* 200.

167 Gilson, *Christian Philosophy of St. Thomas,* 36. (Italics mine.)

Unless it receives it from God, the created universe can have no being at all, but since, in fact, God gives it actual being, each and every created being *owns* the very act *(esse)* in virtue of which it is said to be.'[168]

The idea that real, existing things *owned* their reality was thus born. In the philosophy of Aquinas God does not *lend* to creatures, and specifically to human beings, their *act* of being; he *gives* it to them. That is, the property title passes from him to them when they exercise their act of existence; therefore, once created, they are *autonomous.* The most loyal of modern Thomistic philosophers themselves say precisely as much, openly using precisely the language of 'autonomy' and of God's 'giving' rather than 'lending' to creatures the means to exercise an 'act of existence.'[169] Nor could it be said that when today's followers of Aquinas so aver, they have departed from his teaching; for Thomas's own words are to the same effect: 'every thing whatever has within itself its own existence *[esse proprium],* which is distinct from that of all others.'[170] In the estimation of today's Thomists, therefore, the doctrine of the reality of creatures as their own *actus essendi* meant that '[t]he created universe described by Aquinas is, at one and the same time, both integrally religious and integrally natural.'[171]

That the world as described by Aquinas's original and penetrating existential interpretation was 'integrally natural' is clear; but whether it was quite as hospitable to Christianity as the old one had been is at least debatable. Aquinas's doctrine of existence is by no means incompatible with belief in God, to be sure. But it granted to creatures — including of course to human beings, which is the crucial case — a degree of self-sufficiency that before long made their dependence on God far less obvious than it had been earlier. But more directly relevant to the purposes of our investigation is another consequence of the doctrine: albeit unintentionally, Aquinas's new interpretation of the reality of the world, when conjoined with the defective traditional idea of perception, had the effect of loosening representationism upon our philosophical tradition.

---

168   Gilson, *Elements,* 197. (Italics mine.)

169   For example, Gilson contrasted unfavourably the doctrine of William of Auvergne, a precursor of Thomas, with that of Aquinas on the ground that William's lacked a 'clear conception of the proper autonomy that every particular act of existence has. In the doctrine of William, God lends, rather than gives, existence;' *Philosophie au Moyen Age,* p. 419.

170   Aquinas, *Contra Gentiles,* I, 14.

171   Gilson, *Elements,* 201.

What was the logic of the process that led from one to the other? And how did the process unfold in point of historical fact? These are the two questions to be studied, respectively, in the next two sections.

5. *The existence of the world and the nature of cognition: their relationship*

The position that the world and its objects have 'inherent reality,' or 'existence,' seems obvious to most of us today. But the obviousness of any idea is not necessarily evidence of anything more creditworthy than the fact that the idea has received general acceptance. If we must say, as philosophers, that the doctrine is true, and that its truth is apparent and requires no religious faith, the reason is that it is in accordance with experience. Precisely how does experience reveal it?

We have already remarked on the aspect of our ordinary experience of objects through which we human beings conceive empirically what we today call 'reality' and the 'world.' But another aspect of the same experience results in our experiencing *our* reality as our own, or as our own 'existence.' More particularly, the existence of other existents is revealed to us by our experiencing their 'otherness' to us; our own existence is perceived as real and as our own when we experience our 'otherness' in relation to the objects we experience. The reason is that once we conceive 'existence' as that which makes the world and its objects 'other-than' our experience, we are able to appreciate the difference between *what* we perceive in objects — i.e. their characteristics, properties, and powers, on the one hand — and the fact that they are 'other-than' our experiencing of them. However, knowing the *fact* that the object exists does not necessarily tell us *what* it is; conversely, we may understand a concept without knowing whether it as actually realized in the world. Quite as Thomas said, there is a distinction between the two.

Even newcomers to the world of scholastic thought should have no special difficulty with the foregoing; but there is another aspect of the argument I have developed that may seem strange and require elucidation. For I have proposed that the existential interpretation, which in my view is true and indeed a great discovery, brought about the scourge of representationism and was therefore the precipitating cause of the failure of the philosophical tradition twice in its history. Is this not a self-contradiction? Can the truth of the existence of the world generate the error of representationism?

The answer is: yes, it can, and indeed it did, though only accidentally; representationism is not implied by the doctrine of the inherent reality of the world. But representationism is generated when the doctrine of existence is applied to the prior supposition that perception consists in receiving and possessing mentally the inherently perceptible properties of objects. The historical circumstances in which the discovery of the inherent reality of the world was made by Aquinas created a trap that the scholastics did not manage to escape and which indeed managed to ensnare philosophy later a second time.

The first such circumstance was that, prior to Aquinas's doctrine of existence, the *reality* of objects had been traditionally identified with the 'knowability' of objects; the second was that *cognition,* including perception, had been understood as the effect caused by objects upon the passive and receptive mind. The trap closed when philosophers took for granted that these assumptions regarding cognition and reality should be retained even after the doctrine of existence had been adopted. The truth is, of course, that they may not, because the 'double existence' of perceptions and objects *isolates* each from the other. As Thomas himself said, 'every thing whatever has within itself its own existence' *[esse proprium],* which is distinct from that of all others.'[172]. And so, once the inherent reality of the world is asserted, representationism and existential skepticism follow, if the traditional assumptions regarding perception are retained. The question therefore arises: why did no fourteenth century scholastic jettison the traditional assumptions that to perceive is to receive and possess the knowable 'contents' of objects that have come to exist in the mind?

Apart from historical inertia, in some considerable part, I think, because the roundabout way in which the scholastics came to accept the doctrine of existence tended to obscure the close connection between the concepts of reality and cognition; but probably it was, above all, because Thomas's teaching, when stated in the traditional language of *esse,* was impenetrably obscure. It was only two generations later that gradually philosophers began to use the language of *existere,* which underscored the distinction between cause and effect despite the continuity of the causal process. This was the crux.

---

172   Aquinas, *Contra Gentiles,* I, 14.

Gradually, the truth of the doctrine (so far as it concerned the reality of the world and its creatures) became clear. Eventually some of its theological implications (principally that the existence of God could not be rationally demonstrated) became apparent. But its implications for the philosophy of perception loomed large from an early date. Moreover, the fact that the idea had been first proposed by Thomas did not matter as much as the substance of the matter; the association of his name with the doctrine tended to fade. Modern Thomists themselves knew nothing of what they now call 'the existentialism of Thomas,' until historians of mediaeval philosophy discovered it in the twentieth century.

But perhaps the most powerful single contributory factor to the general lack of awareness of the troublesome nature of the traditional assumptions may have been plain unawareness of the relationship between the concept of existence and the concept of cognition. Let us amplify earlier remarks on the subject of why the two must be mutually consistent.

We learn to think of the reality of the world and of ourselves, and of our capacity for cognition, simultaneously. When we perceive the 'otherness' of objects, we quite naturally perceive 'the world' in contrast to 'ourselves,' our 'perceptions,' and 'our minds.' If we are able to perceive it and speak of it in this manner, it is because our cognition has conscious quality. Our minds are capable to becoming aware of their own activity even as it is exercised — and therefore our minds are able to appreciate *simultaneously* the reality of both our selves and what-is-not-ourselves, namely, the 'world.' Conversely, we do not perceive the existence of existents independently of our perceiving our selves and our existence. And so, we perceive existence as a *relationship* between our conscious selves and the existing world. It is, to be sure, a negative relationship: the world is-not we, and we are-not the world. We perceive the reality of the real by perceiving its non-dependence on our perception of it. All of us have direct empirical evidence of the fact that we *do not* create the world and its objects. It is impossible, and there is nothing we can do about it.

But from the intimate, albeit negative, relationship of opposition between 'self' and 'world' a consequence follows: the interpretations that philosophers may put upon the observable facts that they conceptualize respectively as 'cognition' and as 'reality' must be mutually consistent. Otherwise, given the logical structure of the human mind and the constraints it puts on us, our thinking would be impeded. The existence of the world and the existence of ourselves are thus somewhat like fraternal twins — by no means identical, but sharing a common maternal origin in the womb of the mind. Thereafter, the two must live together as part of a single family of experiences. Adapting to philosophical use a mathematical concept, we may say, therefore, that our ideas of reality and cognition are *covariant*: a change in one demands, under pain of inconsistency, a change in the other. And so, one's affirming the inherent reality of the world could not but impact on one's idea of cognition. The discovery of the former required a change in the latter.

The consistency of our conceptions of 'reality' and 'cognition' should not be confused, however, with their adequacy or truth. In this regard, as in respect of our conception of any other observable fact, different individuals (and different cultures) may conceive 'reality,' 'self,' and 'cognition' more or less adequately, more or less correctly. Nonetheless, misinterpretations of 'reality,' 'self,' and 'cognition' may remain stable and satisfactory to those who hold them, as long as they are mutually consistent. What would be impossible — because logical reasoning would break down — is that one's interpretation of either reality or cognition should change, without either one or the other of two consequences: one will either reason inconsistently or else, sooner or later, realize that a corresponding adjustment must be made to the other.

Well, then, if one assumes, as Aristotle did, (a) that *cognition* is the effect worked on the mind by objects, since it consists in the mind's acquisition of the 'form' of the object; but if one also assumes at the same time, (b) that *reality* is identical with the inherent capacity of objects for becoming known by minds, one's ideas of both cognition and reality may be incorrect, but nevertheless compatible; one's explanation of reality and of cognition can be consistent and stable. The Greek scheme regarding *reality* was modified substantially by Augustine when he superimposed his own Christian assumptions upon the Greek, and therefore explained the reality of creatures as the effect of God's willing that they 'be.' But at the same time, Augustine adjusted proportionally his idea of *cognition*. Human beings gain cognitive possession of objects, he thought, because God gives their mind the 'illumination' whereby to know them. It was a fantastic, totally invented, empirically groundless, but *logically balanced* explanation, and therefore a stable one. It lasted almost a thousand years.

However, when in the thirteenth century Aquinas proposed a different interpretation of the reality of the world, and when in the fourteenth the generality of scholastics accepted it, a correspondingly profound readjustment regarding cognition had become necessary under pain of absurdity in default. Nothing guaranteed, of course, that the philosophers' reinterpretations of cognition must be correct — and in fact they were not. What was assured was that they must either change their idea of cognition sufficiently to harmonize with the new idea of existence or else become utterly perplexed and logically paralysed.

Circumstances conspired to make it difficult for the scholastics to make the transition from a regime of reality as 'being' to reality as 'existing.'[173] It is doubtful whether the participants were aware of the magnitude of the need for reinterpretation in which the idea of existence had plunged them. It was theoretically possible for them to revise the assumptions of the tradition at a fundamental level, but it would have been unrealistic to suppose that they actually could have done so. Even the mere fact that cognition had to be reinterpreted does not seem to have been clear to them for a long time. And they never understood the reason why it had to be reinterpreted, namely, that the reality of the object of cognition had been reinterpreted 'existent-ially.' In short, they laboured hard but without much awareness of the source of the difficulties. What the scholastics of the fourteenth century discovered in the end was that tinkering with representationism was not a cure for philosophy's ailments, but more like a poison pill.

Now, if it is true that the discovery of the inherent existence of the world demanded a change in the traditional conception of perception or else render logical thought impossible, the question may be raised: why did Thomas not feel the need to re-examine his Aristotelian construction of perception? But the answer is clear: he *did* consider the possibility that his doctrine might have consequences for the interpretation of cognition; and what he found was enough to drive him back into an Aristotelianism re-interpreted so as to allow, supposedly, for the distinction between essence and existence. Thus, although Thomas did not use the term

---

173   What matters is, of course, not the terms themselves, but the *meaning* that one has in mind when one uses them. With some idiomatic limitations previously mentioned, we *today* are able to use the terminology of 'to be' with an existential, Thomistic meaning ('there are roses in the garden') as well as with an 'essentialist,' Aristotelian meaning ('the flowers in the garden are roses.')

'representationism' or a synonym thereof, he did speculate on the consequences that would necessarily follow 'if what we understood were only the concepts that are in the soul'[174] (rather than if what we understood were objects directly.) And the consequence, he feared, was that there could be 'no philosophical knowledge *(scientiae)* of things existing outside the soul *[de rebus quae sunt extra animam]* … [that] whatever seems [to be true] is true, and thus that contradictories could be true simultaneously … [and that] all opinions would be true, as well as every apprehension whatever.'[175] Therefore, arguing *a priori*, from the premise that no concept of cognition could be true if it entailed absurdities — which is not the strongest possible argument, but which did yeoman service for him *faute de mieux* — he rejected decisively the supposition that cognition could take place through our knowing 'the concepts that are in the soul *(species quae sunt in anima)*' i.e. representations. But he did not realize that the Aristotelian account of perception was inconsistent with the inherent existence of the world, and that the rejection of representationism entailed a re-examination of the nature of cognition. For he re-read Aristotle as if Aristotle had interpreted the reality of the world and its objects as their inherent 'being' (i.e., existentially). Modern Hellenists themselves used to misread Aristotle in the same way, until they discovered otherwise. Thus, although Aquinas must be said to have rejected representationism, he did so with questionable effectiveness and consistency. As Robert Pasnau has suggested:

> Aquinas's rejection of a representational account appears clear enough. But … later Scholastics questioned whether Aquinas could coherently take such a view. And … Aquinas does in fact treat species as a kind of cognitive object. Although he denies that species are ordinarily the things we see and understand, he tends at the same time to explain cognition in terms of a perceptual-like relationship between our faculties and the species that inform such faculties.[176]

---

174   Aquinas, *Summa Theologiae,* I, 85, 2.

175   Aquinas, *Summa Theologiae,* I, 85, 2.

176   Robert Pasnau, *Theories of Cognition in the Later Middle Ages* (Cambridge: Cambridge University Press, 1997), 15-16.

If Aquinas was not fully conscious of all the necessary implications of his doctrine of existence and specifically not of the danger that it should incidentally lead to existential skepticism; and if, having retained the traditional assumptions about cognition, he could not have explained cognition without lapsing into inconsistencies, it should not astound us. The doctrine of existence introduced a new and unprecedented philosophical regime, and Thomas was navigating uncharted waters.

More important is the contribution of his doctrine of existence towards the awakening of our civilization to the *real* reality of the world and the *conscious* nature of our mental life. The evidence that the doctrine was a factor in such awakening shall be discussed below. As shall be the irony of a system of thought that had hoped to explain the possibility of understanding the world philosophically without resorting to 'revealed truths' and without compromising the Christian faith, but which in the fullness of time not only destroyed philosophy, but weakened faith as well.

6. *The collapse of mediaeval philosophy, and its aftermath*

The Aristotelianism of the thirteenth century in general, but Thomism in particular, provoked an energetic and long-lasting adverse reaction by the Church. From the outset it had 'awakened suspicions'[177] of heterodoxy among the more nervous theologians and ecclesiastics, since it gave off whiffs of excessive and indiscreet interest in the 'natural' world. And as Thomas's project of harmonizing revelation and Aristotle gained adherents, the opposition escalated. The desire of the scholastics to accommodate Greek philosophy had gone too far, it was said, and Thomism in particular simply did not seem to be in keeping with the spirit of the tradition. These were the feelings of many, but particularly the hierarchy. The list of official condemnations of his works by Church authorities is long[178] and began early:

> [T]hree years after the death of St. Thomas some of his teachings were con-
> demned by the bishop of Paris and the archbishop of Canterbury. This con-
> demnation was subsequently lifted, but it reflects the opposition that Thomism

---

177   Gilson, *Philosophie au Moyen Age,* 591.

178   Fernand van Steenberghen, *La philosophie au xiii^e siecle* (Louvain: Publications Universitaires, 1966)*,* 88-100, 487, 488, 495.

met almost from the start … [C]onservative theologians … believed that it gave too much ground to the naturalism of Aristotle and his Arabian commentators, to the detriment of the Catholic faith.[179]

The attitude of the Catholic Church towards Thomism would eventually change and indeed go to the opposite extreme. In 1879 Aquinas's philosophy was proclaimed by the Vatican the model strongly recommended for emulation by Catholic philosophers; Aquinas's thought was elevated for all practical purposes to the status of unofficial orthodoxy. The Church seems to have now felt that a Christianized 'naturalism' such as Thomas's was exactly what was needed to combat the growing influence of science, and the materialism, atheism and other philosophical errors of the modern world. Some of today's Thomists say, therefore, that the original uneasiness of the Church was unreasonable and unwarranted; their usual explanation for its having been such is that:

> [T]he authors immediately after St. Thomas … hesitated to follow him to the end of the novel paths into which he had ventured, and were held back and left behind by augustinian scruples from which they were unable completely to liberate themselves.[180]

The evidence suggests to me rather that the Church's suspicion was amply warranted. But at any rate, the immediate outcome of the events precipitated by the existential interpretation is beyond doubt: that the ambitious hope of integrating faith and reason was abandoned, that scholasticism fragmented along several fault lines, and that philosophical reason was held in contempt. The disintegration of scholasticism took less than a hundred years:

> The distinguishing characteristic of the fourteenth century is to have despaired of the task attempted by the thirteenth, or perhaps rather, to have used philosophy to demonstrate how right had been those theologians who

---

179 Armand Maurer, *Mediaeval Philosophy* (New York: Random House, 1962), 208.

180 Gilson, *Philosophie au Moyen Age*, 621.

in the thirteenth century had denounced the impossibility of supporting [Christian] dogma with philosophy. Better to present faith as such than to base it on pseudo-justifications.[181]

The liquidation of scholastic philosophy was spread over the length of the fourteenth century. In what pertains to the 'critique of philosophy by theology, or by philosophy itself at the urging of theology … [John] Duns Scotus was the first philosopher in which the spirit of the fourteenth century was manifested.'[182] But from the viewpoint of anyone who wants to understand the causes of the failure of modern philosophy, much more significant was the work of William of Ockham during the second quarter of the century; for it was he, not Scotus, who 'exercised a decisive influence over the final stage of development of mediaeval thought.'[183].

Like other scholastics, Ockham had absorbed the idea that worldly objects had inherent reality. For example, the vocabulary of *existere* having by this time been added to that of *esse,* Ockham referred to the beings that populate the world not only as *entia* but also as *existentes*. He may well have realized that the full range of the traditional philosophical and theological questions required thorough reworking — indeed, reformation — and in the end that was what in fact he attempted to do. But whether he suspected that the reason had to do with the assumption that both the perceiver's mind and the object had their own reality is doubtful.

In any event, he took very seriously Thomas's warning against the supposition that representational *species* were 'that which *[id quod]* we perceive.'[184] Also clear is that he was not satisfied that Thomas's positive interpretation of cognition was sufficiently coherent, and that therefore he attempted to correct it. With the clear lenses of historical hindsight, however, we can read his thought as a vain attempt to prevent the disaster that was about to overtake scholasticism. Contrary to his presumable intentions, what he actually achieved was to facilitate the emergence of the open and

---

181 Gilson, *Philosophie au Moyen Age,* 638.

182 Gilson, *Philosophie au Moyen Age,* 638.

183 Gilson, *Philosophie au Moyen Age,* 639.

184 Aquinas, *Summa Theologiae,* I, 85, 2.

acknowledged absolute skepticism from which ultimately followed the scampering, disorderly retreat of cowed reason back into the comforting bosom of faith.

Ockham was in some ways a proto-modern philosopher. To correct Aquinas's account of cognition so as to make it consistent with the existence of the world, Ockham developed an early version of the sort of 'radical empiricism'[185] that would later be rediscovered by some moderns. He recognized no essences, and much as Locke later would, made no distinction between sensible and intelligible forms; all cognition of perceptible objects (as contrasted with intelligible abstractions) was by way of 'sensible intuition.' (The reduction of cognition to perception has endured. The function of understanding, as distinct from perceiving, has tended to be neglected since Locke.) Understandably, in view of such empiricism, Ockham had 'strong opinions on the absolute independence of philosophy as such [from faith], and an extremely sharp tendency to relegate all metaphysics to the domain of theology.'[186] He is sometimes depicted as a 'direct' rather than a 'representational' realist[187] — which is probably true, although in a peculiar sense, but which for reasons I shall explain may not be as significant in his case as may seem at first glance: it did very little to stave off skepticism. He has been described both as a radical and as a moderate skeptic; but he took different positions at different times and it is difficult to determine which, if either, was the dominant one. But it is beyond doubt that Ockham did not only cast aspersions on the reliability of perceptual intuitions by alleging, for example, the false appearance (first highlighted by Plato) of a bent oar immersed in water; he also stirred a veritable hornet's nest when he developed a doctrine that was the mediaeval equivalent of the argument from hallucination, much later to be proposed by some modern philosophers in support of existential skepticism.

A doctrine of Ockham that impacted heavily on later fourteenth century thought seems to have been his remarkable proposal that it was possible for the mind to have perceptions that were not caused by actually existing objects. From this position to skepticism regarding the existence of objects is not an excessively long leap; nevertheless, Ockham refused to take it.

---

185   Gilson, *Philosophie au Moyen Age,* 640.

186   Gilson, *Philosophie au Moyen Age,* 649.

187   Marilyn McCord Adams, *William Ockham* (Notre Dame, Ind.: Notre Dame University Press, 1987), vol. 1, 551-629.

He maintained both (a) that our direct perception of objects could put us in touch with existing objects, but (b) that it should be possible for us, under certain conditions, to have perceptions that appeared to refer to existing objects, but which were not caused by actually existing objects. As Gilson said, to pin down Ockham's theory of knowledge is not an easy task: 'his successive answers have... driven to despair the most conscientious historians.'[188] Fortunately, we need not even try; for we are not interested in Ockham's thought for its own sake, but for the sake of understanding the crisis into which scholasticism was plunged by the Thomist doctrine of existence.

The basis of Ockham's thinking about cognition was his opinion that the difficulties experienced by philosophers when they tried to explain cognition stemmed from inventing fictions; and this was a methodological fault which his well-known guiding principle — that *entia non sunt multiplicanda praeter necessitatem* — should help philosophers avoid.[189] Although the problem of cognition requires that we suppose only 'a knowing subject and a known object ... [philosophers] believe themselves obliged ... to imagine an intermediary between the understanding and things ... [which is] the source of the most abundant difficulties.'[190] The truth, he said, is that mental representations are superfluous: '[i]t is the thing itself, without mediation or intermediary ... that becomes seen or apprehended.'[191] This is why he is often said to have been a direct realist. Which in a sense is indeed true — but which did not solve Ockham's problem. For Ockham's 'direct' perception of reality brings us to the brink of much the same skepticism as representationism does.

The novelty of Ockham's work depended in part upon his having become conscious of an implication of the traditional Aristotelian idea of perception that had long been taken for granted — and which is indeed true — namely that perception is the effect of a cause. No one had denied it was, but no one had perceived as clearly as Ockham did the importance of the fact for an interpretation

---

188   Étienne Gilson, *The Unity of Philosophical Experience* (New York: Scribner's, 1937), 80.

189   I have reproduced the most frequent formulation of the principle, which is not a direct quotation of Ockham's words but a summary of a longer statement to somewhat the same effect. The usual formulation, however, fails to make clear that Ockham's objection was to the introduction of explanatory considerations that were unnecessary not because they were excessively numerous, but because they were not empirically based. Ockham's 'razor' does not actually have to do primarily with 'parsimony.'

190   Gilson, *Philosophie au Moyen Age,* 646.

191   Gilson, *Philosophie au Moyen Age,* 647.

of cognition. It meant that perception had to be explained not only in respects of its 'contents,' but also in respect of its *reality* or *actuality*. But cognition cannot be treated as if objects were optional — which is in effect, what Ockham proposed. Thus, Ockham agreed that the world and its objects caused our knowledge of it; perception was *ordinarily* the effect worked on the mind by the objects that are its cause. And the effect consists in the object's 'contents' coming to exist in the mind — not physically, of course, but 'intentionally,' i.e., by the existence of the mind of the perceiver. Since he also deemed obvious that objects existed, he assumed, in effect, the 'double existence of perceptions and objects.' The same effect, however—i.e. cognition of an object— could exist in the mind, if it were caused by a different cause, for instance, by God:

> [T]he object is normally the cause of cognition of this kind [i.e. direct sensible intuition]; but God can always produce an effect without going through the secondary cause [i.e. the object]; … therefore it is possible to have a sensible intuition of what does not exist … [or at least] a belief in the existence of sensible objects that do not exist.[192]

Of this argument Gilson said that it does not voice Ockham's 'reservations as a philosopher, but as a theologian who is taking care of the possibility of miracles … These theses do not affect philosophical or scientific knowledge directly.'[193] I cannot reconcile this with the fact that Ockham's reasoning presupposes 'the double existence of perceptions and objects,' hardly a theological consideration. Be that as it may, there was in any event another and more fundamental reason why the matter was important to Ockham and why it did affect philosophy directly. Indeed, the text just noted must be said to be part of Ockham's contribution to existential skepticism. For quite apart from any consideration of miracles, his argument depended on the more fundamental possibility of knowing effects without knowing their causes; the possibility of knowing creatures without knowing their creator was only a particular case of the same principle. And this was a consequence of Aquinas's

---

192 Gilson, paraphrasing Ockham, in *Philosophie au Moyen Age,* 654. See William of Ockham, *Commentarium in Libros Sententiarum,* II, 25.

193 Gilson, *Philosophie au Moyen Age,* 654.

doctrine of existence; for the existent is not perceived as real because it has a cause that makes it real, but because it does its own existing.

In short, the lesson of Ockham's argument is that although we may suppose that objects cause perceptions, we cannot establish the causal role of the object merely because we are aware of what we deem its effect, namely, perception. There was no way, therefore, to tell the difference between a perception caused by a real object and a perception that *seemed* to be caused by a real object, but was actually caused by, for instance, God. Hence his insistence that we can perceive objects that do not exist, although ordinarily the objects we perceive actually exist. Ockham 's argument is thus, at bottom, the same as the argument from 'methodical doubt' later made by Descartes, though the latter invoked the agency of a hypothetical *malin génie* rather than God's. And it is essentially the same as the argument from hallucination alleged by some modern skeptics, where the unusual cause of the 'false perception' supposedly involved in hallucinations is not a real object but an organic disturbance.

It is possible that Ockham's purpose in holding onto the twofold possible causation of experience was to develop a conception of cognition that avoided altogether the assumption that objects created representations of themselves in the perceiver's mind. To that end he may have conceived the idea that perception could be understood as the causation of direct perceptual effects by objects, rather than as the causation of representations — a theory of 'direct perception through direct causation,' as it were. But this could not have succeeded. Why not? It should repay us to puzzle out the answer.

Representationism is not a single error, but a complex of errors. One of its sources is the deficient or absent observation of the causation of cognition by the cognizing organism. The projection of the activity onto the object generates the first erroneous element of representationism, namely, the supposition that perception is caused by the action of the object on the senses. This misunderstanding is then further compounded when the need for consistency suggests that the effect of such cause is the transfer of the perceptible 'contents' of the object to the perceiver's mind. The perceiver's possession constitutes perception, because the 'contents' of the mind are (according to one's preferred version) either *like*, or *similar to*, or at the limit, *identical* with, the 'contents' of the object. But this is not enough to amount to representationism. Representationism is reached only when the crowning idea is added to the foregoing that the reality of everything real consists in its inherently 'existing.'

The 'contents' of the mind *exist* in the mind, while the 'contents' of reality continue to *exist* in reality. Perception is now alienated from objects by the 'double [and thus separate] existence of perceptions and objects.' Existential skepticism necessarily follows.

Without the doctrine of existence, existential skepticism is impossible; at most, the accuracy of our perceptions may be doubted, but not whether perception of the externally existing world is possible. For example, Aristotle supposed the causation of perception by objects, as well as the 'likeness' or indeed 'identity' of the sense and the sensed; but he did not develop, and could not have developed, a representationist interpretation of perception, since his view of the nature of reality precluded his thinking of it as its inherent existence.

If, on the other hand, the inherent existence of the mind is supposed and the causation of cognition is vested on the object, then the effect of the object on the perceiver is not merely the possession of the 'contents' that are *similar to,* or *like onto,* or *identical* to the object. The mind now possesses a *duplicate* of an object by means of which it comes, indirectly, into possession of the *duplicated* or *repeated* 'contents' of the object. The latter cannot be perceived directly, because the mind and the object are isolated from each other by their separate and independent existences. Verification of the *reality* of the object cannot be achieved, because it is now impossible to compare the duplicate with the original.

The foregoing breakdown of the elements of representationism should help us appreciate that representationism demands not only the supposition that the 'contents' of perception *represent* the 'contents' of the object. Underlying such requirement is the prior stipulation that the mental representations must be attributable to objects as effects are to their *causes:* mental representations could scarcely be deemed to perform their representative duties unless they were caused by objects. Ockham may have thought he could avoid the representationism that he and Thomas feared by doing away with *representations of objects* and reducing them to *effects caused by objects,* but he did not reckon with the more fundamental supposition that, once the 'double existence of perceptions and objects' is accepted, the *causation* of perception by objects suffices to ensure the imprisonment of the mind within itself. The 'monster' is the 'double existence;' whether objects cause representations or non-representational effects that exist in the mind, makes little difference. Why? Because effects are not known to be effects *a priori*, but only empirically.

The problem that Ockham bequeathed to his successors was that, if it is true (as Ockham believed, and as is indeed true) that causation can be determined only *empirically* — that is, by perceiving the invariability of the absence or the presence of an effect, and the absence or presence of the cause — then it is impossible to tell the difference between a 'normal' perception and one that has been caused by God or by organic malfunction, or by any cause other than an object. Both exist in the mind and both are the effect of an external cause, but the independent existence of the perception means that we can never verify its objective cause. For to verify it, we would have to have a direct perception of its cause; but the cause of such verifying perception would have to be verified by attempting to verify its cause — and so on *ad infinitum*.

And so, once again, when complemented by the 'double existence of perceptions and objects,' the causation of perception by objects is unverifiable, because the existence of each isolates the effect from the cause as surely as representations do. The malefactor of the piece is not simply the representative nature of *species* or other representations, but the unverifiability of the *causation* of independently *existing* perceptions by independently *existing* objects, regardless of whether the perceptions are representative of the objects or not. In sum, underneath representationism, the more fundamental misinterpretation, of Greek origin, is that perception is *caused* by objects.

Well, then, if one is an early fourteenth century philosopher concerned with the dire consequences of representationism, one may want to try the hypothesis that the difficulty might be solved if the *species* — the representations of objects — were done away with. For more fundamental a supposition than *how* objects cause perceptions is the supposition *that* they do. Might representationism not be avoided, therefore, by divorcing the causation of perception from the representational role of *species?* Surely the mere causation of perception by objects is an innocuous hypothesis; besides, there seems to be no alternative to attributing the causation of perception to objects.

One could only estimate, of course, whether this was actually the inspiration that gave us Ockham's work. But the supposition that this was what moved him would account to a large extent for the general scheme of his system. It would also go a fair distance towards explaining the insoluble difficulties into which he ran as he tried to work out a hypothesis that reduced him to having to maintain the somewhat unlikely notion that we could experience both objects that existed as well as objects that did not. And it would tend to make sense of the fact that, after Ockham failed, full-fledged and unapologetic skepticism was the last option available to those who followed him, as typified by the work of Nicholas of Autrecourt.

To recapitulate: what Ockham demonstrated without realizing that he had, was that behind the fallacy of representationism was the fallacy of the assumptions that had led to representationism as soon as the inherent existence of the human mind was glimpsed. Ockham's dismissal of all *species, similitudines,* and sundry intermediaries achieved nothing, because he retained the more fundamental defect: that the causes of experience are the objects that exist in reality as they reproduce their contents in the womb of the mind, whereas the effects of such causes (i.e., the reproduced contents) exist in the mind. His 'direct realism' was a different version of the representationist miscalculation. Philosophy was beginning to go around in circles.

The roundelay has not yet stopped. It is not only the standard varieties of representationism, but also the rendering of the same inadequacy in the form that has become known as 'direct realism,' that remains impotent to account for human cognition. In both instances the same fateful supposition is made: that in one way or another, objects are the cause of experience, and that their effect is that their 'contents' come to exist in the mind and take up residence within it. In the openly representationist versions, objects cause mediating representations; in the crypto-representationist version of 'direct realism' they cause experience directly. But since the effect is in any event other than the cause, it exists independently of the object. In either case, the mind has become shut off within itself, and all extramental reality has become unattainable.

A brief illustration should suffice. Early in the twentieth century, H.H. Price reinvented what was very close to the Ockamist theory of cognition; it became known as 'direct realism.' A few lines after stating that the object 'is "directly" present to my consciousness ... [and that] my consciousness of it is not reached by inference, nor by any other intellectual process,' Price suggested that the 'peculiar and ultimate manner of [objects'] being present to consciousness is called *being given,* and that which is thus present [to the mind] is called a *datum* … [Such data] lead us to conceive of and believe in the existence of certain material things, whether there are in fact any such things or not.'[194] Well, the proposition that we do not reach reality by inference from the *datum*, but by being led to it by the *datum*, asks us to make the proverbial distinction without a difference. And it reaches a reality that 'in fact' may or may not exist — so that Price's 'direct realism,' like Ockham's does not even have the merit of saving philosophy from skepticism. Several proposals other than Price's have been made in recent decades under the label of 'theories of direct realism' that, unlike Price's, have avoided self-contradiction. However, it is debatable whether they can properly be called 'theories,' since they do not actually attempt to explain cognition. Uniformly, they find fault with representationism — which is understandable — and suggest that reality is experienced 'directly.' Quite true, but they offer no explanation of how 'direct experience' takes place, as contrasted with representationism. Besides, they appear to presuppose that perception is caused by objects, and that the effect is that the knowable 'contents' of objects become 'present to consciousness;' or at least, they do not call attention to the causal nature of the perceiving organism's activity. Some of these attempts to develop a theory of direct perception will be discussed in chapter III; none has been more successful than Price's.

Now, before Aquinas made 'existents' out of what traditionally had been conceived as 'beings' in the traditional Greek sense of the term, all creatures were deemed to be the effect of God's creative causation; to know the world was to know it as a sign of the reality and invisible presence of God. What Aquinas did not fathom, but Ockham did, was that if creatures exercised their own existence and made use of their own causal powers, then the signs pointing to a creative divine reality and divine causation were no longer visible in the world. *Perhaps* the world and its objects were created by God; and *perhaps* creatures were only secondary causes whose effectiveness depended on the concurrent will of God. But if they were such, only faith could affirm it. Reason could not know it.

Therefore Ockham rejected the five classical Thomistic proofs for the existence of God; indeed, he said, it was impossible to demonstrate rationally the existence of God by any means. For all such proofs would have to deduce the existence and nature of God from the existence and nature of the empirically-given world — since such world had *its own* inherent reality and *its own* inherent causal

194 H.H. Price, *Perception.* (London: Methuen, 1932), 3, 5.

efficacy. But if the reality of their existence and their powers was their own, they could hardly be indications of the transcendent reality of God and the 'next world.' Ockham's rejection has found an echo in the modern world; the proofs are convincing only on the prior supposition that everything in the world, and the world as a whole, is the *effect* of a cause. The circularity may not be obvious, but is real. The existence of God is demonstrable only in the eyes of those who suppose in the first place that the world's reality is not self-sufficient; the world is only an effect of an antecedent first cause that transcends the world. Thus, once one asks the prejudice-laden question 'Who made the world?' without giving a thought to the prior questions whether the world has been made and why we should think it was, the answer does not matter; one has already fallen into the bottomless pit of circular argumentation. One's distorted idea of the world as less than simply 'real' remains the same, regardless of whether the answer names the Maker or acknowledges that one does not know its name or even whether it actually exists.

It is not certain whether the philosophy of Nicholas of Autrecourt, who taught at the Sorbonne in the early fourteenth century, was derived from that of Ockham or independently arrived at, but in either event its starting point 'is a theory of knowledge that, having been based on principles analogous to those of Ockham, takes them to their most extreme consequences.'[195] Nicholas took for granted that 'in the domain of existents, affirmations are authorized only by experience.'[196] Since existents are known in and of themselves, not as effects of causes, we cannot know the causes of existents simply by knowing the existents. Thus, in Nicholas's own words, anticipating Hume's:

> Because it has been evident to me [in the past] that my hand became hot
> when I put it to the fire, it therefore seems probable to me that, if I should
> now put it [to the fire again] it will become hot.[197]

---

195 Gilson, *Philosophie au Moyen Age,* 665.

196 Gilson, *Philosophie au Moyen Age,* 667.

197 Quoted by Gilson, *Philosophie au Moyen Age,* 669.

It is probable, yes, but it is only a conjecture. Likewise, 'from the fact that one thing exists one may not conclude that something else exists;'[198] therefore the existence of God may not be demonstrated from any consideration about the existing world. Proofs of the truth that God exists 'join the multitude of others that can be demanded only from faith.'[199] And as with causation, so with substantiality; to these concepts nothing corresponds in reality. The idea of substance is formed through association: certain facts having been experienced, whether in relation to the properties of material beings or in respect of mental activities, 'one immediately supposes the existence of a material or a spiritual substance in order to explain them.'[200] Nor could we, Nicholas said, anticipating Hume again, 'have certain and evident knowledge of the existence of any substance other than our own minds.'[201] Indeed:

> We cannot be certain, in the natural light [of reason], when our appearances concerning the existence of objects independent of our own minds are true or false.[202]

Ockham and Nicholas were not the only philosophers who reacted in this manner to the metamorphosis of Aristotelianism by Aquinas's idea of existence. Their numerous followers made up a recognizable school of thought: '[w]hat gave them their family resemblance was that they all laboured, consciously or otherwise, to dissolve the Aristotelian conception of the nature of the world.'[203] The world according to Aquinas — the world made up of entities that existed and caused effects — continued to exist. But the Thomistic marriage of the idea of existence with the presuppositions of both the Greek and the Christian traditions regarding the mind and reality, had come to an acrimonious parting of the ways.

---

198 Gilson, *Philosophie au Moyen Age*, 670.

199 Gilson, *Philosophie au Moyen Age*, 671.

200 Gilson, *Philosophie au Moyen Age*, 668.

201 Quoted by Adams, *Ockham*, vol. 1, 619. Cf. David Hume, *Enquiry*, XII, I.

202 Quoted by Adams, *Ockham*, vol. 1, 614.

203 Gilson, *Philosophie au Moyen Age*, 673.

As existential skepticism ravaged and demoralized scholasticism, the cultivation of philosophy fell to those with less than exemplary aptitude for it. By the fifteenth century, scholasticism had been reduced to trading in verbalisms. The legendary philosophical inquiry into the capacity of pinheads for supporting merry-making angels is apocryphal, but symbolizes aptly the depths to which scholastic philosophy had descended. Nor was that the end of the process. Philosophy having been theologized out of existence, theology itself did not escape the wave of anti-intellectualism unleashed by the Ockhamists. Blowback time had arrived.

An acute manifestation of the 'separatism of faith from reason and of theology from philosophy'[204] that followed Ockham was the movement that some historians call the 'speculative mysticism' of the late fourteenth and fifteenth centuries, which based theology not on philosophy or any form of rational enquiry, but on the attempt to have direct mystical contact with God. Some of the best known practitioners of the genre, such as Meister Eckhart, John Tauler, and Henry Suso date from this period. A different but historically most important manifestation of the same phenomenon was increased reliance on the authority of faith, both by the general population and by its religious leaders. The ancient Christian tradition, reinforced by scholasticism, had long described Christianity as *fides quarens intellectum:* since faith, considered in itself, was an *inferior* form of knowledge,[205] it was proper for faith to seek understanding. This was now turned upside down by 'fideism,' the doctrine that faith should be divorced from rationality, because reason was apt to lead Christians astray in the search for truth. As Thomas à Kempis said, to know all that is truly important — namely, how to be saved from eternal death — all that the Christian need know is God's own wisdom. And such wisdom can be drunk only from the source: it is the wisdom that the Church teaches, who received it from God. However, an alternative supposition regarding the source of the wisdom that takes away the sting of death would soon become available, and roughly half Christendom opted for it.

The strength of the religious reaction against thirteenth century scholasticism and Aristotle can be gauged when we remember that two hundred and fifty years after Aquinas's death, his *Summa Theologiae* unfinished, Martin Luther was still writing his *Contra Scholasticos Sententiam* and his

---

204   Gilson, *Philosophie au Moyen Age,* 659.

205   Aquinas, *Summa Theologiae,* II-II, 174, 2, ad 3.

Disputatio Contra Scholasticam Theologiam, aimed directly at the *antiquos* — that is, the scholastics of the thirteenth century, including Aquinas, whom Luther distinguished from the *moderni,* i.e., the scholastics from Ockham onwards. Nor is it irrelevant towards an assessment of the outcome of scholasticism that Luther's break with Rome centered, so far as concerned dogma, on the moral significance of what human beings were able to achieve by virtue their own inherent causal powers — which according to Luther, speaking for the tradition, was nil. Moreover, so far as concerned Christian practice, the issues for the reformers were naturalism in general, and in particular its inroads into the virtuous conduct of life, as illustrated by the notorious attachment of the papacy and the clergy to the luxuries of 'this world.' All these evils, according to Luther, were largely the nefarious consequence of allowing Reason, 'the Devil's whore,'[206] to lure Faith with false promises of orgasmic truth, ultimately to deliver only *post-mortem tristesse.*

However, as Aristotle said in the *Protrepticus*[207], those who would argue that human beings have no need of reason and that society is better off without philosophy, must resort to reason to reason against reason. Many Christian thinkers of the fifteenth century, and thereafter into modern times, did not become mystics or fideists, but continued to think. Sometimes their thinking was motivated indeed by the apologetic desire to keep faith safe from the depredations that thinking was apt to inflict upon it. For all their thinking, however, it is difficult to classify them in any meaningful way; thinking was in disarray, and improvisation was required. The best known and most influential philosophers of the Renaissance, as well as their pioneer, Francesco Petrarca — that is, Marsiglio Ficino, Pico della Mirandola, Nicholas of Cusa, Giordano Bruno, and Pietro Pomponazzi — agreed on few other topics but were united in their condemnation of scholasticism in general and of Aquinas specifically, and of the ever less effective attempt of the remaining Aristotelians to breathe new life into the ideal of integrating faith and *scientia.*

Nevertheless, to the extent that post-mediaeval philosophers continued to be both Christian believers and rational thinkers, they had perforce to take a position, in practice if not also in theory, on the relationship between reason and revelation. Few went all the way back to what the scholastics

---

206   Brian Gerrish, *Grace and Reason: A Study in the Theology of Luther* (Oxford: Clarendon Press, 1962), 1.

207   Fragment 51.

had called 'Averroism' (i.e. the so called 'double truth' theory that allows contradiction between ratio-nal and religious truths). But many, if they were interested in avoiding heterodoxy, took for granted a pragmatic, milder version of the separation between the two realms of truth. Truth cannot contradict itself, but if scholarly enquiry is confined to what reason teaches us about this world, we are unlikely to run into irresoluble conflicts with faith. This was the position that later, in the sixteenth century, was to be taken by Copernicus and Tycho Brahe, and in the seventeenth by Kepler and Galileo.

A variation of it is still with us today: it maintains that, since neither science nor philosophy can demonstrate that the concepts of God and the supernatural are empty of all meaning, science and philosophy should in all prudence adopt an agnostic position in such matters.[208] But those who reason in this manner do not seem to notice the implication of agnosticism. Namely, that if the possi-bility that God may exist is granted, one's suppositions about the world must be consistent with such possibility. But whether one adverts to it or not, the only supposition consistent with the possibility of God's existence, however hypothetical, is the assumption that the world is not the standard of reality. Under these circumstances, one's suppositions about the reality of the world are much the same as if one positively assumed that God actually existed. One has supposed, in effect, that the world has an insufficient, defective reality; one has posited a world that needs 'the divine.' Blaise Pascal's 'wager,'[209] which is still played today, translates into the realm of practical human life the same sort of *soi-disant* prudence that counsels many of us to seek safety in numbers.

But all that was only after the failure of scholasticism had produced in many quarters a renewed interest in those schools of Greek philosophical thought — Pythagoreanism and Platonism — that had been more attracted to the study of 'the divine' than in the exploration of the material world and its less-than-real reality. Ficino's translation of Plotinus's *Enneads* in 1492 led to his foundation of the influential Neoplatonic Academy of Florence, and eventually to the movement known as Cambridge Platonism. At the other end of the intellectual spectrum of the age, the culture of 'humanism' added another colour to the variegated intellectual palette of the new age. Humanism was not a philosoph-ical movement, though it was not entirely irrelevant to philosophy either; it proposed that scholars

---

208   See Edward J. Larson and Larry Whitham, 'Leading scientists still reject God,' *Nature,* 334 (1998): 313.

209   If one believes in God and obeys him, and the belief is proven true, one wins an eternity of bliss. If it proves false, one loses little or nothing. Believing in God is much the more advantageous wager.

shift their attention from the traditional theological preoccupations of the scholastics, to the study of classical Greek and Roman languages, literature, and cultures.[210]

Listening with half an ear to the Platonizing schools of metaphysically and religiously oriented philosophers, but following Aristotle — adhering, however, not so much to his Philosophy as to his example in later life[211] -were the relatively few scholars — Leonardo da Vinci, Nicholas Copernicus, Tycho Brahe, and William Gilbert are the best known — of the late fifteenth century, but mostly the sixteenth, who, instead of delving into the lofty metaphysical subjects that had preoccupied 'the Schools,' gave their attention to the observation of natural phenomena (or, like Francis Bacon, to theorizing about the observation of nature). They were only practicing what Ockham and Nicholas of Autrecourt had preached; they were taking advantage, in their own way, of the separation of the supernatural from the natural that had been the paradoxical outcome of Aquinas's effort to link them more closely than previously. But hovering over the varieties and mixtures of philosophical opinion was the ever-present threat of skepticism, which flourished in France especially from the mid-sixteenth century onwards, and whose most distinguished patrons were Pierre Charron and Michel the Montaigne — both of them members of the generation immediately preceding Descartes.

The Scholastic tradition had not completely disappeared; but it had gone to ground and had become isolated from the general culture since much earlier. Descartes, however, was about to bring it back from its sickbed. Unfortunately, he had not an inkling of the true aetiology of the illness. And this, at a time when, to make matters even more complicated, the age of modern science had just begun.

---

210   The humanism of the Renaissance is therefore not to be identified with the intellectual movement that nowadays goes by the same name, which actively opposes the religious views that have been retained in modern European civilization.

211   Aristotle wrote most of his biological and 'natural history' treatises during his second Athenian period, which covered the last years of his life: '[t]he general movement [of his thought] … was from other worldliness towards an intense interest in the concrete facts both of nature and history, and a conviction that the 'form' and meaning of the world is to be found not apart from but embedded in its "matter"; Ross, *Aristotle,* 19.

7. The ambivalence of modernity

Aquinas's doctrine of the inherent reality of the world brought about not only the collapse of scholasticism; it also helped trigger a profound change, a veritable tectonic shift, in Western European culture. After centuries of relative stability when cultural change had been slow, though cumulative, the cultural evolution of Western Christendom accelerated during the fifteenth and sixteenth centuries. Countless novelties in the experience and mode of life of its members fairly suddenly burst forth. The 'secular age' had dawned, and the forging of our times and its 'modernity' had begun.

'Modernity' has long been perceived by many, including not a few modern philosophers, as an unalloyed triumph. But it was not; it was more like an opportunity, or perhaps better, a test of the culture's mettle. By almost any standard, however, (other than perhaps that of scientists and science-fiction enthusiasts) the outcome has not been a resounding success — which is not to say that it has been disastrous in every way. The reason why modernity has been of highly mixed value, as I argue, is closely related to the philosophical mismanagement of Hume's most important contribution — his demonstration that representationism necessarily implies existential skepticism — and the challenge it posed. We can best understand the significance of Hume for our civilization and its future, if we first understand the wider cultural context in which the failure of philosophy to deal adequately with Hume took place. This is the topic of this section. Hume, let us remember, did not teach only existential skepticism; he contested the supposition that we lived under a regime of Necessity and drew attention instead to the factuality and contingency of the reality of the real world: '[w]hatever *is* may *not be*.'[212] But his obsession with representationism and his inability to reject it prevented his focusing much attention on the relationship between reality and perception. He felt deeply that philosophy had lost its bearings when it accepted the notion of a 'higher' Mind (and therefore a 'higher' level of reality), but was unable to demonstrate how the misconstruction had been arrived at.

Preliminarily I underline that the concepts of 'modernity' and 'secularity' are closely related but neatly distinct. Their relationship, however, would be misperceived if 'modernity' and 'secularity' were taken simply to refer, respectively, to broader and narrower aspects of European culture — that

---

212   David Hume, *An Enquiry Concerning Human Understanding*, in L.A. Selby-Bigge, (ed.), *Enquiries concerning the human understanding and concerning the principles of morals* (Oxford: Clarendon Press, 1902)*,* XII, 3.

is, as if 'secularity' were but the peculiar form that 'modernity' took in matters pertaining to religion. For it is true that 'modernity' covers a broad range of cultural manifestations the proliferation of which has yet to cease after several centuries of ever accelerating change; but 'secularity' is not well described as a component of 'modernity.' 'Secularity' is rather the foundation of 'modernity;' it is the moving spirit, the soul of modernity, as it were. Or to put it plainly, modernity is the wider *effect* of which the acute *cause* is secularity. For our civilization did not turn to its modern ways whimsically or out of boredom with earlier custom and tradition. The modern ways exhibit, in retrospect, an intelligible pattern and an inner logic that followed upon the shift of perceptions, opinions, attitudes — that is, upon the change in *mentality* — that is most appropriately described as 'secularity.'

Most appropriately, I say, having in mind the etymology of the word. The Latin *saecularitas* means, in effect, 'this-worldliness,' (as contrasted with the 'eternity,' *aeternitas,* of the 'next world'). The word derives from *saeculum,* translatable in various contexts as either 'the times,' or 'the current age' or sometimes as a period of 'one hundred years' (i.e., a very long long time), but usually with reference to the temporality of the 'world,' in contrast with the 'timelessness' or 'eternity' of the 'next world.' Thus, 'secularity' alludes to a more or less consciously professed belief that is typical of (though hardly universal in) modern Western civilization, to the effect that the reality that matters to us human beings is 'this world;' and that indeed 'this world' is (or, according to preference, may be) all that actually exists. For once one supposes that the world carries its own reality within itself, the reality of the 'next world' is, if nothing else, problematic.

Although many moderns go so far as to think that 'this world' is the only world that actually exists, ambivalence and uncertainty characterize the more common variety of secularity in the modern age. Secularity should, therefore, be described in relative terms: it may import greater or lesser awareness and conviction; it may or may not be clearly conceptualized; and its implications may or not be fully adverted to. Moreover, since secularity clearly conflicts with the traditional Western European religious faith, secularity is often taken as a synonym for 'irreligion,' or for 'hostility to religion' by those who identify 'religion' with those specific forms of it which suppose that there is a 'higher' order of reality than that which we find in our world. In fact, 'secularity' is, in a true sense, a *religious* concept, since it is a position taken, whether consciously calculated or inarticulately, regarding the human situation and its mortality.

But if modernity was inspired, channeled, and fuelled by the secular mentality, what caused secularity? Or as Charles Taylor has asked, '[why] was it virtually impossible not to believe in God in, say, 1500 in our Western society, while in 2000 many of us find this not only easy, but inescapable?'[213] After all, disbelief, or at least doubt, regarding the reality of God by isolated individuals is as old as the Old Testament.[214] But as a defining characteristic of an age, disbelief in God had been unknown to our tradition until it appeared in our midst, unheralded and unquestioned, without anyone knowing quite why now it had become possible to doubt what theretofore had been indubitable. But the cause is not difficult to suspect, if we remember, for example, that one of the philosophical consequences ensuing from the Thomistic idea that human beings and their world had inherent reality and causal powers was the impossibility of deducing the existence of God from the existence of the world. The inherent existence of the latter not only took away the possibility of appealing to extramundane causality to account for the world and its events, but rendered the concept of 'other-wordly reality' bereft of all rational support.

And so, the consequences of the existential interpretation of reality were not confined to philosophy. To be sure, the original doctrine was too obscure even for philosophers, let alone for popular consumption; therefore, it worked its effect on the culture only when its technical Latin vocabulary of 'being' and 'to be' had been translated into the terminology of 'existence' and 'to exist.' Slimmed down and extricated from its original theological context, the idea that the world 'existed' became generally and rapidly accepted — albeit, perhaps, with the few minor deviations from what Thomas had intended that we have noted. But certainly with very unanticipated consequences.

But I hasten to make clear: I do not suppose that the teaching of Aquinas on the inherent existence of creatures was the sole cause of the emergence of secularity and the advent of modernity; the process was exceedingly complex, and the factors were endlessly numerous. As Charles Taylor has observed, the question 'is so broad, and so much multi-faceted, that one could write several books

---

213   Charles Taylor, *A Secular Age* (Cambridge, Mass. and London: Harvard University Press, 2007), p. 25.

214   Psalms, 13/14, 52/53.

this length and still not do justice to it.'[215] All the less so in a single volume that is half the length of his, and which unlike his is not devoted to the subject. Nevertheless, the many innovations of modernity point back to the same root; they all manifested and concretized the awakening of Western culture to the *real* reality of man and its world, and to the truly *effective* powers of human and indeed all nature. Human beings were entitled to choose their goals, and indeed might actually achieve them by their own efforts. The doctrine of Thomas may not have been the singular cause of the emergence of secularity and modernity, but it was a singularly important one.

Why was the idea of inherent 'existence' so easily and quietly adopted popularly? And why so readily embraced? Probably, in part, for the same negative reason that it was accepted by philosophers: that it seemed true, but, withal, thoroughly innocuous. It is true, as John Donne eloquently complained, that the new vision of the world and of man's place within it, created cultural stresses that disturbed not a few: '[a]nd freely men confess that this world's spent / When in the planets and the firmament / They seek so many new; they see that this / is crumbled out again to his atomies. / 'Tis all in pieces, all coherence gone.'[216] But the fact that behind 'modernity' lurked the doctrine of existence was not widely recognized; its relevance to religious matters was not generally suspected. Even today it is not, which is why contemporary Thomists praise the existential interpretation of reality and admire its wisdom, seemingly without adverting to its having a sharp second edge. The idea that the real world 'existed' was embedded in linguistic expressions that had gained currency in the usual way — that is, without anyone other than perhaps, professional antiquarians knowing or caring to know where it had come from, but which everyone repeated unhesitatingly whenever one wanted to refer to the reality of the world and of human beings. The vocabulary of 'existence' had become available and was being used simply because it was available and in use. But, also as usual, its implications were subliminally felt just the same.

But there was also a positive and decisive reason why the idea of existence was easily accepted by all. It was because it rang true. By this I mean that the mere suggestion that it might be true created the opportunity for people to *experience*, first, that they owned themselves and their natural

---

215 Taylor, p. 29.

216 John Donne, *An Anatomy of the World,* lines 209-213.

powers — though apparently, it seems, only on condition that they be of the right sex and the right skin colour — and, second, that their causal powers were, of themselves, truly causal and effective. For even if one is not conscious of one's being conscious, one can count, simply by being conscious, on at least a minimal degree of awareness of the reality of both the world and of ourselves. One's recognition of one's ownership of one's reality may be obscured by prejudice, but once the possibility that one actually and truly exists and owns oneself is brought to one's attention — which is what the scholastic debates of the fourteenth century regarding existence ultimately achieved for European culture — one will find it difficult not to give it at least some credence.

Whether one is also able to explain what 'existence' means and why it *belongs* to the existent, is a different matter. Nor will every human being who is exposed to the notion that human beings own themselves experience the fact with the same clarity and conviction as every other fellow human. But the culture will no longer automatically teach them their earlier conviction to the contrary. Many, if not most, believers may well retain the latter, but it will be increasingly difficult for them to base their confidence on the self-evidence of their belief. Thenceforth, in order to believe they will often need more than faith; they may need to appeal consciously and deliberately to what I described earlier as faith in their faith.

Thus, the idea of 'existence' that survived in the common sense of European culture was a decanted form of the original doctrine of Thomas. The theological garnish around the existential interpretation could be discarded without any loss of the main nourishing truth; also inessential and expendable was the characterization of 'being' or 'existing' as an *act*. Sufficient empirical reason to make it obvious that 'existing' may be likened to an activity *done* or *performed* by a creature can be found only in the case of living beings, whose 'existing' is identical with their 'living,' and whose 'life' is indeed characterized by activity. But whereas the responsibility of living things for keeping themselves alive is obvious, the inanimate world is inert. Rocks and stones do not have to *do* anything in order to exist and be real, but they are real nonetheless. If so, existing cannot be comfortably described in all cases and at all levels as an *action* that existents *do* or *perform*.

It is not strange, therefore, that the supposition that existence was an 'act' exercised by the existent held little popular appeal for European culture, and that it dropped out of sight; its vestigial remnant is the grammatically verbal form of 'to exist' (as contrasted with the nominal form 'existence'), which is demanded by Indo-European syntax rather than by philosophical reasons. By default, our culture's common sense seems to have opted for assuming that 'existence' is rather something that is 'had' or 'possessed' by real beings. But this, too, could not be literally true: it would imply that 'existence' itself was an existing reality — a property of the properties of real things, as Gottlob Frege somewhat confusedly thought. The truth is rather, in my estimation, that 'existence' is neither an activity nor a possession of existents: it is a *fact*. Existing is the factual condition or *state* of existents; it is the ground of their finite, contingent, and temporal reality. For finitude and contingency are important aspects of the reality of existents; we cannot very well understand the nature of the reality of human beings unless we account not only for their living, but also for the mortality of their life; not only for their coming into being, but also for their ceasing to be after a time. The question of the literally *factual* —as contrasted with the metaphorically 'active' — nature of reality will be taken up again for its own sake in Chapter III.

The kind of historical transition I have just described — the evolution from ancient-mediaeval into modern culture — was unique. Cultural changes of major importance have taken place at several other times in the European world in connection with other forms of self-discovery, though never of quite the same seismic magnitude as the emergence of the modern conviction that human beings exist and therefore own themselves. In the mid-twentieth century, processes of the sort received the name by which they are now recognized: the 'raising of consciousness.'

Consciousness tends to rise in quantum jumps. Truths that have gone generally unnoticed forever in the past can, within a short span once the right conditions exist, become obvious and liberating. Aquinas pointed to a fact — that the world exists and that we exist — that needs but to be called to the attention of those who had not previously adverted to it before they would most likely apprehend that it was true. They will be inclined to become persuaded of it because they will, with greater or lesser luminosity, appreciate the true and genuine existence of their own experience; they will have learned, therefore, to experience themselves as *real* selves. We should understand easily how the existential interpretation of reality could have 'raised the consciousness' of European culture in the fifteenth and sixteenth centuries, because we who have lived in the second half of the twentieth have had first-hand experience of the same sort of phenomenon in comparably revolutionary issues.

That the two sexes are equal in dignity and rights, and that so are all human races, are the most obvious examples of previously unthinkable ideas that, once society has become ready to listen, even if reluctantly, will fairly suddenly become undeniable. Well, more or less. For this is not to say that they will be universally or even widely accepted in practice; far, far from it. They will be, and they will continue to be, resisted. But the marks of their undeniability are that the troglodytic convictions to the contrary are ordinarily stated only in code, and often in defensive tones, and that the practical denial will usually be surreptitious if not also shamefaced. Well, the idea of existence was of this sort. It made sense. It was undeniable. It might never have survived, but it was likely to. And in fact it did.

In much the same way, the view that the reality of the world was the *norm* of reality was not a philosophical proposal that captured the popular imagination; it was part of the emerging suspicion of many — an anonymous common sense, an upwelling of society's consciousness, a cultural phenomenon for which no one was prepared and which even today is disquieting to many. The same was true of the assumption that when human beings undertook to bring about their objectives, the attribution of the effectiveness of their efforts to themselves was not a delusive appearance that masked the will of God; they felt that their efforts were truly responsible for the effects. But underneath these developments, and implicitly supporting them, was the culture's drowsy awakening to the *activity* and the *creativity* of the human mental functions. Many of the accomplishments of the period were made possible by a profusion of daringly inventive uses to which the human mental powers could be put. At the beginning of the seventeenth century, the conscious nature of human cognition would be adverted to by the culture, though not necessarily well understood by anyone; more about the discovery of consciousness presently. If the world is 'other-than' our experience of it, and if it is 'out there,' then our experience of it is 'other-than' the world, and 'in here.' The 'interiority' of conscious experience received conscious recognition for the first time.[217] But consciousness of consciousness was yet come.

---

217 The publication of Fillippo Brunelleschi's *Rules of Perspective* and Leon Battista Alberti's *On Painting* in 1412, in which they reported their discovery of the techniques of perspectival drawing, illustrates how awareness of one's own existence tended to foster awareness of the conscious nature of human experience. Presumably, when Brunelleschi and Alberti looked

The sentiment first awakened in the fifteenth century by the refreshing newness of the age is manifested by the tags and platitudes by which the period has been described. Alluding to their newly discovered awareness of their inherent reality, people seem to have felt as if they had been 'reborn.' Not even Christianity, theretofore the most stable of all European cultural institutions, escaped the maelstrom of 'revolution.' And 'humanism,' a term that bids fair to be taken 'as a token of the shift in the focus of values to man and his affairs'[218] characterized the new age.

The term 'humanism' was originally assigned to the study of human literary and artistic accomplishments, which was advocated by such Renaissance scholars as Erasmus of Rotterdam, and Walther von den Vogelweide. But humanism in the wider and more important sense emerged in the daylight practicalities of real life more frequently than in the midnight lucubrations of academe. It was to be breathed in, as much as it was to be talked about. At its centre was the idea — a felt conviction rather than a deliberate conclusion — that human beings were capable of affecting definitively the course of their lives, and the path followed by human history. This challenged the assumptions that had ruled in our tradition for more than two millennia. It broke ranks not only with the original Greek belief in the impersonal force of *heimarmene* and *moira* — which the Stoics had also described as a cosmic 'foresight,' *pronoia,* which in literal Latin translation became *providentia*. It also defied the Christian successor of Fate, the 'provident' personal God who 'predestined' human beings in accordance with justice and compassion, but as irrepressibly as *moira* once had:

> Here was the decisive break with the mentality of the Middle Ages, whose
> religiosity and mysticism [had been] reinforced by exactly the opposite
> conviction — that men and women were the helpless pawns of Providence,

upon a scene and then drew or painted it, their visual perception was the same as that of every earlier painter since the artists of Altamira had first tried their hand at depicting what they perceived. If artists had been unable to paint perspectivally before the Renaissance, it was because they did not discriminate, within their experience, between what they actually saw when they looked at reality, and what they judged that the existing world was like when they looked at it. They were conscious, and their visual perception of the world was conscious, but they were not conscious of their perceptual activity as such. Alberti and Brunelleschi, however, were able to paint perspectivally, because they became conscious of the difference between the reality of the world and the reality of their visual perception of it — their own reality as perceivers. Once they grasped the difference, it was only a question of Brunelleschi's working out the geometry of perspective and Alberti's translating it into practical instructions on how to paint perspectivally.

218   W.T. Jones, *A History of Western Philosophy* (New York: Harcourt, Brace, 1952), 561.

overwhelmed by the incomprehensible workings of their environment and of their own nature. Medieval attitudes were dominated by a paralysing anxiety about human inadequacy, ignorance, impotence ... Renaissance attitudes, in contrast, were bred by a sense of liberation and refreshment, deriving from the growing awareness of human potential.[219]

The transition had indeed been 'decisive' — though not in the sense that it was complete, but only to the extent that retreat was not possible. For the new order did not exactly 'break' with the old. To be sure, the citizens of the Renaissance instinctively felt that human beings exercised their own causal powers rather than merely co-opt God's, but they were not altogether sure of it. Strangely and inconsistently, they did not always cease to believe that all human activity and achievement was over-shadowed by the judgment and will of God. And so, their fundamental assumptions were affected, in the sense that their status as indubitable truths could no longer be easily taken for granted; but they had lost much of their self-evidence. Their assumptions did not always change. Thus, they experienced that they owned themselves, but such experience did not harmonize well with their belief that they were God's property; they did not trust their experience. And so, on the one hand, they felt that 'humanity was capable of mastering the world in which it lived,'[220] but they continued, on the other, to recite the Christian creed and to invoke God's help. Their experience and their religious beliefs were, as they have remained, somewhat disconnected. And little useful guidance in the matter came from philosophy; on the contrary, Platonism had been revived and predominated throughout the Renaissance, and under a thin veneer of rationality offered the essentials of Christianity in secular garb. At the very time it was most needed, empirically-based philosophy was scarce.

In brief, underneath the new experience of inherent existence, the traditional attitudes and pre-suppositions remained at work. One would expect quantum jumps in consciousness to be disruptive in any event, but the discovery of the inherent reality of the world and of ourselves has been especially trying for our civilization, because from the outset it was suffused with ambivalence. The political, social, economic, national, and international divisions that were created by the Renaissance attract

---

219 Norman Davies, *Europe: A History* (London: Pimlico, 1997), 473.

220 Davies, *Europe,* 471.

the most attention of historians; the inner division within the mind of individuals are not chronicled very often, but make life for them more difficult than it need be.

Accordingly, the principal cultural division of modern European civilization is not exactly between Christians and non-believers; for as will be remembered, the fundamental assumptions of our tradition had originally taken a Greek form before they were rehabilitated in Christian livery. The more important division of the modern world is different. On one side are to be found those who, be they Christians or not, take for granted that there is a fixed cosmic or 'natural order' that determines the 'truth' and the 'right' way in all human matters, whether political, economic, or social, both in the national and the international dimensions. (Scientists, given the Platonism of the fathers of the tradition, tend to favour the idea of a deterministic 'natural order'.) The other side is occupied by a minority: those who suppose instead that the 'truth' and the 'right way' are not predetermined for us. The former assume that it is up to us to ascertain and abide by the prescribed rules of order; the latter suggest that the rules can only come and benefit us if they are carefully crafted and thoughtfully invented by us. The former believe that the latter position breeds chaos; the latter that the former betrays folly. Worst of all may be the disorientation of a culture that tries to have it both ways.

The 'secularity' that followed from Aquinas's insight that 'reality' inheres in the world has been schizophrenic. Humanism did not replace the faith around which European civilization had revolved since the conversion of Constantine to Christianity thirteen centuries earlier; even today it has not. On the other hand, the humanism of the Renaissance scotched Christianity's 'triumphalism,' the 'sense of invincibility' it had come to acquire. The traditional Christian world-view now had a credible competitor. This is why the typical religious position of Westerners today is neither convinced belief nor settled disbelief in God: it is hopeful-cum-apprehensive agnosticism. It is for the same reason that disaffection with 'organized religion' does not take away popular beliefs in supernatural cosmic forces and in the fearfully uncertain expectation of happy life in the 'next world.' It is sometimes said that we live in a post-Christian world, but in what pertains to our common sense vision of the universe this is not true; we live in a mostly ante-Christian one. With the exception of all that pertains to the dissolution of the human self at death, the decline of Christianity has promoted, in effect, the reversion of many in our culture to the essentials of the civic religion of Greece.

Modern philosophy, for its part, has become divorced from theology and religious belief, but it has no more shed the fundamental assumptions that Greek philosophy imported from Greek religion than our culture at large has. Contemporary philosophers of mind who presumably agree that philosophy should not presuppose or include in its calculations the transcendent reality of God have been known nevertheless to speak of 'laws of nature' that predetermine the way in which the world operates. Indeed, even *materialist* philosophers suppose that individual material entities are compelled to behave as they do by universal '[l]aws of nature [which] are dyadic relations of necessitation … holding between universals.'[221] Apparently, they dismiss the supposition that there is a Ruler of the world, but accept that somehow the rules continue to legislate and enforce themselves. It seems to me that they have adopted an orphan assumption.

Moreover, Aquinas's doctrine of the inherent existence of the world played an important role in the Protestant Reformation. Although from one viewpoint the Reformation aimed at restoring Christianity to its pristine condition, it also adapted many traditional Christian dogmas in ways that manifested much greater awareness of the inherent reality of human beings than had been typical of earlier centuries. The Protestant doctrines of 'the priesthood of all believers' and the 'private examination' of the Bible, but most particularly 'the primacy of conscience' — which to the present spells, arguably, the most truly significant of all the differences between Reformed and Roman Christianity — were among the harbingers of a general trend that has often been described by historians as the shift from 'theocentrism' to 'anthropocentrism.' The reformers blamed scholasticism in general, and specifically Thomas, for its having promoted Greek reason to the detriment of faith.

Nevertheless, and whether one becomes conscious of it or not, if one develops the conviction that human beings can effectively change the world — let us not say 'master' it, as the Renaissance, with adolescent bravado, repeatedly said — one has substantially modified, directly, one's assumptions about human nature, but also, indirectly, one's view of the relationship between the entire world and *ho theos*. More particularly, if one supposes that human beings can actually change the world by virtue of their own powers and in accordance with their own plans — rather than as 'secondary causes' whose effectiveness is not truly their own, but that of the First Cause — one has supposed that change

---

221   David A. Armstrong, *What Is a Law of Nature?* (Cambridge: Cambridge University Press, 1983), 172.

may come to the world from within the world by the power of truly causal worldly causes. But from this follows, if the logic of the thought is followed through to its conclusion, that *ho theos* need no longer be invoked to account for world events. And once God becomes superfluous as an explanatory principle, his existence has become, at very least, a gratuitous conjecture. Understandably, however, given the unthinkability of the latter thought by Christian believers, more than a few generations were to elapse before this implication of humanism began to be widely drawn.

Aquinas had hoped to harmonize faith and reason by liberating reason without inhibiting faith; he surely did not realize that the logical implication of the liberation of reason was to make Christian faith irrelevant to the philosophical and scientific understanding of the world and human nature. But this was, in fact, one of the long-term consequences of the doctrine. The modern idea of a separation of science and religion descends from it. The theocentric view of the world, the ancient supposition of European culture, came to an end as its *typical* assumption, and this title passed to the anthropocentric. And yet, the older view did not disappear. For the inherent reality of the world did not demonstrate the non-existence of God — it only contradicted the idea that the reality of the world was lacking in the dimension of reality. On the other hand, the experience of the inherent reality of the world and of human beings affected the concept of God in a significant way. It made God otiose, a *Dieu fainéant,* as he came to be called by some in the late eighteenth century, a superfluous assumption that might comfort the needy but which was not indispensable for understanding the world. That, as Alexandre Koyré remarked, was exactly what Pierre Simon de Laplace said to Napoleon when the latter enquired why in his *Système du Monde* Laplace had made no reference to God:

> 'Sire, je n'ai pas eu besoin de cette hypothèse.' But it was not Laplace's *System,* it
> was the world described in it that no longer needed the hypothesis God.[222]

Indeed, it was a world that had not needed the hypothesis since much earlier. What is to be marvelled at is, therefore, not this, but why it took so long for modern philosophy and science to begin recognize it, and why the recognition has never been resounding, unambiguous, or complete. The 'new philosophy,' the experimental science of the seventeenth century, was created under the auspices

---

222   Alexandre Koyré, *From the Closed World to the Infinite Universe* (New York: Harper, 1958), 276.

of Pythagoreanism and under the shadow of the 'still pervasive Platonism'[223] of the Renaissance. Even today it is possible for suitably disposed scientists to put a Christian face on science — for instance, by interpreting natural selection as a natural law created by God, or at least, by giving science a generically religious twist, such as has been given to quantum mechanics in recent times by scientists who detect the countenance of God within the mysterious heart of the atom. What Christianity is most truly incompatible with — rather than merely inhospitable to — is not science, but the ordinary person's mundane experience of everyday life.

A natural world with inherent reality and causal powers is not the preserve of scientists and philosophers; it is also the stage of ordinary, day-to-day human existence and the achievement of human purposes. If one is predisposed by faith, one will believe that what happens in the world happens in accordance with God's will, and that miracles are possible. But nothing of what we see happening in the world appears to require God's co-operation, or even his consent. Before the world was held to exercise its own existing, it was perceived as a mirror that showed us the image of God; the world was seen through the same eyes of faith that believed in God. But once the world existed, the world exhibited nothing but itself. One could, if one had faith, see the world *also* in the traditional Christian way. But now one had to look twice before one could see the indistinct shadow of God behind the high-definition screen of the world.

Nowadays, therefore, if my impression is correct, even believers themselves do not always remember clearly — for example, when they read in the newspaper that 'the forsythia spring festival had to be cancelled because of rain' — that God is supposed to be personally involved in the climate of planet Earth. Believers do not deny that he is, and they may even pray for good weather — though hardly always without a dram of realism on the side. But the obviousness of the existence of God and his providence is gone. What is not gone is God.

We still live today by most of the Renascentist convictions — though now somewhat more soberly than when Leon Battista Alberti, the famous Italian artist and architect of the period, one of the two principal creators of the art of perspectival painting, 'proclaimed the Renaissance gospel,

---

223   Burtt, *The Metaphysical Foundations of Modern Physical Science* (Garden City, N.J.: Doubleday, 1954), 54.

"Men can do anything with themselves if they will"[224] More soberly, I say, because in the twentieth century we began to understand what had long remained unapparent about our inherent existence: that although our powers of self-determination are truly effective, they are also limited and hazardous, and subject to being terribly misused. They can, almost without anyone's trying, become self-destructive. The gap between the growth of the modern world's available power and the scarcity of self-discipline, cooperativeness, and wisdom with which to use it, is as wide as a mushroom cloud is high and suffices to demonstrate the point.

Freedom from Fate gives us the power to do as we will, but it does not ensure progress in humane values; indeed, it can also produce the illusion that change in other respects is preferable. Anthropocentrism has not been an unmixed boon; if one ceases to think of human beings as 'a little lower than the angels,' only to suppose that they are definable as naked apes one has not advanced in self-understanding. Awareness of the reality of human existence has played havoc with our civilization, because we learned a great truth, but confusedly; it was like awakening suddenly to a bright light one cannot tolerate without blinking and stumbling and hurting oneself.

Perhaps the deepest ambivalence of modernity is reflected in the peculiar difficulty we experience in managing our lives in an emotionally fully satisfying manner after we became conscious that our reality was inherently our own. We pursue 'happiness,' but it seems to elude us; we achieve our goals, but somehow they do not fulfill what they had seemed to promise. Whence comes such difficulty? More generally, why has our culture's acceptance of our existential reality been ambivalent rather than resolute, unwavering, and a fully self-consistent adoption of it?

Two factors may possibly account for at least part of it. For the first we must go back to the two-fold inaccuracies of the prevailing Greek interpretation of reality we noted in the last chapter for the purpose of setting out the hypothesis of this investigation, namely, (a) that the 'reality' of real objects was reducible to the perceptible and intelligible properties of such objects (which we were directly concerned with), and (b) that their reality was identical with the *inherently* knowable properties of the objects. We set the latter aside, although objecting that, if so, the world would have to be deemed

---

224   Kenneth M Setton, *The Renaissance: Maker of Modern Man* (Washington, D.C.: National Geographic Society, 1970), p. 19.

knowable absolutely — i.e., even in the absence of any mind that might know it. Such absolute knowability would confuse the 'reality' with the 'perceptibility' of the world. The truth in my view is rather that although objects can *be real* regardless of whether they are known by any mind, they can *be known* only by minds.

In other words, the ambivalence of our 'modernity' descends from the ambivalence of our 'secularity.' And to explain the ambivalence of the latter, we might recall the remarks made in the last chapter regarding the *asymmetry* of the relationship between perception and reality. Perception presupposes reality, and can take place only in relation to real objects[225] — but reality does not presuppose relation to any mind and is possible in the absence of every mind. In brief, reality does not need to be *known* in order to *be*. The Greeks, in effect, supposed otherwise when they estimated that the world and its objects were 'watchable.' Projecting their cognition, they seem to have reasoned that (a) if we perceive objects, then objects are perceptible, but that (b) if they are perceptible, yet independent of our perception, it must be because they are perceived by a 'higher' Mind. The concept of 'divinity,' it will be remembered, is the concept of the 'watchability' *(to theion)* of the world.

To this reasoning Christian philosophers added what to them seemed to corroborate the Greek idea, though what it actually accomplished was to rationalize (and thus to reinforce) a misinterpretation: namely, to propose that the world and its reality were created by the thought of the transcendent Mind of God and his Will that they be. And so, the ambivalence of modernity stems from the fact that whereas the existential interpretation of reality corrected the traditional assumption regarding reality, a corresponding interpretation regarding perception — i.e., an interpretation of perception that takes into account the inherent existence of the world — has not superseded the traditional interpretation of perception. Thus, tugged by its conviction of the reality of world, modern secularity tends in one direction, but at the same time it is impelled towards the opposite by its suspicion that the reality of the world is insufficiently solid, as it were; it is less than unqualifiedly real. This conclusion follows from the reasoning that, although it is clear that the world does not need *our* mind, or indeed any *earthly* mind, in order to be itself, its having inherent knowability within itself indicates its relationship to a *non-earthly* or transcendent Mind.

---

225   As previously noted, objects of hallucination are not 'perceived,' but *imagined*.

And so, the persistence of representationism continues to breathe life into the moribund sup-position that the world is less-than-fully real — despite the contrary implication of our conviction regarding the existence of the world.[226] Now, if this is true, it follows that, if modern philosophy should manage to re-orient itself, reject representationism, and develop a sound understanding of human nature and its cognitive powers, our culture might conceivably embrace secularity in a con-sistent and healthy manner and abandon the insanities and idiocies that have been fostered by its confusions about itself and its relationship to the world.

Independently of the first factor that I have invoked to account for the ambivalence of our culture's secularity, the second may be an undesirable side-effect, as it were, of our awareness or our selfhood. Every perception teaches us, in part, that the object is other-than ourselves. And the con-verse of our awareness of the 'otherness' of objects in relation to ourselves is, of course, awareness of the 'otherness' of our perception in relation to the object. Awareness of our inherent reality enables us thus to experience ourselves as 'selves;' that is, as agents and performers of our mental activities, our causal powers, and our living actuality; being a 'self' means being able to do these things deliberately and intentionally rather than as puppets who willy-nilly fulfill the inscrutable will of God. However, awareness of our 'existing' reveals to us not only our 'selfhood;' it also alerts us to our 'individuality.' For if one's existence is one's own, then one's existence is not anyone else's but *one's*. My existence is *mine,* and what is mine is *not yours*. Thus, for the very reason that our existence is our own, our existence is distinct, separate, and as such independent from, the existence of everything else in the world. We are simultaneously 'selves' and 'individuals.' Now, selfhood and individuality are not the same thing. But they are easily confused. And confusion between these two aspects of our nature contributes to the difficulties we experience when we try to conduct our life in accordance with our own best interests.

---

226 Representationism is not the only way in which inconsistency is maintained. Most scientists and many philosophers take an agnostic position regarding the existence of God, but nevertheless have no qualms in supposing that the world is inherently rational and knowable, because there are 'laws of nature' that govern the world. The 'laws of nature' perform the same service as a God whose existence need no longer be affirmed, having been rendered superfluous by recognition of the reality of the world.

The truth of our individuality — the fact that we do not appear to need others in order to exist — may easily mislead us into supposing that we do not need others in order to live our life satisfactorily and enjoy our selfhood; indeed, it may even render such supposition attractive. The truth is otherwise, of course, and is evident at every level of human existence. Perhaps the crudest and most obvious manifestation of our utter dependence on 'others' for the realization of our selfhood is our absolute dependence on atmospheric oxygen from moment to moment in order to live; we depend for our biological life — let alone for our human, conscious life — on our entire environment and its qualities. This is a truth we have long ignored at our peril and disadvantage. Just as necessary, however, in order to manage our lives in a reasonably satisfactory and specifically *human* manner, is our dependence on other human beings for fellowship, for friendship, for sharing both joys and sorrows, for loving and being loved, and most particularly for sharing our existence with a loving and beloved life-partner. The conscious mind *needs* such environment every whit as much as the human organism needs clean air and fresh water to discharge its non-mental functions adequately. Thus, the welfare of human *selves* depends on the co-operation of human *individuals*. Since we cannot do without co-operation altogether, we put up with the minimum we need; but we do not, as a civilization, *cultivate* co-operation or deem it a *necessity* of human life, much less a source of pleasure and well-being. What we openly plant, carefully grow, and sedulously nurture is individualism and competition. The bitter harvest is evident in everyday life.

When our civilization evolved and we developed awareness of our inherent reality, we had achieved the level of mental life that could, by nature and in principle, obtain for itself a previously unattainable high level of self-realization — let us descriptively call it 'contentment' — but on condition that we take *active responsibility* for it. The quality of the world insofar as it is our habitat — not only as our physical environment, but also as conscious selves — depends on the kind of physical and human world we create. It may be significant, however, that our civilization has become more deeply concerned with Human Rights than with Human Responsibilities. Lopsided progress, I suppose, may be deemed better than none. Now, it is not out of the question that we should change course; it is possible that the unprecedentedly global scale of the crisis that our civilization has let loose upon the human species at the beginning of the twenty-first century may be the occasion for our collectively and co-operatively reworking the mode of life we have fashioned for ourselves on the basis of rampant individualism. One looks for signs that we have learned the lesson that human beings must co-operate *globally* in order merely to survive, let alone in order to prosper and enjoy contentment. One watches. And one waits. And one does not give up hope.

Meanwhile we can conclude that our civilization's awareness of our inherent reality was not accompanied by the realization that to stop worshipping God and his providential Fate, only to worship instead human power and the human ability to tame the world's supposed natural determinism, was to exchange a master who at least was said to be kind and compassionate despite the strange ways in which he showed it, for a faceless one who has proven capricious, capable of unspeakable cruelty, uncertain of purpose, unscrupulous as to means, who does not know what it truly wants much less what is good for anyone, and who does not understand its own mind and is even liable to doubt whether it has one.

Conceivably, however, though hardly inevitably, if our civilization survives, an empirically sound philosophy of the future might well accept fully and consistently the idea that the world exists, that *we* exist, and that whereas our selfhood, unlike our individuality, is fulfilled only through co-operation, it is unavoidably corrupted through competition. Easy repetition has rendered platitudinous this thought, weighty though it is nonetheless.

We might then develop our understanding of the world in the light of reasonable alternatives to the aboriginal assumptions of Greek philosophy and Christianity regarding cognition and perception, causality and becoming, and reality and world. Such reorientation of philosophy might then contribute to our civilization's, and indeed our kind's, creation of a less self-tormenting, more human world.

8. *The discovery of consciousness*

Although human beings have been conscious ever since the natural processes of biological evolution gave them the wherewithal to be so, they have not always been conscious of the conscious character of the human mind, much less understood its nature. Consciousness has had to be discovered by those who are already conscious, which is possible only because consciousness has the capability of observing itself. But once again, this is not to suggest that consciousness is constituted by the mind's ability to reflect on its own operations. It is only to note that such reflection is possible and useful. However, we discover the conscious nature of our mental functions only gradually, as self-observation gradually discloses it to us.

The self-observability of the conscious mind has two different but direct and necessary consequences. I have previously mentioned the first: the universal awareness among human beings of their cognitive functions. However, such awareness need not include any understanding of the nature of the functions; a culture would have to generate the practice of philosophy before it could undertake to study and understand them — which is, of course, what actually happened in Greece. But even in Greece, it did not happen immediately after the foundation of philosophy. It was necessary for philosophers first to advert to the self-observability of the mind. But as we have also noted, this did not mean that the Greek philosophers had discovered the conscious nature of the human mental functions. This possibility eluded philosophers, both Greek and Christian, for centuries.

The second direct and necessary consequence of conscious mental life is also universal in human cultures: it is the awakening in human beings, normally at a fairly early stage of their individual development, of what is sometimes called moral sensibility. If one is conscious, one will ordinarily — naturally, and without having to make any special or conscious effort — become aware of one's conduct as one's own. One will then experience, to a greater or lesser degree, self-approval or self-disapproval. This, too, is manifested by the vocabulary of morality that is part of all cultures. In this case, however, the conscious mind's ability to observe itself is not focused on our cognitive functions, but on our emotional reaction to our behaviour and character; it is trained on ourselves. For the self is, of course, a more comprehensive object of observation than the human cognitive activities. The self — that is, the human organism once it has matured into personhood by becoming aware that it functions mentally — is the conscious agent of all its actions, and not only its cognitive activities.

Neither the Greek nor the Christian philosophers neglected the study of moral issues, to be sure, and specifically not those that concerned the rights and wrongs of political, economic, and human social life. But they gave little consideration to the nature of the mental function whereby human beings confronted themselves morally and passed judgment on themselves and each other. They did not make it the object of concentrated study to the same degree to which they did the mental functions of perception, memory, and understanding. Therefore *syneidesis* continued to mean only 'conscience' and not at all 'consciousness.' And so, when European culture eventually recognized the distinctively conscious nature of the human mental functions, the discovery was not the outcome of philosophical inquiry and dialogue. The concept of 'consciousness' was adopted by philosophy only after it had been in common and uncontroversial use for some time, when the vocabulary of 'conscience' was extended from its aboriginal exclusively moral meaning so as to cover the experience of 'consciousness.' How did this come about?

Let us remember the remote background. When Christianity, under the original guidance of the apostle Paul, began to think of itself as a 'Catholic' (i.e. universal) rather than a narrowly Jewish faith, the concepts of *syneidesis* and *conscientia* acquired an importance they had never had for Greek or Roman culture. For according to Paul, the universality of Christianity implied the 'abrogation of the Law,' i.e., the repeal of the moral commands and rituals such as circumcision prescribed for male Israelites in the Old Testament. Christians. Paul said, were 'free from the Law.' This followed from the Christian claim that God's Covenant with Israel had been superseded by the New Testament. And so, when the question arose how Christians could be certain of the correctness of their moral judgments and practices in the absence of written rules such as those previously furnished by the Old Testament, the concepts of *syneidesis* (which is found twice in the New Testament[227]) and *conscientia* in the Latin version were ready at hand to help provide the answer. In the Christian literature, these terms soon came to designate the kind of knowledge about moral matters whose reliability did not depend on the explicit clarity of 'the letter of the Law.' It hinged on the 'spiritual' nature of the moral law 'inscribed by God in the human heart,' as it were, which could be discerned by Christians by listening to the silent 'voice' they heard within themselves. The 'voice of conscience' revealed to them what they must and must not do in order to abide by the will of God. This meaning is preserved, of course, in our English *conscience* and in its counterparts in the other modern European languages.

---

227   2 Corinthians 4:2; Hebrews 10:2.

The historical process whereby Western European culture passed from 'conscience' to 'consciousness' (and to equivalents thereof in the other European languages), remains to be fully studied, but one of its principal strands probably originated when Latin translations of Aristotle's *Nichomachean Ethics* became available in the twelfth and thirteenth centuries and awakened a new and intensive interest among scholastics in the study of moral reasoning; it inspired them, more particularly, to re-examine the doctrine regarding the nature of conscience that had theretofore dominated in the theology of the previous seven centuries, namely, Augustine's.

In accordance with Augustine's 'voluntaristic' inclination to suppose that right moral knowledge depends on right will, moral reasoning was for Augustine almost an oxymoron. Human behaviour is morally good if it follows from love of God; otherwise it is morally evil. Love of God is therefore the guide to right moral decision. If one loves God one will naturally and instinctively know where one's duty lies, because one will know what God wills. *Ama et quod vis fac.* This doctrine is, of course, more likely to appeal to mystics than to philosophers, particularly if, like Aristotle, the philosophers should lean towards the view that human action and decisions follow rather than lead intellectual, cognitive processes. Besides, it is unrealistic; rationalizing one's wishes as love of God is not difficult. The irruption of Aristotelian considerations into the deliberations of the scholastics tended to bring down to earth the root of human morality. After all, the will of God was not supposed to be arbitrary, but highly rational. The rules of moral behaviour were in accordance with God's reason, and therefore were reflected in human nature. Therefore, they could be ascertained by looking into ourselves and learning what our nature demanded regarding our behaviour.

Thus, whereas it was metaphorically true that the voice of conscience was the voice of God informing us of his will, the more literal truth was that the voice of conscience was one's own, and that it told us about ourselves and what our nature required of us. [228] This was the first step towards learning that *conscientia* tells us much more than merely the difference between moral good and moral evil, since it also enlightens us about ourselves and our nature. The trend was of a piece with the change in the climate of philosophical opinion that had allowed Aquinas to propose, in effect,

228   Cf. Timothy C. Potts, *Conscience in Medieval Philosophy.* (Cambridge: Cambridge University Press, 1980); Randall C. Zachman, *The Assurance of Faith: Conscience in the Theology of Martin Luther and John Calvin* (Minneapolis: Fortress Press, 1993).

that human beings 'existed.' The second and decisive step was our culture's awareness of the inherent reality of human beings.

Once it became generally accepted by the popular culture that human beings existed, a parallel change of attitude away from the unremitting theocentrism of earlier times seems to have taken place at the level of common sense regarding the meaning of *conscientia*. Given the 'freedom from the Law' enjoyed by Christians, the Church had long enjoined upon believers the practice known as the 'examination of conscience,' the process of assessing oneself morally, so as to determine with certainty and moral clarity the legislating will of God that Christians must obey.

By the middle of the second millennium, however, the Church's claim to divinely-granted authority over the dogmatic and moral beliefs of its members had increased significantly. Since the Church now considered its voice for all practical purposes to be the voice of God, the believer was expected to examine his or her conscience by going over the well publicized, and largely standard, inventory of 'sins' condemned by the Church, and checking off his or her transgressions against the list. The practice became a pre-requisite of sacramental confession.

Compared with the doctrine of conscience that emerged with the Reformation, the traditional *examen* was a fairly comfortable exercise. With the Reformation, however, the Christian 'examination of conscience' became, for Protestants, a much more demanding and disquieting process. For the Reformation preached 'the priesthood of all believers;' and this meant, so far as concerned moral self-assessment, that the believer was expected to draw up the details and particularities of his or her own most intimate convictions regarding the will of God. The Church advised and criticized, but its voice was no longer identical with the commanding voice of God. The Christian was expected to make his or her own moral decisions — with eternal life at stake, if the decision was not in accordance with the will of God. Throughout the sixteenth century *conscientia* engrossed the attention of Christians to an unprecedented degree, both in their daily lives and in the discussions of theologians. And increasingly, the 'voice of conscience' was heard as what it truly was, namely, the human mental ability to tell ourselves, in our own voice, how we perceive ourselves.

By this time the popular culture of Europe had looked favourably upon the notion that real things 'existed.' But awareness of the inherent reality of the human person may have been the deciding factor in determining whether the scope of the concept of *conscientia* should not be expanded beyond the realm of moral self-awareness so as to cover the full-spectrum of self-awareness of which our cognitive functions are capable. To think of oneself (and indeed of other objects of perception) as real had become part of an everyday experience of people that brought them face to face with themselves. When this eventually happened, European cultures differentiated linguistically between 'consciousness' and 'conscience.'

Whatever considerations may have led to it, the discovery of 'consciousness' as a wider concept than 'conscience' was verbalized, in English, by a newly coined vocabulary that took into account the difference between the moral and the more comprehensive self-observability of the mind. The first recorded step in the linguistic process seems to have been taken by Francis Bacon (in *The Advancement of Learning),* who according to the Oxford English Dictionary (Second Edition) used the adjective 'conscient' in 1605 with much the same meaning as would be carried later by 'conscious.' According to the same source, however, the adjective 'conscious„' conveying the meaning of 'having the witness of one's own judgment or feelings within oneself … [or] knowing within oneself,' was first recorded only in 1620. But of the two, only one would survive: 'conscient' fell into disuse once 'conscious' was coined.[229] By 1625 Bacon himself was using 'conscious' rather than 'conscient.'

We shall probably never know exactly what collective mental processes in the minds of English speakers led to the creation of 'conscious' as a synonym of 'conscient.' But it is a reasonable estimate, I believe, that the emergence of 'conscious' in 1620 as a replacement for 'conscient' was facilitated by the prior appearance of 'conscientious' in 1611 to denote the quality of someone who is guided by 'conscience.' (The latter noun had long been part of Middle English with the exclusively moral meaning it has carried to the present.) The reason is that the adjective 'conscientious,' which is clearly a back-formation from the noun 'conscience,' has patent moral reference. Thus, the coining of 'conscientious' in 1611 would have called attention to the absence of an adjective corresponding to 'conscience' that did

---

229   It is not strange that 'conscient' should have proven less durable than 'conscious' despite the earlier creation of the former; for unlike 'conscient,' the lexical form of 'conscious' paralleled that of 'conscientious,' which had already appeared in 1611.

not have specifically moral reference. If so, the coining of 'conscious' in 1620 pointed to the growing awareness of speakers of English of the difference between the narrowly moral and the more general self-observability of the human mental functions, and to the need for a linguistic means to express it. The last step in the process of differentiating between the two forms of self-observability took place in 1632 — the year of Locke's birth. It was then that the noun 'consciousness' — again, an obvious back-formation from 'conscious' — was recorded. In clear contradistinction to 'conscience,' it meant (according to the *OED)* 'internal knowledge or conviction; knowledge as to which one has the testimony within oneself especially [but not necessarily] of one's own innocence, guilt, deficiencies, etc.'

To sum up, the collective mental process of early seventeenth century English speakers that produced the vocabulary of 'consciousness' may have been stimulated by the culture's suspicion that the self-observability of 'conscience' might extend beyond moral self-observation; but such suspicion would have been promoted by the heightened self-awareness of people who had become aware of their inherent existence and causal powers. 'Conscience' first generated 'conscientious,' through back-formation, with unequivocal moral reference. Since back-formations usually supply a need created by a perceived insufficiency of a primary word, 'conscientious' seems to have been devised for the very purpose of stipulating moral reference. But the coining of 'conscientious' would have highlighted the absence of an adjective corresponding to 'conscience' that did *not* have specifically moral reference. The culture therefore coined the adjective 'conscious' (after having briefly toyed with 'conscient') to specify the wider meaning that was absent from 'conscientious.' From the single noun 'conscience,' a family of two nouns and two corresponding adjectives had been generated, so as to satisfy the needs of a culture whose experience of human nature had expanded as part of the natural process of cultural evolution.

In the other European languages the same differentiation between 'conscience' and 'consciousness' was arrived at during approximately the same period, but not always signified, as in English and the other Germanic languages, by new coinages. In the Romance languages the ancient vocabulary of 'conscience' continued to be used, as it has to the present, but with two quite different acceptations, moral and non-moral. Context is relied upon, and invariably suffices, to make clear which is meant.

At first, the discovery of consciousness went unnoticed by most philosophers. During this period - the seventeenth century before the publication of either the *Discourse on Method* in 1637 or the *Meditations on First Philosophy* in 1641 - philosophy seems to have been mostly in the hands of two quite different types of scholar neither of which was particularly open to new ideas about the mind. The 'new philosophers,' as the pioneers of experimental science were sometimes known, were satisfied with their simplified and philosophically naïve versions of Platonism[230] and Pythagoreanism;[231] these were enough to ground what they were truly interested in, namely, their use of experimentation to discover how the world operated.

They took dualism for granted, and had no difficulty in supposing the strict determinism of Stoic-style 'laws of nature.' The other scholars, until Descartes sought to reform philosophy, were mostly the remnants of scholastic communities who looked back wistfully to earlier glories but frankly admitted, as we know from Descartes, that they did not know how to overcome existential skepticism.

Descartes seems to have been the first philosopher to have taken notice of the discovery of consciousness and put it to philosophical use, even if his interest in it was limited. He knew that philosophy had acquired a bad reputation, but his understanding of the reason for it was garbled. We have seen that, as he erroneously supposed, the problem was that philosophers had neglected to ensure that their conclusions rested on indubitable foundations. What interested him regarding the self-observability of the mind was that it contained an implication — the *cogito* — that refuted the absolute skepticism brought about, as he supposed, by the use of uncertain foundations. For the *cogito* demonstrated the indubitable existence of at least one thing — one's mind — from the existence of which the existence of God and the world could be parlayed.

Nevertheless, discussion of the *cogito* and of the philosophy that Descartes erected upon it, which did indeed attract much attention, brought philosophy in contact with the ragged margins of the topic of consciousness. But consciousness entered into the thick of modern philosophy only in 1690, with Locke's *Essay Concerning Human Understanding.* Fifty years later, Hume brought the

---

230   Cf. Alexandre Koyré, "Galileo and Plato," *Journal of the History of Ideas,* 4 (1943): 4, 400 - 28.

231   Burtt, *Metaphysical Foundations*, 52-54.

Cartesian reform to its penultimate confused condition. The ultimate may have been reached in the twentieth century with the cognitivist denial of the reality of consciousness.

9. *Extraneous contributions to the stagnation of philosophy*

With the facile wisdom of hindsight, we can perceive today what Descartes and his successors did not: that the collective experience of our culture which had at long last produced the awakening of human beings to their existence, consciousness, and selfhood, challenged them to rise to a new level of philosophical thought — and indeed, to a new level of human life. The latter is an almost tangible aspect of the 'modern' experience: even those of us who take little interest in the history of our species in general or of our European tradition in particular, are aware that we live in a new and very different age. Equally patent and common is our awareness of the disparity between the theoretical possibilities for improving civilized human life that are now open to us, and the niggardly paucity of our actual accomplishments in these respects. Today, economic, political, and social welfare for our species on a global scale is theoretically quite feasible — but quite unattainable in practical reality, given the actual conditions in which we exist and the actual assumptions under which we operate. Now, philosophy, being germane to the conduct of human life, is directly relevant to the larger challenges of the modern age. In this work, however, our concern is more modest. Here we are narrowly interested in the inability of modern philosophy to gain much understanding of human nature despite our culture's discovery of the reality of human existence and the conscious quality of the human mental functions.

Our findings in such respects can be briefly summed up: the principal factor and immediate direct cause of the stagnation of modern philosophy is the consensus that emerged among philosophers in reaction to Hume: they accepted representationism in the expectation that it might 'somehow' prove viable without entailing existential skepticism. But there were other important ways in which the traditional ways of thinking were reinforced and perpetuated, and we should review some of them. Few probably suspect that modern *science* was among the sources of the difficulties our culture experiences as it tries to adjust to its discovery of its own inherent reality. But it is true. Science does it unwittingly, to be sure, and in implicit contradiction with some of its other assumptions - but effectively nonetheless.

Let us go back. As the truth of human existence shone forth ever more brightly upon the dawn of the modern age, philosophers failed to revise some of the earlier assumptions handed down from Greece and Christian times. The crucial suppositions, let us remember, were (a) that objects were the efficient cause of cognition (b) that the effect of the object was to bring the mind into possession of the knowable 'contents' of objects, and (c) that objects were knowable because they were inherently thought (or 'watched').[232] But once the evolution of philosophy had reached this stage, nothing short of a critical review and radical revision of the basic concepts of philosophy could have sufficed to redeem the inadequacies with which philosophy had grown from its infancy. Unfortunately, when Descartes undertook the reformation of philosophy, he and the movement he founded were convinced that philosophy had nothing to gain by looking back upon its history. And so, when Hume discovered the antinomies that were at work below the surface of the Cartesian reformation, modern philosophers opted for ignoring the lessons that otherwise might have been taken from Hume.

In the absence of philosophical guidance, if for no other reason, the popular culture of modern Western Europe did not find it possible to accept unreservedly the inherent reality of man and world. The traditional religious beliefs have proven to have had much too firm a hold on the imagination and emotions of people. But our culture's acceptance of what our immediate consciousness reveals was discouraged also by the self-perpetuating vocabulary, idioms and constructions of our speech; it is always difficult for everyone at all times to overrule the connotations and subliminal implications of our linguistic heritage. Our common sense tradition, after two thousand years of having had it dinned in its ears that human beings are only transient occupants of a world that is not real *simpliciter,* but only semi-real, can be forgiven for being a little slow to dare to believe its eyes and unreservedly accept the reality and self-ownership of human existence — nor therefore the full *responsibility* we bear to each other simply because we share with them our conscious life.

---

232   I remind us that only a few Greek philosophers, the best known of whom is Anaxagoras, had dared to conclude that, therefore, the order of the world manifested an actual cosmic but intelligent *Nous.* Later, Christian theologians, of course, identified God as the source of the inherent knowability of the world.

It may be objected that although this conclusion may correctly reflect the situation of philosophy in early modern times, it fails to take into account later developments. Is it not true, for example, that eventually many philosophers acknowledged the incompatibility of religious faith and philosophical reason? Is it not a fact that a clear majority of contemporary philosophers today, and probably as many, or more, scientists, either profess no religious beliefs, or that, if they do, they sedulously exclude non-worldly agencies and causes from their philosophical explanations? Do many of them, indeed, not actually reject the reality of the divine in whatever version it might be proposed? [233] Yes, all this is true. But even those philosophers who do not stop at mere agnosticism and actually reject as false every transcendent reality, are apt to take for granted that such rejection leaves untouched the philosophical enterprise. They appear to assume that the world and its events, insofar as they are the *explicandum* of philosophy, are not substantially affected by whether God exists or not.

This assumption seems to me incorrect. If the underlying perception of the world and its events as self-insufficient is nevertheless allowed to stand unquestioned, the conscious and deliberate rejection of a transcendent reality and the dominion of necessity is ineffective to reorient philosophical attempts to understand the world. The fundamental misinterpretation is not actually the supposition of either *ho theos* or God, or even the lackluster, epicene, colourless 'Higher Power' of much agnostic tradition. What matters is that we have failed to grasp the reality of *the world* — ourselves therein included — as it actually presents itself to us. If one renounces 'the supernatural' and 'the divine,' but continues to make the traditional assumptions about what one is required to explain in order to understand the world, one would have foisted an impossible, self-contradictory task upon oneself.

For philosophers might continue to excogitate ingenious conceptual devices to escape the antinomies they have unwittingly created, and ahistoricism would dissuade them from exploring the radical alternative: questioning their most basic assumptions. It would not be difficult then for philosophers to propose 'naturalized' versions of other-worldly entities and forces upon which to ground

---

233 Surveys of the prevailing opinion of scientists regarding religious beliefs suggest that disbelief in 'a personal God' has steadily increased throughout the twentieth century, and that at the end of the century stood at approximately 75%, while 'agnosticism' has remained fairly steady throughout the period, at about 20% . See the report of Edward J. Larson and Larry Whitham, 'Leading scientists still reject God,' *Nature,* 334 (1998): 313. It is not clear, however, whether in this survey 'agnosticism' envisages a personal God. It is possible that agnosticism regarding a transcendent but impersonal and not necessarily omnipotent force may be higher even among scientists.

philosophical and scientific explanations of the world and its phenomena. Such explanations may not appeal to God or Fate, but to a succedaneum thereof whose other-worldliness is masked.

The role of modern science in providing such substitutes is not given as much attention as it deserves. The discovery of experimentation in modern times as a procedure for obtaining reasonably reliable factual knowledge was so clearly valid, and so obviously a new high mark in the history of human civilization, that the *philosophical* inadequacies of science have tended to escape not only internal criticism by scientists themselves, but also (and much less understandably) by philosophers. On the contrary, in the eyes of not a few philosophers — and endemically among cognitivists — science seems almost like an ideal to be emulated by philosophy. Now, the principal causes of the stagnation of philosophy did not have directly to do with the emergence of science. Nevertheless, modern philosophy's complaisant and uncritical attitude towards the oversimple philosophical assumptions of science has allowed science to lend some credibility to our culture's reluctance fully to recognize the inherent reality and causal efficacy of the world and its objects.

If illustration is required, let us remember the 'determinism' that, even today, most scientists and not a few philosophers deem an indispensable foundation of modern science.[234] This is despite (a) the absence of all empirical evidence to support it, (b) its necessary paradoxical implication that the universe operates as if it were teleologically guided towards a predetermined though unknown end, and (c) its superfluity for determining the actual causes of phenomena, which hinges on observation and experimentation and in no way upon the assumption of the principle of determinism. Scientific determinism is, of course, an orphan assumption, a remnant of the original assumption of the reality of Fate that Greek philosophy inherited from Greek religion. And it is not far fetched to wonder whether Hume's discovery that necessitarian causation is an emperor without clothes, might not have been given more serious consideration than in fact it received, had necessitarianism not been a cornerstone of modern science.

But the principal illustration of my suggestion — that the basic assumptions of the Greek philosophers continue to hold some sway today under the auspices of science — is the concept originally proposed by the Stoics but favoured near-universally by scientists since at least the time of Johannes

---

234   Cf. Roy C. Weatherford, *The Implications of Determinism* (London: Routledge, 1991).

Kepler, from whom it passed unquestioned to much modern science and philosophy. This is the idea that 'laws of nature' preordain with fateful inevitability whatever happens in the world. Modern philosophers have accepted the concept more frequently in contexts other than the study of the mind, but sometimes in the latter as well. For example, according to David Chalmers the ultimate objective of philosophy of mind is to discover 'a set of *psychophysical laws* governing the relationship between consciousness and physical systems … Like the fundamental laws of physics, psychophysical laws are eternal [sic], having existed since the beginning of time.'[235] Now, how did the scientific belief in *eternal* 'laws of nature' that govern a *temporal* world come about?

The early scientists, who for the most part were faithful Christians — and who, given their peculiar interests in concrete phenomena, tended to favour the simplicity of Platonism over the more elaborate and empiricism-tinged Aristotelianism that appealed to most scholastics — devised the technique that is still in use today for solving every possible conflict between faith and reason at the root. They invented a new and improved variation of mediaeval 'Averroism' which avoided the self-contradictory 'double truth' of the original version. They proposed instead, in effect, the division of the scientific mind into religious and secular compartments, respectively concerned with the 'natural' and the 'supernatural' realms. Thus, science was autonomous within its proper sphere, but was not competent outside it; it had no jurisdiction in matters pertaining to either God or the supernatural world, but only regarding the 'laws of nature'. Nevertheless, the early scientists were almost to a man Christian believers, and therefore believed — though hardly for scientific reasons — that the 'laws' had been written by the Will of God, that they existed in the mind of God, and that they were the means through which God governed the natural order of the world he had created. Their acknowledgment of the limited competence of science left them free to alternate at will between premises that at bottom were incompatible. As a rhetorical device, however, it proved most successful.

Nowadays, of course, the proportion of believers among scientists is considerably lower than at the time when the conventional scientific wisdom originated; but in the seventeenth century:

---

235 Chalmers, *Conscious Mind,* pp. 213 , 171. Italics his.

Christians helped the cause of modern rationalism by their jealous determination to sweep out of the world all miracles and magic except their own … In the circle around Mersenne in the 1630's the idea of a complete mechanistic interpretation of the universe came out into the open, and its chief exponents were the most religious men in the group … They were anxious to prove the adequacy and the perfection of Creation — anxious to vindicate God's rationality.[236]

What does not make much sense, in my suggestion (besides the supposition that the 'laws of nature' inscribed in the temporal world are 'eternal') is that such 'laws' should be deemed to exist, notwithstanding the absence of a divine Legislator. Now, a law that constrains the behaviour of natural phenomena under its jurisdiction, that has been thought by an existing Mind, that exists in such Mind, that is eternal because such Mind is eternal, and that is an instrument whereby the omnipotent Will of such Mind achieves its purposes, may be an empirically groundless fantasy, but is self-consistent. Its 'naturalistic' counterpart, however, is a law that expresses the same constraints, but which has been legislated by no one, which is literally a mindless thought, which is immutable and timeless part of the temporal and ceaselessly becoming world, and which indeed exists nowhere in the world but in a Platonic imagination, but whose dispositions are nevertheless, for some mysterious reason, enforced in the world, albeit 'automatically'[237] rather than by the decision of anyone's will. It seems to me, in short, that the concept of 'law of nature' has an intellectual status which must be said to approach that of a superstition. I know of no reason why it should be deemed intellectually preferable to Christian theology.

Some contemporary philosophers and scientists suppose that the 'laws of nature' are only metaphorically so-called. Such 'laws,' they agree, are not 'laws' at all, since they do not truly regulate anything or command obedience by the world. 'Laws of nature,' they recognize, exist only in the thinking of those scientists or philosophers who state them; they actually are either *generalizations*

---

236 Herbert Butterfield, *The Origins of Modern Science: 1300-1800* (London: Bell, 1958), 73.

237 Chalmers, *Conscious Mind,* p. 171.

that encapsulate usefully a multiplicity of concrete and specific observations and measurements made by human minds, or mathematical *idealizations* of such observations.

With the burden of this conception of 'natural laws' I would find it difficult to disagree. But I would object to the appropriateness of using the term 'natural laws' to describe them. For a metaphor that one deems inapplicable in every way to that to which one applies it is, if nothing else, misleading. Calling it what it is, a 'generalization' or an 'idealization.' acknowledges that one is voicing nothing else than one's opinions on the basis of one's observation; it is what *one* says. Calling it a 'law of nature,' on the other hand, tends to promote self-deception; it suggests that it is not one who says it, but that one is merely repeating what the world itself 'says' to us. We fail to advert to this, however, because projecting the generalization onto the object invests it with the false authoritativeness of 'objective truth.' The generalizers have not taken responsibility for saying what, in point of fact, has been said only by them.

But my further and most fundamental objection is that, if one agrees that 'laws of nature' are merely generalizations arrived at by human minds, one must for consistency's sake agree also with the necessary implication thereof: that such 'laws' are neither 'eternally valid' (whatever that might mean) nor 'objective' truths (i.e., that they subsist in the inherent knowability of objects). For the reduction of 'laws of nature' to creations of the human mind implies, for instance, as Martin Heidegger remarked, that:

> Before Newton's laws were discovered, they were not 'true'; it does not follow
> that they were false … [or that] before him there were no such entities as have
> been uncovered and pointed out by those laws. Through Newton the laws
> became true.[238]

Heidegger does not mean, of course, that Newton created the natural phenomena he studied. He means, I take it, that Newton created the truth (that is, the cognitive value *for us*) of our understanding of such phenomena — finite, partial, tentative, and subject to correction and further

---

238   Martin Heidegger, *Being and Time* (London: SCM Press , 1962), 269.

improvement though such truth-value was. Whatever else may be said of it, truth is a quality of knowledge, and knowledge is an activity of a mind. Of course, if one projects onto objects the truth that qualifies the cognizing mind's cognitive efforts, one will imagine that truth resides in the human mind only because it first resides in reality and is merely repeated by the mind. Which, once again, if I may, would make sense only if the truth that supposedly resides in reality and is supposedly borrowed by the mind, was originally thought by an anterior and higher Mind whose thinking creates reality. But not otherwise.

Now, if one holds views such as those expressed by Heidegger one will have to explain, of course, how the nature of reality and the nature of truth should be understood, rather than, respectively, as the inherent knowability of beings and as the correspondence or repetition of such inherent knowability by the mind. But is that not one of the lessons we should take from Hume? That the correct philosophical procedure is to tailor our interpretations to the measure of our observations, rather than the other way about? Our interpretations of truth and reality should conform to what we observe rather than to what we may imagine. And yet, even the latitudinarian versions of modern philosophy's concept of 'laws of nature', much less those that explicitly suppose 'nomic necessity', as D.M. Armstrong's does,[239] retain the questionable assumptions of the Greek and mediaeval philosophical tradition. Modern philosophy has been demythologized only in the limited sense that it has been freed from bondage to the traditional form of ecclesiastically promoted religious belief. However, its dependence on the assumptions that rationalized the common sense beliefs of Greek religion and the authoritative faith of Christianity — the assumptions that made philosophy *theological* in both Greek and Christian times — have not completely disappeared. They remain with us, just below the surface of science.

What allows such premises to remain at work? The single most important reason, I estimate, is oblivion of the history of human knowledge. Ahistoricism explains not only the outcome of the Cartesian attempt to resurrect philosophy, but also philosophy's entering thereafter into a chronic state of seasonally recurring crises, temporarily relieved every so often by springs of enthusiasm and autumns of ultimately dashed hope. This is the cyclical outcome as philosophers devise, in the light of

---

239   In his *What is a Law of Nature*.

previous failures, ingeniously new, laboriously excogitated, and ever more daring and exciting ways to attempt to escape the implications of assumptions that remain in the dark or have acquired the status of self-evident facts.

10. *The reconstruction of philosophy: where to begin, and why*

If the explanation suggested in this chapter has identified at all correctly the fundamental causes of the traditional self-misinterpretation of the human mind and the consequent stagnation of modern philosophy, we should find it possible to avoid making the same miscalculations. And if so, we would be in a good position to undertake the reconstruction of philosophy with the objective of setting it on a course that seems to offer a reasonable expectation of success. But this prospect raises a question. How should we proceed to rebuild philosophy? Exactly what should we do in order to begin? The answer is not obvious. Fortunately, Hume's work, if we read it with this question in mind, offers a few hints.

Hume's acceptance of representationism at the cost of existential skepticism may have been a blunder; but his powers of observation were nonetheless extraordinarily penetrating, as is demonstrated by his having pointed his finger unerringly at the 'monstrous offspring' that was responsible for skepticism. But certain other aspects of his thought also deserve, in my opinion, more credit than he usually receives. I have in mind a facet of his work that seems to me most important, even if it is not as frequently discussed as the substance of his teaching; I refer to the *procedure* to which he resorted in his paradoxical attempt to further the cause of philosophical knowledge while concluding that such knowledge was unattainable.

In both the *Treatise* and the *Enquiry,* Hume was concerned predominantly with three philosophical concepts: cognition, reality, and causality. He thought — quite rightly, in my view — that the traditional understanding of the last two should be rejected; for in the form in which they had always been supposed, they had no empirical grounding. But from this I surmise that, if in his opinion the absence of empirical support should have amounted to sufficient cause for their rejection, his prior assumption would have probably been that such empirical basis should be deemed a *prerequisite* of their acceptability by philosophers. In other words, the traditional concepts of causation and reality were inadequate because they strayed from what experience showed; if so, a sound view of causation and reality was in principle attainable by adhering to what experience revealed about them. This, I think, is true. Now, Hume accepted representationism. But, given his commitment to empiricism, I would estimate that, if he had found that philosophical knowledge was possible, he would have assumed that, as in the case of reality and causality, a viable and empirically justified concept of cognition, too, was required by philosophy in addition to those of reality and causality.

In other words, although Hume did not say so, the concepts of cognition, reality and causality seem to have defined, in his estimation, a certain approach to philosophy — a novel approach. His procedure was predicated, in effect, on the twofold assumption that (a) cognition, reality, and causality were the three principal defining parameters of philosophical reasoning, and (b) that the criterion of their adequacy and admissibility was experience. But this procedure suggests that, if philosophical knowledge had been possible, philosophers would have to reckon *at the outset* with three pivotal concepts — namely, cognition, reality, and causality — so as to ensure that they had been correctly determined. And such determination was to be made by verifying that they were well-grounded in experience.

Thus, if we set aside for the moment all consideration of the nature of cognition, reality, and causality, and attend solely to the role that these concepts play in Hume's thinking about the nature of philosophy, we can appreciate the originality of his vision. Hume seems to have appreciated, more or less consciously, that these three concepts made up, as it were, the portal of philosophy; unless they opened out onto an unobstructed way ahead, the philosophical undertaking must be deemed to have been improperly oriented. It is unfortunate that acceptance of representationism made Hume ineligible to profit from his insight that empirically-supported concepts of cognition, reality, and causality were required as the appropriate entry to the realm of philosophical knowledge. However, if we, unlike him, reject representationism, but nevertheless perceive the wisdom of his procedural insight, we would be well on our way to developing an alternative to the traditional conception of philosophy.

What Hume seems to have glimpsed, even if only from a distance — or at any rate, what we can perceive for ourselves if we agree with him that (a) concepts of cognition, reality, and causality are indispensable for philosophy, and that (b) such concepts can be philosophically admissible and useful only if they are empirically well grounded — is that although philosophical knowledge does have a framework, as it were, and is indeed *constructed*, it is not 'erected,' as the tradition had supposed and as Descartes had repeated, upon 'foundations' or *a priori* 'principles' characterized by their universality, fixity, and dependability. The more appropriate metaphor to describe the nature of philosophy than that of an *edifice* (in which the upper reaches are limited by the logical constraints set by their base), may be that of a *landscape* that will stretch out indefinitely as long as we cultivate it, and which is entered through a *gateway* which is opened with the *key* provided by experience.

In this view, the 'principles' that make up the 'gateway' of philosophy are properly so-called only in the sense that they mark the point at which philosophy *begins,* and thereby help us set the *direction* in which philosophy proceeds. They are not overarching 'universal truths' from which particularities or applications can be logically deduced. If they are appropriately said to be 'fundamental,' it is rather in the sense that they are the simplest, most primitive, and most elementary *observations* from which our further investigation of ourselves and the world can proceed. Nor is their truth guaranteed by their supposed 'self-evidence' or by their certainty. Indeed, they may well be wide off the mark, since the human mind is fallible: no better example of this can be alleged than the traditional, primitive conception of causation according to which causes 'necessitate' their effects. Thus, philosophical knowledge begins with pre-philosophical concepts that *seem* true, and which for the nonce are *assumed* to be true, and which may even appear at first glance to be revealed by experience; but such concepts become *philosophical* concepts only when they are subjected to critical testing by further thought, particularly in the light of further experience, if and when any becomes available.

Philosophy has long been treated as if it were not a human cultural institution, but had a fixed, eternal 'essence.' Its very origin indicates otherwise. The assumptions that launched philosophy in Greece harked back to the common sense constructions that are invariably put by a community on its experience of the simplest, most elementary and general aspects of the world and of human beings themselves. With accumulated experience, a more critical and truer grasp of the same assumptions is possible. Before the idea of philosophy emerges, such assumptions are likely to seem self-evident and certain, simply because we adopt them effortlessly, without any prior inquiry on our part — but above all because we have not questioned them. Moreover, our original perceptions as individuals regarding world and self tend to be solidified by the language in which we think about them, which incorporates the assumptions of the culture's common sense.

But in any event, philosophy begins as an attempt to isolate and examine critically the assumptions of common sense in order to test them and improve upon them. More specifically, if philosophy is to proceed correctly to investigate the world and the position of mankind within it — and to do so more adequately than the various religions have — the concepts of cognition, reality, and causality must be appropriately identified and understood. That is, they must be examined and adjudged to accord with experience. Once these assumptions have become as well-grounded in experience as one can currently best determine, they may be deemed to be true, but only until such time as contrary evidence might appear. And philosophical diligence requires that philosophers actively search for such contrary evidence. In short, philosophy is the *critique* of common sense by empirical reason. And if modern philosophy manages to re-orient itself, it will have to take into account its *evolutionary* nature.

When we look back to the Greek origins of philosophy, we would do well to remember the disadvantage that necessarily accompanies all pioneering efforts: they are unavoidably imperfect. And since philosophy is, of course, a form of *knowledge,* the imperfections of the typical Greek conception of cognition suffice to warn us that their idea of philosophical knowledge must have been correspondingly imperfect.

The original imperfection of the Greek philosophers' conception of philosophy began with a misperception of the relationship of philosophy to common sense. The Greek philosophers thought that philosophy was discontinuous with the latter. Thus, only philosophical knowledge was truly *knowledge;* the convictions of common sense were mere opinions masquerading as knowledge. In many philosophical circles today, the term 'knowledge' continues to be used in this privileged sense; that is, as if 'knowledge' were truly knowledge only if it was true and certain, a 'justified true belief.' (Which is, of course, the origin of the traditional supposition that philosophy could be expected to yield certainty — with little thought having been given to the infallibility that unqualified certainty would require.) And as if our senses and our understanding did not yield any knowledge to other citizens but only to philosophers.

The inaccuracies thus introduced into the philosophical tradition by the Greeks were hardy, and lived through the winter of the fourteenth century, blooming again in the false spring of the mid-seventeenth. But how did they originate? One circumstance that surely did not help prevent them is that, although most Greek philosophers supposed that reality as such was 'divine,' their 'naturalized' idea of 'divinity' brought them into conflict with a culture that was not well disposed towards those who contemned 'the Greek way.' Repeatedly, the philosophers clashed with the popular culture on the very point of the common sense interpretation of 'divinity,' and a good many philosophers were punished in major and minor ways for their dissent; Socrates was scarcely the only victim. The philosophers for their part seem to have been more deeply impressed by the higher reliability of philosophical knowledge over common sense, than by philosophy's origin in common sense. Not all philosophers may have been as extreme as Plato — or as Parmenides had been a century earlier, when he distinguished between 'the way of truth' and 'the way of mortal opinion' — but the philosophers tended generally to separate the two. The stark differentiation between the society at large and the philosophical communities within them — between *episteme* and *doxa* — may well account for the excessive reliance traditionally placed by philosophy on logic to the relative detriment of observation. And, of course, to the complete separation of *aisthesis* and *noesis*.

But common sense and philosophy are not a dichotomy; I remind us again that no one is born a philosopher. No one can begin to practice philosophy without having first become equipped with concepts of 'causality,' 'reality,' and 'cognition' that may or may not be correct, but which in either event define the point from which their critical thinking of these subjects takes its departure. After all, the human mental functions are the same throughout the species, even if, in what concerns knowledge as in every other dimension of human accomplishment, a more cultivated stage of development is continuous with a more primitive one. Philosophy is not, any more than science, a self-contained, privileged realm of knowledge cut off from ordinary human life. It is not a priesthood, and it should not allow itself, as science has, to become one. It is for the sake of philosophy itself that philosophy should recognize its origin in common sense; for when philosophy forgets its origins, it forgets about reviewing and criticizing its assumptions, and risks importing into philosophy, surreptitiously, the mistakes of common sense.

Foundationalism was widely rejected in the twentieth century, but not many viable and clear alternatives to it have been proposed to replace it. 'Coherentism' and 'reliabilism' have found favour with some, but languish and wither. Altogether different is the approach to the nature of philosophy taken by cognitivism: philosophy of mind is, though not a branch of science, at least 'a branch of the philosophy of science.' Now, there are several reasons why these proposals do not seem to me to have been well thought out. One reason is that science depends on philosophical concepts — notably, but not only, the initial suppositions of philosophy — that can be neither determined nor tested by the procedures that define science. Besides, for historical reasons and unnecessarily (rather than because of its nature), science suffers from certain deficiencies which come from its having adopted, during the earliest period of its formation, certain naïve philosophical positions which have, by convention, become *de facto* elements of science. Pythagoreanism, despite the absence of all empirical observations or facts that suggest that reality is ultimately mathematical in nature, is one of these. But also to be cited is a second assumption: the idea of 'objective observation,' which was one of the most important contribution of Galileo to the rationale of 'modern science.' (It will be discussed in the next chapter.) Both these concepts are groundless, as well as quite unnecessary for science, if not indeed a positive hindrance to it.

This is not at all to deny that scientific experimentation is the only way in which we can gain the sort of knowledge and understanding regarding ourselves and the world that science provides, which is now familiar to all of us, and from which we derive much advantage. In sum, nothing can be reasonably said against the validity, usefulness, and benefit of science — although a great deal can be alleged about some of the ways in which our civilization has chosen to use it. But science, of course, is not be confused with scientism. It has been left to some of the more traditional philosophers to reassert, therefore, as P.M.S. Hacker has, the recognizable and unbridgeable differences between philosophy and science:

> Advances in science cannot *in principle* resolve philosophical problems, for the sciences either employ, and hence presuppose an understanding of, the very concepts that give rise to philosophical perplexity; or they employ

different concepts in which case they bypass what puzzles us (and even cheat us out of our puzzlement) and, in some cases, generate fresh conceptual questions.[240]

But the work of Hume, the accidental anti-foundationalist as he may have been, contains the seeds of the concept of the nature of philosophy I have assumed above. It would support E.A. Burtt's suggestion that:

> Philosophers, as philosophers, are not concerned with … the satisfactions of curiosity about specific puzzling occurrences … It is their business to deal with themes of vast and general scope … The scientist, as such, refuses to take the entire universe as his province.… At times he proffers rather general theories … but these theories never claim to embrace everything without exception[241] … When a theory transcends such limited generality, or when it must devise its own method of verification, we have left the realm of science for that of philosophy.[242]

The objective of philosophy, it seems to me, is not simply to accumulate, but above all to *deepen* and *systematize* knowledge. Philosophy is able to do so because it begins with what we experience, but interrogating it at the root. But philosophy cannot come into being without assumptions regarding cognition, reality, and causality; for without them, philosophical questions cannot be asked, much less answered. Together, they sum up the essential subject matter of philosophy and enable it to take the universe for its object: namely, (a) human beings and their conscious life, (b) the reality of the

---

240   P.M.S. Hacker, *Insight and Illusion: Themes in the Philosophy of Wittgenstein* (Oxford: Clarendon Press, 1986), 157-158. This is, of course, hardly all that must needs be said on the subject, which is treated by Hacker at some length at the same location.

241   Since Burtt wrote this, such claims have in fact been made by a number of theoretical physicists, but only by virtue of their reductionistic assumption that, since everything in the world is material in nature, a theoretical explanation of the nature of matter amounts to a 'theory of everything.'

242   Edwin A. Burtt, 'Introduction' to his edition of *The English Philosophers from Bacon To Mill* (New York: Modern Library, 1939), ix, xi-xii.

world of which we are part, and (c) the relationships among the phenomena we witness and among the events that we and the world undergo. This is why a set of such basic concepts had been spontaneously assumed *de facto* throughout the philosophical tradition by all philosophers. What modern philosophers may have failed to advert to, besides the falsity of their version of the concepts, was that philosophy depended on such fundamental assumptions.

Nevertheless, because the basic concepts of philosophy — reality, cognition, and causation — potentially comprise all that philosophy can study; and because they are not derived from other concepts; and because they therefore function as the point of departure of philosophical investigation, such concepts are best denominated by allusion to the role they play in philosophy. Let us refer to them, therefore, as the 'initial assumptions' upon which every philosophical investigation depends.

To call them 'assumptions' does not imply that they are conjectural, but only that they are *presuppositions*. Indeed, they should not be mere conjectures, but should be grounded on sufficient empirical evidence to render them plausible. They are the *Vorverständnisse,* the 'pre-understandings,' on the basis of which philosophical investigation can proceed and philosophical understanding can be hopefully achieved. Nor are they to be arbitrarily or uncritically accepted or postulated. They are to be deemed forever liable to being corrected.

Thus, once we understand the defects that have hindered philosophy, and how they came about, the reconstruction of the discipline should be set in motion with an attempt to revise the traditional assumptions of cognition, causality, and reality in order to align them with what experience reveals. In the next chapter we shall strive to do so.

III

The Initial Assumptions of Post Humean Philiosophy

The principal task before us in this chapter is to try to work out a more adequate version of the fundamental initial assumptions of philosophy interpreting cognition, causality, and reality than our Greek and mediaeval tradition supposed and which modern philosophy appears to have largely retained. To correct them, we shall try to bring our interpretations into line with what we actually observe about ourselves, about the world, and about the way in which changes in ourselves and the world take place. The more difficult part is to make the observations accurately, before we interpret them without distortion. It may help us sharpen our vision if a few preliminary matters are disposed of first.

1. Preliminaries

I assume that human beings do not have innate ideas. The opinion that some of our ideas are not derived empirically, but are built-into human nature is defended by its adherents on various grounds, but its primordial source is the inability of some philosophers to trace the 'contents' of certain ideas to sense perception. When they discover that no counterparts of such 'contents' are to be found in the empirically-given world, the supposition that they are inborn seems unavoidable. For example, the original argument of this type — namely, Plato's, in the *Phaedo* — points out, correctly, that the concept of *'equality'* (or *'sameness,' to ison*) does not correspond to anything we experience in the world. For nothing is absolutely and perfectly 'equal' to anything else; nothing is absolutely the 'same' as anything else, even itself, since it changes. And since the least difference precludes strict equality, *'equality'* cannot admit of degrees. Therefore, the concept is innate.

This reasoning depends on several false assumptions, including the supposition that only external objects can provide the empirical 'contents' of experience. The latter assumption in turn depends on ignoring that the conscious quality of human cognition allows the human mind to become empirically acquainted with its own operations and states. If we advert to this, it is reasonably clear that, even if nothing is exactly 'equal' to, or 'same' as, anything else, we are able to conceive 'equality' empirically: we conceive it when we compare any previously conceived idea with a second instance of it. Concepts, and only concepts, are perfectly self-identical. Likewise, we conceive the opposite of 'sameness,' namely, 'difference,' when we compare any concept with the negation of it. Thus, the concept 'red' is absolutely and perfectly equal to the concept 'red,' as well as absolutely and perfectly 'unequal' (or 'different' from) the concept of 'not-red.'

I have explained how the concepts of 'reality' is arrived at, as the 'otherness' of objects (in relation to our activity of 'experiencing'); it is revealed by the experience of every object. And in the next two sections we shall consider in detail the origin of 'causality' and 'cognition.' Given the importance of the question whether all our concepts ultimately derive from experience, I should mention briefly some examples of other concepts that may appear to be either innate, but are not, as well as concepts that appear to be derived from our experience of external objects but are derived from our experience of our own mental functions. Thus, a concept may be the same as, or different from, another in content, but the second is in any event not the first — for example, 'rose' now is one concept, whereas 'rose' again is another. Each of the two is *one*. Moreover, a concept that is both *one* and *self-same* is a *totality*; for, being the *same* (as itself), it is neither more nor less than (i.e., is *not-different* from) itself. At the same time, being *one*, it holds its self-same contents in itself, rather than both in itself and another. In other words, it is in itself *all* that it is or can be. Whatever coincides with itself, or is self-identical, is also a *whole,* or a *totality*. Likewise, every concept is always identical to itself, and *cannot* be more or less than itself. For if it were, it would be a different concept. Well, then, it is *impossible* to think anything but what in fact one thinks, or to assert what one does not assert; contradictories cannot be held at the same time. The negation of '*possibility*' is of course '*possibility*'. And so on.

The point is that the position is reasonable that all human knowledge begins with, and is derived from, sense perception — although this does not mean that perceptible external objects alone supply the 'contents' of all concepts. The concepts that are the backbone of philosophy, logic and mathematics do not derive from our experience of perceptible objects, but from our experience of the way we think. As contrasted with the perceptible aspects of, say, 'roses,' there is no perceptible object in the world called 'existence' or 'reality' or 'causality' — though in the real world there are events that entitle us to speak and think *truthfully* about 'real' and 'existing' objects and about 'causal' processes. Hence the importance of studying not only their empirical origin, but also what they actually *mean* — or to put it more precisely, what *we* mean when we apply them to the external world. What may we properly and correctly mean by 'reality,' 'cognition,' and 'causality'? These are primordial philosophical questions. If we wish to ensure that philosophy has been re-oriented towards an attainable goal, we must begin by inquiring into their meaning.

Now, we have seen that cognition, reality, and causality are the three parameters that define the fundamental structure of a philosophical *Weltanschauung*. All three concepts are required before philosophical thought can exist; they add up to the basic framework of a systematization of the world which can be perfected and enlarged, and if necessary revised, as new observations and discoveries are made. The three, however, are closely interrelated: each includes reference to the other two.

This should be stressed, because it is the source of much misunderstanding. Observe, then, for example, that *cognition* as traditionally understood is deemed to take place when the mind receives and enters into possession of the knowable 'contents' of *reality*, either by becoming united with the contents when they *act* upon the senses, or by possessing the mental representations of reality that are *caused* by the object to exist in the mind. In other words, cognition cannot be described without reference to reality and causation. Even if this idea of cognition were to be revised, it would have to make reference to its target (i.e., reality) and to its cause (i.e., the organism's active discharge of its cognitive functions).

The interconnection of the three concepts renders them unusually hardy; once they are conceived, they sustain each other rigidly and resist change as a set. If inflated metaphors were not objectionable, one might dare say that they perform as a well-rehearsed and resourceful team of snipers who repel attacks by taking turns at shooting from different directions, disorienting thus the enemy's attempts to respond. Their mutual support may help explain why many philosophers who are aware of the fatal objections that can be brought up against their traditional version, nevertheless continue to assume them. For the assumptions can be criticized only one at a time. The criticism of each, however, fades away soon after it is made, because, as it is impugned, the validity of the other two, which presuppose the first, can be alleged in defence of the first. Conversely, against the revision of each, incompatibility of the revision with the *unrevised* and *uncriticized* version of the other two can be alleged.

For example, if one were to call into question each of the traditional concepts as follows, the suggestion might be dismissed with the aid of the supposition that the other two remain valid:

- Is it possible that **cognition** is not the reception of representations of reality that reality causes in the mind? No, because if so, (a) the knowable 'contents' of **reality** could not be transferred to the mind and cognition would not take place, and (b) reality could not **cause** our cognition.

- Is it possible that **reality** does not contain inherently knowable 'contents' within itself which are cognized when transferred to the mind? No, because if so, (a) there would be nothing to be **cognized** by the mind, and (b) cognition could not be **caused** by objects.

- Is it possible that there is no **causal** power in real objects to create mental representations of reality in the mind? No, because if so, (a) the effect, **cognition**, would not take place, and (b) the knowable contents of **reality** would not be known by the mind.

As we revise the three basic assumptions of the philosophical tradition, therefore, it will be essential to bear in mind that we are not searching for an empirically grounded replacement of each in isolation from the others, but for an alternative to the three interrelated concepts. As I focus on each at a time, I shall make some cross-references to the others, but the validity of the revision can be properly assessed only by considering all three in relation to each other. And in the first place, of course, by paying attention to what observation reveals about each.

A second caution is also in order. I have harped on how easily projection can lead to erroneous conclusions through reasoning processes that do not violate the rules of formal logic but the results of which are fallacious just the same. Well, all three of our traditional initial assumptions of philosophy originate in projection, so that they not only lend each other mutual support, but also seem self-evident; the combination of circumstances renders the assumptions highly misleading. To undeceive ourselves we have to pay close attention to our mental processes. Moreover, no interpretation of anything ever seems true except to those who are open to the possibility that it might be so.

The misperception of cognition, as I have repeatedly noted, begins with defective advertence to our own active and causal role in our cognitive mental processes. In the absence of interoceptive capability in the organs of cognition, our activation of our cognitive functions is especially difficult to detect; to become aware of it we depend mostly on indirect clues. The object, on the other hand, cannot be overlooked: cognizing the object is the built-in purpose of every cognitive function. But this disparity makes it difficult for us to discriminate between what is attributable to the action of our mental powers and what is attributable to the object that the mental process is trained upon: the projection of our cognition onto the object follows. And once we suffer from this confusion, we have not only misunderstood the human mind, but are part of the way towards misunderstanding the nature of the world and its objects, as well as the causation of the changes that both the world and ourselves undergo. These are the concepts of reality and causality that we will then use to buttress the misperception of cognition.

We should also remind ourselves that, as human beings do in every culture, we in our tradition do not gather facts exclusively by making observations ourselves, but also by accepting as normative many observations and interpretations enshrined in our traditional culture and its language. We pick them up mostly in early childhood when, somewhat as marsupials do, we attain to full-term maturity as members of our species outside the womb well after birth. We call it 'socialization,' but it may also be described as a second stage of gestation whereby we are brought to term as constituent members of our speech-endowed species. We then learn not only to speak — a cognitive function that, apparently, does not emerge through organic maturation alone but only in a social context — but we also acquire at the same time the principal current convictions of our culture regarding human nature, the world, and our human situation. This does not necessarily prevent, but it renders difficult, our eventually making, on our own initiative, observations that contradict the opinions of common sense. Not infrequently, therefore, our first impressions are granted immunity from criticism and possible review; they have the built-in advantage that, for the very reason that they are first impressions, they take root. They are much less easily displaced than those convictions which are developed only later and have replaced our original beliefs.

Also to be noted as preliminary is that, in accordance with the trend established by Locke and followed by Hume, human *cognition* has been, for most practical purposes, reduced by modern philosophy to *perception*. The mental functions that involve language — 'speech,' 'thought,' and 'understanding' — are not always considered part of our experiential equipment. And yet, our abilities to speak and think are what make it possible for us to reason and understand; for by thinking and reasoning we can discover what we had not previously known. And when we understand something we had not previously understood, we acquire knowledge and are aware of having acquired it. Or as Galen Strawson, whom I have previously quoted, has suggested, the 'spectrum of experience ranges from the most purely sensory experiences to the most abstractly cognitive experiences.'[243]

Donald Davidson has explained why. It is not only because we use speech (including the silent and purely imaginary form of speech we call 'thought') in order to understand, but also because 'a speaker must himself be an interpreter of others … [A] creature cannot have thoughts unless it is an interpreter of another.'[244] For a speaker must, of course, understand what it wants others to understand; it must understand its own speech before it can make its speech understood by others by saying something that the hearer can be expected to understand.

The idea that the human cognitive functions are exercised at two different levels — sense perception (*aisthesis*) and understanding (*noesis,* which is often translated also as 'thought') — goes back to Greece. But in Greek and mediaeval thought the two levels were discontinuous, because the two functions attained, supposedly, two different objects, namely, the perceptible and the intelligible

243   Galen Strawson, *Mental Reality* (Cambridge, Mass.: MIT Press, 1994)*,* 4, 5.

244   Donald Davidson, 'Thought and Talk,' in Samuel D. Guttenplan, (ed.), *Mind and Language* (Oxford: Clarendon Press, 1977), 9-10.

characteristics of the world. In modern times, however, Hume threw this scheme into question; the absence of empirical support for a distinction between non-perceptible substances and their perceptible qualities resulted in most philosophers' discarding the 'essences' of things, their 'intelligibility.' Understanding has continued to be an object of study, but has tended to be treated as a linguistic and a logical, rather than as a cognitive, phenomenon; it is widely supposed that it has to do with the meaningfulness of linguistic communications and the nature of explanations rather than with cognition of the world.

In my view, the study of the human cognitive functions may not be identified with the study of perception. Nevertheless, in this work, arbitrary and pragmatic considerations persuade me to confine myself to perception, even if it is not an exclusively human mental function, but one that we share with infrahuman animal life. Nevertheless, it is a peculiarity of human perception that normally it is conscious. But the specifically human form of cognition begins rather with speech and thought, and culminates in understanding. However, practicality dictates that in this respect we should follow Ockham: we shall not venture into matters *praeter necessitatem*, but shall confine ourselves to perception.

Finally, the order in which we shall review the concepts of cognition, reality, and causality is dictated by the importance of counteracting the prejudicial effect of first impressions. As I have argued, there is some reason to think that the most primitive and fundamental conscious experience does not generate first of all the concept of the *causation* of effects; it embodies rather our perception of the mutual relationship of *cognition* and *reality*. Disregarding this, however, we shall attempt to revise the initial assumptions of philosophy considering in the first instance the concept of *causality*. There is a reason why this procedure is advisable: that our long philosophical tradition has been indelibly branded by our somewhat confused awareness of our own causal agency in procuring our own cognition and by the consequent projection of our causation of our own experience onto objects. We misconceive causality. It follows that if we do not correct our prejudicial assumptions regarding causality *before* we attempt to determine the nature of cognition, we will find it particularly difficult to entertain the possibility that objects are *not* the cause of cognition. Understanding the nature of causality will help us, on the contrary, to achieve an empirically-supported interpretation of the reason why objects cannot cause cognition, but that cognitively-endowed organisms can.

Of course, even if the weight of centuries has converted the initial assumptions inherited by modern philosophy from Greek and mediaeval thought into deeply embedded prejudices, we are not completely at the mercy of the past. To meet objections raised by prejudice, I resort to the procedure of reconstructing, so far as I am able, the mental processes that produced the inadequate observations perpetuated by the language of the traditional initial assumptions, and contrast them with the observations we can make once we are free from the prejudicial habit of allowing what we customarily *say* to place constraints upon what we, upon reflection, *think*.

2. *The nature of causality*

Be they great or small, minds tend to think alike if they start from the same premises. The traditional assumptions of philosophy having been preserved in modern philosophy, together with the philosophical use of the common sense equivalent of Aquinas's doctrine of the distinction between the characteristics and the autonomous existence of real things, it is not strange that what Nicholas of Autrecourt said at the Sorbonne in the fourteenth century should have been independently rediscovered by David Hume in the eighteenth at — of all places — La Flèche (where Hume wrote most of his *Treatise)*. But it may be a sign of the humanistic direction in which Aquinas's teaching regarding existence biased our culture, that whereas Nicholas perished at the stake for heresy, Hume was only emotionally dispirited when, as he said in his *Autobiography*, his brainchild, the *Treatise of Human Nature,* fell 'dead-born from the press.'[245] What is interesting is that, for all their similarities, their work had very different historical consequences. Both philosophers brought home unwelcome news. One was believed, and for all practical purposes mediaeval philosophy ended. The other was disregarded, and modern philosophy was reprieved.

---

245   Quoted by W.T. Jones, *A History of Western Philosophy* (New York: Harcourt, Brace, 1952), 764,

Hume described causality as 'the cement of the universe.'[246] He was unable, however, to explain precisely how the cement held the bricks together - not because it cannot be explained, but because it can be explained only if we first discard the false assumptions that impede our way.

a) Hume's critique of causality

Few human beings, mostly those of a very tender age, fail to become aware from their own experience that there is a difference between a causal sequence or a coincidence of events, and a non-causal, merely coincidental, sequence of either antecedent and consequent, or coincident, events. For instance, everyone has experienced the difference between, say, one's clapping one's hands to kill a mosquito, and clapping one's hands to kill a mosquito at the same time that the light goes off by reason of a power failure that is causally unrelated to one's action. In the latter case, one may wonder for an instant, but one has enough knowledge about the way in which light bulbs operate to quickly realize that one's actions did not cause the light's going off. It is therefore beyond dispute that, in the absence of any indication of causation besides a sequence of events, it is fallacious to reason *post hoc, ergo propter hoc.* Causality imports *something else* besides a sequence or coincidence of events.

But exactly what? The immemorial tradition of our culture and of philosophy has always iden-tified the difference as some sort of compulsion or force that overcomes a contrary, resisting force: a cause is not a cause unless it *necessitates* the effect. For causes are, supposedly, not only responsible for causing their effects. Causes, when they are actually and truly such, achieve their effect infallibly; when the cause is unleashed, the effect cannot not take place. Conversely, if an effect does not take place, a putative cause was not truly a cause. Causation is thus synonymous with the exercise of over-whelming power; it is the wielding of a force that conquers a lesser force and forecloses the possibility of successful resistance. I mention in passing that anyone who should so conceive causality is likely to assume that the course of world events is determined by the balance of power among its constituent members. Indeed, such view of the world will seem 'natural' and obvious, and one will be tempted at least to respect, if not also to cultivate and worship, the strongest possible Power.

---

246   David Hume, *An Abstract of A Treatise of Human Nature,* (Hamden, CT: Archon, 1965), 32.

In order to make sense, this idea of causality has relied on a further presupposition regarding the source of infallible and unimpeachable causal power. In Greece, the concept was originally kept afloat by the culture's religious belief in Fate, and then by philosophy's relocation of the necessitating power of Fate to the *physis* or *natura* that structured things from within. Christianity did not revoke the Greek relocation of necessity, but with the help of Plato and neo-Platonism (and in the middle ages, Aristotle) added complexities to the system: it assumed the division of reality into our world 'here below,' namely, the 'natural world,' and the world-above-the-world, or the 'supernatural order.' The ultimate source of all causality was the omnipotence of the divine, and alone truly and unqualifiedly real, reality. Worldly causes operated only *deo volente,* with the consent of God.

The advent of modern science modified the Christian causal scheme, but left its heart intact. Nothing in the nature of science was generally held by its founders to require the rejection of the supernatural order; bracketing it was enough. Individuals remained free to compartmentalize their minds into religious and rational hemispheres if they so chose. Scientifically speaking, therefore, it sufficed to suppose, with the later Greek philosophers, that infallible natural causal power was vested in the 'laws of nature.' The question whether such 'laws' required a legislator was, supposedly, a religious rather than a scientific question, and was therefore outside the purview of science. Thus, the supposition that causal sequences were distinguishable from non-causal sequences by the infallibility of the production of effects by their causes remained in force. Hence the scientific assumption of determinism, which later was to foment conflict with Christian advocates of human free will, but which originally (as we noted in the last chapter) had been promoted by the scientists, though motivated by their Christian faith.

This was still the scene in which, one hundred years after Descartes, a philosopher made his debut who, unlike most of his Greek and Christian predecessors, professed not to accept the philosophical validity of extra-empirical evidence, and who did not reserve part of his mind for the use of faith. When Hume applied his talents to the subject of causality, he noted — correctly, thereby rediscovering independently Ockham's insight — that the effects of causes cannot be deduced or predicted strictly by observing their putative causes, or the putative causes by observing its presumed effects. For example, it is a reasonable estimate that when Adam first dipped his toe in the Euphrates, he could not have known that he could have drowned in it; and when he first heard thunder and saw lightning he would have been quite unaware of its cause. We cannot know which effects follow from which causes unless by observing the effects that have actually followed from the causes. And likewise with causes: only experience reveals whether they are such. In other words, we observe causal relationships only as a matter of *fact*. All this seems true to me, and I will take it for granted as I proceed.

But from these observations Hume drew the conclusion that the concept of causation was 'absolutely without any meaning, when employed either in philosophical reasonings or common life.'[247] This referred, of course, to 'causation' as it had always been understood by both philosophy and the culture's common sense. The reason advanced by Hume was that experience disconfirms such idea of causation: '[w]hen we look about us towards external objects … we are never able … to discover any power or necessary connection.'[248] Experience shows sequences of events, but not the bond of necessity that was generally deemed to differentiate between mere sequences and causal sequences of events. Hume then turned his attention to whether the concept of causality might 'be derived from reflection on the operations our minds.'[249] His finding was negative. Since we are conscious, he said, we do know by experience the influence that, for instance, an act of volition has upon the motion in our limbs; but such influence is not foreseeable 'from any apparent energy or power in the cause, which connects it with the effect, and renders the one an infallible consequence of the other.'[250]

We need not analyse the error of Hume's reasoning in much detail. He seems to have thought that his conclusion was supported by the empirical evidence; for it is indeed true that nothing in our experience shows the necessary connection he demanded. His conclusion is nonetheless false, because it is applicable only to a conception of causation that is lacking in empirical support. Once again, as in the case of representationism, he mistook formal validity for material truth.

It is possible to understand causality as a *real* relationship — a true *cause-effect* bond, as contrasted with a mere sequence, conjunction, or coincidence of otherwise unrelated events — without

---

247 Hume, *Enquiry,* VII, 2.

248 Hume, *Enquiry,* VII, 1.

249 Hume, *Enquiry,* VII, 1.

250 Hume, *Enquiry,* VII, 1.

imperilling thereby any of the observable facts. What we have to do in order to understand the nature of causality, however, is to tailor our concept of causality to the measure of what we actually observe in the world. When I crush mosquitos with the palm of my hand, I have empirical evidence that I am the cause of their death; and when I flick the light switch I experience my responsibility for its having been turned on or off. Experience should then begin to teach me what 'causation' means. What Hume did was the opposite; he insisted that causation demands necessitation. Therefore, since experience does not reveal necessitation, it does not reveal causation. Hume's 'empiricism' measured the observable facts by his prior assumptions regarding the nature of causality.

The tangle of truth and falsity is not difficult to unravel. It is indeed true, as Hume alleged, that we do not observe the *infallible* energy or power of our will — or more precisely, of ourselves, our body, our organism. For the effectiveness of one's decision to move one's limbs can be easily rendered impotent by anyone whose causality is more effective than one's. Even mosquitos, which are not generally speaking very powerful, nevertheless often defeat the death-dealing causal efforts of human beings. Dismissing the observable facts, Hume concluded that our decisions yield only 'that vulgar, inaccurate idea'[251] of causality that omits the element of necessitation without which there is no true causation. Vulgar, yes, but why inaccurate? It seems that, for all his empiricism, Hume could upon occasion allow *a priori* argumentation to defeat experience. He chose to place *faith* in the philosophical tradition. His capacity for self-directedness was exceptional in many respects, but seems to have failed him at a certain points.

Subsequently Hume considered in some detail the further possibility that the concept of causality might originate not in the mind's ability to cause bodily effects, but in its ability to create and manipulate its ideas. But the result to which he arrived was the same: the 'command of the mind over itself is limited, as well as the command over the body.'[252] We observe antecedents and consequences, but not the *infallibly* effective 'power or force' whereby they are necessarily connected. Clearly, the ruling premise of Hume was the traditional assumption that causation demands necessitation. The source of his error was his unwillingness to give it up even when the empirical evidence

---

251 Hume, *Enquiry*, VII, 1, footnote.

252 Hume, *Enquiry*, VII.

indicated it was false. It was the same stubborn unwillingness that had won the day in the case of representationism.

The evidence indicates it clearly, I have said, because Hume himself notes that 'the command' we have over our mental and bodily functions 'is limited' — not that it is illusory. That one truly decides to move one's limbs is an observable reality, and so is the motion of one's limbs which is the effect. Nor is it an illusion that the limb's motion *owes* its reality to the reality of one's decision to move them. There is true causal relationship between the effect and the cause, albeit not an infallible one. Thus, the more reasonable conclusion should have been that our 'command' over ourselves and other human beings and other animate and inanimate members of the world is finite and defeasible, but real.

Awareness of ourselves and our activities, and of what happens to us in consequence of the causality exercised by others, teaches us the difference that separates the sequence of events 'A-B,' where something happens *because* we made it happen, from the sequence 'X-Y,' where something happens to us or to something or someone else but we did not make happen. How does it so teach us? Well, in situation 'A-B' we *do* experience a causal relationship when we hold together in our conscious experience (a) awareness of our intending that an effect happen, (b) awareness of the effect that actually takes place, and (c) awareness of the identity between what we intended and what we achieved. The first two items indicate nothing but antecedence and consequence; true causation is experienced by virtue of the third, the identity, within our conscious experience of ourselves, of our striving and our success. This is absent in siuation 'X-Y.'

Such identity is experienced, not guessed at or postulated; experiencing it makes evident to us both *our responsibility* for the effect we experienced, and the *corresponding dependence* of the experienced effect on our decision to cause it. That responsibility is another name for the *cause-effect relationship.* In situation 'X-Y' we experience the sequence of events, but there is no experience of our having done anything to bring about the effect. We may or may not know the cause, but we know that at any rate *we* were not the cause. To discover the cause — which we may or may not be able to do we depend ultimately on inductive inference, though deductive inference may be possible once we have amassed enough knowledge about other causal processes in the world. Thus, contrary to what

Hume thought, conscious awareness of our causal powers generates universally in human beings the concept of causality. What the awareness of the cause-effect relationship does *not* yield is that effects must follow necessarily from the activation of causes.

To reject the assumption that true causation demands necessitation is merely to have escaped the straitjacket of the concept of causality that began with Greek religion and its belief in the determinism of Fate; it is *not* to have explained anything about the nature of causality; it is not even to have established all that the explanation of causality must explain, but only part of it. Perhaps the most obtrusive of all the other facts about causality that have to be explained is the observable *invariability* of certain, but not all, cause-effect sequences. In processes that involve none but *inanimate causal agents,* effects take place invariably — although even in their case, not necessarily. But Hume persisted in identifying invariability and necessitation. Why?

He may have been influenced by more than one factor,[253] but a likely one, in addition to the prejudice already noted, was that when Hume's *Treatise* first appeared, eighty years after Newton's *Principia* had launched the dazzling career of mature modern science, reductionism had already reared its oversimple head. It is possible that Hume assumed that the causality of truly causal processes in the world *at all levels* was reducible to the minimal form of causality that takes place at the lowest. I think, on the contrary, that what follows from the rejection of necessitation is not the rejection of objectively real causality, but acceptance of a non-reductionistic concept of it. However, Hume cannot be blamed for having been born long before Darwin enabled us to reckon with a world that not merely *changes* but which *evolves:* he could not very well have perceived that, in an *emergent* world, causality must be understood to have multiple dimensions. The emergence of material, worldly entities that are subject to biological evolution is the reason why the world cannot be aptly described by reducing all entities to inanimate matter, though they all are material or worldly; it is for the same reason that the operation of the world cannot be described as if there were no differences among the causal processes of the various levels attained by matter as it evolves.

---

253   It is conceivable (though I think unlikely) that he may have been influenced by the supposition that our experience of our mental functions is 'subjective' and therefore negligible. Awareness of our mental functions delivers only the 'appearance' rather than the reality of causality.

An empirically based, post-Humean interpretation of causality would therefore have to give serious consideration to the thought that, if we suppose that life somehow came out of non-living matter, and sentience and consciousness out of life, corresponding emergent levels of causality must be recognized. No causation involves necessitation, but all causes at all levels of causality share the basic element that makes causation objectively real, namely, (a) that the cause is related to the effect as that which *produces* — rather than merely takes precedence over — the latter, and (b) that the latter is related to the cause as that which is produced by the cause. But causes produce their effects in increasingly complex ways as we ascend the scale of evolution. In other words, causality *evolved* as life, and then sentience, appeared.

That causality evolved will seem an unlikely notion to anyone who takes causality for an abstract natural process or 'law of nature' that exists and operates independently of the causality of actually existing entities. But again, I suggest that 'natural laws' make sense only if one further supposes that there is a cosmic legislator who is responsible for enacting them. Apart from that, the only remaining reason to suppose them is not exactly solid: that the Stoics made the concept available, and that Galileo and the early scientists accepted it in order to avoid entanglement in issues they felt unable to cope with. For as Burtt said, with reference to the early scientists, '[m]etaphysics they tended more and more to avoid, so far as they could avoid it;'[254] they were interested in observable facts rather than in philosophical explanations But if we cut the concept of causality to fit the size of our observations, we may agree that causation is not vested in Platonic 'laws of nature' Causation exists only in existing beings and their relationships; things have properties that are causal. But as the universe evolved and life appeared, matter developed new causal properties; and as life continued to evolve, its properties, including their ability to cause effects, continued to evolve. But what did it evolve into?

Let us return to Hume and his treatment of causal agency and 'power or force' as equivalent concepts. The equivalence is questionable. It obscures an important observable fact, namely, that there is a difference between our *ability* to cause effects — that is, our *power* to cause — and our *actual* causation. Every one of us can verify from personal experience that our desiring an effect does

---

254   Edwin A. Burtt, *The Metaphysical Foundations of Modern Physical Science* (Garden City, N.J.: Doubleday, 1954), 306. (Italics throughout in the original.)

not, of itself, suffice to cause the effect; our causal power has to be wielded before it can actually have any effects; conversely, power and force cannot be exercised without their being *activated*. Of course, words mean only what we make them mean: if one wanted to use 'power' and 'force' as a synonym of 'cause,' one could — but in that case one would have to invent a new word for 'cause,' a word that should allow one to take into account that causality can be dormant, as it were, as well as actively at work. Such difference had been implicit in the traditional, ordinary use of the concept of 'power' *(dynamis, potentia)* since the time of Aristotle, who contrasted the 'potential' with the 'actual.' Thus, contrary to Hume, not only must we distinguish between real causation and causal necessitation, but also between causation, on the one hand, and the exertion of 'power' or the use of 'force,' on the other. Some levels of causation involve the exertion of 'power' or the use of 'force,' but not all do.

The difference is important, because it calls attention to an aspect of causality that Hume seems to have ignored. He treated causality as if it were not only of universal application to all processes in the world, which indeed it is, *mutatis mutandis,* but also as if it were *uniform* throughout the entire range of world events. However, if 'power' signifies *potential,* not *actual* causation, then 'power' and 'force' can be found only in agents that are capable of *initiating* activity and *refraining* from initiating it. In other words, the exercise of power and force implies the ability to turn causation on and off. Causal power is, therefore, proper to living organisms only; it is the kind of causation that belongs to entities that are endowed, if not always with a will or a like mental capacity of their organisms for *controlling* activity on the basis of experience, at least with vegetative, automatically regulated, vital functions and activities. There is no doubt that billiard balls can cause effects on each other, but their causality is not the kind that can be turned on and off: it is always on, always ready to bring about their effects automatically as soon as the possibility arises for one to impinge on another. If it is true that 'powers' are properly distinguished from 'acts,' the causality exerted by billiard balls is properly so called, but it is not vested in *powers.*

It would not be objectionable if we attributed power to the causality of non-living entities in a purely metaphorical way; but ordinarily we suppose it literally, and we should ask ourselves why our tradition has done so. The reason, according to those who adhere to the so-called Sapir-Whorf hypothesis,[255] is that we have an inner inclination — if not indeed a compulsion — to do so, because the grammatical properties of the language we use to speak give certain characteristics or 'form' to what we say; they 'shape' it. We use an Indo-European language, and it is a grammatical property of the languages of this family that attributions to subjects are made as if the attribute were the result of the subjects' performance of an action. Thus, in these languages all predicates are verbs — that is, words signifying actions — that are conjugated with the subjects who perform the action; and all subjects are subjects of conjugated verbs. (Even 'to be' is what 'beings' *do).* Now, to discuss at this juncture the role of language in the preservation of cultural assumptions would be an impermissibly large digression; but I will mention briefly that in my view the truth is more complex than Sapir-Whorf supposes. The matter is relevant not only to the case of causality, but also to various other instances previously mentioned where I pointed out how sometimes our speech contains misleading implications regarding the objects of speech.

I point out that verbal predication is not a linguistic universal. Transformational grammarians, cognitivists, and other followers of Noam Chomsky suppose that it is;[256] but other linguists agree that the Indo-European languages are unusual (though not absolutely unique), since the way in which Indo-European speakers make attributions is different from the way in which attributions are made in most other linguistic families. In the latter, predicates are cast in the grammatical form of verbs only when they attribute actions that the subjects actually perform; otherwise the predicates function grammatically as nouns and adjectives. The compulsion of Indo-European speakers to project activity onto all objects is manifested by their use of the verb 'to be' even when no activity is involved.

---

255   The gist of the Sapir-Whorf hypothesis is that 'the background linguistic system (in other words, the grammar) of each language is not merely a reproducing instrument for voicing ideas but rather is itself the shaper of ideas… [Therefore,] all observers are not led by the same physical evidence to the same picture of the universe, unless their linguistic backgrounds are similar, or can be in some way calibrated,' Benjamin L. Whorf, *Language, Thought and Reality: Selected Writings* (Cambridge, MA: MIT Press, 1956), 212, 214. At the turn of the century Friedrich Nietzsche had advanced somewhat the same possibility in his *Beyond Good and Evil: Prelude to a Philosophy of the Future* (Cambridge: Cambridge University Press, 2002), Aphorism 20; but Nietzsche did not attempt to develop or to substantiate this view.

256   They reason *a priori* and ethnocentrically. From the fact that our languages use verbal predication, they suppose that all do.. When it is pointed out to them that verbal predication is absent from the majority of languages, they dismiss it with the assertion that it is implicit in the 'deep structure' of the language, although the only reason for so supposing is the assumption that verbal predication is a linguistic universal.

And yet, the use of the 'verb " to be" … is almost confined to Indo-European languages.'[257] Most other linguistic families lack a verb discharging the function that 'to be' satisfies among the Indo-European, namely, to ensure that all predication assimilates the relationship of the predicate to the subject as an activity performed by the subject. And activities result from the exercise of powers, since they can be turned on and off.

My supposition is therefore more complex, and in part is the opposite of, the Sapir-Whorf hypothesis. If the perception of the members of certain early human communities as they were developing speech should have been defective (for instance, because they projected human characteristics such as active causality onto inanimate objects), their defective perception would have been enshrined in the anthropomorphic assumption that, even in the case of inanimate subjects, predicates should be attributed to subjects as what the subjects *do.* Thereafter, every new generation having learned to speak using the community's language, would have had no option but to predicate actions, and nothing but actions, in relation to subjects. This is the position in which we, Indo-European speakers, exist today. If this is true, the characteristics of languages do not inhere in the language itself, but depend on the mental processes of speakers through which they learn to speak. The constraint supposed by Sapir-Whorf does not originate in the properties of speech, but in the misperception of the world that in the course of human evolution entered into the creation of certain specific languages whose syntactic properties follow from faulty observation of the world.[258] The misperception generated languages that enshrine an inadequate observation of the world.

The point is that we can be enslaved by our language only as long as we allow it to do so; awareness of the nature of the mental activity of 'speaking' may liberate us from bondage to the implications of our idea of how we relate ourselves to the world when we speak of it. If we speak thoughtfully enough, we may observe that inanimate nature is not active: indeed, its distinctive feature is its inactivity. The very word we use to refer to it indicates that its peculiarity is that it *does not perform* any

257   Angus C. Graham, '"Being" in Linguistics and Philosophy: a Preliminary Inquiry,' Foundations of Language, 1 (1965), 223-31, p. 223; see also Ernst Locker, 'Etre et Avoir: leurs expressions dans les langues,' Anthropos, 49 (1954), 481-510.

258   In *Evolution and Consciousness: The Role of Speech in the Origin and Development of Human Nature* (Toronto: University of Toronto Press, 1989), I discuss the peculiarities of the Indo-European languages and their differences from the languages of most other linguistic families.

activities: it is non-animate. And experience confirms it. For example, there is no question but that the earth moves, but what does a planet have to *do* to swing in orbit or to rotate on its axis? What power does a river activate when it turns a turbine, which it deactivates at other times? Nothing in the world stays the same, but this hardly means that everything in the world is always *acting*. 'Becoming' and 'changing' should not be confused with 'doing.'

Thus, if we do not project onto inanimate nature the sort of causality that we derive from observing our own activities and the changes that follow from them, we shall experience no compulsion to suppose that causes are necessarily active or that they necessarily involve the exertion of power. We may interpret the causation of events by inanimate entities as their bringing about change *without acting* in any but a figurative way; inanimate entities cause their effects simply by being themselves. And since they are themselves continuously, the world is in a constant state of becoming. This, too, is among the considerations that define the *explicandum;* it is part of what an explanation of the nature of causality must actually explain.

Another implication of the difference between power and causation is relevant not only to the causation of worldly events by worldly causes, but also to the wider topic of the nature of the world. If power is a capacity for actively causing effects, then causal power is necessarily finite; the concept of causal omnipotence is self-contradictory. We human beings can be said to have power because we can activate a *capacity* for causing effects that otherwise remains latent. Unless we activate it, we bring about no effects. But power cannot be infinite, because if it were it would not *bring about* effects: the effects would be coextensive with the cause. And if so, there would be no change — and therefore no causes of it. An omnipotent cause would have nothing to *do*. It would be at best an indolent omnipotence — which is to say, a self-contradiction.

And yet, some scientific cosmologists propose that some real and material worldly entities — not purely ideal mathematical entities, but actual *physical*, bodily entities — can have truly *infinite* physical power.[259] But if infinite *divine* power is at least somewhat problematic, as Aquinas realized

---

259   For instance, according to Stephen W. Hawking, at the time of "the big bang the density of the universe and the curvature of space-time would have been infinite … and the universe is thought to have been infinitely hot," *A Brief History of Time: From the Big Bang to Black Holes* (Toronto: Bantam, 1988), 117. In this case infinity does not seem to be simply a mathematical abstraction; it is attributed to the world as a real characteristic of it. But experience suggests that the world and everything

when he inquired into the nature of God's omnipotence,[260] infinite *physical* power should be rather more so. Omnipotence is rather the imaginary negation of power as we actually experience it in ourselves, that is, as inherently finite. The mental process that issues in the concept of omnipotence is the same as that by means of which we confect the concepts of 'immateriality,' and 'other worldliness.' Without much difficulty — simply by manipulating mentally our empiri-cally-derived concept of 'power' — we can conceive a causal agent that does not need to act in order to cause and who does not even have to wish in order to command; for one can wish only for what one lacks. An omnipotent Power would be an agent that had already achieved, from all eternity, and merely by existing eternally, everything that can be achieved. But such omnipotent agent could not cause a world that was distinct from it, a world that had come into being, a world that existed in time and changed, and least of all a world that should be *truly real,* yet not-God. Of course, if the world is only quasi-real, this problem would disappear. But in its place would arise the stultifying problem of how to make sense of a real world that was not really real.

Laplacian mechanism has been deemed by some scholars a plausible interpretation; the world is ruled by the resultant of deterministic forces that inflexibly bring about their effect. Before one accepts this possibility one should consider at least one of its implications: namely, that a deterministic world proceeds, however automatically or mechanically, towards a specific end. For a world that proceeds so as to bring about predetermined effects would be a world that unfolds according to a pre-established sequence of events: causation would be the unfolding of a *plan*. But planning requires a mind. To say that no Mind plans the plan that realizes its predetermined results would add obscurity to what was already obscure. The notion of a providential divine plan seems to me inconsistent with what we know about the world, but it makes, in my opinion, somewhat more sense than a plan that no one has planned.

---

within it is finite. The contrary assumption may not blandly be assumed without so much as an attempt at explanation and justification. It is no less objectionable than appealing to miracles or to divine intervention.

260   Thomas Aquinas, prompted by some of the same considerations I have alleged, raised the question whether it should not be *denied* that power was among the attributes of God; see his *De Potentia Dei*, I,1. He concluded that God did have infinite power, which is not especially surprising. But to conclude as he did he had to make a number of questionable distinctions *ad hoc,* including one between 'acting' and 'operating;' it seems that God did the one, but not the other. In my view the distinction is meaningless; but in any event, it is clear that Aquinas did not think that the omnipotence of God was as obvious and unproblematic as it is generally assumed to be.

Let us recapitulate. The foregoing analysis supports certain negative conclusions. An empirically grounded understanding of causality would have to *reject* all of the following positions:

- *That* causes necessitate their effects,

- *That* the concept of cause is not derived from our experience of our own causation of effects,

- *That* causality is a universally uniform relationship between causes and effects,

- *That* all causation involves the exertion of power or the use of force,

- *That* all causes produce invariable and predictably regular effects,

- *That* the causation of effects by inanimate entities is the paradigm to which all causation is reducible and

- *That* such causation depends on the power exerted by natural forces that act upon inanimate entities from without.

We are now ready to try to determine positively the nature of causality.

b) The relativity of causality

The conviction of nineteenth century positivism that science should rid itself of whatever religious and metaphysical assumptions it may have carried from its past, was the origin of 'the modern trend toward eliminating the concept of force from the conceptual scheme of physical science.'[261] 'Trend,' however, may not describe well the project of eliminating the concept of force; 'ideal' would be more accurate, since this objective has been achieved by theoretical physics, so far, only in the case of gravitational phenomena.

---

261   Max Jammer, *Concepts of Force: A Study in the Foundations of Dynamics* (New York: Harper, 1962), viii.

A few years after Albert Einstein proposed his General Theory of Relativity and its explanation of gravitation, Bertrand Russell took it as evidence of the existence of the kind of natural causal process involving physical entities that did not involve force or necessitation. Russell continued to assume, however, that the causality involved in physical changes was the paradigm of all causality. In a work popularizing Einstein's theory, he devoted a chapter to 'The Abolition of "Force"'. It was a historic event, he thought, when Einstein proposed that:

> Causation, in the old sense, no longer has a place in theoretical physics. There is, of course, something else which takes its place, but the substitute appears to have a better empirical foundation than the old principle which it has superseded.[262]

Russell seems to have assumed that the concept of causation without force should be deemed to have general application, and not restricted to the inanimate world:

> If people were to learn to conceive the world in the new way, without the old notion of "force," it would alter not only their physical imagination, but probably also their morals and their politics.[263]

However, the universal applicability of the concept should not be confused with the uniformity of its applicability; Russell seems to have identified the two. On the other hand, his estimate of the scope of the concept of causality, I think, was not exaggerated. (But I would have insisted on adding philosophy to the list.) General relativity, however, was not of itself a contribution to philosophy. It is doubtful whether Einstein estimated that his theory made use of a new concept of causality, since he continued to profess his faith in determinism to the end of his life. But what he did propose was relevant to philosophy. A comparison of the type of explanation given by Newton of the phenomenon we still call 'gravitation' with that given by Einstein should explain Russell's enthusiasm.

---

262   Bertrand Russell, *The ABC of Relativity* (London: Kegan Paul, Trench, Trubner, 1925), 225.

263   Russell, *ABC,* 196.

Newton assumed that material particles move along 'natural' paths. For Newton, however, the natural path of bodies in motion was an inertial one; it was the straight-line path described by bodies in undisturbed, natural motion in Euclidean, common sense, absolute space. The 'force' of gravitation — no longer, as with Aristotle, a property of matter, but an external agency that acted on matter from without — was invoked by Newton to account for deviations from the natural inertial path. Heaping fantasy thus on top of fantasy, a force was gratuitously imagined by him in order to account for an event (namely, the deviation of a body in motion from its natural inertial path) that had been gratuitously imagined by him to have consisted in the force's compelling the body to undergo a change that, left to its own devices, the body would not have undergone. The underlying premise was of course, that causes compel their effects: gravitation makes bodies do what they would not do of their own accord. And so, as a contemporary scientist has aptly said, in Newton's theory of gravitation 'the acceleration of an object … may be regarded as a miracle,'[264] an intervention into the mechanics of the universe from somewhere outside the universe. And indeed, Newton himself hinted as much:

> It is inconceivable, that inanimate … matter, should, without the mediation
> of something else, which is not material, operate upon and affect other matter
> without mutual contact, as it must be, if gravitation … be essential and inher-
> ent in it … Gravity must be caused by an agent … but whether this agent be
> material or immaterial, I have left to the consideration of my readers.[265]

For behind Newton's science there was the *sotto voce* assumption that nature reflected the supernatural order. The separation of science and religion does not always mean the liberation of science from religious prejudice; sometimes it is rather the screen behind which originally religious

---

264 Jammer, *Concepts of Force*, 258. It might be objected against Jammer that a miracle is the supposed intervention of God outside, or contrary to, the otherwise invariable course of natural events; and that therefore acceleration is in no way a miracle, since it happens normally and invariably. However, the point is rather that Newton's explanation involves the self-contradiction of a supposedly natural force that acts contrary to nature, and ascribes to the world capabilities that are otherwise said to define the nature of God. It is an instance of how the attempt of science to manage without God, while retaining the premises that produce the concept of God, leads to the divinization of the world.

265 *Letter III to Richard Bentley*, quoted by Jammer, *Concepts of Force*, 139.

assumptions that eventually become scientific prejudices can be made invisible to one-self. On the other hand, for Einstein, too, there was a natural path along which bodies move, but:

> [T]he 'natural path' … [is] a geodesic[266] … [in] a non-Euclidean space-time of variable curvature … Only in the absence of … matter does … space-time become Euclidean and geodetic lines degenerate into the straight lines of Euclidean geometry. Thus, gravitation in general relativity has not the character of a force. It is a *property* of space-time. Mechanical events are thus accounted for by purely geometrico-kinematic conceptions.[267]

In this scheme, force does not have to be supposed, because the motion of bodies is always 'natural;' it is never compelled to be different from what it spontaneously is. Gravitational phenomena are nevertheless accounted for, but the explanation 'lies now in the *functional relation* between the space-time structure and the mass-energy distribution.'[268] In other words, it lies in the way in which material entities function, in accordance with their spatio-temporal relations and their relative properties. Thus, Einstein, whose preoccupation with Hume's philosophy is not likely to have been habitual, or deep, may or may not have realized it, but in point of fact he implicitly distinguished between true causation and causal necessitation or force.

This was what Russell perceived and found significant — as indeed it was — although it was overoptimistic of him to have imagined that science would thenceforth dispense with the 'old' and 'superseded' idea of causality. For more than a century the General Theory of Relativity has remained an anomaly that cannot be integrated into the general corpus of physics or reconciled with quantum

---

266   A geodesic, or a geodetic line, is the shortest possible line between two points on a curved surface; for example, the shortest path that an aircraft can take to fly from one point on the surface of the earth to another is of course not a straight line in Euclidean space, which would go through the earth, but a geodesic line along the surface of the earth, which would be a curved line.

267   Jammer, *Concepts of Force*, 260. (Italics mine.) The expression 'a non-Euclidean space-time of variable curvature' conjures the image of a flexible, substantive, bodily entity called 'space-time' There is, of course, no such entity, although 'space-time' is real, not a mathematical or other abstraction. But its reality is that of the real (but variable) spatio-temporal relationships among material entities.

268   Jammer, *Concepts of Force*, 261.

mechanics. These continue to depend on the concept of force, either in its unadulterated Newtonian sense, or in the form of the necessitation produced by the 'interaction' of bodies.

It is not my suggestion that philosophy should accept from theoretical physics that causation need not involve necessitation or force; the fact is philosophically ascertainable, as previously noted. My point is rather that Einstein's example might inspire philosophy to try to determine the nature of causality, as Einstein did, in terms of the relational properties of things. For motion is not the only characteristic of real entities of which it must be said that it is relative to the characteristics of other entities, rather than their absolute possession. Much the same may be said of all the other characteristics of all entities in the world.

Contrary to the monadic interpretation supposed by the philosophical tradition that reached its culmination in Leibniz' thought, reality is a real characteristic of real entities — but it is not a characteristic that they have independently of other entities and which isolates one from another. Nothing in our experience indicates that it should be. On the contrary, to identify, for example, the chemical properties of a given substance we test its interrelations with other substances; to identify those of organisms we observe how they relate themselves adjustively to their environment. But perhaps the clearest example is cognition. Cognition is not found in a human being as its absolute possession of a function which it might exercise independently of the world; cognition exists only in relation to objects of cognition. If reference to objects of cognition were taken away, cognition would be inconceivable; it would be an absurdity, much like taking nourishment without reference to food, or breathing without reference to our atmosphere. To be sure, a thing affects other things by virtue of *its* being such as it is; it acts upon others as it does because of characteristics that belong to *it*. In other words, its characteristics are truly real. But we can say that it is such as it is, and that it is real, only because its properties are relative to the properties of other things.

The causal relationship among things is, accordingly, the obverse of their reality. Just as the other properties of things are intelligible only by reference to the properties of other things, their ability to cause effects is intelligible only by reference to the differences that they make to each other. Let us argue *per impossibile:* if a thing were totally unrelated to all other things in the world, we would have no warrant for calling it real or for supposing that it could have any effects on anything else in the world. But among the differences that manifest the relativity of the characteristics of things are to be included the differences that one characteristic of a thing can make to other characteristics of the same thing. For things can act causally upon themselves as well as upon each other; that is, things can make a difference to themselves by virtue of the mutual relativity of their properties. At all levels of causality, causal processes are intelligible only by reference to the differences that things are apt to make to each other and upon themselves because each one is as it is.

Thus, effects are never caused at random or capriciously at any level of causation. If sodium and chlorine come into each other's presence under the appropriate requisite conditions — which include the spatio-temporal range of effective presence to each other that their nature defines — they will combine to make up table salt. And water will always freeze when sufficiently cooled. Genetic accidents and like circumstances aside, the interaction of the gametes of sparrows, whales, or human beings will predictably produce sparrows, whales and human beings respectively; the outcome is scarcely left to chance. Why may these *regularities* be counted upon? Not because anything preordains or necessitates the results ahead of time, or because natural forces prevail over the supposed natural inertia of things, but because of the simple *fact* expressed by the tautology that the properties of all things, both inanimate entities and living organisms, remain the same as long as they do not change. Since sodium retains the properties of sodium as long as it remains sodium, and since the properties of sodium include its capacity for interrelating with chlorine in a certain way, every time that sodium and chlorine interrelate, the same effects will follow. The constancy of the properties of the causes explains the constancy of the properties of the effects.

Accordingly, the absence of force in causal processes does not mean that conjunctions or sequences of events are inexplicable: they are explicable in principle as cause-effect processes. Causal explanations can be found by learning how the interrelations among the various characteristics of objects, whether animate or inanimate, produce the effects they do. But whereas the way in which inanimate entities interrelate is, under normal conditions, invariable, other causal processes are not reducible to those of inanimate entities, and their effects are variable: the causes *tend* to produce certain effects. The degree of tendency is itself variable. Causality, however, if understood as a relationship that accounts for the various ways in which the characteristics of things are interrelated, enables us to understand why both kinds of processes are properly described as causal, as well as why the latter are not reducible to the former.

We may further refine our understanding of the relativity of causation if we note that although Einstein's general relativity was the first, and so far the only, time when physics had emancipated itself from necessitarianism, there had been an earlier instance of the same scientific achievement, though it had taken place in biology and without much advertence on the part of scientists to its implications for their (and for philosophers') understanding of causality. I have in mind Darwin's theory of evolution by natural selection. Russell does not seem to have understood that in this respect Darwin had anticipated Einstein and had indeed provided an even more striking and useful instance of causation-without-necessitation than Einstein.

Natural selection is not often described as a causal explanation, but that is exactly what it is: natural selection is the *cause* of the emergence of new species. And natural selection works its effects without the intervention of any force. Like Einsteinian gravitation, natural selection explains the evolution of life as the regular, natural, and invariable outcome of the interrelationship among the properties of living beings. But Darwinian selection shows a more elaborate form of causality than that which takes place at the inanimate level; for it operates, of course, exclusively at the level of life.

Natural selection operates its effects solely by virtue of the interrelationship between the adjustive and the reproductive functions of organisms. These two types of biological functions are altogether different: every organism's vital functions are adjustive, but reproduction is not an adjustive function. Of itself it does not contribute to the survival of the organism that exercises it, but only to the survival and further evolution of the species. Nevertheless, the two types of functions are present in the same organism and therefore interrelate; indeed, they are able to *interact*, since the characteristics in question pertain to active organic functions. But how do they do so?

Well, if the adjustive functions of living organisms operate according to their nature and ensure the survival of the organism until it reaches reproductive age; its survival makes it possible, in turn, for the reproductive functions to discharge *their* evolutionary role. Without reproduction, the genetic advantages of the organism would not be preserved and passed on to a new generation. Thus, as some biologists have recommended, the much misunderstood traditional reference to the 'survival value' of certain characteristics — which so easily lends itself to being misconstrued as if new characteristics were selected *because* they have survival value — would be less ambiguously described as their 'reproductive advantage.' The result of the interaction is that the peculiar advantages, if any, of the adjustive functions of individuals would be enjoyed automatically by the succeeding offspring resulting from the exercise of the organism's reproductive functions.

Unlike gravitation, moreover, natural selection demonstrates that among the changes that can be caused without necessitation are to be included those differences that one characteristic of a thing can make to other characteristics of the *same* thing. Things can act causally upon themselves; that is, things can make a difference to themselves by virtue of the relationships among their properties. The causal mechanism of natural selection, moreover, operates within the relationship between the organism and the organism's 'environment.' Of course, this refers to an environment that has no more absolute, independent reality than does the 'organism.' Just as the organism's 'adaptability' is constituted by the organism's relation to its environment, the environment is constituted as environment by the relation that entities other-than the organism, and the events they cause, bear to the organism. [269]

At the level of inanimate entities, their mutual relativity makes the world a mechanically and physically — but even in their case, not deterministically — integrated, orderly, and normally inflexible unity. But the universe of causal inanimate entities is a universe that becomes. Moreover, becoming, too, becomes. The 'becoming' of inanimate matter became the 'evolution' of life. Somehow — unfortunately, we have no idea how, though wild guesses abound — living material entities emerged out of non-living matter. And when they did, so did the way in which they caused events by virtue of their new, emergent properties; the fact that they have emergent properties manifests their new form of causation. Once life arose, the outcome of many of the events that made a difference to them depended, in part, on what they *did* and not merely in what they *were*. Only in part, I say, because

---

269   The work of Timo Järvilehto on the nature of the relationship between the organism and its environment is helpful towards understanding the nature of Darwinian evolution. See his 'Theory of the Organism-environment System;' 'Part I: Description of the theory,' *Integrative Physiological and Behavioral Science,* 33 (1998): 321-324; 'Part II: Significance of nervous activity in the organism- environment system,' 33 (1998): 335-342; 'Part III: Role of efferent influences on receptors in the formation of knowledge,' 34 (1999): 90-100; 'Part IV: The problem of mental activity and consciousness,' (2000): 35-57.

of course, they did not lose their materiality. They remained subject to the same causal processes as inanimate entities were. This is why, when bodies fall to the ground after being thrown from the Leaning Tower of Pisa, the acceleration in a vacuum is the same for steel balls, heliotrope blooms, three-toed sloths, and suicidal philosophers.

The supposition of some scientists and even a few biologists that evolution involves some sort of 'enormously creative force'[270] seems to me, therefore, incorrect. Evolution is indeed creative, but it is not a force; quite the contrary, what is striking about it is that it is *not* a force. Like Einsteinian gravitation, it does not compel anything to do what it would naturally not do. Natural selection follows *effortlessly,* from the mere *fact* that the antecedents of the process are such as they are. The *factuality* of causality thus interpreted — the superfluity of finality, necessity, compulsion, and force for the purpose of understanding causality — was remarked upon by Russell (though not with reference to evolution) in a memorable phrase:

> The physical universe is orderly, not because there is a central government,
> but because every body minds its own business.[271]

The nuances of Russell's intended meaning, however, are not completely transparent to me. It is clear that he excluded the possibility that the causation of events might depend upon the policies and decisions of a transcendent Governor of the world. Did he also intend to exclude an impersonal 'government' such as the rule of abstract metaphysical 'laws of nature'? To be consistent, he should have. But in view of his life-long scientism, I would need further evidence before I concluded that he did. Some philosophers seem to think that they disbelieve in God, when in truth they disbelieve in the religious trappings in which the concept has come down to us, but have no objection to the infinite, omnipotent, and eternal power and truth that are the substance of our traditional religious belief in God.

---

270   Charles J. Lumsden and Edward O. Wilson, *Promethean Fire: Reflections on the Origin of the Mind* (Cambridge, MA: Harvard University Press, 1983), 53.

271   Russell, *ABC*, 197.

Russell's metaphor is somewhat ambiguous also insofar as it could be taken to imply that every body, at all levels of causality, fares well by going its own way without reckoning with the rest of the world. On the contrary, it seems to me that (a) since there is no government of the world from without things themselves, and (b) since no one component of the world can govern every other, the most likely possibility is that the world as a whole can be governed only by the mutual relativity of its members. My point, more exactly, is that the world is supervised neither by a *Governor* nor even by a *government* of natural laws and regulating forces that maintains order and co-operation in the rest of the world. The mutual relativity of the multiplicity of component members of the world results in the *governance* of the world as a whole by the whole of the world.

The nature of causality also explains, moreover, why no effect is absolutely predictable from its causes, although all effects are explicable, in principle, *by* their causes and as following *from* their causes. Retrospective logic does not imply prospective necessity.[272] Least reliable are those predictions that are based simply on the historical record of correlations between causes and effects; for such correlations may or may not indicate coincidences rather than truly causal processes. However, if an observer can establish that a certain sequence of events depends on the properties of the entities involved, the observer may be able to predict effects, though the prediction will be more or less reliable in accordance with the level of causality involved. Predictions of human behaviour are, of course, notoriously unreliable, notwithstanding the true causality of human decisions — though a few can be made with reasonable expectation of some accuracy, especially if they do not extend very far into the future. The reason for such unpredictability has to do with the ability of conscious agents to experience their own causal agency and thus to modify it. For this implies that the conditions under which they can exercise their causal powers are indefinitely variable.

Much more reliable would be predictions made regarding causal processes that involve less complex levels of life; but even in the case of the simplest, a margin of error can be counted upon.

---

272   For example, after the human or any other given species evolves, we can in principle explain its emergence causally; it was the logical outcome of the series of events that led to it. But before it happened, we could not have predicted its emergence — not simply for lack of knowledge of all the factors involved, but because the conditions under which natural selection operated were themselves not predetermined, since they depended on prior interrelations that could have had a multiplicity of different outcomes.

For example, many bacteria produce gyrase, an enzyme that they require to reproduce themselves. Ciprofloxacin is a synthetic compound that blocks the formation of gyrase in bacteria. When it is administered to a person infected with susceptible bacteria, a prognosis of recovery can be made that in most cases will be verified within approximately two weeks; the prediction depends on a prior determination of a causal relationship of the properties of certain entities and how they relate to each other; one therefore knows of the likelihood that the drug will interfere with the multiplication of the bacteria and thus cause the colony to die out.

But certain strains of the bacterium have greater resistance to the drug than others; they may even have *acquired* such resistance by adaptation to antibiotics such as ciprofloxacin. This may cause the drug to work more slowly, or in some cases not at all. If one knows that one is trying to cure a particularly resistant strain, one's prognosis will be modified accordingly. The prediction, however, will never be absolutely certain. Not all patients are identical, and neither are all strains or even all specimens of a bacterium: since living beings are individuals with individual origin and individual histories, differences among individuals are found in all forms of life.

Other things being equal, therefore, the more detailed one's knowledge of the causal process, the more reliable one's predictions; but the more complex the causal process and the form of life involved, the less reliable the predictions will be. However, the predictions are somewhat uncertain not only because one's knowledge of the process is often less than complete or fully accurate, but, more fundamentally, because even in the simplest cases individual differences in the characteristics of reality will be at work. It is the causal process itself that is more or less uncertain.

At the lowest rung in the causal scale — the behaviour of inanimate entities — effects are for all practical purposes as good as absolutely predictable in principle. However, even in their case the possibility of novelty cannot be absolutely excluded without transgressing the boundaries of empiricism and relapsing into *a priori* thinking. This is the conclusion we must reach if, after supposing that causation does not take place through the imposition of forces on inanimate bodies from without, but follows from the relations among the properties of things, we pay attention to a fact that stares us in the face at every moment of our lives — but which, perhaps for that very reason, we take for granted: that the universe is not homogeneous. Matter is unevenly distributed throughout the entire world. The cosmos is inwardly differentiated in every conceivable way. Everywhere we look in both the heavens and on earth, we see a multiplicity of *different* things.

In Laplacian determinism, the heterogeneity of the world can be ignored: the causation of effects is vested in natural forces that operate with unfailing regularity because they obey universally operating 'laws' that necessitate their proper effects. The universality of the 'law' suffices to account for the invariability of effects. Conversely, absence of uniformity in the constitution of the universe is irrelevant to the perfect uniformity of the natural forces and laws that, supposedly, yield absolute determinism; the mutual relationship among real beings that we call their 'reality' is irrelevant, since beings are deemed to act on each other from without. But in a universe where causation is multiform in accordance with the interrelations among the properties of things, the heterogeneity of the world means that the relations among the properties of things are subject to local and temporal variations; the environment that their mutual relativity creates for each of them is not necessarily uniform throughout the universe. And from this follows that unusual conditions — an unusual environment — under which inanimate entities interrelate can always emerge, with proportionately unusual results. Such conditions do not emerge necessarily or predictably, but they *can* in principle emerge. Perhaps the origin of life, which is hardly a quotidian occurrence in the universe could one day be understood as having taken place in accordance with the properties of inanimate reality.

For if the suggestion I have advanced is well taken, the fact that causation takes place with endless regularity in processes involving inanimate entities exclusively does not take away the possibility that there may be completely natural configurations of causal factors that at present we cannot even imagine, under which the interrelation of, say, sodium and chlorine will produce effects that have never happened before in our experience — or perhaps at all — and which therefore we have no reason to suspect. For perhaps there are conditions under which the properties of sodium and chlorine will change; and if they were to become different from what they ordinarily are, they will interrelate differently. This is the best estimate of which we are capable at present. It is only an estimate, and it may not be correct; but it is the best, because it is based exclusively on what we can observe about the way in which causality actually operates in the world. The assertion that, on the contrary, the world is a deterministic system, has no empirical support; it follows from the gratuitous and anthropomorphic assumption that causes operate by overwhelming opposition to them — that is, by necessitating their effects.

The nature of causality, if understood as I have proposed, affects philosophy's treatment of a question that did not arise in our philosophical tradition until the confluence of Greek philosophical reason and Christian faith took place, namely, what is the cause of the world's 'being there.' The first article of the Christian creed is belief in God, and the substance of the second is that God is the cause of the world. For according to Christianity the ultimate explanation of the world's causal processes is to be found in God as the anterior and external (or transcendent) cause of the world's causal processes. This explanation is questionable.[273] But, more important, the question itself is questionable, because it rests on the assumption of causality as necessitation. This is why some philosophers who do not believe that God exists persist in asking the Leibnizian question: *Why is there something rather than nothing?*[274] Popularly, the question is not usually formulated in these terms; it is framed as an inquiry regarding the cause of the existence of reality. 'Who or what made the world? Who, or what, and why, made us?' But if disbelief in the transcendent reality of God is not accompanied by disbelief in necessitarian causation, the question is unanswerable: it amounts to the so-called fallacy of 'complex question.' The question presupposes, circularly, that the world has been 'made,' and thus that its cause transcends the world.

If it is true that causality is correctly described as the multiform interrelation among the characteristics of things, then the causal explanation of the world and its events can be found within the world itself. Since everything in the world is related to everything else *inherently* — that is, simply by being itself — and since interrelation among the characteristics of things causes things to change, it follows that everything in the world is a cause of change and that the world is in a perpetual state of becoming. Its reality — its being — is its becoming. This interpretation forecloses any question about the cause of the world as a whole. It means that causality, as well as space, time, and reality, arises

---

273   It fails to take into account that there is a reason why we explain phenomena by ascertaining their causes, namely, that our mind (including its finding explanations in terms of causes) is itself the outcome of causal world processes: the human mind has evolved in and from a world that (as we can appreciate once we have come to be) changes and develops causally. Thus, our thinking in causal terms *does* have a cause that is anterior to our thinking (namely, the world's causality); but projecting this feature of our own mind onto the world results in our searching for the world's anterior cause.

274   Leibniz, *Principles of Nature and of Grace*, 7; in Wiener, *Leibniz*, 527. Italics in the original.

only within the world and by virtue of the characteristics of the world itself. Nothing we observe in the world suggests that the world must have a cause from without itself, or that there is a reality other than the mutually relative reality of the things that make up the world.

And so, the question whether God (or any impersonal and abstract equivalent thereof) exists is possible only because, once we learn to think of events and changes in the world as the effects of causes, we arbitrarily imagine a world outside the world in relation to which the world as a whole would be as an effect is to a cause. But it is only once we exist in space and time and are real — and after we become conscious of space, time, and reality — that we can arbitrarily imagine a location outside the world, a time before and after all time, and a reality other than reality, in relation to which the world would move and endure, and in relation to which the reality of the world would be real. The plain fact and the simple truth — and it is indeed simple — is that the world is real *tout court,* without more, and that temporality, spatiality, and causality are the warp and woof of the real world.

Let us sum up. The relativistic concept of causality enables us to explain: (a) how there can be real relationships between causes and effects in which the effect follow from the cause but only as a matter of *fact,* that is, without the cause's having compelled the effect; (b) why some effects are more or less variable whereas others are invariable; and (c) why predictions are, accordingly, of variable reliability but never absolutely reliable.

Causality, therefore, as it actually and observably operates in the world, works as follows:

- Real beings are constituted by certain characteristics;

- Their characteristics are self-consistent and coherent;

- The characteristics of real beings are relative to those of other real beings, as well as mutually relative within the same real being;

- When real beings interrelate (or interact, if they are capable of acting, as is the case of living beings), they are mutually affected by each other's characteristics and in proportion to them;

- The same is true of the interrelation (or interaction) of properties within the same real being;

- The causal efficacy of living beings is not reducible to the causal efficacy of non-living beings, as the former can cause not only transitive effects on others but also immanent effects on themselves, and can initiate as well as discontinue causal activity;

- Causes produce invariable effects only in the simplest cases of causality, namely, causal interrelations involving none but inanimate entities; otherwise they are defeasible in principle;

- Since the world is heterogeneous, causal regularities do not imply absolute determinism even in the case of inanimate causation, though the invariability in the latter form of causation is, for all practical purposes, equivalent to determinism.

To re-conceive causality in this manner amounts to re-conceiving the way in which the world operates. It would be an open world, a world whose possibilities are never closed. It would be a world where nothing necessitates anything — a world in which causation need not involve compulsion or the exertion of force. But withal, it would be a world where billiard balls bounce off each other and where water, as long as it remains water and nothing interferes with its normal causality (as changes in atmospheric pressure do), will always boil when it reaches a certain temperature. It would be a purely factual — that is, non-necessitated — utterly contingent world, a world that is not ruled by inherent rationality, but to which *we,* who are rational, can relate ourselves rationally and understand it just the same. More on this when we come to the nature of reality and why it can be understood, despite the fact that, contrary to our philosophical tradition, its reality is not identical with its supposedly inherent intelligibility.

The foregoing interpretation of the true nature of causality applies to all causal processes, but in this work we are especially interested in two narrow manifestations of it. First, if the foregoing interpretation is not altogether incorrect, it should have a bearing on our understanding how sentient organisms can become informed *of* objects, without being informed *by* objects. The causal relationship among objects — all of which, of course, are material and capable of physical causation — is the precondition of the cognitive activity of sentient organisms whereby the organism becomes related to such objects. Invoking thus the idea of causality proposed above, the causal explanation of the nature of experience I shall propose in the next section does *not* suppose that experience is caused by the activity of objects upon sensitive receptors. Second, the same is true of the phenomenon of consciousness: interrelation among the properties of sentient organisms can be expected to explain how consciousness is caused by organic processes in suitably equipped sentient organisms. And it should enable us to erase once for all the 'explanatory gap' between the properties of the biochemical causes of our cognitive processes, and the properties of the conscious experience that is their effect.

3. *The nature of perceptual cognition*

If we are to understand the consciousness that ordinarily characterizes the exercise of the human mental functions, the first of several pitfalls we must avoid is to suppose that consciousness is a mental function. Scant observation should suffice to verify that it is not. The evidence is that, however closely we might examine our mental functions, 'being conscious,' or 'having consciousness' is not to be found among them. 'Seeing consciously,' 'hearing consciously,' and so on, are mental activities: we *do* our 'seeing,' our 'imagining,' and our 'understanding.' But to perform these activities consciously we do not have to *do* anything besides 'seeing,' or 'hearing,' and so on. We do not *do* 'being conscious.' If one pays attention to, say, an object currently before one's eyes, and one becomes visually aware of it, one will see it consciously; seeing it in a specifically conscious way looks after itself. This is one reason why it is easy to suppose that all cognition is conscious. A second indication pointing towards the same finding — that consciousness is not a mental function — is that conscious status is common to various cognitive functions. For if it is common to several, it cannot be one of them.

On the other hand, we never 'are perceptually conscious' unless in respect of 'seeing,' or 'hearing,' or 'understanding,' or some other mental function. Consciousness is not among our mental functions, but accompanies our mental functions and activities and characterizes the mental states that result from the activation of our mental functions. Consciousness should be described, therefore, as a *quality* that modifies our cognitive activities and states; it is the quality that makes a cognitive act or state to have the features that make it, specifically, a *conscious* cognitive act or a conscious state. The fact that consciousness is not a mental function is one reason why we cannot treat the terms 'cognition' and 'conscious cognition' as if they described the same sort of activity. I underline: the quality of consciousness accrues *only* to cognitive activities, not to the 'contents' of perception that, supposedly, exist 'subjectively' or 'intentionally' in the mind.

The difference between cognitive activities and their conscious quality requires that we adopt a correspondingly clear-cut terminology. 'Conscious cognition' refers to a more elaborate mental activity than mere 'cognition;' the former has peculiar features that are not present in all cognition. When it is enhanced by the quality of consciousness, the activity is no longer simply 'cognition,' but 'conscious cognition.' And when cognition is enriched by consciousness, it exhibits additional features, but retains those of mere 'cognition.' Thus, if the cognitive process continues beyond mere cognition, the result is 'conscious cognition;' if the process of cognition does not develop conscious quality, it stops at 'non-conscious cognition.'

The distinction between conscious and non-conscious cognition accords with the assumption that consciousness is part of the outcome of human evolution. The human species shares cognitive functions with the remainder of the animal kingdom, but evolution did not cease when animals first appeared. Many widely different levels of cognition are present in today's fauna; some animals that undoubtedly sense their environment are not capable of learning or problem-solving, whereas many of the more evolved species are. It is also a safe estimate that at least the simpler animals — say, insects — are not conscious; the simplicity of their 'nervous systems,' if they can be called such, and of their consequent behaviour, would lead one to suspect it. And if so, non-conscious cognition should be possible. But this is not important; since we are narrowly interested in human cognition, we can ignore most of the forms of cognition that have emerged at earlier stages of animal evolution, including those forms of animal life, if there should be any, that might have developed an infra-human level of consciousness: what matters is that *we* are conscious. Although we can, therefore, put aside the question whether a primitive form of consciousness actually appeared in other animals before the human species evolved, we cannot ignore, first, that when the human species appeared (if not also earlier), cognition had evolved into the kind that typically has the quality of consciousness that we recognize in ourselves. And, second, that, nevertheless, there is evidence that not all human cognition is conscious.

It may seem strange that human beings, who typically are conscious, should at the same time be capable of experiencing but not consciously. Should the more evolved form of cognition not have supplanted the earlier? Not necessarily; for as we learn about the nature of consciousness we should understand that consciousness is not an improved form of the perceptual capabilities of human organisms; indeed, many infrahumans have more powerful hearing, vision, and smell than human beings. What consciousness added to cognition was a new *dimension* of experience. An indication of this is that consciousness accrues not only to perception, but also to the abilities to speak and understand. Indeed, these functions, unlike perception, demand consciousness, and cannot take place unless consciously. If evidence of this is needed, we need only consult our experience of speaking and understanding and ask ourselves what speaking non-consciously would be like; or what would understanding be like, if it were not done consciously. Speech is not mere communication, the sort of function that is found even in insects; speech is *conscious* communication. And human beings can communicate, both to themselves and to others, not only the perceptible facts that describe a certain phenomenon, but also the *explanation* of the phenomenon. Could one explain it without being conscious of the explanation?

In this section we shall therefore study perceptual cognition separately from the conscious quality it typically has in human beings; what we discover regarding perception should apply to both conscious and non-conscious perception, but will tell us nothing about the peculiarities of conscious cognition. First we shall consider the cause of perception; then we shall inquire into the nature of the process through which perception comes about and its consequences. Only then we shall ready to investigate the quality of consciousness that perception develops ordinarily in human beings, as well as its causes and consequences. Additional remarks will then be made on two questions that are not usually discussed in the same breath as consciousness — namely, the fallibility of the human mind, and the nature of truth and falsity. Both are directly relevant to a correct understanding of the nature of consciousness.

The procedure to be followed in order to investigate human cognition should be justified. The fact that much of our cognitive life takes place below the level of consciousness has been difficult to detect; traditionally, therefore, cognition and conscious cognition have been deemed synonymous. The reason is that organisms endowed with cognition have the capability of observing themselves only when their cognition is qualified by consciousness. But this remains true even after one recognizes the reality of non-conscious cognition. The latter cannot be observed directly; we depend on deduction from what we observe consciously. Such deduction is both possible and procedurally acceptable, once we determine (as we shall) that sometimes we perceive objects consciously, whereas at other times we perceive them without our perception's acquiring conscious quality. Because the fundamental features of cognition are common to all cognition; they are found in conscious as well as in non-conscious cognition.

a) The cause of perception

We have already seen some reasons why we must say that reality does not depend for its being real on our cognition of it, either for its characteristics or for its existing; the Greeks made no mistake in this regard. And we shall find additional reasons later. It is a different matter whether our intellectual ancestors correctly estimated that, since our awareness of reality does not cause reality, we must say that reality causes our awareness of it. There can be no doubt, of course, that objects play an indispensable role in the causation of experience; no one but Buddhists and other mystics would claim that it should be possible to know without knowing something that serves as the 'object' or 'subject matter' of cognition. However, taking 'causation' strictly — i.e., as efficient causation — there are reasons to think that although objects have a causal role in the mind's causation of experience, the effect they cause is not our cognition. Precisely what effects are caused by objects and how objects contribute to the process of cognition should become apparent as we proceed.

Both the predominant Greek tradition and our own modern representationism have alleged some observations that qualify their depiction of the mind's role in cognition as fundamentally passive and receptive. The classical Aristotelian metaphors will be remembered. Sense perception comes about 'in the way in which a piece of wax takes on the impression of a signet ring without the iron or gold;'[275] and our understanding — our perception of the supra-sensible or intelligible content of objects — is like 'a tablet on which nothing has yet been written.'[276] But no philosopher who thinks that objects cause our experience will fail to add, on the other, that objects can have such effect only upon a suitably sensitive organism. Seals impress their shape only on wax that is sufficiently soft; objects impress themselves only on receptive experiencers. Sensitivity and impressionability, however, are not active capacities, but capacities to *undergo* causation and *suffer* effects.

Nor have many philosophers failed to recognize the active *reaction* of human beings to the knowledge caused in the mind by objects. Once objects have generated mental representations of themselves in the mind, the mind contributes its own activity to the process; it reaps the benefit of the causal activity of the objects by appropriating and using the knowable 'content' that structures the object. Thus, representationism grants that, in this limited sense, the mind *actively* knows; it makes use, applies, and enjoys the benefits of its knowing. But for representationists the mental activity of knowing is only the mind's *response* to the causation of cognition by object.

What I suggest goes beyond this. The cognizer causes its own cognition. Now, if there is any difficulty in maintaining this, the problem would be the causation of, specifically, *cognition;* so far as concerns the organism's causing an effect *on itself,* there should be little to cavil about. For it is an observable fact that causation can be immanent as well as transitive. If I throw an object, the effect is the motion of the object, and my causation of the effect is transitive; when I walk or run, the effect is my own motion, and my causation of it is immanent. But granted that immanent causation is possible, can it be true that we cause our own cognition?

Before I call attention to the evidence that so indicates, we should consider briefly some of the efforts that were made at various times throughout the twentieth century to understand the human mind by escaping representationism, but which usually retained the supposition that sufficed to

---

275   Aristotle, *On the Soul,* 2.12.424a20.

276   Aristotle, *On the Soul,* 3.4.430a1.

nullify such efforts, namely, that the cause of cognition was reality, and that the effect was the 'appear-ance' of reality to the mind.

Much discussed at the turn of the twentieth century were the movements known as the 'new realism,' and 'critical realism,' of Ralph Barton Perry and others, such as G. Dawes Hicks, who insisted that perception took place 'directly,' but who did not provide a positive explanation of the nature of 'direct perception.' Perry accepted[277] that perception cannot take place by means of mental duplicates of objects, but at the cost of adopting 'neutral monism' — a fantastic, wholly *a priori* creation of the philosophical imagination — and omitting from consideration the conscious quality of perception. And Hicks argued that no interpretation of the mind that introduced mediating appearances between reality and the mind could be correct. For example, alluding to the reasoning of such philosophers as Bertrand Russell, Hicks pointed out the paradox that:

> [A] line of reflection which took for its point of departure the necessity of dis-tinguishing the act of consciousness from its object, and which emphasized the duality between sensing and *sensum,* between perceiving and percept, between thinking and thoughts, ends by reaching the conclusion that there is no such distinction, that seeing just means colors occurring ... [and] think-ing means thoughts occurring.[278]

In the absence of the mediating representations of reality that had been rejected, neo-realism and critical realism defaulted to the idea that reality appeared directly to the mind, but left unques-tioned the supposition that reality causes the 'appearances' of itself in the mind. The 'appearances' of objects thus caused by objects to exist in the mind are, of course, the traditional representations under a new name. Several variations of the direct apprehension of reality by the mind, which came to be known as the 'theory of appearing,' have been proposed since. I have already criticized (in chap-ter II) H.H. Price's inadequate version of the same idea. Better, but incomplete attempts were made

---

277   Edwin B. Hold, Ralph Barton Perry, et al., *The New Realism: Cooperative Studies in Philosophy* (New York: Macmillan, 1912).

278   G. Dawes Hicks, *Critical Realism: Studies in the Philosophy of Mind and Nature* (London: Macmillan, 1938), 36-37.

later in the century, for example, by W.H.F. Barnes, who proposed 'the theory of appearing … [that is] implicit in common sense.'[279] He argued that if 'we are content to talk in terms of appearance or, better still, of things appearing, we shall not have pseudo-problems'[280] such as haunt representation-ism. But whereas Barnes explicitly assumed that things appear to the mind, he offered no theoretical explanation of how they do so; his 'theory' explained only why theories of *indirect* or *representative* appearance could not possibly be correct. More recently Harold Langsam has proposed that the 'phe-nomenal features [of cognition] are relations between material objects and minds,'[281] contradicting thus the view that they are 'intrinsic properties of mental objects.' In my view, this is true. He did not explain, however, how the cognitive relation comes about, or why cognitive states should be ascribed 'phenomenal features,' or how such features can be had by organic functions; most of his paper is devoted to explaining how the indistinguishability of hallucinations from veridical perception did not stand in the way of the 'theory of appearing,' and in meeting other possible objections to it.

Among the most recent contributions in this vein is William P. Alston's. Like his predecessors, Alston restates why mediated cognition cannot be correct, and affirms instead that 'perceptual con-sciousness is an *awareness of* objects, which are, in normal cases, *physical objects in the environment*'[282]. This proposition seems to me unquestionably true, and is an important part of what philosophy of mind is required to explain; but it does not of itself explain what cognition is or how it takes place. Like others of the type, Alton's critique of representationism reaches the valuable and true conclusion that an adequate theoretical explanation of cognition must recognize and respect the elementary facts of cognition. But recognition and respect of the facts do not of themselves explain anything.

Two final preliminary observations are particularly to be taken into account as we study why the causation of cognition should not be ascribed to the object, but to the organism. One is that we do not actually perceive 'objects' one by one, as if they acted upon our senses one by one; the supposition that we do is not borne out if we pay attention to what actually happens when we perceive. What we

279   W.H.F. Barnes, 'The myth of sense-data,' *Proceedings of the Aristotelian Society* 45 (1944-45): 89-117, 111.

280   Barnes, 'The myth of sense-data,' 115.

281   Harold Langsam, 'The Theory of Appearing Defended,' *Philosophical Studies* 87 no.1 (1997): 33-59, 36.

 See also his 'Why I believe in an external world' *Metaphilosophy* 37 (2006): 652-672.

282   William P. Alston, 'Back to the theory of appearing,' *Philosophical Perspectives* 13: 181-203, 183.

in fact do is to perceive a complex *totality* of a given sensory dimension (i.e. visual, or auditory, or tactile, and so on). We may *attend* to individual 'objects,' but we do not see, hear, or otherwise *sense* individual 'objects.' We sense an *integrated whole* we usually call the 'world' or the 'environment.' Within the perceived visual, auditory, or other sensible 'world' we then distinguish or focus upon individual 'objects' — say, a flower, an apple, a bush, a leaf, or a petal. Bowing to convention, however, I shall express myself here as if our sense perceptions were built up out of distinct 'objects,' though in fact they are not.

A second misunderstanding of the *explicandum* of perception abets the first; it consists in supposing that our perceptions are built up out of sensing distinct 'objects' by means of distinct 'acts,' quite as if they were comparable to photographic snapshots caused by objects acting on photographic film. In fact, perceptions are 'processes,' in the same sense in which our other organic, vital activities are processes — although perception, unlike our vegetative vital processes, starts and stops and is interrupted by sleep. Taken together, these two misinterpretations of our sense perception facilitate the supposition that perception is the effect of the activity of 'objects' upon our sense organs, one individual 'object' and one individual 'act' or 'moment' at a time.

In outline, the decisive argument that supports attributing the causation of cognition to the cognizing organism, and denying it to the object, is simple; we observe, albeit with difficulty, the causal activity of the mind, whereas we do not observe the causal activity of the object that has the specific effect of rendering us cognizant of the object. That objects can have effects on us, I repeat, is not in question; the issue is whether they cause *our cognition*. On the other hand, we *can* observe our cognizing activity, even if only with some difficulty. We are able to experience our *doing* our experiencing — though admittedly, we may become confused and fail to observe it. But we have no reason, and certainly no empirical evidence, to suppose that objects as such — a category that includes, of course, inanimate objects — *do* anything whose effect might conceivably be that we experience the object.

For example, what happens when Adam, walking about Eden, is attracted by an apple dangling before him at tempting eye-level? What happens is, of course, that Adam sees it. But what has the apple *done* to cause Adam's seeing that it was not already doing (if anything) before Adam came within sight of the apple and saw it? Or that the apple did not continue to do (if anything) long after

Adam departed for sadder shores and the apple ceased to be seen? Without an existing apple there can be no 'seeing' of an apple. But once the apple (and whatever else may be relevant) exists and is *there,* within spatio-temporal range of the eye, all the requirements that must be met *by the apple* before it can be experienced have been satisfied. However, when cognition takes place, objects as such — the paradigmatic, elementary case of which is, of course, the cognition of inanimate objects — do not change. Objects may be active, of course, if they are alive (but not otherwise, since causal *action* has to be initiated and can be discontinued); but an object as such, or as that-which-is-known, does not *do* anything in order to become known. Only the cognizer changes. Only the cognizer is the efficient cause of its own cognition.

But does the apple not *act* causally upon Adam, bringing about, for example, a change in his retinas? Actually, and to put a fine point on it, no. For as we saw when we studied the nature of causality, entities below the level of life cause effects without performing any *action.* Apples can cause change, as well as undergo causation, but do not act at all. Objects cause effects on other objects, including on the human organisms, but as passive causes; they have effects by virtue of the relationship that their properties bear to the properties of other entities. Active causality, by contrast, has to be turned on and off; it is possible only in living entities. Thus, the apple does not *do* anything that has for its effect a change in Adam's retinas. However, the apple has certain characteristics, such as a certain reflectance, and therefore, when light is reflected by the apple and captured by Adam's eyes, Adam's retinas change in proportion to the colour of the apple. But the colour of the apple is not turned *on* by the apple when Adam approaches, and *off* in his absence; the apple has neither changed nor initiated any action; Adam experiences the colour because the apple has certain characteristics that automatically interrelate causally with the characteristics of Adam's retinas so as to change the latter. The apple has such characteristics before, during, and after the time when Adam experiences the colour of the apple. There is no reason to suppose that the apple has done anything to cause the experience.

In other words, inanimate entities are never active causes; their causality is always passive, spending no energy and exerting no force or necessitation. But even if the apple and its colour actually were causally active, the activity is not directed specifically towards Adam or confined to him. We cannot seriously suppose that inanimate objects lie in wait for cognizers to arrive on the scene and then spring into action and cause their cognition. The apple's peculiar reflectance affects everything within range, and not only Adam's retinas. The apple does indeed cause a chemical change in the retina, but the change thus caused is comparable to the change that takes place in a photographic film exposed to the apple — or for that matter, upon anything else in the vicinity that is capable of being affected by light. It is not a change from 'not-seeing' to 'seeing.' If apples could cause cognition, photographic films would *see* apples as well as Adam can.

The alternative to making assumptions that lack all empirical foundation is to accept that experiencing is caused exclusively by the experiencer. When cognition takes place, we gain knowledge of the world about us; we become informed *of* reality. But the informing is not done to us, or for us, *by* reality. Given the well established conventions of our European languages, it would be unreasonable to forbid ourselves every metaphorical ascription of human characteristics to things, but we should be careful that we do not allow our figurative words to take the bit between their teeth and, taking advantage of our difficulty in perceiving our own mental activity, drive us to distracted conclusions of their own. We may choose to speak of real objects as if they actually handed over information to us; but we should not confuse the true fact — that we inform ourselves of them — with the supposition that they provide, and transmit to us, information about themselves.

The observations I have alleged seem to me sufficient support for the conclusion I have drawn; but it is possible to describe the same observations in terms that underline other important aspects of the causation of cognition. For cognition may also be said to consist in the cognizer's creation, within itself, of a peculiar *relationship* to the world — the cognitive *relationship* of knower to known that Langsam recognized. Cognition may be described in terms of such relationship. But before I do so, I acknowledge the principal assumptions regarding the nature of 'relationships' I bring to the subject.

The concept of 'relation' has an empirical basis. We perceive that events and things sometimes 'have to do with each other.' They are not disconnected; for example, one calls to mind the other; it 'refers' us (i.e. 'carries us over') to the other. Because we develop the concept of 'relation' in this manner, we are tempted to suppose that relations are created when *we*, as observers of the world, compare or otherwise *refer* one thing to another. The very terms 'relation' and 'reference' make use of such metaphors. And indeed, some relations are creatures of the human mind; they are purely 'logical' relations. Mathematical relations are the clearest example of the kind; for mathematics does not have to do with reality (though it can be applied to reality) but solely with the relationships among concepts insofar as they fall under one or another mathematical category such as 'one,' 'plus,' 'minus,' 'equal' and 'whole.' However, other relations are real — quite as objectively real as reality itself. Spatial and temporal relations are of this kind. The 'distance' that relates A and B spatially is real; it is a feature of the world, and is whatever it is regardless of whether anyone perceives it. The time it takes for a traveler to traverse the distance from A to B is not imaginary, but real. (A human mind's *measure* of the distance, however, is created by the mind that measures it, and exists only in a human mind; it is no part of the extramental world.)

Moreover, a relationship deserves being called 'real,' if it has implications or consequences that affect the real world and do not depend on their being noticed or experienced. Now, real relationships are usually bilateral (or multilateral); and if so, they may also be mutual, such as the parent-child relationship. This is an example of an asymmetrical mutual relationship, since the relationship is created by the active, transitive causality of parent and passively undergone by the transitively generated child — whereas the relationship among sibs, for instance, is real, mutual, and symmetrical.

But relationships need not always be bilateral or mutual. This is true in the case of the relationship between the knower and the known, a relationship that is generated by cognition which is a causal process. We would not have suspected this *a priori*; we discover it empirically by examining our cognition. Cognizers relate themselves to objects, and the relationship is caused by cognizers themselves, but the relationship they thus develop affects only themselves. It creates cognition only in the cognizers. The relationship neither creates nor changes the objects. For cognizers do not act causally upon the object but only upon themselves; their causality is immanent. The result is that the cognizer, by virtue of its immanent causal activity, develops a relationship that is real on the part of the knower, but which is only logical on the part of the object. That is, it is not real part of the real object, though the human mind can think of it as if it were real. Why should we say so?

Well, the assertion that on the side of the knower the relationship is real rests on observation: there is a real difference between a knower's state of 'knowing an object,' and the state of 'not-knowing it.' That the relationship of the object to the knower is not real, but purely logical, is also empirically based; it is supported by observing what happens to an object when it is known. And when an object becomes known, what happens to it *itself*, as we have already noted, is precisely *nothing*. The object does not change. The only observable change is in the experiencer. To be sure, if the object is a fellow human, the difference between 'being known' and 'not being known' may be real and important. But if it is, the reason would be, of course, that in this case the object is not merely an object of cognition; it is a person. To objects *as such* it makes no difference whether they are known or not. Indeed, unless the object is capable of cognition and can find out, it would not *know* that it has been known.

It might be objected that when we know an object, we are entitled to say, quite truthfully, that the object has 'become known.' Does this not mean that the object has changed, and that it has a real relationship to us? Well, we can say it — indeed, our Indo-European syntax leaves us little alternative to our saying it, if we want to speak of it — but it would not be true. We can trace our inclination to say it to the fact that, when we learn to speak using an Indo-European language, we are taught to suppose, first, that everything in the world — every subject of predication — is the agent of an active process; and, second, that every active process can be both performed and undergone.[283] But our syntax cannot be reasonably supposed to compel reality. The object exhibits no observable change consisting in its having acquired the status of 'being known.' If we imagine otherwise, it is because our projecting onto objects the active causation of cognition suggests to us the further projection of our real change (from 'not-knowing' to 'knowing') into the falsely supposed change of the object (from 'not-being known' to 'being known.')

If the mind causes its own experiences, it follows that the mind is not well conceived as something that *has* experiences, or that *undergoes* experiences, or that *contains* experiences. The mind *experiences.* Or more exactly, the *organism* does something called experiencing. (But again, we need not flout the linguistic conventions of our culture merely to make a philosophical point.) For as I have insisted from the outset, the 'mind' is not an agent, but an action, or an active process: it is an activity of the organism as it discharges the cognitive functions with which evolution has endowed it. The agent is the organism, and its action — its active causality — is the physiology of the organism. The

---

283   Or in grammatical terms: every subject of predication is a verb, and verbs may normally be conjugated with subjects either in the active or in the passive voice. Not all languages require these presuppositions. For example, Indonesian does not.

effect is the achievement of cognitive states. This may well be what John Dewey had in mind when he said that '[m]ind is primarily a verb.'[284] Properly speaking, human beings (and other animal organisms) should not be said *to have* a mind, but *to mind*. Or *to mentate*, I would add, were this not too ugly a neologism to be seriously entertained.

b) *The nature and finality of perception*

If we accept that the cause of cognition is the cognizing organism, the question then arises how the organism causes its knowledge of the object. The organism does so in somewhat the same way in which it nourishes itself. To nourish itself, the organism makes use of food. Food is indispensable for nutrition, but the efficient cause of nutrition is not food; it is the operation of the organism's nutritive functions exercised upon the food in order to incorporate it into the organism. Chemical interrelations between the characteristics of food and the characteristics of the digestive system enable the organism to nourish itself. Well, cognition is not the incorporation of objects into the cognizer's mind, whether representatively or otherwise; but in other respects the process is, fundamentally, like nutrition. The knower gains knowledge of the object by making use of the object; that is, by taking advantage of certain characteristics of the object — characteristics that, of themselves, do not have to do with cognition, but with the ordinary causal interrelations among objects. For objects, even when they are inanimate, cause physical effects on other objects, including human organisms. Human organisms take advantage of the physical changes caused in them by objects, in order to bring about in themselves the organic state of knowing the object: when the state is achieved, the cognizing organism has established a cognitive relationship with the object. Thus, cognition of reality is an effect caused upon itself by the organism when it exercises its cognitive functions. This, however, is only the general explanation of the nature of the process. We need to examine it in somewhat finer detail.

We can best understand what the activity of human mentation consists in, if we keep in mind its evolutionary origin. Our philosophical tradition has tended to follow the supposition of Aristotle

---

284 John Dewey, 'Mind and Consciousness,' in Joseph Ratner, (ed.), *Intelligence in the Modern World: John Dewey's Philosophy* (New York: Modern Library, 1939), 812.

and others that inanimate nature exhibits not only passive, but also active characteristics, but nothing in experience justifies it. Below the level of life, the world is 'inert,' so to speak, in the sense that it is utterly passive. This is not to deny that inanimate entities work effects on each other and bring about changes in the world; for as we have seen, causation need not be an active process. Non-living beings have the capacity to work effects without having to *do* anything to cause them. A further reason why we must differentiate between the active causality of living beings and the 'inertial' or passive causality of inanimate nature, is that active causation, as we observe it in ourselves and in all other living beings whether animal or sub-animal, is vectorial. It has not only magnitude — a degree or finite amount of effective causal power — but also direction. All activity properly so called is relative to a specific end that the action naturally *tends* to bring about as its effect.

The causality of inanimate beings, on the other hand, results in effects, but *achieves* nothing; this is why I have called it 'inertial' causality. If only living beings may be correctly said to 'act,' the reason is that only living beings behave *so as to attain* an objective. Sentient beings may also *seek* to attain it, and human beings may even seek it *on purpose,* or consciously; these are further evolutionary developments of the *active* nature of life. However, anthropomorphism is so deeply embedded in our idea of causality that we may find it difficult to abstain from projecting activity, power, and force into all causal processes, including those that involve none but inanimate entities. We have to think hard before, overcoming our habitual inclination, we can recognize that there is no 'heaviness' in stones; however, to watch a volcano in full eruption spewing molten lava, but without our projecting activity, power, and force into the phenomenon, may be more than most of us can contemplate. Nevertheless, to project power, force and activity onto inanimate nature would be a misconstruction of what actually takes place.

That causality should not be uniform throughout the universe runs against the grain of our prejudices, which treat causality as if it were a 'principle' or 'law' that the world was required to obey. But as we have seen, causality is not a Newtonian-style universal principle — that is, a 'force' that, like 'gravity,' is distinct from things and acts upon things from without. Causality is rather a manifestation of the properties of things; or more exactly, a manifestation of the relativity of the reality of real things to each other, which accounts for the mutual relativity of their properties. Now, worldly entities do not exhibit homogeneity as to properties; we do not demand, for instance, that all things in the world be alive, or that all be inanimate: we accept the observable fact that some are alive and some are not. Why should philosophy demand uniformity in causation? (Indeed, why should philosophy *demand* anything, instead of merely *observing* and *noting* all it can?) Since living and sentient entities have emerged out of non-living reality, our expectation should be, if any, that they may cause effects in emergently different ways from the way in which inanimate nature does. Even *a priori*, we might suspect that different things are likely to have different causal properties.

Well, when life emerged, entities had come into being whose functions exhibited a more elaborate level of causation than that which is observable in inanimate entities. For the emergence of living beings was the emergence of beings characterized by 'finality' — beings that were capable of activities through the exercise of which they might procure (though not infallibly) 'advantages' and 'benefits' that ultimately redounded in the enhancement and preservation of their own life. The finality of living beings is not merely one of their components, but is identical with what we also call their *life*. To understand the nature of life, therefore, we have to study the finality of the functions — i.e., the causal powers — discharged by living beings in order to live; we have to determine what such functions achieve and how they achieve it. By the same token, to understand the nature of cognition we have to observe what the cognitive powers of animal organisms achieve, and how.

The significance and the *novelty* of the evolutionary emergence of life and its inherent finality have been memorably described by Daniel Dennett:

> When an entity arrives on the scene capable of behavior that staves off, however primitively, its own dissolution and decomposition, it brings with it into the world its 'good.' That is to say, it creates a point of view from which the world's events can be roughly partitioned into the favorable, the unfavorable, and the neutral.[285]

---

285   Daniel C. Dennett, *Consciousness Explained* (Boston: Little, Brown, 1991), 174.

Staving off death is impossible for the non-living, of course. And to be sure, only conscious experiencers are able to *evaluate* the world's events in relation to themselves and from their 'point of view'; only they, as already noted, are able to cause advantages and benefits to accrue to them afore-thought, or intending to obtain them, or aware that they seem 'good.' The events themselves, however, are in fact always either favourable, unfavourable, or neutral for all living beings, even when those who undergo the events are unable to know that they are good, bad, or indifferent. Thus, whenever they act, all agents — that is, all living beings, all organisms — act for an end. To repeat, hardly all do so intentionally, or 'on purpose.' But all their activities invariably *have* a built-in purpose: they *accomplish* something. It is not an antecedent, but an inherent, end: it is built into the nature of the activity. And all the accomplishments of the activities of living agents converge on procuring the self-preservation of the organism. Which is why absence or presence of activity is the most obvious difference between inanimate beings and living organisms — and why, conversely, to ascribe active causality (let alone 'mentality') to non-living beings amounts to erasing the principal difference between life and absence of life.

Misunderstandings about the nature of evolution sometimes overtake even its ardent and otherwise knowledgeable proponents. (The SETI project, to be briefly discussed below, is a striking illustration of this.) Some philosophers cavil at the suggestion that cognition, being a biological activity — and specifically, an *adjustive* activity — is rooted upon the finalistic tendencies inherent in the nature of life. For instance, John R. Searle has taken the position that, since biological functions are the product of Darwinian evolution, which aims at no purpose, 'biological functions … are entirely devoid of purpose.'[286] I think that Searle may be forgetting that what is true of the evolutionary process should not be confused with what is true of the living beings created by the process. Biological functions achieve no antecedent purpose of evolution, but they achieve inherent purposes; the discharge of their functions leads to the achievement of goals that are built-into the nature of the function. This is crucial for understanding the nature of cognition; we shall have to discuss it in some detail.

Searle's lapse is akin to supposing that, since nothing in the universe moves in absolute space, nothing in the universe is truly in motion. But this would be a *non sequitur:* although the motion of

---

286   John R. Searle, *The Rediscovery of the Mind* (Cambridge, Mass.: MIT Press, 1992), 52.

bodies in relation to each other is not absolute, their motion is none the less real for its being relative. Likewise, evolution is devoid of an antecedent purpose; it does not tend to achieve, or to prefer, predetermined outcomes. But the vital functions of the living beings that are generated by evolution do fulfill purposes that are *immanent* in the nature of life. Thus, there is no reason to think that purposive agents appeared on Earth by virtue of an antecedent purpose that determined the nature of the universe or the course of its becoming. Searle is right in thinking that whatever the evolving universe may bring forth, its being brought forth is never more than a matter of fact. Or as Hume insightfully put it, '[w]hatever *is* may *not be*.'[287] On the other hand, it is a matter of observable fact that on at least one occasion the universe brought forth life, and that living beings function, observably, *so as to* protect their life. As Dennett has put it, every organism 'staves off … its own dissolution and decomposition.'

The confusion can be avoided. To do so, we need to refine our observations and differentiate between the peculiarly human sort of purposes and the kind that human beings share with infrahuman life; for purposiveness, or finality, emerged together with life, but life and its purposiveness continued to evolve. The specifically human purposes presuppose consciousness. Since they are consequent upon *awareness* of the desirability of their being attained, they can be intended. But purposes need not be intended; they can be achieved unintentionally. By contrast, however, the purposes or goals that are typically built into the functions that we share with infrahuman life do not necessarily depend upon their being known, foreseen, or intended. Unlike the invariable effects brought about by inanimate causes, these purposes, on the one hand, merely *tend* to achieve certain effects; but like our human, consciously sought purposes, on the other, are defeasible. Accordingly, notwithstanding their not always achieving intended purposes, the biological functions we share both with other animals and with sub-animal life always *serve* certain purposes: they have observable built-in tendencies to bring about certain results. Every organ functions for a purpose that is relevant to the survival of the organism; so to function is what defines its nature as a vital function of the living organism. We live only as long as our organism functions so as to keep us alive.

---

287 David Hume, *An Enquiry Concerning Human Understanding*, in L.A. Selby-Bigge, (ed.), *Enquiries concerning the human understanding and concerning the principles of morals* (Oxford: Clarendon Press, 1902), XII, 3.

Now, the purpose of the vital functions of organisms is, in general, to maintain the life of the organism and to facilitate its adjustment to the world as it actually is. To say this is merely to say that living beings function so as to tend to repair and preserve themselves, even if their capacity for self-preservation is, of course, exhaustible. It follows, therefore, that the purposiveness of the vital functions of organisms is not merely compatible with evolution, but is indeed an indispensable component of the mechanism of evolution. For, reifying the evolutionary process, we say that a certain trait *has* something called 'survival value' or 'disvalue;' although in reality, if we were to express ourselves with precision, what we should say is that the trait increases or decreases the organism's capacity for self-preservation. Without self-preservation — and therefore without purposive functions — there could be neither survival values nor disvalues, and natural selection could not operate.

I digress for a moment to underline the importance of the topic under discussion — the inherent purposiveness of the vital functions of organisms — by noting that it is directly relevant to, among other philosophical issues, a sound understanding of the nature of morality, of the possibility of moral progress, and of the practical question how to educate ourselves, individually and collectively, so as to fulfil adequately our need for moral self-approval. The need is generated by the fact that consciousness makes human beings aware of, and able to exercise a degree of deliberate control over, some of their causal powers. We can therefore *steer* ourselves towards goals we value not only when their value or disvalue affects our experiences of pleasure and pain and ultimately our biological survival, but also when it affects our character and selfhood. The evidence of it is that human beings have, and sometimes exercise, the power to choose to die for the sake of values that, rightly or wrongly, they deem preferable to the continuation of their existence: morality is generated by consciousness. Correspondingly, our decisions can have not only of the sort of value that is relevant to natural selection — namely, pleasure and pain, and ultimately the biological health or unhealth of the life of the human organism — but also the kind that affects the *moral* health or unhealth of the conscious mode of life that characterizes the same organism.

In other words, since consciousness renders human beings aware of their existence, of themselves as owners of their reality, and of their causal powers and activities, consciousness renders human beings worthy or unworthy of their own existence in their own eyes. We can experience shame, just as we can take pride in the self or person into which we fashion ourselves. Evidently, however, as with every other human skill — and we should think of the moral character of human beings as a more or less adequately developed human skill rather than as a static property — individual variations in the depth of such feelings, in the realism and accuracy of our self-evaluations, and in the degree to which we develop moral awareness and maturity, are very wide.

I am hardly the first critic to point out that our culture has fostered grossly inadequate moral sensibilities; for instance, it urges us to abide by *duties* instead of facilitating our living up to our *responsibilities,* to substitute the experience of *guilt* by that of *shame,* and to distort legitimate *self-satisfaction* into *self-righteousness.* Given these conditions, it should not astonish us that our modern culture has had only slight success as it has tried to make the transition from the morality of resignation to Fate or obedience to God, to the morality that our ownership of our existence should have brought about: the morality of honour, nobility, self-respect, fidelity to our nature, and solidarity with our species. The task of creating wise customary norms of individual behaviour, of political and economic relations, and of social regulation, is infinitely more difficult than merely conforming to authoritative formulae, or to wise traditions, or even to reasonable customs. Nor should we be surprised if some modern philosophers, having discovered the vacuity and groundlessness of the traditional morality, have philosophized reactively and have developed no more civilized alternative to our traditional religious morality than the morality of the jungle. For example, alleging the fact that evolution obeys no purpose and does not tend to bring about either the human species or any other preferred outcome, coupled with a travesty of Darwinian evolution according to which there is no significant difference between man and beast, the controversial British philosopher John Gray has sought to justify a radical nihilism that asserts the emptiness of human values, the illusoriness of human morality, and the impossibility of mankind's making any true moral progress. Human beings are the 'straw dogs' of the universe.[288]

---

288   John Gray, *Straw Dogs: Thoughts on Humans and Other Animals,*(London: Granta, 2002). The title of this book alludes to a passage from Lao Tzu, which in one translation reads: 'Heaven and earth are ruthless, and treat creatures as straw dogs.' This classical Chinese expression is said to describe the treatment of someone deferentially as long as may be convenient, but contemptuously otherwise.

It is true that, as best we can tell, evolution operates at random; when it brought human beings into the world, it did not do so in fulfillment of any purpose, tendency, or built-in bias, much less because either a personal God or an impersonal cosmic force determined that it should. Nevertheless, we may be glad that, as it happens, we human beings came to be. All the more so because we came to be *gratuitously:* but for the random and unlikely coincidence of a large number of evolutionary events, we would never have come to be. But the fact that human life and behaviour do not have a transcendent value or fulfil a transcendent purpose hardly means that human beings can *achieve* nothing, or that our efforts cannot be evaluated as *progressive* or *regressive* in relation to the possibilities that are open to us as a result of our having evolved into experiencers who are conscious. Because we are conscious, we can confront ourselves; our actions and the events we cause are valued or disvalued *by us,* and this is enough to ensure that they have moral significance *for us.* Although there is no reason to think that evolution and history tend to bring about ends of their own, whether supra- or intra-cosmic, there is abundant empirical reason to observe that what we do with our lives carries, besides pleasure or pain, moral value and disvalue in our own eyes.

But moral issues lie beyond the boundaries of this investigation; I return to the purposiveness that characterizes the functions of living entities. I have argued that their generic purpose — self-preservation — is achieved by specific functions in specific ways. And this brings us to the question: specifically in what way do the cognitive functions realize the generic adaptive purpose of human life?

The concepts of adaptation and self-preservation do not convey vividly enough the active *self-determination* implied by life, much less the sort of self-determination that is possible for cognitively active organisms — and least of all, the kind that is possible for conscious organisms. But even the most elementary form of life plays a role in determining what happens to it — not absolutely, to be sure, but to a degree — insofar as it participates in the processes whereby it is related to other beings. Its activities contribute to its condition, its health, and to its configuration or 'shape,' at any given time: the events that befall it are not caused exclusively by its environment but by the interrelation of the two. For the environment is reacted to by the organism, and the latter's response is determined not only by the nature of the stimulus but also by that of the organism itself. Correspondingly, a living being may be said to *take advantage,* for its own purposes, of the properties of other things.

At the lower levels of life, an organism takes such advantage mostly by incorporating others into itself and by shedding, or by ceding to its environment, whatever may be superfluous or harmful within itself. Organic life cannot be maintained by any entity except through the consumption of foreign substances that it appropriates and processes, and the elimination of what may be unhealthy for it. Adjustment at this level is identical with physical change in what Timo Järvilehto, in the work previously cited, calls 'the organism-environment system.' At the more elaborate level of evolution reached by sentient life, however, the organism's role in determining its life unfolds in a novel, immanent way; not only does it maintain its own existence as best it can, but it also contributes to the shaping of the events that will befall it as it navigates the sea of time. Sentient living beings, as such, take advantage of other entities, whether living or inanimate, but not in the crude manner that consists in appropriating them bodily; they benefit from others, but not at the expense of the other. They benefit in a peculiar manner that is characteristic of cognition. In what manner?

To begin with, we might describe it resorting to paradox: cognition may be said to amount to 'digesting' the object without ingesting it. But let us describe it more accurately and literally, even if in order to do so we have to turn to negative terms: cognitive agents make use of the presence and characteristics of objects, but without changing the object; cognition brings about a change only in cognizers themselves. This is, indeed, the reason why cognition is biologically advantageous and a candidate for natural selection: that it takes place immanently, entirely within the experiencing organism.

Without cognition, an organism has no control over the consequences of its encounters with the entities that make up its environment: the organism is affected, for good or for ill, only if, when, and as, the encounter takes place — and thus, when it is too late to prevent the bad consequences of the encounter or to take advantage of its favourable ones. Cognition is biologically valuable because cognition takes place *ahead of* the behavioural or other reactions to the environment that need take place to achieve adjustment to it. Cognition offers a *prior* alternative: it inserts a sort of *interval* or *distance*, so to speak, between the organism and its world that buffers the organism from the direct and immediate impact of the latter. The animal can then, with the benefit of cognition, behave so as to avoid what is 'bad' before it happens, or else actively to procure what is 'good' for it. Because the animal can count on sentience, it does not have to wait until the environment acts upon it. It need not wait until events should or should not happen. Cognition enables animal life to respond to its environment *preveniently,* ahead of time.

This is not to suggest, of course, that a trilobite drifting in the ocean stops abruptly upon coming into hailing distance of plankton, meditates whether to ingest it or to swim away, and after some prudent hesitation chooses wisely. Prevenient responses to the environment need not rise to the level of foresight and conscious anticipation, though in the random course of evolution they eventually did. But however simple and biologically automatic might be the quasi-mechanical, infra-conscious, non-deliberate, protoneural mechanism whereby the most primitive arthropod makes its 'choice' before it commits itself to a course of action, cognition is the ground of new, advantageous, organism-empowering capabilities that exceed, and are irreducible to, those of the more primitive, vegetative forms of life.

Granted that cognition even in its simplest form offers to sentient organisms the opportunity to respond preveniently to the hazards of the environment, *how* does it do so? By enabling the animal, I suggest, to *differentiate* itself from the rest of the world. In relation to the world they know, knowers are 'other-than' the world. Again, I do not mean that even the most primitive animals are able to *signify* to themselves the fact that they are 'other-than' the world. Infrahuman animals would be able to know that this fact is a fact, and that a reality is real, only if they were endowed with consciousness. What I mean is that cognition enables them to reap, blindly and without the benefit of consciousness if in no other way, the advantage of the individuality that in point of fact *distinguishes* them, as living beings, from all other individuals in the world. Every living being, and not only every animal, is, to a degree, a distinct, self-enclosed, unitary entity that is 'other-than' everything else in the world. But cognitively-endowed living beings are able to take advantage of the fact by behaving accordingly (and, if they are conscious, also in more elaborate ways). Thus, at all levels of life the *difference* between what is 'good' and what is 'bad' affects the organism; but if an organism is more that simply alive, and is endowed with cognition, it can also *discriminate* — functionally and automatically, if in no other way — between what is 'good' and what is 'bad' in relation to itself, and therefore behave accordingly.

To put it conversely, cognition enables human and infrahuman animals to react to others in accordance with the cognizer's inherent 'criteria' of what may be 'healthy' and 'unhealthy' for it. But however we may put it, the point is that, at all levels of animal life, cognition renders the animal's behaviour a function of the relationship of 'otherness-to' that mutually binds it and the world. The simplest forms of animal life suffice to demonstrate, therefore, the general principle that cognition is the very opposite of both the Aristotelian *union* of knower and known, and of the more modern 'intentional' or 'subjective' or 'representative' *possession* of the latter by the former. On the contrary, cognition enhances the self-containment that defines the organic unity of every living being. (But self-containment should not be confused with self-sufficiency.) Cognition depends upon the relationship of opposition — the *otherness-to* — that relates knower and known. The knower *is-not* the object, and the object *is-not* the knower. Cognition overcomes the difference without destroying it, because it is a real relationship on the side of the knower but only a logical one on the side of the object.

The purposiveness of cognition is fairly easily recognizable; we should not have needed a Francis Bacon to remind us that 'knowledge is power.' Nevertheless, with exceptions such as John Dewey and the pragmatists, who did take it into account, the finality of cognition is not given as much attention as it might be given in the standard syllabus of philosophy of mind. Pragmatism, however, distorted such finality by construing it much too narrowly, as if human, conscious cognition had no other value than directly or indirectly to enhance organic health and survival. This may have been true at the lower levels of evolution, but we should recognize that, once conscious cognition emerged, its value ceased to be tied exclusively to the direct or indirect service of the biological criterion of natural selection, namely, survival to reproductive age.

In what pertains to survival over a dangerous, possibly hostile environment, consciousness has overkill capacity; this is important for understanding consciousness, which would be underestimated if it were construed as extraordinary intelligence or craftiness. Consciousness is superfluous for human survival; indeed, it is apt to create perils of its own, such as those that for the last hundred years or so have become serious enough to evoke the realistic fear that our species might, either deliberately, negligently, or accidentally, destroy itself. Besides, our collective conscious existence makes life less pleasant than it might be, when the ingenuity that comes with the ability of consciousness to direct and manage its cognition is not appropriately directed. Consciousness was built upon the inherent tendency of life to preserve itself; but it also created its own finality, which is amply and equally well manifested by the paradoxical conscious endeavour of human beings sometimes to prolong, but at other times to bring to an end, their lives. Or to take a less stark manifestation of the supererogatory, non-practical value of consciousness: with consciousness the sort of cognition emerged that was its own value. Consciousness brought about the desire to learn for learning's sake, and the desire to live for living's sake. When consciousness appeared, survival ceased to be merely 'instinctive' (i.e. automatically regulated by the organism), and became also a conscious and deliberate purpose that human beings are able to affirm or deny — and which, upon not so rare occasion, they both affirm and deny at the same time.

Once we recognize that cognition conforms to the finalistic nature of all organic activities, we may proceed to observe the essentials of the cognitive process. What does it achieve? How do cognizers reap the prevenient advantages of cognition? Well, so far as concerns perception,[289] they reap it, as it appears, by taking advantage of the effects caused upon them by the causality — 'inertial causality,' as I have called it — that objects as such, and as material entities, exercise in the ordinary course of events when they encounter other objects in the world, regardless of whether the latter have cognitive powers or not.

c) The process of perception

The philosophical tradition has always described the process of cognition in terms of 'information' — but invariably, of course, in the light of the traditional initial assumptions about cognition and reality. 'Information' is nevertheless a useful concept, and can be rehabilitated by recasting its meaning so as to conform with what we actually observe. In its traditional form, the concept harks back, of course, to the supposition of Plato — systematized, rationalized, and shorn by Aristotle of the grossest, but not all, of Plato's fantastic interpretations — that cognition is the process whereby

---

289   But let us not forget that perception is only the lowest degree of cognition. Thinking and understanding require explanation also, but shall be studied later.

cognizers *acquire* the 'form' of 'beings.' According to the Aristotelian tradition, the form is the 'content' of reality that becomes possessed by the mind when the mind and the object become 'one;' according to representationists, the 'content' of reality becomes known by the mind upon being imprinted on the mind by the object. Both interpretations suppose that reality is constituted in itself by an inherent knowability or cognoscibility that is possessed, transferred, or conveyed to the mind when cognition takes place.

I do not question, of course, that real things have real properties, and that we are capable of perceiving and understanding them and their properties. But I do suggest that there is nothing in any being or in its properties that is *inherently* knowable or that has an *inherent relationship* to anyone's mind. If it does become related to a mind, it is because the mind creates the relationship. The relationship of real beings and their properties to a mind that knows them, is not a real, but a purely logical, relationship. For, to repeat, objects are not changed when they are experienced. Both the cause and the effect of cognition are to be found entirely within the mind.

The reasoning that produces the supposition that knowability inheres in reality implies that reality is naturally apt for mental consumption: it is mind-like, since it is fully primed, as it were, and ready to exist mentally when it is cognized. And this has been taken at various times by various philosophers to imply one of three things. One possibility, the option of most Greek philosophers in one version or another, was to suppose that the mind-like content of the objects that make up the world indicated that the world was 'divine.' A more concrete version of this idea was the possibility ventured by Anaxagoras: that a mental force or cosmic condition that, by analogy with the human mind, was describable as 'Mind' *(nous),* was required in order to explain the world. The third possibility, a further concretization of Anaxagoras's proposal, was the Christian theological version, which overlaid Anaxagoras's mythological notion with a veneer of rationality by explaining that worldly reality was knowable because real things were, literally, the concretized, existing 'thoughts' or 'ideas' of the concrete Mind known as God. The world was created by God's thinking it up, and therefore enjoyed the rationality and intelligibility of the divine Mind itself.

The predictable objection to the position that the world is not inherently knowable is that it would amount to declaring reality absurd. And this would be unacceptable, because the human mind needs to experience meaningfully; if we were to accept that the world is absurd, it may be said, we would have to accept also Sartre's evaluation of human existence as nauseating. In his view modern philosophy avoided such evaluation by continuing to assume that the world was inherently rational and intelligible -while abstracting, at the same time, from the supposition that the world and human existence were God's creation. But this, he suggested, is self-contradictory. It is true, he counseled, that we should discard all thought of God; but if so, we should accept the consequence, namely, that the world is meaningless and human existence absurd.

I think that Sartre was in part quite correct. But only in part. The traditional assumptions of philosophy include, and modern philosophy has retained, the assumption of a mind-like, inherently rational and intelligible world, while setting aside the Greek and the Christian beliefs that supported it. And it is indeed true, as Sartre said. that this is self-contradictory. (Or in other words, the inherent intelligibility of the world is an orphan assumption.) What is not true is that a world that is *not* inherently intelligible must be deemed absurd. For in fact, it can be understood. And human existence is not absurd; it, too, can be understood and perceived as 'making sense.'

Some of those who do not understand why this is so, reason that, since it would not make sense to suppose that reality is absurd, we have to believe in God despite the absence of all evidence of his existence. Sartrean existentialists reason inversely: since God does not exist, we must agree that human existence is absurd. What this dilemma demonstrates is that if one's reasoning begins with projecting onto the world the active causality of the mind, one is likely to end by having to accept one or else another absurdity. One's choice will be limited mostly to determining which — unless perhaps one would prefer to indulge one's perplexity and refuse to make up one's mind. But to all of these suppositions there is, I think, an alternative: to diverge from the controlling assumption at the root of the dilemma, and to recognize that the world is *in itself* neither intelligible nor absurd, neither inherently intelligible nor refractory to being understood. The meaningfulness of human experience is created by the mind by relating itself to the world. Now, once we refrain from projecting mentality onto objects as such, we have to answer the question how the nature of reality should be interpreted accordingly. This will be considered in a separate section at the end of this chapter, though some aspects of it will be mentioned presently.

Meanwhile, let us return to cognition. Nowadays few philosophers other than Aristotelians and neo-scholastics would say that 'forms' inhere in objects. But the same general idea — that our minds become informed when they acquire the knowable content that originally resides in objects — is preserved under a different terminology by those philosophers who refer, for example, to the 'intentional content' of mental states, or to the 'mental representations' which repeat 'subjectively' an 'objective content' existing in reality. Still more obviously a descendant of the ancient views of cognition is the explicit supposition of information theorists and some other philosophers that information is 'physically realized' in objects, whence it 'flows' to the mind wherein it becomes 'phenomenally realized.'[290] Such philosophers do not hesitate to suppose that there can be 'physically realized' information even in the total absence of any mind that knows it. They do not seem concerned that such supposition may pose the problem of how there can be knowledge in the absence of anyone who has it or exercises it.

Projection allows some philosophers to go so far as to say that the physically realized information contained in, say, a book, may be treated as a 'commodity' — a suggestion that provokes an uncouth thought: if the information is as real as a pork belly, it would have to be present in the book as fat is on bacon, namely, irrespectively of anyone's perception or consumption of it. Predictably, however — because ingenious logic is a soldier of fortune, always ready to take any philosopher's shilling — information theorists retort that the physical realization of information should not be gracelessly understood. A book, they grant, contains nothing but words. The information is nevertheless physically realized in the book, because the information is *carried* by the words. (Actually, the information is not *in* the words; the information is in the *meaning* of the words, and meanings inhabit only *minds.*) Therefore, they say, one should not expect bloodstains in a book about the Iraq war. Now, this is undoubtedly correct; blurbs to the contrary, books are never actually explosive. Now, not only is it true that words carry information only by meaning what they mean. Words do not mean anything *to* themselves; they mean whatever they mean, only to the minds that utter or understand them. If books contained physically realized information, they should be able to read themselves.

---

290   See, for instance, David J. Chalmers, *The Conscious Mind: In Search of a Fundamental Theory* (New York: Oxford University Press, 1996), 277 ff.

In line with the position I have taken above regarding the cause of cognition, I would reject the idea that we obtain the information originally contained by objects within themselves. I would affirm instead that animal organisms become *informed of* objects, or *informed about* them, by virtue of their own activation of their own organisms. How does this come about? The information does not exist within reality; the information is the effect that the mind procures for itself by means of its cognitive activity.

I have already quoted one of the analogies proposed by Aristotle to illustrate his understanding of cognition: it is, he said, somewhat like the shaping of wax by the action of a seal. Well, if we wanted an analogy that performed the same service for the foregoing interpretation of sentience, we could do worse than to repeat Aristotle's ingenious trope with but one change. In Aristotle's figure, the passive, soft wax stood for the mind, and the hard seal was actively manipulated so that it should impress its shape on the malleable wax. Let us, however, invert the metaphor, and suppose that the seal, standing for the object, is inert and immobile and does not change shape — whereas the wax, standing for the mind, is alive and endowed with causal powers which it activates so as to adapt to its environment — in this case, the seal. Thus, when the wax comes within the causal range at which the mutual impenetrability of the two can be effective, the wax adapts by activating its malleability — that is, putting it to work so as to take advantage of the characteristics of the seal. Meanwhile the seal does nothing; it simply continues to be itself. What is the result?

That the wax, acting on its own initiative, has become in-formed of the shape of the seal. It has taken on a shape or form that conforms to that of the seal. And the wax is the sole cause of its having become so informed. And since the wax is, according to my analogy's supposition, alive, it can thereafter use such information to preserve and enhance its life. Observe, however, that nothing has been transmitted from the seal to the wax: the seal retains *its* shape, and the shape that the wax has taken on — or rather, given to itself — is, likewise, its own, and never was the seal's. To give itself its new shape, the wax took advantage of the passive characteristics of the seal; otherwise it could not have given itself any shape. But its new shape did not pre-exist either in the seal or in the wax before the wax gave it to itself. The wax's process of informing itself in relation to the seal is adaptive not because the wax has received anything from, or because it has united itself with, the seal, but because the shape it has given to itself is *proportioned* to the shape of the seal. This is of course only an analogy; but as an analogy it may be closer to the truth than Aristotle's.

The point of the analogy is that the experiential activity of the organism achieves the *proportioning* of the experiencing organism to the object. The relationship of proportion that the sensing organism has to the object sensed is ensured by the process I have described. For the proportionality is achieved by the organism as it takes advantage, for its own adaptive purposes, of the non-cognitive effects passively caused by the object's properties on the properties of the organism. The result is that although nothing has passed from the object to the organism or been reproduced or repeated in the latter, the organism has become, by none but its own actions, 'imprinted' *with* the object, as it were. But it has not been imprinted *by* the object; the organism has imprinted the object on itself. The object is not affected by the process. Having proportioned itself to the object, however, the organism's subsequent activities will be affected by the fact that it has so proportioned itself. If metaphor were desired, it would be better to say that the mind reaches out and grasps the object, than to attribute to the object the cognizer's enrichment by appropriating the object mentally.

But let us put metaphor aside and describe the process literally. Real objects and real experiencers have the real and mutual physical relationship noted above, the kind of relationship that enables material entities to have effects on each other without either of them putting forth activity, energy, or necessitation. Simply by existing, the object interrelates with the experiencer in accordance with the relationship that their respective physical characteristics bear to each other; the object does so in the same way in which it interrelates with everything else in the world that might be within the effective causal range of their mutual relationships. For example, under ordinary conditions of illumination, and if the reflected light is suitably focused, and so on, the object interrelates with a human eye's retina in much the same way in which it interrelates with photographic film: the pattern of changes that results from the interrelation of the object with the film will be comparable to that which results from its interrelation with the retina. Thus, a sentient organism's visual experience of an object requires both the existence of, and causal interrelation with, the object, in exactly the same way that a camera's photographic record of the object does. In this respect there is no difference between a camera and a living, seeing eye. Nor is there any difference between the object's relation to the eye and its relation to the camera; exactly the same inertial causality is in play when light is reflected from the object to the camera and from the object to the eye.

But of course, when the pattern is registered by photographic film, no experience takes place. The same effect upon the retina, however, provides the opportunity for the human being (and/or any other sentient organism) to inform itself of the visible object. Objects play an indis-pensable role in the causation of experience, because their causation of effects (on the organism) is what makes them actually and immediately *available* to the experiencer; this is a necessary condition precedent to the experiencer's causation of its cognitive relationship to the object.

We have been discussing cognition before it develops conscious quality. Becoming informed of the object does not yet mean, for instance, awareness of the fact that the object has been perceived. The organism becomes informed of the object only in the sense that, since it is a sentient organism, then, once it knows, it is primed to react in response to the object's characteristics as they actually are. It is primed, in the sense that it is now equipped to behave adjustively in relation to, *specifically,* the object. And its reaction, if it does behave in reaction to the stimulus, will not be random, but an *informed* one. That is, it will bear proportion to the actual characteristics of the object. Adjustive behaviour in response to non-conscious cognition cannot be consciously determined or directed, of course; it is controlled by automatic biological mechanisms ranging from simple reflex behaviour to complex instinctual patterns of stereotyped behaviour. Inanimate objects such as photographic film undergo effects, but do not adjust to them experientially, or indeed in any other way.

d) *The effect of the process of perception*

To forestall a possible misunderstanding, I underline that we continue to be concerned with the causation of *perception,* not specifically with the causation of the *conscious* quality of perception when perception is conscious. But since we cannot examine our cognitive processes when they do not attain to consciousness, we have no option but to study the nature of perception by analysing instances of conscious perceptual cognition. Nevertheless, it is possible to differentiate between per-ception and its conscious quality, and I shall try to make the difference clear as we proceed.

The effect of the process of cognition has traditionally been understood as the knower's vicarious mental possession of the 'contents' of objects when they are transferred from the latter and received by the mind. But the only thing that might be properly said to be the 'content' of cognition does not exist in the mind and is not mental, but real. It is the object itself, in its full reality. In other words, cognition may not be analysed in terms of 'act' and '[mental] content,' but only in terms of 'act' and '[real] object.' There is nothing between the cognitive activity and the object. Why must we say this?

A minor and *a priori* reason is that it alone is consonant with the immanence of the causation of cognition by the human organism. But the more important reason is that it is observable. Of course, it is observable only when cognition is conscious. But the relationship of the knower to the known is common to all cognition; the fundamental characteristics of the relationship are not taken away when the experience is enhanced by its developing conscious quality.

To verify that nothing mediates between the mind and the object, it may be useful to perform once again the exercise conducted in the last chapter. You are at this moment looking at an object of the kind known as a book. Where is the object you are seeing? It is, of course, 'out there,' approximately twenty-five centimetres from your nose. It exists outside you. And where do you see it? You see it exactly where it itself is; you see it 'out there.' And you see it *nowhere* else. Most particularly, you do not see it in your mind. It does not exist in your mind. You do not confuse it with yourself or your experience of it. You perceive the book *at* the book, and *only* at the book. And you perceive it as something that is *other-than* yourself and your mind; the book is not a creature of your mental processes. This may be puzzling, perhaps — and even unintelligible, if one is accustomed to thinking that cognition brings reality *into the mind* — but it is glaringly factual in any event. Thus, quite the opposite of our usual assumption (namely, that cognition brings the world into the human organism's mind), cognition *takes the mind into the world*.

The fact that objects do not exist 'in the mind' when they are known — neither representatively nor 'intentionally' — is the reason why in this work I have always used quotation marks around the term 'contents;' I wanted to dissociate myself from the supposition that what we know is not the object, but the 'contents' of the object. Objects have indeed characteristics that we know when we know the object. But they do not become the 'contents' of cognition. *What* we know is the object itself.

Not even skeptics fail to experience that external objects are 'out there', beyond oneself, and that even internal objects are 'other-than' our experiencing of them. For skepticism is not based on any information that skeptics obtain regarding objects; it is based, *a priori* and dogmatically, on the inability of skeptics to interpret their own experience at all adequately. Instead of rejecting their assumptions, they reject their experience and heed instead what Hume described as the 'extravagant attempt … to destroy *reason* by argument and ratiocination.'[291] This is why Heidegger, commenting on Kant's complaint that it is a scandal of philosophy that there is no cogent proof of the existence of external reality, remarked that the scandal 'is not that this proof has yet to be given, but that *such proofs are expected and attempted again and again.*'[292]

Does the 'otherness-to' or externality of objects in relation to our experience of them mean, however, that there is nothing mental *within* us? Not at all. But what is *in* us and *in* our mind, however — that is to say, in our organism insofar as it is endowed with mental capabilities that are currently at work — is our *activity* of perceiving (or imagining, or understanding) the book. If one perceives such activity, it will be because one is conscious. If one were not conscious, one could not be aware of one's mental activities, though one might well have non-conscious cognition of the object just the same. On the other hand, one may be conscious but nevertheless fail to perceive one's own mental activity.

This is, indeed, what may confuse us when we try to understand our mind. On the one hand, one is clearly and forcefully aware of *what one perceives* and *understands*, as well as the fact that one's organism has achieved the state of *actually and currently perceiving* or *understanding.* But on the other, one is not at all, or only dimly, aware of *one's activity of perceiving* or of *one's activity of understanding* what one perceives or understands. The responsibility for putting us in this disadvantageous position lies on our physiology — i.e., on the absence of interoceptive capability in the brain and other components of our cognitive apparatus. But we do count on a few vague and indirect empirical indications of mental activity. For example, one can get a headache from intense mental function.

---

291   Hume, *Enquiry,* XII, 2.

292   Martin Heidegger, *Being and Time* (London: SCM Press, 1962), 249. Italics in the original.

And beginning students of philosophy not infrequently report that prolonged reading of philosophical texts 'makes their heads swim.' Philosophers themselves can become physically tired, indeed, exhausted, if they spend too many sedentary hours thinking and writing philosophically. And during such times they may feel that the apical end of their body seems busier than the rest. In any event, our activities are truly *within* our organisms. What is invariably *without* — without the act at least, if not also without the organism — is *what* one perceives, imagines, or understands. Namely, the object itself. The object is *always* other-than the activity.

It follows that the effect achieved by the process of perception is to establish the relationship previously mentioned, the *cognitive* relationship of cognizer to cognized, otherwise describable as the organism's *state* of perceiving or understanding. The *relativity* of cognition — the fact that it consists in a relationship — imposes itself on us. The relationship, as we have seen, is unilateral; it makes a real difference only to the cognizer; the cognized is not affected simply because it has been cognized. Skipping ahead to conscious perception just for a moment, however, I add that when perception is conscious, a further relationship is created by the perceptual process, namely, the relationship that knower and known bear to each other insofar as both are real; for all real beings are other-to-each-other. We should describe it, therefore, as an *ontological* relationship. And it is not a unilateral, but a mutual, relationship. This relationship becomes known to the knower when the knower establishes its cognitive relationship to the known, though only if the experience is conscious.

Thus, if our perception of an object is of the conscious kind, we know, in addition to the object, the fact that the object is real. And this is important because it helps us understand a little about the nature of reality as well as about the nature of consciousness. The fact underlines that reality is not exactly a feature of objects over and above their characteristics and properties — or a 'property of their properties' as Gottlob Frege and Bertrand Russell thought. The truth is rather, as Thomas taught, that the existence of the object is distinct from the properties of the object. If it were a 'property of the properties,' the object would exist necessarily; it could not not-exist. Existence, as we shall consider more fully in the next section, is rather what makes the object an actual participant in the world; it describes the *fact* that real beings are other-to-each-other. The further fact that *we* can understand it (by measuring it using units of measurement provided by our own mental functions) does not require that the world be *inherently* intelligible, even in the absence of a mind that relates the world as a whole to itself.

Thus, when cognition is less than conscious, the knower and known *are* ontologically related, but the knower does not know that they are so related. In this case, the cognitive relationship is definable by the behavioural dispositions and possibilities that have been created in the organism; that is, the organism becomes capable of taking into account, behaviourally, the reality of the object. When cognition is conscious, on the other hand, the knower is aware of both its ontological and its cognitive relationship to the known. The perceiver can then not only adjust to the information it has gained about the world, but it can also grasp that the object exists and is part of the real world.

We cannot leave the subject without commenting on one of the most controversial aspects of the extremes to which modern philosophers have had to go in order to support the traditional assumptions. If one's analysis of the perceptual process and its causation begins with the usual representationist assumptions, the effect of the process is turned inside out; the knower ends up knowing not reality, but at best a succedaneum of it, such as 'sense data' — or 'qualia,' the favourite conundrum of philosophers only few years ago. For example, the winey taste of wine and the creamy taste of ice cream, it is said, are 'subjective,' although in reality, or 'objectively,' neither has any taste. But if so, where does the taste we taste come from? One of the attractions of cognitivism was precisely that it allowed philosophers the option of retaining, if they wanted to do so, the essentials of representationism without having to trade in the sort of mental 'contents' that had no counterpart in reality. Philosophers could then say that:

> Philosophers have adopted various names for the things in the beholder …
> that have been banished from the 'external; world … [such as] 'raw feels,'
> 'sensa,' 'phenomenal qualities,' 'intrinsic properties of conscious experiences,'
> 'the qualitative content of mental states,' and of course 'qualia' … I am denying
> that there are any such properties … [T]he very idea of qualia is nonsense.[293]

---

293 Dennett, *Consciousness Explained,* 372, 390.

The rejection of subjective qualities, or 'qualia,' like the discarding of dualism, is entirely justified. However, the reinstatement of representations under cover of the 'multiple realizability' of mind created a new, but even less credible, reinterpretation of representationism. There may be a better way.

Quale is, of course, Latin for 'how,' and 'quality' means 'howness.' If one holds, as I have proposed, that the real redness of really red objects is what we in fact perceive when we perceive 'red,' then 'red' is a real *quale,* and it is not at all 'subjective.' It is *how* things that are really red actually look to us, not because our mind has made it up, but because that is *how* they actually are *in relation to us.* And so, apples actually have the properties or *qualities* by virtue of which they reflect light in such manner that they look red to us. The question for philosophy is how to explain facts of this sort, while respecting simultaneously the fact that experiencing does not create reality, and that what the mind experiences is not a mental counterpart of reality, but reality itself.

To do so, we need to remember that the effect of cognition is the relationship I have described — real on the side of the cognizer, logical on the side of the object. It may be useful if I illustrate the point by retrieving the second favourite subject of table talk among first-year undergraduates after they have exhausted the one about the Contest for Primacy Between the Chicken and the Egg. I refer to the Riddle of the Tree that Crashed in the Forest. When a tree comes down in the depth of a forest beyond hearing range of any hearer, does it make a sound, or does it make only compression waves in the atmosphere?

The question poses false alternatives; to choose either would be a mistake. A correct reply would have to begin by stressing that, on the one hand, objects exist and are what they are regardless of whether they are experienced; but also that, on the other, objects cannot very well be *experienced* in the absence of experiencers and their experiential activities. Reality is not inherently knowable; it is knowable only in relation to knowers. (Do not confuse this with the very different, and needless to say, false, supposition that reality can *be real* only in relation to knowers, which would imply that reality depends on our cognition of it.) For experience is a relationship between experiencer and object, of which the experiencer alone is the cause and sole beneficiary. Therefore, on the one hand, an unheard sound cannot be a sound that *sounds* like a heard sound although no one heard it. This would imply that objects can be experienced even when no one is experiencing them. But on the other hand, objects do not *do* our experiencing for us. The experiencer alone experiences; and it does so by taking advantage of the effects that objects have on experiencers, for instance, when objects create compression waves in the atmosphere that may (or may not) physically press against other entities, including experiencers' eardrums.

Therefore, trees crashing in the forest do not merely make compression waves in the air; when they make compression waves, they make something that is *audible;* it can be heard. But only *by a hearer,* of course. Whether the audible sound also is — or has been, or will become — an actually heard sound is a different matter. A compression wave (of the right frequency and volume) is properly called an audible sound, because it already possesses, objectively and in itself, all that it needs before a hearer can hear it. For it is not a sound 'in itself,' but only relative to a hearer. Thus, crashing trees broadcast audible sounds — audible compression waves — which hearers can hear, if there should be any within hearing range. If a hearer hears them, the hearer has not created the audible sound; the hearer actually hears the audible sound made by the crashing tree. If there are no hearers, the audible sounds are, of course, not heard, and amount to compression waves. And so, audible sounds can be made by many sources, but sounds can be actually heard only by hearers. This is hardly a profound observation; it is merely a particular instance of the truth that all experiences must have not only objects, but also experiencers by whose agency the objects become known. Sounds are not *inherently* audible, though they are truly audible *in relation to* potential hearers just the same. (Robert Pasnau has taken a position in this matter that, if I understand it correctly, overlaps considerably with mine.[294])

The point is perhaps more easily grasped in the case of tactile perception, where no distance intervenes between the touching activity of the organism and the object that is touched. When a person touches sandpaper, is the felt 'roughness' in the sandpaper, or is it in the mind of the person? Well, the characteristics of the sandpaper, including its gritty surface are *objectively* in the sandpaper, of course, just as the tactile power of the touching organism is an *objectively* possessed characteristic of the organism. But the person cannot perceive the 'roughness' of the sandpaper unless by actively

---

294   Robert Pasnau, 'What is Sound?', The *Philosophical Quarterly,* 49 (1999), 309-324.

touching it — while sandpaper and its gritty surface, for its part, does not feel 'rough' unless to someone who is endowed with tactile sensitivity and actively touches it. Now, the touching is done solely by the toucher. But what the toucher touches (when he or she touches it, but not otherwise, and only while he or she is touching it) is the 'rough' surface that characterizes the sandpaper. The toucher has related itself tangentially, if I may so put it, to the objectively existing and unchanging reality of the sandpaper.

The prejudice that cognition brings reality into the mind runs deep and turbulent and is not easily diverted from its destructive course. When we imagine something that does not exist in reality, it might be argued, does not the act of imagining have some mental 'content'? And since the content exists in the mind, must we not say that it is a mental or intentional object? No, an act of imagining *does* indeed have an object, but the object is not in the mind. Even in this case the supposed 'content' of the mind is the recalled, actual reality of physically existent objects that had been actually perceived in the past. That is, all the *elements* of anything we imagine, no matter how fantastic, are derived from objectively existing and previously perceived reality; the luxuriant imaginations of a Hieronymus Bosch and a Salvador Dalí are bound by the utter impotence of human beings to 'picture to themselves' anything that is not made up of recognizable aspects of the world that they have actually experienced. The ability to imagine is not the ability to create perceptual objects that do not exist; it is the ability to retain, recall, reproduce, and mentally manipulate — to divide and sub-divide, to combine and recombine — what we have experienced in reality, albeit in ways that need not be found in the world and that may indeed be physically impossible in the real world.

But that is the extent of the originality of our imagination: fantasy never invents the tesserae, only the mosaic. What exists *in* the mind when we imagine anything is not an imaginary object, but the organism's *activity,* and the organic *state* thereby achieved, of imagining the imaginary object. It is therefore not particularly striking that human beings should *imagine* something that does not exist and even something that cannot exist. *Perception* of what does not exist is something else: it would be a miraculous feat. There is no reason to suppose that we ever perform it.

But the objections may persist, and we may be reminded of hallucinations: are they not the perception of something that does not exist? No, it is true that hallucinatory experiences take place; but to call these abnormal cognitive phenomena 'perceptions of objects that do not exist,' or 'false perceptions' — as psychologists often do — is a confused way to describe them. They are not perceptions at all; they do not involve our senses; they are rather a dysfunctional use of our imagination. Their abnormality does not consist in the fantastic nature of what is imagined, but in the hallucinator's inability to advert to the imaginary nature of imagined objects. How can this be explained?

It is an observable feature of the normal human mind that its cognitive activities include information about the *kind* of activity it is. Pathology aside, none of us has any difficulty telling the difference between seeing an apple and tasting an apple. And when we imagine an apple, the experience of the imaginary apple includes reference to its being an imaginative experience. However, like some (but hardly all) dreams, in which indication of the oneiric, imaginative quality of the cognitive experience is either missing from the experience or so vague that we are not sure whether we are dreaming or not, hallucinations are activations of the imagination where a functional or a structural abnormality of the organism prevents the experiencer's correct identification of the kind of experience it is. The hallucinator usually, and the dreamer sometimes, misinterprets its imaginative activity for a non-imaginative sense perception of a present reality. Those who observe this phenomenon may then contribute their own further misinterpretation, and say that the hallucinator has *perceived* an object that does not exist.

e) The nature of consciousness

Let us put aside the question whether consciousness is a peculiarity of our species; in any event, we can be reasonably certain that not all animals are conscious. Mosquitoes and other insects behave differentially towards their environment in accordance with information they 'receive' from the world; they are animals and have cognitive capabilities.[295] But we cannot seriously entertain the possibility, I suggest, that when they strike they know what they do, much less that they do it after reflecting and deliberating, as ordinarily human beings do. Thus, the differentiating characteristic of animal life cannot be consciousness; it is cognition. But evolution did not stop when primitive forms

---

295   In the popular acceptation of anglophone cultures, 'animals' is often restricted to vertebrates, and sometimes even to mammals. This usage is, of course, biologically indefensible.

of cognition appeared, and at some point it developed the specific type of cognition - conscious cognition -that we recognize in ourselves. We share cognition with all other animal species, but we do not recognize consciousness in any other species but our own - though our nearest animal relatives may well approach it. Be that as it may, what bears on the issue I raise is that the difference between a mosquito's cognition and that of a human being suffices to assure us that the term 'cognition' may not be properly used as if it were synonymous with 'conscious cognition.' Cognition may be non-conscious as well as conscious.

If so, we can be reasonably confident that cognition can take place in the absence of consciousness, as is the case in the simplest forms of animal life. However, the fact that there is a difference between the non-conscious cognition of some animals and the conscious cognition of human beings does not of itself answer the question whether all human cognition is conscious. For conscious cognition might well be a highly evolved form of cognition that had replaced altogether the more primitive form of cognition evident at an earlier stage of animal evolution; for aught we know, we might have evolved into animals that were capable of none but conscious cognition. The question I bring up is rather whether consciousness necessarily qualifies every human mental activity. Is it true that some human experiences are non-conscious?

The proposition that human cognition can lack consciousness is frequently greeted with skepticism; and even when it is entertained, its importance tends to be underrated. The reason, in part, is that the possibility that some human cognitive processes may be non-conscious has been given earnest consideration by philosophers only since the turn of the twentieth century, after Sigmund Freud proposed the concept of the 'unconscious' as part of his highly controversial psychoanalytic theory. Many philosophers and even more psychologists have objected to the theory principally on the grounds that it is not 'scientific.' In my view, however, that the nature, the epistemic status, and the validity of psychoanalysis and its concepts are irrelevant to the philosophical issue. One could set aside — as we shall in the present context — every consideration of Freud, psychoanalysis, and the Freudian 'unconscious,' and the question would remain open whether the human cognitive processes are necessarily qualified by consciousness.

But another factor has also been at work keeping alive the identification of all human experience with consciousness. Old habits of speech — and therefore of thought — die hard. Since consciousness first figured in the calculations of philosophers late in the seventeenth century, 'conscious cognition' has been treated, with but rare and unproductive exceptions,[296] as a pleonastic synonym of 'cognition.' It is therefore not difficult to read 'non-conscious experience' as a self-contradictory concept. And besides consuetude, crypto-dualism may be also at work. Crypto-dualists are sometimes unaware of the dualistic implication of the supposition that 'subjectivity' characterizes our mental processes while 'objectivity' characterizes the brain's physiological processes; some crypto-dualists therefore conclude that consciousness can qualify only truly mental (that is, 'subjective') processes. According to Searle:

> When you make a claim about unconscious intentionality, there are no facts that bear on the case except neurophysiological states and processes describable in neurophysiological terms.[297]

Now, if all cognition were conscious, it would follow that, since every animal is capable of cognition, then every animal, even a trilobite or a mosquito, was conscious; if it were not conscious, it would want cognition altogether. I think this is at least doubtful. There are, of course, many physiological processes that do not issue in consciousness, but they are non-conscious only in the sense that they are not *cognitive* processes at all.

Our habits of speech and thought, however, are grounded on certain characteristics of *our* language. (I am not suggesting that it is a characteristic of every language, as if it were of the very nature of language.) I refer to our atavistic tendency to identify reality with 'that which *is*,' or with 'being,' as contrasted with 'becoming.' If one thinks that reality as such does not 'become,' but merely 'is,' one

---

296   The distinction between conscious and non-conscious experience seems to have been first proposed by G.W. von Leibniz in *The Principles of Nature and Grace,* 14, and *The Monadology,* 24. See Philip P. Wiener, (ed.), *Leibniz Selections* (New York: Scribner's, 1951), 530, 537. Leibniz's distinction, however, is not particularly useful for our purposes, because (a) it was not empirically based, and (b) it presupposed dualism. It had to do with the spirituality of the 'rational soul' and with the superiority of the human over the 'simply bare monads'.

297   Searle, *Rediscovery,* 161.

has excised and discarded the temporality of reality. The real as such is timeless and inactive — and we therefore tend to misconstrue our mental *activity.* We have difficulty believing that when we say that the discharge of our cognitive functions delivers 'experience,' we fail to notice that what it delivers is nothing but an *active relationship,* a time-bound mental state that consists in our actively *experiencing* the world. To 'experience' perceptually is not to project a static, unchanging 'picture' of the world upon the inner screen of consciousness: it is to relate oneself temporally to the temporal world in a unique manner that enables the experiencer to *live with* the world. If the experience is conscious, moreover, the activity of 'experiencing' enables the experiencer not only to share in the temporal events that happen in the world, but at the same time to experience its own temporal agency as the agent that procures the experiencing, and thus enables the experiencer to experience its relationship to the world. When we misidentify 'reality' as 'that which *is,*' our understanding of our own perception is distorted beyond recognition.

A further contributory factor to the reluctance of some philosophers to reckon with non-conscious mental processes may be the fact that human beings do not have the power to decree that their mental activities shall be conscious. It is possible for us to refuse to see the scene before us not only by closing our eyes, but also by deadening our consciousness, or through self-deception; but we cannot control our physiology so as to impose consciousness upon a non-conscious mental state. It is easy to assume, therefore, that all cognition is conscious.

The difference between cognition qualified by consciousness, and cognition in the absence of consciousness, is not always rejected as an absurdity; sometimes it is explained away, for example, by invoking 'inattention.' There are countless ways in which stimulation impinges upon the experiential faculties of the human organism, affording it the possibility of gaining the same information as when the experience becomes conscious, but without consciousness arising. To explain this by saying that the organism is 'not attending' is not incorrect; but it would be vacuous and misleading, if what one really meant was that the organism had not raised its becoming informed to the level at which the experience had become conscious. What we may not say is that before 'attention' was turned to it there was no cognition at all; for information had been acquired through sense organs and might well have been used by the organism. Stimulation of the organism, say, by the weight of one's glasses on the bridge of the nose, does not begin when one 'attends' to it. One had been informing oneself for some time, but one's cognitive organs had not been operating at the level of functioning that resulted in conscious experience. Much the same thing is observable when human beings are stimulated lightly during sleep. Responses such as brushing away at a tickle leave no doubt that sleepers have received sensory stimuli, though they make no conscious motor response and do not later report having had any conscious experience at the time.

Hypnosis may illustrate the difference between conscious and non-conscious experience in humans. The subjects are, apparently, not conscious of the obstacle they have been instructed not to see, yet do not stumble over it; they do not *see*, though evidently they 'see.' The hysterically blind and the somnambulist do likewise. Their disability need not be faked; there is some reason to infer that there are cases when they actually 'see,' but that somehow, at the same time, they do not really *see* — consciously. The explanation may be that a sort of self-prohibition produces a purely functional 'blindness;' the conscious quality of the visual experience is either blocked or in some way nullified, though non-conscious visual experience continues.

But hypnosis and mental disorders are unusual phenomena, and we would be justified if we did not deem their evidence sufficiently reliable; let us set it aside. Familiar and difficult to explain away, however, is a phenomenon of which all of us have had first-hand experience. It consists in arranging to receive stimulation while one is not conscious (which one will, experience at first, if at all, non-consciously), for the very purpose of becoming conscious when the information is further processed by the brain and we awaken. What I have just described is what we otherwise call 'setting one's alarm clock.' If we did not 'hear' the sound non-consciously before we awakened and became conscious, we would not be awakened by the sound and thereby become able to *hear* it consciously. Conversely, if non-conscious experience were not possible, the attempt to awaken someone through sensory stimulation could never succeed: the person would have to be awake and be conscious before it could experience the stimulus. Note, however, that the quiescence of the brain during sleep is not identical with loss or diminution of consciousness; on the one hand, animals sleep, and, on the other, human sleep is not always completely bereft of consciousness. But sleep affects the experiential faculties of the organism, which in man include the brain's ability to function in the way required for consciousness. Nor can non-conscious experience be equated with sleep, since non-conscious perception can occur in the waking state.

We have already dealt with the first of the two basic questions that arise from the obser-vation that human experience can be non-conscious as well as conscious, namely, what charact-erizes cognition, if it is not identical to consciousness. Now we face the second: what characterizes consciousness, if it is not identical to cognition What accounts for the difference? And most particularly, what is the cause of the acquisition of the quality of consciousness by cognition?

The next pitfall we must avoid may be the most pernicious of all; historically it has been the one that has exacted the highest toll. I mentioned it in the last chapter, but now I refer again to the concept of consciousness that entered into modern philosophy principally through the work of John Locke. He, and thereafter most modern philosophers, understood consciousness as if it referred simply to our self-observability, our ability to introspect by 'looking into' our minds and beholding its contents. Or to describe it more technically, in this tradition consciousness is our mind's ability to reflect upon, and thereby perceive, by means of a sort of 'inner sense,' as Locke called it, the products of the mind's own cognitive processes or its mental representations of reality, otherwise known as 'ideas.' Now, it is true that the human mind is equipped with the ability to become informed of its mental activities and to use its memory and its imagination to reflect on its prior mental activities and states; but this truth can also throw us off the scent regarding the nature of consciousness. For consciousness is not reducible to such self-observability.

The first philosopher to have pointed this out was, so far as I know, Jean-Paul Sartre, when he proposed that:

> [W]ithout a doubt, consciousness can [both] know and know itself. But consciousness itself is something other than cognition turned back upon itself.[298]

For there is reason to judge that no amount of reflection can impart consciousness to a non-conscious experience. To reflect is to re-experience a *prior* act of experience; one remembers an earlier

---

298   Jean-Paul Sartre, *L'être et le néant* (Paris: Gallimard, 1943), 17.

experience and reproduces it in imagination, making it thus the object of a second cognitive act. We can indeed do so. But this cannot describe the nature of consciousness; for either the original experience was conscious from the outset. or it was not. But if it was conscious, a subsequent act of reflection would be unnecessary for making it conscious; and if it was not conscious from the outset, a subsequent experience could hardly operate retroactively so as to make the earlier to have been conscious.

Moreover, if the second, reflexive act were needed to make the first conscious, what would make the second act conscious? Either the reflexive act is conscious by itself, and from the outset — without the need for yet another act — or else an infinite series of reflexive acts would be required before the original act could acquire consciousness. Thus, if a mental process is to have conscious quality, the conscious quality must be its own; and it must be its own prior to all reflection. Likewise, if the reflexive process itself is conscious, it is because *it* has conscious quality — not because another act has such quality. This, incidentally, should be enough to dispose of all the so-called 'higher order' theories of consciousness.[299] All of them, which tacitly or otherwise presuppose (in addition to representationism) the Lockean interpretation of consciousness, invoke a second cognitive act to account for the conscious quality of a first act.

We may conclude that consciousness is not conferred on cognition by reflection, but that it accrues to the act of cognition itself. This accords with what we can observe in our actual conscious life. Ordinarily we are conscious of objects immediately upon perceiving them; we do not have to wait until we think back about our having experienced them. We are conscious from the outset. But just as we need not be conscious of the fact that we are conscious, we can be conscious of an object without being conscious of the fact that we are conscious of it. Indeed, we are conscious continuously during all our waking hours, but we are conscious of our being conscious only rarely. And when we become conscious of it, there is usually some special reason why we do. Moreover, once we have had a conscious experience, if we remember it later, we remember it as an experience that was conscious at the time, regardless of whether we originally were conscious of its being a conscious experience.

---

299 A survey of the principal 'higher order theories' is available in Peter Carruthers, *Phenomenal Consciousness: A Naturalistic Theory* (Cambridge: Cambridge University Press, 2000).

Thus, consciousness is not equivalent to awareness of one's awareness — although after one experiences an object consciously, one can become consciously aware of such experience. There is a clear-cut difference between consciousness and awareness of awareness. It is the difference between conscious experience of a real object without, and consciousness of the object with, one's being *also* aware of one's prior experience of it. If we take this as a fact, however, the question arises: if self-observation is not a necessary and invariable concomitant of conscious cognition, what is?

Again, the answer is given by experience. Whenever we know an object consciously, we know not only the object, but also that it is an *experienced* object — an object that has the status of being experienced. This is the basis of our experiencing the object *as real*. For the objects we call 'real' or 'existing' are experienced as 'real' or as 'existing' not because they have some property in themselves called 'reality' or 'existence' which we perceive with our senses. (As we have seen, reality is not a property of real things; it is their factual state or condition.) We experience external objects as real, only because we perceive them as independent of our experience. Or more precisely, as *other-than* ourselves and our experience of them: we did not create them, and we are not responsible for their 'being there.' They themselves are 'there.' Thus, conscious cognition is necessarily and invariably the cognition of the *reality* of the object. That is the first defining aspect of it.

But conscious cognition is also, of course, cognition of the *unreality* of the object, if the object is a purely imaginary one. For, whenever we imagine an object, we experience that we are imagining it (just as we experience that we are perceiving it, in the case of perception). Therefore, unless our mental processes are affected by abnormalities such as organic disease or functional impairment caused, for instance, by certain drugs, we imagine the imagined object, but we do not imagine it as a real object. The *absence* of reality in the object is revealed by the difference between experiencing a real object and experiencing an imaginary one. When cognition lacks the quality that makes it conscious, however, neither reality nor the absence of reality comes into play; the cognizer has become informed of a real object, but reference to either its reality or its unreality is no part of the experience.

Of course, otherness-than is a reciprocal relationship. Implicit in the experience of the real as real is therefore a reference to the perceiver's mental activity. An experience could be conscious and could yield the reality of the object only if the experiencer has become informed of not only the object, but also of its own experiential activity. This is the second defining aspect of consciousness. The conscious experiencer is aware of not only the reality of the object, but also of the fact that the object has been experienced — and thus of the reality of the experiencer and of its being the agent of the experience (otherwise known as one's 'self.') On the other hand, as we have repeatedly noted, the degree to which conscious experiencers appreciate their own active causal role in the production of cognition is variable. To the very degree that conscious experiencers are unable to perceive their experiential activities, they will project onto the object the activity that is truly their own. However, their inability to recognize that in fact it is they who *do* their perceiving, does not take away their recognition of the otherness of the object. The experience will in any event remain a conscious one.

To sum up, then, the essential and necessary feature of experience, when it is conscious, is that it yield not merely experience of the object, but experience of the *reality* and *in-itselfness* of the object — as well as, thereby, also experience of the *reality* and *in-itselfness* of the experiencer. That is, one experiences *simultaneously* the reality of oneself and the reality of what is not-oneself, but is itself. We may also refer to such in-itselfness and such reality as the *objectivity* of objects, but only on condition that we remember that the objectivity of objects does not isolate them from the *objectivity* — that is, the undeniable and true *reality* — of the mind. The mind is, after all, an integral part of the one world and its objects. The true objectivity of objects is identical with their reality; it is not identical with their supposed inherent cognoscibility. Why are we apt to suppose otherwise?

If recognition of the role of the experiencer's agency in the procurement of cognition is absent, the nature of consciousness will be misperceived — although such misperception does not change the conscious nature of the experience. (Again, perception can be conscious without being necessarily accompanied by awareness of its being conscious.) On the other hand, once we are conscious of an object, we are in a position to become conscious of the fact that we have become conscious of it; indeed, we can become conscious of ourselves and our being endowed with conscious cognition. We can achieve this by recalling an earlier conscious process and making it the object of a new conscious mental activity — or in other words, by reflecting upon a prior conscious act of perception. Such 'reflexive consciousness' — the conscious mind's ability to observe itself consciously — is indispensable for philosophers who wish to study the conscious mind: it enables them to analyse the human mental processes. And such reflection is possible even if one has misunderstood the nature of consciousness and supposed, as Locke did (and as others have repeated), that it consists in the ability of the mind to reflect upon itself and observe the products of its mental operations.

Thus, it is clear that consciousness comes in degrees of intensity. Beyond the ordinary, everyday conscious perception of objects, we can become aware of the fact that our awareness of objects is conscious. Such awareness, however, does not necessarily imply awareness of the nature of consciousness. And awareness of the nature of consciousness is itself possible in various degrees: one may have a more or less correct understanding of the nature of consciousness. Consciousness develops, and indeed evolves — or in the idiom of today, it can be 'raised.'

The fact that we can have conscious experience of objects without being aware that the experience is conscious can be illustrated by an imaginary 'experiment' that should underline such divergence in an extreme case. Suppose a person who is astounded and dazed while facing imminent death upon being caught in a firestorm during the atrocities of Coventry or Dresden. If someone speaks to him, he does not hear; if he has been wounded, he feels no pain. He is consciously aware solely of the events that spell disaster and destruction. He is conscious; he is aware of the events, but is unaware of his being aware of them. He is aware of what is happening, but is not observing it. Eventually, however, he comes back to the everyday world and someone asks him: 'Why has your hair turned white?' He looks back, remembers his experience, and answers without hesitation: 'I had a harrowing experience, living through an air raid.' And if the questioner persists, 'Yes, but were you conscious when it was happening?' he will reply: 'Of course I was. Did you think I would have slept through it?' He is telling the truth, because at the time of the events he was aware of their reality and their in-itselfness — that is, the fact that the real events were happening to him — although he was not aware of his being conscious of it. He was too busy consciously experiencing the awful reality to reflect on and observe what he was experiencing.

This is exactly what one should expect, if consciousness is not identical with self-observability. The person recalls *later* not only the sounds, sights, and pain that provoked his terror, but also that he was conscious of them, and of his emotions at the time — though *at the time* he was not aware of being conscious of them. He was not observing himself or his mental activity. Understandably, in view of the circumstances, he paid no attention (i.e., was not conscious) of the fact that he was nevertheless fully experiencing the events and their reality. We may conclude that although the conscious mind is able to observe itself, consciousness is not reducible to the self-observability of the human mind. Self-observability is a consequence of consciousness. Or as Sartre put it in his idiosyncratic (and, to me, not fully satisfactory[300] terminology: 'there is a pre-reflexive *cogito* that is the pre-condition of the [reflexive] Cartesian *cogito*.'[301] (Indeed, if my interpretation of certain neuroscientific experiments is correct, there is scientific evidence of the distinction between pre-reflexive and reflexive consciousness, and the temporal priority of the former over the latter.)[302]

---

300   It may suggest, misleadingly, that there are two kinds of consciousness, which is not true. I would refer to distinguish between 'consciousness' and the 'self-observability' of consciousness that results from reflection upon a prior conscious act. What Sartre means, which I think is true, is that 'consciousness' should not be confused with the 'self-observability' of the conscious mind when, at a second moment, the conscious mind reflects upon itself. Consciousness provides awareness of objects and awareness of the activity of the mind *simultaneously,* not successively. One may be conscious (of objects) without being self-conscious. But one cannot be conscious of oneself without reflecting on one's consciousness (of objects).

301   Sartre, *L'être*, 20.

302   Benjamin Libet and his collaborators are well known for a series of experiments the central findings of which may be summarily described as follows. Subjects were asked to decide, at a time of their own choosing, to press a button while watching a clockface — an oscilloscope on which a dot described an orbit — and to take note of the position of the dot when they were first aware of deciding to press the button. The time when the button was pressed was recorded automatically. EEG records of brain activity were kept while the subjects followed the instructions. The results, which have been replicated by other scientists, showed, in Libet's words, that '[f]reely voluntary acts are preceded by a specific electrical change in the brain … that begins 550 ms before the act. Human subjects became aware of intention to act 350-400 ms [after the change in the brain],' Benjamin Libet, 'Do we have a free will?,' *Journal of Consciousness Studies* 6 (1999): 47-57. See also Libet, *Mind Time: The Temporal Factor in Consciousness* (Cambridge, Mass.,: Harvard University Press, 2004).

Interpretations of the results, however, have been numerous and varied, though one of the most common (and the favourite among mind/brain identity theorists) has been that free will is a delusion; see, e.g. the commentaries collected in *Philosophy, Psychiatry, and Psychology,* 3, no. 2 (1996). Supposedly, the results indicate that the decision is made non-consciously by the brain, before the subject becomes conscious of making it. But if so, human beings are actually robots controlled by their brain's independent and non-conscious decisions. This interpretation, however, fails to take into account the elementary observation that human brains do not go about issuing random decisions to press buttons; strangely, the subjects' brains seem to have made their supposedly independent non-conscious decision only after the subjects accepted consciously the experimenter's instructions to make a decision. Others have held that the temporal gap is between two consecutive conscious acts — deciding to press the button, and *then* noting the time. This seems to me closer to the truth, but an oversimplification. My own interpretation takes into account that consciousness is a continuous temporal process, not a succession of discrete acts. In this case, the first stage of the process was a decision (to press the button) that the subject made consciously and deliberately by activating his brain, as recorded encephalographically. This was followed by a conscious reflexive awareness of the consciously made decision, which was in turn followed by conscious awareness of the time, and then by a conscious decision to press the button to report the time. If this is correct, it confirms Sartre's insight that consciousness takes place prior to reflexive consciousness and is distinct from the latter.

Let us recapitulate. To understand the nature of *cognition* (as contrasted with *conscious cognition,* which has all the features of cognition, but is further qualified by *consciousness)* we undertook to determine (a) its cause, which we found to be the activity of the cognizing organism rather than that of the object, and (b) how the organism's activity brings about the cognitive effect that consists in the organism's having become cognitively related to the object. More precisely, the organism becomes so related to the object by taking advantage of the object's passive causation of changes in the physiology of the organism; for such changes enable the organism to take the object and its characteristics into account as it performs its own organic functions. In other words, the changes enable the organism to function in a manner that is proportionate to the object, or adequate to it, and preveniently.

But now, in order to understand the nature of, specifically, *conscious* cognition, we have to establish how its conscious quality is caused, as well the additional benefit it confers upon the cognizer. We have seen that such benefit is, in the first place, that the cognizer becomes aware of the reality of the object, as well as its own reality, and thus, that the organism awakens to its mental life and to the experiential character of its experience; and second, that the cognizer becomes able to observe itself, its awareness of objects, and its own mental functioning, and thus, becomes able to 'manipulate' its experience, i.e., to speak and think about it, to analyse it, and to try to understand and explain it, More particularly, we have to determine: (a) what the organism (which presumably means mostly the brain) would have to do, in order to cause an act of cognition to develop conscious quality, which otherwise would remain non-conscious, and (b) how biological processes in the brain can procure the effect of giving conscious quality to cognition. Certain widely accepted neuroscientific findings, if interpreted in the light of the foregoing philosophical understanding of what constitutes the conscious quality of conscious experience, may help us understand, in principle, how the brain can procure such effect. We should then understand also why there is no 'explanatory gap' between the human mind and the human organism.

f) The causation of consciousness and the illusion of the 'explanatory gap'

Assuming that the human organism causes cognitive states -both those that ultimately become conscious states, as well as those that do not — in the manner that has been suggested above, we now wish to determine the further effect that the organism must work into the process of cognition in order to make the resulting cognitive state to be, specifically, a conscious cognitive state. If one rejects dualism, of course, one would expect such further effect be the outcome of nothing but a further biological process. The question is, therefore: what is added to the biological process that otherwise would stop at mere (i.e. non-conscious) cognition, that renders it conscious cognition? The addition cannot be in respect of the object: the object remains constant, regardless of whether our cognition is conscious or not. But when cognition is conscious, part of what we experience does not have to do with the object, but with the cognitive activity of the organism. And this may be the clue to determining the nature of the additional processing that accounts for the difference between cognition that does not develop conscious quality, and cognition that does.

I have already referred in other contexts to the facts that suggest such additional cognitive processing; we now meet them again, but with a new purpose in mind. The first fact is that, when cognition is conscious, one is aware not only of the object, but also of the fact that *experiencing* is taking place: when experience is conscious, one experiences not simply an object, but an object that, at the same time, is known either to have been perceived, or currently to be in the process of being perceived. This is why, when one has an experience, one can be unclear about precisely *what* has been perceived (and indeed, under certain conditions may even wonder whether it is real or imaginary), but one cannot entertain any doubt regarding *whether* something has been perceived. Or which is the same, when one's experience is conscious, one can never be in doubt that a cognitive process is under way. As we have seen, when this happens one need not, and ordinarily one does not, consciously remark to oneself or reflect upon it. But regardless of whether one remarks upon it or not, it is possible, as we have seen, to recall the experience, upon reflection, as a conscious one.

In other words, we may have a conscious experience without becoming consciously aware of the conscious character of our experience. This is the key observation that led Sartre to differentiate between consciousness (which is a quality of every conscious perception, or of every conscious awareness of an object) and 'reflexive consciousness' (which is the quality of our conscious reflection upon a prior conscious perception, or of our conscious awareness of our conscious awareness of an object). Even in the case of reflexive consciousness, however, the experience will include information regarding the reality (or non-reality) of the object; that is, either the object is experienced as other-than ourselves, or as not other-than ourselves and our mind. In either event, the experience will be a conscious one.

The significance of this is that, therefore, to transform an experience that otherwise would remain non-conscious, into one that has become conscious, all that is required is simultaneous information about the experiential nature of the activity — even when such activity is projected onto the object rather than recognized as one's own. Nothing else is needed — and certainly not reflection. Becoming informed simultaneously of both the object and the mental activity of experiencing the object is the exact point at which the cognitive *process* acquires conscious quality. Thus, when one experiences an object, but experiencing (i.e. being informed about) at the *same time* and by virtue of the *same activity* that the experiencing (of the object) is taking place, the experience necessarily has the characteristics of a conscious experience. Or, to describe the same experience, but from the opposite viewpoint: when one experiences the *object* as other-than *our experiencing* it, the acquisition of conscious quality by the cognitive process coincides with the same activity's recognition of the reality of the object (i.e. its otherness-to our mind, if the object is real), or else its non-reality (i.e. its being not-other-than our mind, if the object is not real). It is, therefore, as part of one and the same event, by one and the same active process, and at one and the same time, that cognition becomes conscious, and that it becomes conscious of the reality of what we perceive (or the non-reality of what we only imagine).

It is not directly relevant to present purposes, though it bolsters the foregoing explanation of the cause of consciousness, that normally conscious experience includes information about the specific sense modality of the conscious perceptual activity involved. If we *see* the object, we know we have *seen* it rather than *heard* it, and so on. I am not referring to the fact that it is easy to learn that one's eyes are involved in 'seeing,' and our ears in 'hearing.' A conscious visual experience is different, *as experience,* from a conscious auditory one. Likewise, no one confuses the activity of *understanding* with the activity of, say, *touching.* It is somewhat different in the case of *imagining;* ordinarily one can tell whether one's experience is that of imagining, but hallucinations do happen; one may think one is perceiving what in fact one is only imagining. Even in the absence of the gross organic abnormalities that account for psychotic hallucinations, the degree of creative freedom that our imaginative powers are allowed, and the variability in self-awareness that consciousness permits, account for the frequently realized possibility that one might be unable to discriminate between what one imagines and what actually is. Likewise, if one is only semi-conscious, whether because of the normal quiescence of the brain during sleep or because of abnormal impediments with the physiology of consciousness, one may remain totally or partly unaware of the information about one's cognitive activity that ordinary, normal conscious experience includes. This does not diminish the conclusion we have reached. The simultaneous conjunction, in the unity of a single active event of cognition, of (a) our informing ourselves about the object and (b) our informing ourselves about our cognitive agency, renders it an act of conscious cognition and accounts for the peculiarities of cognition when it is conscious.

It is understandable and makes sense — though it was not inevitable — that evolution should have created a process that results in the availability to the organism of information regarding its cognitive activities, in addition to information regarding objects. For consciousness can be described, in a sense, and in part, as a unique form of proprioception. Proprioceptive capability can be found in many higher species to provide information regarding non-mental functions. For example, we have the ability to move our limbs as antagonistic muscles pull in different directions; we can control a limb's motion nicely and efficiently, even in the absence of all other clues such as visual information about their position, because we are proprioceptively informed at all times of the activities of the muscles that push and pull the limb. Well, consciousness is somewhat like proprioception, but in respect of our mental activities. One of the consequences of consciousness is that it enables the organism to exert a degree of control over its cognition, as it becomes informed not only of the object to which it attains, but also about the activity of attaining it.

I comment briefly that the ability of human beings to direct their cognitive functions is so useful a consequence of consciousness, that some authors assume that consciousness was selected by evolution *because* of its high survival value. This cannot be true in any event, because evolution does not tend to bring about traits that have survival value *because* of their survival value; this is probably the most common misunderstanding about natural selection. But the further error in this case would be to suppose that consciousness has high survival value. Much of what can be accomplished by conscious experiencers by virtue of their consciousness is deemed highly desirable by us (for example, labour-saving devices, and longevity), but is not relevant to the *biological* survival of human beings to reproductive age, which is what ordinarily counts as survival value so far as concerns natural selection.

Indeed, much of what consciousness procures is ambivalent rather than unequivocally valuable. The ability of consciousness to direct itself and to multiply the power of human ingenuity is a thoroughly mixed blessing, fraught with risks that our species does not always manage to avoid, and with challenges it almost routinely fails to meet with as little as elementary adequacy. The possibility should be entertained, therefore, that when consciousness appeared the reason why it was selected by evolution (i.e. survived), was not related to its supposed survival value. This would not necessarily take consciousness outside the purview of natural selection; Darwinian evolution allows for the so-called selection of characteristics that have no survival value in themselves, if they are incidental to, but genetically accompany, other characteristics that do have survival value. There is no reason why consciousness could not have evolved accidentally. In a sense, every evolutionary change is an accident.

For evolution does not seek survival values; variations do not appear *because* they have survival value, but at random. Natural 'selection' 'selects' or filters characteristics with reference to their survival value, only *after* they appear. But *once they appear,* certain characteristics — or certain packages of characteristics — may have, as it turns out, survival value. Which means, more precisely, that having such characteristic enhances the likelihood that the organism will reproduce itself before it dies. When the affected organisms reproduce themselves, their novel characteristics become incorporated into the genome of the species. Thus, nothing predetermines the course taken by evolution; the surviving characteristics might never have emerged in the first place.

Therefore, no one can consistently accept Darwinian evolution and suppose — as some contemporary *scientists* do — that 'intelligence' (which is their name for the type of mind that is typical of human beings) was predestined to emerge on Earth, and is likely to have emerged, or to emerge in the future, in many other planets where life has emerged. Indeed, they say, 'evolution is such an enormously creative force [that] there are probably also advanced [extrater-restrial] civilizations.'[303] The suppositions that minds of the same (or comparable) nature as ours are plentiful in the universe, and that we can therefore communicate with them, are necessary premises of the Search for Extraterrestrial Intelligence, as well as a firmly held view of many other scientists who do not seem to advert to the, literally, astronomically large unlikelihood of evolution repeating itself.[304] Their supposition is incompatible with Darwinian evolution.

Once we accept that the cause of the conscious quality of conscious cognition is the inclusion of information about both the cognitive activity and the effects of objects on the organism, we are ready to face the question how the two are integrated in the biological functioning of the brain so as to bring about the morphing of non-conscious into conscious cognition. Now, when we inquired into the question how non-conscious cognition is brought about by the organism, we were able to count on scientific assurance of the correctness of the important philosophical point — namely, that the ordinary, inertial causality of the material properties of objects produces effects on the cognizing organism that proportion the organism to the object. We do not have parallel scientific assurance regarding the biological process that produces the conscious quality of conscious cognition. Although neuroscientists have done much research on the subject, they have not come to a stable explanation

---

303   Charles Lumsden and Edward O. Wilson, *Promethean Fire* (Cambridge, MA: Harvard University Press, 1983), 53.

304   The practicality of SETI depends on estimates of the likelihood that human-type minds might be found elsewhere in the universe besides Earth. If such estimates were to comply with the principles of Darwinian evolution, they would assign an infinitesimally small probability to human life having emerged on Earth. Even smaller, in the absence of other evidence, would be the probability of the emergence of a species comparable to the human in another planet with similarly favourable conditions. The SETI enthusiasts assume, however, that once life had appeared on Earth, it was predetermined that sooner or later our human species would appear in our planet, and indeed in other planets: 'a factor of one should be assigned to the emergence of [human-type] intelligence — meaning that it would arise, eventually, on virtually any planet where there is life', Walter Sullivan, *We Are Not Alone* (New York: New American Library, 1966), 250.

But why do those who so reckon not assign a factor of one also to the emergence of Monarch butterflies and ladybugs in virtually any planet where there is life? They do not say — although as simpler forms of life than the human they are somewhat less unlikely to be repeated at random in the course of natural selection, than human beings. Evolution tends to radiate, and is practically certain not to repeat itself. Some well known biologists have therefore commented on the baselessness of the SETI calculations; see Ernst Mayr, 'Are we alone in this vast universe?' in his *What Makes Biology Unique: Considerations on the Autonomy of a Scientific Discipline* (Cambridge: Cambridge University Press, 2004). But the SETI scientists have not been deterred. The emergence of creatures with human - type mental processes throughout the universe is now widely deemed a scientific near-certainty, although it flies in the face of the Darwinian theory of evolution. It is ironic that such scientists have succeeded in reviving in the popular imagination, and even in certain scientific circles, the same supposition that formerly was held on religious grounds; namely, that mankind owes its existence to predilection by a creative force.

about the neural mechanisms involved in the production of consciousness. The reason may well be that they often approach the subject in the dim light of questionable (usually dualistic) assumptions about consciousness, e.g., that consciousness is the 'subjective' 'correlate' of the 'objective' physiology of the brain. If one does not understand well enough what requires explanation, one approaches the subject preconditioned by the expectation of an 'explanatory gap.' One may then fail to recognize the right explanation even when it stares one in the face. The alternative is to realize that in the absence of dualism there can be no 'explanatory gap.' That is, a description of the conscious quality of experience is a description of a *biological state* of the organism that is the effect caused by a *biological process.*

The difference between conscious and non-conscious experience to which I have called attention suggests what the physiological difference between these two kinds of experience may well be. If the difference depends, as I have explained, on the superimposition and integration of information about the cognitive activity upon information about the object — that is, if it depends on the addition of further information (regarding the cognitive activities of the organism) to the information gained regarding the object — and on the integration of the two, certain well and long-known physiological facts regarding the human brain seem the most likely explanation of how the biological functioning of the human organism transforms mere cognition into conscious cognition. For as Francis Crick put it years ago, and as remains true today:

> There is more than a suspicion [among neuroscientists] that such phenomena [as conscious perceptions] result from the [brain's] computation pathways acting in some way on themselves, [though] exactly how this happens is not known.[305]

---

305   Crick, 'Thinking about the Brain,' *Scientific American* 241 (1979): 221. See also Gerald M. Edelman, *Bright Air, Brilliant Fire: On the Matter of the Mind* (New York: Basic Books, 1992), who has proposed one of several current versions of the theory that consciousness results from certain activities of the brain upon itself. If it were confirmed that the physiological cause of consciousness is the sort of activity of the brain upon itself I have described, and if such functioning could somehow be monitored, it should be possible to put to scientific experimental test the hypothesis that the ability to experience consciously is not present at birth, but emerges during the early stages of post-natal development of the human organism.

If I understand Crick's statement correctly, it means that although neuroscientists have observed that conscious perception takes place when certain computation pathways in the brain act upon themselves, neuroscientists do not know how such action of the brain produces conscious perception. But if this is what Crick intended to convey, then his meaning was not well expressed. For what neuroscientists do not know is *not* exactly 'how this happens' — i.e. how conscious perception is produced. They know, as Crick himself says, that conscious perceptions 'result from the computation pathways acting in some way on themselves.' What apparently neuroscientists do not know, is that, when this happens, what happens is consciousness. They have discovered the fact that consciousness is 'correlated' with the action of certain pathways on themselves, but do not recognize that such events are the *cause* of consciousness. Which suggests that the reason why they fail to recognize the explanation when they come upon it, is that they are unaware of precisely what requires explanation.

What requires explanation is the difference between non-conscious and conscious experience. And the difference is that conscious quality accrues to experience when the experiencer gains information simultaneously about its mental activity as well as information about the object, and integrates both. Without such additional information, there is cognition, but no conscious cognition. It follows that nothing else need be done by the brain in order to produce conscious perception, besides acting upon itself appropriately — that is, providing to itself not only information about the object, but also information about the mental activity of obtaining such information, and integrating the two. The conditions that make the experience to have conscious quality have been satisfied. Of course, further neuroscientific studies would be required to fill in the biological details of the process. This would be of great interest to neuroscientists and probably of much practical importance; but once the biological cause of consciousness has been determined in principle the biological details are of secondary philosophical value.

This brings up a question; if it is true that neuroscientists do not grasp correctly the *explicandum* of consciousness, what do they suppose it to be? The answer will differ from one neuroscientist to another, of course. In some cases it may be a deliberate assumption of dualism. More often perhaps, it may be crypto-dualism: The contrast between 'subjectivity' and 'objectivity' makes it impossible to understand how 'objective' events, such as biochemical processes in the brain, could be responsible for something so elusive, if not ethereal, as conscious experience. The classical expression of what is nowadays called the 'explanatory gap' separating biochemical events and states of consciousness goes back a century and a half to the eminent British biologist, T. H. Huxley:

> But what consciousness is, we know not; and how it is that anything so remarkable as a state of consciousness comes about as the result of irritating nervous tissue, is just as unaccountable as the appearance of the Djin when Aladdin rubbed his lamp.[306]

The gap does not exist; it is an illusion created by prejudice. The prejudice is that the difference between 'irritating nervous tissue' and a 'state of consciousness' indicates a difference between an 'objectively *observable*' reality and a 'subjectively *observable*' reality. And the root of this prejudice, *pace* Searle[307], is the supposed difference between 'objective observation' and 'subjective observation.' (an issue that will be discussed in detail below). The difference that is actually observable is rather the difference between the *organic cause,* namely, a biological process of the organism such as 'irritating nervous tissue,' and the biological, *organic effect* thereof, namely, the organism's 'state of consciousness.' A 'state of consciousness' is a bodily state of the human organism. But this is precisely what dualists and crypto-dualists fail to recognize.

To perceive the difference between the organic, bodily cause and the organic, bodily effect, however, it is necessary to take into account the temporality of organic (and indeed all) world processes. On the one hand, effects are neither identical with their causes nor reducible to them. Nonetheless, between a cause and its effect, on the other hand, there is no gap. The causation of effects is not a sequence of static events — as if, first, the cause causes, and then, once the cause has finished causing, the effect takes over and does its part of the job. Causation is a continuous process whereby a given region of the world *becomes* different from what it was at an earlier time. Cause and effect are different moments or aspects of a single continuous process. The integration of the information regarding

---

306   Huxley, *Elementary Physiology,* quoted by Güzeldere, in 'The many faces of consciousness,' in Ned Block et al., *The Nature of Consciousness: Philosophical Debates* (Cambridge, Mass.: MIT Press, 1998), 47.

307   Searle, *Rediscovery,* 19, 65.

the object, and the information regarding the organism's own activity of informing itself regarding the object, ensures the result, namely, not merely a cognitive state of the organism in relation to the object, but also, and at the same time, a cognitive state of the organism in relation to its own cognitive activity. In a word: consciousness.

The illusion of the 'explanatory gap' is responsible for the false disjunction posed by some philosophers: that we must choose between dualism and 'mind/brain identity.' Both should be rejected. The objection to the former has been noted above; the objection to the latter is that it negates the very difference that requires explanation, namely, between 'irritating nervous tissue' and 'experiencing consciously.' It reduces the latter to the former. But this is illogical and arbitrary; reductionism explains differences by erasing them, and it explains effects by declaring them identical with their causes. In my view, this is not a philosophically permissible procedure; it yields only the illusion of truth.

g) The consequences of consciousness for the human mode of life

Consciousness is the foundation of the human mode of life. Nevertheless, consciousness is sometimes treated, even by those who do not contemn it, as if were one among the many issues into which 'the problem of human nature' may be divided. Actually it is, in a sense, the only one; all other questions about the specificity of human nature are particular aspects of it. For, without exception, all that makes our life what it is, either is conscious experience or affects — or is capable of affecting — our consciousness. Without consciousness, neither our existence nor our experience could be of any value or importance to us. *All* that matters to us is our conscious life. Of course, there is more to living the conscious life than perceiving the world consciously: conscious perception is hardly the only human biological function, or even the only cognitive function. But the other biological processes of the organism have no value in the absence of the capacity for conscious experience. Human beings are definable as organisms that are capable of consciousness.

The direct consequences of consciousness for the human individual are two; they are closely related, and they have a common source. As will be remembered, all cognitive activity transcends the cognizer and reaches something that is 'other-than,' or 'other-in-relation-to,' the cognizing organism

— or at least, in the case of internal objects, 'other-than' the cognizer's act of knowing it. At every level of cognition, the cognizer makes contact with reality, but in the case of non-conscious cognition, the cognitive activity relates the organism simply to an object that in fac*t is* 'other-than' the experience. Conscious cognition, however, includes information about the cognizing organism's cognitive activity, and therefore relates the organism to an object that *is experienced as* 'other-than' the experiencing organism. [308] (The *mutual* relationship of the reality of the mind and the reality of the object, i.e. the *ontological* relationship, should not be confused with the *unilateral* relationship of cognition to the object we encountered above i.e., the *cognitive* relationship. The latter relationship is relevant to understanding the nature of *cognition*; the former is relevant to understanding the nature of *reality*.)

The difference between experiencing something that *is* 'other-than' the experiencer, and experiencing it *as* 'other-than' the experiencer, is the difference between experiencing objects that in fact are real, but without experiencing that they are real, and experiencing them with awareness of their being real. Or as the case may be, that they are 'not real', but that they are rather a creature of our imagination crafted out of our relived and manipulated experiences of the real world. Well, when we become aware of such difference, we have become aware of what by another name we call the 'reality' (or the 'existence') of the real. Conscious cognition is the kind of cognition where objects are experienced in the dimension of reality-unreality. Nothing guarantees, of course, the infallibility of any given perception of reality, and least of all, the correctness of one's portrayal and interpretation of it; delusions, and especially illusions, regarding what is real and what is not real are not uncommon. Experiencing the real as real, and the unreal as unreal, and to discriminate between the two, is at the heart of our human, conscious life.

If the foregoing account of how we learn to perceive the reality of the real is correct, it is not true, as it is sometimes assumed, that before we experience real objects we are already in possession of the concept of 'reality' and that we then discover that real objects fit the concept. Nor is it true, as

---

308 The alienation of the mind from its objects was explicitly noted by the later Scholastics at least as far back as the seventeenth century, when John Poinsot (frequently referred to by historians by his religious name of John of St Thomas) said that to know was 'to become the other than self… as other than self' (*On the Soul*, IV, 1). But this formula served only to perpetuate the representationism that underlay it. To experience consciously is not to *become* the other as other, but to *experience* the other as other.

others suppose instead, that there is something in objects that is usually called their 'reality' or 'existence,' which we capture with our minds in somewhat the same way we capture its other properties. The viable and empirically defensible alternative is, in my view, that what we call the reality of the real *is* the *relationship* of 'otherness-to' that binds together all real things into a real world. We begin to grasp this when we experience the relationship of 'otherness-to' that objects have to the cognizing organism. And we continue to grasp it when we observe that the same 'otherness-to' also describes the 'reality' of the mind in relation to real objects. For the mind, too, is an object, an *objectively* real constituent of the real world. Thus, reality *is* the mutual relationship that characterizes the individuals that make up the world. (Again, the *mutual* relationship of the reality of the mind and the reality of the object should not be confused with the *unilateral* relationship of cognition to the object we encountered earlier.)

Of course, if one presupposes that what we experience is a representation of reality that exists within the mind, one will have reason to wonder whether the 'otherness-to' of objects is not created by the mind and is indeed part of the mind.[309] Otherwise one will have no difficulty observing that the externality of objects in relation to the cognition (and to the human organism) is not the only externality of objects. All things are related to each other, and not only to human beings, by being 'other-than' each other. This interpretation of the nature of reality will be expanded when we take up for its own sake, in the next section, the topic of the nature of reality.

The second consequence of conscious life (or rather, the second aspect of the same consequence we have been studying) is the correlative of the experience of the real as real; it is the sense of *self* that corresponds to the sense of the *world*. All cognition demands, of course, a cognizing organism as well as a cognized object; but when cognition is conscious, the cognizing organism acquires information regarding the cognizer itself — that is, regarding the mental functions of the organism itself. This is why the immediacy of the experience of selfhood is striking. I cannot begin to imagine what it would be like to suppose that my cognition was done by, or happened to, someone other-than me, or that it was not done by anyone. And I do not believe I am alone in finding it impossible to image it. Least

---

309   That is, one will confuse the relationship of the cognizer *as cognizer* to the object cognized (which is real on the side of the cognizer, but only logical on the side of the object), and the relationship of the cognizer *as a real being* to the real object (which is real on both sides, and mutual).

of all can I imagine that 'it knows' is an objectively existing 'occurrence' that, like 'it rains,' simply happens, without its happening to, or its being done by, anyone. If I refrain from commenting that a person would ordinarily have to be deranged before it could seriously entertain this thought, it is because I am also aware that self-deception can impersonate rationality.

The foundation of the sense of selfhood is the mutual relationship of object and cognizer. As we have repeatedly noted, nothing can be merely 'other;' whatever is 'other' is 'other-than' something else. Thus, the necessary counterpart of the sense of *world* is the sense of *self*, because to experience the other *as other* is to experience it as other-than something else, or as other-to-another. And since to experience an object consciously is to be aware of it as other-than the act whereby it is experienced (or as other-than the experiencing organism), it follows that to be conscious of an object is the same as to experience it as relative to, or as other-than, the 'something else' that is the act of experience (which is performed by the experiencing organism). This 'something else' is what eventually the conscious organism learns to call *me*.

But only eventually. For what we call *I* or *me* — the self that experiences consciously — is originally devoid of all personal identity; it comes into being bereft of almost all positive content. (It counts, of course, on a genetic endowment that conditions its development, but that is a different matter.) We can understand why, if we reflect upon the process I have just described. The conscious organism awakens to its own reality by experiencing itself merely as the 'something else' to which the real objects it experiences are relative; the self is, to begin with, nothing but that which is 'other-than-the-object.' It is, indeed, if I may awkwardly but exactly put it, nothing but 'the other-that-the-other-is-other-than.' So far as concerns its conscious life as a self (and apart from the limitations placed upon it by its genetic endowment), a human being is, therefore, born as a purely negative reality; it is merely that-which-is-*not*-the-world. Selfhood begins as a mere capacity of the organism for acquiring identity — a capacity that is grounded on the fact that information regarding the organism's experiential activity (namely, that the experiencer is *not-the-object)* has been made part of the conscious experiencing of the object. Thus, conscious organisms possess their own identity only because they construct it; they are persons only because they develop personhood. Selfhood is the quality that conscious cognition earns for the cognizing organism in consequence of the organism's becoming acquainted — more or less well, of course — with its cognitive agency. In other words, it is the outcome of the infusion of conscious quality upon cognitive processes that otherwise would remain non-conscious.

What I have just proposed runs counter to some of our common assumptions, which suppose that the self is an aboriginal substantive reality. According to preference, the *ego* may be identified with the organism (or at least with its immature, genetic potentialities) or with a non-organic soul or mind, or else with the composite of organism plus mind, or body and soul; but, in any case, the human person supposedly pre-exists its development. The *self* is, therefore, deemed the subject of events and operations; after it has human reality and existence it activates its faculties and obtains experience. Among other experiences, so runs the argument, it experiences its own reality and conscious nature, eventually becoming conscious of its consciousness and of the selfhood that it possessed at least in immature form even before it was conscious.

This construction, however, is not justified by any empirical evidence. It is indeed self-contra-dictory, if one accepts the fact that one is *really* whom one experiences oneself to be. For the most fundamental empirically given characteristic by which one can identify one's selfhood is: being the experiencer who performs one's conscious acts. To be oneself is above all to be the agent and the owner of one's own experience. Of course, one may have a tighter or looser grip on one's self-pos-session. One may also deceive oneself about one's identity; one may even do so deliberately. Self-appropriation is achieved by individual human beings to very different degrees. But the self could perceive itself as the performer of its conscious acts, or as the owner of its own experience, only *after* the organism had performed conscious acts and only *after* there was conscious experience that could be owned. The interpretation of selfhood according to which the existence of the self is antecedent to its mental life, implies dualism.

Selfhood, as I understand it, is not the antecedent, but the consequent, of conscious experience; the only antecedent required by selfhood is an organism that that has the organic, physiological capa-bility of functioning mentally at the level of consciousness, though it is not yet a person.[310] But con-

---

310   Its aboriginal lack of selfhood, however, does not prevent its having the inborn, genetically determined dispositions that will later condition the self-identity that it will give itself.

sciousness personalizes itself; or more exactly, the human organism creates its personhood by means of its ability to function consciously. As it accumulates its experiences of its own cognitive agency, it creates its self. This is not to forget, however, that we do not choose the specific world into which we are born, nor therefore the range of objects and events that we shall experience. Whether we realize it or not, we create ourselves, but not out of nothing; we create ourselves out of the specific and limited resources that we find in ourselves — and in our communities and our species, — as we live out our lives and interact with other human beings and with the world.

h) The fallibility of the human mind

On several occasions above I have drawn attention to the fallibility of the human mind. It may be wondered whether the matter is of much relevance to the problem of why philosophy has stagnated and what it should do in order to recover. Besides, everyone knows that 'to err is human.' Has any philosopher proposed that the human mind is infallible? To bring up his topic for philosophical discussion is unusual enough to call for justification.

Well, ideas, especially the fundamental kind, tend to have consequences not only when conscious ratiocination about them leads to conscious conclusions. Ideas also have implications that philosophers might not become fully aware of, or at all, but which are apt to influence their thinking just the same — if in no other way, by generating subliminal attitudes and unacknowledged expectations. One of the fundamental ideas that has been with us ever since the Greeks, was that cognition is caused by objects. And one of the remote implications of this, of which we may become only dimly aware, or not at all, suggests that normally we should not make mistakes. (How could we, if we are not the cause of our cognition?)

The implication comes about because part of the same *Weltanschauung* that assigns to objects the causation of knowledge is the supposition that objects are knowable because of the necessity that inheres in their nature. Thus, the causation of cognition by reality is, otherwise described, the necessitation of the mind by the nature of the objects it knows. But if so, what is the cause of mistakes? Since objects cause our knowledge, they could not be the cause of error; they could not act so as to frustrate their own causality. On the other hand, it cannot be denied that we make mistakes. But if so, how do our mistakes fit within our traditional philosophical interpretation of cognition? And in what sense are they *our* mistakes?

Plato's identification of reality and the 'divine' and the stark opposition between the 'divine' and the material led him to propose, in effect, that when the soul in an earlier life beheld the Forms directly, its knowledge was infallible. At the other extreme, once the soul was embodied in matter, it had only the illusion of knowledge; the best it could aspire to were the faint 'reminiscences' of is originally infallible knowledge. And thus, in effect, either one has infallible knowledge, or else no knowledge at all, but only the illusion of it. Knowledge that is truly knowledge is necessarily knowledge that is true.

Aristotle's reformation of the Platonic scheme was much more realistic, and did not have to suppose the mythological elements required by Plato's. And so, although both perception and understanding (at least to the extent that the latter is 'passive') are, according to Aristotle, the effect of the object, it is clear that the mind may contradict the message sent by the object. If so, its knowledge is false: 'to say of what is that it is not, or of what is not that it is, is false; while to say of what is that it is, and of what is not that it is not, is true.'[311] But why would any sane human being say of what is false that it is true, or of what is true that it is false?

Aristotle left it at that; he did not explain what the mind had to do in order to contradict the truth that otherwise the object would have caused. He seems to have assumed that a mistake happened when cognition (which *as such* was invariably true, since it was caused by the object) failed to be accorded recognition by the knower. (But how, or why?) Error was the purely negative absence of such recognition. It did not have to be explained as part of the interpretation of cognition, because it took place beyond the strictly delimited cognitive process. But however it may have come about, a lasting bias or predisposition against the *positive reality* of error entered into the philosophical tradition at a relatively early stage in the history of philosophy. In modern philosophy it is manifested, for instance, in the search for 'theories of truth' — rather than 'theories of truth *and falsity*.'

---

311 Aristotle, *Metaphysics*, 4.7.1011b26-7.

The bias reinforced the classical belief that, unlike the common sense of the culture, philosophical knowledge could be relied upon to deliver truth. Since philosophical knowledge reveals the inward necessity of things, and since its further conclusions are backed by logical demonstration, philosophy is characterized by *episteme,* 'trustworthiness' or certainty. More exactly, it is characterized by *warranted* certainty. For certainty can be either imprudent or prudent. The certainty that accompanies philosophical knowledge is warranted, because it results from logical demonstration; the truth is 'proven' before it is accepted as such. The warranted certainty of philosophical knowledge contrasts with the pseudo-certainty of the pseudo-knowledge of common sense, namely, the belief that the truth has been attained, despite the absence of good reason to suppose as much. The dichotomous opposition of philosophy and common sense as truth and falsity has survived to the present — even if, for reasons I have explained, it does not work to the advantage of philosophy. Philosophical knowledge is not esoteric. It ignores its continuity with common sense at is peril — as well as the continuity of falsity and truth.

The bias against the fallibility of cognition influences us also in other respects; for in order to treat cognition as if it were infallible, it is not necessary to say explicitly that the human mind is infallible. Our bias may merely incline us to take no interest in why and how it is possible for us to make mistakes. The tacit *expectation* amongst us is not rare, that cognition should, by virtue of its nature, invariably attain to truth; in the normal course of events we should not make mistakes. The human mind was made for knowing truth; in the absence of truth there is no knowledge, but a travesty thereof. Conversely, an aura of abnormality clings to error, as if making mistakes subverted the use of our mental powers.

Contrary to this, there is some reason to argue, I think, that the fallibility of the mind is quite as normal as its ability to know truthfully. And it is important to know why we must say so. The reason is that certitude would be possible only to a mind that existed outside time and worldliness; awareness of our mind's fallibility should bring us, on the contrary, face to face with the temporality and historicity — and thus with the worldliness — of the human mind. Now, I stress again that neither the Greek nor the modern philosophers have ever denied that, *as a matter of fact* all human beings, including philosophers, are liable to make mistakes. But the ordinary supposition has nevertheless been that although human cognition is *de facto* fallible, philosophical knowledge as such and *de jure* — that is, by *nature* and *ideally* — should be infallible.

Surely, it will be objected, this is factually untrue: surely philosophers have never made so obvious a mistake as supposing themselves infallible. Has anyone actually suggested it? Well, not often explicitly. But one can also suppose it implicitly, for example, by supposing that philosophy can attain to unqualifiedly certain knowledge. For what is dogmatism, if not the manifestation of the unacknowledged assumption of infallibility? To believe that one's knowledge is certainly true is the equivalent of believing that it is impossible that one has made a mistake. Besides, on some occasions infallibility has been explicitly supposed to be a normal attribute of human nature.

The opinion that the human mind was *naturally* infallible, although it makes mistakes extra-naturally, so to speak, was actually drawn by some scholastics. According to Thomas Aquinas, 'as truth is the good of the intellect, so falsehood is its evil.' Therefore, he concluded, at the time when God created human nature 'it would have been impossible for the human intellect to assent to falsehood as if it were truth.'[312]. Not only philosophical reason, but every level of knowledge, would have been infallibly true by reason of the nature of the mind.

The reasoning of any scholastic theologian who so concluded would have been facilitated by Christianity's having ready at hand an explanation for what otherwise would have been a baffling disparity between the natural infallibility of the human mind and its factual fallibility. But the discrepancy was explained satisfactorily by the Christian doctrine that human beings do not actually exist in a 'state of nature.' According to Christianity, Adam's disobedience 'disfigured' or 'wounded' human nature, and one of the consequences of the 'state of fallen nature' in which Adam's descendants thereafter were born was the 'darkening of the intellect' that makes understanding difficult and learning laborious, and which renders human beings liable to make mistakes. Note, however, that in Aquinas's argument, Christian doctrine is invoked only as the explanation of the *factual* fallibility of the mind. Thomas's basis for supposing the *natural* infallibility of the mind is not religious faith. It is the nature of the mind as traditionally conceived: the natural and normal function of the human

---

312 Thomas Aquinas, *Summa Theologiae,* I, 94, 4.

mind is to attain to true knowledge, not to falsehood, because 'as truth is the good of the intellect, so falsehood is its evil.'

However subliminally, the supposition that the human mind should ideally not make mistakes has constrained philosophy to try to understand a mind that in fact operated in time and space and in history, but which, to judge by some of its supposed properties, was better suited to sojourn in the realm of the divine and the eternal. For example, although no one can say with much confidence what Aristotle meant when he described the office of the so called 'agent intellect,' there is no question regarding what he *did* say about it, namely, that of all the aspects of the human soul, it 'alone [was] immortal and eternal.'[313] However unintentionally, the assumption that the human mind was capable of warrantedly reaching unqualified certainty and unmixed truth, implicitly ascribed immateriality to the human mind. And however indirectly and remotely, this assumption could not but have contributed to the ultimate failure of philosophy. Therefore, if we are to overcome it, we have to get to the bottom of the issue. Is the human mind capable of achieving unqualified but *warranted* certainty? And if it is not, what does it tell us about the nature of the mind? And about the nature of human error? And — perhaps most important of all — how mistakes can be redeemed once they are lapsed in?

Let us begin to explore these questions by remembering that the temporality of the world encompasses, of course, the temporality of the human mind and its processes, including philosophical thought. That human knowledge is inherently time-bound, historical, and worldly, and therefore inherently fallible, is not an *a priori* conclusion. Observing how the human mental life actually unfolds provides the empirical evidence of it.

In Chapter I we touched on the difference between the experiences of 'being right' or 'being correct,' and 'being wrong' or 'being mistaken.' From an early stage in life, human beings have occasion to experience that their cognitive activities seem to have met with success. But the contrary sort of experience sooner or later catches up with them: their perceptions or their understanding have failed to achieve their purpose. Our received linguistic conventions, however, do not do justice to the imbalance between what we usually describe as 'being right,' and what we call 'being wrong.' The

---

313   Aristotle, *On the Soul*, 3.5.430a23.

truth is that no one ever experiences *'being* wrong' or *'being* mistaken,' i.e., now, at present. What we experience sometimes is *'having been* wrong,' or *'having been* mistaken.' Errors never show themselves up until they have ceased to be such, because what we had deemed true, but mistakenly, has been replaced by what we *now* deem true. To be sure, the consequences of our mistake may very well remain to the present, and even pursue us into the future, but that is a different matter. The point is that, try as we might, we cannot think that the truth is the opposite of what we at present think.[314] We can never experience our errors as such unless in retrospect.

The nature of truth and falsity will be further discussed presently. At the moment let us pause to note that truth is the normal outcome of our cognitive efforts, because we discharge our mental functions for the purpose of becoming informed of the world. But let us also observe that this does not imply that error is abnormal; making mistakes is every whit as normal as achieving truth. The explanation is that our mental functions, having acquired through evolution the capacity to bring off cognition by their own causal efforts, are oriented towards the attainment of cognition, but have limited causal power to accomplish it. Thus, we cannot understand our cognitive powers well, unless we *positively* understand that they are fallible. A theory of truth *and falsity* should have something to say about the fallibility of the mind and the fact that we make mistakes.

These suggestions are in part close to the teaching of C.S. Peirce, who in the late nineteenth century, taking a different route from mine, arrived to what he called 'fallibilism.' His proposal, however, seems to have been shunted aside by the philosophical mainstream. Nevertheless, study of our experience shows that, since human cognition is fallible, both truth and falsity are normal and both are possible; what is not possible is *cognitio certa,* cognition that is supposed to justify undisturbed and unqualified confidence in one's having reached the truth of the matter. Let us mark well the logical property of the human cognitive processes that results in our thinking, at any given time, that whatever we are perceiving or understanding is to be deemed true; otherwise, we would not think it. It follows, as Peirce also noted, that this property of the human mind is dangerous to human intellectual health. It is a principal reason why it is so easy for human beings to be dogmatic. Philosophers

---

314   One can lie, of course, by misrepresenting what in fact one thinks is the truth; but one cannot very well simultaneously lie and think that the lie is true. One can, however, persuade oneself that one is not lying, though in fact one is. In other words, self-deception is perfectly possible. But it does not affect my suggestion that the experience of error is always retrospective.

should warn themselves that, as Peirce said, 'the first step towards *finding out* is to acknowledge that you do not satisfactorily know already; so that no blight can so surely arrest all intellectual growth as the blight of cocksureness.'[315] John Dewey, too, advised philosophy to beware of certainty and to refuse to join in its pursuit.[316] It may have been unhealthy for our civilization that this has not always been clear. Sometimes we pass judgment on the opinions of others by determining whether they confirm our own. Not all philosophers seem to realize that, whereas I must willy-nilly think that you are mistaken if you disagree with me, I am not entitled to think that you are mistaken just because you disagree with me. The difference seems to escape them.

We can, of course, become aware of our mistakes and errors. But only in either of two ways. Primarily, as already noted, we can experience 'being mistaken' as a condition in which we actually existed in the past, but in which we no longer exist (for *now* we judge that it was a mistake). The second way is derivative: it is possible only after we have perceived our having made mistakes in the past, and consists in imagining a hypothetical condition of our minds in which, as we foresee, we may possibly exist in the future, if we should eventually discover that when we had previously thought we were right we had in fact been mistaken.

But if it is true that we can be conscious of our mistakes only retrospectively, it follows that a human being who has experienced his or her fallibility even once could not thereafter, justifiably, discard the possibility that despite his or her reasonably judging (at present) that he or she was right,[317] he or she might in fact have made a mistake but had not yet recognized it as a mistake. And if so, every claim that one's knowledge is *certainly* true, or that one is sometimes entitled to have *no doubt* that one is right, is dogmatic. What may be warranted is rather the estimate that one's knowledge enjoys a *degree* of reliability — though to be sure, even this more modest claim is not warranted simply because the claim is made, but only if one has good and sufficient reason for judging that it is warranted. Nor is the question what constitutes such 'good reason' beyond debate.

---

315   C.S. Peirce, *Collected Papers,* vol. I, 1.13; quoted by Nicholas Rescher, 'Fallibilism,' in Honderich, (ed.), *Companion to Philosophy*, 268.

316   Cf. Dewey, *The Quest for Certainty: A Study of the Relation of Knowledge and Action* (New York: Putnam's, 1929).

317   The judgment that a certain conclusion one has reached is correct can be reasonably or unreasonably made. The judgment can be reasonable if it makes allowance for one's fallibility and is therefore made only after self-criticism.

Absolute certainty in this respect is as impossible as in any other. And the warrant is always issued by oneself, who is fallible.

The fallibility of the human mind should affect profoundly our conception of philosophy. It demonstrates once again not only that foundationalism cannot be correct, but also that its basis — the supposition that the human mind can enjoy warranted certainty, and that philosophical knowledge is indeed characterized by such certainty — is false and misleading. Certainty could be warranted only in Cartesian minds, whose understanding of objects was instantaneous and exhaustive, 'clear and distinct,' instead of having to be developed and improved upon a little at a time. We neglect our fallibility at our disadvantage. We may rest assured, however, that fallibility entails no skepticism. The truth of our knowledge depends on our exercising our cognitive functions appropriately; it does not depend on our thinking that our knowledge is true, or in our assessing it as such. The sincere admission to oneself of the possibility that one may be mistaken is compatible with a reasonably and cautiously made — but of course, fallible — assessment of one's judgments as probably true.

One's assessment of the truth of one's opinions may be reasonable if the likelihood of their truth is measured by reference to the procedures through which one arrived at them. Not every doubt is reasonable; only a philosopher intoxicated with logic will actually think that, since there is no empirical evidence that causation involves the necessitation of effects; next time the ice-cube tray is placed in a freezer the water may well boil. On the other hand, one's opinions are never true *because* one thinks they are. What our fallibility implies is rather that there is no way in which we can ensure beforehand that we shall not make mistakes. Awareness of our radical fallibility entails recognition of the hard fact that there is no device, no formula, no mechanism, no method, no magic charm whereby our knowledge can be guaranteed at any time to be error-free. To accept the temporality and fallibility of the human mind is not to give up a privilege or advantage we have hitherto enjoyed. It is only to reject a delusion that has tended to hobble philosophy's understanding of the human mind by promoting dogmatism.

It also follows that the correction of errors cannot be itself explained correctly as long as we suppose representationism and the passivity of a human mind which supposedly makes mistakes because it failed to conform to, or be moulded by, the active causation of experience by objects. We cannot correct our mistakes as long as we do not acknowledge our active responsibility for having *committed* them. As long as we suppose that the error resulted from our not having received reality 'as it is' — which is to say, as long as we suppose that we *suffered* or *underwent* the error when our mind failed to reflect reality faithfully — we are not open to correcting the error by our own renewed activity, as best we can, and if we can.

Likewise, since one cannot experience one's mistakes except in retrospect, human beings cannot come to believe that anything is true unless they are open beforehand to the possibility that it might be so. We all have had the experience of witnessing the dogmatism (always someone else's, of course) that will not accept the plainest evidence to the contrary, and we find it difficult to understand why. But unreasoning dogmatism is grounded on self-misunderstanding; it is a consequence of the fact that human knowledge is time-bound, qualified by historicity, and that therefore our present experience is always deemed true. Unless we quite clearly, deliberately, and fully consciously conceive our mind as an inherently fallible active and creative power, we will lack the disposition that is required in order to be open to changing our minds. Only then is it possible for us to take, as we say, 'a fresh look' at the evidence and to entertain a new truth.[318]

i) The relativity of truth and falsity

The account of cognition I have proposed has been confined so far to human sense perception; the question how sense perception is augmented by understanding has been pragmatically excluded from the scope of this chapter. But what we have already learned suggests that even now we may round out our study of the rudiments of conscious perceptual cognition by examining the nature of truth and falsity principally at the level of perception, though our findings should generally apply to understanding as well.

An important difference between the concepts that make up the initial assumptions of philosophy — cognition, causality, and reality — and the concepts of truth and falsity should be noted at

---

318   I specify for clarity's sake that I have been arguing in favour of 'fallibilism' and against dogmatism in the context of *knowledge*, particularly of course scholarly knowledge. Faith is appropriate, of course, and indeed, indispensable, in the sphere of personal relationhips.

the outset. The former are primary and underived, whereas the concepts of truth and falsity presuppose, and are shaped by, our prior conceptions of cognition and reality. If one accepts the traditional assumptions that objects cause cognition and become part of the mind, one cannot very well avoid supposing that truth is the valuable quality that enhances the mind when its cognition corresponds to, mirrors, repeats, or otherwise *conforms* to the reality cognized. Somewhat different versions of truth as the correspondence of mind and reality follow from different views regarding which aspect of the human mental life — sentences, propositions, or statements — is the 'bearer' of truth. But the differences are not important for our limited purposes. Revised assumptions of cognition and reality, however, demand revised notions of truth and falsity.

The experience that the activation of one's cognitive functions is sometimes more successful than at other times is implicit in the characteristic of the mind previously discussed: sometimes we find it necessary to change our minds. We so find when we experience that our earlier cognition was not true, but false. The experience of truth and falsity in this sense is universal in the species. After enough ordinary experience, every human being perceives the difference between truth and falsity, as well as the value of one and the disvalue of the other. Valuation is necessarily involved, because cognition is valuable; the cognitive functions are discharged for the ultimate purpose of achieving an adjustive relationship to reality. But of course, the precise meaning of the concepts of truth and falsity depends in large part on one's prior conception of cognition and reality. All human beings are conscious of truth and falsity as values and disvalues that their cognition has at different times, but their concepts of truth and falsity may be more or less correct. They may be quite mistaken, and at the limit they may even be absurd.

Having already discussed why representationism is untenable, there would be little point in showing in any detail why the conception of truth as the conformity of the mind to reality, or its correspondence to reality (and of falsity as the absence of truth), is self-contradictory. Two remarks should suffice. The first is that the 'correspondence' conception of truth is vitiated not only by representationism, but also by the mistakes that precede representationism, in particular the attribution of the causation of knowledge to objects, and the assumption that objects are inherently knowable. When these suppositions are coupled with the fact that our knowledge of objects is conscious — and that therefore we become aware not only of objects, but also of their reality — it is not difficult to become confused. We then suppose that representations have (or lack) truth, to the extent that they represent reality accurately or faithfully (or fail to do so). That is, truth and falsity have to do with the extent to which our mental representations of reality coincide (or fail to coincide) with reality. But this cannot be true, because the accuracy of mental representations could be evaluated only by comparing reality and our knowledge of it. And this is not only impossible but absurd. This conception of truth invites us to know an object without our availing ourselves of a representation of it, after supposing that we can know objects only by means of a representation.

The second remark is that the 'correspondence' or 'conformity' concept of truth supposes that the truth value of knowledge, which is variable (i.e. true or false), depends on whether it meets the fixed requirements of the object. The mind is expected to 'conform to,' or 'to mirror' the object, saying, as Aristotle said, 'of what is that it is, and of what is not that it is not.' It is as if the mind owed a duty of justice to reality, an obligation to acknowledge exactly what it owes to reality. Which would imply the absurdity that the benefit of true cognition and the disadvantage of falsity accrue to objects rather than to cognizers. When we depict the world correctly, we do what is right by the world; when we make a mistake, we fail to give it its due.

To understand the nature of truth and falsity we should begin by remembering that the cause of cognition is the discharge of our organism's cognitive powers, and that the effect that the cognitive activity seeks is a cognitive state of the organism; such state consists in one's being informed of the objects on which the powers have been trained. Since the cognitive function is purposive, the resulting state is valuable to the degree that the functioning accomplishes its purpose. Given the knower's responsibility for knowing whatever it knows, truth should be deemed, therefore, the valuable quality that the cognizer acquires when the resulting cognitive state achieves the purpose for which the cognitive activity has been undertaken. But the cognizer's activities can be more or less successful, since its causal powers are finite. Falsity is, therefore, the disvalue that follows from insufficient or inadequate exercise of the cognitive powers. And so, truth is relative to the cognitive causality that creates the more or less valuable cognitive effect. For the achievement is not procured by (or the defect attributable to) the object, but by and to the mind. As effects are relative to their causes, cognitive states are relative to the cognitive activities that create them.

The truth of our cognition is, accordingly, a matter of degree; truth and falsity are not digital but analogical. The truth value of cognition depends on the degree to which the specific purpose envisaged by the cognizer — which varies over time, even in relation to the same object — is achieved. For example, the most detailed and exhaustive perception of an object is not necessarily the truest. For, if account is taken of what one seeks to know, which may not depend on detail or completeness, an 'overview' may be cognitively more valuable (i.e. truer) than a more complete perception. Truth is greater or lesser in relation to what one wants or seeks to

know, not in relation to what can be known. Thus, truth and falsity are bestowed by the mind on itself as it performs its cognitive functions more or less adequately, given its purposes.

Now, in some of my preceding remarks I have gone along, for the sake of the argument, with the usual supposition that truth and falsity are a dichotomy; but this, too, cannot be true. Since the mind is the cause of both its success and its failures, falsity is as much the *effect* of the mind's activity as truth is; and it is as *real* as truth is. Falsity is not the mere absence of truth, but a real disvalue of cognition, of which the mind is the responsible cause. And since, moreover, the success and the failure of the mind obtain in degrees, it follows that truth and falsity make up a spectrum. Somewhat like health and unhealth, truth and falsity are the poles of a continuum; they add up to a single parameter of cognition that measures the effectiveness of our mental activities. Truth and falsity are therefore relative not only in the basic sense already noted — namely, that they are relative to, and dependent upon, the cognitive activity — but also in the sense that they are mutually relative. The cognitive achievements of the mind are never absolutely and perfectly true, or absolutely and perfectly false. There is no true perception so true that it could not be improved upon, nor falsity so false that it is absolutely meaningless and bears no relation to the truth.

A comparison of truth and falsity with health and sickness — or rather, health and unhealth — is instructive. In both cases it would be a distortion of the observable facts if the two were dichotomized. When the organism's functioning becomes impaired, we become aware of the state of health we ordinarily enjoy, and are likely then to conceive 'sickness' as the absence of 'health,' although in reality health and unhealth describe the single continuously variable effectiveness of the organism's discharge of its vital activities. Likewise, the usual dichotomous concepts of truth and falsity mislead us into supposing that falsity is abnormal and should not be, just as health and sickness, if dichotomized, mislead us into supposing that mortality is abnormal and should not be — and indeed, ought not to be.

Our fallibility manifests thus the same finitude of our human nature that is demonstrated by our mortality; and it is to our advantage to recognize both. And just as we take health for granted until we are brought up short by a malfunction of our organisms, we take it that our cognitive activities have been successful until we should discover that they have not been as successful as we had assumed. We cannot experience '*being* mistaken,' but we are able to recognize our fallibility. Our power to gain knowledge would be enhanced if we did so. It is for an analogous reason that we cannot experience '*being* dead' — though somehow we find it easy to suppose that eventually we shall experience it, a prospect that evokes the direst fears in us. What we can truly do instead is rather to recognize our mortality; and if we do so, we have received the benefit of a most important and consequence-laden truth.

In the climate created by representationism, the word 'relativity' evokes strong negative emotions in the coolest brows. Therefore, I stress that what I have suggested is only that truth and falsity are relative to the mind and its purposes; and I have suggested it on the ground that they are qualities of the mind and of the mind's greater or lesser achievement of its purposes. I have not suggested that truth is relative to, or depends on, our wishes, or on our imaginative inventions, or on our 'subjectivity.' Nothing I have said casts doubt on the fact that, if one fails to perceive a stumbling block across one's path, reality will impose its hard, sharp, and painful edges on one's misperception. The same is true at the level of understanding: if one misjudges the speed of an approaching vehicle as one crosses the street, one will suffer the predictable consequences; and if one is convinced that arsenic is a harmless condiment, one would be well advised to stick to a bland diet.

My suggestion, quite to the contrary, is that the truth and falsity of our knowledge do not affect reality; they affect *us* and matter to us, because they measure our cognition of reality. But of course, there can hardly be cognition by cognizers unless *in relation to* objective reality: the active causality of our cognitive functions *presupposes* an object on which it is exercised, and the object is not affected simply by being perceived or understood, any more than by being misperceived or misunderstood. Clearly, when cognition is exercised, it must *abide by* the reality of the object. But *not* because objects of cognition have any claims on our cognition and should be given their due– as if the world and its objects had an inherent right to be perceived and understood and in the age of global egalitarianism we had to guard against lapsing into 'thingism.' The reason is that, if we want to enjoy the benefits of true knowledge and avoid the disadvantages of error we must abide by what the reality actually is. But it is *we,* the knowers, who should so abide.

If we have difficulty understanding the nature of truth, it is not only because we misidentify the cause of cognition, but also the nature of the reality that is the object of cognition. We shall deal with the latter question in the next section, but some cross-reference to it at this time may be useful.

Let us observe that our knowledge of the world would not be true unless it was *warranted* by the objective reality of the world. But there is a difference between the world's being real and its being constituted by an inherent truth. Once more, the latter supposition makes sense only on the assumption that the world's reality consists in its being thought by God, or reflects a 'higher' or a 'divine' Mind. Some philosophers seem to think, as Hilary Putnam has remarked, that, absent such assumption, reality must be said to be constituted by an inherent truth that is created either by the individual mind, or our language, or our culture. But to suppose so, Putnam comments, is in effect to 'view the world ... as a *product*. One kind of philosopher views it as a product from a raw material ... The other views it as a creation *ex nihilo. But the world isn't a product. It's just the world* ... [and to] deny ... that there is a "ready-made world" is not to say that we make up the world.' [319]

I agree. Although the objective reality of the world is indeed what we can aspire to know truly, truth has to do solely with the reality of the mind and its functional adequacy. The reason is that the characteristics of cognition do not come from the objects of cognition, but from the nature of the mind: whether the mind works well or not depends on the mind and how it is used. There is no question but that our cognition does not create the reality of its objects, but it *does* create the relationship

---

319   Putnam, *The Many Faces of Realism* (La Salle, IL: Open Court, 1987), 30.

that our mind has to its objects. Truth can be reasonably understood only as a quality of our *knowledge* of reality — a quality that depends solely on how well *we* exercise our cognitive functions.

That cognition is required to abide by reality before it can be true is therefore beyond question. But the object determines only what cognizers should *take into account,* given their purposes, if their cognition is to have the quality of truth. Truth can be construed as the accurate representation, reproduction, or repetition of reality, only if one presupposes that cognition is caused by the objects of cognition and consists in the mind's 'subjectively' representing, reproducing, or repeating what is cognized. That the mind's causation of its cognition must abide by reality is an entirely different proposition, for the validity of which there are almost tangibly clear reasons: if the mind's cognitive activity did not abide by reality, the cognitive state it procured for itself would not satisfy the purpose of the activity — namely, to know *the object.* But *abiding* by reality has nothing to do with reproducing the object within ourselves.

Therefore, abiding by reality and respecting it does not exclude treating it and making use of it *creatively.* This is why our perception of the world generates, collaterally, major and minor forms of art, games, and entertainment, by means of which we embellish reality, to our benefit and enjoyment. It is for the same reason that understanding can be aided by wondering, theorizing, and hypothesizing, and not simply by observing perceiving and understanding. But the compelling fact remains: our cognitive efforts are effective only to the degree that they abide by reality; otherwise their effectiveness is illusory. For unlike reality, the truth is *created* by the mind, and the goal of the mind is not to create reality any more than to repeat it; it is to perceive and understand the reality that we find in the world.

Moreover, apart from the fact that there is some truth in every mistake, and vice versa (which is simply to recognize the finitude of our cognitive powers), when we treat error as a privative concept — that is, when we think of falsity as the absence of cognitive value — we implicitly reject the useful role that mistakes, errors and other deficiencies of our cognitive performance can play in human cognition. The experience of having made a mistake accomplishes for human beings a comparable service to that of physical pain. Pain is, of course, not desirable of itself, and we rightly seek to avoid it. But pain is not necessarily unhealthy. Often it is a means whereby our organism alerts us to organic conditions that, if left unattended to, would be deleterious to the health of the organism; pain creates the opportunity to *correct* such conditions. Likewise, the errors and mistakes we make, warn us, when we become aware of them, about the defects or insufficiencies of our cognitive activities. Awareness of them offers not simply the opportunity to rectify them, but indeed the *possibility* of doing so. For as long as we are unaware of the inadequacies of our knowledge, we would find it satisfactory and would not actively search for the truth. When we make a mistake, we *need* to know it. The ahistoricity that has prevailed in modern philosophy illustrates how unawareness of the role of error in human cognition retards, and may even altogether prevent, the advancement of knowledge.

Since truth and falsity are, if rightly conceived, mutually relative, the retrospective nature of error points to the prospective character of truth: truth creates the possibility of more truth. It also follows that there can be no criterion whereby to secure the truth beforehand as one strives to reach it, any more than there can be any reasonable hope of ascertaining 'the whole truth.' I do not mean that 'the whole truth' is a desirable but unattainable ideal, but that it is an absurdity, like 'seeing beyond the horizon.' Awareness of one's ability to experience truthfully should normally be accompanied by the humbling realization of one's fallibility. The best practical safeguard against error in everyday matters is to heed one's experience; in philosophical matters it is a keen and respectful recognition of the inherent fallibility of the human mental functions and the consequent need for self-criticism.

j) The phenomenon of 'absent-mindedness'

According to my explanation, the root of the defective assumptions of our philosophical tradition regarding our typically conscious human cognition is the difficulty that our cultural and philosophical traditions have experienced as their members, living in the world, observed their cognitive functions in action. We then fail to appreciate that our experience is rendered conscious by the inclusion and integration, within the unity of experience, of information regarding our organism's cognitive activity and information regarding the object. But there is a reason why we fail to appreciate it. Namely, that on the one hand, no experiencer can be altogether unaware of the *object* (since to know it is the direct and inherent purpose of cognition), whereas, on the other, the *activity* of the organism whereby the object becomes known is difficult to detect. It is all the more so, I have repeatedly suggested, because the brain and the other organs in which the cognitive functions are vested do not have interoceptive capabilities. Therefore, the organism's mental activity, unlike the object, tends to escape our notice; at best it is dimly perceived, and it is always easily ignored.

Moreover, when our mental activity is then projected onto the world, confusion inevitably ensues. Our perception of the conscious quality of our cognition is distorted, and our conception of consciousness (if we have become conscious of it) is correspondingly faulty. Thus, whereas the experiential process normally yields relatively sharp, unambiguous, explicit, definite, and specific information regarding the object, the information it provides about the cognitive process and its conscious quality is none of these. (We have already seen that our defective assumptions regarding causality have the same source; in the next section we shall verify that the same is true of our usual assumptions regarding reality: lack of clarity regarding our mind's relationship to its objects interferes with our perception of it.)

The difficulty I have described is the cause of much grief, philosophically and in every other human respect. It is surely not by mere coincidence that the vain striving of modern philosophy for understanding the world and human nature is paralleled by the vain striving of our modern civilization to manage its human affairs in a reasonably orderly and satisfactory manner. To refer to such difficulty economically, we should give it a convenient and telling name. I propose to describe it as the 'absent-mindedness' that is apt to cloud the human organism's awareness of the process whereby it bestows the quality of consciousness upon its experience. When the human mind operates in this way, the organism's cognitive functions develop conscious quality, but its awareness of what in fact it is doing is not vivid or distinctive enough to enable the experiencer to make the discriminations without which confusion — and projection — will unavoidably follow. It is as if the conscious mind were not fully 'there,' fully present to itself; it is, so to speak, distracted or inattentive, and easily confused. One is 'absent-minded.'

René Magritte, the Belgian painter of the last century, seems to have observed the phenomenon of absent-mindedness and expressed his vision of it (or so I take it) with a dramatic graphic illustration of the phenomenon. I do not know, of course, what Magritte actually intended to call to the attention of the viewer of his *La Réproduction Interdite*; it may have been an altogether different meaning from that which I take from it. But on its face the painting does seem to portray some sort of obfuscation or flawed vision that may afflict human beings not unlike that which I have described as 'absent-mindedness.'

Magritte's picture shows a man facing a mirror and looking at himself in it. Now, in real life a photograph of a man standing in front of a mirror and looking at himself in it, would show in the foreground the back of the man standing before the mirror, while the mirror would show, of course, a mirror image of the man. That is, the mirror image would show a frontal aspect of the man. Thus, the photograph would represent a man who, by looking in the mirror, would see himself looking at himself. In Magritte's painting, however, the man is indeed facing the mirror, so that the painting depicts him from the back. But strangely, the image in the mirror also portrays him from the back. Thus, although the man is in a good position to see himself looking at himself, the painting shows him as unable to do so. The painting shows him instead as seeing himself as a stranger would — or as would every museum-goer looking at Magritte's painting in real life. That is, from behind. And so, the painting exhibits to the viewer a man who would like to behold a *réproduction* of his experiencing himself, but is barred from doing so. The picture shows *La Réproduction Interdite.* We are not told what forbids the man's perceiving his perceiving himself; the picture merely records the strange, almost self-contradictory fact that he is unable to perceive what he is actually doing, namely, perceiving himself.[320] Which describes accurately the self-defeating nature of 'absent-mindedness.'

One of the most important practical consequences of absent-mindedness is that it tends to impair the ability of human individuals to cooperate and even tolerate and live at peace with each other. In his novel *Blindness,* José Saramago, the Portuguese winner of the Nobel Prize for Literature for 1998, traced what happens to ordinary people when their 'blindness' renders them unable to see the humanity of others, who in turn suffer from the same disability; what happens is that they become blind to their own humanity, which crumbles bit by bit until they revert to the grossest animality. The vulnerability of human nature to absent-mindedness is especially unfortunate, because consciousness puts much greater social demands on human beings than on infra-human animals,

---

320   Further speculation on the meaning of the work is possible. For example, the title of the painting may allude to the 'copyrighted' individuality of the conscious self whose mental activities some human beings cannot experience clearly.

whose social behaviour is ruled mostly by genetically programmed instincts that can be modified by the individual animal's experience only to a small extent, if at all. Since human beings are conscious, however, much of their behaviour is deliberate rather than stereotyped, especially in what concerns their consciously managed relationship to other human beings. Absent-mindedness brings to all of us, to some degree or other, difficulty in experiencing - I do not merely say difficulty in *understanding*, but difficulty in experiencing — our own experienceing activity. Our difficulty in experiencing the experiencing that goes on in the mind of others is all the greater, of course, because we cannot experience it in the direct way we can experience our own; we can experience it only to the degree that we are able to communicate with them.

Consciousness is, in a way, the ability to *empathize* with oneself. Since we experience our experiencing, we develop feelings about it. For example, we can be glad we are listening to beautiful music; we even develop feelings about our feelings (for example, we can feel guilty because we hate someone who has done us no harm). And of course, absent-mindedness lessens our capacity for identifying our feelings correctly, especially if they are ambivalent to begin with. And, naturally, it interferes even more pronouncedly with our ability to empathize with fellow humans, since we cannot experience their experiencing directly, but depend on communication with them. We tend therefore to experience them as *objects,* rather than as *experiencers* (or as 'selves' like onto ourselves). We then feel what they feel not so much by feeling it as if for ourselves, but rather by *interpreting* as best we can their behaviour and their communications. As we all know, even among people with the highest empathetic capacity and mutual love and affection, 'misunderstandings' are not rare.

What is the cause of absent-mindedness? The absence of proprioception in the brain and our cognitive organs must be genetically conditioned, and may well be a factor; but nevertheless we can, if we pay close attention, perceive our cognitive efforts, more or less indirectly and more or less clearly; lack of proprioception could not by itself fully account for absent-mindedness. Other genetic factors can be suspected that would affect the physiology of the brain in some manner, for instance by interfering with, but not preventing altogether, the integration of the two information streams (about the object and about the experiencer's activity) that, when integrated, add up to consciousness. Moreover, the organization of the brain is known to depend to a considerable extent on the culture within which the brain grows to maturity during the first few years of life. The properties of one's culture's language could conceivably promote absent-mindedness.[321] Absent-mindedness may or may not have a genetic origin, but in either event it has cultural manifestations.

Moreover, absent-mindedness seems to affect in significant ways the initial presuppositions with which human beings become equipped early in life, especially regarding their cognitive agency, the world, and the causation of changes in themselves and in the world. Convictions in these matters are held by them more or less consciously, but tend to be constant, generation after generation; individual differences are filtered out of the culture by the prevailing common sense. However, there is some anthropological evidence that absent-mindedness is not uniform throughout our species. For a society's initial assumptions regarding the human mind, the nature of reality, and the causation of events, are revealed in the earliest religious beliefs of human cultures. And the study of primitive religions shows that not all cultures seem predisposed towards making the same initial assumptions we Europeans do. Most of mankind's primitive religions exhibit somewhat different attitudes towards the human situation from those which have ruled in our tradition, and in particular on whether human beings exist under a regime of Necessity (and thus, whether the world is a cauldron of competing causal forces), and whether the world we inhabit is the measure of 'reality,' or whether there is a viewpoint external to the world from which the world is 'watched.'

As noted in chapter II, the beliefs of Greek and Roman religion in Fate, and Christianity's in God, and in the relativity of the visible world's reality to a 'higher' and 'really real' reality, are fairly rare. They are found in the ancient and modern religions of all the Indo-European cultures, but outside these only in a very few other cultural streams. They characterized the religions of Sumer and its succeeding Akkadian and Assyrian civilizations, and that of the Hebrews and their descendant Israelites; they are found also in the cultures spawned by the religions generated by the Biblical tradition (including, of course, Islam and Christianity). But they are not readily found in the native religions of the other civilizations that have flourished in the past, or in those of the primitive cultures that have survived to, and been studied in, modern times.

---

321   See Atuhiro Sibatani, 'The Japanese Brain,' *Science 80* 3, no. 3 (1980): 24-30, 24.

If this is not readily evident to us, the reason may be, in part, plain ethnocentrism. We tend to assume that all religions are like those we are already familiar with. Besides, the history of mankind since the beginning of historical times has been ever increasingly determined by the growing power — and above all, by the attitude to power — that seems endemic among the Indo-European peoples and among those that have become acculturated to it or to a biblical religion. With but relatively few exceptions, the handful of great empires that have emerged during the five thousand years of recorded history have been either Indo-European, or erected on much the same assumptions of the Indo-Europeans regarding the world and the human situation that have animated the Indo-European cultures. In the last five hundred they have usually been, more specifically, Western European; modern Western European civilization now dominates, albeit uneasily and precariously, the entire human species; and it has gradually marginalized, or crowded out of existence, or otherwise annihilated all but a very few of what were probably thousands of originally distinct human cultures in prehistoric times, along with their languages and religions.

The possibility should not be discarded offhand, therefore, that 'absent-mindedness' appeared at a very early stage of human evolution and differentiated some cultural streams from others, perhaps by virtue of genetic differences which made it difficult for human beings in some

societies to become fully and clearly aware of their mental activities, as contrasted with their awareness of objects and events.

k) A collateral note on 'objectivity'

One of the most consequential missteps of modern philosophy goes back to the seventeenth century, when early modern science supposed that the reliability of all knowledge — but crucially that of scientific knowledge — was contingent on its 'objectivity.' Behind this was, of course, the traditional assumption that knowability inhered in the world. As an explicit position, the doctrine that the value of scientific knowledge depended on its objectivity had no precedent in the history of philosophy; it was an original contribution of the early scientists — although it could be argued that it was implicit, at a very deep level, in the Platonic supposition that philosophy provided *episteme*. At any rate, so far as I know, the earliest expression of it in modern times is to be found in Galileo's justification of the truth of his findings on the ground that they enjoyed, in his own words, the 'objective certainty'[322] that only observation, and in particular experimental and quantified observation, could provide. Quantification was ideal, since Pythagoreanism was also assumed.

In the background of the doctrine that science provided 'objective certainty' was the historical fact that neither Galileo nor his contemporary scientists were vitally interested in the usual philosophical issues, and that therefore they tailored their philosophical work to their needs using the least possible amount of philosophical cloth. As Burtt pointed out in his classical study of the origin of the philosophical foundations of science, the early scientists took little interest in metaphysics and tried hard to avoid it.[323] Nevertheless, they were being attacked on matters philosophical and epistemological and had little option but to reply in kind. Their principal self-defence appealed to experience: if only their opponents deigned to look through a telescope, or watch steel balls rolling down an inclined plane, they would have known that the scientists were right. But they had to explain what they meant by 'experience'. And so, the scientists developed oversimple interpretations of the nature of cognition that have nevertheless proven hardy. None hardier than Galileo's doctrine of the 'objective certainty' that follows upon 'objective observation'. Such certainty was the mark of the 'objective knowledge' that soon was to lend authoritativeness to science.

The concept of 'objective knowledge' — that is, knowledge resulting from 'objective observation' — passed into the ideology and everyday speech of our common sense, and took root in our popular culture, which increasingly vested prestige and influence in science during the nineteenth and twentieth centuries The respect of science by philosophy of mind having eventually become deference, the concept of 'objective knowledge' now entrenches confusions that prejudice the study of the mind and shackle philosophy. It is mostly for this reason that a discussion of the matter is apposite to this work, rather than for its direct relevance to my principal theses regarding the challenge of Hume and the causes of modern philosophy's stagnation, which is scant.

---

322   Galileo Galilei, *Dialogue Concerning the Two Chief World Systems, Ptolemaic and Copernican*, Stillman Drake, (trans.), (Berkeley: University of California Press, 1967), 103. The terms 'objective observation' and 'objective knowledge' are not found in Galileo himself, though the concepts are implicit in his explicit concept of 'objective certainty', the warranted certainty that scholars may legitimately enjoy if their knowledge depends on 'objective observation' and is therefore 'objective.'

323   Burtt, *Metaphysical Foundations*, 306.

The doctrine begins with a twofold confusion. First, it confuses the *objectivity of reality* with the supposed *objectivity of knowledge,* also known eponymously as *scientific objectivity.* Objective knowledge is obtainable under certain conditions, but not under others. Its opposite is, of course, 'subjective knowledge.' And whereas the former is reliable, because it results from 'objective observation,' 'subjective knowledge' is the product of 'subjective observation' and is altogether unreliable. Now, what is the difference between 'objective' and 'subjective' knowledge? Supposedly, that the former is the cognition of reality from the object's own viewpoint, whereas the latter is the cognition that takes place from the viewpoint of the cognizing subject.

Thus, the second and deeper confusion is the supposition that perceivers can experience objects from either of two different viewpoints, not only from their own but also from that of the object — the 'subjective' and the 'objective' viewpoints — and that only the latter provides knowledge about the object as it itself actually is. It seems to me, however, that this is absurd on both counts. It is self-contradictory to suppose that when we perceive objects 'subjectively,' or from our viewpoint, we do not actually perceive them, but only think we do. It is also self-contradictory to suppose that we can perceive objects from the viewpoint of objects; for our perceptions are done by us, not by the objects we perceive. But to be clear, I add: there is no question that it is possible for us to understand and even imagine how an object is perceived by a *perceiver* other than ourselves; it is called 'sympathy.' The self-contradiction lies in attributing a viewpoint to *objects* of perception — although objects of perception as such do not perceive, but are perceived. The attribution is a projection.

To begin to clear the confusion, let us distinguish between the objectivity *of reality* and the objectivity of *knowledge.* The former is a valid notion; I have resorted to it in this work repeatedly without any qualms or explanation; for this concept merely asserts what experience teaches us when we perceive the 'otherness' of objects. It merely underscores the empirically given fact that the reality of the world is not created by our minds. Conversely, the 'objectivity of reality' merely restates that reality is whatever *it itself* is. 'Objective knowledge,' on the other hand, is best characterized as an oxymoron, while 'subjective knowledge' is its Siamese twin. The opposition of the objectivity of reality to the objectivity and the subjectivity of knowledge is a direct consequence of representationism.

The snarled thread of thought that leads to the doctrine can be unraveled. As is often the case, a misconception has been crafted out of true facts. One such fact is, of course, that neither our immediate observation of reality by means of our senses, nor any of our other mental processes directed at the reality thus observed — thinking, judging, reasoning — is what makes reality real or to have whichever characteristics it has. To note this is merely to restate the objectivity of reality. A second true fact can be derived from the accumulation of nothing more recondite than a little practical experience in human affairs: that biases, assumptions, prejudices, and prior convictions are liable to interfere with one's observation of, and reasoning about, reality; they may disrupt our cognition and prevent us from learning what we otherwise could learn. Equally evident is the third, which blends the truth of the first two: when knowledge of reality is filtered through prejudice, it is of course unreliable; knowledge can be reliable only if we attain to objective reality, to reality as it itself is, rather than as we would prefer that it be. Knowingly to allow one's prejudices or passions to interfere with one's acquisition of knowledge would of course be the height of folly.

Since early times, therefore, modern scientists were conscious, and rightly so, of the importance of methodology. Rules of procedure help us guard against prejudice. However, the rule of 'scientific objectivity' does not actually protect science against unjustified opinions and judgments; it is useless in practice, and theoretically serves only, if at all, to rationalize representationism by supposing 'subjectivity' in parallel to 'objectivity.' The idea of 'scientific objectivity' was nevertheless arrived at when a fourth consideration suggested one way in which science might take advantage of the first three in order to increase the reliability of scientific observations; it, too, derived from some correct observations about the way in which the human mind works.

Our senses divide aspects of reality in accordance with their peculiar sensitivities; but the various senses can be activated separately and we can exert some control over whether we use one or another sense in relation to the same objective reality. Our thinking is even freer: our concepts slice and package *ad libitum* the information we gain about reality through perceptual experience. Thus, it is perfectly possible for human observers to perceive and think about one fact in abstraction from another, even if in reality the two are inseparable. For instance, one can observe a solid's weight paying no attention to its bulk; and in reality a rose petal and its colour cannot be separated, but one can consider, observe, and reason about rose petals in abstraction from their colour, or vice versa; and so on. Well, then: although no object can be observed unless an observer observes it, nothing forbids observers from considering exclusively the object under observation while ignoring the fact that they, the observers, are observing the object; this is true. Therefore, if what we are interested in observing is the object rather than ourselves, observers may quite properly subtract themselves and their observing activity from their observations.

The doctrine of scientific objectivity is arrived at by drawing an unwarranted conclusion from the foregoing true premises. The reasoning is that, if reality exists in itself, and if its characteristics are not determined by the mind that perceives it, and if our biases and prejudices are to be avoided so that our knowledge will attune us to what reality itself is, what we must do is to ensure that our prejudices and biases from our observations are removed from our observations and judgments, so that we may consider solely what the objective reality itself is. But how can we achieve the observation of reality as it itself objectively is, rather than as one might think, imagine, prejudge it, or wish it to be? Very simply: by observing reality while abstracting from the fact that we are observing it. One observes it as if one were not making the observation, or indeed as if one did not exist. Therefore — and this is the unwarranted conclusion — the solution consists in restricting ourselves to the use of *objective observation*. Objective observation consists in observing reality from *the viewpoint of objective reality itself* rather than from our own viewpoint — which is subjective, which may well be biased, and which is unreliable.

Needless to say, the rule of objectivity does not suppose that observers actually cease to exist or that they in fact discontinue their observing activity when they observe or think objectively. The idea is rather that they must observe *as if* they were not observing, or *as if* they did not exist. Therefore, objectivity should be considered an ideal to be approximated rather than one that is invariably achieved. The rule of objectivity does not include a guarantee that each and every observer will abide by the rule of scientific objectivity; it guarantees only the general principle that no observation or judgment should be deemed reliable unless it was made from the viewpoint of the observed reality itself.

We have noted already why this thinking is self-contradictory: objects as such have no viewpoint. Only observers have a viewpoint. For cognition is not caused by objects, but by ourselves. Like the power of a hunting gun, which does not depend on whether it is used on an elephant or else on grouse, the quality of experience does not depend on what we exercise our experiential functions upon; it depends only on the nature of the mind and how its functions are discharged. Any observation I make will be made exclusively by me, and therefore will always remain an observation made from my viewpoint. Objective reality as such has no viewpoint. Only a mind can have a viewpoint. In brief, 'objective certainty' and the 'objectivity' of 'objective observation' are a mirage.

If the point is not clear, consider the common acceptation of 'subjectivity' as reported by the *Oxford English Dictionary*: 'subjectivity' is the 'quality or condition of viewing things exclusively through the medium of one's own mind.' But through what medium other than one's mind does one, or could one, ever view anything? Exactly what would one have to do, in order to use the objects we experience as the medium through which to experience them?

Rebuttal might be attempted by alleging that 'objective observation' demands only that observers observe objects *as if* they were not observing them. What is wrong with this? Nothing. The pretense is not only permissible, but usually necessary. If one wants to study apples and therefore observes apples, one must attend solely to the apples and abstract from the fact that one is observing apples; otherwise one would end up observing the nature of observation rather than apples. Of course, the latter is possible too. The objection to 'objective observation' is not the pretense that the observer is not observing; it is that the doctrine of objective observation tries to say, self-contradictorily, that when observers pretend that they are not observing, the *effect* of the pretense is that the observation *truly* takes place from the viewpoint of reality itself and no longer from the observer's. But pretenses, even when they are useful, do not become true simply because pretenders forget that they have been pretending.

The doctrine of scientific objectivity thrives on a diet of equivocation: the term 'objectivity' is applied ambiguously to both the true objectivity of 'objective reality' and to the self-contradictory objectivity of 'objective observation.' The mistake, as John McDowell has put it, consists in thinking 'that reality is objective, in the sense of being fully describable from no particular point of view.'[324] But I wish McDowell had omitted the adverb: no object is even *partially* describable from no particular viewpoint — and least of all from *its own* viewpoint.

Support for the possibility of objective observation is perhaps most frequently sought in a true fact. There are clear differences between the procedures and observational techniques — and the instrument and devices, if any — that we need to use in order to observe objects external to our organisms, and those procedures which are appropriate to the observation of our own mind. Gregor Mendel would have been foolish to try to study the inherited characteristics of peas by introspecting or by examining his concept of 'pea,' whereas Aristotle would have been unwise to investigate the paralogisms of reason by trying to use litmus paper to detect a fallacy. Does it not seem, therefore, that certain objects can be observed only subjectively, whereas others may be observed objectively as well as subjectively?

What is true is rather that we cannot use the same techniques to study the mind and to study extramental entities, including our own bodies.[325] But this does not demonstrate that mental processes can be either objective or subjective. It is evidence that the objective characteristics of objects determine the objective (i.e. actual and real) conditions under which they can be observed, and that therefore the nature of the object to be observed limits the procedures and techniques of observation that *observers* can use to observe them. Objects do place constraints on observers, in the sense that, in the absence of compliance with the real requirements imposed by real objects, the observer will not be able to observe them at all. For instance, there is no way we can observe the various stages of stellar evolution without telescopes; but telescopes are worse than useless to observe amoebas. That objects determine the *characteristics* of the observing function, however, would be an unwarranted inference from this fact.

The most obvious and general requirement of observation is that the observed object be, or be made, present to the observer in one or else another sense in which one thing can be present to

---

324   McDowell, 'Functionalism and anomalous monism,' 395.

325   To observe one's own body, one must take it as the object or target of our mental activity of observing; one's body, as object of obsevation, is thus *external* to the mental activity.

another. And so, for instance, the size and luminosity of objects determines under what conditions, and even whether, objects can be observed by visual organs with the characteristics of human eyes. Accordingly, some objects are visible with the naked eye, others only with the aid of appropriate telescopic or microscopic or other instruments, and some not at all unless perhaps indirectly. This does not mean, however, that human visual observation is of four kinds, macroscopic, telescopic, microscopic and indirect — the first three being, respectively, astronomically reliable, required by biologists, and indispensable for theoretical physicists interested in observing the tracks of sub-atomic particles in a cloud chamber. By the same token, the location of objects determines where we must look for them and the direction in which we must train our observational apparatus and our eyes. Obviously, to observe external objects we must look externally; that is where external objects can be expected to be. To observe our minds we must, for an analogous reason, introspect.

This indicates not that our *observations,* but that the *objects* of possible human observation fall into two categories. One includes the mind and its operations, characteristics, and manifestations; the other is the world external to the mind. But our observation of external objects is 'subjective' in exactly the same original sense of the term that would be applicable to the observation of our own mind (namely, in the sense that it is performed by a human subject). Likewise, our observation of our mind is as 'objective' as our observation of the world, in the sense that it pertains to an object. It is one and the same mind, making use of one and the same set of mental characteristics, that observes the world and that observes itself.

Now, there is no doubt that when we wish to know the length of a certain object and we use a ruler to measure it, our judgment should be deemed much more reliable than when we simply estimate the length. But the reason is not that the former is an objective judgment whereas the latter is subjective. The reason is that in the former instance the unit of measurement, being an objectively existing ruler, is the same for all measurers and for all instances of measuring; whereas the purely imaginary ruler used to estimate the length varies from one individual measurer to another and from one occasion to another. An existing ruler is an objective ruler; an imaginary ruler is not an objective existent. The judgment, however, is in either case no less 'subjective,' and no more 'objective,' than in the other.

Although the concept of 'objective observation' is to be rejected, the problems that the doctrine of objective observation was intended to help solve cannot be belittled. However, the remedy prescribed by science is not only false but naive. For surely we have amassed in this century, if not from an earlier time, enough collective experience in the human ways of self-deception to realize that few tricks are more easily played upon ourselves, by all of us, to our own detriment or that of others, than to become blind to our biases and prejudices - or else to ration-alize them, if they knock so insistently at our back door that we cannot manage to ignore them altogether. To enjoin others or oneself to 'be objective,' in the expectation that calling our obser-vations 'objective' will make us free from prejudice, is to believe in the incantatory power of words. Objectivity is about as useful a piece of methodological advice as would be to recommend to the morally perplexed that they do only what is right while carefully avoiding evil; objectivity is the philosopher's bargain-basement emulation of the cheap politician's motherhood.

There is no amulet called 'objectivity' that can protect us against either our prejudices or our fallibility. What sound scientific observation and reasoning require is better called honesty, fair-mindedness, and truthfulness. But this is hardly to say that we can do nothing to overcome personal dispositions that may impede the correct observation of reality, What one should do, however, is to make a deliberate and usually costly effort to confront and acknowledge to oneself one's prejudicial disposition and one's inherent, natural, and unavoidable fallibility — and one's society's and culture's.

But if scientific objectivity is as confused and useless a notion as I have argued, why is science as intellectually and technologically successful as it is? The reason is that the success of science has nothing to do with the validity of its doctrine of objectivity. In fact, it has nothing to do with several of science's traditional philosophical assumptions, such as its Platonic epistemology and Pythagorean metaphysics, the falsity and naiveté of which fail to harm science seriously only because they are superfluous to the adequate discharge of science's tasks. It would be useful for science, I think, if scientists generally had a philosophically sophisticated understanding of the nature and justification of science as a form of knowledge. But the accuracy of, say, a research oncologist's observation of cancerous cells, and of the inferences to be drawn therefrom concerning the causes and treatment of cancer, does not depend on what the scientist may think about the nature of observation — or the nature of truth, or of the human mind, or of reality, or the meaning of life and death.

The success of science depends on several things. One is the high value that science places upon precise observation, quantification, and experimentation. Another is the amazing ingenuity of the scientific techniques of experimentation and other forms of observation that scientists have developed. Success is the due reward of scientists' having honed the art, the instruments, and the procedures of exact, reliable, minute, and seemingly endless, fact-finding. Science requires more than observation; but it excels at observing before it proceeds to relate and reason about large numbers of observations and to understand the pattern they make.

But the success of science is promoted above all by the happy fact that most scientists are genuinely interested in obtaining true knowledge rather than in feeding their prejudices. If scientists were generally unscrupulous, science would be in disrepute and would probably have achieved little. But by and large scientists are intellectually honest and are able to control their biases without excessive difficulty. To the extent that freedom from bias has a bearing on the success of science, what counts is the personal integrity of scientists, not the validity of the idea that we can observe reality from reality's own viewpoint.

4. *The nature of reality*

Since the initial assumptions of philosophy are closely interconnected, the study of our concepts of cognition and causality and how they are affected by our projections has already made apparent some of the inadequacies of the traditional concept of reality and has touched on some of the revisions it should undergo. Now, however, we face the topic squarely and for its own sake.

Two brief preliminary remarks will open the topic. The first is to remind us of the quasi-geological layers of the conventionally sanctioned language we use at present to refer to reality. We can expect to avoid confusion only if we keep in mind that they reflect the three principal stages in the history of philosophy's concern with the 'reality' of the 'real' world. The latter terms, 'reality', and 'real', are standard in modern times to refer to the totality of existing things as well as to any one of the many individuals that make up the world. 'Existing' and 'existence' recast the older concepts of 'to be' and 'being' so as to include reference to that which accounts for the difference between real and purely imaginary things; only real beings 'have existence,' or 'exist.' But we also use 'to be' existentially, much as Aquinas often did, though most often we use it in this manner only in conjunction with 'there,' the so-called anticipatory adverb. Now, when Thomas's interpretation of reality as inherent existence filtered down to common sense, it was not explicitly accompanied by the Thomistic formula that there was a 'real distinction between essence and existence.' However, the practical equivalent of it became an unacknowledged assumption embedded in the linguistic usages of European culture. Hardly anyone today in our civilization would disagree with Thomas's teaching that, whereas we may or may not understand the nature of any given being, all of us know that *what* a thing is is not the same as *whether* it exists: the distinction between 'essence' (i.e. knowable characteristics) and 'existence' is only implicit in this, but amply clear. What we now want to know is: what is there in reality that explains what 'to be there' — or 'there to be' — means? How should we best understand the nature of reality, if we understand that it inheres in the real world?

But I also remind us, second, that when philosophers undertake to examine the concept of 'reality' and attempt to determine its nature, they are already equipped with a common-sense concept of reality; they conceived it at an early stage of their mental development simply because they are human beings and therefore do not merely experience the world, but are aware that they do so. As they attend to each of the two poles of the single event we call 'perceiving an object,' they conceive both 'perception' and 'reality' — though not necessarily using such language, of course, and not necessarily with either clarity or precision, but forcefully and with conviction just the same. For every one of our perceptions reveals the object as *not-ourselves*. We cannot perceive as if it were part of oneself. Rather, it is itself, and its 'itselfness' is what we in often refer to as its 'reality.' However, as we proceed to inquire into the nature of reality, 'absent-mindedness' may distort our vision of its nature. We should therefore consciously mark the fixed point from which we should proceed and to which we should remain anchored: the experience of the 'otherness-than' that characterizes the objects of perception. We have met it several times already, but we shall now study certain aspects of it in finer detail. And the first question to consider is how the distorted perception of reality comes about?

We already know that it is the outcome of a simple projection: the inadequacy of our perception of our own reality in opposition to the object is attributed to the world, where it becomes the inadequacy of the reality of the world and its objects. But now, first, we shall analyse the process; and then, second, we shall examine how our distorted conception of reality has fared in the history of our tradition. Answering these two questions should facilitate, third, our attempt to arrive, as we may hope, at a more perspicuous understanding of the reality of the world of which we are integral part — and therefore also of our own reality.

a) *The experience of reality, and its distortion.*

Once we project our cognitive activity onto the object, we must suppose that cognition, the effect of the activity of objects on the mind, is brought about by our mental possession of objects when they imprint themselves on the receptive mind. But this supposition further implies that the world and its objects are inherently knowable: when we know the world, we know what it itself *already* is. Thus, the world is inherently 'watchable;' objects are, in themselves, apt to be known by a mind. Of course, we do not necessarily describe this experience to ourselves in the terms I have used. We are apt to describe it, for example, in emotional terms of the Kantian 'awe' that is evoked in us when we behold the 'majesty' of the universe.. But the outcome is the same: the independence of the object's reality from our knowledge of it, has been converted into the *dependence* of the object's reality on its being known independently of oneself. Thus, the inadequacy of our perception of our reality has been *projected* onto the object as the inadequacy of its reality. More precisely still, when we so project our own otherness-to the object, after having recognized the otherness-to us of the object, the sum of the two amounts to our perceiving not only the object as real, but also its reality — that is, its knowability — as relative to a viewpoint beyond the object itself. Thus, the reality of the empirically-given world and its objects is a qualified sort of reality; it is the sort of reality that can be experienced by us. Fully real reality is beyond the reality we experience; the latter is only like a shadow of the former.

The distortion of the reality of the world does not *necessarily* lead to the supposition that the reality of the world and its objects depends on a 'higher' Mind (or an abstract 'mentality') who thinks up the world — although once we suppose that the reality of the world is defective, or less than really real, it is a very short step to the further inference that such Mind (or 'mentality') must exist. This step was taken by a few Greek philosophers (notably by Anaxagoras); but hardly by all, perhaps because such inference goes beyond what the premises most strictly imply. Our distorted perception of reality simply tells that the world can be perceived from its own viewpoint; it is a *watched* or *observed* world, even when no human being is watching it. Whether a supra-human Mind is actually watching it, is a different matter. On the basis of the premise it is reasonable, but not an apodictic, implication that there is a Watcher or Observer, or Thinker of the world. This may be why affirmative answers to the question *Utrum Deus sit* — both before and after the question was understood to mean 'Does God *exist*,' but especially after — have always been controversial. The premise in either case is that the reality of the empirically-given world is less than simply real.

What matters to philosophy, therefore, is whether the reality *of the world* is reality pure and simple, reality without further qualification or restriction — reality *comme il faut*. For what detracts from the reality of our world is not exactly the supposition that there is a 'higher' reality than that of the world; it is the supposition that the reality of the empirically-given world is imperfect, or less than fully real — and thus, 'lower' than a thereto unknown level of reality. Thus, atheists are right when they say that belief in God indicates a distorted view of the reality of the world, but they do not always make clear which is the cause and which is the effect, and therefore waste much time attempting to persuade others that God does not exist. What we need to learn is rather that the *world* exists, and that it does so *truly* and *unqualifiedly.* The world is the standard of what 'reality' and 'existence' mean.

For the conception of the world which assigns to it a deficient reality is not the result of supposing the existence of God. On the contrary, supposing the existence of God results from the misperception of the empirically given reality of the world as lacking in reality. And the latter misperception is the outcome of absent-mindedness. In other words, the idea of God is created by the human mind when it functions under the handicap of an imperfect, flawed self-perception which in turn distorts our perception of the world and leads us to suppose that its reality is imperfect and flawed. Therefore, the only way in which this misperception of the world can be avoided is by correcting our self- perception. It is for the same reason that mere agnosticism regarding a supra-worldly level of reality, changes nothing of much importance; it does not bring us nearer to the truth concerning the reality of the world. For agnosticism makes allowance for the possibility that God may exist. At bottom it amounts to a tentative or uncertain theism; it presupposes much the same misperception of the world as theism. In either case, the world lacks inherent reality.

And so, the absent-minded perception of reality does not necessarily generate belief in God; but if not in God, at least in something else that transcends the world of which we are native citizens. Accordingly, the large segment of our contemporary culture that has long been alienated from all the usual religious beliefs and is skeptical whether God or any entity of the sort actually exists, nevertheless usually deems it possible that he does. Since their distorted understanding of the reality of the world prevents their perceiving the world as unqualifiedly real, they are ready to suspect, if nothing more concrete, that a 'mysterious' and 'occult' realm lurks 'just around the corner' from our ordinary experience, as it were, where 'strange things happen' that are 'beyond human ken.' And the credulous are always ready to believe such suspicions, just as the unscrupulous are to exploit it. Spiritism, fortune-telling, and numberless other popular superstitions depend on the premise that 'things are not what they seem,' and that there is more to reality 'than meets the eye.'

In our scholarly tradition, the absent-minded perception of the world has generated not only crude superstitions, but sophisticated self-contradictions that are not adverted to as such. I have already mentioned the distortion that lives on in philosophy and science under the label of the 'objectivity' of the world, if such 'objectivity' is misunderstood and contrasted with the 'subjectivity' of experience. Likewise, the objective reality of the real has traditionally been hidden under its perceptible subjective appearances. But Hume was right: there is no empirical support for the proposition that a trans-empirical level of reality underlies its appearances of objects. However, the presupposition that it does is required in order to support, for example, the Pythagoreanism of modern theoretical physics, which takes for granted that the real reality of the world is mathematical in nature, and that to understand the true and fundamental nature of phenomena it is necessary to determine their mathematical structure. The same assumption is required by the supposition that the unfolding of world events is regulated by 'laws of nature' that determine the interaction of all the individual particles of matter and the aggregates thereof that make up the world.

The contradiction would have been perhaps less blatantly absurd when, as in the early days of modern science, the 'objective' viewpoint was avowedly 'God's viewpoint,' and when, as the early scientists said, science consisted in our recognizing for ourselves the thoughts that God's mind had inscribed in things in order to give them their existence and properties. Nowadays, when God is no longer invoked or presupposed by science, 'the viewpoint of reality itself' is held to be no mind's viewpoint, but the 'view from nowhere.'[326] The supposition that there is a viewpoint that is no one's viewpoint and is 'from nowhere,' is entertained by most scientists, and even by many philosophers, with amazing tranquility of mind.

b) The concept of reality in historical perspective

The idea that a real object is real, but *not really* — or that it is both 'being' *(to on)* and 'non-being' *(to me on)* — is of course a self-contradiction. But that was the very idea introduced, in those very terms, into the philosophical stream by the Greek philosophers: the suggestion was that the world *seemed* real, and up to a point *was* real, but that nonetheless it was less than fully and simply real. This view is most familiar to us in its extreme Platonic version, but it did not begin or end with Plato. It had been adumbrated since the early stages of philosophy by the teaching of Milesian 'physicists' such as Anaximander and Anaximenes to the effect that 'worlds arise … elsewhere than with us.'[327] By definition, such worlds were 'watchable;' they were under the supervision of the 'divine.' To be sure, in the thought of the philosophers the mythological 'gods' were only the crudest, grossest manifestations of the 'divine,' and deserved being so classified only because their powers exceeded ours, albeit not by much. In a few interpretations the 'divine' constituted a separate world of its own, anticipating thus what only Christian theology would eventually maintain resolutely. Later, however, after Greek philosophy had developed the more sophisticated thought of Parmenides and Heraclitus, and 'physics' had ripened into *theologia,* or metaphysics, Plato proposed a simplified version of the doctrine and made it more coherent by reinterpreting the multiplicity of worlds. As Burnet noted, Plato 'was led to substitute for this old doctrine the belief in a single world'[328] — but a single world

---

326 Thomas Nagel, *The View from Nowhere* (New York: Oxford University Press, 1986).

327 John Burnet, *Greek Philosophy: Thales to Plato* (London: Macmillan, 1950), 23.

328 Burnet, *Greek Philosophy,* 23

that included various levels of reality, ranging upwards from the level of material reality at which we live and experience. As the *Phaedo* explains, human immaterial souls pass back and forth from one to another level as human beings die and are reborn.

However, even after Aristotle's reform of Platonism, the cogency of Plato's world was still questionable. Not least objectionable were Plato's methodological shortcomings; he depended on the Parmenidean equivalence of concept and reality, and at key points resorted to mythological notions such as metempsychosis and the immortality of the human soul. It fell to Aristotle to offer a much less fantastic, more enduring, non-mythological, and more empirically based philosophical interpretation. Nevertheless, it was an interpretation that was rooted in the supposition that reality obtained in degrees, in accordance with the immateriality and mind-like nature of the real. In Aristotle's *theologia*, as he himself said, 'there cannot be more worlds than one.'[329] But the one world was, as Ross describes it:

> [A] hierarchy reaching continuously from the lowest beings, those most immersed in matter, up to man, the heavenly bodies, the intelligences [i.e. disembodied minds], and God [i.e., *to theion].*[330]

If evaluated from their viewpoint, the interpretation of the nature of reality on which the Greek philosophers gradually tended to converge was a long stride along the road of demythologization. By finding a place for the reinterpreted versions of Fate and the divine within a single *scala naturae,* Aristotle did much to rationalize such religious beliefs. But by that very fact he also enhanced them; for to the degree that he 'naturalized' them, he gave them respectability and stability. The doctrine of the multiplicity of worlds did not rise to prominence again until it was restored by Christianity and justified by appeal to a faith that was itself justified, circularly, by its being the gift of God to man.

The natural and the supernatural Christian realms were not only distinct levels of reality, but distinct worlds. One was temporal, material, and changing; the other was eternal, immaterial, and immutable. Not only immaterial souls, but bodies, too (if suitably transformed or 'glorified' by God),

---

329   Aristotle, *On the Heavens,* 1.8. 276b22.

330   W.D. Ross, *Aristotle* (London: Methuen, 1949), 153.

could dwell in eternity. The reality of the material world was relative to that of God, who was the measure of true reality. But only God was absolutely and unqualifiedly real, and therefore unrelated to creatures. According to theologians, it might seem paradoxical that whereas creatures were 'other-than' God, God was not 'other-than' the created world. But that was because he was absolutely 'other,' *totaliter aliter*. (The methodology of theology allows illations of this paradoxical form.) And so, since God was absolutely transcendent, theologians attempted to declaw the paradox of a creator God who was unrelated to the world, by adding the contradictory thereof: that God was also totally immanent in the created world. Human beings, for their part, were in a sense deemed native to the material world, although from the outset they had been intended to leave it and to migrate to the final destination that had from all eternity been destined for them.

The Greek philosophers' misinterpretations of reality had further consequences. Two should be noted, because they have survived. Even those modern philosophers who have rejected — or as is more likely, profess agnosticism about — higher levels of reality beyond that of the world we inhabit, are influenced by the ancient beliefs. Both consequences make it difficult for us to understand that, as I suggest, the reality of real things is best understood as a form of reciprocity, the benefit that the constituents of the universe procure for each other by virtue of their causal relations. Since their causal relations account for the ceaseless becoming of the world, we may conclude that the reality of the world consists in its becoming. Its becoming is what makes it 'to be there.'

One consequence of the inaccuracy of the Greek trend of thought was the reduction of reality to the knowability — the perceptibility and the intelligibility — of the world. We have seen already the reasoning through which this conclusion was logically arrived at, but now we should consider the inspiration behind the reasoning. Let us remember that the relationship of reciprocal reality (i.e. otherness-to-each-other) between ourselves and the world is not a cognitive relationship — though it is, of course, a relationship of which we have knowledge, given the conscious quality of our cognition. But the Greek philosophers treated the reality of the real as if human beings were related to the reality of the world exclusively by knowing it. Which is clearly not true: for example, we live in constant biological exchange with, and dependence upon, the world. Why did they think so nonetheless?

The process that inspired their efforts began with their use of the term 'being' to refer, as we ourselves sometimes do today, to the real. They assumed everything we experience is a 'being.' And they did so, because theirs was an Indo-European language, and as we have previously noted, in these languages whatever is to be asserted (a 'predicate') in relation to anything else (a 'subject') can be asserted of it as 'what it *is*.' To put it more accurately, it is invariably asserted as 'what it *is*' only in the case of a quality or property it exhibits; if it is an action, then it is usually asserted as 'what it *does*.' Thus, reality is always predicated by means of a verb. And since 'what a thing *does*' is reducible to 'what it *is* doing,' it follows that predication can always be done by means of the verb 'to be.' Hence, everything in the world is a 'being,' and their reality is their 'beingness.'

Therefore, if a society learns to speak using an Indo-European language (or one of the very few other languages that share the trait of verbal predication), the society thereby learns to assume (a) that to assert anything in relation to something else, a verb is indispensable, and (b) that 'to be' is the indispensable, all-encompassing verb, since (c) all other verbs are particular manifestations of 'to be.' Therefore, all reality is 'being,' and all predicates can be attributed to subjects as 'what they are.' However, there is some reason to think that these assumptions interfere with our appreciation of the nature of reality; for they lead to the very confusion of the Greek philosophers we have previously encountered: the supposition that reality is inherently knowable.

How does such interference come about? Well, if all that is attributed to a being is attributable to it as 'what it is,' and 'what it is' is what our minds perceive and attribute to it, then the 'beingness' (*ousia,* or *essentia)* or reality of beings (i.e., the feature of beings whereby we experience them as 'other-than' ourselves), is identical with what the being shows to us about itself when it causes our perception. This is why the Greek philosophers saw no distinction between the 'beingness' of a real object and its substantial or accidental 'essence.' In short, 'to be' was the same as 'to be something' (namely, whatever was predicable of an object as its substantial or accidental 'essence.' Conversely, if the reality of a being was the same as its knowability, reality was mind-like and inherently apt to be known. Every idealism ever conceived in our philosophical tradition is the more or less direct descendant of the supposedly inherent cognoscibility of reality according to the Greeks. Thus, the identification of reality and knowability lent verisimilitude to the idea that reality obtained in degrees; the reality of the world we experienced was relative to that of a higher 'mentality.' Christianity then added the final corroborative detail: the creatures that integrated the material and temporal world were thoughts in the Mind of God. Moreover, the converse of reducing the reality of the real to its knowability was the supposition that the 'being there' of every being in the world was unrelated to the 'being there' of everything else.

Actually, knowability does not inhere in real beings; the reason we should say so is that things themselves are not responsible for their becoming 'known.' They become 'known' only because 'knowing' is a wholly immanent activity of knowers in relation to them. 'Becoming known' does not change objects of knowledge at all. But the Greeks taught us to suppose, on the contrary, that when an object becomes 'known,' it is because it has acted upon the human organism to communicate its contents and its reality to us, and has communicated to us the mind-like 'content' it holds in itself. In other words, to become 'known' is in its nature; its causing knowledge is the natural consequence of its knowability. Thus, the identification of reality and knowability meant that the reality of each object isolated it from the reality of every other object. It was its 'in itselfness.' Reality was, in effect, the boundary that *separated* every real thing from every other. (More about this when we consider the second consequence of the failure to perceive the reciprocal otherness-to-each other of the knower and the known.)

We have inherited this perspective on reality; it seems self-evident and undeniable, though actually it is contradicted by experience. For this prejudice implies that real objects are, for the very reason that they are real, *unrelated* to each other. And this is the opposite of what we actually see when we look at the real world, in which *everything* depends, directly or indirectly, for its being and for its continuing to be, on the existence and functioning of the world as a whole. But we see it only if our vision is not obscured by prior difficulty in observing the reciprocity — the mutual otherness-to-each-other — of object and cognition.

The one aspect of Aquinas's teaching on the creation of the world that impacted on the popular imagination was, of course, the suggestion that reality or existence inhered in the world and its objects. Human beings not only had their own reality, but by virtue of their awareness of their reality they also owned themselves. On the other hand, Thomas's explanation of how existence worked its realizing effects on things — namely, as an 'act' of the creature — was hardly of much popular interest and tended to fall by the wayside. It would have been difficult for philosophically unsophisticated citizens unambiguously to suppose that existing was 'done' by existents. Instead, and notwithstanding that reality was said *to exist* (which is of course a verb and therefore connotes *activity),* the usual and somewhat equivocal assumption was, as it has remained, that *existence* was 'had' (rather than 'done') by existents. Much the same was true of the esoteric notion of the 'distinction between essence and existence.' This formula was indispensable for Aquinas's doctrine of the creatureliness of an inherently knowable and efficacious created world, but it would have been meaningless to any but persons versed in theology and philosophy. However, as noted above, the substance of it survived in the distinction between *what* a thing is and *whether* it is. And so, our common sense today supposes that, in addition to having certain properties, beings have something else, namely, existence; otherwise they would not be real.

Between the end of the middle ages and the age of Descartes, little empirically-minded philosophy was cultivated. And when Descartes founded modern philosophy he simply took over, without change or elaboration, the popular notion of 'existence' as 'something' that real beings 'had' which made them real. 'Existence' and 'reality' were known to him and to succeeding modern philosophers (including Hume, of course) only as part of the culture's lexicon. They were not terms of art; for as a subject of inquiry, the nature of reality had long ceased to be among the preoccupations of philosophers The subject was important mostly to those who were inspired, as Spinoza and Leibniz were, respectively, by their religious beliefs and their scholastic education. They wanted to ensure that modern philosophy corrected Descartes and that it give a thoroughly rational, if not a quasi-mathematical, form to the ancient Judaeo-Christian tradition about the nature of the world and its relation to God.

In the late nineteenth century, however, the topic of existence was brought up by Gottlob Frege as a collateral issue arising from his ultimately failed attempt to develop a mathematical logic. It is unlikely that he was sufficiently well acquainted with the history of mediaeval philosophy to understand why the concept of reality accepted by contemporary European culture's common sense exhibited ambiguities that in his opinion should be corrected; but in any event he observed that such was in fact the case. But he did not appreciate that the common sense idea of reality already distinguished, albeit vaguely and inarticulately, between the knowable characteristics and the existence. of beings. Assuming otherwise, he thought, correctly, that it made no sense to think of existence as a property of existing things; it would be a featureless feature, a property with no specific characteristics, and, withal, common to all real existents. But since it was somehow 'had' by existing things, it must be in a sense a property after all. The best Frege could do was, therefore, to excogitate *a priori* a distinction between 'first level' and 'second level' properties, and to classify existence in the latter category: existence was not a property of things, but a property of the properties of existing things. Of course, a property of its properties is a property — or so one would think. The conundrums were not dispelled. Frege did not perceive that a viable, empirically-grounded conception of reality would not treat existence as any kind of property, whether 'first' or 'second level.'

After Frege, Bertrand Russell adopted the same distinction between levels of property, and then W.V. Quine continued the study of existence from the viewpoint of logic. There it has remained mostly, a casualty of the 'analytic philosophy' inspired by Wittgenstein's unfortunate conclusions about the nature of philosophy, according to which philosophy was not expected to solve problems but to 'dissolve' them. Thus, according to one of the few recent works on the subject, '[t]he problems of existence … are problems whose solutions are provided by logic … [T]he only sensible way to tackle the question 'What is existence?' is to investigate what might be meant by saying that certain things … exist.'[331] Apparently, the 'existence' that is the object of philosophical study has nothing to do with the reality of the world; the problems are created by the vagaries of speech, and are dissolved by learning, through the use of logic, how to use the vocabulary of 'existence' consistently.

By way of exception, the various 'existentialisms' of the twentieth century took 'existence' with reference to the real world — but only up to a point. For in their treatment of it, 'existence' was narrowly circumscribed for the most part to the reality of human beings. Now, it is true that 'being-there' matters only to us, human beings; but human beings are not all that matters to philosophy. At any rate, the well-established trend was not reversed by existentialism, and today the study of the nature

---

331   C.J.F. Williams, *What is Existence?* (Oxford: Clarendon Press, 1981), x, 1.

of reality does not excite much interest. This is understandable, since in contemporary philosophy the concept of reality still seems to have little to do with the real world.

The second principal misconception that hinders our attempts to understand the nature of reality — the first being, as noted, the identification of reality and knowability — can be briefly dealt with, though it is crucial. It is the supposition that originally generated 'atomism' among the Greek 'physicists,' but which ultimately became the wider *metaphysical* concept that, in memory of Leibniz and his taking atomism to its logical conclusion, should be better described as 'monadism.' By this term I refer to the supposition — which in my estimation is lacking in all empirical justification — that reality comes in individual portions or in self-contained, self-sufficient units called, at various times, 'beings,' or 'atoms,' or 'monads.' In this view, the 'world' as such is not real; 'world' is merely the name we give to the sum total of real beings. For only individual beings are real. Now, there is no question that individuals exist; my objection is only to the assumption that their reality belongs to them as individuals and is to be found *in* them individually, and that therefore the 'world' is nothing but a *number* of real things, their *total*. The possibility we should explore is rather that the reality of anything that may be truly called real is the fundamental reciprocal relationship it bears to all the other things that make up the world. But this is better put conversely: reality is most properly perceived as pertaining to the world as a whole; it is the integration of the individuals that make up the world. The truth, if so, is the very opposite of what we usually continue to suppose. In my suggestion, reality can be truthfully ascribed to individuals only if, and to the extent that, they are members of, and occupy a position within, the one world. Existence, if I may borrow an expression of Heidegger and put it to my own use, is the 'worldliness' of the world.

c) *The relativity of reality and the factuality of the world*

Since it is next to impossible to rebottle genies once they have breathed fresh air, it is unlikely that our civilization will be so foolish as to renege on its earth-shaking recognition, at the dawn of modern times, of the inherent, existential reality of the world in general and of conscious human beings in particular. However, the ambivalence of our culture's recognition of this truth is not likely to be dispelled in the foreseeable future either; for even if the increasing disaffection of our culture with Christianity should continue to accelerate, it would not, of itself, diminish the deeply-seated difficulty that we experience in perceiving the world as unqualifiedly real. Theism is not the cause of our confusion, but a symptom of it. Nor is science likely to contribute to our culture's better understanding of the nature of reality — it is not a scientific question — but least of all as long as it retains its Pythagorean and Platonic assumptions. Philosophy, however, could so contribute, if it should apply itself to the task and developed a concept of reality firmly based on empirical observation. Whether it actually does so remains of course very much to be seen.

We have already noted in various contexts what experience demonstrates regarding the nature of reality. Now we need only bring it together and systematize it. Thus, that reality and existence are not to be found *in* real existing things can be verified by examining a real existent — say, an apple left over from our earlier experiments — and noting that we perceive only its red colour, its smooth skin, its fragrant aroma, and so on, but that we do not perceive its reality or existence. But let us be precise: we do not perceive any reality or existence *in,* or as a *property* of, the apple — or as a property of its properties. Nevertheless, we certainly *do* experience real things *as* real, and existents *as* existing. Apples *do* exist, and we know it. How do we learn that they do?

Well, let us conduct a variation of an earlier 'experiment.' If one holds a book approximately twenty-five centimetres from one's nose and looks at it, one does not see merely a 'book.' One sees (if I may use this typographical artifice) a '[real] book.' That is, *what* one sees is only the book, the object or target to which the cognitive activity has been aimed; but besides perceiving *what* the object is (namely, a 'book'), we also perceive the fact *that it is,* or the fact *that it exists.* We have seen why this is so, and what it means. It is *not* because the 'existence' of the book exists either in the book or somewhere else, or is one of its characteristics. It is because we experience it as *other-than* our own experiencing and thus as *other-than* ourselves. Moreover, this 'book' is other-than the 'table' from which I took it. Things are not only other-than experiencers: all things in the world are 'other-to' each other. Well, such mutual *relationship* of 'otherness-to' *is* what we can rightly conceive as the empirically-given 'reality' and 'existence' of things. If we conceive reality and existence as somehow part of things in themselves and apart from the reality of everything else, it is because we have failed to observe the mutuality of the relationship.

Note well: I have not said that the book *exists* because we experience it as other-than ourselves. What I have said is that *we know* that the book exists, because we experience it as other-than-our-selves, and because we experience it as other-than-everything-else. What I have suggested is indeed the opposite of the idea that the reality of objects depends on their being experienced, whether by us or by a Higher Mind. Objects, I stress, *are* 'other-than' our experience of them: what could be a plainer rejection of the supposition that our minds create their objects? But I have also said that the *reality* of real objects can *be perceived* only in and through our perception of the object — which is trivially true and almost tautological, but which is important just the same, because it safeguards the truth that existence is not a property of existing objects, but the relationship that they bear to other objects, including their relationship to mentally active human minds.

Thus, Aquinas was right not only when he thought that the reality of the real inhered in the real, but also when he further grasped that 'being real' was not a property of the real; it was distinct, he said, from the properties of the being. It is indeed possible that he so thought not merely because he reasoned *a priori* so as to construct a theological doctrine that legitimized the autonomy of rational knowledge, but because it seemed observably true to him. One hopes this was so. But be that as it may, what matters is that it was true. We say that the object 'is there,' in part, because we perceive its relationship of otherness-to our experience; and this suffices to assure us that the object is not the creature of our experience. We also observe that real objects are 'other-than' each other, since they interrelate with each other and not only with us. We thus experience not only the reality of individ-ual real objects, but also the reality of the *world*. But we should further observe that 'reality' may therefore be described as the fundamental reciprocal relationship of all things in the world. This is in accordance with what we actually observe from moment to moment. Existence is the relationship of every real being to the environment in which it is situated — an environment that is integrated by all other real beings. Reality is, therefore, also describable as the spatio-temporality of all things, and of the world as a whole (but provided we keep in mind that space and time are not entities, but relationships). Reality is the characteristic of the world as such; reality is 'worldliness,' and to affirm the worldliness of the world is merely to be *realistic*. It is to abide by reality in respect of its most fun-damental characteristic.

And incidentally, since 'otherness' is a relationship, nothing can be 'other' by itself; if it is 'other,' it is 'other-than' something else (which in turn is 'other-than' it). But if this is true, it follows that absolutely nothing can be absolutely 'other.' A being that was, as some theologians say, *totaliter aliter,* would be a self-contradiction. However, the reason why we are obliged to admit that nothing can be absolutely 'other' should be made clear. It is not that the concept of 'otherness' is either self-evident, or innate, and that its logical properties imply reciprocity. The reason we think of 'otherness' as requiring reciprocity, is that we can *experience* such reciprocity; we experience it, first in the relationship between objects and ourselves, and then in the relationship among all objects as 'other to each other.' The compulsion comes from the twofold fact that we are *unable* to experience objects unless as 'other-to-each-other,' and that we are *unable* to create real objects by force of mind and will. The *logical* impossibility implied by the concept depends upon the *physical* impossibility of our experiencing either the world or ourselves otherwise.

But if is true that we necessarily experience the world as other-than our experience, how is it possible for anyone to fail to recognize the inherent reality of the world? The answer closes the explanatory circle that binds together cognition, causation, and reality. The reason is that nothing obliges human beings to advert to the active nature of their experience; they may fail to become sufficiently well aware of it. But if they so fail, they will reduce experience to the subjective counterpart (or 'picture,' or 'image,' or 'representation,' or other *repetition)* of the object, which supposedly 'exists' in the mind. The experiencing activity vanishes. The object is seen to be real, but its relativity to the experiencer's own reality has disappeared, along with the experiencing activity. Again, note well: I have described the relativity of the object to the experiencer's *reality,* not its relativity to the experiencer's *experience,* a relativity that is indeed wholly dependent on the experiencer. But perhaps the point should be further explained.

At the beginning of this chapter I cautioned ourselves against the mistake of attempting to judge the truth of each of the initial assumptions of philosophy in isolation from the others. A further caution should be issued at this time. The reciprocal relationship of mind and object that we discover empirically should not be confused with the unilateral relationship of mind to object we studied earlier. The latter was a *cognitive* relationship — that is, a relationship between the object *known,* and the *knowing* mind — and was not reciprocal. It was asymmetric. For only knowers know; objects as such do not know, but are known — though not necessarily, but only if a knower actually proceeds to know them. The relationship of 'otherness-to-each-other,' on the other hand, is between (a) oneself as one of the constituent individual members of the world, and (b) the world of objects as the milieu within which we live out our reality. This is not a cognitive but an *ontological* relationship — a relationship that concerns the reality of objects. It is only because we are conscious that we are capable of apprehending the 'otherness-to-each-other' of everything in the world. Cognition is involved in the *discovery* of the relationship of 'otherness-to-each-other' of ourselves and the world; but the relationship we thus discover is not cognitive, and should not be mistaken for one. Our consciously cognitive relationship to objects of experience is only one manifestation of this more basic relationship.

Recognizing the relativity of reality is only the first step we can take towards revising our conception of the nature of reality. To take the next, let us pursue the opportunity opened up by Aquinas's hypothesis that the world has its own reality, but taking care that we are not tripped up by the Greek assumptions that would interfere with that very hypothesis. The possibility of avoiding the assumptions was first broached by Hume, who with uncanny insight understood that the world and everything that exists is neither contingent on God nor necessary in itself, but radically contingent, a mere matter of *fact*. Anticipating Sartre's stock remark that the world was *de trop,* Hume pointed out that:

> Whatever *is* may *not be.* No negation of a fact can involve a contradiction. The non-existence of any being, without exception, is as clear and distinct an idea as its existence. The proposition, which affirms it not to be, however false, is no less conceivable and intelligible, than that which affirms it to be.[332]

The evidence of this truth, however, is not to be found in any *a priori* idea of reality, but in experience. No existent can claim existence as of right, or by nature. Every attempt to justify the reality of the world — or to inquire, with Leibniz, why there should be 'something rather than nothing' — rests on the false presupposition that *something* — that is, if not God, then the world — has to exist necessarily and as of right. Hume was the first modern philosopher to glimpse the *factuality* of — the

332 Hume, *Enquiry,* XII, 3.

absolute contingency, the absence of all justification for — the reality of the world. But being altogether unprepared for it — that is, being unaware of the irrationality of the contrary expectations and incapable of conceiving an alternative to them — his philosophical reflections reduced him 'almost to despair.'[333] Sartre's would later dismay him too. Neither he nor Leibniz seems to have eked relief out of the truth that real life does not depend on philosophy's attempt to understand it, but the other way about. There is no need to think, just because one learns that the world was not created by God's thinking it up, that philosophy is responsible for doing what God no longer does.

Although we are not responsible for making the world rational, we owe it *to ourselves* to try to understand it — and to understand it, indeed, as it actually is. But this is because our nature — our cognitive powers — makes it possible for us to perceive the world consciously, and thereafter to *understand it* as well as to perceive it. The obligation to understand is much like the duty to have good manners: one does not behave as a gentleman because others deserve it (which may or may not be true), but because in any event *one* does. The world is not owed our understanding of it. Since it is our nature that makes it possible for us to understand, we owe it to ourselves to try — and to reap the rewards of success. We are bound to want to understand, because we *can* understand. What we do not need in order to understand the world, is a world that has already been understood by a transcendent Mind but who takes a perverse delight in making riddles out of the world's supposedly inherent rationality and wisdom.

The trite objection to the position I have taken is that, if the world is not inherently rational, it is absurd. But if one understands that inherent rationality should not be confused with inherent reality, one will see through this *non sequitur*. The reality of the world and the eventuation of world events do not have to be *intelligible in themselves* — whatever *that* might mean — in order to be *intelligible to us*. The latter is the intelligibility that counts, which depends upon ourselves and the cognitive powers that evolution has wrought in us. We can understand both the characteristics and the existence of the world. The characteristics are intelligible because the causation of world events is intelligible as the factual and contingent causation of the world's becoming. And the existence of the world and its objects is intelligible as the factual and contingent reality of the characteristics of

---

333 Hume, *Treatise,* I, iv, 7.

beings, because such reality is not the absolute possession of each monadic entity, but relative to the reality of other existents.

If we should understand this, but our habitual assumptions should nevertheless so disquiet us that we persist in asking ourselves 'why is there something rather than nothing,' we might bring to mind the nature of reality as the mutual relativity of everything in the world. The relativity of reality means: to be real is, for any given entity, to be not merely itself, but to be other-than — i.e. distinct-from but inherently related-to — other real things. Relative reality is the difference *from* one being to another that makes it possible for one to make a difference *to* the other, and vice versa. Therefore, if a definition of nothingness that did not depend on the classical assumptions were required, it would not make reference to the absence of reality or existence or being, which would only bring us back to the beginning of the repetition-compulsion cycle of modern philosophy. The definition would be: nothing is that which makes no difference to anything. Reality, on the contrary, as observation demonstrates, is what does. Note the implication. There is no such thing as nothingness. Nothingness does not exist, since it makes no difference to what does exist. There is no need to be frightened by it. Or to take it into account as we try to understand ourselves and the world.

Now, our reality situates not just our mental functions, but the whole of ourselves, within the reality of the world; the conception of reality I have been proposing should have practical consequences for the adequate performance of the entire range of human activities and behaviour, and not only for our understanding of the world — just as the traditional ideas on the same subject may be suspected of having taken their toll upon all aspects of human life and not only on philosophy. For it is probably not by pure coincidence that the assumptions that have governed our cultural and philosophical traditions parallel the unsatisfactory state of human affairs that we have brought upon ourselves from as far back as records have been kept — and even upon our biological and physical environments. But if not by coincidence, why?

Well, it is almost certainly because of a fundamental truth about human nature that has been captured (but which has also been misused) by the Judaeo-Christian religious tradition, but which explains much of our history. The truth is stated by Christianity in mythological terms explaining why there is 'something wrong' with the human species. But it is true nonetheless: there truly is an imperfection or flaw in the construction of our human nature that originated at an early state of human evolution, which is endlessly passed on from parent to child and which makes human existence for all of us, at very least, much less pleasant than it could be. Indeed, for a good many of us, the consequences are dreadful and intolerable. And yet, we seem unable to do anything to remedy it, even when we try to do so with the best and most earnest will in the world.

Contrary to the biblical tradition, however, there are indications that the 'original disfigurement' of human nature may not have afflicted the entire human species but only some branches of it — or if it blighted all, not all to the same degrees. In any event, what is 'wrong' with our human nature is not the condition of 'sin.' It is the condition of 'absent-mindedness,' which in practical terms is synonymous with the diminished ability of human beings to *empathize* with fellow humans, which is in turn a consequence of their diminished ability to empathize *with themselves*. The behavioural manifestation of diminished empathy is difficulty in cooperating with others. On the whole we can work together with other human beings bearably well when we deal with few individuals or with small groups. In the case of large communities, lesser or greater trouble of some sort is commonplace and usually to be expected. And at the level of ethnic and national societies, we often seem incapable of recognizing the humanity of other human beings *at all*. We do not hesitate to oppress and steal from each other, and sometimes to maim and murder perfect strangers on a mass scale, while deeming virtuous the most barbaric atrocities, including assassination, torture, and inflicting overwhelming carnage on weaker peoples on the ground that we have to protect our right to self-defence. We never lack for ingenious self-justification. Racial superiority, divine election, patriotism, and if nothing else comes to mind, the right to look out for number one, are invoked to explain why one's group is exceptional and entitled to deem itself worthier than all others.

Nevertheless, human societies have long existed whose fundamental beliefs and self-definition demonstrate that they perceive the world with the benefit of reasonably clear awareness of the reciprocal 'otherness-to-each-other' that we find foreign to our thinking. It is an easily verifiable fact by reference to the historical record, that some peoples are less paranoidal and bellicose than others. And not all worship power, either finite or infinite — much less both, as we do. But the number of reasonably peaceful societies has decreased in modern times, as European and earlier civilizations of like aggressive disposition have exterminated them. No one, however, has perfected the arts of premeditated and merciless infliction of pain, death and destruction to the degree that we have. Such other societies may have been primitive in many ways, but they also seem to have known a few basic truths that we come by, if at all, with great difficulty. Absent-mindedness, it seems, can affect different cultures to varying degrees.

The interpretation of the nature of reality I have proposed rests on my prior conclusion that an empirically well grounded conception of cognition must reject the fantastic supposition that cognition transfers to the mind, or duplicates within itself, the characteristics of reality. However, the inclination to project our mental processes onto the world is so strong in most of us that it is possible for a philosopher to discover the falsity of representationism but nevertheless fail to advert to its true implications regarding the knowability of the world. It should be a lesson to us all that no less talented a thinker than Jean-Paul Sartre did so fail.

Sartre was well aware that when we experience reality, it is the reality itself that appears to us — because *we* make it appear — and that experiencing consists in our making the world apparent to ourselves: an existent, he wrote, is reducible 'to the series of appearances that manifest it.'[334] He knew, therefore, (a) that cognition does not take place through representations of objects that exist in the mind, (b) that intelligibility is not pre-contained in the objects we understand, (c) that understanding cannot consist in the mind's acquisition and possession of such intelligibility, and (d) that therefore 'the first step of any philosophy should be to expel things from consciousness.'[335] For Sartre was the compleat anti-essentialist, far more acerbic in his condemnation of 'essences' and necessary properties than Wittgenstein at his most obsessive-repetitive. But Sartre does not seem to have had, any more than Wittgenstein did, as much as an inkling of the historical reasons why philosophers had ever been essentialists. Silently echoing, therefore, the tradition that unless reality contained intelligibility in itself it could not be known by us — but assuming at the same time that the reality we understand is not constituted by inherent intelligibility — Sartre was reactively driven to the fundamental position that thereafter defined his 'existentialist' philosophy: that the world was absurd.

334   Jean-Paul Sartre, *L'être et le néant* (Paris: Gallimard, 1943), p. 11.

335   Sartre, *L'être*, p. 18. This is true, but perhaps it would have been better to say that they should be expelled from the mind and its cognitive states, be they conscious or non-conscious.

The correct conclusion, I think, should have been that reality cannot be said to be either intelligible or absurd *in itself*; both intelligibility and absurdity imply relationship to a mind. And the cognitive relationship is the effect of the mind's activity exclusively — an effect that remains within the cognizer alone and does not touch the object. Thus, the world does not need the human mind in order to be itself; things do not exist for the purpose of being known and admired by us, any more than for the purpose of making life difficult and unpleasant for us. Or if I may paraphrase Freud, the intention that the world should make sense, just so that human beings could take delight in understanding it, is no part of the scheme of creation.

What Sartre misperceived as a philosopher, others who were not philosophers have misperceived also, because they, too, have been caught in the clash between their semi-awareness of the conscious quality of the human mind and our culture's traditional common sense. Not a few sensitive poets, dramatists, novelists, and essayists of the twentieth century have written in the same existentialist vein that characterized Sartre's philosophy. And reasoning with their solar plexus, as he did, they have arrived at much the same conclusions he did. If God were in his heaven, all would be right with the world; but without God there is no choice other than to deem our existence absurd and nauseating. This is a false disjunction. The corollary of the conclusion that the world is not inherently rational is that understanding cannot consist in taking advantage of the world's inherently intelligible constitution. Understanding is something that *we* do, if we can, with a world that can be understood *by us,* although it is not a world that is intelligible either 'in itself' or 'for itself.'

Since the fundamental presuppositions of both our common and our philosophical tradition are deeply seated, when we say that through the use of reason we can understand reality although it itself is not rational, our thought refuses to follow our tongue. Once again, we allow our vocabulary and our syntax to dictate to us what we should think today, because it is what we have thought in the past. But should it not be reason that leads, and words that follow?

To assert this is not to explain what it is that we do when we understand anything, or why the objective reality of the real does not demand the self-contradiction of the concept of 'objective truth' (or even why this is a self-contradiction). To assert it is only to state part of what is to be explained about the higher, plus-quam-perceptual cognitive functions of the human mind. It is merely to open up for ourselves the possibility of understanding the mind free from one of the principal impediments to philosophy's normal progress.

This should suffice to explain also why the supposition that science or philosophy might one day be 'complete' cannot be true. Knowledge is not our mind's extraction of the wisdom precontained in the world. Knowledge is something that *we* do with, and in relation to, the world. The idea that human knowledge might one day know all that there is to know is as ill-considered as would be the idea that one day the repertoire of human music-making will have been exhausted, because all possible combinations of a finite number of musical notes had been reached; or that writing will come to end when the last possible combination of words has been used in a novel, in the last poem, and in the last essay, and nothing remains to be said. After all, we do not say what we say because it can be said, but because we want to say it. The day may indeed arrive when science, poetry, and art — and philosophy — have come to an end. But if this comes to pass, it will be because there are no human minds to cultivate them. Which at the most recent rates at which human self-destruction has been taking place may well be sooner than one would otherwise calculate.

Meanwhile we need only accept that the contribution that reality is required to make towards our understanding it, is simply that it be a *fact:* that it *be* there, and that it *be* itself. This is enough: a world whose existence and reality are neither more nor less than a matter of fact. What we make of it, and what we make with it — which *for us* may be intelligible or absurd, good or evil, happy or tragic, ugly or beautiful — depends exclusively on us.

Since a world that does not hide behind our visible world or behind the world's visible appearances is a purely factual world, it carries neither a certificate of fitness to exist, nor a warrant or other legal title justifying its appearance to us. On the other hand, it does not need either. Since it is the only real world, it sets the standard of what a true and genuine world should be like; it alone defines the conditions under which a real world can exist. Nor does it have to produce a license reassuring the curious, or the suspicious, or the paranoid that it has been authorized to be. It is a *fait accompli;* it cannot be sent back to wherever it came from with the request that it should be properly reissued. In short, there is no alternative to it: it is the only real world. We would be well advised to accept it as such, and then try to make it as comfortable and pleasant an abode for all of us as we, in our more rational moments, fervently desire and anxiously hope.

5. Addendum: Understanding a world that is not inherently intelligible

The proposed investigation of the causes of the stagnation of modern philosophy has now concluded. But only because the Agenda we adopted restricted its scope by accepting, for the sake of argument, what I called the eclipse of understanding by perception by Locke's oversimple empiricism. But in fact, understanding is not a higher or elaborate form of perception; it is irreducibly distinct from perception, as a little reflection upon our experience suffices to demonstrate. For example, anyone can, merely by lifting an automobile's hood, perceive a four-cycle internal combustion engine and watch it run. But to perceive the engine is not the same as to understand why it can move the automobile and how it does so. When we perceive, we learn 'facts;' when we understand, we gain an 'explanation' of the facts.

The difference between these two cognitive functions was recognized by philosophy in Greek times. But after Locke conflated perception and understanding — perception yields 'ideas,' and ideas are compounded by reason into 'knowledge' — understanding ceased to be normally treated as a distinct function of the human mind. Nevertheless, in time, and under the influence of science, a new version of the inherent intelligibility of the world became widely accepted by modern philosophers— namely, that the world processes are predetermined and regulated by 'laws of nature.' Acquaintance with such laws replaced in scientific circles, in effect, the function of understanding. From this perspective, the human mind does not actually explain the world's phenomena to itself; instead; it discovers and takes note of the 'laws' that explain them; the human mind simply repeats to itself the explanation it reads in nature. The mental function of understanding is, therefore, no longer a live philosophical question.

To study the nature of understanding as a distinct cognitive function would take us beyond the limits of our undertaking in this volume. But I am obliged to comment, if only very sketchily, on one aspect of the matter. For in the course of this investigation I have taken the position that, although our tradition has projected both the perceptual and the intelligent mental activities of human beings onto objects, the world is neither inherently perceptible nor inherently intelligible. That is, I have already argued how perception takes place even if the world is not inherently perceptible, but I should now explain, if only schematically, the fundamental reason why the same should be said of understanding. In other words, in the absence of a transcendent Mind that should make the world inherently intelligible, the vital question arises: how do we understand the real and existing world, if it is not inherently intelligible?

Understanding the world is the outcome of systematizing — that is, giving order and integration to — our perceptions. Understanding is possible only because we have the ability to speak, and thus the ability to think.[336] Now, speech (and therefore also thought) hark back, as we can presume, all the way to the ability of some organisms (already present at the early level of insect life) to make their experience known to conspecifics. Speech, however, is a highly evolved form of animal communication; it is not reducible to communication to others. For when we speak or think, we communicate in the first place with ourselves. We hear — and, as Donald Davidson has stressed,[337] we *understand* — what we say. But as we think about what we perceive or have perceived, if we do so adeptly, then, as the words come and the sentences flow, somehow the information we had already perceptually

---

336 I take 'thinking' to be identical with the mental activity of speaking, but with the difference that the *thinker* merely imagines the sounds instead of actually making them, as the *speaker* does. This implies, of course, that wordless thought is impossible. Some philosophers believe, on the contrary, that 'wordless thought [is] possible, as when we think how a room would look with the furniture rearranged,' Bede Rundle, 'Thinking,' in Honderich, (ed.), *The Oxford Companion to Philosophy,* 872. Now, in my view it is beyond doubt that to *imagine* such rearranged scene wordlessly is perfectly possible. But if one calls it *thinking,* one has thereby assumed, whether wittingly or inadvertently, that there is no difference between the use of our imagination to confect *imaginary perceptions,* on the one hand, and *imaginary speech,* or *thought,* on the other. The two should not be equated. Whereas imaginary perception is the recall, reactivation, and imaginative tinkering with our remembered perceptions (e.g., imagining the rearranged room), the latter is the aboriginal activation of newly and currently imagined speech (e.g., in Rundle's example, describing to ourselves in imaginary speech the rearranging of the room).

337 For the speaker must, of course, understand what it wants others to understand when they grasp what we mean; in other words, the speaker must understand its own speech before it can make itself understood by others by saying something that the hearer can understand. Thus, a 'speaker must himself be an interpreter of others … [A] creature cannot have thoughts unless it is an interpreter of another. [This] imputes no priority to language … [and] allows that there may be thoughts for which the speaker cannot find words, or for which there are no words,' Donald Davidson, "Thought and Talk," in Samuel D. Guttenplan, (ed.), *Mind and Language* (Oxford: Clarendon Press, 1977), 9-10. Thus, to communicate with others, we must communicate to ourselves — i.e, in the sense that we must be conscious of — what we want to communicate to others. We could scarcely fail to be aware of what we wanted others to become conscious of as a result of our saying it. However, not every modern philosopher before Davidson had observed this, and some appear not to have noticed it even now. The reduction of speech to 'language,' and of 'language' to a means of communication, is in part the result of failing to observe the thoughtfulness of speech.

obtained is *processed*. As we say, the facts 'fall into place.' They become *interpreted* facts. For when they are integrated into a 'narrative,' they begin to 'make sense.' The sound they make as they mesh smoothly and click softly is somehow pleasant and soothing; it yields the easy breathing, the comfort, the delight — and even the excitement, if the matter is important — with which one experiences one's experiencing of what one perceives. But what is the nature of the process that yields the state of understanding?

To achieve such state, we perform a mental activity that is like perception in the limited sense that it consists in our actively *relating* ourselves to the characteristics of objects. But in the case of perception, as we have seen, such active self-relation takes advantage of the causal relativity of the characteristics of objects to the characteristics of the perceiving organism; the activity of understanding, on the other hand, takes advantage of the characteristics of speech. (I underline that in this context 'speech' is to be understood as including the soundless form of self-communication we call 'thought.') Speech and thought enable human beings to 'handle' objects mentally, as it were, by relating the *concepts* we derive from our perceptions of objects to each other. And our mental 'manipulation' of our concepts as we relate them to each other, produces understanding when we follow a procedure that is comparable to the (direct or indirect) physical manipulation of objects to which we usually refer as *measuring* them, in the ordinary, literal, and mathematical sense of the term.

To measure an object mathematically, for example, in the dimension of length, we compare the object with an arbitrarily predetermined or pre-defined 'standard' or 'unit' of length. Thereby we gain knowledge of the *relationship* of the object to the unit. Such knowledge is useful because it 'translates' or re-states the unknown (i.e., the length of the object) into the familiar (i.e., the length of the unit). Thus, measuring the length of a field we wish to traverse to reach a goal enables us to conceive (and thus to re-state to ourselves) the field's real and inherent length in terms that describe its relationship to the unit of length we have previously and arbitrarily defined. The field is 5,262.4 meters long. Note well; the definition of the unit of measurement is arbitrary, but the length to which the definition of the unit refers is real and independent of the mind that measures it; indeed, we must be familiar with such real length before we use it as a standard of measurement. Unless you know what 'meter' means, the above information regarding the length of the field is meaningless. However, if we are familiar with what 'meter' means (i.e., if we have sense experience of the length to which the concept of 'meter' refers), then, when we learn that a certain goal is 'x meters' away from us, we can anticipate the effort and time needed to reach it. Without some such comparison, we would not know. Measurements can be useful, therefore, because they enable us to extend the range of our practical adjustment to the world beyond what it would otherwise be. But unless one has previously accepted the empirically groundless, quasi-mystical supposition of Pythagoras and Philolaus — that 'being' (i.e., reality) is eternal and divine, but is nevertheless knowable because it is constituted by 'number' — the usefulness of measuring mathematically the world does not amount to an *explanation* of anything. Mathematical measurements, like perception, deliver only knowledge of facts.

Well, understanding is somewhat like taking a mathematical measurement, but with some differences; it is a measurement at a more basic level and with superior results. For understanding depends on our first conceiving certain 'units' or 'standards' of intelligibility, as it were, by reference to which we can 'measure' the world *interpretatively* (rather than *mathematically)*; that is, in terms that 'make sense.' Such concepts are derived empirically, but not from our experience of the world; they come from the mind's immediate experience of itself. The mind's conscious nature enables it to adopt its own constitution and the ways in which it operates and describes itself to itself, as standards for measuring all things interpretatively — even itself. The speaker's statements regarding the world are meaningful — they help us 'make sense' of the world — because they relate our perceptions of the world to what is immediately and directly familiar to us— namely, our own actual and immediate characteristics as conscious experiencers and thinkers. The 'measuring' of the perceived world by such 'measures' or 'standards' of intelligibility is an 'interpretation' of the world. How do such interpretations come about?

Speech and thought enable us to conceive whatever we consciously observe. But speech is complete, and apt to produce understanding, only when we assert concepts in relation to each other — that is, when we assert 'theses' in relation to specified 'themes.' Now, our assertions take the general form 'A is B.' But whereas there is an unlimited number of concepts that may fill in for 'A' and for 'B,' the number of *ways* in which 'B' can be related to 'A' is fairly small; for concepts may have very different significations in relation to objects, yet have exactly the same function in relation to other concepts.

For instance, when the concepts of, say, 'toad slime' and 'the prime minister' are considered simply as organizing perceptual information supplied by reality, they are utterly different; they have as little in common as, say, the concepts of 'giving you warts' and 'corrupting the rule of law.' When the same concepts are used as theses and themes, however, a similarity appears. In the assertion 'toad slime gives you warts,' the relationship between the concepts that signify the thesis and the theme is the same as that which is found between the thesis and the theme in the assertion 'the prime minister has repeatedly corrupted the rule of law.' In the case of the two themes, two concepts that by themselves mean very different things have a common function: both signify a *causal agency*, (the slime that causes warts, in one case, the willful official who causes governmental corruption, in the other). Likewise, the two concepts used as theses have different meanings in themselves, but share the meaning of 'effect' in relation to their respective themes. Thus, whereas concepts organize information in patterns, assertive speech organizes and elaborates it into patterns of patterns. This level of organization is the basis of 'understanding,' that is, the conversion of merely perceived facts into intelligible, 'sense-making' facts. Let us see how the conversion comes about.

It was well over twenty centuries ago that our philosophical tradition became aware of the fact that our assertions are classifiable into *categories* (literally, 'ways of holding forth'). Since the meaning of these various ways of making assertions about the world can itself be, upon reflection, conceptually asserted, we may say that our assertions organize theses and themes in accordance with concepts such as 'reality' and 'unreality,' 'cause' and 'effect,' 'subject' and 'process,' 'unity' and 'multiplicity,' 'sameness' and 'difference,' 'quantity' and 'quality,' and so on. Even today the precise number and description of the categories are not universally agreed upon — which is understandable, since the degree to which human beings grasp accurately their own mental activities is highly variable — though it is common coin that they are of the order of a dozen or so. Since it is ambiguous to refer to the categories simply as *concepts,* we should draw a distinction between *ordinary concepts* and *categorical concepts.*

Like ordinary concepts, the categories are conceived empirically. But unlike ordinary concepts, which are derived from our experience of the world, the categorical concepts are derived from the mind's immediate experience of itself — or more exactly, from its immediate experience of the way in which it experiences objects consciously. The categories are thus the conceptualization of contents provided not by objects in reality, but by the reality that is the conscious mind itself. They are generated when consciousness organizes the factual information that it provides to itself about the characteristics of its own activity of experiencing consciously. Only consciousness, the presence of the human mind to itself as it learns to assert theses in relation to themes, makes this possible. The contents thus conceived are therefore the formal properties of consciousness. Or which is the same, they are the categorical concepts that underlie the overt and specific meaning of our assertion of theses in relation to themes.

Thus, once we have learned to speak assertively and have conceived the various 'ways of holding forth,' we *presuppose* one or else another of the categories whenever we assert specific theses in relation to specific themes. Conversely, the assertions we make using ordinary concepts, are structured by *underlying* categories that determine their interpretative meaning of the assertion. This is what enables us to systematize and integrate our perceptions, and thus interpret the world, discriminatingly organizing perceptual information that is anterior to them and that they in no way change, filter, or distort. Nor do the categorical concepts add any contents of their own to the contents of reality. For, as with ordinary concepts, once the meaning of a categorical concept has been established (because it has been asserted with such meaning), the concept may be used to organize our perceptions. We organize them by measuring them against the meaning that the concept already has. Thus, the assertion 'toad slime gives you warts' states a cause of a certain effect. It explains how warts come about. And the assertion about 'the prime minister' explains how his autocratic ways perform a gross disservice to the nation. The explanation 'makes sense.' Whence comes its 'making sense'?

It comes from the peculiarities of the categorical concepts. Ordinary concepts express reality as we experience it in real objects themselves. However, when we conceive a category such as 'causality' and then apply it to certain events, we measure the latter by a 'standard' that we have derived from our own nature; we assimilate the world to what we have already learned to think of as 'causality' in ourselves. Of course, we may misidentify the nature of causality, supposing, say, that it involves necessitation; if so, the explanation will be erroneous to the very degree that the concept is faulty. But if we did not observe our own causality at all, we could not think of real events at all, even incorrectly, in terms of cause and effect. The result is that, by implicit reference to the categories, our experience of the world can be cast in *familiar* terms: if we can 'make sense' of the world by making causally structured assertions, it is because we can relate the causality at work in alien events to our real and familiar causality in ourselves. In other words, we have interpreted the world in terms that are meaningful to us. It 'makes sense.' We *understand*.

The categories are, therefore, not innate (as Kant supposed), but empirically acquired. They are *a posteriori* ways of organizing information conceptually — though in relation to the objects measured by them they are *a priori*, or preconceived. And unlike the 'units' used to measure objects mathematically, they are not arbitrary. For we do not determine arbitrarily what we shall experience when we, for instance, become conscious of our own causal efforts and conceive 'causality.' Our 'causality,' our 'activity,' our 'reality,' and so on, are *real*; they are not created by our perceiving or imaging them, and do not depend for their existence on our arbitrarily defining them.

The basic categorical concepts assert the fundamental characteristics on which conscious life is established: reality, efficient causality, and finality. We hardly need consider how we conceive 'reality' or 'causality,' since these topics have been repeatedly discussed already; and the derivation of 'finality' from our own conscious strivings is as easily surmised as that of 'activity' and 'passivity.' Not as obvious, however, is the mental process that results in the concepts of 'necessity' (and 'contingency') and 'possibility' (and 'impossibility.') Like *sameness* and *unity*, which will be considered in a moment, *necessity* is conceived when we experience the identity of the act of consciousness (which is the cause of the conscious state of experiencing) and the corresponding conscious state (which is the effect). Since the cause and the effect coincide, we cannot both experience and not experience at the same time, or experience anything but what we actually experience. This is the way in which, as a matter of fact, consciousness operates: the experiencer must *necessarily* experience whenever it experiences, and it must *necessarily* experience whatever it in fact experiences. The alternative would be an 'impossibility.'

There cannot be any exception to an impossibility, because the standard of possibility and impossibility is the self-identity that conceptual thought in fact exhibits.[338]

Special mention should be made of the categorical concepts that allow us to take mathematical and logical 'measurements' of the world — principally, 'equality,' or synonymously 'sameness' and 'identity,' followed by 'unity' and 'totality' (and of course their negations: 'difference,' 'multiplicity' and 'partiality,' and their synonyms. As previously mentioned in another context, a concept may be the *same as,* or *different from,* another in respect of content; but in any event the second is not the first; for example, 'rose' now is one concept, whereas 'rose' again is another. Each of the two is *one.* Moreover, a concept that is both *one* and *self-same* is a *totality*; for, being *same* (as itself), it is neither more nor less than (i.e., is *not-different* from) itself. At the same time, being *one,* it is in itself *all* that it is or can be: whatever coincides with itself is also a *whole* or a *totality.*

Given that these categories underlie a speaker's or thinker's assertions of theses in relation to themes, a thinker would experience its attempt to assert a self-contradiction such as 'A rose is not a rose' as meaningless. The reason is not that things in themselves are self-identical — actually, they are not — but that *concepts* are. Likewise, a syllogism makes no sense if neither premise is universal; for this means that the middle term would be undistributed (i.e., *not-a-totality*) twice, and equivocality would result; a seemingly constant term would have *different* meanings in each of two premises. By the same token, *one* plus *one* is *equal* to a *total* called two. The total is neither more nor less, but exactly equal to the sum, as mathematics supposes — although in the real world (as Plato noted in the *Phaedo),* nothing is truly equal to anything else, not even itself (since it changes). Nor can 'one' real thing be actually added either to itself or to another in order to make 'two.' When I count the

---

338   This does not imply that the possibility or impossibility of real events depends on whether they are actually conceived; it means that we **think** of an event as possible or impossible depending on whether we find it conceivable or not. Nor does the absolute character of the category of necessity imply that the reality of consciousness is absolute; this is why I have stressed that the self-identity of thought, which is the ground of the concept of necessity, is itself nothing but an observable **fact**; that is, thinking must abide by necessity in the sense that one of its characteristics is, **as a matter of fact**, to be self-identical. Indeed, all the categories have a perfection or absoluteness that the real world seems only to approximate; the reason is of course that in the categorical measuring of reality by consciousness, the nature of consciousness is adopted as the unit of measurement. For instance, the self-coincidence of every concept is perfect because the self-coincidence of **acts of conceiving** is what provides the contents of the definitions of 'self-coincidence,' 'self-identity,' and 'sameness.' Likewise, the characteristics of consciousness that are conceived as its 'unity,' its 'finality,' and so on, are no more absolute than those of other entities. Only the categorical **concepts** are absolute.

oranges in a basket and call the total 'twelve,' in reality each orange remains 'one,' and the 'twelve' exists nowhere but as a concept in my mind.

Thus, unlike those assertions that ascribe 'reality' 'causality' and 'finality,' 'quantity,' 'quality,' and so on, assertions that are structured by the logical and mathematical categories do not describe any property of the real world, though they are nevertheless applicable to it. The real world is neither logical nor mathematical in itself, but can be interpreted by means of logical and mathematical thought — and of course, by means of scientific and philosophical thought as well. Its contents are not distorted simply by being interpreted. But they would be, if the logical and mathematical properties of thought were projected onto the world's objects and ascribed to them as their own. The human mind is perceptive, but the world is not inherently perceptible. And the human mind is rational, but the world is not.

The foregoing interpretation of the nature of understanding cannot but bring to mind the teaching of Protagoras that 'Man is the measure of all things, of the things that are, that [or how] they are, and of things that are not, that [or how] they are not.'[339] This opinion is commonly reviled under the label of 'relativism.' Should it be?

'Relativism' has been in disrepute since as far back as Plato's *Theaetetus,* in which Socrates offers several refutations of Protagoras's opinion. The principal and most memorable argument concludes not simply that Protagoras's doctrine was wrong, but that it was absurd and self-refuting. For in Socrates's depiction of it — as in the usual modern versions of 'relativism' — Protagoras meant that a person's beliefs were true for the person who held them, but not necessarily for others. And this did not mean simply that different persons might deem their own opinions were true despite other people's disagreement — which is of course perfectly possible, and indeed a common occurrence. Protagoras was painted by Socrates to mean rather that a person's beliefs actually could be true, even when they conflicted with the beliefs of other persons who, likewise, did not merely take their own

---

339   Diels-Kranz 80B1. The interpolations in this translation are necessary because, in view of the Greek idea of reality, Protagoras cannot be supposed to have meant that the human mind is the measure of the *existence* of things (i.e., 'of the things that are, that they are') but at most that it is the measure of their *characteristics* (i.e., 'of the things that are, how they are.')

opinions to be true, but correctly deemed that they were true. This is what has come to be known informally as the 'true-for-me' reading of Protagoras.

If this was what Protagoras in fact meant, then, for the very reasons given in Socrates' squelching refutation, to say that Protagoras was mistaken would be an understatement; more to the point would have been to question Protagoras's sanity. However, modern opinion has been fairer to him than the tradition. Although Protagoras's true intention is still not beyond some dispute among today's Hellenists, it is now granted by many that Protagoras's 'bon mot is striking but susceptible of many interpretations,'[340] and that more than one such interpretation could be sensible and intelligent. On the other hand, 'relativism' — the word — has not fared as well as Protagoras, the 'relativist.'

Words, including terms of art, are more often debased by general than by technical use, but upon occasion by the hand of philosophers. 'Relativism' is a case in point. It is ironic that Protagoras is known to have been deeply concerned with the consistent and precise use of technical terms, and with the adverse consequences for philosophy of the careless use thereof. For the meaning of 'relativism' has become narrowly circumscribed in modern times and is now automatically taken to imply some version or other of the obtuse interpretation of the nature of cognition ascribed to Protagoras in the *Theaetetus,* the 'true-for-me' idea of relativism.

This unthinking prejudice against 'relativism' does not seem to me to be justified. Every philosophical interpretation of cognition involves some form of relativity; it has to, because cognition *is* a *relationship* between a cognizer and a cognized. Representationism, for example, assumes tacitly the relativity of representations to the represented. Its mistake does not lie in this, but in the kind of relationship between cognition and reality that it supposes — namely, a *representational* (or 'double existence') relationship. If we make allowance for the causation of cognition by the cognizing organism rather than the object, we should have no objection to maintaining both the relativity of truth to the mind, and the relativity of cognition to reality. My position may be deemed a form of 'relativism,' but it is hardly akin to the self-refuting 'true-for-me' doctrine of the Socratic Protagoras.

---

340   Coady, 'Relativism, epistemological,' in Ted Honderich, (ed.), *The Oxford Companion,* 757.

To sum up, my 'relativism' supposes that understanding may not be construed as the mind's inward repetition of the meaning or explanation objectively contained in the thing; it is rather the mind's interpretations of reality when it relates itself to reality by means of the categorical properties of speech. Understanding consists in the human mind's taking the measure of reality using standards provided by our conceiving the various ways in which the conscious mind actually operates. Such units of measurement are conceived empirically and are familiar to us. We have no innate ideas of the sort, and specifically none of reality, causality, or self. And so, regardless of whether Protagoras thought so or not, I suggest that although the human mind does not create the reality of the world, it has the capability to make the world intelligible to the human mind.

IV

Living Consciously: Speech, Thought, and Understanding

We do not know how life on Earth began, but it is a reasonable estimate that it appeared as a natural development of non-living matter. But then, as life evolved, it took on various guises, each of which built on the previous one, but adding unprecedented variations on the theme of life. Eventually, life took human form. What characterizes the level of life at which we human beings exist and operate is that it is conscious.

Unless one professes an ideological commitment to the reduction of evolutionary differences to similarities — a commitment that is incompatible with Darwinian evolution through the natural selection of irreducible *differences* — one will deem the uniqueness of animal organisms to depend on their having cognitive, mental functions; and one will deem the uniqueness of the human mental functions to be literally self-evident. A little thinking and a few observations are enough to teach us that we have a 'novel' form of mind. Biologically, we are just another ape. Mentally, we are a new phylum of organisms.[341] Indeed, it could be argued with not a little plausibility that conscious life constitutes by itself a distinct biological kingdom, since it adds consciousness to the characteristic that defines the entire kingdom of animal life, namely, sentience. However, the precise taxonomy of the human species is of relatively little weight; what matters to philosophy is whether the peculiarities of human nature are recognized and respected. Consciousness cannot be treated by philosophy simply as one among other characteristics of the human mental functions, since it is the one that throws into relief the distinctive features of the human mode of life and the source of its value to us.

---

341   Terence W. Deacon, *The Symbolic Species: The Co-evolution of Language and the Brain* (New York: Norton, 1997), 23.

For example, once a human organism has irreversibly lost all its capacity for living at the level of consciousness, the human being has ceased to be: it has died, even if the formerly human organism should retain an infrahuman level of life. And when we say that we 'enjoy life' — or for that matter, that we do not — what we actually have in mind is not the biochemistry of our organisms for its own sake or that of the brain in particular; what we prize is the conscious outcome of our organism's mental operations and their consequences for the entirety of the human organism. Without consciousness, we would not know that we were conscious or that we existed; our existence and our mental life would be worthless to us. In short, consciousness suffuses the typically human mode of life. We *live* consciously, and to understand our human nature we must gain at least a basic understanding of all the essential features of our conscious cognitive life. To complete our study the latter, so as to round out our overview of human cognition, is the objective of this chapter.

Our investigation of the conscious life of human organisms, therefore, would be doomed to fail from the outset, unless the first observation we took into account were that conscious cognition comprises more than the one aspect of it — namely, conscious perception — we have studied so far. If this has to be pointedly remarked upon, the reason is not that it is inherently difficult to observe, but that modern philosophy of mind has tended to focus most of its attention on perception at the expense of other aspects of the mind. This has probably been related to the absence of stable, time-tested explanations of the nature of conscious perception; attention has had to be focused where it was most obviously needed. But a less obvious, though more decisive consideration may have been the trend initiated by Hume's pointing out the vacuity of the supposition that had traditionally reigned in philosophy, to the effect that non-perceptible, intelligible 'substances' underlay the perceptible 'accidents' of beings. However, doing away with the inherent intelligibility of the world does not do away with the fact that we are somehow capable of understanding: all of us have direct experience of it. (One is puzzled when the car will not start, until the mechanic points out that the ignition switch is defective; one ceases to be puzzled, and the explanation 'makes sense.') The demise of essences notwithstanding, philosophers continued to study the nature of understanding, but under the assumption that it is probably related instead to speech and communication. In any event, understanding had little to do with perception. Perception stands by itself.

In my view, this assumption is not correct. If the rudimentary explanation we have developed of the simpler, perceptual level of consciousness is reasonably plausible, it frees us further to observe that, as Charles B. Daniels has remarked, 'there is [no] such thing as purely perceptual knowledge or belief … that is not infected by inference or memory … [T]he bits of information … which we get by virtue of sense alone, even the senses jointly, is severely and surprisingly limited.'[342] The life of consciousness begins with conscious perception, but comprises more than perception. But precisely what?

As we try to answer this question, I suggest that we heed Isaac Newton's warning about premature theorizing.[343] We should consult our experience before we attempt to develop hypotheses that might explain what we observe. For hypotheses are not mere conjectures for which we seek support or disconfirmation in facts pro and con; to imagine they are is to risk mistaking rationalizations for evidence. Hypotheses deserve entertaining only if they grow out of observation. This more strict procedure is especially important in complex cases like that at hand, where a multitude of issues intersect. Besides, the very concept of 'living consciously' has no established philosophical currency: our study must begin with a description of the phenomenon to which this concept refers. As its meaning becomes clear, we shall see problems arising, and it is only then that we shall then try to solve them. If the observations that have generated our questions have been adequate, our efforts will have been aimed at the right target. That is, we shall seek to explain the true *explicandum* rather than one we invented ourselves.

1. The phenomenon of 'conscious life'

It is not at all difficult for us to observe the facts, and to appreciate the value of the facts (a) that we live in a world that offers colours, sounds, textures, flavours, and smells for our enjoyment, benefit, and safety, and (b) that our organisms are equipped with the mental functions whereby to experience them. We do not quite as often remark on the extraordinary circumstance to which Terence

---

342   Charles B. Daniels, 'Perception, Thought, and Reality', *Nous* 22 (1988): 455-464, 455-6. The same position had been taken earlier by George Boas, 'The Perceptual Element in Cognition.' *Philosophy and Phenomenological Research* 12 (1952): 486-494.

343   See his *Principia Mathematica Naturalis Philosophiae,* (Second edition), Bk. III, General Scholium; Eng. trans., *The Mathematical Principles of Natural Philosophy* (New York: Philosophical Library, 1964), where he made his famous but frequently misunderstood statement, *'hypotheses non fingo.'*

W. Deacon has eloquently drawn our attention: that, on the one hand, we live in a perceptible world we share with those other animal species whose perceptual cognitive powers are comparable to ours, but that, on the other:

> [W]e also live in a world that no other species has access to. We inhabit a world full of abstractions, impossibilities, and paradoxes. We alone brood about what didn't happen, and spend a large time of each day musing about the way things could have been if events had transpired differently. And we alone ponder what it will be like not to be. In what other species could individuals ever be troubled by the fact that they do not recall the way things were before they were born and will not know what will occur after they die? We tell stories about our real experiences and invent stories about imagined ones, and we even make use of these stories to organize our lives. In a real sense, we live our lives in this shared virtual world. And slowly, over the millennia, we have come to realize that no other species on earth seems able to follow us into this miraculous place.[344]

Daniels is indeed right; perception provides only a small fraction of the totality of our conscious cognitive life; it is a crucial fraction, because it provides empirical facts, but hardly the whole of it. However, some aspects of Deacon's description of our mental life in 'this miraculous place' require further explanation and some qualification. For example, the world 'that no other species has access to,' is said to be a 'virtual world;' in the absence of further clarification, Deacon's words might yield the impression that the 'world' in question is an unreal, imaginary world, distinct and separate from the actually existing world, a world of make-believe and illusion that exists only in our minds. But how could we be truthfully said to 'live our lives' in such a world 'in a real sense'? Surely our human life does not consist in perceiving the world and then retreating into daydreaming and fantasizing within ourselves. This is not to deny, on the other hand, that sometimes we *do* construct illusions and pipe-dreams; and as Deacon reminds us, we also tell 'stories about our real experiences,' and indeed

---

344   Deacon, *Symbolic Species,* 21-22.

we 'invent' imaginary experiences. Deacon's description of the sort of the uniquely mental process that is superimposed upon human perception is enlightening, but it could be usefully expanded and refined.

a) The twofold employment of the human imagination

The second observation we must record concerns, therefore, a distinction that helps us bring precision to Deacon's remarks. When at an earlier stage of this investigation I listed the various cognitive functions of human beings, I mentioned that in addition to our ability to remember, recall, and revisit many of our previous perceptions, we also possessed a mental power that is quite distinct from sense perception, but which enables us to exploit and, as it were, manipulate at will, our recalled perceptions. It is the power of *imagination.* We have the ability to bring back our perceptions in the shape of conscious 'images,' and to proceed thereafter to break them up arbitrarily into elements that we can configure and reconfigure without regard to the constraints of reality, possibility, or truth. With our imagination we can indeed create many 'virtual worlds.' To the imagination insofar as it enables us to *isolate* ourselves from the real world and to construct a fictitious counterpart of it, I shall refer as *fantasy.*

Now, many of the higher infrahuman animal species are able to store and recall their experiences. But the memories of animals not capable of consciousness would not be conscious, of course; nor could such memories be consciously manipulated at will. Whether any species besides our own can therefore rework their perceptual memories, seems to me unlikely; but in any event, it is certain that *we* can. We are able to manhandle at will the perceptual memories that we consciously experience as 'images.' Using our fantasy we can indeed *retreat* into an imaginary sphere of our own making. And we do so for a variety of purposes, which range from the useful, through the frivolous, to the positively harmful. But in any case, when we use our imagination in this manner, we leave behind the real world. In fact, sometimes we deliberately resort to fantasy in the form of day-dreaming (or consume what is significantly called 'escapist' literature or performances), for the very reason that it enables us to evade, albeit ephemerally, the unpleasant realities that sometimes are integral part of the real world.

But this is only one way in which we can use our power to imagine. We can use it also in a very different manner and for very different purposes — namely, in order to advance our *knowledge* of both the *real* world and ourselves, and to reap a deeper *awareness* of them than mere perception alone affords us. If exercised in this peculiar way, the human imagination performs a *cognitive* function — a mental function whereby we can become aware of certain aspects of the *real* world that mere perception cannot deliver. The fantastic use of our imagination is to be contrasted with our employment of it to achieve the very opposite of retreating from reality. We can use it to *explore* the real world as well as ourselves. Whereas perception yields awareness of perceptible facts, the appropriate use of our imagination can procure for us the level of knowledge that reaches into the implications of facts and into the significance that the perceived facts hold for us.

To achieve this, however, we have to apply our imagination not simply to our recalled prior perceptions; we must use it to *assert* our perceptions mentally — that is, to give them *worded* form, by imagining the vocal sounds we originally learned to make in order to *speak*. We store auditory memories of our speech just as we do visual and others. But when we recall them in imaginary speech, we do more than create auditory images of the sounds: imagining the sounds enables us to *reassert* the meaning we originally learned to *assert* by making the sounds. When our imagination is used in this way, it is sometimes referred to as *cogitation*, but more commonly, as *thought*. We can, of course, if we so wish, vocalize the words at the same time as we think them; but we are likely to do this only if we want to let others know what we are thinking. The important point is that what we thus do, which I have called 'thinking,' is not to be confused with fantasizing. Thinking, as I use the term, is imaginary speech.

We need go no deeper into the subject before we risk confusion. In the popular terminology of English speakers (or for that matter, in at least the principal modern European languages), 'to think' covers a wide range of mental operations, and not only the imaginary speech I have referred to as 'thought.' This has been true since at least the time of Descartes, when he used the word *cogito* to cover mental processes omnicomprehensively. Today, for example, one could say 'I am thinking' to describe one's fantasizing about one's forthcoming beach holidays, as well as one's attempt to reason regarding the nature of the mind; and most of us use the expression 'I think so' as readily to signify an unshakeable conviction as a highly doubtful conjecture. As I shall use the term here, however, it will inflexibly refer to our *speaking* without making any audible vocal sounds, but simply imagining the sounds and asserting their meaning mentally so that only we ourselves are aware of what we think.

But it is not only the popular usage that we should beware; that of many philosophers, also, is often imprecise. Absence of due discrimination between *fantasizing* and *thinking* accounts for the position taken by the many philosophers who would agree with Bede Rundle that

'thinking is seldom … a matter of an inward dialogue carried on by the mind with itself … [W]ordless thought [is] possible, as when we think how a room would look with the furniture rearranged.'[345]

Well, it is beyond doubt that to *imagine* such a scene wordlessly is perfectly possible. But if one calls it 'wordless thought' one has thereby assumed, wittingly or otherwise, that there is no difference between *imaginary perception,* on the one hand, and *imaginary speech,* or *thought,* on the other. One has ignored the peculiarities of imaginary *speech* and reduced it to imaginary *perception;* one has equated the two, as the language of common sense does, under the common heading of 'thought,' despite their being observably different. Whereas fantasy or imaginary perception is the recall, reactivation, and imaginative tinkering with our remembered perceptions, imaginary speech, or thought, is the aboriginal activation of currently imagined speech by means of which we can become aware of aspects of reality that perception alone does not reveal. When we exercise our fantasy to create an 'image,' what we imagine is invented by us out of the constituent elements of what we have previously *perceived* with our senses. What we imagine when we exercise our thinking so as to create a 'thought' and record an observation, is made up from the constituent elements — not merely sounds, but *meaningful* sounds, or words — that we have previously *said.* We first learned to say the meaning, of course, by making vocal sounds that asserted our experience in audible speech; but we soon learned to say it in imagination only, inaudibly. Fantasy and thought are two different ways to use our imagination.

---

345   Bede Rundle, 'Thinking,' in Ted Honderich, (ed.), *The Oxford Companion to Philosophy* (Oxford: Oxford University Press, 1995), 872.

If this is not readily observed by every one of us, the explanation may be found, in part, in the traditional view of the mind as *undergoing* its mental processes. But the active nature of the mind should not be forgotten; our mental activity does not stop at perception. Thus, the imaginary speech of thinking would be misconceived if it were deemed a sort of dialogue where one passively 'hears' what one's imagination 'says.' It is more like an inward monologue in which one actively makes assertions to oneself. And this is exactly what existing or living consciously ultimately implies: not simply experiencing the world and ourselves, but actively asserting our experience to ourselves, appreciating thus its experiential nature, and building it up into 'constructions' that reveal the *relationships* among the aspects of reality with which we become acquainted through sense perception. The slightest and most trivial generalizations, for example, such as 'plants need water to grow' would be impossible without words. Much less could a complex deduction or a theoretical explanation drawn from perceived facts be accomplished, in the absence of a means to gain more information about the world than our senses alone can provide.

My objection to the absence of distinction between fantasy and thought is not, of course, that the term 'thinking' inherently means 'to think' and may not be used to signify anything else. I demur rather at the erasing of the difference between two different types of imaginative mental activity, regardless of the means by which the equation of the two should be assumed. Fantasy, in which we shall take no further interest, must be carefully distinguished from imaginary speech; I so distinguish it by reserving for it the title of 'thought.'

Now, *how* imaginary speech enables us to reach a deeper, less conspicuous level of knowledge than mere perception affords us, is of course not at all obvious; it is one of the principal issues to be investigated here. But *that* it so enables us, is on its face not subject to much doubt. For it is an empirical fact that, for example, we think up questions about the world we perceive, and about ourselves, and that we try to obtain answers, sometimes successfully, by thinking about what we perceive. But to ask questions and to answer them, we have to use words; this, too, is a fact. Moreover it is another fact that, besides asking questions of ourselves, silently, we can ask our questions of others, if our words are audibly sounded. And it is yet another fact, and a most important one, that we cannot ask questions of others unless we also ask them of ourselves — though we can do the latter without doing the former as well. Thus, everyday experience teaches us — but philosophy is required to establish critically — that cogitation, or thinking, is a mental function whereby we interact cognitively with the world, including ourselves, at the level of consciousness. (And with each other, if we think audibly, and not only for our own 'hearing.') Thinking is the process whereby we put our perceptions in the service of living our lives in the real world insofar as we are conscious beings. The world we fantasize about does not exist in reality; it is, as Deacon says, a 'separate' and 'virtual world.' The world we can think about is the real world. The thinking — the activity of thinking the real world — is of course the thinking organism's activity, and part of the organism.

Moreover, thinking is not merely an activity we perform now and then in our spare time. We do it constantly. Thinking is the way in which we exist, the way we *live* the conscious life. We can hardly conceive what human life would be like if we were unable to think and were confined to perceiving, to reliving our perceptions in memory, and to fantasizing. We would have lost our ability to evaluate what we perceive. We could not grasp its significance, or inquire into it when we did not. We could not relate anything to anything else, or make comparisons, or think of events as causes and effects. The simplest reasoning would be beyond us. Our experience would be so confusing we would not even know that it was confused. Thinking so perfects and elaborates our perceptions that, quite possibly, we might not be able to perceive consciously unless we could also think. For it is not out of the question that learning to assert our sense experience by signifying it through the instrumentality of either audible or imaginary vocal sounds is what educates the brain of the young child simultaneously to experience objects and its own activity of experiencing objects.[346]

And so, we think throughout our waking hours, in conjunction with actual and recreated perceptions, and as the enlightening complement of perception, in order to reach the level of consciousness that we all take for granted. The 'stream of consciousness,' as we sometimes describe the complex mental process whereby we simultaneously perceive, imagine, and think, never stops as long as we live: we may sleep, but as William James remarked long ago, our consciousness is 'sensibly continuous,'[347] and the 'stream' picks up, without a break, where it had left off upon our falling asleep. Well, it

---

346   I have discussed this possibility in *Evolution and Consciousness; The Role of Speech in the Origin and Development of Human Nature* (Toronto: University of Toronto Press, 1989).

347   James, *Principles of Psychology,* vol. 1, (New York: Macmillan, 1891), 146.

is only when our perceiving is processed by our thinking (whether we share our thinking with others or keep it to ourselves), that we have transcended mere *conscious perception* and begun to lead a *conscious life*. We are then conscious in the full sense of the term. The literal and important truth behind Deacon's metaphorical 'enchanted place' is thus not merely that other species cannot follow us into the internal world of human *fantasy*, but that they cannot follow us when, by means of thought, we penetrate deeper into the real and external world than they can ever go.

Thinking reveals itself to our introspective observation in a range of specific modalities which we variously describe as to *opine, believe, surmise, deem, calculate, estimate, judge, wonder, deliberate, argue, demonstrate, ponder, excogitate, consider, study, reason, reflect, meditate, speculate, explain, suppose, examine,* and so on. Each of these terms, like countless similar others I have not listed, emphasizes a peculiar nuance that thinking exhibits in the various contexts and for the various purposes in which we exercise it. But the many variations of 'thinking' all tend in the same direction — namely, towards our *interpreting, explaining,* and *understanding* the world and its objects (including, of course, ourselves and our fellow humans).

Thus, the third observation without which we are not likely to understand the fundamental features of thought is that thinking is the means whereby, transcending mere perception, we rise to *understanding* what we perceive — though to be sure, we achieve understanding neither infallibly nor universally. But thinking enables us to investigate the world and to ferret out some answers to our questions about it. Unlike fantasizing, understanding is very much concerned with grasping the truth regarding the real world. Thinking can lead to the sort of knowledge that puts us in possession of not only facts, but also their *explanation*. And as Roger Squires has remarked, the human ability to understand, puny though it may be, is nevertheless wondrous, because it is so 'far in excess of what we need in order to get by … The most astounding thing in the world, it may seem, is that we can understand it and the creatures within it.'[348] Not merely perceive it, but *think* about it and *understand* it.

We are most often motivated to think for the sake of reaching mental states that satisfy our desire — and often enough our urgent need — to find our perceptions. of both external objects

---

348   Roger Squires, 'Understanding,' in Honderich (ed), *Oxford Companion to Philosophy,* p. 886.

and of ourselves, 'meaningful.' For all of us are aware that although our perceptions usually 'make sense,' sometimes they do not; and if they do not, we feel uncomfortable. Thus, most of the time our exchanges with the world and our confrontations with ourselves are uneventful; if so, our ordinary thinking is desultory and humdrum. But thought it is not less important for all that, since the desultory and humdrum thinking of our ordinary stream of consciousness carries our conscious human life. Even in our minor encounters with reality (say, when we go to the market), we want to understand what we perceive and therefore interpret it: we tell ourselves 'what it means.' It is not only at special times or in especially important matters, but always, that we expect to find the world reasonably predictable and intelligible — though it is when we do not so find it that we direct ourselves towards the objective of making it so. (If the market is closed during its normal hours, we want to know why, and we seek an explanation.)

Thus, understanding does not invariably require much wit or sophistication. For we not only inquire into tricky and knotty matters such as the evolution of stars and the nature of the human mind; we are also curious about trivialities, such as the reason why the bus to the market was delayed. But in every case, though we may not always advert to it, the activity is cognitive in nature; for thinking elaborates, through imaginary speech, the knowledge that we gain through conscious perceptual experience — both as we obtain it at the time we think it, and as we recall earlier perceptions. We need thought in addition to perception in order to arrive at musings, opinions, questions, conclusions, evaluations, convictions, explanations, interpretations, and sundry cognate states of mind, that make up the stuff of our daily experience. The results of thinking can then be applied, directly or indirectly, to the conscious and deliberate conduct of our lives.

Understanding is therefore not a distinct mental function in addition to thinking: it is the end-state of thinking when thinking reaches the objective it naturally seeks. We want to understand, because we can understand; and it is only because we engage in 'thinking' that we understand whatever we understand. The ability to live at the level of *conscious perception, thought, and understanding* is the hallmark of humanity; it defines the human specificity.

We have yet to determine why and how words, whether imaginary or sounded, can help us not only structure our conscious life, but also contribute to its becoming 'meaningful,' by bringing about changes in our experience so that it 'makes sense:' We want to learn how the processing of conscious perceptions through thinking brings about our conscious life, and thereby ultimately acquire a degree of understanding of world and self. And we want to understand why the world and its objects need not be inherently intelligible in order to be understood by us. But meanwhile, from preceding remarks a question arises. Clearly, there is a very close relationship between thought and speech. But precisely how are they related?

b) The functional equivalence of speech and thought

I have called attention to the observable fact that when we 'think' we speak with the aid of our imagination, although we can also speak audibly, using our vocal apparatus. This could be taken to indicate that, although speech and thought are two distinct and separate functions, thinking presupposes (and to that extent depends on) speaking, whereas speaking is independent of thought. In my view, however, although this is a fairly common assumption of common sense and of some philosophers, and although it has superficial plausibility, it is incorrect; indeed, the separation of speech from thought into distinct functions is one of two presuppositions that are guaranteed to derail the study of the conscious mind's ability to understand. (The other is the supposition that speech is reducible to the communication of thought.)

My contrary view is that, from the viewpoint of cognition, thought and speech are functionally equivalent; we cannot think without performing the same mental operation we perform when we speak audibly; nor can we speak audibly without performing the same mental operation we perform when we think, speaking inaudibly. It may not be readily apparent, but careful observation suggests that thinking and speaking are two different modalities of what in all fundamental respects is one and the same mental function; to think is a particular way to speak, and to speak is a particular way to think. The obvious difference between them — that speech is audible, whereas thought, of course, is not — does not amount to a difference between two functions, but to two different ways of discharging one and the same function. No doubt, it is puzzling that it should be so, and we would like to know why. And there is an explanation, which as we shall see has to do with the way in which evolution seems to have brought about the function of thinking and understanding out of the infrahuman ability to communicate. But at the moment we continue to be concerned with what we can observe — which we should therefore respect as a fact, until such time, if ever, as we should have good reason to deem it a mistake. The problem is how to solve, rather than, as Wittgenstein would say, how to dissolve, the puzzle.

To argue that neither the function of thought nor the function of speech can be understood unless in relation to the other, I appeal again to experience. Since thinking requires the use of imaginary speech, we cannot expect to understand the nature of thought unless we understand at the same time the nature of speech. Much less clear to most of us, however, is that the converse is also true: that we cannot conceive speech unless as part of our conception of the nature of thought and cannot expect to understand either without reference to the other. Thinking is wordly; it requires words, though not necessarily sounded words. Speech, for its part, is thoughtful, it has to be thought; otherwise it would be plain noise and babble. If we do not advert to this, we may overlook the empirical fact that thinking is done using one or else another language; we will insist that either thought has no linguistic form (i.e. it is not worded), or that, if it has linguistic form, it is in the sense that it is cast in the native and universal human 'language' of raw cognition, as it were — the so called 'language of thought' — a paradoxically universal language that no one can understand until one's brain translates it into an ordinary language actually spoken by a human community. But nothing in our experience supports this opinion.

If we consult our experience, we may verify that to speak without thinking is impossible; we cannot do it. It is true that, resorting to a graphic figure of speech, on appropriate occasions we can say, with reason but hyperbolically, that someone's speech is 'thoughtless.' We are justified when we so call it in order to signify that the speaker's thinking of what was said was foolish or ill-considered — but it cannot be said literally. It would be a contradiction of what we experience. When someone speaks 'thoughtlessly,' what would have to be thoughtless is the person's *thinking* of what the person says audibly. But neither could we think, if we did not know how to speak audibly. If someone were to think "wordlessly,' what would have to be wordless is the thinker's concepts — that is the *imaginary words* — thought by the thinker.

Now, why is this not obvious to all of us? Aside from absent-mindedness (more about which will be said below), it is because when we speak audibly, our thinking coincides with our making the vocal sounds of speech: we think what we say by making actual vocal sounds. We therefore hear — we literally *hear* — the sounds we make when we speak audibly; we hear them by means of the same auditory organs by which we hear other sounds. (For as it happens, human vocal sounds are produced mostly by the activity of the laryngeal muscles; however, proprioceptors 'are absent from… [these] muscles, and feedback control [in vocal sound-making] comes by way of the ear.'[349]) The vocal activity therefore masks the thinking activity, in much the same way that a soft sound close to one's ears mask a much louder sound farther away. We are vividly aware of our sound making, but do not advert readily to the fact that we also *think* what we say — despite the fact that, if we did not think it, we would not *mean* what we say.

If confirmation that speech demands thinking is required, let us remember that anyone who knows how to speak knows how to lie: children discover how to do it after having barely learned how to speak. Instead of saying what one actually thinks, one says what one pretends to think, namely, the lie. But lies cannot be told unless they are thought. If speaking did not involve thinking, it would be impossible for speakers to tell a lie. It would not be possible for them to say what they falsely thought while hiding what they thought was true.

Donald Davidson is among the few philosophers who have expressed what I take to be some-what the same recognition of the fundamental thoughtfulness of speech, by insisting that:

> [A] speaker must himself be an interpreter of others … [A] creature cannot
> have thoughts unless it is an interpreter of another … [This] imputes no pri-
> ority to language … [and] allows that there may be thoughts for which the
> speaker cannot find words, or for which there are no words.[350]

---

349 Bernard G. Campbell, *Human Evolution: An Introduction to Man's Adaptations* (Chicago, 1966), p. 308. Thus, human beings cannot learn to control vocal sounds — and therefore cannot learn to make vocal signals —unless they can hear the sounds that they make. This is why congenitally deaf children do not ordinarily learn to make vocal signals, though they can learn to use other means to assert their experience and communicate it to others.

350 Donald Davidson, 'Thought and Talk,' in Samuel D. Guttenplan, (ed.), *Mind and Language* (Oxford: Clarendon Press, 1977), 9-10.

The reason is that the speaker must, of course, understand what it wants others to understand; it must understand its own speech before it can make itself understood by others by saying something that the hearer can understand. If no words already exist to mean what one wants to mean, one will invent them; if nothing else, one can always call it 'it.' (In colloquial English, 'whatchamacallit' is also available, since the ability to speak and think is the ability to determine what vocal sound *shall* mean.) For as previously noted, to communicate with others, we must communicate to ourselves — i.e., we must be conscious of — what we want to communicate to others. We could scarcely fail to be aware of what we wanted others to become conscious of as a result of our saying it. However, not every modern philosopher before Davidson had observed this, and some appear not to have noticed it even now.

Part of the difficulty we may have in grasping the functional equivalence of thought and speech is, again, our received vocabulary. Lexical awkwardness, however, most often masks insufficient or inaccurate observation. In the invariable usage of our culture — but also, frequently, in that of philosophy — the terms 'thinking' and 'thought' carry a heavy load of imprecision and equivocality. If their meaning were not suitably harnessed, they would be useless for philosophical purposes. The so-called 'wordless thought' involved in *thinking* is not actually wordless, but *soundless.* Confusing the use of *words* (which may be either actually sounded or soundlessly imagined) with the use of *vocal sound*s, is among the shoals on which the study of the conscious mind has sometimes foundered.

In contrast, the Greek philosophers had at their disposal a verb, *legein,* that signified the human activity of *saying* or *affirming,* or *meaning* something, regardless of whether it was said or affirmed vocally or in silent imagination only. (Heraclitus depended on this for developing his doctrine of the mind.) This is why *legein* and its derivatives, such as the noun *logos* ('what is said'), are sometimes translated into English as 'thinking' and 'thought,' but at other times, according to context, as 'speaking' and as 'speech' or as 'word.' The closest to such ambivalence that English allows may be the verbs 'to assert,' 'to say,' and 'to mean.' Aristotle, however, as noted earlier, swayed perhaps by the fact that speakers of different languages used different vocal sounds to refer to the same objective reality (which as will be remembered, he identified with its meaning), seems to have been among the first Greek philosophers to have separated speech and thought. The tradition of ignoring the thoughtfulness of speech and the wordliness of thought is long; speech and thought have therefore been most commonly treated as separate functions. Thought is 'inner' and private, whereas speech is 'outer' and public. (To be precise, speech is not necessarily, but only *potentially,* public; but it is widely assumed that this is irrelevant to its characterization, although in fact it is an indication that communicativeness cannot be an indispensable component of speech.)

The separation having been taken for granted, the philosophical study of speech in modern times has usually supposed that speaking — or rather 'language', a term that omits reference to activity — consisted in transforming or 'translating' our inner thoughts, which were inherently wordless, into worded 'expressions' of the thoughts. As a well-known and not atypical linguist put it, there is a distinction between the conceptual 'purport' of the speaker, which is linguistically 'amorphous', and the concrete linguistic 'form' that it has in any given language; for example, if we consider a variety of sentences such as 'I do not know', *'Je ne sais pas',* and *'No sé',* we may observe that 'despite all their differences, [they] have a factor in common, namely, the purport, the thought itself.'[351] Of course, 'the same purport is formed or structured differently in different languages ... [But the form] is independent of, and stands in arbitrary relation to, the *purport.*'[352] Thus, thought is wordless, and speech is thoughtless.

Actually, the truth is that the three sentences of the foregoing example are three different thoughts. There is a common element to the three assertions, of course, but it is not a thought: it is the objective reality of which I am speaking, my state of ignorance. Because the factual reality of which I speak is the same in all three cases, all three state the same thing in three different languages. But only the 'thing' is common. The three assertions are three distinct thoughts about one and the same reality.

The assumption that thought is wordless and speech is thoughtless has retained the allegiance of some, but is no longer as widely accepted by philosophers as it was as little as a generation or two ago. It fell into disfavour in the light of the critique to which it was subjected during the second half of the twentieth century by several Continental philosophers, most notably perhaps Maurice

---

351   Louis Hjelmslev, *Prolegomena to a Theory of Language* (Madison, WS: University of Wisconsin Press, 1961), p. 50.

352   Hjelmslev, *Prolegomena,* 52.

Merleau-Ponty, and in anglophone circles by Ludwig Wittgenstein. To Wittgenstein we owe the negative but most valuable insight that:

> [L]anguage is misrepresented as a vehicle for the communication of language-independent thoughts. Speaking is not a matter of translating wordless thoughts into language, and understanding is not a matter of interpreting — transforming dead signs into living thoughts.[353]

But Wittgenstein does not seem to have pursued the thoughtfulness of speech that his criticism of the more traditional views implies; he stopped short at allowing that 'language' has consequences for thought. Consistently with his failure to recognize the cognitive function of 'language,' he also denied the cognitive nature of philosophy. He thought that language is apt to create insoluble problems; as previously noted, philosophy can only explain them away by showing how they are created by language.

In what pertains to recognition of the active and cognitive nature of speech, the rejection of the first assumption — the separation of speech and thought — has proven to be a sideways step. It has not been taken advantage of. And the second assumption — namely, that the essential and primary function of speech is to communicate one's thoughts — has not been easily shed. But once it is assumed, the truly primary cognitive function of speech — the features that render it incommensurable with communication of the sort that we detect among infrahumans — is likely to be ignored. In the result, the 'philosophy of language' as it has been cultivated by modern philosophy, and in particular as practiced under the auspices of analytic philosophy and cognitivism, does not seem to me quite relevant to the study of speech as one of two modalities in which human beings can exercise a single cognitive power of the mind

The reduction of speech to 'language,' and of 'language' to a means of communication, is in part the result of failing to observe the thoughtfulness of speech[354] and the corresponding failure to

---

353   P.M.S. Hacker, 'Wittgenstein, Ludwig,' in Honderich (ed.), *Oxford Companion to Philosophy*, 915.

354   The reduction of speech to making vocal sounds provides the grounds for a spurious objection to the functional equivalence of thought and speech: that it would deny the ability to think to 'those who cannot in fact speak,' (Rundle, 'Thinking,'

observe the wordliness of thought. A more fundamental cause of such reduction, however, may be the same absent-mindedness we encountered above when we studied our perceptual function. In the case of speech, however, the misunderstanding is a little different. The reason is that the human organism's agency in perception can be easily overlooked, whereas it is impossible for speakers to fail to observe altogether that they play some sort of active role when they speak. If nothing else, speakers make the vocal sounds that, upon being heard by a communicand, are said to function as signs that convey the meaning carried by the signs. Absent-mindedness nevertheless tends to prevail, as speakers fail to detect the mental activity of *thinking* what they say: they do not advert to their own causal activity of *meaning* the meaning they want to communicate. Speaking tends to be deemed active, therefore, only insofar as it requires making sounds. And so, absent-minded speakers tend to project their own causal agency onto the words they use to speak (and ultimately onto the reality signified by the words).

Consequently, speakers may easily suppose that cognition transfers to the mind the meaning that inheres in reality, that the meaning is then transferred from the mind to the words, and that words are the carriers of the meaning from the speaker to the hearer. We have already noted all this in earlier contexts. Of course, every philosopher — though hardly every speaker — is aware that the words themselves cannot carry their meaning simply by virtue of their specific characteristics as sounds (or as visible marks, in the case of writing). For every philosopher is aware that any sign whatever can be used to signify anything whatever. Words are nevertheless deemed apt to carry meaning by virtue of their *conventional* reference to things. Speakers will grant that the reference of the words is arbitrary, but they will also suppose that upon the communicand's hearing the words that carry the conventional meaning, such meaning will be received by the communicand and cause its understanding of the words and of the reality signified by the words.

---

872). This expression refers, I take it, to deaf-mutes and aphasics, but if so, the objection is fallacious. The functional equivalence of thought and speech would be contradicted if there were reason to think that there were human beings who had never become able to communicate with other human beings using any medium whatever, but who nevertheless were able to think. This is not the case of either deaf-mutes or aphasics. The latter do not lose the ability to think when they lose the ability to make vocal sounds; and deaf-mutes are able to communicate using a non-audible medium. Vocal sounds are the usual, and normally the basic, medium of human communication, but not the only one. Young children before they have learned to speak should indeed be deemed unable to think.

The cruder versions of this misinterpretation will suppose that the conventional meaning of words reflects the meaning that inheres in reality; words are like labels we apply to reality. (This false comparison overlooks the fact that in reality we do not apply labels to objects to assert their identity, but only to remind us of their previously determined identity. The label 'strawberry jam' is attached only to jars that one knows to contain strawberry jam, and would be meaningless to anyone who did not already know what 'strawberry jam' was.) The more sophisticated versions recognize that speech refers to reality only indirectly; what we communicate by means of speech is not reality, but our *experience* of reality. This is true and important. But in either event, speakers will be puzzled by what they take for a marvel: that vocal sounds (or other signs) should *mean* anything.

Actually there is no marvel— or rather, if there is, it is not in the words — because it is *speakers*, not the words they use, who *mean* whatever is meant. For the same reason, if speech is deemed to be independent of thought, speech cannot be envisaged as a cognitive mental function of living human organisms, but only as 'language,' i.e., a mechanism or device whereby communication can be achieved.

Our misunderstanding of the thoughtfulness required by speech, and of the wordliness required by thought, however, begins with misunderstanding the communicativeness of speech. It is possible that somewhat the same confusion we noted earlier regarding 'information' may be at work in the case of 'communication.' Fundamentally the same projective reasoning that leads some philosophers to propose that information can be 'physically realized,' might lead others to suppose, in effect, that vocal sounds suffice to communicate — as if communicativeness were 'physically realized' in certain sounds. But just as there cannot be information in the absence of a mind that can entertain it, communication in the human sense is possible only among minds; it requires the reciprocal interaction of minds.

When I speak to you, and you hear and understand what I say, it is my mind that communicates with your mind. But 'mind,' let us not forget, is shorthand for the mental functions of human organisms. To say that 'my mind communicates with your mind' actually means: 'my organism's mental functions affect your organism's mental functions,' and vice versa. It is my mind — my thinking what I say — that makes itself available to your mind to share what I mean when I speak. Correspondingly, it is your mind that understands my mind. But of course, my mind makes itself available to your mind by making its thoughts audible. For to communicate with each other, our minds need a *medium* or instrument. The reason is, of course, that our minds are functions of our organisms. Therefore, your mind and mine are separated spatio-temporally by the spatio-temporality of our organisms. Vocal sounds (or other perceptible signs) are needed as a means whereby to render one organism's mind (i.e., its mental functioning) perceivable by the mental functioning of other human organisms.

If such other organisms have human mental powers, they will be able to understand what speakers mean when they make the product of their mental functions available to others by means of such words or signs. And so, when you talk to me, I want to understand what *you* mean, not what your words mean (or what reality dictates that your words should mean). *They,* the words, do not mean anything; it is you who means what you say. Which is why, if your words betray me, I blame you, not your words.

Let us accept that speech and thought perform one and the same mental function in either of two different modes. What is the nature of such function? And why should it have come about that it can be exercised in two different modes?

2. The assertiveness of speech and thought

Just as it is clear that thinking has close relations with speech, little observation is needed to realize that speech has to do with communication. But if one's observations stop after this has been noted, one is apt to reduce speech to communication. Many linguists do so. They say, for example, that:

> [Language] is human vocal noise … used systematically for purposes of communication. Occasionally language is used for purposes other than communication — for example, to let off steam…or to give delight…or as a vehicle for our own thoughts when no one is present. But such uses of language are secondary.[355]

---

355   David Crystal, *Linguistics* (Hammondsworth, Eng.: Penguin, 1971), 243.

Now, there can be no reasonable objection to the study of language as the typical mode of human communication, but the reduction of speech to a medium of communication is short sighted. What we do when we speak in fact includes, but is not limited to, making available to others what we have in mind when we speak. The crucial part is, to begin with, 'having it in mind' and thinking it. The key to understanding both speech and thought is to grasp the empirical fact that we can communicate with others in the *conscious* manner that is typical of human communication, only if at the same time we communicate *with ourselves*, as it were— that is, only if we *think* what we audibly say. But let us begin by remembering that the human ability to communicate by means of vocal sounds developed out of a much earlier and vastly simpler evolutionary accomplishment: surely human communication exhibits more complex features than that of ants and bees. What is the difference?

a) The differences between human and infrahuman communication

If one were to argue that when one billiard ball hits another, the one 'communicates' motion (or if not motion, energy) to the other, one would have failed to take into account the difference between metaphor and literality. Nor is there communication, in the usual human sense we shall assume here, simply when a sentient organism perceives an object and appears to take it as a 'sign' of something else. For instance, when a herbivore avoids a poisonous mushroom upon seeing the white-dots-on-red (or smelling its scent, or whatever), all the animal has done, so far as we can reasonably estimate, is to perceive something that the animal has been genetically programmed to avoid instinctively; there has been no communication, but only perception. An infrahuman mind that is conditioned to spurn mushrooms, or a human one that knows enough about mushrooms, may perceive a poisonous mushroom and be warned off by the *signs* of poison, but the mushroom has not sent a *signal* communicating the information. The difference between signs and signals, in the ordinary usage of these terms, is that signs may either happen or be made, whereas signals are sent.

Therefore, if understood in a sense that bears comparison with what humans do when they speak with others, 'communication' imports two requirements. First, there must be some sort of propagation of information — which presupposes cognition, and therefore animal life. What human communicators communicate is their perceptual experiences, whether current, remembered or thought about. Second, it must be a bilateral process. The information is sent, and is apt to be received. It is propagated from one sentient organism (a communicator) to another (a communicand) — or, of course, to many. Thus, communication takes advantage of the perceptual abilities of animal organisms. Evolution superimposed communication on perception at a fairly early stage: communication can be found even in some insect species. We can understand why biological evolution should have protected communication. It was because communication extends the reach and heightens the survival value of sentient life; it amounts to the capacity to obtain the benefit of someone else's sense experience vicariously. The receiver of the communication can react adjustively to what the sender experiences, without having to experience it directly.

I note in passing, in order to avoid possible confusion, that although thought is not cast in audible vocal sounds, it is nevertheless 'communicated' — namely, to oneself. For it is always done consciously; when thinkers think, they are necessarily aware of what they think. In a peculiar sense, therefore, they may be said to 'communicate' their thoughts to themselves. But not, of course, in the sense that they have to wait until after they have thought a thought, and then communicate the thought to themselves. Simply by thinking a thought they become aware of the thought. 'Communication' in the usual and conventional sense refers to communication *to others,* but every conscious communication to others is communicated to oneself.

Since the meaning carried by a signal does not depend upon the nature of the signal itself, the signals that animals can make are no more inherently limited, in what pertains to their contents, than human signals: a chirp or a certain bodily gesture can carry any meaning whatever, for the very reason that it has no necessary connection with whatever it might signify. Animals could, therefore, in principle, communicate whatever they experience. And yet, though animal 'vocabularies' are enormously richer and subtler than had been realized in the past, their signals are invariably related to a fairly narrow set of contents. Animals keep to themselves most of what they experience — whereas human beings communicate almost all of it (though not necessarily widely). Of course, only human beings can value privacy; for only those who are conscious can distinguish between themselves and others, and their private individuality from their social life. But the life of consciousness is much more public than we ordinarily realize; it is lived by individuals largely outside themselves, in the more or less extensive network of communicative relationships created by the need of human beings to learn what fellow-humans think and feel, and to share with others what they themselves do.

That evolution should have favoured the ability to perceive not only signs, but also the signals made by others, makes sense. But why did evolution favour the transmission of signals? The values that evolution 'rewards' with survival are those which accrue to the individual itself — whereas the capacity for sending signals seems, on its face, to be of little benefit to the sender. A signaling bee's signaling behaviour does not increase its store of information: it is the communicand that obtains the advantage of receiving information it would otherwise lack. However, a bee that survives as a result of another bee's transmitting proficiency is thereby in a position to transmit valuable signals to the bee that helped it survive. Once communication had appeared in sentient organisms, the transformation of the species — to the limited extent to which communication had a role in it before it became speech — no longer depended only on the contribution of the best adapted individuals, but also on that of the best adapted team.

Clearly, therefore, there are points of contact between infrahuman and human communication — but also unbridgeable differences. A few years ago, a widely discussed paper of ethologist Robert Seyfarth and his colleagues[356] reported that vervet monkeys consistently produced different alarm calls for different predators, and that the calls seemed to function as so many distinctive names given to various predators. The alarm calls were clearly useful in any event, of course, but it was especially useful that the monkeys issued different calls for different predators, because different predators (say, eagles and snakes) were best evaded by different techniques (e.g. hiding as contrasted with climbing trees). To those critics who approached communication strictly as a form of behaviour, this seemed to be evidence of a simplified form of non-vocal but speech-like communication of basically the same sort that is observable in young children beginning to use single words to name objects. But others took into account the peculiarly mental function involved in speech and therefore concluded that 'the example of vervet alarm calls offers a false lead'[357] for understanding speech. Why?

---

356 Robert Seyfarth, Dorothy Cheney, and Peter Marler, "Monkey Responses to Three Different Alarm Calls: Evidence of Predator Classification and Semantic Communication" *Science* 210, no. 10 (1980): 801-803.

357 Deacon, Symbolic Species, 59.

Because human communication demands more than a communicator's sending a signal containing information, plus a communicand who perceives it and thereby reaps the benefit of information gained not from its own experience but from that of the communicator. Infrahuman signals are 'sent,' only in the sense that they are produced by the communicator in response to its own experience: when it perceives a predator, it makes the sounds of the alarm call; when no predator is perceived, it does not make the call. The call is simply the animal's behavioural, adjustive response to its perception. But since the alarm call is perceptible by a conspecific, the communicand is able to share vicariously in the experience of the communicator. There is, however, no reason for us to suppose that the animal *intended* to send the signal, or was *aware* that the signal, if received by a conspecific, would enable the latter to share in the experience of the communicator.

And yet, to send a signal intending to produce an effect in the recipient — namely, that the recipient should share in the experience of the sender — and with awareness of the aptness of the signal for producing such effect, is exactly what human beings do when they communicate, either through speech or through a derivative of speech. This is possible only to conscious experiencers, since it requires awareness of the experiential nature of one's experience.

By contrast, the phenomenon reported by Seyfarth can be interpreted as evolution's having bred into vervet monkeys the adaptive response of making certain sounds whenever they perceive certain other animals. By so responding the animal, broadcasts its experience. We can properly say that the animal has 'communicated' and 'signaled' it, provided we do not thereby suppose that it has done anything other than to *behave* as it has. By the same token, the reception of the communication by the communicand means simply that the second animal, upon perceiving the behaviour of the first, responds adjustively to what it has experienced; and it so responds because natural selection has programmed it to do so when it hears the call. No more intent to communicate, no more awareness of the signal's communicative powers, and no more consciousness are required for this than for the same communicand to respond adjustively to any other perceivable object of experience.

At the higher levels, animals can improve their native communicative behaviour through learning. This is most obvious when they do so under human tutelage, but can happen also as the result of natural selection under ordinary environmental pressures 'prompting' the species to adjust. But though natural selection improved and enlarged the *languages* of animals, the nature of animal *communication* remained essentially unchanged until the appearance of mankind. The 'vocabularies' of, say, dolphins and anthropoids may be superior to those of ants and bees — not least strikingly because that of the former can be enlarged through either artificial or natural conditioning and training whereas that of the latter cannot — but my description of animal communication applies to all communicating animal species equally well.

We can also understand why evolution has not given to animals the communicative freedom it has to human beings, who can speak about each and everything in the world, and make up names at will, and assert, in relation to named objects, whatever their sense perceptions may sanction — whereas only those signals the transmission and reception of which was apt to be rewarded with a survival advantage could have become incorporated into the genetically programmed repertoire of adjustive responses by infrahumans. The individual animal does not have to learn to transmit and receive signals; it is the species that 'learns' to do so, under the 'tutorship' of natural selection. The wonder is not, then, that animals communicate as frequently as they do, but that there is an abysmal disparity between their high receptive and their low transmitting capabilities — a disparity that reflects the fact that human speech (and other human communications) are under conscious initiative and control, whereas infrahuman communications are not. The same disparity accounts for the fact that animals can be trained to receive and act on cues sent by humans that animals themselves do not transmit to each other. Amazingly, horses can be trained to perform what to all superficial appearances looks like arithmetical operations by obeying instructions contained in the trainer's surreptitious, barely perceptible signals. But the explanation is clear: there could not have been many opportunities (or much point) for natural selection to produce amusement show horses, or dogs genetically programmed to sit up and beg on command.

One more difference should be noted. Among infrahuman animals, as we have seen, evolution favoured the emergence of communicating teams. But when bilateral communication became more than genetically programmed signal transmission — amounting instead to mind-to-mind communication — communication transformed collectivities into human-type societies and group life into consortium, i.e., life in a group that shares its fortunes (the information received) for better or for worse. It would be insufficient, therefore, to say that human communication holds societies together, as if societies, like mere colonies, were constituted by individuals entering into collective relationships that communication helps maintain. Rather, human signal-transmission generates social relationships. Human communication does not arise in a social context, it creates a social context. The conscious life of human beings is a common life, a shared life. This property of human nature is not always given due recognition or accorded due importance. It cannot be ignored with impunity, but is inescapable in any event.

b) The assertion of experience and its cognitive consequences

Let us draw some conclusions from the foregoing comparison of human and infrahuman communication. The critics of Seyfarth were right to point out that an essential characteristic of speech seemed to be absent from the communicative behaviour of vervet monkeys; the latter did not appear to obey either an intention to communicate, or awareness of the possibility of communicating, with their conspecifics. But there is a further consideration the critics do not seem to have taken into account.

The intention to communicate and the communicative potential of speech have to do with the *communication* of what the speaker thinks. However, speakers can intend to communicate, and be aware of the communicative possibilities of their signals, only if, in the first place, they are also aware of what they intend to communicate. To be precise, it is not enough that they perceive objects; in order to communicate what they perceive, they have to perceive it consciously. If the reason why this is so is not clear, a simple experiment will demonstrate it: one might try to communicate something of which one is not conscious. One will find that it is impossible. Thus, behind the obvious communicativeness of speech may hide the less obvious fact that by means of speech we can communicate only that of which we are conscious. The communicativeness of speech camouflages, so to speak — it draws attention away from — the *thinking* of what is communicated by speech.

To illustrate the point: before vervet monkeys could be deemed able to perform an activity comparable to speaking, they would have to do more than to send signals corresponding to different predators, intending to warn conspecifics of a danger, and aware that their calls were apt to have such effect; for in order to be able to do as much, the animals, apart from perceiving the predators, would have to be aware also that their alarm calls referred to the predators, that the reference could be apprehended by conspecifics, and that thereby their communicands might share in their experience. In short, the monkeys would have to be conscious.

From this follows that to understand the nature of speech, we have to understand not only what speech achieves in what pertains to communication, but also what it adds to communication, with the result that speech is irreducible to any form of communication - not only to infrahuman animal communication, but also human communication. I have already suggested that what it adds is a form of *cognition* that builds upon perception but transcends it. But now I must explain why we must affirm it, as well as the peculiarities of such form of cognition, and the cognitive benefits that it achieves that perception does not. We should then have no difficulty in perceiving that such form of cognition is common to both speech and thought — i.e., it operates in the same way regardless of whether it makes use of perceptible signs or not.

Preliminarily, let us note briefly a feature of speech and thought that we shall study in more detail later, when we focus on the question how speech and thought operate so as to issue in understanding and explanation. At this time we need only note that here are two different forms or levels at which we speak and think. The second is more complex than the first, and virtually includes the first,; this suggests that the second accumulated upon a prior stage in the evolution of the human mind and its cognitive functions. In any event, we retain the ability to use both, and actually use both, though perhaps mostly the second.

The simpler level of speech and thought consists in doing what ordinarily we call *naming* the objects we experience — but which would be more accurately said to consist in naming *our experiences* of objects. This precision is required because the mental operation of our ability to name does not change reality, although it does make a difference to our experience, as I shall explain presently. This is one reason why the mental function is cognitive: it affects our experience of reality. The second level of speech consists in what we usually call *attributing* one named object of experience to another — but which, again, should be more properly described as attributing *what we experience* regarding a named object, to our experience of another named object. For, like naming, attributing cannot change reality; it can change only our experience of reality. Thus, the mental function common to speech and thought, whether it be discharged merely to name, or to make attributions to what we have named, must be said to have cognitive value: it can make a difference to our experience of reality. For by speech and thought we cannot change reality; but we can change our experience of reality. That is, we can learn. Through the instrumentality of naming and attribution we transcend the limitations of mere perception. The reason why naming and attribution have this effect should be clear, if we examine what we do when we perform these operations.

When we give a name to our experience of an object, we do not give it its identity; the object's identity is what we experience, and what we name is our experience of its identity. Conversely, what we do is to *impose* a name on our experience of the object, thereby asserting its identity. Naming is asserting what a certain sound *shall mean,* namely, that which the name identifies. It is not important, but interesting enough to make passing mention of it, that there is a passage in the Old Testament that conveys the assertive nature of naming with admirable clarity and simplicity: '[a]nd out of the ground the Lord God formed every beast of the field, and every fowl of the air; and brought them unto Adam to see what he would call them: and whatsoever Adam called every living creature, that was the name thereof.'[358] Adam had asserted the meaning of the sound, and consequently fixed the meaning that the sound should thereafter bear for him and for anyone else who accepted that the sound should have such meaning.

Of course, the mental activity of naming is performed not only when one coins a name. Since we are born and learn to speak in interaction with a community that has long been in possession of speech, individual speakers impose original names on their experiences only rarely; in most instances individuals simply accept, with or without modification in respect of connotations, what has already become the socially conventional name of the experience. But in any event, the result is the same. Naming our experiences enables us to *process* them; we can, as it were, 'manipulate' or 'handle' them. This opens up new possibilities for our cognition to develop and improve it; it is no longer static and fixed; we can direct it. Naming enables us to isolate and focus on selected experiences of what is named; it enables us, therefore, to take the reality we experience out of its own context and attend

---

358   Genesis 2:19 (Revised Standard Version).

to our experience of. And to do so is, in other words, to conceive reality; the name we impose on it identifies our conception of the object. Thus, the difference between perceiving reality and naming it (which we can do either, at first, by means of audible words, or thereafter by merely imaginary words), is to *assert* or *affirm* our experience of reality. Asserting our experience is the common function of speech and thought, regardless of whether the signs used to assert it are perceptible or not. We may also describe it as *meaning* the meaning of what we mean, and *saying* what we say.

I mention only in passing, since the issue lies outside the scope of this work, a possibility I have considered elsewhere in some detail:[359] that the child's learning to assert its experience of an object by naming the experience that identifies the object, precipitates the organization of the brain that brings together, into the unity of a single process, information regarding the object, and information regarding the activity. In other words, it may be that we begin to learn to experience consciously by learning to assert our experience. The infusion of conscious quality into human perception would be complete, however, only after the child has mastered the higher level of assertive speech that we are about to study.

The cognitive possibilities open to the speaking and thinking mind are multiplied when the speaker develops the further, more complex ability to assert its experience of the relationship between (or among) the experiences it is already able to name. Naming extends, by itself, the cognitive range of the human mind, but in a more limited way than does the ability to relate experiences. The latter renders possible the mental, vicarious exploration of reality by exploring the implications of a variety of perceptual experiences when we establish how they are related. Perceptions reveal facts, but the ability to speak and think of how the various aspects of reality we experience are related, reveals what perception alone cannot. Why is this so?

Let us go back to the power of imagination we can use either to fantasize or to think. Both ways to use our imagination are anchored in reality; both depend upon the use of certain 'materials,' so to speak, namely our perceptions of reality, whether recalled or current. And both depend on breaking down and reconstituting the components of such materials. Thus, the fantastic imagination works on perceptions — for example, visual perceptions — which even at their simplest are highly complex.

---

359 In my *Evolution and Consciousness.*

Even the smallest visual field or visual memory includes dozens of objects, innumerable shapes, a multiplicity of colours, shades, and textures, which persist for various times as we shift our gaze, and which change rapidly over time. We fantasize by *selecting* either at will or at random one or more aspects of one or more such perceptions and *organizing* them as we may wish.

The thoughtful use of our imagination is in part the same as the fantastic; it depends on selecting and organizing the elements of prior perceptual experiences. But in the case of speech and thought, before we process our perceptions we introduce a condition that distinguishes, once for all, thinking from fantasizing. What acts as a filter, as it were, whereby to separate fantasy from thought is that the recalled experiences to be thought, have been asserted with reference to reality. By that very fact, the focus of our consideration of our experience has been narrowed down, in somewhat the same way as looking through a powerful microscope narrows down the scope of our visual perception. Let us compare, for instance, the number of objects one may visually distinguish within the scene covered by one's current field of vision, with the almost unlimited number of assertions that could be made affirming the various elements included in the same experience. When we think or speak, we *select*, out of all we experience or have experienced, what we want to say; for we speak and think in *units* of limited compass devoted to specific microscopic takes that are culled from our global perceptual experiences. Even at their most complex and convoluted, such units — complete 'sentences' — focus on no more than a few of the extraordinarily large number of element that are included in every perception.

For example, consider the room where Bede Rundle has rearranged the furniture, and count how many different sentences may one utter, describing what one has seen, as compared to the global perception of many different objects but all at the same time. With the aid of words, we can look at the world in infinitesimal detail, and therefore at almost inexhaustible length. For one sentence follows another, and soon a 'picture' emerges. Now, a 'picture' emerges also when our fantasy puts together elements of our perceptual experience. But there is a difference between the 'picture' that is painted by our imagination and the 'picture' that coalesces before our eyes when our perceptual experiences are asserted by means of words. What is the difference?

That, willy-nilly, and whether we advert to the fact or not, the wordliness of speech and thought inserts into our mental processes the parameter of cognition we call *truth* — the relationship of our experience of reality to reality. Neither speech nor thought can function in the total absence of every consideration of their adequacy (or lack thereof) in taking into account the reality of reality and its independence of ours (or indeed, any) mind. Truth is to speech and thought as temperature and humidity are to climate, a defining variable without which the *definiendum* cannot be defined, an aspect of speech and thought that is integral part of their relating us to reality. But more specifically, they relate us to reality insofar as we are conscious experiencers. That is, they relate us to reality by the kind of relationship that takes into account the fact that, unlike infrahuman animals, we do not only perceive reality, but also perceive the fact that we perceive reality. Conscious experience necessarily includes reference to the dimension of truth-falsity, because conscious experience, even at its most absent-minded, includes awareness of the reality of the real as 'other-than' ourselves and our experience.

Fantasies are in themselves neither true nor false; they are divorced from the reality from which they descend: they are what they in fact are, in defiance of reality. Nor are perceptions as such true or false; they may be more or less partial, and they may be easily contaminated by our imagination, especially when we indulge in what is commonly called 'wishful thinking.' But what our senses perceive is what they have perceived, not what we have imagined. By contrast, what we say when we think or speak, however, is *affirmed* — positively or negatively —in relation to what one communicates to others or notes for oneself. Unless one is lying, one must think that what one says is true; and even when one says what is untrue, one thinks what is true. The affirmation or assertion that is the heart of speech and thought is embodied in the speaker's intentional voicing of the audible (or in the thinker's imagining the inaudible) words of speech and thought.

Speakers and thinkers, therefore, simply by speaking or thinking, implicitly hold out (to themselves, if they think it, and to other also, if they vocalize it), that their assertions are actually or at least potentially true. Speech may be sincere or mendacious, categorical or doubtful, and irresponsible or deliberate, but in any event includes taking a stand towards the truth of what-is-said. Truth is always in the background of speech and thought. Which is why, as noted in chapter I, we can never experience the erroneous nature of our errors unless in retrospect. Thus, what introduces the dimension of truth and falsity into our speech and thought is the *assertiveness* of speech and thought. Without assertiveness there can be neither the truthfulness nor the lack of it that is a typical and necessary part of speech and thought.

How does the introduction of the necessary consideration of truth and falsity into our speech and thought affect human cognition? Well, once truth is a consideration, the *selection* of what we say when we speak or think takes a very different form from that which is characteristic of fantasy. The elements of a fantasy are chosen either arbitrarily or at random. Since truth is not a consideration in fantasizing, there is no 'logical' (i.e. speech-like) way to compose a fantasy. 'Logic,' however (i.e., the relationship that obtains among the asserted elements of speech and thought, signally the relationship of implication) applies to speech and thought, simply because speech and thought are characterized by truth and falsity. Thus, speech and thought should not be said merely to result from selecting, out of one's experience of reality, what one says. More precisely, speech and thought enable us rather to *analyse* our experience of reality. For the same reason, the compilation of the elements of a fantasy is arbitrary and thus unlike the *synthesis* that is possible in the case of speech and thought. The synthetic aspect of speech and thought aims at discovering the deeper truth that is implied in the directly accessible sensory experiences that perception suffices to reveal.

In other words, the analysis of our experience of the world and of ourselves permits, though it does not infallibly secure, our drawing out conclusions; 'taking one consideration with another,' as the common expression goes, enables us to reach a third. This is what enables us, by means of speech and thought, not merely to assert what we already know as the outcome of our perceptions, but to deepen our knowledge, or to give it the additional dimensions of *continuity, logic, process,* and *explanation* that yield the cognitive state of *understanding,* Which as suggested in the first section of this chapter, is the end-state which is the goal to which speech and thought are aimed. Moreover, saying to ourselves what we think, like saying it to others, introduces the possibility of 'discipline' and 'method' into our thinking. Speech and thought enable us, quite literally, to *experiment* with the world of perception in order to understand what perception alone cannot teach us. Speech and thought are the built-in mental *laboratory* of philosophy and all scholarship, and the prototype of a scientific installation. Scientific experimentation and scientific methods are possible only because they apply the more fundamental experimentation and methodology that is built into the nature of speech and thought.

The final conclusion we may draw, once we understand the difference between infrahuman communication and human speech, should enable us to make sense out of a fact that seems strange at first blush, but which is eminently intelligible: why is it that human beings are able to assert their experience in either of the two modalities in which we can assert our experience, which we distinguish as thought and speech?

Speech evolved presumably out of the infrahuman ability to communicate; it preserves the infrahuman ability to send signals that enable the recipient to benefit vicariously from the experience of the communicator. We know indeed that among the higher infrahuman species such as vervet monkeys, communication had advanced to the point where animals were capable of issuing signals that differentiated among various kinds of experiences, in somewhat the same way as the 'names' used by human speakers do. Different signals therefore had corresponding effects, in somewhat the same way as the various signals sent by human beings have different meanings. Speech, however, is not reducible to communication; it requires awareness of its potential effects on communicands, and of its power to have such effects.

It is possible, therefore, that just before speech and consciousness appeared in the first truly human species — by which I mean, a species endowed with speech and consciousness — prior developments in respect of brain power, as well as the emergence of a vocal apparatus that permitted human beings to make an extraordinarily wide range of vocal sounds, had brought about a species that used an extensive repertoire of sounds that were available for a wide variety of useful purposes besides warning each other of predators. The survival value of communication and of the co-operation that communication facilitates, would have 'protected' their evolution along these lines, and as a result they had probably become the proto-human equivalent of extraordinarily accomplished vervet monkeys. But they had not yet taken the decisive step across the threshold of humanity. They had not yet acquired the ability to *assert* their signals, or to *mean* what they meant, or to apprehend that, when they said what they said, their communicands knew what they knew. Acquiring it consisted in making the same vocal sounds they had long made, but assertively. Thinking silently what they asserted would come naturally thereafter; it added nothing new to the function, but simply suppressed its audibility. Well, speech is necessarily communicable to others (and therefore, perceptible by them) because it is the ability of human beings to assert their experience preserved, and was superimposed upon, the infrahuman ability to communicate; but because its evolution added assertiveness to the mere ability to communicate, it can take place in the absence of all communicability. Thus, unlike infrahuman animals, which can neither speak nor think, but nevertheless are able to communicate, we can both speak and think, and we never can do one without doing at the same time the other, though we need not always communicate what we think, nor prevent its communication to others unless by thinking inaudibly.

To become speech, all that had to be added to proto-human communication was, when the occasion arose, to take advantage of characteristics that had emerged earlier in the course of evolution, and put them to a new, unprecedented use. This is one way in which evolution sometimes takes place — that is, opportunistically. For instance evolutionary biologists have attributed the emergence of wings in some insects to the development of organs whose original service was thermal control. Now, precisely how the earliest humans developed speech out of a highly proficient but infrahuman system of communication, we can only speculate.[360] That in fact they developed speech, however, as well as thought, is scarcely in doubt.

When they did develop speech and thought, however, we can be reasonably certain that it was not because speech (as contrasted with mere communication) and thought (as contrasted with mere perception) had *biological* survival value. From the viewpoint of survival to reproductive age, which is what counts as 'survival value' subject to 'natural selection,' both speech and thought are utterly

---

360   The possibility I have considered in *Evolution and Consciousness* is that assertiveness accrued to the vocal communications of proto-humans by virtue of the fortuitous circumstance that the human vocal organs lack interoception. Human vocal signals are produced mostly by the activity of the laryngeal muscles; however, interoceptors 'are absent from…[these] muscles, and feedback control [in vocal sound-making] comes by way of the ear.' Thus, human beings cannot learn to control vocal sounds — and therefore cannot learn to make vocal signals — unless they can hear the sounds that they make. (This is of, course, the reason why congenitally deaf children do not ordinarily learn to make vocal signals.) The absence of proprioception in vocal signalling facilitated enormously, perhaps decisively, the speaker's identification of what he heard with what his listener heard; it made possible for him to hear the sound of his voice in the same way as his listener did, and to hear the sound of another's voice in the same way in which he did his own.

superfluous. Consciousness, indeed, like the civilization it naturally tends to promote, has positively dangerous aspects as well. It is easy to lapse into the assumption that the human species is intended by nature to ascend 'higher' than it prehistorically did, but nothing (other than religious faith) so suggests. A mankind definable by reference to speech and consciousness might never have emerged: we might well have remained naked apes. But we did not. The question of the origin of the speech and conscious thought that distinguish our species remains.

Natural selection, however, is not limited to the selection of genes. Most scientist recognize, as Deacon does,[361] that socio-cultural inheritance has almost certainly played a role in human evolution; this form of inheritance is responsible for the amended form of Darwinian evolution known variously as 'gene-culture co-evolution' and 'Baldwinian evolution,' the latter having been named after the early twentieth century psychologist who first proposed it.[362] Although the idea of Baldwinian evolution is fully a century old, it still meets with some resistance — possibly, at least in some cases, for the same reasons that have kept the traditional reductionistic materialisms alive to the present: panic fear of dualism, and reckless anti-dualism. Since speech is learned, rather than genetically inherited, it is a particularly good example of how socio-cultural inheritance can operate with the same inflexibility as genetic inheritance. Children are constrained to discover speech by unrelenting environmental pressure; they cannot but acquire speech, and they cannot function in the human world unless they do. This inheritance mechanism seems to operate alongside genetic selection as a component in the evolution of the *functions* of organs whose *structure* remains unchanged and genetically reproduced. It is possible that continued awareness of the *cognitive* role of speech and the inseparability of speech and consciousness may result in greater attention being given in the future to the Baldwinian evolution of what we may well call the trinity of consciousness: namely, speech, thought, and understanding.

In this section I have dealt only with the general principle that the discharge of the function common to speech and thought — namely, the *assertion* of experience, the *meaning* of what is meant, and the *saying* of what is said — has cognitive consequences. We have yet to examine the matter in

361   Deacon, *Symbolic Species,* chapter 11.

362   Namely, James Mark Baldwin, in his *Development and Evolution.*

detail, in order to understand what to understand is, how the assertion of experience can procure understanding, and why reality need have no inherent intelligibility before we can understand it. This we shall do in the concluding section of this chapter a final preparatory discussion of why we tend to misunderstand the nature of speech.

c) The temporality of human nature and the generation of the human mind

Although there is no valid reason to suppose that communicating with other minds suffices to define the nature and principal purpose of speech, more than one circumstance misleads us into thinking that it does. One is the simple fact that speech includes, whereas thought excludes, the making of vocal sounds. Thought may well seem, therefore, somewhat like speech *manqué.* This impression is reinforced when we consider that in order to develop the ability to assert their experience, children can learn to *speak* only through interaction with those who already know how to speak, whereas they are wholly responsible for learning to think — which they appear to learn automatically and by themselves, simply by learning to speak. Traditionally, therefore, the relationship between speech and thought has been conceived as the priority and independence of speech, and the posteriority and dependence of thought. But if so, it would follow that 'the only route to the analysis of thought goes through the analysis of language.'[363] Much less obvious, however, than the absence of sounds in thought, is the fact that *what is communicated* by means of sounds is a 'meaning,' and that the absence of actual sounds does not affect the meaning: all that is affected is whether it is communicated to another. When the sounds are only imagined, the sounds have been dispensed with, but without loss of the speaker's actively meaning what he or she means.

Especially misleading, however, is another circumstance, an orphan assumption of Greek parentage that may well influence modern philosophy below the level of consciousness. Typically, the Greek philosophers assumed that reality as such, or as 'being,' was outside time and becoming, Even those philosophers who, like Aristotle, recognized the reality of the empirically-given world, vested the necessity, stability, and intelligibility of 'beings' in their 'beingness,' that is, in their *ousia,*

---

363   Peacock, 'Concepts Without Words,' in Richard G. Heck, (ed.), *Language, Thought, and Logic: Essays in Honour of Michael Dummett* (Oxford: Oxford University Press, 1997), 2. Peacock is among those who question this estimate.

essence, or nature. They assumed that the intelligible constitution of human nature, like the nature of everything else, was timeless; individual humans were young or old, but human nature was neither. For individuals concretized the essence of humanity in matter; therefore, they changed in other respects, but their nature did not. It was eternal. To be precise, it was not quite 'eternal' in the strict Christian sense (which requires simultaneity of perfections), but it was eternal in the sense that it was *everlasting*. It had neither beginning nor end. The humanity of human beings was not subject to time and change.

Now, in the twentieth century most modern philosophy professed 'anti-essentialism.' And in the absence of 'essences,' the temporality of human nature should have been recognized. But it was not; anti-essentialism has not been consistently held, and reality has continued to be frequently identified as 'that which is' rather than as 'that which becomes.' Inattention to the *process* through which we human beings *become* human has been part of modern philosophy's ahistoricist bias. We are inclined to omit from our considerations the fact that human nature is acquired by human beings as the outcome of a temporal, gradual, and indeed long drawn-out, process of *becoming* human.

If we take into account the *development* of the human mind, we should find, on the one hand, that to acquire the ability to speak what one thinks is, in principle, identical with acquiring the ability to think what one says. On the other hand, the two modalities of the assertion of our experience are related differently *at different times*. While one is still in the process of learning to assert one's experience — and thus, learning to speak and think — one can think what one means only if one also says it by making the appropriate vocal sounds. The two modalities of the same function have *not yet* become differentiated; one can only think by thinking aloud (much as children do at an early stage of the process of learning to speak and think). But human beings acquire the ability to think as they acquire speech, and they do so to the exact degree to which they have acquired speech. Their acquisition of speech does not *precede* their acquisition of thought, but it *leads* the simultaneous acquisition of the ability to think. Speech, therefore, has no priority over thought, but is nevertheless the foundation, the model, and the mould of thought. Without speech, thought could not exist. Without thought, however, communication by means of speech could not exist — though vervet-style communication could nevertheless exist.

Inattention to the fact that we are human only as the outcome of the process of *becoming* human, has a further consequence. So far as I am aware, no philosopher — apart from the Catholics among them, of course — has explicitly taken the position that humanness is acquired by human beings instantaneously. For the latter, however, at time 't[1]' there are two cells, and at time 't[2],' a millisecond later, there is a human being; an immature one, they allow, but a fully human one. But others who are not swayed by religious beliefs sometimes take for granted for all practical purposes much the same position, albeit by unwitting implication rather than deliberately; for they assume that an understanding of the temporal, developmental process that generates human nature is irrelevant to the philosophical study of human nature. The notion might even seem a little bizarre to them that we human beings should first come into existence at a level below the human, and that we then *ascended* to the human level of life as we *developed* our humanity, by *acquiring* the specifically human cognitive functions of conscious perception, thinking, and understanding as we acquire speech. It may come as a surprise to them, but it should be reasonably obvious that birth does not yet bring into being the human being. But astonishing or otherwise, that is exactly what seems to be suggested by the relationship between thought and speech. Actually, we should have expected it. For it is generally recognized that the non-mental functions and structures of human organisms go through an epigenetic process. Why should the mental functions and associated brain structures of the same human organisms not go through their own epigenesis?

We have long known that the absolute beginning of the reality of human beings takes place at conception. But at what point does the generation of the human person satisfy the criteria of humanness, so that the individual actually begins to exist humanly? And after going through what stages? The answers are obvious only to those who abdicate their reason in favour of faith, or who are just plain unaware of the issues. And yet, it is curious that in the past, even during those ages that in other respects were unenlightened, philosophers managed to recognize that the humanity of human beings was the outcome of a transition from pre-human to human status[364] — though the transition, they thought, was complete before birth. And indeed, some informal and ambiguous recognition of the

---

364 See Pasnau, *Thomas Aquinas on Human Nature: A Philosophical Study of* Summa Theologiae I, 75-89 (Cambridge: Cambridge University Press, 2001), chapter IV.

fact that the transition is not complete even at birth has long been implicit also at law, politically, and in many social respects, as part of our culture's eminently practical decision to withhold the status of full human persons from children before a certain arbitrarily and crudely defined age. This is one more instance of the unwisdom of condemning the culture's common sense as a matter of principle, or of prejudice, rather than because philosophical thought can offer a more rational alternative.

If the foregoing remarks are true, they may have some implications for our interpretation of the evolution of human nature. They suggest that the acquisition of the ability to speak by primitive humans implied the emergence of the ability of the human mind to be aware not only of objects, but to be aware also and simultaneously of its own mental activity. In other words, it suggests that when human beings acquired the ability to speak, however it may have come about, the assertive communication of their experience put them in a position to confront the reality of their experience. To study this possibility, however, would be well beyond the scope of this work and shall not be pursued.

3. The nature of speech and thought

The human mind may be said to develop gradually not only because human organisms take a good deal of time to traverse the epigenetic journey from unicellular origins to the crossing of the threshold of humanity, but also because even the last step of the process, acquiring the ability to assert their experience — and thus, the ability to speak and think — is not taken all at once but has two distinguishable, though continuous, stages. For as already noted, we perform the activity of speaking or thinking in two different ways, or at two different levels of assertive-ness. The two are different procedures by which human beings can exercise their ability to assert their experience, and by means of which they achieve somewhat different cognitive results. The difference between them is obscured by the usual terminology of both philosophy and common sense; for if one is not well and clearly aware that speech and thought discharge one and the same cognitive function, one will not devise a term to signify what I have called the 'assertion of experience' that is the heart of the mental function discharged by speech and thought.

We begin to characterize the two levels of assertion by describing them more carefully than previously. For reasons that will become clear, I shall refer to the two levels of assertion, respectively, as *non-thematic* (or *pre-thematic)* and *thematic* assertion.

a) The two levels of assertion

Philosophers and other students of 'language' make frequent use of a distinction between 'words,' the meaningful elements of spoken communications (and of derivatives thereof), and 'sentences,' a set of words that convey an affirmation or statement. This distinction is proper and true, and applies also to thought. It concerns, however, the grammatical structure of language, and therefore the structure of thought. It enables linguists and philosophers to observe, for example, that in children the 'first stage of [speech development] is one in which the maximum sentence length is one word; it is followed by a stage in which the maximum sentence length is two words.'[365] But words are words regardless of whether they are audible or not, so the same is true of the development of thought. Now, non-thematic assertion is often expressed by single words (or by a succession of single-word expressions), whereas thematic assertion uses at least two related word-elements. But the difference that matters to us is not in respect of the length of the sentence as such, but in the functioning of the speaking and thinking mind in the two cases.

Let us suppose that you raise your arm threateningly against me. I may, speaking (and thinking) non-thematically, yell at you the single word 'Don't! or I may call out a warning to others using a series of discrete locutions or single words: 'Look out! Danger! Run!' Or to take a different example, I may hang up on a telemarketer saying: 'Go away and get a real job!' However, when I tell you that 'the cat is on the mat,' or when a friend inquires after my two pets and I say: 'Unfortunately, the cat suffer

---

365   B.A. Moskowitz, 'The Acquisition of Language,' *Scientific American* 239 (1978): 95-99, 95. Thematic speech does not consist in arranging two or more words together, but in making assertions integrated by two functional elements, thesis and theme; but since the thesis and the theme must be signified separately, a thematic assertion must be at least two words long. Of course, a string of two or more words, each asserted non-thematically, is also perfectly possible. A child's two-word assertion — say, 'doll, pretty' — could be either a simple thematic assertion or a complex non-thematic assertion; knowledge of the contents alone would not enable us to determine which it was. It is possible, if not indeed probable, that children normally pass through an intermediate stage of two-word non-thematic assertion before they begin to make simple two-word thematic assertions. But in any event, the first stage in their speech is non-thematic, since it uses single words.

from neurotic fits,' I am speaking and thinking thematically. I also speak and think thematically when as part of a lecture I say to my students: 'The cat had a religious significance in Orphism.' Now, what is the difference between the two kinds of mental process involved?

We have seen that the mental process that produces my non-thematic warning to others is radically different from the infrahuman animal's alarm call, because it is made assertively. On the other hand, my warning someone of danger, like an expostulation with an annoying and mendacious salesman, is quite like the infrahuman call insofar as the speaker asserts its signal with *immediate*, direct reference to an outer or inner object of perception that is experienced (or recalled), and which constitutes, in its own reality, the context or object of the assertion. That is, the warning and the complaint are about the immediately experienced or recalled object. Correspondingly, when speakers think in this way, they can communicate only the kind of experience (or remembered experience) that takes place with *immediate* reference to the thinker's situation — that is, within the context given to the thinking speakers by their situation in reality. (Unless someone is threatening or annoying you, you will not call out, or think of calling out, a warning, or issue a complaint.) Thus, the context of both (a) what the assertion in my mind asserts, and (b) what the assertion is about in reality, is *given to*, rather than *determined by,* the speaker. This is why non-thematic speech is adequate mostly for communicating to others (as contrasted with asserting exclusively for our own benefit) our conscious perception (or recollection) of reality and our immediate reaction to it. Thematic speech and thought do not operate under the same limitation, which is why they can rise to the level of reasoning and understanding. To signify the higher forms of cognition that mature human beings normally achieve, we need thematic assertion.

Nevertheless, even the basic, non-thematic, level of assertion confers upon experiencers a privilege that the infrahuman communication of experience does not provide: the freedom to determine how the information they receive shall be envisaged, and to what extent. What humans speak or think about non-thematically, and what they shall say, are determined for them by their situation, in the sense that the content of their speech or thought is furnished by reality. But precisely how they will encompass it, or handle it. or refer to it (e.g., as 'cat' rather than as 'pet,' or as 'flower' rather than as 'rose') is determined by them, not by reality. In other words, non-thematic assertion suffices to allow the human mind to *conceptualize* its experiences of reality in different ways, and to select in which way. One *conceives* real things as one does, and one means what one means when one conceives then, by asserting one's experience of objects in accordance with one or else another vocable in the repertoire at one's disposal — or if no other word is available, by making up one's own. For if one can speak at all, one can make up words. To know how to speak is to be aware of the possibility of using anything to signify anything.

Thus, concepts refer to reality as one experiences it (or as one remembers or imagines it), because concepts are conceived so as to mean what 'they' mean. But as I have repeatedly noted, it is not *they*, the concepts, that actually *mean* it, though it is difficult to avoid altogether our customary habits of speech. The concepts one uses mean what *one* means. And conceivers mean them *ad libitum*, since the sounded or soundless vocabulary at their disposal is neither furnished to them by reality nor genetically programmed, as it is in infrahumans. The signals are determined by the speakers themselves. Or to be precise, they are determined in the first instance by the community that teaches the individual to speak (for the apprentice speaker does not invent, but mostly accepts, the language through the use of which it acquires speech, and therefore thought) — although eventually the language can be determined also, to some extent, by the individual speaker itself, who occasionally coins words or uses them idiosyncratically. This freedom is undoubtedly a closely delimited one; it only means that the speaker or thinker can decide, within the limits of its received or created conceptual repertoire, the specific way in which it will attend to the reality it experiences. Nevertheless, this is more than any infrahuman animal can do. The ability to mean what one thinks, even if only non-thematically, implies the ability to select, designate and delimit, in the specific way in which one means it, the reality 'one has in mind' when one thinks or speaks.

Now, a person who is able to speak and think at all, even if only non-thematically — such as a child who has just begun to acquire speech — is necessarily conscious (though possibly to a degree only, and perhaps intermittently), but therefore may, in time, become consciously aware of its speaking and thinking. Once it does, it will be in a good position to bring its assertive powers under a measure of conscious control. And if so, after enough experience in asserting its experience non-thematically, the child will develop its ability to make assertions not only when prompted to do so by its immediate situation, but also to make it on its own initiative: it will have developed the ability to determine what its assertions are made in relation to. And once the child has become able to do this, it will have become a thematic asserter. Being able to determine arbitrarily the context of its assertions suffices to make it one.

For a thematic speaker is one that has become able to speak about an experienced reality not only as *given*, but also as *stipulated,* or *proposed,* or *supposed*. For example, a speaker can advance 'the cat' as an *object of speech*, a topic in relation to which it intends to affirm, for instance, that it 'is on the mat.' Eventually, after enough experience, it could also say, for example, that 'the cat suffers from neurotic fits,' and that 'the cat had religious significance in Orphism.' When an asserter makes thematic assertions regarding 'the cat,' the asserter does not necessarily — though it may — mean the kind of feline object that can be given in conscious perception. (It does in the first of the three instances just mentioned; it may or may not in the second, depending on whether the asserter has in mind an existing cat, or else felines in general; and it does not in the last.) The reason is that reality as immediately given in actual or recollected perception is not the context of assertions made thematically. The context of 'is on the mat,' 'is neurotic,' and 'had religious significance in Orphism' is precisely the *object of assertion* signified as 'the cat.' And such object of speech or thought may or may not exist in reality.

But did I not suggest earlier that truth is a parameter of speech and thought? That neither speech nor thought can abstract from every consideration of their adequacy for relating us to reality? Am I contradicting myself?

b) *The relationship of thematic speech and thought to reality*

Needless to say, thematic speech and thought would be useless if they were to result in our having knowledge that had no relation to truth; and if the knowledge we gain by means of speech and thought is to be true, it must be anchored in reality. Nevertheless, the assertion of experience in speech and thought does not have to be true in order to be useful and to fulfil the objective of procuring true knowledge. This is not self-contradictory. The artificiality of an experiment in a scientific laboratory does not prevent the determination of true knowledge if the experiment is well designed,[366] so why should the artificiality of the laboratory we carry entirely within the mind in the form of thematic assertiveness be much different?

For at its most accomplished, speech is able to *remove* reality altogether out of its own context in the real world, and allow the speaker to speak and think about reality creatively — that is, in the context created and stipulated by the speaker. This allows the thinking speaker, for example, *wonder* about what is true and what is not, and to *inquire* and *speculate* into the nature of reality. It may even invent reality, as young children notoriously do — and mistake it for the real reality, if the apprentice speaker does not handle prudently its newly found freedom to make assertions about whatever it wishes to propose. Of course, the speaker may also learn to discipline its assertiveness, so as to ensure that its creative speaking and thinking shall procure true understanding instead of delusions and insanities. But it is when the asserter becomes able to assert thematically that it can, for example, 'brood about what didn't happen, and spend a large time of each day musing about the way things could have been if events had transpired differently.' Only thematic speakers and thinkers are allowed to inhabit Deacon's 'miraculous place.'

When one becomes able to speak or think in this way, one's assertion of one's experience is not merely *thetic*, as all assertion is, but also *thematic*; for a specified context to which assertions refer, or a designated subject to which the meaning of a thesis relates, or a selected topic in relation to which one's affirmations are to be understood, is what we ordinarily call a *theme*. Thematic speech or thought is an assertion in which a thesis — *what* is asserted — is asserted in relation to a theme, and in which the theme is asserted merely as the *context* in relation to which the speaker means what he says. When one says 'the cat is on the mat' one speaks thematically, because one speaks of an experienced reality only through the mediation of one's *thematization* of it. I stress that the world *about which* one speaks or thinks thematically may well be the same world *to which* one might speak or think non-thematically; the difference does not depend on the reality that provides

---

366   For example, to study the acceleration of falling bodies, Galileo found it was impractical to drop bodies down from a height; they fell too fast to allow measurements to be taken. So instead, he rolled steel balls down a slightly inclined place, where the motion was slow and measurements were manageable. Experimentation normally requires the creation of a situation that is removed from reality but which nonetheless makes it possible to gain true knowledge of reality.

the objects of speech and thought but on how the asserter uses its ability to assert its experience of it. Confronted with the same situation in which a non-thematic asserter might say, 'No! Please! Stop!' or 'Danger! Run!' I speak thematically if I say, for instance, 'Your behaviour is reprehensible, and you should desist,' or if I yell out 'The enemy is at the gates!' The contrast is not in respect of what is audibly said or inaudibly thought (although thematic assertion lends itself to saying it in a highly nuanced way), but in level of assertiveness — and in the consequences thereof, yet to be considered (such as its enabling the asserter to deal with vast amounts of information all at once — and indeed, to reason and to understand.) For example, since 'the cat' signifies directly an object of assertion, and an experienced reality only indirectly, one and the same concept, 'the cat,' is equally apt to signify not only the concrete, individual animal lying before me on the mat, but also the intangible, generic feline nature that, for instance, according to a fanciful opinion held a certain religious significance for some Greeks.

Very little of what human beings say thematically asserts an experienced reality in its immediacy; we speak mostly in 'sentences' about 'the cat' rather than in comminations such as 'Scat!' However, non-thematic assertions need not absolutely consist in isolated single words or convey a simple message. Nor are they restricted to signifying emotional states of mind or inner objects; when I say, for instance, 'someone, please, call a physician!' I am not speaking about my emotions (though I may reveal them), but about an emergency. Moreover, I may or may not have strong feelings about the matter; and if I have them, I may or may not intend to communicate them. And of course, I may convey emotional states thematically: 'I am utterly disgusted with your behaviour!' The telling differences are: whether the experienced reality is taken out of its own context as an actual reality by the very speech that asserts it, and whether one speaks about reality with, or else without, implicit reference to the fact that the reality is being experienced and spoken about. To thematize an experienced reality is thus to lift it out of its situation in real life by means of speech; it is to pick it up with the discriminating pincers called concepts, and to hold it out as the object of one's assertiveness. Whereas the non-thematic speaker is simply a communicator who has learned to assert an experienced reality, thematic speakers have learned also to remove it or *abstract* it from its immediacy, so that they can affirm it as experienced and as signified.

Let us further contrast the two. Non-thematic, unlike thematic, speech and thought contain a single though not necessarily simple element, a *thesis*, which simultaneously asserts and signifies the experienced reality. Though it has an object — namely, a reality as such (rather than as a stated object of speech) — it lacks a *theme*. Non-thematic speech corresponds thus to the level of conscious experience that, like an irate victim's accusing finger, does not merely point or refer, since it also affirms, but which does so bluntly and inarticulately. Its obtuseness is what limits it to making affirmations only in relation to those experienced realities that, by their immediacy, lend themselves to being pointed to.

However, non-thematic assertion is not restricted to the signification of objects experienced at present through external sensation; it may refer to the imaginative recollection of an object previously sensed but no longer before one. Even the latter experience, however, must be said to take place *immediately* (i.e., with direct reference to reality). For, since it consists in imagining a reality precisely as having been given to the experiencer in sensation, albeit at an earlier time, even such experience would be asserted by the non-thematic asserter without the mediation of a theme.

In short, the *immediacy* of non-thematic speech should not be confused with the spatial or temporal *proximity* of the speaker to the object. It is perfectly possible to speak non-thematically of absent objects, as in the fanciful example of a hypothetical early primitive and exclusively non-thematic speaker saying to fellow hunters 'Deer! Big! Many! Watering-hole! Come! Quick! Spear! Encircling-strategy! Hurry! Food!' It is equally possible, however, as I have mentioned, to speak and think thematically of present and currently sensed objects. The difference has to do with whether the relationship of speech to the experienced objects is or is not mediated by the thematizing and thesis-making that characterize thematic speech and thought. Likewise, the immediacy of conscious sense perception to reality should not be identified with spatial proximity; we can be immediately conscious of imagined as well as of sensed objects. Even immediate consciousness of sensible objects does not require either spatial proximity or temporal co-existence, as in the case of the visual consciousness of heavenly constellations. But immediate conscious experience interposes no sign — neither audible nor imaginary speech — between the experience and the object, whereas the mediated form of consciousness we call thinking and understanding does.

Since thematic assertion *separates* the signification of the object of assertion from the activity of asserting it, it can never consist in fewer than two words (though some words may be tacitly understood rather than expressed). For the same reason, it involves the twofold aspects of *thematization*, as I have called the first, and *thesis-making*, as we may refer to the second. But by being separated, the two aspects of the assertive signification that begins with non-thematic speech become transformed. The experienced reality becomes an object of speech when the speaker, holding back his assertiveness as a sparring prize-fighter would his punch, affirms the theme with a force so measured that the theme will directly signify only the object of speech; the theme is designated, so to speak, as the target of the assertion that the thesis will *then* bring down upon it. The thesis, for its part, has to be made to bear not upon reality directly, but upon the theme: an experienced reality is made into a thesis by its being asserted, specifically, in relation to the theme.

The superiority of thematic over non-thematic assertion should be evident: it allows the asserter to determine and precisely delimit what the asserter will speak about. And such precision is important because, although conceptualization begins with non-thematic speech, to be able to conceptualize without being able to thematize is like having an unlimited charge account in a shop that has only poor-quality merchandise and little stock. Before speakers develop thematic assertiveness they can differentiate between, say, 'rose' and 'flower,' 'petal' and 'leaf,' and 'red' and 'green.' But *which* of these they will actually speak about will not depend solely on them; it will be determined above all by their immediate situation, which will call one rather than the other to their attention and create in them the need to make assertions about it. When a dangerous fire threatens, the fire 'prompts' one to speak and 'tells' one what to address one's speech to (though it does not determine how one must conceive what one needs to say). The thematic asserter, however, can made assertions even when the situation does not demand it, and when one has none but an inner motive for speaking — such as the need to understand oneself, or others, or one's world. Or to luxuriate in the beauty of language as an art form.

Thus, out of the 'rose' given to me in experience, I, a thematic asserter, can choose either 'red' or 'petal' as the object I shall make assertions about, and indeed can decide whether to make any at all. Of course, I also have the freedom to place the empirical information I receive from the object within the wider context of many other experiences by signifying it as 'flower.' This means that I can analytically slice the universe of my experience as nicely or as coarsely as I will, dealing mentally with an 'atom' as easily as with the entire 'universe' simply by conceiving and thematizing the theme of my speech accordingly. By the same token, I can synthetically choose to thematize the 'red' dispersed in a multiplicity of red objects and not only in red flowers, as well as the 'flower' that comprises all of them, not only roses. Thus, through thematic conceptualization I transform the whole universe into an endless series of possible objects of assertion that I can either dissect or bundle as my own purposes rather than external events may require. The thematic asserter, to be sure, does not determine what the object so delimited shall contain; it nevertheless determines what the *object* of speech shall be, in the sense that the asserter selects the specific reality that will be marked off as the object that the speaker 'has in mind.'

c) The creativity of thematic assertions

But the creativity of thematic assertion culminates in thesis-making, which requires using assertive power in a new way. Since the object of thematic assertion is signified separately from what-it-is-asserted-about, the latter too must be separately signified; it no longer rides free upon the signification of the object of assertion. Quite as an experienced reality has been made into a theme, another experienced reality, or another aspect of the same one, is made into a thesis. Let us, therefore, refine our terminology. Non-thematic assertion may be said to *assert a thesis* only in the sense that it signifies an experienced reality thetically. Since pre-thematic asserters assert theses only with direct reference to reality rather than in relation to a stated theme, they do not assert a thesis *as such*, or with consciousness of its being what-they-say. Thematic asserters, on the contrary, have to signify the experienced reality separately, or as what-they-assert; they must *make* the experienced reality into a thesis, and therefore asserts theses *as such*. The final result of the separation of assertion and signification in thematic speech is that thematic speakers can say whatever they select, conceived in whichever way they select, in relation to whatever they select, conceived in whichever way they select, out of whatever information they have received in any way at any time. The world created by the assertive signification of our perceptual experience is truly a 'miraculous place.'

But we have not yet exhausted the creativity of thematic assertion. Thematic asserters can make thematic assertions repeatedly, limited only by the amount of information they have empirically received and by their thematic skill. To the extent that their experiences may be organized with reference to a common theme, they can hold together in speech and thought a number of more or less systematically concatenated assertions that make up a sense-making narrative telling a more or less meaningful story. The story is meaningful to the degree that it relates a multiplicity of experiences into a pattern that unifies them all. Organizing their experiences in this way satisfies a profound need in human beings. If they cannot do it, they feel anxiety; and if the disorganization of their experience is severe enough, they may be driven to extremes. We shall take up in the next section the question why this should be so; but the brief answer is that human beings need to make sense out of the multiplicity of their experiences of reality, because by so doing they can situate themselves within a conceptually organized world and thus acquire self-identity; and they need self-identity in order to be satisfied with themselves. The narrative capability of thematic speech is what enables the conscious experiencer to create its selfhood.

With thesis-making, consciousness can become — if one chooses, and if one can learn how to do it properly — somewhat like a prosecuting Crown attorney. Prompted by the 'curiosity' that inheres in the mind's capacity for understanding, the mind compels reality to appear before the bar that separates the true and the false, and subjects it to a judicial process. A case is now to be made — and if the trial is fair, supported by evidence — so that a 'truth-saying' or verdict can be pronounced. Prosecutors operate, however, within the framework of an established law; their point of departure is what society has previously defined as admissible and normal behaviour. The conscious asserter does not, through its judging of reality, construct its world-interpretation and its self-identity strictly by itself. The conscious life of individual asserters is played out against a cultural backdrop that is already part of the stage when the individual first comes upon the scene; the backdrop is the lexicon and the more or less well-integrated system of propositions that add up to the society's accumulated lore, parts of which all individuals acquire as they learn to speak and think, becoming thus inducted into their culture and its ways of perceiving man and world.

The system is actually a system of systems; ultimately it comprises all that society can teach to the individual — plus the contribution to it, if any, that individuals might offer to it. The system is synonymous with the entire culture in which the asserter lives. Of course, individuals eventually becomes able to develop novel concepts and acquire original convictions about themselves and the world. Having learned how to conceive and narrate, they can create new ways of organizing their empirically received information. These concepts and assertions may or may not be valuable to others; new ways to mean what one says and new ways to understand what one means may or may not survive. And they may be, of course, more or less true, more or less new, and more or less useful. But if individuals had to develop their conceptual apparatus and accumulate thematic assertions about self and world starting with nothing, they would make as little headway in their short lifetimes as if they had to invent speech all by themselves.

The acquisition of understanding by individuals — the emergence of their ability to experience reality with a degree of *meaningfulness* — is thus an essentially socio-cultural process. Culture contributes to the generation of consciousness in individual human beings not only by transmitting the vocabulary and the stories (mythical, scientific, philosophical or in-between) that attempt to make sense out of experience, but by transmitting in the first place a syntax and a logic, and a narrative ability to make assertions in accordance with them. After they acquire the techniques of world- and self-definition, individuals can participate in their culture's definition of man and world and in their society's and their own definition of themselves; they have, however, no more choice about the world— and self-understanding from which they can begin to develop their independent interpretations — if they develop any — than a child has to choose its genetic endowment. The marvel is not, therefore, that human beings are culturally programmed as strictly as they are, but that they can, at least theoretically, rewrite their programmes. Even a moderate amount of creative self-definition, however, can never be achieved except by dint of self-discipline, arduous labour, and the passage of time. It is a strange fact that human beings find it difficult to be themselves.

4. The nature of understanding

Our intellectual tradition since Greek times has tended to interpret sense perception and understanding as two different experiential faculties that capture two distinct aspects of reality, namely, its sensible, perceptible appearances and its intelligible, deducible meaning. Some empirical observations seem to support this view; for example, there is a very clear difference between perceiving, say, a human being, and understanding human nature. If cognition is understood as a passive, receptive function, the double dichotomy — two distinct and separate mental functions, perception and understanding, and two corresponding objects in reality, sensible and intelligible — is unavoidable. To escape it, we have to recognize, as discussed in chapter III, the active nature of cognition and perceive that it consists in relating ourselves to reality rather than in possessing it. Cognition is the way in which cognizers live in and with the world, the way in which they wend their adjustive way within the world. If we take this position, however, we still have to explain the empirically observable differences between perceiving and understanding.

a) The emergence of understanding

The explanation is based on what we have already determined about the cognitive role of the assertion of experience: thematic speech and thought vault the human mind above perception, and liberate it from bondage to the concrete reality of the world afforded by mere perception. Thematicity opens up the possibility of understanding the world as a whole. By this I do not mean: understanding the whole world (which is a notion of questionable cogency). I mean: understanding our various concrete, discrete, and partial perceptual encounters with the world (and with ourselves) in relation to each other. For to 'make sense' of what we see, hear, and touch, is to grasp how it is *connected* to whatever else we see, hear, and touch. Understanding is systematized, organized knowledge. As we think about what we perceive and have perceived, and the words come and the sentences flow, the mere information we had already obtained is organized and systematized: as we say, the facts 'fall into place.' They become *interpreted* facts. The soft sound they make as they mesh and click is somehow pleasant and soothing; it yields the easy breathing, the comfort, the delight — and even the excitement, if the matter is important — with which one experiences one's experiencing of the world.

The organization of cognition begins, as we have seen, at the humble level of perception, i.e., with the conceptualization of our perceptual experience. The bare essentials of interpretation are present by our speaking of anything assertively; for we assert what we say in a specific sense. Our words have a meaning. Experiencers are conscious of the object of experience in the particular guise that they now conceive it to be, only because they learned to use the words of speech and thought to assert it — and thus, to *mean* it — in the very sense that the experience now 'states.' For example, objects always have names; if nothing else, a consciously perceived object is 'it,' or 'something,' or 'that.' Thus, the conscious mind is interpretative even at its simplest level of operation, because human beings can perceive reality consciously only in those ways in which they have learned to speak and think of it. On the other hand, information that has not been processed conceptually will, of course, be received just the same, but one will not realize that it has been received. One will experience — but not consciously.

An illustration may be useful. Two baskets of apples lie before me on the grocery counter, selling at the same price. I cannot choose what information reality will appear to broadcast, but depending on what I am able to say about it I can select and organize in various ways the information I gain from what I see. For example, since I can think of 'apples' in particular, and not only of 'fruit' in general, I can treat all other baskets but those containing apples as if they did not exist; I have the power to decide which stimuli shall be allowed to remain operative and which shall be shut out; I can channel my attention at will. Moreover, because I can package the information in alternative ways — for instance, I can perceive some of the empirical facts as 'ten' in one basket and 'twelve' in the other, and think 'Delicious' in one and 'Spy' in the next — I am able to make certain discriminations that otherwise would be beyond me. Therefore I can use the information in ways that otherwise would not be open to me. To make apple sauce I choose 'Spy' regardless of the number; to take for lunch I buy 'Delicious,' though I get fewer for my money; to give away at Hallowe'en, silently giving away thereby an aspect of my character, I pick any 'twelve' rather than 'ten' at the same price.

My ability to organize the information in these various ways, however, is nothing but my ability to conceive it specifically as I do, by my actual or potential use of audible or imaginary words to signify it as I do. If I am unable to count, I see exactly the same ten apples as a mathematician does, but I cannot see them as 'ten.' Of course, I can lack the ability to count and nevertheless be able to think of apples as 'Delicious,' 'Spy,' and so on — or, vice-versa, I may be able to count but not to discriminate among varieties of apples. But if I lacked both types of conceptual instruments, the range of my conscious experience and my behavioural repertoire would be correspondingly restricted. They would be yet more limited if I could not even conceive an apple as 'apple,' but only as, say, 'food,' or 'missile,' or 'it.' Suppose, however, that I lacked the ability to conceive them at all, or to signify objects of experience assertively in any way whatsoever (and there was a time in the life of all human beings when they were in this very position, namely, before they learned to speak and think). What then? Well, although I would receive the same sense information as I do now (and would therefore experience it non-consciously, and be able to react to it accordingly, as animals do), I could hardly experience it consciously at all. It was only as I learned to speak of reality assertively, conceiving it in various ways, that I acquired the conceptual lexicon that I would thereafter have ready at hand to apply to reality whenever the concept might fit. And if this is true, then it seems to imply that the human mind's ability to give conscious quality to its perceptions is generated by the acquisition of the ability to speak and think.

To say that conceptualizing reality amounts to interpreting it may seem an exaggeration: surely not much interpretation is involved in packaging information as 'petal,' say, rather than as 'flower,' or as 'blue' rather than as 'blue-green,' or vice versa. And it is true, not much indeed. What justifies calling conceptualization an 'interpretation' is the fact that although no specific way of packaging information conceptually is necessitated by the reality itself, the information is conceptualized just the same. This fact reveals creativity, even if not a great deal of it; it manifests the conscious experiencer's budding ability to manage its experience; it amounts to a rudimentary ability to interpret reality, since it enables us to make use of our perceptual experience in accordance with specifically human cognitive needs or wants. Of course, since every reality has its own characteristics, no reality can be adequately manipulated conceptually as if it had characteristics other than its own: if 'red' means a colour like that of a ripe Delicious apple, no amount of creativity could justify saying that bananas are 'red.' Nevertheless, all things whatever, even bananas, may be organized in accordance with the concept 'red,' since they all may be spoken and thought of as either 'red' or 'not-red.' The interpretative quality of even the simplest level of speech lies in the freedom of experiencers to organize the information in accordance with the way in which *they* signify it.

As we have seen, a vastly superior kind of interpretation is afforded by thematic speech. Of course, the interpretative value of thematic assertions is highly variable; some types of thematic assertion contribute more than others to our understanding of the world. But such value tends to rise, and is most obvious, when discrete thematic assertions are in turn organized into logically coherent narratives such as the mechanic's relatively simple 'diagnosis' of why the car will not start or the sociologist's highly analytic 'report' explaining simultaneously both why the peace talks have once again failed and why the rich continue to victimize the poor — namely, because power does not remove paranoidal fears, but allows one to indulge them. At yet higher levels of interpretation we find ambitious, far-reaching *Weltanschauungen* such as the 'system' of Copernicus, Newton's 'theory' of gravitation, Freud's 'psychoanalysis' of human nature, and Christianity's 'idea' of mankind and its situation in the world. The simple thematic assertion is only the basic unit of human understanding. But how does the assertion of theses in relation to themes organize factual information so as to enable us to make sense out of the facts?

Although all thematic assertions take the general form 'A is B,' there is an unlimited number of concepts that may fill in for 'A' and for 'B,' However, the number of *ways* in which 'B' can be related to 'A' is relatively very small; for concepts may have very different significations in relation to reality, yet have exactly the same function in relation to other concepts. For instance, when the concepts of, say, 'toad slime' and 'hunger and oppression' are considered simply as organizing conceptually perceptual information supplied by reality, they are utterly different; they have as little in common as, say, the concepts of 'giving you warts' and 'driving people to revolt.' When the same concepts are used as theses and themes, however, a similarity appears. In the thematic assertion 'Toad slime gives you warts,' the relationship between the concepts that signify the thesis and the theme is the same as that which is found between the thesis and the theme in the assertion 'Hunger and oppression drive people to revolt.' In the case of the two themes, two concepts ('giving' and 'driving'} that by themselves mean very different things, have the common meaning of 'causing'; likewise, the two concepts used as theses have different meanings in themselves, but share the meaning of 'effect' in relation to their respective themes. Thus, whereas non-thematic speech organizes information in patterns, thematic speech organizes it into patterns of patterns. But why does this higher level of organization convert mere facts into 'sense-making' facts?

It was well over twenty centuries ago that our philosophical tradition became aware of the fact that thematic assertions are classifiable into *categories,* as the Greeks called them. The English adaptation of the Greek word is colourless: 'ways of holding forth' would be a more idiomatic yet more literal rendering.) Since the meaning of these various ways of speaking thematically can itself be, upon reflection, conceptually asserted, we may say that thematic assertions organize the thesis and the theme in accordance with concepts such as 'reality' and 'unreality,' 'cause' and 'effect,' 'substance' and 'accident,' 'unity' and 'multiplicity,' 'quantity' and 'quality,' and so on. Even today the precise number and description of the categories are not universally agreed upon, though it is common coin that they are of the order of a dozen or so. I also mention that it is ambiguous to refer to the categories simply as *concepts,* the same term by which we refer to the concepts that even non-thematic speech uses; the least we should do is draw a distinction, as I shall here, between *ordinary concepts* and *categorical concepts*. In any event, in the wake of Immanuel Kant's struggle with Hume's skepticism, the following questions come up: (a) how do we conceive the idea of relating theses and themes in the ways in which we do? (b) how is the meaning of the categorical concepts related to reality? and (c) what is therefore the validity of the categories as means of interpreting reality? What we have studied regarding the nature of conscious perception and the nature of speech and thought, suggests what the answer may be.

In my suggestion, the categorical concepts, like ordinary concepts, are conceived empirically. That is, we have no innate idea of 'reality' or 'causality,' and so on. The categorical concepts are derived from the mind's immediate experience of the way in which it itself experiences objects consciously. The categories are thus the conceptualization of 'objects' provided not by external reality, but by the reality that is conscious experience itself. They are generated when the conscious mind organizes the factual information that it provides immediately to itself about the characteristics of its own activity of experiencing consciously. Only the self-coincidence of conscious experience — the presence of consciousness to itself as it learns to assert thematically — makes this possible. The contents thus conceived — 'conceived' in the sense that they constitute the essential components of the 'idea' of speaking thematically[367] — are therefore the formal, logical properties of consciousness. Or which is the same, they are the properties exhibited by ordinary concepts precisely insofar as they function in thematic assertions, in relation to each other, as theses and themes (i.e. regardless of their actual and concrete contents). Conversely, to 'conceive' the categories is the same as to discover the key 'idea' that defines thematic assertion, or to learn to relate experienced objects in accordance with the various characteristics that consciousness perceives immediately in itself. The categories emerge at the borderline between mere conscious perception and the level of consciousness that is beginning to acquire thematic speech, thought, and understanding.

But after conscious experiencers have learned to make thematic assertions — because they have 'conceived' the 'ways of holding forth' — the categories can be used over and over again to classify experiences and interpret the world, discriminatingly organizing sense information that is anterior to them and that they in no way change, filter, or distort. Nor do they add any contents of their own to the contents of reality. For, as with ordinary concepts, once the meaning of a categorical concept has been established (because it has been asserted with such meaning), the concept will be found to be either applicable, or else inapplicable, to sense information. In other words, the categories are like ordinary concepts in that they can be used to organize the experience of all objects whatever by measuring them against the meaning that the concept already has; the difference is that in the case of the categories the units of measurement are the characteristics of consciousness itself. As I have

---

367   Children, I think, do not learn to speak by understanding what to speak is, but by learning in a practical way to *do* what is needed in order to speak. Likewise, categorical *concepts* are, to begin with, merely implicit in our practice of thematic speech; it is only after we are able to use the categories that we can, upon reflection, make assertions about them; and it is only then that we may properly refer to the *concepts* of 'reality', 'causality', and so on. In other words, the assertion of the properties of consciousness that enables the speaker to 'conceive' the categories is an *immediate* assertion; it does not pertain to the order of thematic assertion. For the ability to speak thematically develops out of immediate consciousness and non-thematic speech; it cannot very well precede itself. Moreover, since reflection can take place in a practically infinite variety of degrees, the categories may be conceived at many different levels of reflexive thought. Long before human beings refer to concrete things as 'real' or as the 'causes' of certain effects — let alone speak of the abstractions called 'efficient causality', 'reality', 'existence', and so on — the categorical concepts of *reality* and *efficient causality* have been conceived and have been effectively at work in thematic assertions that speak of things as being, for instance, 'there', or as 'happening', or as being 'given', and as 'doing' certain things, or as 'bringing them about' (as toad slime supposedly does warts), and the like. We may, however, ignore the differences between the more and the less abstract forms of the categories; I shall ordinarily speak of them here only in the highly abstract form that is familiar to philosophers.

suggested, therefore, the categories are not innate, but empirically acquired. They are *a posteriori* ways of organizing information thematically — though in relation to the objects organized by them they are *a priori*, or preconceived.

This interpretation of the nature of understanding explains why the world can be understood despite its not being inherently intelligible, and without supposing that if it were not inherently intelligible it must therefore be inherently absurd. The world is intelligible only in the sense that, in point of fact, *we* can understand it. But our understanding of it does not make it intelligible in itself. To suppose otherwise is possible only if we project our understanding onto the objects understood.

To be sure, our traditional prejudices are well rooted, and we find it difficult to believe that our knowledge and understanding are exclusively *our* affair. We are accustomed instead to suppose, quasi-mystically, that the 'pursuit of truth' brings us closer to the awe-inspiring secrets and arcana of the universe; we may therefore, contemn the suggestion that truth exists only in a knowing mind, and that in the absence of a Higher Mind, only our earthly minds remain to cultivate, produce, and harvest knowledge. This scarcely minimizes, I stress once again, the fact that our knowledge can be true only on condition that it should abide by the *factuality* of reality. But our knowledge remains nevertheless exclusively our own achievement. And it is truly creative; obtaining it requires ingenuity and initiative. In short, knowledge and understanding are not the human repetition of a pre-existing knowledge inscribed within reality, much less immanent in 'laws of nature' that the world is obliged to obey. Our knowledge and understanding are not imported from the world, but manufactured at home for domestic consumption.

It may be useful to compare the foregoing with Kant's doctrine of the categories. His profound insight, the fountainhead of most of what is truly novel in modern philosophy, was in effect that the conscious mind is interpretative. It does not merely 'read' what is pre-written in reality, but 'translates' it, as it were, into the kind of language it can understand. But Kant was unable to shed the traditional presupposition that experience must be in some sense representative as well. Thus, according to Kant the concepts used in 'judgments' as theses and themes have an empirical content, or 'matter,' which derives from reality; at the same time, however, the 'understanding…introduces a transcendental [i.e., non-empirical, innate] *content* into its representations.'[368] That is, the empirical content of experience is organized in accordance with the 'transcendental content' provided by the categories.

Conversely, the categories are the organizational patterns of the propositions that represent the world in speech and thought, and which may be otherwise described as the various ways in which subjects and predicates can be related. These are 'pure' conceptual forms, i.e., they are not derived empirically, but are the innate dispositions of the mind to speak and think in certain patterns, and are part of the necessary structure of the mind. They constitute, therefore, the antecedent conditions of the possibility of understanding what we sense. In Kant's own words, the human ability to understand is governed by certain 'rules…[that operate] prior to objects being given to me…[which] find expression in *a priori* concepts to which all objects of experience necessarily conform, and with which they must agree.'[369] Therefore, the conscious mind receives not simply the information given by reality, but an information that has been modified, in respect of its *contents*, by the information that the human mind contributes to the final outcome of the experiential process. But by the very fact that the categorical concepts give to the *contents* of experience a 'form' (i.e., a non-empirical *content*) that is foreign to them, they affect the *contents* that they represent. And this is why for Kant reality cannot be experienced consciously 'as it is in itself.'

The possibility explored here is very different. Neither conscious sense perception nor understanding represents reality, although both are interpretative; and neither level of interpretation contributes anything to the *contents* of experience. Interpretation may be said to contribute the 'form' of experience only in the sense that it determines the conscious quality of conscious experience; it gives it its assertive form, both at the level of immediate, perceptual consciousness and at the level of understanding. The difference between these two levels of experience depends on the kind of processing to which the information 'received' by the senses has been subjected. But at both levels, to give assertive form to the experience of certain contents is to make it a conscious experience of the *same* contents; it is not to make it an experience of different, or modified, or hybrid contents.

---

368   Immanuel Kant, *Critique of Pure Reason*, A 79, B 105; Norman Kemp Smith, (trans.), (London: Macmillan, 1950), 112; italics mine.

369   Kant, *Critique of Pure Reason,* B xvii; Kemp Smith, 28.

An objection might be raised: if a categorical concept is formed by conceptually organizing information pertaining to the conscious mind itself, how can it thereafter be *validly* applied to information received from the world? And what could be the *usefulness* of so applying it? To learn the answer we need but to remember that the function of even ordinary concepts is not to represent reality, but to organize it. The fact that a child has derived its concept of 'red' from its experience of apples and cherries does not prevent the valid application of the concept to the *rambutan* that the child first saw only years later, when he travelled to Indonesia as an adult. The concept is validly applied because its meaning is constant. For the same reason, the fact that one first learned of 'reality' when one experienced the mutual otherness-to-each other of self and world, or that one learned of 'causality,' when one first experienced one's own causation of effects, and so on, does not prevent the valid application of the same concept to quite different causal events and real realities. Although the content of every category comes from the charac-teristics of conscious experience itself, what is measured by the categories is not one's experience but the objects or events that inform one's senses in accordance with what reality itself is.

Now, does the foregoing interpretation of the nature of interpreting and understanding not imply that, as Protagoras said, 'Man is the measure of all things, of the things that are, that [or how] they are, and of things that are not, that [or how] they are not,'[370] a doctrine commonly reviled under the label of 'relativism'?

'Relativism' has been in disrepute at least as far back as Plato's *Theaetetus,* in which Socrates offers numerous refutations of Protagoras's teaching. The principal and most memorable argument concludes not simply that Protagoras's doctrine was wrong, but that it was absurd. For it was self-refuting. As Socrates paints him, Protagoras meant that a person's beliefs were true for the person who held them, but not necessarily for others. And this did not mean simply that people may have contradictory opinions which they continue to hold despite other people's disagreement — which is of course true. Protagoras was held by Socrates to mean rather that a person's beliefs actually *had* the quality of truth, even when they conflicted with the beliefs of other persons who, likewise, did

---

370   Herman Diels and Walther Kranz, *Die Fragmente der Vorsokratiker* (Zurich: Weidmann, 1985), 80B1. In view of the Greek idea of reality, Protagoras may in no event be supposed to have meant that the mind determined the existence and non-existence of reality, but at most that it determined the characteristics of reality.

not merely take their own opinions to be true, but correctly thought that they were true. This is what has come to be known as 'relativism;' or sometimes, more informally, as the 'true-for-me' reading of Protagoras.

If this is what Protagoras in fact meant, then, for the very reasons given in Socrates' squelching refutation, to say that Protagoras was mistaken would be an understatement; more to the point would have been to question his sanity. However, modern opinion has been fairer. Although Protagoras's true intention is still not beyond dispute among today's Hellenists, it is now granted by many that Protagoras's *'bon mot* is striking but susceptible of many interpretations,'[371] and that more than one interpretation could be sensible and intelligent. On the other hand, 'relativism' — the word — has not fared as well as Protagoras the 'relativist.' Words, including terms of art, are more often debased by general than by technical use, but upon occasion by the mangling hand of philosophers. 'Relativism' is a case in point. It is ironic that Protagoras is known to have been deeply concerned with the consistent and accurate use of technical terms, and with the adverse consequences for philosophy of the careless use thereof. For the meaning of 'relativism' has become narrowly circumscribed in modern times and is now automatically taken to imply some version or other of the obtuse interpretation of the nature of cognition ascribed to Protagoras in the *Theaetetus* — the 'true-for-me' idea of relativism

The unthinking prejudice against 'relativism' is not justified. *Every* philosophical interpretation of cognition involves some form of relativism; it has to, because cognition *is,* by everyone's reckoning, a *relationship* between a cognizer and a cognized. Representationism, for example, assumes tacitly the relativity of representations to the represented. Its mistake does not lie in this, but in the kind of relationship between cognition and reality that it supposes — namely, a *representational* relationship. If we make allowance for the causation of cognition by the cognizing organism rather than for causation by the object, we should have no objection to maintaining both the relativity of truth to the mind, and the relativity of cognition to reality. My position may be deemed a form of 'relativism,' but it is hardly akin to the self-refuting 'true-for-me' doctrine of the Socratic Protagoras

If what I have proposed above regarding the nature of human understanding is correct —in particular, if it is true that understanding anything may not be construed as the mind's inward repetition

---

371   Coady, 'Relativism, epistemological,' in Ted Honderich, (ed.), *The Oxford Companion* 757.

of the meaning or intelligibility physically contained in the thing, but as the mind's interpretative self-relation to reality by means of thematic speech and its categories — then it *does* follow that understanding consists in the human mind's *taking the measure of reality.* To measure something is to relate it to a standard or unit of measurement. And in the case of understanding, the *standard of measurement* is provided by the various ways in which the conscious mind operates. Our human mind provides us with units of measurement, as it were (i.e., categorical concepts), by reference to which we understand reality and explain it to ourselves. And the human mind conceives such units of measurement empirically. We have no innate ideas of the sort, and specifically none of reality, causality, or self.

The meaning of this suggestion may be further clarified, and its validity tested, if we compare the function of ordinary concepts and that of categorical concepts. Ordinary concepts measure reality by a standard given to us by objects themselves; by means of such standards we therefore take the measure of things by reference to each other. For example, we measure objects as 'red' or 'not red' by reference to the conventional meaning of 'red,' which accepts the colour of ripe cherries but not that of bananas as the informal and imprecise standard of 'red.' But standards may be quite precise: in a lumberyard the length of pieces of lumber are measured fairly exactly by reference to a measuring tape that is calibrated, in turn, by reference, ultimately, to a platinum rod kept under glass in the French Academy of Sciences in Paris. Likewise, when we conceive a categorical concept such as 'causality' and then apply it to objects and events, we measure the latter by a unit that we have derived from our own nature; we then assimilate the world to what we have already learned to think of as 'causality' in ourselves. The result is that by implicit reference to the categories (that is, by asserting our experiences thematically) reality can be cast in *familiar* and *homely* terms — in *our* terms — in propositions and narratives about a world in relation to which we can experience ourselves as ourselves. For example, we can assert not simply certain observable facts about "A and "B" but also draw from them the conclusion that 'A is the cause of B.' We *understand* what this means, because even before we observed the actual relationship between 'A' and 'B,' we already knew (though we might or might not have *understood* or interpreted correctly) what 'cause' and 'effect' meant. And we knew it from our own experience of ourselves. Once we conceive (or for that matter misconceive) causality, assertions affirming or denying causality are always meaningful. We always understand what they mean.

b) The categorical concepts

Finally, let us attempt to reconstruct summarily how the specific categorical concepts that function as the practical tools of understanding may be generated. We are on reasonably firm ground in the case of the three basic — or *constitutive* — categories, the first of which is 'reality.' The information asserted by this concept is the fact that consciousness opposes the object of experience to the experiencing of the object, discriminating thus between self and not-self. But since the mind of human beings is conscious, they are not only aware of the object, but also of this fact — i.e., of the difference between the object and the activity of experiencing it. And so, by the very fact that experiencers are conscious, they can experience the 'otherness' of objects (in relation to their experiencing of the object), as well as their own otherness (in relation to the otherness of objects of experience). Thereafter, every experience of theirs will be apt to include a sense of the *otherness-to* that characterizes both objects and the conscious experiencing of objects.[372] And when they learn, as part of their acquisition of the ability to assert their experience, to relate theses to themes as having (or, as the case may be, as not-having) such otherness to each other, they have implicitly 'conceived' what by another name we call 'reality.'

---

372   The same sense of *otherness-to* that enables the conscious mind to perceive real things as real, also enables it to differentiate its assertiveness into, more particularly, the abilities to affirm and to deny. For every assertion is other-than every other assertion. But, if so, what one assertion asserts can be other-than what another asserts. Now, if what the first one asserts is merely other-than what the second asserts, the assertions are simply different; if, however, they are different assertions in respect of the same contents, then the one is not simply different from the other, but contradicts it — or *counterasserts* it — and vice versa. Out of the ability to assert develops the ability to assert either positively or negatively.

Moreover, upon reflection they can explicitly conceive[373] such relationship precisely as *other-ness-to,* whether in these or in equivalent terms such as *actuality, objectivity, existence,* and so on.[374] Thus, consciousness does not create the reality of the real — but neither does the idea of reality mirror or repeat what the real first 'told' us about the reality it possessed absolutely within itself. Whether clearly and fully consciously or dimly and confusedly, the conscious mind is aware of the fundamental relationship of *otherness-to* that every thing bears to every other thing, namely, 'reality.'

Moreover, the same conscious experience that reveals otherness-to also shows that such relativity is not restricted to otherness-to-experience (and much less to otherness-to-*my*-experience). For the same objects that are other-than my experience of them are shown, by experience, to be also other-to each other; likewise, not only my act of experiencing objects, but also my organism and indeed my selfhood are experienced as other-to such objects. Thus, the supposition that the reality of anything could consist in its being perceived *by oneself* is naturally repugnant to all of us. But this is not because some instinct or irrational feeling so disposes us; it is for the very sound reason that our immediate conscious perception contradicts it. Besides, each one of us also knows, through experience, that the relation of otherness-to-one's-experience may be potential as well as actual, and indirect as well as direct. Many things I have never experienced may well be real — though if they are real it is inherently possible that, directly or indirectly, they could be experienced by me.

Now if reality is not an absolute characteristic of objects in themselves, the question may be raised again, but this time with specific reference to *reality,* how this categorical concept may be

---

373   But even after they have conceived the categories, experiencers will not necessarily *understand* what the categories mean, or how they came to use them with the meaning they intend. This would require application, skill, and a high level of reflection. Thus, most people can use meaningfully the concepts of, *reality, causality, sameness, difference* and so on, but would be hard pressed to explain what these mean; they are also likely to imagine that they learned the meaning of these concepts by experiencing their counterparts in the world.

374   However, not all conceptualizations of *reality* will be equally adequate. It is only when the meaning of *reality* is asserted as *otherness-to* — which is possible only to the degree that consciousness is not absent-minded — that the reality of real things will be experienced adequately, as a relationship; it will mean indeed nothing but the fundamental relativity towards each other that is exhibited by all real things. The absent-minded, too, will perceive the otherness of objects; but since their own experiencing is not clearly felt, such otherness will be mistaken for a characteristic that objects hold absolutely, or in themselves. But *absolute reality* — that is, *absolute otherness* — is a self-contradiction: nothing can be other without being other-than. Absent-mindedness affects the conception of all the other categories analogously: the absent-minded tend to project onto objects the absolute or ideal character that the categorical concepts can have only in human thought.

validly ascribed by consciousness to objects. Perhaps this analogy will be useful. An audience does not perform; it only watches the actors' portrayal of the characters that they alone create: their art is their own and not the audience's. Though strictly by watching, however, the audience is what enables the actors to perform as such; without an audience there can be only a rehearsal or a would-be performance, not an actual *exhibition* of the artists' skill. Well, likewise, the properties of real things and the real events constituted by the real interactions among real things need no consciousness in order to take place. But the real does not enter into that particular sort of interaction we call 'being experienced as a reality' unless there should be a consciousness by which it can be experienced 'as a reality.' And this means: a consciousness for which the real can 'perform' not only *because* it is real, but also *in the role of* 'being real'; not only *because* it is itself and is what it is, but also *in the role of* 'being itself' and 'being what it is.' When the real so 'performs,' however, it is only because consciousness had created the role — the category — into which the real as such could be fittingly cast. And, as it turns out, the real is a natural for the part. This should be hardly astonishing: the role had been written by consciousness with the real in mind.

The empirical ground of the concept of *efficacy* or *causation* is the fact that consciousness *does* its own experiencing. Being conscious consists in *doing* something; for unless one's experiencing be done, one will not experience at all. More particularly, conceiving is an act, because a concept is conceived by the mind's assertion of it. However, even before *conceiving* and *being conceived* are themselves conceived by consciousness as *doing* and *being done* (or as *activity* and *passivity*), they are conceived as *causing* and *being caused.* The basis of this category is the relationship between the 'doing' of one's experiencing, and the 'experiencing' that is achieved by the 'doing.' One and the same conscious mind that appears to itself in the former guise also appears to itself in the latter, since these are but two ways in which consciousness can be present to itself. Thus, the activity and the outcome correspond perfectly, and cannot but so correspond. The categorical concepts of *activity* and *passivity* assert each of the two aspects separately, in abstraction from each other, whereas the concept of *efficient causality* asserts them in the first place as mutually related, or as found in real conscious life; it signifies the mirror-image proportion between 'doing' and 'what is done,' or between 'cause' and 'effect.' Of itself, the category of *causality* includes no reference to *necessity,* the negation of *factuality* or *contingency.*

We may speculate also that the active constitution of the conscious mind has another side, which is the basis of the categorical concepts of *finality* and *purposiveness.* When we do our experiencing, we do it *wanting* or *intending* to experience what in fact we do, or else despite our *not wanting* to do it. What no one can do as long as he or she experiences consciously is to take no interest whatever in its experience. At the bottom of this phenomenon is the fact that all life has needs. The higher animals, however, experience their needs; they have *wants.* Being able to experience both their wants and the objects that satisfy them, they learn to behave so as to attain such objects. The self-presence of consciousness means, however, that human beings not only want and not-want; they also experience the facts *that* they want and *that* they do not. They there-fore not only seek objects that satisfy their wants and reject those that frustrate them, but experience some objects as desirable and others as undesirable. In other words, a human being, un-like an animal, not only takes advantage of the relationship between satisfaction and the means to attain it, but also experiences this relationship as such. The deliberate postponement of gratification is only one of the many possibilities opened up by this conscious experience. Once the conscious experiencer has learned to relate means and ends, it has discovered its finality and can thereafter organize sense information in terms of *desirability,* *value, purpose, intention,* and so on.

Together with *otherness-to,* or however we may conceptualize our experience of reality, the constitutive categories of *efficacy* and *finality* assert the *ante-logical* properties of consciousness. For even before our speech develops thematicity, the conscious mind is aware of itself, if only dimly, as other-than its objects, as causing its own states, and as undertaking to achieve goals. The *logical* properties of the conscious mind arise only with thematic speech and thought. There is, thus, a second type of category, which asserts the *necessity* and *contingency,* the *impossibility* and *possibility,* the *sameness* and *difference,* the *similarities* and *dissimilarities,* the *unity* and *multiplicity,* and the *totality* and *partiality* that consciousness can perceive in its own concepts when the experience of thinking and speaking include the meaningfulness that is typical of understanding. Since these categorical concepts determine the rules of logic, they may be called the *regulative* categories.[375] Of course, the 'rules' of logic merely describe how the conscious mind in fact works when it speaks and thinks thematically,[376] not how it must willy-nilly work — as if the rules existed first and consciousness had then been designed in accordance with the rules. But absent-minded students of the mind may well imagine otherwise — just as it may mistake mathematical, and sometimes even grammatical, 'rules' for objective constraints that determine from without how human beings may and may not think.

Necessity and *contingency* (and *possibility* and *impossibility)* and the other 'regulative' categories reflect different aspects of the same experience, which is made possible by the ability of the conscious mind to reflect upon its own experience. If I conceive 'rose,' and then I conceive 'rose' again, and compare the later to the first concept, I will experience their *sameness;* they are absolutely identical. Now, in reality, as Plato quite correctly observed — though drawing therefrom some incorrect conclusions[377] — nothing is absolutely the same as itself, much less absolutely the same as something else, since everything in the world is a state of becoming. In reality we can detect only greater or lesser *similarities*. By contrast with reality, however, every concept is always perfectly identical to itself, and *cannot* be more or less than itself. For if it were, it would be a different concept. Well, then, it is *impossible* to think anything but what in fact one thinks, or to assert what one does not assert; contradictories cannot be held at the same time. This is the way in which, as a matter of fact, the conscious mind operates, given its presence to itself. This impossibility — or its diametric opposite, necessity — is absolute. There cannot be any exception to it, for the very good reason that the stan-

---

375   The relation between the constitutive and the regulative categories may require some elucidation. The most fundamental properties of consciousness — reality, efficacy, and finality — are enjoyed by consciousness, of course, even before it develops *thematicity*, though it is only when it learns to speak thematically that it conceives the corresponding constitutive categories. It is, however, only when it acquires narrative ability — and for that very reason — that consciousness develops logical properties, becomes able to experience logically, and conceives the categories that regulate its narrative, logical processes. Thus, both the constitutive and the regulative <u>categories</u> appear at the same stage of evolution; but the former assert the ante-logical, whereas the latter the logical, <u>properties</u> of consciousness.

376   Although all thematic speakers are 'ruled' by the logical properties of thematic speech and thought, they do not all take the same advantage of their capacity for learning to reason consistently with the logic of their thought. Likewise, not all cultures develop logic — or mathematics, or grammar — to the same degree, or at all, by reflecting upon the properties of their speech and thought.

377   Namely, that the concept of *sameness* represents the absolute self-sameness of a reality beyond the empirical world; see Plato, *Phaedo*, 75A ff.

dard by which possibility and impossibility are measured by consciousness is the self-sameness that conceptual thought *in fact* exhibits.[378]

Necessity is, therefore, not a logical property of the *reality* interpreted by thought, but only of the *thought* that interprets reality. This is true even when the reality interpreted by thought is thought itself (or more generally, the processes of consciousness). In short, necessity has a purely 'logical' reality — that is, as a property of the organization that the thematic consciousness gives to its own processes. Efficient causality does not imply the necessitation or compulsion of the effect by the cause. It would be easy for an absent-minded consciousness, however, to imagine that it did, projecting thus onto all causal processes a characteristic that only logical thought showed.

Sameness or *equality*, and its opposite, *difference*, and *inequality* also arise empirically when conscious experiencers assert to themselves the fact that every concept coincides with itself. If I think 'rose,' and then think 'rose' again, I experience that the concept 'rose' is the same as itself; whereas if I think 'rose,' and then 'red,' the two do not coincide. They are *not-same*, but *different*. It is thus an empirical fact that, although no concept can be more or less than itself, nothing is ever exactly the same as anything else; indeed, nothing is quite the same as even itself, since it is always changing. But it does not matter that, in the real world, sameness is relative to difference, and differences are relative to sameness. By means of the categories of *sameness* and *difference* we are able to relate ourselves to reality precisely insofar as real things are relative to each other and to us.

Other facts of the inner life of consciousness provide the original meaning of the categories of *unity* and *totality*. A concept may be the same as, or different from, another in content, but the second is in any event not the first — for example, 'rose' now is one concept, whereas 'rose' again is

---

378 This does not imply that the possibility or impossibility of real events depends on whether they are actually conceived; it means that we think of an event as possible or impossible depending on whether we find it conceivable or not. Nor does the absolute character of the category of necessity imply that the reality of consciousness is absolute; this is why I have stressed that the self-identity of thought, which is the ground of the concept of necessity, is itself only an observable *fact*; that is, thinking must abide by necessity in the sense that one of the characteristics of concepts is, *as a matter of fact*, to be self-identical. Indeed, all concepts have a perfection or absoluteness that empirical reality seems only to approximate; the reason is of course that in the categorical measuring of reality by consciousness, the nature of consciousness is adopted as the unit of measurement. For instance, the self-coincidence of every concept is perfect because the self-coincidence of *acts of conceiving* is what provides the contents of the definitions of 'self-coincidence,' 'self-identity,' and 'sameness.' Likewise, the characteristics of consciousness that are conceived as its 'unity,' its 'finality,' and so on, are no more absolute than those of other entities. Only *concepts* are absolutely self-identical.

another. Each of the two is *one*. Moreover, a concept that is both *one* and *self-same* is a *totality*; for, being the *same* (as itself), it is neither more nor less than (i.e., is *not-different* from) itself. At the same time, being *one*, it holds its self-same contents in itself, rather than both in itself and another. In other words, it is in itself *all* that it is or can be: whatever coincides with itself, or is self-identical, is also a *whole*, or a *totality*. Thus, given the regulative categories, a thematic thinker would experience his attempt to assert a self-contradiction such as 'A rose is not a rose' as meaningless. The reason is not that things in themselves are self-identical, but that *concepts* are. Likewise, a syllogism makes no sense if neither premise is universal; for this means that the middle term would be undistributed (i.e., *not-a-totality*) twice, and equivocality would result; a seemingly constant term would have *different* meanings in each of two propositions. By the same token, *one* plus *one* is *equal* to a *total* called two; this assertion does not correspond to any property of the real world, though it is nevertheless applicable to it. Thus, reality is neither logical nor mathematical in itself, but can be interpreted by means of logical and mathematical thought. Its contents are not distorted simply by being so interpreted. But they would be, if the logical and mathematical properties of thought were projected onto objects and ascribed to them as their own.

Categories of a third type conceptualize the *post-logical* characteristics of thematic speech. Their list may not be closed; for it is possible that, as consciousness evolves, new categories of this sort may be conceived. They measure the experience of thinking and speaking, as conceived in accordance with the constitutive categories, by the units provided by the regulative categories. Since they unfold before one's own eyes the ways in which one has elaborated one's thematic abilities, they may be called the *descriptive* categories. The most likely to be developed in the majority of cultures, because they are the most elementary, are *quantity* and *quality*, *structure* and *function* (or *subject* and *accident*), *space* and *time*, and *absoluteness* and *relativity*. Since the meaning of these categories depends not only upon the nature of consciousness, but also upon the categorical thinker's prior perception of his reality and his efficient and final causality, the misinterpretation of the latter categories by the absent-minded will compound their misunderstanding of the former. Since their handicap prevents their appreciating the relativity of reality, they will inevitably assume that only one of the terms of each pair — that is, *quantity*, *subject*, *space*, and *absoluteness* — is truly and unqualifiedly applicable to reality. The prejudice that *quality*, *event*, *time*, and *relation* are somewhat less real than the forego-ing is among the most deep-seated that the human mind can acquire as it develops thematic speech.

c) The construction of the self

But how does thematic speech generate not merely conscious experience, conscious thought, conscious inquiry, and conscious understanding, but also an inwardly unified set of experiences — an experiential life — that is present to itself *as a self*? For discrete acts of consciousness are an abstraction; they are never found in real life, which is a continuous *process*. Once the human organ-ism becomes a self, consciousness is a continuous process in which reality, ourselves, and our situa-tion within reality are forever being adjudicated upon. In short, we come once again to the realization that consciousness is not simply a quality of sense experience, but above all the typical quality of the human life of a human self. And thematic speech, I have said, is responsible for this characteristic of human life. But why?

The reason is that the organism I call *myself* is, by virtue of its exercise of its cognitive powers, the narrator of the narrative I call my conscious experience of the meaningful world; and the self is the counterpart of the world as organized by means of thematic assertions. Conversely, if a human being is capable of speaking and thinking thematically — and thus with consciousness of its own speech — its narrating is present to itself. Narrating the narrative automatically converts a conscious organism into a narrator, a 'first person' who is the subject who speaks. But narrating the narrative, moreover, makes it possible for narrators to become meaningful to themselves (though it does not automatically ensure the realization of this possibility). The reason is that narrating the narrative it enables them to derive their own meaning from their self-perception as part of a meaningful world — and, indeed, as the narrator of a meaningfully narrated world. Thus, the ultimate significance of the emergence of thematic speech is that, rendering consciousness discursive and interpretative, it makes possible the kind of consciousness that can experience itself as a sense-making, identifi-able self. The thematic assertion of experience, unbidden and almost mechanically, creates, not long after it comes into being, incipient, sketchy selves who thereafter may craft themselves into adult, mature persons through the conscious use of the very thematic assertiveness that generated their embryonic selfhood.

Admittedly, the world- and the self-understanding of human beings and their conscious life are not always original, or methodically created, or deep, or valid, and in many of us cease to develop altogether at a relatively early age — so that thereafter every new experience that fails to tally with their world- and self-concept is either denied out of existence or else distorted so as to make it fit. Human nature decrees that every individual and culture shall be appointed a judge of reality and an executive officer in charge of itself, but it cannot legislate the responsible exercise of the human self-governmental powers. Not infrequently, therefore, human beings can be observed presiding over kangaroo courts and administrative tribunals where the rules of evidence are laughed at and where the measures of truth are the smirk of the peer group and the fury of the mob. But the experience of reality as world, and of one's own conscious experience as self, need not be original, or methodical, or deep, or true, nor must it fulfil its potentiality for lifelong development, before it can discharge its most fundamental role: to enable consciousness to assert meaningfully what otherwise would be a disintegrated multiplicity of meaningless transient impressions, and to bring to life the conscious self. Experience of the world without the unity of self-organization — without its being integrated as *my* experience of the world — is possible only below the human level, where the totality of experiences can be organized without the benefit of consciousness. If human experience is to have the unity and integrity that come to it from being a self's experience of its world — an experiential life and not a mere congeries of physiologically connected events — it must organize and unify itself.

Thematic assertion is what empowers consciousness to do so; it is by interpreting the world that we can learn to interpret ourselves as interpreters of the world. And this requires thematic assertiveness, because reality cannot be said to be organized — or for that matter, disorganized — in itself. Unless one were prepared to say, gratuitously, that reality exists for the sake of serving mankind's experiential or other needs, one should admit that reality can exhibit coherence and pattern only if it is given conceptual organization by asserters. Asserters do not, of course, 'give' it such organization within itself, but within their mind. However, the possibility of arranging and rearranging reality physically — for instance to take advantage of its properties — follows therefrom.

One may be able to make thematic assertions, however, without being necessarily very clear about what to make thematic assertions is; absent-mindedness makes it hard for us to realize that thematic assertion abstracts reality from its own context, and that, unlike the non-thematic, the thematic asserter asserts the experienced reality precisely as experienced and as asserted. Thus, everyone in our culture knows that, when we speak and think about reality, reality has, *of course*, been spoken and thought about. But most of us fail to realize that we speak and think about it under the very guise of its being spoken and thought about, or as object of speech and thought. We assume instead that, when we assert a thesis in relation to a theme, reality has been spoken about directly; we misconstrue thematic speech as a complicated form of non-thematic speech. And since in non-thematic speech reality determines what the speaker shall be conscious of and speak about, confusion between the two levels of speech yields the familiar delusion: a thematic assertion repeats what reality 'asserts' to us about itself. This mistake implies in turn the classical misinterpretation of reality as a sort of solidified thematic assertion, an objectively existing message or 'word' — a *logos*, a *ratio* — which is the original that experience and speech merely repeat. Reality itself is deemed to contain an inner meaning, a logical organization, that meaningful experience simply mirrors, duplicates, or represents.

Even non-thematic assertions are not a repetition of what reality first 'tells' speakers; for what reality 'says' to them is, to be exact, not what they must say but only what they must address themselves to. All the less so thematic assertions, in which reality does not 'tell' the speaker even what to speak about, which is determined solely by the speaker. However, quite as the presence of consciousness to itself may escape the notice of human beings who are undoubtedly conscious, the assertiveness of thematic assertions may not reach the ears of those of us who are absent-minded. It would then seem incredible to us that speech should be valuable, and that it should account for the typical characteristics of human life, for the very reason that it speaks directly about what speech itself proposes and only indirectly about reality itself. And yet, quite as the value of consciousness is that it can differentiate itself from the world and acquire the perspective that enables it to experience the real as real, the advantage of thematic speech is that, being the kind that is consciously undertaken, it can distance itself from reality and organize it in the form of a narrative and as whole. To be sure, the thematic consciousness can, by the same token, alienate itself from reality. The possibility of failure inheres in every possible success. This, too, is part of the finitude of human nature.

Epilogue: The Future of Philosophy

Historical determinism receives little support from experience; one would be hard pressed to point to anything we actually observe in the world that leads us reasonably even to suspect, much less positively affirm, that historical events are fated, either for better or for worse. Yet it is likely to be empirically discovered in evidence that scholarly knowledge is destined to progress indefinitely. The record seems to me to demonstrate that philosophy, specifically, has failed in the past, and that it has not overcome the mistakes that brought it down.

The degree of historical perspective that is already available today suffices for us to appreciate not only why mediaeval philosophy came to a bad end, but also why Descartes's valiant but misconceived attempt to reform philosophy succeeded only in one respect. For Descartes's initiative may not have prevented a repetition of the mediaeval failure, but it did bring about, at the very time that philosophical skepticism and the reliance of scholars on religious faith were at their height, the revival of Europe's cultivation of rational thought. Descartes not only gave us back our earlier belief that philosophical knowledge and understanding of the world and of human life were attainable; he also improved upon the tradition in one respect, by teaching the modern world, despite his own religious belief, that philosophical reason ought not be made to depend on theology or religious faith.

This is one lesson the superficial meaning of which has been learned reasonably well by philosophy. But, being unaware of the connection between traditional religious beliefs and some of our fundamental assumptions about the world and our mental functions, modern Western culture and its philosophy have not completely shed such assumptions; this implicit self-contradiction creates unnecessary difficulties for us. For it seems almost as if it were a feature of human knowledge, fallible and finite as it is, that the discovery of every truth comes to us wrapped in several woolly layers of possible ways to misunderstand it. As Pope said, ' a little learning is a dangerous thing,' which is demonstrated by our having learned of our inherent existence while having remained insufficiently aware of the implications it holds for our understanding of our situation in the world and for the conduct of our lives — and therefore also for our adoption of the means to ensure the adequacy of such understanding.

Now, cultivated, disciplined, and systematic knowledge about the world and ourselves can be obtained by us only by means of two rational methodologies, science and philosophy; if other ways to procure reasonably reliable knowledge are possible, we have yet to discover them. The differences that in fact obtain between them, which at the time of Galileo and Descartes had been no more sharply delineated than by references to the 'new philosophy' and the 'old,' during the seventeenth and eighteenth centuries began to impose themselves, but gradually, upon the consciousness of scholars. Thus, as late as the end of the Age of Reason one could have met a renowned philosopher — namely, Kant — who had made important contributions to science. By the middle of the nineteenth century, however, the mere distinction between philosophy and science had become the fairly complete separation we take for granted today; science and philosophy had become two independent scholarly communities, each with its own culture and ethos, sharing fairly little besides their dedication to the disciplined use of the human mind to enlarge our knowledge of reality. But as science had ascended, philosophy had declined: 'Hume's problem' was working its mischief, and by the end of the nineteenth century philosophy had lost most of its Enlightenment sheen. The resuscitation of rational scholarship in modern times had reached different outcomes in science and in philosophy.

In comparison with science, philosophical reason has contributed little to our modern civilization. It has not been in a good position to do so; it has had enough predicaments of its own to keep it occupied full-time with its own survival — at about the same time that the triumphs of science encouraged optimism among scientists. The realistic expectation that methodically used reason would make knowledge attainable, morphed into the attitude that scientific understanding was omnicompetent and would inevitably continue to expand indefinitely into the future. Belief in steady and unending scientific progress having soon whetted the appetite of the culture for novelty, and expanded so as to encompass every sphere of human life to which scientifically-based technology could make a profitable contribution, our civilization eventually felt entitled to expect that wisdom, along with knowledge, would continue to be amassed indefinitely by science as long as our determination to obtain it persisted.

The expectation was presumptuous. Scientific knowledge is not the same as wisdom, and whereas science has procured for us the exponential growth of human power, it has not taught us — because it cannot teach us — how to wield it without doing severe, possibly mortal, harm to our civilization and to our species, and indeed to our planet. To achieve soundness of life, the least we need is a sound understanding of our own human nature, most particularly our mental functions, our inherent existence, and our finitude, and a reasonably firm grasp of the true situation in which we actually exist — namely, in a world that is, simply and without qualification, real. But in the absence of effective philosophical criticism, the accomplishments of science have been thoroughly ambivalent, and the delusion persists that the world of which we are integral part is only a pale, defective version of true reality. The illusion that we have made wondrous progress has displaced the more realistic truth that we have made some modest moral advances, though not particularly because of science.

Thus, at one point in recent history, during a brief attack of lucidity, and for once recognizing instead of glorifying the folly of record levels of mutual human extermination during the first half of the twentieth century, the generation to which I belong dared to suppose that mankind had at long last acquired a rudimentary level of mental stability. Technologically proficient means of mass murder would cease to be resorted to by the civilized world as a means of settling disagreements. Provisions were to be made not only for governing the entire world through reason, negotiation, and co-operation instead of competition, but also for sharing our wealth on a global scale. We expected to reshape social, economic, and political relations in our communities not only so as to live in reasonable harmony, but to derive the positive benefits and pleasures of human fellowship. Indeed, many of the political, social, and economic institutions whereby to achieve all this were actually created. But no sooner were they established than they were subverted. Myopia prevailed, and self-interest reigned. We did not follow through for many reasons, but at least in part because the only solutions we are good at devising are scientific — and there are no scientific solutions to the problems that assail us when we misunderstand our nature as conscious beings, and when, therefore, we cannot control our mode of life so as to further our true best interests. Without self-understanding, empathy is impossible, knowledge is madness, and lunacies become the beacon of truth. And so, we are now in the twenty-first century and have to admit we have regressed. We are no longer certain that barbarities are barbarous, and deem it a sign of good breeding — rather than of the degeneracy it truly is — that we can coolly debate just how barbarous barbarities have to be before they should be considered barbarities.

It would be quixotic to suggest that philosophy can aspire to redeem the human species from its insanities. But the globalization of our species has brought about the globalization of irrationality, and cultivating reliance on reason cannot be deemed altogether irrelevant to the welfare and perhaps the survival of mankind. Thought is what makes us human, and thought might conceivably bring us nearer to fulfilling the possibilities inherent in conscious life. However, philosophy could help human beings look at themselves and perceive more than what lies on the surface only if it took account of its history, surmounted its failures, and reoriented itself.

I am not the only contemporary philosopher who thinks that the typically modern trends in philosophy betray disorientation and indicate a failure of the tradition in basic respects; I have referred to a few of the few others who are like-minded. But since their reasons for their discontent are different from mine, they may well judge that my explanation of the historical causes of the failure is partly or altogether incorrect, and that my recommendations for the reconstruction of philosophy are therefore largely, if not wholly, useless.

Nevertheless, if Peter Hare is right, 'an increasing number of philosophers are coming to recognize that 'doing philosophy historically' is possible, [and] that the purism of both the analysts and the historicists is misguided.'[379] It is not out of the question that in the future there should be other attempts, besides mine, to understand the historical causes of the failure of modern philosophy, and to attempt to remedy them. And if such attempts reach the correct conclusions that may have escaped me, they should yield more adequate proposals than mine. It could very well be, however that no effort to renew philosophy will be deemed necessary and that none will be made. This is true. But it is also true that reason may eventually prevail.

---

379 Hare, *Doing Philosophy Historically,* 12.

Works Cited

Ancient Sources

Aquinas, Thomas. *Commentarium In XII Libros Metaphysicorum.*

———. *De Ente et Essentia.*

———. *De Potentia Dei.*

———. *De Veritate Catholicae Fidei Contra Gentiles.*

———. *Quaestiones Disputatae De Veritate.*

———. *Summa Theologiae.*

Aristotle, *Metaphysics.*

———. *Nichomachean Ethics.*

———. *On Interpretation.*

———. *On the Heavens.*

———. *On the Soul.*

———. *Posterior Analytics.*

John of St. Thomas (John Poinsot). *Cursus Philosophiae: De Anima.*

Plato. *Phaedo.*

———. *Republic.*

William of Ockham. *Commentarium in Libros Sententiarum.*

Modern Sources

Adams, Marilyn McCord. *William Ockham.* 2 vols. Notre Dame. Ind.: Notre Dame University Press. 1987.

Alston, William P. 'Back to the Theory of Appearing.' *Philosophical Perspectives* 13 1999: 2. 181-203.

Armstrong, David M. *What Is a Law of Nature?* Cambridge: Cambridge University Press, 1983.

Audi, Robert, ed. *The Cambridge Dictionary of Philosophy.* Cambridge: Cambridge University Press, 1995.

Baldwin, James Mark. *Development and Evolution.* New York: Macmillan, 1902.

Barnes, W.H.F. 'The myth of sense-data.' *Proceedings of the Aristotelian Society* 45 1944-45: 1. 89-117.

Block, Ned, Owen Flanagan, and Güven Güzeldere, eds. *The Nature of Consciousness: Philosophical Debates.* Cambridge, MA.: MIT Press, 1998.

Brandon, S.G.F. *Man and His Destiny in the Great Religions: An Historical and Comparative Study.* Manchester: Manchester University Press, 1962.

Brentano, Franz. *Psychologie von Empirischen Standpunkt.* Leipzig: Felix Meiner, 1924.

Britton, Karl. 'Portrait of a Philosopher.' *The Listener* 53 1955: 1372, 1072.

Brown, Roger W. *Words and Things.* Glencoe, IL.: Free Press, 1958.

Bultmann, Rudolf. *Jesus Christ and Mythology.* London: SCM Press, 1966.

Bunge, Mario A. *Philosophy in Crisis: The Need for Reconstruction.* Amherst, NY: Prometheus, 2001.

Burnet, John. *Early Greek Philosophy.* London: Black, 1920.

———. *Greek Philosophy: Thales to Plato.* London: Macmillan, 1950.

Burtt, Edwin A. ed. *The English Philosophers from Bacon To Mill.* New York: Modern Library, 1939.

———. *The Metaphysical Foundations of Modern Physical* Science. Garden City, N.J.: Doubleday, 1954.

Butterfield, Herbert. *The Origins of Modern Science: 1300-1800.* London: Bell, 1958.

Carruthers, Peter. *Phenomenal Consciousness: A Naturalistic Theory.* Cambridge: Cambridge University Press, 2000.

Chalmers, David J. *The Conscious Mind: In Search of a Fundamental Theory.* New York: Oxford University Press, 1996.

Chomsky, Noam. *Cartesian Linguistics: A Chapter in the History of Rationalist Thought.* New York: Harper & Row, 1966.

———. *Problems of Knowledge and Freedom.* London: Barrie & Jenkins, 1972.

Cohen, Avner, and Marcelo Dascal eds. *The Institution of Philosophy: A Discipline in Crisis?* LaSalle, IL: Open Court, 1989.

Cohen, David. *The Secret Language of Mind: A Visual Enquiry into the Mysteries of Consciousness*. London: Duncan-Baird, 1998.

Cohen, L. Jonathan. *The Dialogue of Reason: An Analysis of Analytical Philosophy*. Oxford: Clarendon Press, 1986.

Copleston, Frederick C. *A History of Mediaeval Philosophy*. London: Methuen, 1972.

Cornford, Maurice. *From Religion to Philosophy: A Study in the Origins of Western Speculation*. New York: Harper & Row, 1957.

Crane, Tim. *The Mechanical Mind: A Philosophical Introduction to Minds. Machines and Mental Representations*. London: Penguin, 1991.

Crick, Francis H. 'Thinking About the Brain.' *Scientific American* 241 1979: 3. 221.

Damasio, Antonio R. *Descartes' Error: Emotion. Reason. and the Human Brain*. New York: Putnam, 1994.

Davidson, Donald. 'Thought and Talk' in Samuel D. Guttenplan ed. *Mind and Language*. Oxford: Clarendon Press, 1977.

Davies, Norman. *Europe: A History*. London: Pimlico, 1997.

Davis, K. 'Extreme Social Isolation of a Child' *American Journal of Sociology* 45 1940: 4. 554-65.

———. 'Final Note on a Case of Extreme Social Isolation.' *American Journal of Sociology* 52 1947: 3. 432-7.

Dennett, Daniel C. *Brainstorms: Philosophical Essays on Mind and Psychology*. Cambridge, MA.: MIT Press, 1978.

———. *Consciousness Explained.* Boston: Little, Brown, 1991.

Descartes, René. *Dioptric* in Norman Kemp Smith ed. *Descartes' Philosophical Writings.* London: Macmillan, 1952.

———. *Discourse on Method* in Norman Kemp Smith ed. *Descartes' Philosophical Writings.* London: Macmillan, 1952.

———. *Meditations on First Philosophy* in Norman Kemp Smith ed. *Descartes' Philosophical Writings,* London: Macmillan, 1952.

Dewey, John. 'Mind and Consciousness.' in Joseph Ratner ed. *Intelligence in the Modern World: John Dewey's Philosophy.* New York: Modern Library, 1939.

———.*The Quest for Certainty: A Study of the Relation of Knowledge and Action.* New York: Putnam's, 1929.

Dewart, Leslie. *Evolution and Consciousness; The Role of Speech in the Origin and Development of Human Nature.* Toronto: University of Toronto Press, 1989.

Diels, Herman and Walther Kranz. *Die Fragmente der Vorsokratiker.* Zurich: Weidmann, 1985.

Duddy, Thomas. *Mind. Self and Interiority.* Aldershot: Avebury. 1995.

Durkheim. Emile. *The Elementary Forms of the Religious Life.* London: Allen & Unwin, 1964.

Edelman, Gerald M. *Bright Air, Brilliant Fire: On the Matter of the Mind.* New York: Basic Books, 1992.

Freeman, Kathleen. *Ancilla to the Pre-Socratic Philosophers: A Complete Translation of the Fragments in Diels.* Fragmente der Vorsokratiker. Oxford: Blackwell, 1948.

———. *The Pre-Socratic Philosophers: A Companion to Diels.* Fragmente der Vorsokratiker. Oxford: Blackwell, 1949.

Fromkin, Victoria et al. 'The Development of Language in Genie: a Case of Language Acquisition beyond the "Critical Period"'. *Brain and Language* 1 1974: 1. 81-107.

Galilei, Galileo. *Dialogue Concerning the Two Chief World Systems, Ptolemaic and Copernican.* Stillman Drake (trans.) Berkeley: University of California Press, 1967.

Gardner, Howard. *The Mind's New Science: A History of the Cognitive Revolution.* New York: Basic Books, 1985.

Gerrish, Brian. *Grace and Reason: A Study in the Theology of Luther.* Oxford: Clarendon Press, 1962.

Gilson, Étienne. *Being and Some Philosophers.* Toronto: Pontifical Institute of Mediaeval Studies, 1949.

———. *Elements of Christian Philosophy.* New York: Doubleday, 1960.

———. Études sur le rôle de la pensée médiévale dans la formation du système cartésien. Paris:Vrin, 1930.

———. *History of Christian Philosophy in the Middle Ages.* New York: Random House, 1955.

———. *Introduction a l'étude de Saint Augustin.* Paris: Vrin, 1949.

———. *La philosophie au moyen age: des origines patristiques a la fin du XIVe siècle.* Paris: Payot, 1947.

———. *Reason and Revelation in the Middle Ages.* New York: Scribner's, 1948.

———. *The Christian Philosophy of St Thomas Aquinas.* London: Gollancz, 1957.

———. *The Spirit of Mediaeval Philosophy.* New York: Scribner's, 1949.

———. *The Unity of Philosophical Experience.* New York: Scribner's, 1937.

Graham, Angus C. "'Being" in Linguistics and Philosophy: a Preliminary Inquiry.' *Foundations of Language.* 1. 1965. 223-31.

Gray, John. N. *Straw Dogs: Thoughts on Humans and Other Animals.* London: Granta, 2002.

Greene, William Chase. *Moira: Fate. Good. and Evil in Greek Thought.* Cambridge. MA.: Harvard University Press, 1944.

Guttenplan, Samuel D. ed. *Mind and Language* Oxford: Clarendon Press, 1977.

Güzeldere. Güven. 'The many faces of consciousness.' in Ned Block, Owen Flanagan, and Güven Güzeldere (eds.) *The Nature of Consciousness: Philosophical Debates.* Cambridge, MA.: MIT Press, 1998.

Hacker, P.M.S. *Insight and Illusion: Themes in the Philosophy of Wittgenstein.* Oxford: Clarendon Press, 1986.

Hanna, Alastair. *Human Consciousness.* London: Routledge, 1990.

Hare, Peter H. ed. *Doing Philosophy Historically.* Amherst. NY: Prometheus, 1988.

Hawking, Stephen W. *A Brief History of Time: From the Big Bang to Black Holes.* Toronto: Bantam, 1988.

Heidegger, Martin. *Being and Time.* London: SCM Press, 1962.

Heck, Richard G. ed. *Language. Thought. and Logic: Essays in Honour of Michael Dummett.* Oxford: Oxford University Press, 1997.

Hicks, G. Dawes. *Critical Realism: Studies in the Philosophy of Mind and Nature.* London: Macmillan, 1938.

Hold, Edwin B., Ralph Barton Perry et al. *The New Realism: Cooperative Studies in Philosophy.* New York: Macmillan, 1912.

Honderich, Ted ed. *The Oxford Companion to Philosophy.* Oxford: Oxford University Press, 1995.

Hume, David. *An Abstract of A Treatise of Human Nature. 1740: a Pamphlet Hitherto Unknown.* Hamden, CT: Archon, 1965.

———. *An Enquiry Concerning Human Understanding.* in L.A. Selby-Bigge ed. *Enquiries concerning the human understanding and concerning the principles of morals.* Oxford: Clarendon Press, 1902. and in Edwin A. Burtt ed. *The English Philosophers from Bacon to Mill.* New York: Modern Library, 1939.

———. *A Treatise of Human Nature.* edited by L.A. Selby-Bigge. Oxford: Clarendon Press, 1960.

Huxley, T.H. *Lessons in Elementary Physiology.* London: Macmillan, 1866.

Hyland, Drew A. *The Origins of Philosophy: Its Rise in Myth and the Pre-Socratics.* New York: Putnam, 1973.

Jaeger, Werner. *The Theology of the Early Greek Philosophers.* Oxford: Clarendon Press, 1947.

Jammer, Max. *Concepts of Force: A Study in the Foundations of Dynamics.* New York: Harper, 1962.

Järvilehto, Timo. 'The Theory of the Organism-environment System.' 'Part I: Description of the theory.' *Integrative Physiological and Behavioral Science* 33. 1998: 3, 321-324; 'Part II: Significance of nervous activity in the organism-environment system.' 33. 1998 3, 335-342; 'Part III: Role of efferent influences on receptors in the formation of knowledge.' 34 (1999): 90-100; 'Part IV: The problem of mental activity and consciousness.' 35. 2000: 1. 35-57.

Jaynes, Julian. *The Origin of Consciousness in the Breakdown of the Bicameral Mind.* Toronto: University of Toronto Press, 1976.

Jones, W.T. *A History of Western Philosophy.* New York: Harcourt Brace, 1952.

Kemp Smith, Norman ed. *Descartes' Philosophical Writings.* London: Macmillan, 1952.

Kim, Jaegwon. *Supervenience and Mind: Selected Philosophical Essays.* Cambridge: Cambridge University Press, 1993.

Koyré, Alexandre. 'Galileo and Plato.' *Journal of the History of Ideas.* 4. 1943: 4, 400-28.

———. *From the Closed World to the Infinite Universe.* New York: Harper, 1958.

Kretzman, Norman, Anthony Kenny, Jan Pinborg eds. *The Cambridge History of Later Mediaeval Philosophy: From the Rediscovery of Aristotle to the Disintegration of Scholasticism.* Cambridge: Cambridge University Press, 1982.

Langsam, Harold. 'The Theory of Appearing Defended' *Philosophical Studies.* 87. 1997: 1, 33-59

———. 'Why I Believe in an External World.' *Metaphilosophy* 37. 2006: 652-672.

Larson, Edward J. and Larry Whitham. 'Leading scientists still reject God.' *Nature.* 334. 1998: 313

Leibniz, G.W. von. *The Monadology.* in Philip P. Wiener ed. *Leibniz Selections.* New York: Scribner's, 1951.

———. *The Principles of Nature and of Grace Based on Reason* in Philip P. Wiener ed. *Leibniz Selections.* New York: Scribner's, 1951.

Lenzer, Gertrud ed. *Auguste Comte and Positivism: The Essential Writings.* Chicago: University of Chicago Press, 1983.

LePore, Ernest and Brian McLaughlin eds. *Actions and Events: Perspectives on the Philosophy of Donald Davidson.* Oxford: Blackwell, 1988.

Libet, Benjamin. 'Do We Have a Free Will?' *Journal of Consciousness Studies* 6. 1999: 47-57.

———. *Mind Time: The Temporal Factor in Consciousness.* Cambridge, MA.: Harvard University Press, 2004.

Locke, John. *An Essay Concerning Human Understanding* in Edwin A. Burtt ed. *The English Philosophers from Bacon to Mill.* New York: Modern Library, 1939.

Locker, Ernst. 'Etre et Avoir: leurs expressions dans les langues.' *Anthropos* 49. 1954. 481-510.

Lumsden, Charles J. and Edward O. Wilson. *Promethean Fire: Reflections on the Origin of the Mind.* Cambridge, MA: Harvard University Press, 1983.

Lycan, William G. *Consciousness and Experience.* Cambridge, MA.: MIT Press, 1996.

Malson, Lucien. *Wolf Children.* London: NLB, 1972.

Maritain, Jacques. *A Preface to Metaphysics: Seven Lectures on Being.* London: Sheed & Ward, 1948.

Martin, C.J.F. *An Introduction to Medieval Philosophy.* Edinburgh: Edinburgh University Press, 1996.

Maurer, Armand A. *Mediaeval Philosophy.* New York: Random House, 1962.

Mayr, Ernst. 'Are We Alone in this Vast Universe?' *What Makes Biology Unique: Considerations on the Autonomy of a Scientific Discipline.* Cambridge: Cambridge University Press, 2004.

McCarthy, Michael M. *The Crisis of Philosophy.* Albany: State University of New York, 1989.

McDowell, John. 'Functionalism and Anomalous Monism.' in Ernest LePore and Brian McLaughlin eds. *Actions and Events: Perspectives on the Philosophy of Donald Davidson.* Oxford: Blackwell, 1988.

———. *Mind and World.* Cambridge, MA.: Harvard University Press, 1994.

McGinn, Colin. *The Problem of Consciousness: Essays Towards a Resolution.* Oxford: Blackwell, 1991.

McLuhan, Marshall. *The Gutenberg Galaxy.* Toronto: University of Toronto Press, 1962.

Merleau-Ponty, Maurice. *The Phenomenology of Perception.* London: Routledge & Kegan Paul, 1962.

Mondin, Battista. *A History of Mediaeval Philosophy.* Rome: Urbaniana University Press, 1991.

Moskowitz, B.A. 'The Acquisition of Language.' *Scientific American* 239. 1978: 95-99.

Nagel, Thomas. *The View from Nowhere.* New York: Oxford University Press, 1986.

———. *Mortal Questions* Cambridge: Cambridge University Press, 1974.

Newton, Isaac. *The Mathematical Principles of Natural Philosophy.* New York: Philosophical Library, 1964.

Nietzsche, Friedrich. *Beyond Good and Evil: Prelude to a Philosophy of the Future.* Cambridge: Cambridge University Press, 2002.

Oates, Whitney J. 'Introduction' to *The Basic Writings of Saint Augustine.* New York: Random House, 1948.

Olafson, Frederick A. 'Brain Dualism.' *Inquiry* 37. 1994: 3, 253-265.

Owens, Joseph. *The Doctrine of Being in the Aristotelian 'Metaphysics:' A Study in the Greek Background of Mediaeval Thought.* Toronto: Pontifical Institute of Mediaeval Studies, 1948.

Pasnau, Robert. *Theories of Cognition in the Later Middle Ages.* Cambridge: Cambridge University Press, 1997.

———. 'What is Sound?.' The *Philosophical Quarterly* 49. 1999: 309-324.

Peacock, Christopher. 'Concepts Without Words.' in Richard G. Heck ed. *Language, Thought, and Logic: Essays in Honour of Michael Dummett.* Oxford: Oxford University Press, 1997.

Pitcher, George. *The Philosophy of Wittgenstein.* Englewood Cliffs. N.J.: Prentice-Hall, 1964.

Potts, Timothy C. *Conscience in Medieval Philosophy.* Cambridge: Cambridge University Press, 1980.

Price, H.H. *Perception.* London: Methuen, 1932.

Putnam, Hilary. *The Many Faces of Realism.* La Salle, IL: Open Court, 1987.

———. *Realism with a Human Face.* Cambridge, MA: Harvard University Press, 1990.

———. *Renewing Philosophy.* Cambridge, MA: Harvard University Press, 1992.

———. *Words and Life.* Cambridge, MA.: Harvard University Press, 1994.

Quine, W.V.O. *Ontological Relativity and Other Essays.* New York: Columbia University Press, 1969.

Reid, Thomas. *An Inquiry into the Human Mind: On the Principles of Common Sense.* University Park, PA: Pennsylvania State University Press. 1997.

Rorty, Richard. *Consequences of Pragmatism: Essays. 1972-1980.* Minneapolis: University of Minnesota Press, 1982.

———. *Philosophy and the Mirror of Nature.* Princeton, N.J.: Princeton University Press, 1979.

Ross, W. D. *Aristotle.* London: Methuen, 1949.

Russell, Bertrand. *The ABC of Relativity.* London: Kegan Paul, Trench,Trubner, 1925.

———. *The Analysis of Mind.* London: Allen & Unwin, 1921.

Santayana, George. *The Life of Reason: or The Phases of Human Progress,* vol. 1. New York: Scribner's, 1906.

Sartre, Jean-Paul. *L'être et le néant.* Paris: Gallimard, 1943.

Searle, John R. 'Consciousness and the Philosophers.' *The New York Review of Books*. 44. 1997: 44. 43-50

———. *The Rediscovery of the Mind*. Cambridge, MA.: MIT Press, 1992.

Selby-Bigge, L.A. ed. *Enquiries concerning the human understanding and concerning the principles of morals*. Oxford: Clarendon Press, 1902.

Setton, Kenneth M. *The Renaissance: Maker of Modern Man*. Washington, D.C.: National Geographic Society, 1970.

Sibatani, Atuhiro. 'The Japanese Brain.' *Science 80, 3*. 1980: 3, 24-30.

Steenberghen, Fernand van. *La philosophie au xiiie siècle*. Louvain: Publications Universitaires, 1966.

Strawson, Galen. *Mental Reality*. Cambridge. MA.: MIT Press, 1994.

Sullivan, Walter. *We Are Not Alone*. New York: New American Library, 1966.

Taylor, Charles. *A Secular Age*. Cambridge, MA.: Harvard University Press, 2007.

Weatherford, Roy C. *The Implications of Determinism*. London: Routledge, 1991.

Whorf, Benjamin L. *Language, Thought and Reality: Selected Writings*. Cambridge, MA: MIT Press, 1956.

Wiener, Philip P. ed. *Leibniz Selections*. New York: Scribner's, 1951.

Williams, C.J.F. *What is Existence?* Oxford: Clarendon Press, 1981.

Wippel, John F. 'Essence and existence.' in Norman Kretzman, Anthony Kenny, Jan Pinborg eds. *The Cambridge History of Later Mediaeval Philosophy: From the Rediscovery of Aristotle to the Disintegration of Scholasticism.* Cambridge: Cambridge University Press, 1982.

Zachman, Randall C. *The Assurance of Faith: Conscience in the Theology of Martin Luther and John Calvin.* Minneapolis: Fortress Press, 1993.

Zingg, Robert M. *Wolf-children and Feral Man.* New York: Harper, 1942.

Curriculum Vitae & Publications |
Leslie Dewart

Biographical

1922   Born in Madrid, Spain

1942-47 Royal Canadian Air Force. Pilot, bomber-reconnaissance operations

1951   B.A. (Honour Psychology), University of Toronto

1952-54 Teaching Fellow, Dept. of Philosophy, St. Michael's College, U. of T.

1952   M.A. (Philosophy), University of Toronto

1954   Ph.D. (Philosophy), University of Toronto

1954-56 Instructor, Dept. of Philosophy, University of Detroit

1956-61 Assistant Professor, Dept. of Philosophy, St. Michael's College, U. of T.

1961-68 Associate Professor, *ibid.*

1961-68 Associate Professor, Dept. of Philosophy, School of Graduate Studies, U. of T.

1964-70 Associate editor, Continuum

1967-74 Associate editor, Internationale Dialog Zeitschrift

1968 Member, Societé Europeénne de Culture

1968-75 Professor, Dept. of Religious Studies, St. Michael's College, U. of T.

1968-88 Professor, Faculty of Theology, St. Michael's College

1968-70 Associate Editor, Concurrence

1969-79 Professor, Institute of Christian Thought, St. Michael's College

1970-80 Member, Editorial Board, Studies in Religion—Sciences réligieuses

1970-71 Chair, Combined Departments of Religious Studies, U. of T.

1974-78 Member, Advisory Board, Journal of Ultimate Reality and Meaning

1975-88 Professor, Dept. of Religious Studies, U. of T.

1976-88 Professor, Centre for Religious Studies, School of Graduate Studies, U. of T.

1979   L.l.B., Faculty of Law, U. of T.

1981 Barrister-at-Law, Osgoode Hall, Toronto

1981 Member, Bar of the Province of Ontario

1982-83 Member, Advisory Committee on the Future of Education, Ministry of Education of Ontario

1988 Professor Emeritus, St. Michael's College, U. of T.

1988 Professor Emeritus, University of Toronto

1995-2005 Senior Research Associate, Faculty of Divinity, Trinity College

Books

1. *Christianity and Revolution,* (New York: Herder & Herder, 1963), pp. 320 (Translations: Spanish, Catalán).

2. *The Future of Belief,* (New York: Herder & Herder, 1963), pp. 223. (Translations: Dutch, French, German, Spanish, Italian, Portuguese).

3. *The Foundations of Belief,* (New York: Herder & Herder, 1966), pp. 526. (Translation: German).

4. *Religion, Language and Truth,* (New York: Herder & Herder, 1969), pp. 174.

5. *Evolution and Consciousness: The Role of Speech in the Origin and Development of Human Nature,* (Toronto: University of Toronto Press, 1989), pp. 399.

Contributions to books

1. "Some early historical developments of the New Testament morality," in William Dunphy, ed., *The New Morality*, (New York: Herder & Herder, 1967), 83-106.

2. "Education and political values," in Abraham Rotstein, ed., *The Prospect of Change*, (Toronto: McGraw-Hill, 1965), 286-307.

3. "Foreword" to Gabriel Marcel, *Problematic Man*, (New York: Herder & Herder, 1967), 7-12.

4. "Neo-Thomism and the continuity of philosophical experience," in Gregory Baum, ed., *The Future of Belief Debate*, (New York: Herder & Herder, 1967), 211-229.

5. "God and the supernatural," in Martin Marty and Dean Peerman, eds., *The New Theology*, (New York: Macmillan, 1968), 142-155.

6. "Metaphysics and the concept of God," in Christopher Mooney, ed., *The Presence and Absence of God*, (New York: Fordham University Press, 1969), 87-108.

7. "The fear of death and its basis in the nature of consciousness," in Florence M. Hetzler and Austin H. Kutscher, eds., *Philosophical Aspects of Thanatology*, vol. 1, (New York: Arno Press, 1978), pp. 53-63.

8. "Properties of speech and ideas of reality," in Bruce Alton, ed., *Religions and Languages*, (New York: Peter Lang, 1991), 67-83.

Articles

1. "Existentialism and the degrees of knowledge," *The Thomist*, XIX (1956), 2, 193-218.

2. "American leadership and the future of the West," *Liberation*, VII (1962), 5, 23-28.

3. "War and the Christian tradition," *Commonweal*, LXXVII (1962), 6 , 145-148.

4. "The prospects of peace," *Liberation*, VII (1962), 10, 5-10.

5. "Modern war and Catholic morality," *Current*, III (1962), 3, 182-193.

6. "Christianity's vocation in the nuclear age," *Blackfriars*, XLIV (1963), 512, 57-62.

7. "Christians and Marxists in dialogue: possibilities, prospects, and perils," *Continuum,* I, 2 (Summer, 1963), 139-153.

8. "Is this a post-Christian age?" *Continuum,* I, 4 (Winter, 1964), 556-567.

9. "Academic freedom and Catholic dissent," *Commonweal,* LXXX (1964), 2, 33-36.

10. "A comparison of the concepts of 'peaceful coexistence' in John XXIII's *Pacem in Terris and in Soviet-American diplomacy,"* Co-existence, I (1964), 1, 21-38.

11. "Pacem in Terris and Soviet-American relations: a comparative analysis of the basis of international peace," *Cross Currents,* XIV (1964), 3, 287-312.

12. "Neo-traditionalists and pseudo-progressives: a note on recent conflicts within the Catholic Church," *Continuum,* III , 1 (Spring, 1965), 121-123.

13. "Les bases morales de la paix," (1re partie), *Comprendre,* XXVIII (1965), 137-154.

14. "The school of conformity: a phenomenological critique," *Continuum,* IV, 2 (Summer, 1966), 171-177.

15. "Catholic philosophy and the socialization of the intellect," *Ecumenist,* V (1967), 4, 52-55.

16. "Les bases morales de la paix" (conclusion), *Comprendre,* XXIX (1966), 85-102.

17. "Wahrheit, Irrtum, und Dialog," *Internationale Dialog Zeitschrift,* I, 4 (1968), 330-345.

18. "Towards a new form of faith," *Ferment,* II (1968), 2, 10-12.

19. "On transcendental Thomism," *Continuum,* VI, 3 (Autumn, 1968), 389-401.

20. "The meaning of religious belief," *Commonweal,* XC (1969), 1, 15-17.

21. "The nature of truth in relation to language," *Continuum,* VII, 2 (Summer, 1969), 332-340.

22. "The fact of death," *Commonweal,* XCI (1969), 7, 206-208.

23. "A response to J. Donceel," *Continuum,* VII, 3 (Autumn, 1969), 453-462.

24. "Hope and immortality," *Agora,* XII (1970), 12-16.25.

25. "Unité et vérité," *Lumière et Vie,* XX, 103 (Juin, 1970), 70-89.

26. "Sprache und Wahrheit," *Theologie der Gegenwart,* XIV (1971), 4, 198-202.

27. "Christianity and the philosophy of language," *Drijarkara (Indonesia),* I (1972) 4, 96-102.

28. "Der Zustand der römisch-katholischen Kirche," *Wort und Wahrheit,* XXVII (1972), 2, 116-119.

29. "Language and religion," *Philosophic Exchange,* I (1972) 3, 35-44.

30. "The relevance of Thomism today," *Proc. Am. Cath. Phil. Assn.,* XLVIII (1974), 308-317.

31. "The grounds for observing the law: a critical analysis of H.L.A. Hart's foundations of a theory of law," *Queen's Law* J., V (1979), 1, 116-152.